Good Growth and Governance in Africa

THE INITIATIVE FOR POLICY DIALOGUE SERIES

The Initiative for Policy Dialogue (IPD) brings together the top voices in development to address some of the most pressing and controversial debates in economic policy today. The IPD book series approaches topics such as capital market liberalization, macroeconomics, environmental economics, and trade policy from a balanced perspective, presenting alternatives, and analyzing their consequences on the basis of the best available research. Written in a language accessible to policymakers and civil society, this series will rekindle the debate on economic policy and facilitate a more democratic discussion of development around the world.

OTHER TITLES PUBLISHED BY OXFORD UNIVERSITY PRESS IN THIS SERIES

Fair Trade for All
Joseph E. Stiglitz and Andrew Charlton

Economic Development and Environmental Sustainability
Ramón López and Michael A. Toman

Stability with Growth
Joseph E. Stiglitz, José Antonio Ocampo, Shari Spiegel,
Ricardo Ffrench-Davis, and Deepak Nayyar

The Washington Consensus Reconsidered
Narcis Serra and Joseph E. Stiglitz

Capital Market Liberalization and Development
José Antonio Ocampo and Joseph E. Stiglitz

Industrial Policy and Development
Mario Cimoli, Giovanni Dosi, and Joseph E. Stiglitz

Time for a Visible Hand
Stephany Griffith-Jones, José Antonio Ocampo, and Joseph E. Stiglitz

Overcoming Developing Country Debt Crises
Barry Herman, José Antonio Ocampo, and Shari Spiegel

Debates in the Measurement of Global Poverty
Sudhir Anand, Paul Segal, and Joseph E. Stiglitz

Good Growth and Governance in Africa
Akbar Noman, Kwesi Botchwey, Howard Stein, and Joseph E. Stiglitz

Good Growth and Governance in Africa

Rethinking Development Strategies

Edited by
Akbar Noman
Kwesi Botchwey
Howard Stein
Joseph E. Stiglitz

OXFORD
UNIVERSITY PRESS

OXFORD
UNIVERSITY PRESS

Great Clarendon Street, Oxford OX2 6DP

Oxford University Press is a department of the University of Oxford.
It furthers the University's objective of excellence in research, scholarship,
and education by publishing worldwide in

Oxford New York

Auckland Cape Town Dar es Salaam Hong Kong Karachi
Kuala Lumpur Madrid Melbourne Mexico City Nairobi
New Delhi Shanghai Taipei Toronto

With offices in

Argentina Austria Brazil Chile Czech Republic France Greece
Guatemala Hungary Italy Japan Poland Portugal Singapore
South Korea Switzerland Thailand Turkey Ukraine Vietnam

Oxford is a registered trade mark of Oxford University Press
in the UK and in certain other countries

Published in the United States
by Oxford University Press Inc., New York

British Library Cataloguing in Publication Data

Data available

Library of Congress Cataloging in Publication Data

Data available

Typeset by SPI Publisher Services, Pondicherry, India
Printed in Great Britain
on acid-free paper by
Clays Ltd, St Ives plc

ISBN 978–0–19–969856–1 (Hbk.)
        978–0–19–969857–8 (Pbk.)

1 3 5 7 9 10 8 6 4 2

Acknowledgments

The book is the outcome of the research of the Africa Task Force of the Initiative for Policy Dialogue (IPD) at Columbia University, directed by Kwesi Botchwey, Akbar Noman, and Joseph E. Stiglitz. IPD is a global interdisciplinary network of over 250 leading social scientists, policymakers and civil society representatives committed to furthering understanding of the development process. We would like to thank all Task Force members, whose participation in provocative dialogues and debates on development issues in Africa informed the content of this book.

In addition to the contributing authors, we gratefully acknowledge the comments of a long list of friends who participated in various capacities to the gestation of this enterprise (without of course committing them to our analysis or conclusions) and in particular to Padraig Carmody, Mamadou Diouf, Ben Fine, Howard French, Antoinette Handley, Morten Jerven, Raphie Kaplinksy, Machiko Nissanke, Carlo Petrobelli, Robert Pollin, Ian Taylor, Rolph van Der Hoeven, Sam Wangwe, and John Weeks. We are very grateful to the two anonymous referees who provided insightful comments on the manuscript. This work would not have been possible without the professional dedication of IPD's Publications Coordinator Farah Siddique and former Program Manager Eva Kaplan who helped arrange the Africa Task Force meetings and coordinated the various stages of production of the book. Other former IPD staff whose valuable contributions are gratefully acknowledged are Sheila Chanani, Siddhartha Gupta, and Sarah Green. IPD also expresses its gratitude to Tyra Walker and Rebecca Wilson.

Finally, we are most grateful to the Brooks World Poverty Institute at the University of Manchester and Japan International Cooperation Agency (JICA) for funding the work of the IPD Task Force on Africa.

Preface

Akbar Noman, Kwesi Botchwey, Howard Stein, and Joseph E. Stiglitz

When the countries of Sub-Saharan Africa (which, for shorthand, we will simply refer to as Africa) achieved independence in rapid succession starting with Ghana in 1957, there were high hopes for the region. At the time, incomes in some countries actually exceeded some East Asian nations. A group of outstanding leaders would, it was hoped, inspire a new era in a subcontinent long suffering from colonial exploitation and developmental neglect. Whilst generalizations about a region as vast and varied as Africa must be made with circumspection, overall what has happened since has been disappointing, though there have been notable successes in different countries, time periods, and dimensions of development.

These outcomes have been particularly disappointing given the predictions of standard economic theory. There should be a *convergence* in economic outcomes, with those countries with lower per capita incomes growing faster than those with higher. Poor countries face a scarcity of capital, which implies that the returns to capital should be higher, and capital should flow toward these countries. As it does so, incomes there should increase relative to those in richer countries. By contrast, there has been divergence between Africa and other regions of the world including developed countries. Incomes per capita rose fairly rapidly from independence through the mid-1970s, but plummeted after 1980, a period that witnessed the imposition of the now widely criticized policies that came to be known by the shorthand of "Washington Consensus" (see Chapter 1 in this volume). Gross National Income per capita fell by more than 30 percent between 1980–2002 for Africa as a whole and more than 40 percent if you exclude South Africa (World Bank 2005). By contrast, in the rest of the world per capita incomes more than doubled and in some of the most successful developing countries increased four-fold or more (see the figures in Chapter 1 in this volume).

The resulting situation for Africa's poor has been dismal. Whilst poverty estimates are subject to limitations of data and to differences in definitions, there is little doubt that taking into account the overall trends there was a substantial increase in poverty. One highly regarded estimate indicates that the percentage of the region's population in poverty went from nearly 52 percent to nearly 60 percent between 1981–99 before declining to levels similar to 1981. However, the absolute numbers have continued to grow and by 2005 the population living under $1.25 per day had reached 390.6 million people, an 83 percent increase over the twenty-four-year period. The percentage of the world's poor living in Africa went from 11 percent in 1981 to 28 percent in 2005 (Chen and Ravallion 2008).

Only the few years before the global economic crisis of 2008 brought respite to this unimpressive picture for Africa. Annual GDP growth soared to 6.4 and 6.5 percent during 2006 and 2007 respectively, with only the East and the South Asian regions exceeding it by a significant margin. But even this period of optimism appears fragile, built on soaring resource prices as much as anything else and without much improvement in other measures of performance such as economic structure and savings or investment rates that would suggest a sustained transition to a higher growth path (see Chapter 1 in this volume).

This naturally raises the question: Why has the economic growth performance of Africa overall been so disappointing during the past fifty years? More importantly, what are the policy options for reversing that trend, and for sustaining and improving upon the growth experienced in the years before the crisis? What are the possibilities and policies for Africa to achieve sustained, rapid economic growth, poverty reduction, and associated structural transformations and begin to catch up?

These were the questions posed to a diverse group of experts on development, including many specialists on Africa, convened as the "Africa Task Force," by the Initiative for Policy Dialogue (IPD) with the support of the Japan International Cooperation Agency (JICA) and Brooks World Poverty Institute (BWPI) at the University of Manchester.[1] The first two meetings of the Task Force were in 2006 and 2007 at the University of Manchester, hosted by BWPI. The third meeting in Addis Ababa was supported by JICA and organized jointly with the Ethiopian Development Research Institute (EDRI), as was the fourth in Pretoria, in collaboration with the South African Government's Department for Trade and Industry and the African Center for Economic Transformation (ACET—headquartered in Accra). In addition to academics, staff members of the IMF, World Bank, and other UN agencies, the meetings were attended by government ministers (including an African head of government), NGOs, and corporate sector representatives. This volume draws on a set of papers mostly presented at the first three meetings.

The overview in Chapter 1 (Noman and Stiglitz) aims both to pull together the main threads of the other contributions in this volume as well as reflect some of the rich policy-focused discussions at the meetings. Of course, it would be impossible to do full justice to either but many of the other chapters capture more of the complexities and nuances of both the literature and the discussions at the meetings. While there were disagreements, and even heated exchanges, there was a general consensus on several points: a disappointment with past strategies and the need for fresh approaches adequately informed by the lessons of success both in and out of Africa, particularly drawing on the experiences of Asia; and the need for greater bilateral and multilateral agency flexibility to allow the policy space to formulate and implement these new approaches. There was consensus too on the enormous challenge facing Africa. Faster growth is necessary if Africa is to reach the Millennium Development Goals (MDGs) even a few years after 2015—a sustained annual growth rate of around 7 percent is called for, a number that corresponds to the *best* average performance that Africa has been able to achieve.[2] New strategies have to be placed on the policy agenda for African countries if the region is to achieve such growth, breaking out of its "low-growth-and-low-expectations equilibrium."

The objective of this volume, a selection of the papers presented at the Task Force meetings,[3] is to broaden the policy debate, expand the policy options, and propose alternative development strategies. Our focus is on those countries whose governments are reasonably serious and committed to pursuing a developmental agenda and either have or are quite capable of acquiring the capacity to do so. There are many such countries in Africa that received wide acclaim in the discussions of the Task Force. (See also the contributions to this volume, in particular those of Mushtaq Khan, Thandika Mkandawire, and Meles Zenawi.) There are, of course, states that are mired in serious armed conflict or with severe problems of governance, and we have little, if anything, to say for such contexts.

Perhaps the most salient, overarching message of this exercise is that at the center of the policy missteps in Africa was a failure to get the balance right between the state and the market. There is no simple formula for getting that balance right; what it entails is contingent on a detailed understanding of the preconditions and limitations of any new policy approaches and the circumstances in the country.

Notes

1. Core institutional funding for the Initiative for Policy Dialogue (IPD) was also provided by the Hewlett Foundation. The work of the Africa Task Force overlapped with work of IPD Climate Change Task Force, supported by the Rockefeller Brothers Fund, and the Financial Markets Reform Task Force, supported by the Ford Foundation.
2. Africa's GDP growth averaged at least 7 percent in three years since 1960: 7 percent in 1969, 7.8 percent in 1970, and 7.2 percent in 1974.
3. The papers have been revised, both in response to the discussion at the Task Force meetings and to comments from referees who remain anonymous to the authors. For that reason we cannot name them but would like to express our deep gratitude to them.

References

Chen, S. and Ravallion, M. (2008). "The Developing World is Poorer Than We Thought, But no Less Successful in the Fight Against Poverty." World Bank Policy Research Working Paper No. 4703. Washington, DC: World Bank.

World Bank (2005). *African Development Indicators*. Washington, DC: World Bank.

—— (2010). World dataBank, World Development Indicators (WDI) & Global Development Finance (GDF). Online database available at <http://databank.worldbank.org/ddp/home. do?Step=12&id=4&CNO=2>.

Contents

List of Figures	xiii
List of Tables	xvi
List of Boxes	xix
List of Contributors	xx

Part I: Introduction and Overview

1. Strategies for African Development   3
   Akbar Noman and Joseph E. Stiglitz

Part II: Governance, Institutions, and the State

2. Governance and Growth: History, Ideology, and Methods of Proof   51
   Mushtaq H. Khan

3. Institutional Monocropping and Monotasking in Africa   80
   Thandika Mkandawire

4. Governance and Growth Challenges for Africa   114
   Mushtaq H. Khan

5. States and Markets: Neoliberal Limitations and the Case for a
   Developmental State   140
   Meles Zenawi

6. The African Economic Growth Record, and the Roles of Policy
   Syndromes and Governance   175
   Augustin Kwasi Fosu

Part III: Technology, Industrial, and Trade Policies

7. Dynamic Capacity Development: What Africa Can Learn from
   Industrial Policy Formulation in East Asia   221
   Izumi Ohno and Kenichi Ohno

Contents

8. How can Low-Income Countries Accelerate their Catch-Up with
   High-Income Countries? The Case for Open-Economy Industrial Policy   246
   Robert H. Wade

9. Institutional Capacity and Policy Choices for Latecomer Technology
   Development   273
   Banji O. Oyeyinka and Padmashree Gehl Sampath

10. State–Business Relations, Investment Climate Reform, and
    Economic Growth in Sub-Saharan Africa   303
    Kunal Sen and Dirk Willem te Velde

11. Africa, Industrial Policy, and Export Processing Zones: Lessons
    from Asia   322
    Howard Stein

12. South African Post-Apartheid Policies Towards Industrialization:
    Tentative Implications for Other African Countries   345
    Nimrod Zalk

13. Issues in Africa's Industrial Policy Process   372
    Matsuo Watanabe and Atsushi Hanatani

14. Tiger, Tiger, Burning Bright? Industrial Policy "Lessons"
    from Ireland for Small African Economies   406
    David Bailey, Helena Lenihan, and Ajit Singh

Part IV: Employment and Human Capital

15. Employment in Sub-Saharan Africa: Lessons to be Learnt from
    the East Asian Experience   437
    Azizur Rahman Khan

16. Skills Development for Economic Growth in Sub-Saharan Africa:
    A Pragmatic Perspective   462
    Yaw Ansu and Jee-Peng Tan

Part V: International Context

17. Economic Liberalization and Constraints to Development in
    Sub-Saharan Africa   499
    Jomo K. S. and Rudiger von Arnim

18. The Emerging Asian Giants and Economic Development in Africa   536
    Deepak Nayyar

Index   565

List of Figures

Figure 1.1 Africa GDP per capita trend 9

Figure 1.2 Africa GDP and GDP per capita annual growth rates 10

Figure 1.3 GDP annual growth regional comparison 10

Figure 1.4 GDP per capita annual growth rates: regional comparisons 11

Figure 2.1 Growth requires specific growth-enhancing governance capabilities 60

Figure 2.2 The liberal/good governance approach 62

Figure 2.3 Theoretical linkages underpinning the good governance agenda 63

Figure 2.4 The good governance and anti-corruption agenda 64

Figure 2.5 An example of the evidence: "rule of law" and growth, 1990–2003 67

Figure 2.6 Governance characteristics of growth economies 68

Figure 2.7 The Acemoglu et al. version of colonial history 69

Figure 2.8 Colonial history's inconvenient truths 71

Figure 3.1 Relationship between governance and per capita income 87

Figure 4.1 Steps in developing a national growth strategy 132

Figure 6.1 Half-decadal mean annual SSA GDP growth rates (%), 1961–2005 181

Figure 6.2 Evolutions of syndrome-free (SF) and executive constraints (XC), 1960–2004 200

Figure 6.3 Evolutions of syndrome-free (SF) and state breakdown (SB) regimes, 1960–2000 (%) 204

Figure 7.1 Different speeds of catching-up 223

Figure 7.2 Malaysia: overlapping policy structure 233

Figure 7.3 El Salvador: the Japanese aid package around La Union Port 240

Figure 10.1 Higher SBR scores for groups of faster growing countries 309

Figure 10.2 Private-sector organizations membership across African countries 310

Figure 10.3a Value of services by business associations to firms in Zambia 310

Figure 10.3b Value of services by business associations to firms in Ethiopia 311

Figure 10.3c Value of services by business associations to firms in South Africa 311

Figure 10.4 The effect of business association membership on productivity
is greater in countries that are better prepared for effective
state–business relations   316

Figure 12.1 Investment by public corporations and value-added in metal
fabrication, capital equipment and transport equipment (R'm 2000),
1970–2007   351

Figure 12.2a Components of annual GDP growth (R'm 2000)   357

Figure 12.2b Cumulative components of GDP (R'm 2000)   357

Figure 12.3 Growth in GDP by nine broad sectors (R'm 2000)   358

Figure 12.4 Gross fixed capital formation to GDP versus share of finance
and insurance sector in GDP (R'm 2000), %   359

Figure 12.5 Employment growth by nine broad sectors (R'm 2000) 360

Figure 12.6 Employment growth in private services   360

Figure 12.7 Index of real value-added growth of merchandise sectors by
sectoral grouping (R'm 1994=100), 1970–2007   362

Figure 12.8 Real export growth of merchandise sectors by sectoral grouping
(R'm 2000), 1970–2007   364

Figure 12.9 Real investment by sectoral grouping (2000), 1970–2007 364

Figure 12.10 Employment by sectoral grouping, 1970–2007   365

Figure 13.1 GDP growth of developing regions, 1990–2007   373

Figure 13.2 GDP growth of African countries   374

Figure 13.3 Income level: 2000–7 average   375

Figure 13.4 Africa's growth and commodity prices   375

Figure 13.5 Manufacturing share in GDP   376

Figure 13.6 ASEAN dependence on foreign capital   387

Figure 13.7 Malaysia growth of GDP and FDI   392

Figure 13.8 Malaysia GDP structure and trade   392

Figure 13.9 Development of manufacturing   393

Figure 16.1 Skills development to support FDI-led industrialization 466

Figure 16.2 Education profile of the non-school population ages 25–34,
circa 2003   467

Figure 16.3 Evolution of Singapore's industrial phases and skills development,
1960–2000   472

Figure 16.4 Education profiles of the working population in Korea and Ghana,
1960–2000   477

Figure 16.5 Coverage in secondary and tertiary education in Sub-Saharan
            Africa and other world regions, 1999 and 2007   479

Figure 16.6 Student learning outcomes in primary education in Africa,
            1996–2005   480

Figure 17.1 Total offical aid flows: regional composition, 1970–2005   508

List of Tables

Table 1.1 Africa: Average annual growth in real GDP per capita, 1961–2004
(percent)   15

Table 6.1 GDP growth (annual %), five-year averages   177

Table 6.2 GDP per capita growth (annual %), five-year averages   179

Table 6.3 Half-decadal mean annual SSA GDP growth rates (%), 1961–2005   181

Table 6.4 Annual growth of real GDP per worker, SSA versus other regions:
mean and variability measures, 1960–2000 (percent)   182

Table 6.5 Growth decomposition for Sub-Saharan Africa   183

Table 6.6 Evolution of policy syndromes in Sub-Saharan Africa (half-decadal
relative frequencies)   190

Table 6.7 Five-year panel estimation with country and time fixed effects
(sample period = 1960–2000)   197

Table 6.8 Five-year panel estimation with country and time fixed effects
(sample period = 1981–2000)   198

Appendix Table A Growth-accounting decomposition, African economies,
1960–2000   207

Appendix Table B.1 Summary statistics (sample period = 1960–2000)   209

Appendix Table B.2 Summary statistics (sample period = 1981–2000)   209

Appendix Table C.1 Correlogram of variables (sample period = 1960–2000)   209

Appendix Table C.2 Correlogram of variables (sample period = 1981–2000)   209

Table 7.1 Japan: policy menu for enhancing industrial capability in East Asia   236

Table 7.2 Japan–Vietnam Bilateral Policy Dialogue for Industrial Competitiveness   238

Table 9.1 R&D spending as a percentage of total revenues of the top five
firms from 2003–6 (excluding Cipla)   284

Table 9.2 Comparing Bangladesh and India's policy regimes for
pharmaceutical self-sufficiency   286

Table 9.3 Investment in human capital and R&D 1995–2002
(RMB ten thousand)   288

Table 9.4 Comparative R&D intensity in the manufacturing, high-technology, and electronics industry   289

Table 9.5 2001 global EMS contract manufacturers' production locations in China   290

Table 10.1 Effective state–business relations and economic growth: regression results   313

Table 10.2 Effects of different services of business associations on productivity   315

Table 12.1 Regional shares in manufacturing value-added US$ (percent), 2004   345

Table 12.2 Regional shares in world trade US$ (percent), 2006   346

Table 13.1 Classification of industrial policies   377

Table 13.2 Transformation of trade and investment regime   389

Table 14.1 Per capita GDP growth by region and economic grouping, 1981–2007 (percent)   411

Table 14.2 World primary commodity prices, 2002–6 (percentage change)   411

Table 15.1 Some aspects of labor force and employment in Sub-Saharan Africa and contemporary developing Asia   439

Table 15.2 HIV, income level, and LFPR, circa 2006   442

Table 15.3 Growth in the SSA countries, 2000–6 (annual percent)   449

Table 15.4 Median monthly incomes/wages in Kenya (in Ksh), 2005–6   455

Table 16.1 Distribution of out-of-school population ages 15–59 by employment status, 23 SSA countries, circa 2003   468

Table 16.2 Employment status by age cohort and educational attainment, average for 23 African countries, circa 2003   469

Table 16.3 Indicators of educational coverage in low-income Sub-Saharan Africa, 1990, 1999, 2005, and 2009   478

Table 16.4 Eighth graders' performance on international tests in Africa and other selected countries, 2003 and 2007   481

Table 16.5 Share of tertiary students enrolled in science and technology disciplines, Africa, 1980–2003/4   482

Table 17.1 GDP per capita in constant 2000 US$ 501

Table 17.2 Real GDP growth   502

Table 17.3 Percentage of population below poverty line, 1981–2004   502

Table 17.4 Africa's share in inward foreign direct investment   504

Table 17.5 SSA economies with the highest shares in the region's total FDI   505

Table 17.6 Net debt transfers of selected regions   509

Table 17.7 African shares of world manufacturing exports, 1995–2006   510

Table 17.8 GDP components of SSA excluding South Africa, 1970–2006   512

Table 17.9 GDP components of major petroleum exporters in developing Africa, 1970–2006   520

List of Tables

Table 17.10 Destinations and sources of SSA trade with selected regions, 1960–2006   521

Table 17.11 Africa's export composition, 1995–2006   522

Table 18.1 China, India, and Africa in the world economy (percentage share in population and income)   537

Table 18.2 GDP, population, and GDP per capita China, India, and Africa, 2000 and 2005   539

Table 18.3 Growth performance of China, India, and Africa: 1951–80 and 1981–2005. Comparison with country groups (percent per annum)   540

Table 18.4 China and India: trade with Africa   544

Table 18.5 Africa's trade with China and India   544

Table 18.6 Composition of China's trade with Africa and the world (in percentages)   546

Table 18.7 Composition of India's trade with Africa and the world (in percentages)   548

Table 18.8 Composition of Africa's exports to China, India, and the world (in percentages)   549

Table 18.9 Composition of Africa's imports from China, India, and the world (in percentages)   549

Table 18.10 Foreign direct investment: China, India, and Africa: stocks and flows ($billion)   550

List of Boxes

Box 9.1 Government initiatives for ICTs in South Africa   291

Box 12.1 Main elements of the GEAR strategy   353

Box 12.2 Sectoral groupings   363

List of Contributors

Yaw Ansu Chief Economist, African Center for Economic Transformation

David Bailey Professor of International Business Strategy and Economics, Coventry University

Kwesi Botchwey Executive Chairman, African Development Policy Ownership Initiative (ADPOI)

Augustin Kwasi Fosu Deputy Director, United Nations University World Institute for Development Economics Research (UNU-WIDER)

Atsushi Hanatani Head of Japan International Cooperation Agency (JICA) South Sudan office

Azizur Rahman Khan Emeritus Professor of Economics, University of California, Riverside

Mushtaq H. Khan Professor of Economics, School of Oriental and African Studies (SOAS), University of London

Helena Lenihan Senior Lecturer in Economics, University of Limerick

Thandika Mkandawire Professor of African Development, Department of International Development, London School of Economics and Political Science

Deepak Nayyar Professor of Economics, Jawaharlal Nehru University

Akbar Noman Senior Fellow, Initiative for Policy Dialogue and Adjunct Associate Professor of International and Public Affairs, Columbia University

Izumi Ohno Professor, National Graduate Institute for Policy Studies

Kenichi Ohno Professor, National Graduate Institute for Policy Studies

Banji O. Oyeyinka Professorial Fellow, United Nations University Maastricht Economic and Social Research Institute on Innovation and Technology (UNU-MERIT)

Padmashree Gehl Sampath Researcher, United Nations University Maastricht Economic and Social Research Institute on Innovation and Technology (UNU-MERIT)

Kunal Sen Professor of Development Economics and Policy, University of Manchester

Ajit Singh Emeritus Professor of Economics, University of Cambridge

Howard Stein Professor, Department of Afroamerican and African Studies, University of Michigan

Joseph E. Stiglitz University Professor, Columbia University

Jomo K. S. Assistant Secretary-General for Economic Development, United Nations Department of Economic and Social Affairs (UN DESA)

Jee-Peng Tan Advisor, Education Department, Human Development Network, World Bank

Dirk Willem te Velde Programme Leader, Investment and Growth Programme, Overseas Development Institute

Rudiger von Arnim Assistant Professor of Economics, University of Utah

Robert H. Wade Professor of Political Economy and Development, Department of International Development, London School of Economics and Political Science

Matsuo Watanabe Faculty of International Studies and Regional Development, University of Niigata Prefecture

Nimrod Zalk Deputy Director-General, Industrial Development Division, South African Department of Trade and Industry (DTI)

Meles Zenawi Prime Minister of Ethiopia

Part I
Introduction and Overview

1

Strategies for African Development

Akbar Noman and Joseph E. Stiglitz

Objectives of this volume

Why has the economic performance of Sub-Saharan Africa (which we will simply refer to as Africa from here on) been so disappointing? This is an important question, but our real objective is not so much to understand what went wrong, as to assess how Africa can change its course: What are the policy options for a sustained reversal of that trend? How can Africa catch up with developing countries in other regions, some of which have had spectacular successes in the very period during which Africa was stagnating?

It is worth recalling that as Africa emerged from colonialism, East Asia was the region in trouble and turmoil. Its extensive involvement with and destruction in World War II was followed by the Chinese Revolution (1949), the Korean War (1950–2), insurgency in the Malay Peninsula in the 1950s, the bloodbath in Indonesia (1967–8), and the Vietnam War that spilled over into Laos and Cambodia and continued for over three decades. A widely held view at the time contrasted Africa's promise with Asia's pitfalls. Thus, just a half century ago, Nobel Laureate economist Gunnar Myrdal visited Asia—whose economies then were doing little better than those of Africa have since that time. Even his rich and sophisticated work shared the view that that continent's prospects were dismal.[1] History, of course, proved that consensus view to be wrong: Much of the continent was just beginning the most rapid period of sustained growth seen anywhere in the world at any time. Stiglitz was one of the leaders of the early 1990s World Bank study *The East Asian Miracle*[2], undertaken to understand the factors responsible for Asian countries' success. The study described the important role that government had played in promoting savings, education, technology, and entrepreneurship as well as regulating finance and ensuring that financial markets served the needs of society—a view markedly different from that embodied in the

3

market-fundamentalist version of the "Washington Consensus,"[3] which entails a very limited role of the state and was the prevailing doctrine in the World Bank and the IMF at the time. (The financial crisis that broke out in 2008 and the ensuing recession has, of course, bolstered the critique of market fundamentalism.[4]) These ideas—that the government can play a central role in the promotion of development and *govern* markets—have been encapsulated in the notion of the *developmental state*.

Given the disappointing results of reforms that relied excessively on markets, one of the central issues addressed by the chapters in this volume[5] is, *could government play a more active role in promoting development? If so, what should it do? What are the governance requirements of a more activist state? How could one mitigate the risks of government failure? What lessons could Africa glean from the experience of Asia?* There are, of course, many differences between the two regions, leading some to suggest that the experiences in one are of little relevance to the other. Most of the participants in the meetings of the Initiative for Policy Dialogue's Africa Task Force in Pretoria, Addis Ababa, and Manchester (where various drafts of these papers were presented and where these ideas were hotly debated) disagreed with that conclusion.

There was one fundamental issue that clearly had to be addressed, and that was governance: Do at least some of the states of Africa have the capacity to play the roles that they would have to play? How could one square accusations of corruption, one of the standard explanations for Africa's failures, with the tasks to be performed by the developmental state or its more common and feasible variant, the "developmentalist state."[6] That is why the Task Force addressed not only the economics of the developmental state, but also its institutional and political dimensions. The predominant view of the Task Force had a strong note of optimism: governments could actively promote development—and some in fact were doing so. Full success was not around the corner; many difficulties lay ahead; but, especially with well-designed assistance from the more advanced industrial countries and international organizations—and a favorable global economic environment—there were good prospects for sustained growth and poverty reduction in several African countries.

The puzzle of Africa's growth has, of course, been a subject of intense debate and alternative views that blame poor governance, an unfortunate location (geography), or history (colonial legacy), especially after the failure of the simplistic formula of "get prices right, privatize, and liberate the magic of the market." As we explain below, most of the members of the Task Force found these explanations or, at any rate, the importance often accorded to them, unpersuasive. Unfortunately, too much of the policy discourse on Africa has been too dominated by these perspectives.

The need to widen the policy debate and space in Africa and suggestions for some crucial ways of doing so are the dominant themes of the collection of chapters that follow. In this introductory chapter, we will not only draw on them, pulling together many of their threads, but also supplement them, notably by trying to reflect some of the highlights of the rich and wide-ranging discussions that took place in meetings of the Task Force.[7]

There was, of course, no unanimity of views, and later in this introduction, we comment on one key debate. The discussion was lively and at times contentious. But what was clear was that it was imperative for new strategies to be placed on the policy agenda for African countries, if the region is to break out of its "low-growth-and-low-expectations equilibrium" and if the growth achieved in the decade before the 2008 crisis is to be sustained and enhanced.

Complexities of African development

The question of interpreting Africa's developmental experience is not as simple as was starkly posed above, because of the diversity of African countries and their experiences. The region includes the fastest growing economy in the world during 1960–2000: Botswana. It also includes the long-standing success story of Mauritius, as well as other countries that have experienced fairly rapid growth, of 5 percent or more, over the fairly long-term period of a decade or so, countries such as Mozambique, Ethiopia, Tanzania, Uganda, and Ghana. There is also great diversity when it comes to factors such as size, natural and human resources, ethnic configurations, and regime types.

There are a myriad of country-specific or idiosyncratic factors that affect economic performance. The crucial factors determining economic outcomes may have little to do with economic policies. In particular, states mired in civil conflicts and states that have failed are not contexts that are amenable to the sort of policy solutions we are seeking to illuminate. Economic difficulties and mismanagement may contribute in varying degrees to such political meltdowns in particular cases; but beyond a point, political failure rules. Economic success may prevent political collapse but it cannot cure it. We have little, if anything, to say for contexts such as today's Somalia and Eritrea or Mugabe's Zimbabwe or Mobutu's Zaire (or, for that matter, the contexts of Burma, North Korea, Haiti, and elsewhere). However, for such post-conflict states as Liberia or Ethiopia, the policy options we propose are likely to be of relevance, as serious, committed, developmental regimes embark on rebuilding their economies or moving beyond reconstruction and toward accelerated development. At any rate, it is the economic policy options for these types of regimes—whether post-conflict or not—that we are concerned with. Today, Africa has many such regimes—something that is ignored by sweeping generalizations about problems of governance in Africa.

But still, there is a stylized or "average" African case, which can be useful for engaging in the sort of broad discourse on development strategies that we aim for. (Much of what we have to say is also relevant for low-income, least-developed, or latecomer economies in other regions of the world.)

5

The fact that so many of the countries have succeeded in creating reasonably "good governments" and adopting reasonably "sound policies" (at least as defined by conventional standards) and yet have failed to attract non-extractive foreign direct investment, or even to promote domestic investment, has been a major source of concern. Some investments in natural resources may simply reflect the fact that those countries willing to give away their resources for a low enough price can always find some company to take them. But these typically bring relatively few jobs, and often bring harm to the environment as well as leading to suboptimal use of depletable resources. Similarly, if a country gives away a telecom concession at sweet enough terms, it can find an interested investor. The concern is that there has been too little of the kind of investment in manufacturing or service sectors that would give rise to sustained growth and job creation.

In this introductory chapter we describe and explain Africa's growth, putting its experience within a global context. The next section discusses Africa's "lost quarter century." The following section explores the relationship between the state and the market, in theory and in practice, noting that in almost all successful countries, government has played an important role. Part of the reason is the presence of pervasive market failures. This section thus reinforces the conclusions of the previous. Policies which eviscerated this state contributed to Africa's lost quarter century. The next section then focuses on one key set of policies for Africa: Learning, industrial, and technology policies. This is followed by a discussion of governance. Deficiencies in governance are often cited as the reason why policies that were so successful in East Asia won't work in Africa. We explain why that view is too simplistic and misses the point. We suggest that, instead, the right question to ask is: *In which contexts could which particular mix of measures improve governance and markets?* And, *how can markets and government work together to best enhance economic performance?* We then expand the discussion to explore the "Development State" in general, and in Africa in particular. We conclude with two sections, one dealing with the impact of globalization on Africa, the other with a brief sketch of some important, related topics.

Before beginning our analysis, there are two more preliminary notes: Discussions of policy, especially those from the international economic institutions (the World Bank and the IMF) typically talk about "good policies" and "good institutions." The failure to have good policies and institutions is usually given center stage in the explanations of Africa's failures. But the global financial crisis has shed new light on these long-standing platitudes: Before the crisis, defining a "good" institution or a "good" policy may have been difficult, but if asked to give an example, a common response would have been to cite those of the US as exemplary—though, to be sure, its persistent deficits would have meant that it would not be given an A+. Indeed, during the East Asia crisis, the countries of that region were told to adopt American-style capitalism, with its bankruptcy, corporate governance, and financial regulations. Now, most observers would have to admit that there were major deficiencies in both US policies and institutions. Critical institutions—including its central bank—were captured by special interests. The policies adopted—and which were advocated by the international financial institutions and many government agencies, most notably the US Treasury— contributed to creating the crisis and its rapid spread around the world. The faith in independent central banks has come under attack because of their lack of transparency and deficiencies in the ways in which some key officers are chosen in the case the US resulting in disturbing conflicts of interest; the system of self-regulation is a model of what should not be done. The lesson here is that we should be less confident in what we mean by good policies and institutions; we should be even more modest in our belief that exactly replicating institutions and policies that may have worked in one context will be as successful in another.

The second observation is that neither the recent growth rates nor the changes in economic fundamentals and structures in Africa that have accompanied this higher growth are adequate in relation to both what is needed and what has been achieved in successful cases, including the African star, Botswana. And Africa remains too dependent on what happens outside of its borders, as the recent slowdown resulting from the global financial crisis illustrates.

This book suggests a set of policy reforms that we believe may be able to meet these higher ambitions. It is based on the notion that long-term success rests on societies' "learning"—new technologies, new ways of doing business, new ways of managing the economy, new ways of dealing with other economies. The "old" policies (which we glibly refer to as Washington Consensus policies, described at greater length below) focused on improving economic efficiency *within a static framework*. But the essence of development is dynamic. What matters, for instance, is not comparative advantage as of today, but dynamic comparative advantage. If South Korea had focused on its static comparative advantage, it would arguably still be a country of rice farmers.

We also argue that we need to think about governance in a way that is markedly different from how it has been thought about in the past. Successful development requires that the state play an important role. Failed or failing states with dysfunctional and egregiously corrupt governments obviously cannot do that. But much of the discussion on governance has focused on restricting and restraining the state, rather than strengthening and enabling it to perform the roles it needs to perform as a catalyst for growth and development.

These are the two simple but powerful messages of this book.

A disappointing record

On average, in most African countries, per capita income in 2000 was not much above that of 1960 and lower than that of 1975. Even with the improved growth performance of the region after 1995, at the onset of the Great Recession, on average per capita income had barely reached the level of the early 1970s. (See figures 1.1–1.4 at the end of this section. Other features of this disappointing performance are noted below.) But the reasonable average annual growth of around 5 percent that was achieved during 1960–75, and the acceleration of growth in the past decade or so to roughly that level once again, shows that Africa is not doomed to the economic stagnation or decline that characterized the quarter century or so that these periods of reasonable growth bookend. This is the more so, given the ample scope for improving policies, as suggested by the papers in this volume. The case that growth can be substantially increased is made more compelling, not only by the modesty of the growth itself—even the accelerated growth of 1995–2005 remains below the rates achieved during 1960–80 or 1965–75—but also by the scope for structural improvements, notably the lack of economic or export diversification (see below).

Indeed, the share of manufacturing has been generally declining steadily since 1980 (as has employment in the formal sector): At 12.9 percent on average, the share of manufacturing in GDP in 2009 was actually lower than the 17.5 percent reached in 1965.[8] There has also been little success in exporting manufactures and in attracting foreign direct investment (FDI) in non-extractive industries. Much of the growth of the past decade or so is accounted for by extractive activities in non-renewable resources—metals, minerals, and, above all, oil. Such growth won't be sustainable, if all or most of the income generated by using non-renewable resources is consumed or wasted rather than used to create productive assets. Yields in agriculture have also stagnated, and this has had important adverse implications for the reduction of poverty. But the stagnation in agriculture is not a surprise, given the low levels of investment. The level of irrigation remains far below that of Asia: Only 4 percent of arable and permanent cropland, compared with 39 percent in South Asia and 29 percent in East Asia. Related: Fertilizer use of 13 kilograms per hectare in Africa contrasts with 90 kilograms in South Asia and 190 kilograms in East Asia.[9] Africa is still to benefit from a "green revolution."

Whilst it is difficult to directly measure learning and the acquisition of technology[10]—which we argue is central to sustained growth—these trends suggest that there has been precious little of that. Moreover, the global crisis that broke out in 2008 highlights the vulnerabilities of commodity-dependent African economies and the importance of breaking out of the "structural stagnation" of Africa.

There are, of course, a myriad of country-specific factors that affect economic performance. Learning lessons of success and failure involves not merely documenting and interpreting policy lessons but also adapting them to particular country contexts. This is as true in Africa as it is in East Asia, where the mix of policies varied considerably across countries and over time (as emphasized, for example, in the contributions by Hanatani and Watanabe and by Ohno and Ohno). There are controversies in interpreting lessons and on the need to reform the reforms.

There is, for instance, a broad consensus that some of the policies pursued by many African states contributed to the problems facing them by the late 1970s or early 1980s: Highly overvalued exchange rates, macroeconomic instability, irrational and extreme protection, un- or counterproductive rent-seeking, bloated bureaucracies and public sectors, and dysfunctional financial sectors. Frequently, extensive and excessive interventions were undertaken without regard for the capacity to design and implement them effectively.

To the extent that the Africa version of the Washington Consensus served to highlight these deficiencies and tilt the balance toward the market, it served a useful purpose. But it went too far in the other direction. From a neglect of government failure, the policy pendulum swung to the other extreme of neglect of market failure. As discussed further (especially in the fifth section below), neither economic theory nor history provide a case for unfettered markets. When government programs were cut back, markets often did not arise to fill the gaps; when regulations were stripped, market performance often did not improve in the ways predicted. In many cases, welfare was reduced, growth impeded, and poverty increased.

Global experience: The cases and ingredients of success

Africa's poor performance is especially disturbing when seen in a global perspective. The period of African stagnation corresponded to a period of rapid growth in East Asia. The causes of that growth have been the subject of extensive discussion, including the aforementioned World Bank study, *The East Asian Miracle*.

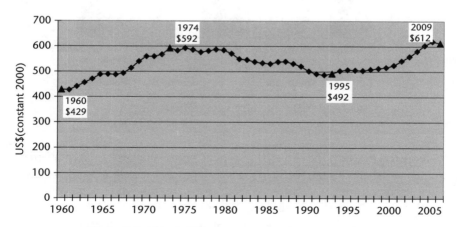

Figure 1.1 Africa* GDP per capita trend
*Referring to Sub-Saharan Africa
Source: World Bank, World Development Indicators database

9

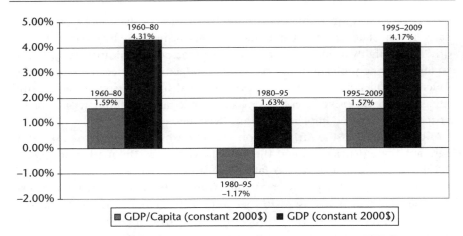

Figure 1.2 Africa* GDP and GDP per capita annual growth rates
*Referring to Sub-Saharan Africa
Source: World Bank, World Development Indicators database

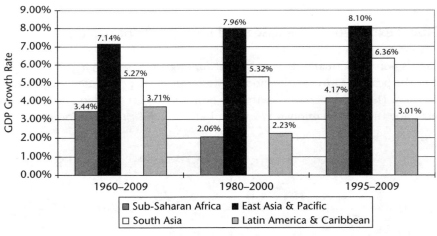

Figure 1.3 GDP annual growth regional comparison
Source: World Bank, World Development Indicators database

A more recent study, the Growth or Spence Commission (as it is often referred to and that we label GSC) has revisited the issues on a global scale and seeks to extract policy lessons from the experience of thirteen countries that achieved annual growth rates of 7 percent or more for at least twenty-five years.[11]

The countries and their periods of sustained growth at the rates that GSC concerns itself with are as follows: Botswana 1960–2005; Brazil 1950–80; China 1961–2005; Hong Kong 1960–97; Indonesia 1966–97; Malaysia 1967–97; Japan

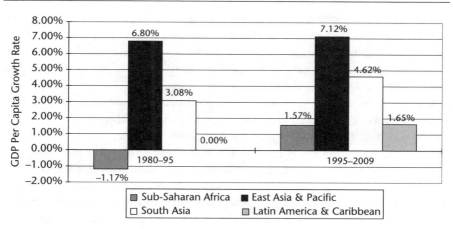

Figure 1.4 GDP per capita annual growth rates: regional comparisons
Source: World Bank, World Development Indicators database

1950–83; S. Korea 1960–2001; Malta 1963–94; Oman 1960–99; Singapore 1967–2002; Taiwan 1965–2002; and Thailand 1960–97. Nine of these thirteen countries are East Asian. Of the remaining four, only one is of significant size (Brazil), only one is African (Botswana), and two are in distinct circumstances: One is on the border of Europe and tiny (Malta), the other an oil sheikdom (Oman). In its own words, the Report "is about sustained, high growth of this kind: its causes, consequences and internal dynamics."[12] In a sense, the Spence Commission reinforced the motivation of the African Task Force: Were there lessons from that experience (or more accurately, those experiences) that were applicable to Africa, with appropriate adaptation?

The Commission's analysis is wide-ranging, highly nuanced, eclectic, and context-sensitive in a very marked and possibly deliberate contrast to the oversimplified certainties of the Washington Consensus (see the discussion below). Its broad canvass and the diversity and distinction of its membership[13] are amongst its virtues but they do inevitably tend toward "two-handedness." Nonetheless, it also has some clear and potentially strong messages; perhaps the central one being the context-specificity of what constitutes good and bad policies (though it does identify some that are *always* good or bad without sacrificing much of its non-dogmatic character). Its unorthodoxy even goes so far as not rejecting outright the case for industrial policy in all circumstances.

GSC notes the diversity of the experiences of the thirteen countries, but adds that "A close look at the 13 cases reveals five striking points of resemblance: 1) They fully exploited the world economy; 2) They maintained macroeconomic stability; 3) They mustered high rates of savings and investment; 4) They let markets allocate resources; 5) They had committed, credible, and capable governments."[14] The markets that it speaks of, though, were not unfettered and GSC adds

11

that aside from Hong Kong, "Other governments in our list were more hands-on, intervening with tax breaks, subsidized credit, directed lending, and other such measures. These interventions may have helped them to discover their comparative advantage . . . But they did not defy their comparative advantage . . . This process of 'self-discovery' may have been helped along by the government's hand."[15]

These can also be said to be among the lessons of *The East Asian Miracle*. In a sense, the Spence Commission reinforced the findings of the earlier study—not surprising given the dominance of the East Asian countries among the success cases.[16] The GSC, though, is refreshingly free of the encumbrance of trying to make its analysis conform to institutional positions, something the final version of *The East Asian Miracle* study tries to do.[17] Adding Brazil and Botswana enhances, of course, the importance of the perspective advanced in this book, one which we refer to as *the developmentalist state*, which takes an active role in promoting development. In both of these countries, governments played a central role in promoting growth. Brazil adds one important wrinkle: It pursued what was essentially an import-substitution policy, as opposed to export-led growth (though it did not neglect exports), during the period of rapid growth that the GSC focuses on. (There is one other way in which Brazil changes the picture presented in *The East Asian Miracle*. That book emphasized the importance of education and equality. Through most of this period, Brazil performed relatively poorly on both counts; more recently, it has performed better on both.) What is essential is "learning"; and an appropriately designed import-substitution policy can be the basis of technological advances and export diversification, as Brazil has repeatedly shown. (The Spence Commission seems to implicitly disagree with the Washington Consensus view of Latin America's "lost decade": that it was the inevitable result of flawed import substitution policies. As Stiglitz,[18] Rodrik,[19] and Ocampo[20] have argued elsewhere, it was mainly the result of the macroeconomic disturbance brought to Latin America by US monetary policies, sometimes referred to as the "Volcker shock."[21])

Botswana brings to the fore another lesson of especial importance to Africa: Natural resources do not have to be a curse. If appropriately managed, they can be a blessing. But the fact that there are so few natural-resource-rich countries on the list of success cases is a reminder of how difficult that is.[22]

On the list of policies leading to sustained growth, a few strategies are notably absent. The "expanded" Washington Consensus policies (expanded beyond the list of prescriptions formulated for Latin America in Williamson's original paper defining the Washington Consensus[23]) did not include capital and financial market liberalization—something that most of the success cases treated with caution; and it did not include clear systems of property rights—how could it, when among the most successful cases was China, where property rights are just now becoming more precisely defined. Indeed, contrary to the "property rights school," several of the success cases began with large land reforms. But while property rights may not play the pivotal role that Hernando DeSoto has suggested, deficiencies in the property rights system can be a hindrance to growth, and that may be the case in some African countries.

Finally, the Task Force discussions noted that there may be more agreement about what should be on the list of policies that contribute to growth than the specifics: Everybody can agree that good macroeconomic policy is not only desirable, but almost necessary. Growth is impossible with Zimbabwe's levels of runaway inflation. But, beyond avoiding such extremes, what constitutes "good" macroeconomic policy is a subject of intense debate. To many central bankers, it has meant focusing on keeping inflation rates low. While the fad among central bankers twenty-five years ago was monetarism, which has faded and been replaced by inflation targeting, many of the success cases took a very different tack. They realized that what mattered was the real economy—stability of growth as much as that of prices—and good monetary policy entailed having access to an adequate supply of capital. As Stiglitz et al. argue in *Stability with Growth*,[24] policies that tolerate low to moderate levels of inflation may actually lead to more stability of the real economy and higher rates of growth.

Interpreting the African experience

There are three strands of work that interpret Africa's experience that respectively focus on Africa's distinct circumstances (its geography or its natural resources); what has been done to Africa and the global environment in which it finds itself (changes in international prices, IMF programs); and its own policies (the failure of governance). This book takes the view that while geography may affect levels of per capita income, or even growth, geography is not destiny. So too failed states have played a role—but arguably they can be as much of a consequence as a cause, a consequence of low and falling or stagnant income and of policies that argued for a minimalist state. *At any rate what we are concerned with are the policy options for African states that have not failed and that have or can have reasonably adequate governance.*

The role of geography

An important strand of research has emphasized Africa's geography as an impediment to its growth. This is even echoed, albeit somewhat faintly, in the report of the Growth Spence Commission. The argument[25] is that landlocked countries are at a disadvantage because of a lack of access to global markets and trade, and that isolation is even more acute for mountainous countries. Tropical countries have the further problem of a disease burden. Every country begins life with advantages and disadvantages. We noted that many African countries have a rich endowment of resources, which on average has served as an impediment to growth. But that need not be the case, as landlocked Botswana shows so forcefully. By the same token, the example of Switzerland shows that landlocked mountainous countries can perform well. Nor is it likely that Mongolia would have grown more rapidly if this landlocked country had had a corridor to the sea.

Countries cannot, moreover, change their geography. The relevant question is: *Given their geography, what policies and institutions can best promote growth?* Indeed, in the light of the improvement in African growth performance since the late 1990s, with a number of landlocked countries recording annual growth rates of some 5 percent or so, there is the question of the significance of the whole geography debate.

The passion generated by the debate is reflected in one African participant being moved to comment that "in the '80s we were told to get our prices right; then we were told to get our policies right; then to get our institutions right; then to get our history right; and now we are being told to get our geography right but where on earth can we move Africa to?" The example of Ethiopia was cited, where the new, rapidly growing exports of flowers and leather goods are based around Addis Ababa rather than cities much nearer the coast, so that "geography doesn't even work within a country." Resource-poor, landlocked Ethiopia was attempting to emulate East Asia with some success, and its policymakers did not consider geography to be an insuperable or even all that important a barrier (Prime Minister Meles Zenawi and his economic adviser, Ato Newai Gebre-Ab, participated in two meetings, though not in their official capacities).

The position of the "geography-growth skeptics" is more precisely interpreted as follows. Geography is, of course important: It affects the availability of natural resources, transport costs, irrigation potential, infrastructure costs, disease burden, and so on. But geography is multidimensional, and simply focusing on one or the other element, such as being landlocked, is too simplistic. Geography may well provide an important explanation of why some countries are poorer than others. It may have even played a role in past growth or technical change. Indeed, there may well be some validity to the Jared Diamond view[26] that in the distant past, the East-West Axis and contiguous land mass of Eurasia facilitated trade and knowledge flows as compared with the North-South axis and physical barriers of Africa and the Americas.

But *so what* in terms of current policies and future growth potential? Are transport costs that important and measures to reduce them that difficult or expensive to implement? At worst, being landlocked means a somewhat higher requirement for investments for any given growth, as well as lower wages and land rents. It may well argue for aid donors to provide more assistance for investments to overcome such infrastructural barriers in landlocked countries, *ceteris paribus*. And once these "adjustments" are made, even if levels of income are lower, why should *growth* be lower? Indeed, if changes in technology that reduce transport costs will

Table 1.1 Africa: Average annual growth in real GDP per capita, 1961–2004 (percent)

	Mean (unweighted)	Median
Coastal Resource-Rich (9 countries)	0.86	0.86
Coastal Resource-Poor (15 countries)	0.88	0.70
Landlocked Resource-Rich (2 countries)	2.89	...
Landlocked Resource-Poor (14 countries)	0.79	0.76
All Coastal (24 countries)	0.87	1.33
All Landlocked (16 countries)	1.05	1.02

Source: Ndulu et al. (2008)

differentially benefit geographically disadvantaged countries, that will allow them to have growth rates that are higher than average.

The danger of an excessive focus on geography is that (a) it distracts attention away from the policies and institutions needed to realize a country's growth potential; and (b) it camouflages the past failings of policies and reform conditionalities inspired by the Washington Consensus.

The view that geography has, at most, limited relevance for determining growth would seem to be supported by the following estimates based on the data in the book by Benno Ndulu and his co-authors (see table 1.1).[27]

On the face of it, this particular cut at geography suggests that geography does not make much of a difference, or at least is not the *determining* factor. If anything, the most notable feature of these data is that the average growth rate of landlocked countries was significantly faster than that of coastal countries in Africa for 43 years! Amongst the subcategory of resource-poor countries, whilst the average growth rate for the landlocked ones is slightly lower than for the coastal ones, the median is higher. Of course, the hypothesis that geography is important maintains that *holding everything else constant,* countries with "adverse" geographies perform worse. Ndulu et al. use econometric techniques to conclude that geography plays a more important role than is suggested by this data.[28]

At any rate, no matter how, to what extent, and in what ways geography is important, it does not eliminate the need for development strategies or policies. Geography may pose special issues: What can such countries do to compensate for these disadvantages most effectively? There is ample scope for such societal choices to make a difference in the growth performance of African countries. The analysis and the policy options presented in this volume are just as applicable to landlocked countries as they are to others.

Africa in the global context

The second strand of explanations focuses on what has happened *to* Africa. At independence, it was left with little human or physical capital; the colonial experience arguably weakened its institutional and social capital. Some suggest that Botswana's success is not an accident: During the colonial period, it was bereft of resources, so benefited from benign neglect, which put it in a better position to grow when colonialism ended. In these interpretations, after independence, political colonialism was replaced by economic colonialism, as Western powers took resources, paying a fraction of what they were worth. The international economic institutions are alleged to have helped manage this new economic exploitation. Whatever the merit of such views, they are usually accompanied by another perspective. The development strategies foisted on Africa emphasized liberalization and privatization, as well as static comparative advantage with its corollary of reliance on natural resources whilst neglecting structural transformation. In this view, it is these policies that account for the de-industrialization of Africa, noted in the statistics in the previous section, and led to heavy dependence on commodity exports, which made the countries of Africa vulnerable to global commodity prices. When prices were weak, as they were in the 1980s, Africa performed poorly. When prices were strong, as they were in the middle of this decade, Africa performed well.

These development strategies also included an almost exclusive focus on primary education at the expense of higher education, which inhibited the region's ability to close the knowledge gap—as important as the resource gap in explaining the low level of per capita income. Adjustment programs often excessively limited public investment in a region that was suffering greatly from inadequate infrastructure. If East Asia's success was partly because of the role of the state in promoting development—the developmental state—structural adjustment policies weakened the state, and hence the ability of the state to perform these vital functions.

Governance

The third strand of explanations of Africa's growth experience focuses on governance and what Africa did to itself through flawed policies and weak institutions. It was perhaps not surprising that the adherents of the policies and conditionalities that failed would try to shift the blame for Africa's failure to grow to Africa itself. There is a general consensus today that the Washington Consensus policies have failed, not only in Africa, but around the world. As a package, they were neither necessary nor sufficient for growth;[29] and too often, even when they brought a modicum of growth, it was not inclusive with the benefits going to relatively few. One of the objectives of this book is to explain why, in the African context, these policies failed. Rather than enhancing long-term sustainable growth, they may have had just the opposite effect.

When it became increasingly apparent that the policies were failing, the adherents of neoliberalism or the Washington Consensus increasingly focused on "governance," or institutions. They had, of course, a hard time defining what was meant by good institutions.[30] They have an even harder time defining how one creates and maintains good institutions. As we explain below, the papers in this volume argue that the standard discussion of "good governance" is as misdirected as that of "good policies."

One contribution in this volume, in particular, offers a fundamentally different perspective from the dominant one that informs most of the chapters: The one by Augustin Fosu. His paper and the first of the two contributions by Mushtaq Khan make for a particularly interesting contrast. We included Augustin Fosu's contribution as one of the more thoughtful elaborations of the alternative to the dominant perspective in this volume. That, we believe, is the spirit in which scholarly debates should take place.

Analytic studies: Explaining variability and differences in growth performance

Whilst both on average and in most countries, performance in the areas of growth, structural change, and poverty reduction in Africa has been disappointing in the "lost" quarter century, the reversal of the trend of falling per capita income in the past decade or so has raised the question of whether this recent acceleration is mainly another turn in the familiar African cycle of boom and bust, reflecting trends in commodity prices and the international economy, or as some have argued, representing a belated vindication of the Washington Consensus or at any rate, its reformed version. The latter view implies that the dominant policy agenda does not need to be altered in any particularly radical manner. If there is a failure, it is because there has been an inadequate commitment to adopting Washington Consensus policies.

This volume contains several studies that try to parse out the relative roles of the various factors affecting African growth. The answers have strong policy implications. Augustin Fosu's contribution to this volume argues that growth is the result of policy reforms. His paper arose out of a major research project, "Explaining African Growth," of the Africa Economic Research Consortium (AERC).[31] The work places considerable emphasis not only on the role of geography but also on what the AERC project refers to as "syndromes" in the growth experience of African countries.

Noting the stop-go history of growth in Africa, one strand of the AERC growth project seeks to look at what explains the ending and beginning of growth episodes.[32]

The anti-growth syndrome is said to consist of some combination of (a) excessive regulation (e.g. the "bad old days" in Ghana and Tanzania); (b) inappropriate redistributive policies (e.g. once upon a time in Burundi); (c) suboptimal intertemporal allocation of natural resource rents (e.g. Nigeria); and (d) state failure (e.g. Zaire, Liberia). Avoiding this syndrome is deemed to be a "near necessary" condition for growth and "near sufficient" for preventing a growth collapse. And it was estimated to add two percentage points to per capita growth.

Whilst this analysis was of considerable interest, several commentators questioned its value in providing answers to how to get on the path of sustained, rapid growth. One comment was that what we need is a better understanding of how to get and stay on the path of rapid growth, whilst what the anti-growth syndrome showed was that "if you stop doing stupid things you could get an extra 2 percent growth." The "explanatory" variables, the components of the anti-growth syndrome, were themselves endogenous. A second critique emphasized the need to parse more carefully the different elements of the anti-growth syndrome. Many of the fastest growers in East Asia could be said to have at least some elements of the anti-growth syndrome, such as "excessive regulation" (unless "excessive regulation" is defined tautologically as regulation that adversely affects growth). Extensive regulation marked not only the original four East Asian "miracle" economies but also latecomers such as Malaysia, Thailand, and Indonesia. And perhaps this was the case even more so in the biggest and brightest growth star, China, and the other two great success stories of the past twenty-five years or so, India and Vietnam. The World Bank's business environment surveys, which focus on many aspects of the syndrome, consistently rate these countries poorly; China and India were ranked 91st and 115th, respectively, out of 155 countries in 2006. Moreover, in light of the global financial crisis, or even the East Asian crisis a decade earlier, insufficient regulation can be as much of a problem as too much regulation, so the issue is not so much whether regulation is excessive or not, but rather what constitutes an appropriate regulatory framework.

The other aspect of the AERC project that received a great deal of attention was the distinction it made among different African countries based on geography and resources. This strand of the AERC project is also reflected in the Ndulu et al. book referred to above.[33] It distinguished three groups of African countries: (a) resource-rich; (b) resource-poor landlocked; and (c) resource-scarce coastal. Each of them roughly accounts for about one third of Africa's population. For the first group, the central issue is said to be how to manage public expenditures and deal with the resource curse. The second group was said to be pretty much a distinctive African phenomenon with no particularly promising prospects. Their growth is especially dependent on their neighbors: they need to get their neighbors to get their act together. The third group was deemed to be the one with the option of attempting to emulate East Asia or pursuing "non-natural-resource-export-led" growth. While such taxonomies may be useful, they must be used with care. Ethiopia is among the landlocked resource-poor countries, and yet its growth in recent years—averaging about 11 percent during FY2003–9—has been among the most impressive in the world.

Two of the chapters in the recent anthology on Africa, edited by John Page and Delphin Go, support the view that policy reforms were central, though obviously high export prices helped: "The analysis confirms a trend break in the mid-1990s, identifying a growth acceleration that is due not only to favorable terms of trade and greater aid, but also to better policy.... As a result the likelihood of growth deceleration has declined significantly. Nonetheless, the sustainability of that growth is fragile, because economic fundamentals, such as savings, investment, productivity, and export diversification remain stagnant."[34]

The Go and Page analysis is an important contribution to the debate on the relative roles of endogenous (policy) and exogenous (commodity prices) factors in the acceleration of growth in the region, prior to the global crisis that broke out in 2009. The study focuses on the period 1975–2005 in identifying a break in the growth trend after 1995. It ascribes key importance to the policies; but the picture is likely to get muddier if one goes back to 1960 or 1965: 1960–75 was a period of reasonably good growth followed by a growth collapse in 1975–95, and then a resumption of fair growth after 1995. Over this longer period the story appears more complicated: The policies in the earlier period were "bad" (according to the standard classification) and yet growth was good. There are also more technical issues. In the shorter period of 1975–2005, there is a "trend break" in commodity prices corresponding to that in GDP, and that clouds the analysis.

In many countries, there have, of course, been important "improvements" in policies, notably with respect to macroeconomic stability and exchange rates. The two relevant policy questions are: (1) is the improvement in growth rates a result of the elimination of distortions caused by previous policies—implying a one-time gain—or the result of a policy environment that is more conducive to *sustained* faster growth (to the kind of learning that we focus on below); and (2) can the policies be further "bettered" (whatever that might mean)?

Suffice it to say that at this juncture, there is little consensus on these matters. The standard methodology used by economists for ascertaining quantitatively the relative importance of different factors has, itself, come under attack. Such studies look at the differences in performance (for instance, as measured by growth rates) in different countries and different periods and relate it to different "explanatory" factors. Critics focus on deficiencies in measurement both of the performance variables (GDP)[35] and the explanatory variables, the problem of causation (does trade cause growth or growth, trade?), the problem of simultaneity (the oil price shock of the 1970s lowered the real income of oil-importing countries and resulted in inflation), and the problem of "omitted variables" (some third factor explains why some countries responded to the oil price shock by allowing more inflation; it was not the inflation itself, but this omitted third factor which is to blame for the poor performance). Advocates of the methodology say that, notwithstanding these concerns, it is the best or "least-worst" way of sorting out the relative roles played by different factors.

The state and the market in theory and practice

Development policy has been the subject of intense debate over the past quarter century. As we have seen, policies advocated by one group are seen by its critics as actually hindering growth. There are many issues in this debate (e.g. what are good macroeconomic policies?). But one overriding issue is the role of the state. What has been variously termed as "market fundamentalism," "neoliberalism," or the Washington Consensus saw the government more often than not as an impediment to growth. Its advocates worked to limit its role, and to strengthen markets. In its almost exclusive focus on government failure, it neglected market failures.

Indeed, as we noted in the preface, the standard "neoclassical growth theory" that underlay these policy prescriptions argued that markets by themselves would lead incomes of poorer economies to converge toward that of the richer ones. The scarcity of capital in the poor countries will attract investment, to the point where differences in returns—and per capita output—are eliminated.

Both theory and evidence have not been kind to the neoliberal version of the Washington Consensus. The underlying model was based on assumptions of perfect information, perfect competition, and a full set of markets (perfect capital and risk markets). None of these assumptions are good even for a developed country; they are particularly ill suited for most developing countries. More to the point, research during the past three decades showed that the results of the analyses—including the policy implications—were not robust. Even a small amount of imperfect information had very large consequences for the functioning of markets. Markets are not even in general constrained Pareto-efficient. In practice, convergence remains the exception rather than the rule.[36]

Governments, of course, need to play some role in all markets—creating the rules of the game that allow markets to function, including a legal system that enforces property rights (appropriately defined), and contracts (appropriately circumscribed) that ensure competition and that regulate financial markets. East Asia's experience is similar to that of the countries that are now developed: The state has played a much more activist role than allowed by the neoliberal perspective.[37]

Advocates of the minimalist role for the state might agree on the *theoretical* importance of the government in dealing with externalities and providing public goods, but even these roles are often downplayed. (Coase, for instance, argued that these could be dealt with through bargaining arrangements.[38]) And the critics of government worry at least as much about government failure as about market failure; government interventions should, in their view, be exercised with great circumspection, and in general, the less the government does to hinder the "invisible hand" of the market the better.

We agree that, yes, governments can fail too, but a "minimalist" role for government does not follow. The right question to ask is what sort of intervention is appropriate in what context—for governments of particular capabilities and for markets characterized by particular failures—and what should be the priorities of governance reforms to enhance the ability of government to perform various roles.

In the neoclassical models underlying the policy analysis or conditionality that became so influential in Africa during the lost quarter century, there is no room for technology acquisition or learning since technology and knowledge are assumed to be exogenous and freely available to all economies; hence the structure of the economy is irrelevant: Whether an economy produces computer chips or potato chips does not matter.[39] But if an essential part of development is closing the "knowledge gap" that separates developed and less developed countries, then what countries produce or export matters a great deal. Different activities have differing learning and technology intensities and linkages with the rest of the economy. Learning and acquiring technology is central to "catching up." The externalities associated with learning and the public-good dimension of knowledge mean that the market will be inefficient: there will be too little investment in "learning," and especially learning with significant spillovers. The potential returns to state interventions to correct this inherent deficiency of markets can be and often have been extremely high.

Thus, while the post-1980 policies focused on ensuring that a country's resources were efficiently allocated—given a particular level of knowledge (and even here, the conclusions were also flawed because of the failure to take into account market imperfections), the impacts of economic structure on societal learning may be far more important, especially in the long run. Solow argued, for instance, that some seven eighths of all the increase in per capita output was the result of improvements in efficiency. There may be trade-offs between dynamic growth and static inefficiency. The Washington Consensus models were framed in such a way that the issue was never considered.

Given the pervasiveness and seriousness of market failures both in theory and in practice, the continued influence of the overly market-friendly orthodoxy in one of its many variants (emphasized, in particular, by the contributions of Wade, Mushtaq Khan, Meles Zenawi, and Jomo K. Sunderam and Rudiger von Arnim in this volume) is typically justified by the judgment that the risks and costs of government interventions to correct market failures, whether through restrictions (regulations) or through market-fortifying interventions (such as assistance in finance or technology) are greater than those of market failure.

The fact that the most successful countries have in fact used government intervention to increase growth implies that the conclusion that government failures inevitably trump market failures is simply wrong. Parsing out the extent to which advocates of market fundamentalism have had their judgments influenced by ideology and interests need not concern us. But we should note that it is not just policies of interventionism but also of "non-interventionism"—market liberalization, deregulation, and privatization—that are susceptible to the political economy of "capture":[40] In the end, governance rules.

At any rate, when government intervention makes matters worse than they otherwise would be and what constitutes an appropriate balance between the roles of the market and the state is contextual: It depends above all on the type and varieties of market failures to be addressed, the particular policy of intervention, and the institutional framework, especially pertaining to governance. In countries at early stages of development, both market and government failures tend to be more common and more serious than in more developed countries.[41] This suggests that there are both higher risks and rewards to correcting the errors of markets in such economies. Foregoing the rewards is hardly likely to be the answer to rapid development; rather, how to minimize the risks and maximize the rewards should be a central issue for policy design.

That this is an important lesson of history is one theme running through many of the essays in this volume. Another is that despite the recognition of its limitations and failures and attempts to curb some of its excesses, the Washington Consensus retains enormous influence. A radical overhaul of the policy options on the table and the perspectives that inform them is necessary if African countries are to have the option of achieving sustained rapid economic growth and associated structural transformation. Beginning such an overhaul was indeed one of the objectives of the IPD Africa Task Force.

As noted above, Africa's economic crisis did originally reflect, in large measure, mistaken policies that often went to the extreme of neglecting such fundamentals as a modicum of macroeconomic stability, avoidance of highly overvalued exchange rates, inappropriate and counterproductive interventions in markets, bloated public sectors, and disregard of government failure. In the end, "African socialism," in most of its variants, was also disappointing. It did not bring the hoped-for benefits. As pointed out previously, to the extent that the African variant of the Washington Consensus served to correct these deficiencies and tilt the balance toward the market, it served a useful role, but it went too far in the other direction. Worse still, it undermined important capacities of the state, weakening its ability to perform the roles that it must in early stages of development.[42]

Whatever the content or merit of specific policy measures, the sequencing, packaging, and speed with which they are introduced are crucial for their success. The reform packages that were imposed as conditionalities were also wanting on that critical dimension. In particular, they were prone to undertaking too many policy measures too quickly, overwhelming the capacity of the governments that were to implement them and of economic agents to absorb the signals and adding to uncertainty and to risk of investment. The 2008 global financial crisis underlined the importance of sequencing and packaging. Excessively rapid liberalization of finance without attention to regulatory reforms contributed in no small measure to the crisis.

Overly ambitious and poorly sequenced policy packages became all too common in Africa. Thus liberalizing interest rates in the absence or thinness of financial markets that could provide useful benchmarks often led to very high interest rates—often exceeding 15 percent in real terms—and they combined with the absence of long-term credit to dampen investment and overwhelm the effects of reforms aimed at improving the business climate. Similarly, the liberalization of agricultural prices typically was not accompanied by measures to increase the supply elasticity, measures such as provision of credit, improved seeds, fertilizer, and rural roads.

The dissatisfaction with the results of market fundamentalism and the ensuing debates are not, of course, confined to Africa. A new strand of literature was born out of the disappointing growth in many countries, especially in Africa and Latin America. We previously noted the earlier World Bank study on *The East Asian Miracle* (which itself was a slightly toned-down version of the background work by outside experts)[43] and the Growth/Spence Commission report. Another important contribution to this literature is the World Bank study, *Economic Growth in the 1990s: Learning from a Decade of Reforms.*[44]

However, the extent to which these studies are having an impact on the dominant policy discourse and practice, especially in IFIs, remains an open question. There is a risk that it might meet the same fate as the World Bank's study on the East Asian miracle,[45] whose implications for Africa were ignored in the policy prescriptions and conditionalities following its publication (see Chapter 8 by Robert Wade).

Other recent publications that have contributed to advancing the debate on policy options for sustained growth and structural transformation in Africa include the report of the Commission for Africa initiated by the UK government (also known as the Blair Commission;[46] three of its members participated in meetings of the Task Force) and a study by JICA on Asian lessons for Africa[47] (several of whose authors also participated in the Africa Task Force).

The Commission for Africa included a heavy representation of African policymakers and sought to mobilize increased aid, less conditionality, and an eclectic policy agenda in support of a more ambitious growth effort for Africa. The JICA report was prepared in the context of the Fourth Tokyo International Conference on Development (TICAD IV) in 2008, where there was also renewed interest in accelerating growth in Africa and the lessons for Africa from Asian experiences.

Our focus in this book is more narrow and selective, focusing on some key overarching issues for Africa's growth agenda, especially (1) the appropriate role of "industrial policy" (or more accurately, learning, industrial, and technology policies); and (2) governance.

23

The state and the market: Learning, industrial, and technology (LIT) policies as an option for Africa

In the fifty-odd years since Solow showed that the bulk of growth in advanced economies was accounted for by productivity increases, very little work has been done on learning, especially on how societies learn while in the process of developing and how that can be accelerated.[48] This neglect is in marked contrast to the attention given to allocation of resources; and the neglect is particularly significant in policy analyses.

The nexus of issues around learning, technology transfer, the infant industry and infant economy arguments, externalities associated with "discovery" of what can be produced competitively in a particular context[49] were all part of the rationale for state intervention designed to promote growth (as opposed to, for instance, state interventions to prevent adverse consequences of unfettered financial markets). Perhaps the neglect of learning reflects the fact that state-sponsored efforts to do so have been often related to or manifested in industrial policies, a term that has acquired a bad name, partly because industrial policies have become associated or equated with the "loser" policy of picking winners and of private rents without social rewards.

There are many dimensions to what is called "industrial policy" and it has taken markedly different forms in different countries. Learning, industrial, and technology (LIT) policies are not focused on picking winners or providing indiscriminate, unconditional, or everlasting rents. Rather, LIT policies focus on learning, especially by infant industries and economies; they focus on externalities and knowledge spillovers; they typically (especially in Asia) consist of promoting exports and the private sector. They apply not only to manufacturing, but also to other sectors, such as agriculture, and to modern services, such as information technology or finance. In most cases, such policies are the result of government action; occasionally, non-governmental actors, and in particular foundations and universities, have played a key role.

Arguably, virtually every country that had achieved substantial development used some variant of LIT policies, not only Japan and some other East Asian countries.[50] In the US such state interventions led to the development of the telegraph, the Internet, and such successful companies as Federal Express (which started with financing from a government-sponsored program of loans for small businesses).

Indeed, the green revolution in South Asia could also be said to be a prime example of LIT policy. (This highlights the broader meaning of industrial policies. While we prefer the terminology *LIT policies*, many of the authors use the older term.)

In Africa, there were also examples of accomplishments with LIT policies. Ethiopia has enjoyed significant success in promoting exports of leather goods, flowers, and sesame via instruments of industrial policy. The success in promoting leather is particularly noteworthy because it involved using policies that are highly controversial. The government banned exports of raw hides and skins[51] and took additional measures to encourage a supply response through a package of support, including access to term credit at reasonable interest rates, infrastructure, and the establishment of a leather institute to promote acquisition of technological capability and skills. The government is now seeking to reinforce early successes by promoting further value addition by moving up the chain from processed leather to footwear exports. Similar comprehensive packages of support had spurred rapid growth in the non-traditional exports of flowers. As a result of industrial policies, the share of "high-technology exports" in manufactured exports, though still tiny, had gone up from zero to 3 percent between 2000 and 2007.[52] Kenya too has had successful LIT policies, both in horticulture and tea,[53] and Mauritius in promoting manufactured exports.

Other African examples of LIT policies are discussed in other chapters in this volume. For instance, the South African government's efforts at LIT policies are the subject of Nimrod Zalk's paper.[54] Sen and te Velde discuss state-business relations, an important aspect of East Asia's successful industrial policies, in several African countries. (There is a simple rationale for this coordination: With market imperfections, prices do an imperfect job at "market coordination."[55] Other contributions in this volume that emphasize consultative mechanisms for exchange of information and coordination between the state and the private sector include the contributions of Oyeyinka and Sampath, Bailey, Lenihan and Singh, Ohno and Ohno, and Hanatani and Watanabe.)

What lessons can be learned from these experiences in Africa and East Asia? Under what circumstances or for what types of states, should what sort of LIT policies be put on the menu of policy options? What sort of "health warning" should they carry? How can one reduce the risks of picking losers? Is it better to focus on broad-based policies—promoting all exports through exchange rate policies—rather than particular sectors, let alone particular firms? Several aspects of Africa's distinctive situation, noted earlier, give particular salience to these issues. Is it possible, for instance, for Africa to reverse de-industrialization and increase employment opportunities in the industrial or formal sectors without some form of LIT policy? Indeed, can Africa narrow its agricultural productivity gap with other regions without an LIT policy for agriculture? These are the sorts of questions on which several of the papers in this collection aim to shed light.

Broadly speaking, the conclusion of these studies is that *Africa can benefit from appropriately designed LIT policies*. These contributions, whilst calling for care and caution, illuminate ways in which the high rewards of LIT policies can be reaped and the risks reduced in countries that have the requisite governance capabilities or the ability to acquire them. More targeted policies may yield better benefits, but risk greater abuse. (The critical issue of governance is discussed in the next section.) Even if the degree of success achieved in the best-performing, full-fledged East Asian developmental states such as Korea or Taiwan may be difficult to replicate, the policies may enhance African growth. For a whole range of countries have managed to benefit from such policies; there have been notable successes in quasi-developmental or developmentalist states, such as those in South and Southeast Asia, including the post-1980 "miracles" of China, India, and Vietnam. The question is, how can some African countries join this list of successes?

Market failures as a rationale for LIT policies

Among the keys to success are understanding the rationale for industrial policies, on the one hand, and the downside risks of industrial policy on the other. There are several "market failures," which explain why there is a role for government. It is widely recognized that when markets are incomplete, information is imperfect, and when there are externalities, markets may not work well. All of these factors are relevant for an economy in the process of "learning." First, as we have already noted, knowledge itself is a public good; restricting the use of knowledge introduces an inefficiency. The potential conflict between dynamic and static efficiency is illustrated by patents. Patents restrict the use of knowledge; even worse, they can give rise to monopoly power. We accept (even "encourage") these static inefficiencies because it is believed that they can give rise to "dynamic gains" by inducing firms to invest more in research. There are, of course controversies around patent policies centered on the best way of striking the trade-off. Neoliberal policies focused on the inefficiencies associated with, say, tariffs, without ever asking the question of whether there might be dynamic gains.

Even with patents, there is incomplete appropriability of the "learning" that occurs when a firm develops or introduces a new product in a country. There is thus an externality—an important externality that is at the center of development—and whenever there are such externalities, markets will not be efficient. But much of the learning that is associated with development is not patentable. A worker who is trained in the techniques of modern manufacturing can use this learning in another firm. A farm that discovers that the soil of the country is well suited for a particular crop for which there is a good market can easily be imitated. Indeed, matters can be even worse: If his "experiment" is successful, he will be imitated, to the point that profits may be driven down to zero; thus, he may face a no-win situation—if he is successful, entry will drive down profits; if he fails, he bears the loss. (See Hausmann and Rodrik 2003, and Hoff 1997 for the development of these ideas.[56])

The same is true for a bank that is trying to identify who is a good entrepreneur. If someone proves himself to be good, he will be poached away by rival lenders—or the threat of doing so will drive down the interest rates charged. But the bank may be limited (by risks of moral hazard—high interest rates can induce excessive risk-taking[57]) in the interest rates it can charge, so that it can't capture from good entrepreneurs enough returns to offset the losses from bad loans.[58]

In each of these cases, private returns are not commensurate with social returns.

The "infant capitalist" argument is of special significance for Africa, where the organized/formal private sector is not only sparse but also heavily dominated by ethnic minorities of relatively recent vintage and by foreign investors. On this view, there is much to be said for the creation or strengthening of a class of indigenous African entrepreneurs.[59] In this context, Malaysia's experience may well be of relevance.

LIT policy can be a powerful instrument for socializing the risks of private investment. Such risk amelioration—important because of the imperfections of markets for key risks, even in advanced industrial countries—played an important part in Asia and is particularly salient in early stages of development, when a nascent class of proto-capitalists must be nurtured or created. This risk socialization function may be even more important in Africa, which is said to have an inherent particularly high-risk environment because of its vulnerability to exogenous shocks of weather and commodity prices. Is there a case for paying systematic attention to socializing risks? If so, what are the implications? Does that bolster the case for stylized East-Asian-type interventions of the trade, industry, and finance variety? *Again, the answer provided in this collection of essays is broadly "yes," but not in all cases; they have to be carefully tailored to specific country contexts and the existence or creation of relevant governance capabilities.*

The critique of industrial policies

The neoliberal or Washington Consensus reforms have been particularly hostile to the sort of activist trade and other interventions that are the stuff of LIT policies and that were so widely used in East and South Asia. Whilst there is much to be said for doing away with irrational, highly distorted structures of protection that serve little purpose other then engendering rents to some privileged elites, LIT policies can be very effective in promoting technological change and encouraging shifts in production structures in agriculture, among other ways.

To be sure, while LIT policies have been at the center of sustained growth and successful development, there have been many failures. But failure is by no means unique or even distinctive to such policies. Bad design and poor implementation can trump policy in any area. There have also been, for example, many failed programs of stabilization, agricultural research and extension, and financial reforms. That does not mean we give up on macroeconomic stability or improvements in agricultural productivity and in finance. The point

27

is to learn lessons of both successes and failures in elaborating policy options and to examine how the risk–reward ratio can be improved.

Critiques of LIT policies focus on three issues: (1) learning doesn't require government intervention; (2) government intervention to promote learning distorts resources by creating rents; and (3) special interests capture industrial policies, so that in the end, they serve those interests rather than the general interests, and so that the distortions outweigh the benefits.

LIT policies are unnecessary

There has long been a discussion of government interventions to promote industries based on the "infant industry" argument.[60] A criticism of that argument is that a firm, knowing that it will be more productive in the future as a result of "learning" today, could borrow—financing today's losses with tomorrow's profits. But this argument fails if there are capital market imperfections—as there are, inevitably, given information imperfections.[61] But matters are even worse because of coordination failures and other externalities. Some of the learning of one firm spills over to others. Greenwald and Stiglitz argue that all economic policy should be shaped by how policies affect the ability of economies to learn. For instance, if some sector (say the industrial export sector) has greater capacity to learn technology from abroad, and some of the benefits of that learning spill over to the rest of the economy, then the government may wish to "distort" the economy toward the industrial sector. They refer to this as the infant economy argument for protection. By encouraging industrialization, growth can be enhanced as many examples, not just in East Asia, demonstrate. The static inefficiencies were more than offset by the dynamic gains (just as they are with well-designed patents).[62]

This discussion highlights the point that the interactions of market failures provide much of the impetus for these policies.

Creating rents

A recurring theme of the critics of interventionist trade policies aimed at promoting development is that they created rents. Some of the trade distortions failed to promote dynamic industries. Trade reforms in Africa often took away such distortions, but replaced them with nothing. The result was not an elimination of rents but their diversion to other less useful or "growth-unfriendly" forms such as kickbacks on government contracts. Moreover, rents are not exclusive to industrial policy or interventionism. Neoliberal reforms—and especially privatizations and concessions—also give rise to rents. The issue was not whether or not there were rents but how those rents are used or what activities they encourage; and what institutional arrangements minimized agency costs. Markets are not "technology-friendly" (for one thing technology is a public good) and rents are essential for the acquisition or development of technology.

A more nuanced policy would have asked: How does one prevent the associated rents from becoming a permanent subsidy to inefficient, uncompetitive enterprises that become addicted to the rents rather than growing up?

The political economy of LIT

The fact that LIT policies are associated with the creation of rents leads to the danger of "capture" by special interests who will seek out these rents for themselves, cloaking their argument in the language of industrial policy. Such a danger exists, of course, not just in developing countries but also countries such as the US where the subsidy to biofuels could be seen as an example of "capture." The trick is to combine carrots with sticks and to cut one's losses early rather than allowing permanent subsidies to inefficiencies. Being clear about the purposes and pitfalls of LIT policies is crucial, as is having the requisite governance capabilities.

Opponents of industrial policies argue, moreover, that while there is the downside of capture, there is no upside: Governments are unlikely to do a better job than the private sector in picking winners. But this way of putting the argument misses the point—the reason for government involvement is because of the externalities and other market failures. The case for government intervention is to support investment projects with large spillovers, which the private sector would not take into account in their investment decisions. (Wade makes a distinction between the state acting as a "leader" and trying to pick winners and as a "follower" that seeks to encourage nascent activities that have shown promise.) But clearly LIT policies have to be cognizant of the danger of lapsing into picking losers: the price of good economic management is eternal vigilance.

The risks of the absence of LIT policies

The consequences of abjuring any form or degree of LIT policy proved disappointing. They were reflected in the de-industrialization of Africa, manifested in the falling share of manufacturing in GDP that has been widespread over the past three decades or so. (Of course not all industry is desirable and the returns on investment in the sector may be negligible or even negative if value-added at world prices is minimal or negative.) Concomitantly, formal-sector employment has fallen as a share of total employment, often quite sharply in the face of rapid population and labor force growth (see the contribution of Azizur Rahman Khan).

Some success cases

These questions inform the discussion of "industrial policy" that is the center of attention of several of this volume's papers; Ohno and Ohno, as well as Hanatani and Watanabe aim to draw lessons from East Asia for Africa. They both emphasize the diversity of circumstances and LIT policies in East Asia and stress that there is no one-size-fits-all LIT policy.

A large part of the East Asian lesson is the method of policy formulation rather than specific measures. This style of policymaking is characterized by pragmatism and flexibility. As Ohno and Ohno note in such an approach, "the problem of weak policy capacity is overcome through focused hands-on endeavors to achieve concrete results, which we call *dynamic capacity development,* rather than trying to improve governance scores, generally vis-à-vis the global standard" (italics in original). This "dynamic capacity development" is akin to the "growth-enhancing governance" that we emphasize in the next section.

Bailey, Lenihan, and Singh underline the variety of LIT policies by extending the analysis of LIT policy to Ireland and arguing that that too has useful lessons for Africa. They remark that "Commonly adopted definitions of industrial policy are too narrow where the prime focus ... has been on subsidizing firms and [on] interventions with respect to particular sectors.... good-practice industrial policy is in fact much more 'holistic' in its approach and focuses *simultaneously* on both demand and supply side factors ... on microeconomics as well as macroeconomics" (italics in original).

The contribution of Sen and te Velde focuses on experience in several African countries with a vital element of LIT policy, state-business relations (SBR), and shows not only the possibilities but also successes that have resulted from such policy. More precisely, they find that there are a number of cases of varying degrees of success with establishing the sort of SBR that were so central to LIT policy success in East Asia and that these had a favorable impact on private investment and growth.

Nimrod Zalk's case study of LIT policy in South Africa makes a case for such policy, paying attention to both the pitfalls and potential of LIT policy. The essays by Wade and by Oyeyinka and Sampath also serve to highlight the possibilities and potential for success of LIT policies in low-income or "latecomer" countries in general, which is of special relevance for Africa. Oyeyinka and Sampath emphasize ways to strengthen institutional capacity for LIT policy, whilst Wade examines the ways that LIT policy can help with "catching up" in today's globalized world by making a case for open-economy LIT policy. Stein examines the African experience with one important tool of industrial policies, export-processing zones, that have had such success in some countries but have had only limited success in Africa. He attributes that to the fact that such economic zones in Africa have not been part of a broader LIT policy as they have in countries where the zones have been particularly successful.

Governance

A central question repeatedly raised with respect to the applicability of LIT policies that were so successful in East Asia to Africa is "governance." The lack or inadequacy of governance capabilities is held to be a major, if not the central, cause of the poor economic performance of Africa. By the same token, the problem of governance is said to preclude Africa from successfully emulating many of the interventions that proved so effective in other contexts, notably of the East Asian variety. Credible sunset clauses on rents are, it is argued, rare and difficult—beyond the governance capacity of most African countries.

This is one of the pivotal issues addressed in this volume; indeed it could be said to be at the heart of the constraints to and possibilities of economic growth and transformation in Africa. (Most of the papers in this volume touch, in one way or another, on governance. It is the focus of the contributions of Mushtaq Khan, Thandika Mkandawire, and Meles Zenawi. The nexus of governance and the state also feature significantly in the contributions of Fosu, Hanatani and Watanabe, Ohno and Ohno, Oyeyinka and Sampath, and Sen and te Velde.)

While the "governance" discussion is important—it is clearly one of the critical issues facing the countries of the subcontinent (and, in one form or another, virtually all countries around the world)—we argue that the "good governance" agenda as it has come to be defined and pursued in Africa has itself become a part of the problem. We propose a radically different approach—what Mushtaq Khan's paper refers to as "growth-enhancing" governance and which is closely allied with the call for a focus on "transformative" rather than "restraining" institutions in Thandika Mkandawire's contribution. We consider this to be necessary for Africa to achieve sustained, rapid, poverty-reducing growth.

Of course, corruption and lack of competence of state institutions can result in poor economic performance. However, the standard good governance package that has emerged confuses ends with means and, in as much as it is about means to development, it can be misleading and diversionary. There is no gainsaying that appropriately designed anti-corruption efforts, democracy, the rule of law, clear and credible property rights, and related elements of good governance are desirable in themselves. But such words often hide as much as they enlighten. As legal scholars have pointed out, there is more to the issue of property rights than the simplistic formula "defining clear and credible property rights" might suggest.[63] Often these "prescriptions" have been used to promote a particular view of which institutions are the most important for development and how they should be designed, a view that is embedded in neoliberalism and its excessive faith in markets.[64]

The first of the two contributions by Mushtaq Khan traces the roots of the good governance agenda and relates it to the wider literature on institutions and development. He finds a conflict between the conventional good governance agenda, which he calls "market-enhancing governance," and what should be the agenda from a developmental perspective: What he refers to as "growth-enhancing governance." He attributes the former as emanating from a particular methodology and view of history. This view is in fact profoundly ahistorical and conforms to the neoliberal take on the relative roles of the market and the state, e.g. by focusing on institutions that are deemed to be hindrances to markets performing in the way they are presumed to in neoliberalism (e.g. property rights) to the neglect of other forms of government interventions to improve on or substitute for markets (e.g. by solving coordination problems). The standard argument for the importance of good governance is based on a statistical relationship between a measure of governance and a measure of performance. Mushtaq Khan points out that if you take developed countries out of the econometric study of the relationship between growth and governance, as measured by the standard indicators, there is no meaningful statistical relationship between governance and growth. More particularly, countries can be divided into high-growth economies and low-growth economies; and within each category, there is no relationship between growth and governance.

The conventional governance agenda starts with the question, *why do markets fail?* The answer it gives is, *because of weak property rights, bad interventions, and high transaction costs.* Given the seeming obviousness of the desirability of, say, having good property rights, the question arises: *Why have so many countries failed to do what would seem to be in their interests?* The answer given is because of corruption and rent-seeking. And to solve this problem, it is suggested that you need sweeping reforms and democracy to ensure accountable governments.

These are all highly desirable ends in themselves and may well facilitate and in turn be an outcome of development, but they are neither necessary nor sufficient for development (and they beg the question of priorities). For developing countries, this may be welcome news, because this good governance agenda may not be feasible, especially in countries at an early stage of development. No country has ever implemented the current good governance agenda before embarking on development—not the now-developed countries nor the rapidly "catching-up" countries of Asia, a point emphasized by several of the contributions to this volume.

So what should developing countries be doing? The answer is that successful development requires governance reforms focused not on this particular good governance agenda, but on "growth-enhancing" governance. It will certainly entail *ex post* flexibility and dealing with constraints as they arise. This more pragmatic approach would focus on a small number of measures at each stage directed at the governance capabilities required for dealing with the critical market failures holding back growth in a specific context.

In some instances in the past, growth-enhancing governance even entailed the protection and creation of property rights for the productive groups in society, at the expense of undermining the rights of unproductive groups. This happened commonly in settler colonies, where not just the property rights but often the lives of "pre-capitalist" indigenous groups were eliminated. In today's world, such policies may neither be sustainable nor even feasible, without a level of oppression that would itself impair development.

Thandika Mkandawire's essay argues that in the African discourse, the importance of institutions had long been recognized but the particular form that "institutional reform" took was counterproductive. It was only after the "good policy" agenda of "getting prices right" had failed that the multilateral institutions and donors turned to the "institutional" agenda. This disappointment was attributed to the failure of "governance." The "new paradigm" defined institutions and approached institutional reforms in an excessively narrow way. There emerged a "one-size-fits-all" approach to institutions or what Mkandawire calls "institutional monocropping." This "monocropping" itself became part of the problem: The institutions focused on were not the appropriate ones; they had not been integral to the development of the rich countries and were not so for Africa. The emphasis had been almost exclusively on "restraining" institutions to the neglect of the "transformative" institutions that development requires.

At the same time, there were increasing expectations of governments and a mismatch between institutions and tasks: Governments deemed to be unable to intervene properly in markets are deemed to be capable of effectively implementing a highly demanding set of institutional reforms. Moreover, impractical and inappropriate institutional "imports" neglect to make use of and build on institutions that exist in a society—contrary to one of the lessons of East Asia for Africa.

Thandika Mkandawire and Mushtaq Khan's essays complement each other. They both worry that, the pursuit of overly ambitious and complex governance agendas risks making the pursuit of the best an enemy of the good. Khan and Mkandawire draw attention to and shed light on such questions as: What policies mitigate the developmental impact of corruption? Are there systematic ways of changing the way rents are accrued and shared in a manner that promotes or at least does not hinder growth? Are there ways of designing, for instance, systems of checks and balances, of monitoring, which reduce the scope for corruption? What governance capabilities need to be prioritized, when, and to what end?

The developmental state

The experiences in East Asia and elsewhere show that states can intervene with reasonable efficacy and can, for instance, influence the use of rents in the right direction. As we noted earlier, countries such as Indonesia, Malaysia, and Thailand did not have a developmental state with as much scope as that of Korea or Taiwan, but still succeeded in accomplishing rapid development. They intervened with a wide range of instruments. More complex was the "developmentalism" of South Asia: India, Pakistan, and Bangladesh at various points had achieved substantial success with developmentalist interventions, notably including the spread of the "green revolution."

The full-fledged developmental states of Korea and Taiwan did not emerge out of nowhere in a complete form. As several of the essays in this volume emphasize, the construction of the developmental state is a deliberate, messy, and complex affair. For example, Korea in the 1950s could be termed a highly incompetent, dysfunctional, and corrupt polity. Also, China could be thought of as having made a transition from an ideological, revolutionary state to a developmental one. And so could Vietnam. Being developmental or not is not a binary choice but there is a continuum, and states can aim to move up the chain rather than face the stark and impossible choice of being either developmental and able to intervene or non-developmental and confined to the minimalist roles assigned to them by neoliberalism.

The African development state

Mkandawire's and Khan's essays partly echo and also serve to lay the groundwork for Meles Zenawi's contribution and his call for the pursuit of a developmental state paradigm in Africa. That is in contrast to the neoliberal paradigm with its limited or "nightwatchman" state. If Africa is to catch up, it will need to go beyond this limited vision of the state. Whilst it is too early to declare success for Ethiopia's developmentalist strategy, there are positive signs as illustrated by the encouraging results of export growth and diversification aided by industrial policies; and by the fact that GDP growth exceeded 7 percent per annum during 2000–7, accelerating to 11.5 percent in 2006–8.

Ethiopia is not alone. African leaders and scholars have emphasized both the feasibility and desirability of a developmentalist state in Africa. In an earlier piece published elsewhere, Mkandawire comments, "most arguments raised on the impossibility of developmental states in Africa are not firmly founded either in African historical experience or in the trajectories of the more successful 'developmental states' elsewhere. Africa has had examples of countries whose ideological inclination was clearly 'developmentalist' and that pursued policies that produced fairly high rates of growth and significant social gains and accumulation of human capital in the post-colonial era."[65] Botswana's success is perhaps the most notable. A developmentalist state cannot, of course, be imposed from outside; it has to emerge from within the political economy of a country. Even in Ethiopia, the project of building one has had to contend with divisions amongst the political party in power.

The right questions to focus on are what sort of state is able to intervene and in what manner? What are the critical requirements of governance and how does one go about acquiring them? What are the requirements and prospects of moving toward a developmental state? How can the risks of government failure be mitigated—failures that might make matters worse than market failures? How can countries ensure that they do not repeat the errors of failed etatism of the past?

Whilst mistakes are unavoidable, it is important to emphasize the East Asian lesson of abandoning failures quickly; of constantly reviewing and modifying policies, as emphasized by several contributions to this volume, including those of Ohno and Ohno, of Hanatani and Watanabe, and of Bailey, Lenihan, and Singh who remark that the "key is to adapt and tailor policies holistically to [the] stage of development." At the very least, the options for an African government wishing and able to take the route to the developmental state paradigm and undertake the necessary governance reforms should be elaborated and put on the table, albeit with a warning about potential dangers.

The promise and possibilities in Africa are indicated by Sen and te Velde who conclude—in line with the case for a state that is "growth-enhancing" and "transformative"—that "our research shows that the creation and sustenance of effective state-business relations...may have a stronger impact on economic growth in Sub-Saharan Africa than the conventional measures of governance reform such as improvements in the rule of law and stronger anti-corruption measures that have been stressed in the literature and the policy debate."

Pro-poor growth and human capital

A developmental state is concerned not just with promoting growth for its own sake, but because it can enhance the well-being of its citizens, especially the poorest.[66] For Africa, increases in agricultural productivity have to be a central element of poverty reduction. Employment is another key issue, particularly in urban areas. In this volume, the paper by Azizur Rahman Khan notes that employment generation is perhaps the most important characteristic of pro-poor growth. Analysis of labor markets in Africa is hindered by paucity and indifferent quality of data. Nonetheless certain broad trends are fairly clear. Self-employment in family and subsistence activities hides unemployment, and low productivity in these activities means that the incidence of the working poor is very high in the region. In Africa, 55 percent of employed people earn less than PPP$1 a day, compared with 34 percent in the region with the next highest proportion, South Asia, and a range of 3–12 percent in other developing regions.

Whilst making employment in agriculture more productive and lucrative has to be an essential element of poverty-alleviating growth, it is unlikely that agriculture can provide reasonably high-productivity employment to perhaps even all the labor force already in the sector, let alone the additions to the labor force in the pipeline in the foreseeable future. This implies that reasonable progress in reducing poverty will require Africa to replicate what Azizur Rahman Khan labels as one of the most important lessons of East Asian development, viz. "rapid structural change leading to a transfer of labor from agriculture to industries and modern services by means of very high rates of growth of these sectors brought about by support for these sectors on a very broad front." Sustained, rapid growth and structural change then is particularly important for poverty reduction in Africa.

We have focused on some fundamental policy requirements for such outcomes in Africa. Azizur Rahman Khan notes several others, including the importance of public investment in providing infrastructure and human capital.

Critics of "pro-poor" growth worry that the focus on poverty will reduce the overall growth rate, and thus long-term prospects for poverty reduction. This raises the question of whether countries with particularly poor growth and essentially stagnant or falling per capita incomes, should focus first only on growth. Is that a challenging enough task without overburdening the agenda, one that also influences the pattern of growth to ensure that it is pro-poor?

The experience of East Asia suggests that simultaneously focusing on distribution may actually contribute to sustained growth. Indeed, one can ask whether some African countries can afford to neglect the issue of making growth pro-poor. "Shared growth" facilitates, and may even be essential, for political sustainability of reforms.

Indeed, in low-income African countries, rapid growth in the initial stages, unless based on natural resources, is almost necessarily pro-poor: It is not possible to have strong overall growth without healthy growth of agriculture and small-and-medium enterprises (SMEs), precisely where the jobs for the poor are. The distributional impact of growth in low-income Africa should be of central concern where it is fuelled by natural resources. In such countries, inequality cannot be justified as a necessary consequence of providing incentives. It is striking that, nonetheless, such countries are typically marked by high levels of inequality.

The objectives of making growth pro-poor and acquiring technological competence may conflict: Some technical change may even hurt the poor. Hence it is also important to have the impact on poverty as an element of LIT policies, e.g. in the case of Africa paying particular attention to LIT policies that increase agricultural productivity and employment and encourage labor-intensive industrialization (as in East Asia).

Another essential ingredient of making growth pro-poor is, of course, investment in the human capital of the poor. That health, education, fertility reduction, and poverty alleviation are a seamless web has gained widespread recognition since this nexus was emphasized in *The World Development Report 1980*,[67] the World Bank's first such report on poverty. Since then these issues have received much attention in the literature. *The World Development Report 1998*, focusing on knowledge in development, acknowledged that it was a great mistake to neglect post-primary education in Africa. Investment in human capital of the poor is vital both as an end and as a means.

The paper by Ansu and Tan looks at the issue of higher-level skills for growth. In Africa there is the anomaly of a shortage of high-level skills, even though the region is a significant exporter of these skills; moreover those who remain in their countries are often underutilized, with high rates of unemployment for those with higher education and many of those employed being engaged in activities other than those for which they were trained. A two-track approach to be pursued simultaneously is proposed. One is for quick results, utilizing those with higher education, and another is a longer-term effort at a systematic transformation of the education system.

A World Bank team working on this issue, looking at the experience of several East Asian countries, found much of relevance for Africa in adopting a short-term, quick-results strategy linked to attracting direct foreign investment in non-extractive activities. Singapore provides an example. The government invited India's Tata Industries to invest in Singapore and offered to subsidize or pay for much of the costs of training whilst Tata supplied the equipment and trainers. It also worked with the French and Japanese governments to establish an electronics training and a higher technology institute, respectively. Malaysia and Ireland were also examples of countries that had successfully pursued public-private partnerships and established and subsidized technical training for skills needed by the private sector. In Africa there are beginnings of this type of approach, e.g. in Ghana, Mozambique, and Nigeria. There are then the longer-term challenges of raising the quality of training and relating the supply of trained people to the demand for them.

International context

Africa's development, like that of so many developing countries, is greatly affected by globalization: Both flows of goods and services, capital, and labor, and ideas about how development should proceed. "Impact of Globalization and Liberalization on Africa" is the subject of a wide-ranging review by Jomo K. Sunderam and von Arnim. The issues raised included the problems of declining terms of trade for primary exporters (the Singer-Prebisch thesis), market access, capital outflows, debt, aid, and direct foreign investment. In their view, globalization and liberalization have not been nearly as beneficial to Africa as they could have been; indeed, it was not entirely clear that their impact on Africa had been positive.

There are two sets of questions: One is how to make the international system more Africa-friendly (e.g. by improving the quality and quantity of aid); the second is how Africa should respond to the changing global context.

A major change in the global economic scene in recent years has been the growth of China—now the world's second largest economy—and India. The global financial crisis accelerated a trend already under way. Deepak Nayyar examines the growing importance of China and India as aid and trade partners of Africa, and the implications for Africa of the rising importance of China and India in the world economy. On the trade front, there are both substantial challenges and opportunities; they are formidable competitors as well as large and growing markets. China has also become a major source of foreign assistance, and though Western governments have expressed unease about the seeming lack of concern over human rights and governance issues, China's commitment to non-intervention and its willingness to provide funds without the conditionalities that are typically imposed by Western donors has not only made such assistance particularly welcome, but in some instances, may have made it more effective.

Issues to be explored and concluding comments

A single volume, even one as wide ranging as this, cannot touch upon all of the issues that are of importance to transforming Africa and enhancing growth and poverty reduction. Particularly significant omissions concern (1) finance, (2) agriculture, (3) climate change, and (4) aid.

Sustained and reasonably rapid growth is hardly possible without businesses having adequate access to credit at reasonable real interest rates. The absence of such access to credit in Africa is in marked contrast to East Asia, and has been, arguably, one of the chief inhibitors of growth. In East Asia, governments took an active role in helping to create effective financial sectors. At critical stages in the development of the region, the government played a crucial role in allocation of finance—one of the main tools of LIT policy was access to finance, provided, for instance as a reward for success in exports. Governments often exercised financial restraint—limiting entry, controlling interest rates—though they did so carefully, ensuring positive real interest rates.[68]

In Africa, dysfunctional, decrepit financial sectors that were common in the pre-reform period have been the subject of protracted reforms since 1980. A high degree of financial repression, often with negative real interest rates, was not uncommon. Nor was the abuse of development finance and other state-owned financial institutions by the politically powerful. Invariably, the reforms have been mainly about liberalization, deregulation, and privatization of the financial sector. The results have been disappointing, though not surprising to those not wedded to the neoclassical models that assume perfect information and perfect markets.[69] Financial markets are especially prone to failure, particularly given the salience of information asymmetries and moral hazard in such markets.

The Washington Consensus reforms have often led to persistently high real interest rates (frequently in double digits), and huge spreads between deposit and lending rates, without a major improvement in access to credit and without significant increases in savings rates. The "reformed" financial sector was neither doing a good job of mobilizing savings nor of allocating them. Excess liquidity was common; high yields on government bonds reduced the banks' desire to supply term credit to businesses. The rural areas, by and large, remained starved of banking services. This has led to a revival of interest in the role of the state in the provision of credit: Is there a role for development banks or directed credit that played such a vital role in accelerating growth not only in East Asia, but also at different times in different countries of South Asia (e.g. Pakistan in the 1960s) and Latin America (e.g. Brazil in the 1950s and 1960s and again more recently)? How might the details of policy design guard against relapse into the bad old ways of state involvement in the financial sector in much of Africa and elsewhere?

As noted above, agriculture is vital not only for growth but also for making growth pro-poor. This is another area where the insights of the successful developmental states of East Asia may be of relevance to Africa: Many of the East Asian countries began their successful developmental efforts with land reform.

Climate change is already having a large impact on many parts of Africa. Ultimately the sustainability of rapid growth and poverty reduction will depend on how this issue is addressed. Given Africa's low income, widespread poverty, and small carbon footprint, any equitable sharing of the remaining carbon space ought not to constrain the region's growth. Moreover, substantial monies need to be provided by the international community to help Africa adapt to climate change, as recognized at the Copenhagen summit on climate change in 2009.

Many African countries are highly dependent on aid, but there is a controversy over whether such aid is growth-enhancing. Some worry about aid dependency. Others about excessive and inappropriate conditionality. But there is no gainsaying that an adequate response in Africa to the challenge of climate change will require considerable foreign assistance, both financial and technological. Strong growth in the future will require that the developed countries not only live up to their commitments to provide aid, but redesign aid in a way that better supports the countries' development strategies.

Concluding comments

At the time of the first meeting of the Africa Task Force at the Brooks World Poverty Institute in Manchester, the sense of the meeting was that whilst the recent revival of growth was welcome, it partly reflected the familiar African cycle of rising and falling growth, susceptible to changes in the external environment, particularly commodity exports and prices. That meeting concluded that there was little room for complacency: There were concerns about the sustainability of the higher growth path and that 5 percent was not nearly good enough, especially in light of continuing rapid population growth in the vicinity of 3 percent per annum. The last meeting of the Task Force prior to the publication of this book occurred after the global financial crisis,[70] and reaffirmed the Task Force's concern about sustainability: Africa had been badly hit, through no fault of its own. It appeared likely that the growth of the subcontinent's economy would be lower than that of its population in 2009. South Africa was especially badly hit, as GDP fell by some 2 percent.[71] The rebound since then provides cause for optimism.

Africa has been afflicted with low growth expectations—and these expectations may have contributed to the subcontinent's poor performance. The Task Force's emphasis on the need to break out of the "low growth expectations equilibrium" has received support from virtually every study of Africa's future. Africa should be aiming for growth in excess of 7 percent.[72] As we noted earlier, growth on this level will be necessary if the region is to achieve the Millennium Development Goals—aspirations that it is not on target to meet.[73] In light of the standards set by the successful developing countries in recent decades, including the African star, Botswana, such aspirations are not unreasonable. The recent improvement in growth in the years before the global financial crisis does not diminish the importance of the issue of enhancing sustained growth in Africa; and the impact of the global financial crisis has reemphasized the need to break out of its dependence on the export of natural resources.

It is our hope that this book illustrates how the experiences of the successful countries in other parts of the world may be of relevance to Africa as it seeks strategies for growth and poverty reduction that are more effective than those that have dominated in the past. There are no simple answers. We also hope that the outcome of that debate or ideas propounded and the policies recommended in this volume are not reduced to a formulaic fad. One of our messages is the importance of avoiding the sort of "absolutism" that previous strategies have been prone to. There is no policy package that fits all sizes.

Notes

1. Myrdal (1968).
2. World Bank (1993).
3. As Kwesi Botchwey has remarked, "John Williamson . . . has said that he did not intend for the policy prescriptions he called the Washington Consensus to become a definitive, exhaustive framework to be applied in all developing countries. But quick fixes have a universal appeal and brilliant summaries and intuitions tend to be turned into broader formulas—often over the protests of their inventors . . . so it was that in Sub-Saharan Africa . . . development strategies in the 1980s and 1990s were defined by structural adjustment programs based on the policies that came to be known as the Washington Consensus" (Botchwey 2005: 44).
4. See Stiglitz (2010a).
5. And the Task Force of the Initiative for Policy Dialogue, which organized the conference at which these papers were first presented (see the Preface).
6. The full-fledged development state refers to the state that governed the market—in Robert Wade's memorable phrase—extensively and refers to Korea, Taiwan, and Japan. Other countries have grown rapidly with a less stringent version of interventionism (e.g. Malaysia, Thailand, Brazil) and could be referred to as "developmentalist states."
7. These meetings benefited not only from the participation of the authors of the papers included here, other scholars, and staff of development agencies, but also from a number

of distinguished past and present African policymakers. One of them, Kwesi Botchwey, formerly finance minister of Ghana, is a co-chair of the Task Force.

8. World Bank's World Data Bank, which can be accessed on the World Bank's website: <http://www.worldbank.org>.

9. Refers to 2002, whilst in 2000 the area under cereals using improved varieties was 24 percent in Africa, 77 percent in South Asia, and 85 percent in East Asia. All these data are from World Bank (2007).

10. Total factor productivity growth (TFPG) is one indicator that could be used in principle, but in practice it is fraught with serious problems of data, especially in least developed countries, and is also sensitive to the specification of the production function. It is highly doubtful that reasonably reliable estimates of TFPG can be made in most, if any, African countries (with the possible exception of South Africa).

11. Whilst GSC devotes a chapter to country contexts, which looks at the implications of its analysis for Sub-Saharan Africa, small economies, and those rich in natural resources, it does so in a rather broad-brush manner (e.g. only seven pages on Africa), especially in comparison with its carefully detailed and nuanced general discussion of growth issues. The Report does not aim to fully engage directly with the growth debate in Africa; for example on the role of geography, it simply notes that many countries are landlocked, a muted suggestion that that is part of the reason for Africa's disappointing growth performance, but does not examine the issue in any detail (we examine this issue later). This reflects the fact that its focus is broad, ambitious, and general—or at any rate considerably more so than that of the Africa Task Force. The Commission's report is mindful of the dangers of excessive or excessively rapid capital account liberalization but does not pay much attention to other aspects of the financial sector (e.g. domestic financial restraint, directed credit, or the role of DFIs) (Commission on Growth and Development 2008).

12. Commission on Growth and Development (2008: 1).

13. In the GSC Report's own words: "It reflects the views of 19 well-known and experienced policy, government, and business leaders, mostly from the developing world, and two renowned economists" (p. 1).

14. Ibid., p. 21.

15. It is not clear what this means, of course, given that long-term comparative advantage is itself endogenous. See Stiglitz (2010b).

16. See also Stiglitz (1996).

17. The published report appears to try to make its analysis conform as much as possible to the then-prevailing orthodoxy in the World Bank by going to great lengths to emphasize the difficulties for other countries in emulating East-Asian-style interventions (they were deemed to be particularly daunting for Africa) and to downplay the role of some interventions. For example, it argues that industrial policy did not make much of a difference in East Asia.

18. Stiglitz (2003, 2006: 36).

19. Rodrik (1999: 75).

20. Ocampo's many relevant writings include Cárdenas (2000).

21. This refers to Paul Volcker's role, as Chairman of the US Federal Reserve Bank, in the sharp rise in interest rates in the US in the later part of the 1970s to fight inflation.

22. For a more extensive discussion of these issues, see Humphreys, Sachs, and Stiglitz (2007).

23. Williamson (1989).

24. Stiglitz et al. (2006).
25. This is discussed further below where we comment on the AERC research project that has spawned amongst other publications, Ndulu et al.(2008). See also Augustin Fosu's chapter in this volume and Sachs and Warner (1997).
26. Diamond (1997).
27. Ndulu et al. (2008).
28. Presumably, the "geography school" would have a similar explanation for why land-locked countries performed better than the coastal ones during the global recession in 2009. Alternatively, because such countries were not as globally integrated, they were less buffeted by the global storms. See Kasekende et al. (2010).
29. This also seems to us to be a clear implication of the Growth/Spence Commission Report (GSC) discussed above.
30. Before the crisis, if one had asked most IMF economists whether the central banks and regulatory agencies in the United States and Europe were good institutions, they would surely have said yes—so would many, if not the majority, of other economists. After-ward, as we have noted, it was clear that these institutions failed to effectively perform their central tasks. One of the explanations commonly put forward is that they were captured by financial interests. Capture is, of course, a mark of "failed" institutions.
31. Paul Collier, who also played a key role in this project, also made a presentation to the first meeting of the Task Force.
32. In addition to Augustin Fosu's chapter here, see also Fosu and O'Connell (2005).
33. Reproduced in summary form in the Commission on Growth and Development (2008: 74–5).
34. Go and Page (2008: 2–3).
35. See, for instance, the recent report of the International Commission on the Measurement of Economic Performance and Social Progress, appointed by President Sarkozy and published as Fitoussi et al. (2010).
36. See the contribution of Robert Wade in this volume. A more detailed discussion of the facts and implications of divergence in the world economy is found in Pritchett (1997).
37. See Chang (2002) and (2008). Chang also argues that even in the case of Britain's industrial revolution the role of government was much more extensive than allowed in the interpretation of history that makes it conform to the neoclassical or neoliberal view.
38. Coase (1960).
39. A quote, apocryphally attributed to Michael Boskin, Chairman of the Council of Economic Advisers under the first President Bush: "It does not make any difference whether a country makes computer chips or potato chips."
40. This is a common allegation of the root causes of the financial crisis that erupted in 2008; there is a consensus that there was too little regulation of derivatives and that the policy of not regulating derivatives was a result of political capture of regulatory agencies, the Administration, and legislative processes. In many countries, privatizations represented large transfers of wealth from the state to particular individuals, and helped create new oligarchs. See Stiglitz (2002).
41. Some might dispute this claim, looking at say, the contrast between the US and Asia in contributing to both the current economic crisis and to the recovery from it.

42. The orthodoxy did, on occasion, recognize market failures; but typically the market failures were blamed on government: *If governments would only get out of the way, markets would work as they were supposed to.* Thus, on this view, the absence of competitive middlemen in buying and selling agricultural products was seen to be the result of government marketing boards, which had "crowded out" the private sector. But when government marketing boards were abolished, the result often was that they were replaced by local monopolies; before, farmers were squeezed to help support the state, now they were squeezed, but by local mafias.

43. See, for instance, Stiglitz and Uy (1996).

44. World Bank (2005).

45. World Bank (1993).

46. Commission for Africa (2005).

47. Hanatani and Kuroki (2008); also see Kuroki and Hanatani (2008).

48. In the years immediately after Solow's classic study (Solow 1957), there were a number of studies analyzing "endogenous" determinants of the rate of technical progress and the allocation of resources to research and development. These include Kenneth J. Arrow (1962a, 1962b) and work by Uzawa, Shell, Nordhaus, Atkinson, and Stiglitz. In the late 1970s, there was a resurgence of interest in these topics, and in Schumpeterian innovation theory more generally, focusing on the integration of growth theory with the theory of industrial organization, with work of Mansfield; see, for example, Mansfield (1980), Stiglitz (1987), and Dasgupta and Stiglitz (1980a, 1980b). A second revival occurred with the work of Romer (1990). Much of this work, though, was focused on innovation in advanced industrial countries. The process of learning and adaptation facing developing countries remained relatively undeveloped (see, e.g. Sah and Stiglitz 1989).

49. The importance of "discovery" had been emphasized in particular in the works of Karla Hoff (1997) and of Ricardo Hausmann and Dani Rodrik (2003).

50. See, for example, Chang (2002).

51. It was noted that restrictions on exports of raw materials can be used to offset the disincentive effect on processing in developing countries on account of tariff escalation in developed countries, though it can't, of course, substitute for doing away with such tariff escalation.

52. These are defined as "High-technology exports are products with high R&D intensity, such as in aerospace, computers, pharmaceuticals, scientific instruments, and electrical machinery." World Bank, World Development Indicators database, April 2009.

53. Industrial promotion combined with agricultural extension worked very well in Kenya, as did the partnership between the public and private sectors. Smallholders were persuaded to grow tea, a long-term investment, by a combination of extension services and roads (public-sector actions), whilst the private sector took up tea processing and marketing activities. This started in the 1960s and blossomed in the 1970s.

54. Also relevant are the efforts of a private firm, South African Breweries—sometimes working with the government—which claims to adapt to and encourage production of local raw materials in countries it had invested in, according to a presentation at one Task Force meeting of a representative of the firm.

55. This market failure provides the rationale for the indicative planning that was much discussed in earlier decades.
56. See note 49 above.
57. See Stiglitz and Weiss (1981).
58. See Emran and Stiglitz (2009).
59. A lack of understanding of the depths of market imperfections may play an important role in some of the failures of industrial policies. Weakness or absence of critical support rather than culture or capture or governance accounted for some of the failures of industrial policy.
60. See Chang (2002).
61. See Stiglitz and Weiss (1981). For a related argument, see also Dasgupta and Stiglitz (1988).
62. See Greenwald and Stiglitz (2006).
63. The property rights agenda has been at the center of the work of Hernando DeSoto. For a critique of these views, see Kennedy (2003: 17–26) or Haldar and Stiglitz (forthcoming).
64. This is not to deny the vital importance of institutions; indeed it may well be that "institutions rule" as Rodrik et al. (2004) famously remarked. As Mkandawire reminds us, development economics from its inception in the early post-war years has emphasized the role of institutions.
65. Mkandawire (2001).
66. The issue of pro-poor growth received more attention in the discussions of the Task Force than it does in this volume.
67. World Bank (1980).
68. See Stiglitz and Uy (1996) and World Bank (1993).
69. See World Bank (1999).
70. The meeting took place in Pretoria, on July 9–10, 2009.
71. IMF (2009), World Economic Outlook, October 2009.
72. This is the sort of growth that the Growth/Spence Commission focuses on. The Commission for Africa speaks of growth targets of 7+ percent in the region.
73. UN Economic Commission for Africa and African Union Commission (2008): "The continent's average annual growth rate of approximately 5.8 percent still remains significantly lower than the 7 percent annual growth rate required to reduce poverty by half by 2015." "It shows that progress is being made in a number of areas such as primary enrolment, gender parity in primary education, malaria deaths, and representation of women in parliaments. If this rate of progress continues, the continent will be on course to meet a significant number of the MDGs by the target date. This will still be disappointing since the objective is to reach all the targets by 2015."

References

Arrow, K. J. (1962a). "The Economic Implications of Learning by Doing," *Review of Economic Studies*, 29: 155–73.
—— (1962b). "Competitive Stability under Weak Gross Substitutability: Nonlinear Price Adjustment and Adaptive Expectations," *International Economic Review*, 3 (2): 233–55.

Botchwey, K. (2005). "Changing Views and Approaches to Africa's Development," in T. Besley and R. Zagha (eds.), *Development Challenges in the 1990s: Leading Policymakers Speak From Experience*. Washington, DC: World Bank.

Cárdenas, E., Ocampo, J. A., and Thorp, R. (eds.) (2000). *An Economic History of Twentieth-Century Latin America, Volume 3: Industrialization and the State in Latin America: The Postwar Years*. New York: Palgrave Macmillan.

Chang, H.-J. (2002). *Kicking Away the Ladder: Development Strategy in Historical Perspective*. London: Anthem Press.

—— (2008). *Bad Samaritans: The Myth of Free Trade and the Secret History of Capitalism*. New York: Bloomsbury Press.

Coase, R. (1960). "The Problem of Social Cost," *The Journal of Law and Economics*, 3(October): 1–44.

Commission for Africa (2005). *Our Common Interest: Report of the Commission for Africa*, March, available at <http://www.commissionforafrica.org/english/report/introduction.html>.

Commission on Growth and Development (2008). *The Growth Report: Strategies for Sustained Growth and Inclusive Development*. Washington, DC: World Bank.

Dasgupta, P. and Stiglitz, J. E. (1980a). "Industrial Structure and the Nature of Innovative Activity," *Economic Journal*, 90 (358): 266–93.

—— (1980b). "Uncertainty, Industrial Structure and the Speed of R&D," *Bell Journal of Economics*, 11 (1): 1–28.

—— (1988). "Learning-by-Doing, Market Structure and Industrial and Trade Policies," *Oxford Economic Papers*, 40 (2): 246–68.

Diamond, J. (1997). *Guns, Germs, and Steel: The Fates of Human Societies*. New York: W. W. Norton.

Emran, M. S. and Stiglitz, J. E. (2009). "Financial Liberalization, Financial Restraint, and Entrepreneurial Development." Columbia University, New York, available at <http://www2.gsb.columbia.edu/faculty/jstiglitz/download/papers/2009_Financial_Liberalization.pdf>.

Fitoussi, J.-P., Sen, A., and Stiglitz, J. E. (2010). *Mismeasuring Our Lives: Why GDP Doesn't Add Up*. New York: New Press, also available at <http://www.stiglitz-sen-fitoussi.fr/en/index.htm>.

Fosu, A. K. and O'Connell, S. (2005). "Explaining African Economic Growth: The Role of Anti-Growth Syndromes." Africa Task Force, Institute for Policy Dialogue, Columbia University, New York, available at <http://www0.gsb.columbia.edu/ipd/pub/ABCDE_FosuOC_revised.pdf>.

Go, D. S. and Page, J. (eds.) (2008). *Africa at a Turning Point?* Washington, DC: World Bank.

Greenwald, B. and Stiglitz, J. E. (2006). "Helping Infant Economies Grow: Foundations of Trade Policies for Developing Countries," *American Economic Review*, 96 (2): 141–6.

Haldar, A. and Stiglitz, J. E. (forthcoming). "Analyzing Legal Formality and Informality: Lessons from the Land—Titling and Microcredit Programs," in D. Kennedy and J. E. Stiglitz (eds.), *Law and Economics with Chinese Characteristics: Institutions for Promoting Development in the 21st Century*. Oxford: Oxford University Press.

Hanatani, A. and Kuroki, M. (2008). "Asian Lessons for Africa and TICAD IV." Unpublished presentation at IPD Task Force on Africa in Addis Ababa, July 10–11.

Hausmann, R. and Rodrik, D. (2003). "Economic Development as Self-Discovery," *Journal of Development Economics* 72(2): 603–33.

Hoff, K. (1997). "Bayesian Learning in an Infant Industry Model," *Journal of International Economics*, 43: 409–36.

Humphreys, M., Sachs, J., and Stiglitz, J. E. (eds.) (2007). *Escaping the Resource Curse*. New York: Columbia University Press.

IMF (2009). *World Economic Outlook, October 2009*.

Kasekende, L., Brixiova, Z., and Ndikumana, L. (2010). "Africa: Africa's Counter-cyclical Responses to the Crisis," *Journal of Globalization and Development*, 1(1), article 16, available at <http://www.bepress.com/cgi/viewcontent.cgi?article=1048&context=jgd>.

Kennedy, D. (2003). "Laws and Developments," in A. Perry-Kessaris and J. Hatchard (eds.), *Law and Development: Facing Complexity in the 21st Century*. London: Cavendish.

Kuroki, M. and Hanatani, A. (2008). *Role of Government in Promoting Sustained and Accelerated Growth in Africa and Lessons from Asian Experiences*. JICA/JBIC International Workshop Report, available at <http://www.jica.or.id/english/publications/reports/study/topical/aid/aid_02.pdf>.

Mansfield, E. (1980). "Basic Research and Productivity Increase in Manufacturing," *American Economic Review*, 70 (5): 863–73.

Mkandawire, T. (2001). "Thinking about Developmental States in Africa," *Cambridge Journal of Economics*, 25 (3): 289–313.

Myrdal, G. (1968). *Asian Drama: An Inquiry into the Poverty of Nations*. New York: Twentieth Century Fund.

Ndulu, B. J. (2007). *Challenges of African Growth: Opportunities, Constraints, and Strategic Directions*. Washington, DC: World Bank.

Ndulu, B. J., O'Connell, S. A., Azam, J.-P., Bates, R. H., Fosu, A. K., Gunning, J. W., and Nijinkeu, D. (eds.) (2008). *The Political Economy of Economic Growth in Africa 1960–2000*. Cambridge: Cambridge University Press.

Pritchett, L. (1997). "Divergence, Big Time," *Journal of Economic Perspectives*, 11 (3): 3–17.

Rodrik, D. (1999). *The New Global Economy and Developing Countries: Making Openness Work*. Washington, DC: Overseas Development Council.

—— Subramanian, A., and Trebbi, F. (2004). "Institutions Rule: The Primacy of Institutions Over Geography and Integration in Economic Development," *Journal of Economic Growth*, 9 (2): 131–65.

Romer, P. (1990). "Endogenous Technological Change," *Journal of Political Economy*, October, 98 (5/2): S71–S102.

Sachs, J. D. and Warner, A. M. (1997). "Sources of Slow Growth in African Economies," *Journal of African Economies*, 6 (3): 335–76.

Sah, R. K. and Stiglitz, J. E. (1989). "Technological Learning, Social Learning and Technological Change," in *The Balance between Industry and Agriculture in Economic Development*, S. Chakravarty (ed.), MacMillan Press/IEA, pp. 285–298.

Solow, R. M. (1957). *Learning from "Learning by Doing": Lessons for Economic Growth*. Stanford: Stanford University Press.

Stiglitz, J. E. (1987a). "The Wage-Productivity Hypothesis: Its Economic Consequences and Policy Implications," in *Modern Developments in Public Finance*, Michael J. Boskin (ed.), Basil Blackwell, pp. 130–165.

—— (1987b). "On the Microeconomics of Technical Progress," in *Technology Generation in Latin American Manufacturing Industries*, Jorge M. Katz (ed.), MacMillan Press Ltd., pp. 56–77.

—— (1996). "Some Lessons from the East Asian Miracle," *World Bank Research Observer*, 11 (2): 151–77.

—— (2002). *Globalization and its Discontent*. New York: W. W. Norton.

—— (2003). "El rumbo de las reformas. Hacia una nueva agenda para América Latina," *Revista de la CEPAL*, 80 (August): 7–40.

—— (2006). *Making Globalization Work*. New York: W. W. Norton.

—— (2010a). *Freefall: America, Free Markets, and the Sinking of the World Economy*. New York: W. W. Norton.

—— (2010b). "Rethinking Development Economics," *World Bank Research Observer*, Published online, July 19, 2011, hard copy forthcoming.

—— Ocampo, J. A., Spiegel, S., Ffrench-Davis, R., and Nayyar, D. (2006). *Stability with Growth: Macroeconomics, Liberalization and Development*. Oxford: Oxford University Press.

—— and Uy, M. (1996). "Financial Markets, Public Policy, and the East Asian Miracle," *World Bank Research Observer*, 11 (2): 249–76.

—— and Weiss, A. (1981). "Credit Rationing in Markets with Imperfect Information," *American Economic Review*, 71 (3): 393–410.

United Nations Economic Commission for Africa and African Union Commission (2008). *Assessing Progress in Africa toward the Millennium Development Goals Report 2008*. New York: United Nations, available at <http://www.uneca.org/cfm/2008/docs/AssessingProgressin AfricaMDGs.pdf>.

Williamson, J. (1989). "What Washington Means by Policy Reform," in J. Williamson (ed.), *Latin American Adjustment: How Much has Happened*. Washington, DC: Institute for International Economics.

World Bank (1980). *World Development Report 1980, Volume 1*. New York: Oxford University Press.

—— (1993). *The East Asian Miracle: Economic Growth and Public Policy*, World Bank Policy Research Report. Oxford: Oxford University Press.

—— (1999). *World Bank Development Report 1998–99: Knowledge for Development*. Washington, DC: World Bank.

—— (2005). *Economic Growth in the 1990s: Learning from a Decade of Reforms*. Washington, DC: World Bank.

—— (2007). World Development Report 2008: Agriculture for Development. Washington, DC: World Bank.

Part II
Governance, Institutions, and the State

2

Governance and Growth: History, Ideology, and Methods of Proof

Mushtaq H. Khan

There is a broad consensus that sustaining growth in poor countries is a challenge not only because the right economic policies have to be identified but also because policies have to be supported by appropriate governance capabilities, which in poor countries are correspondingly weak. Weaknesses in governance have therefore received a great deal of attention in Africa and other poorly performing areas of the world. However, there is much less agreement about the specific governance capabilities that are required to trigger and sustain growth in countries at different levels of development and facing different development problems. This chapter points out ideological, methodological, and historical differences in the ways that governance is understood by making a distinction between the dominant liberal approach to governance, which we call "market-enhancing" governance (and which is generally referred to as good governance), and an alternative view of governance appropriate for developing countries that draws on the historical evidence of catching up. We describe the alternative approach as "growth-enhancing" governance.

The divide between these approaches is not just about the underlying economic theory and reading of history. Their differences touch on broader differences within economics and the social sciences about how relevant knowledge about social change and policy can be acquired and tested with data and historical knowledge. As such, the debate about governance also flags deeper differences within the social sciences that policymakers need to be aware of. Methods of research and testing of hypotheses are not "right" or "wrong" because it is very difficult to disprove the validity or otherwise of broad analytical methods. Instead, we can at least make policymakers aware of the differences between methods, the strengths and weaknesses of each, and allow them to assess the plausibility of competing explanations and their applicability and appropriateness for their particular context.

Governance refers to how state and society interact. Therefore questions about governance cannot be separated from broader questions about the economic role of the state in sustaining growth. Many of the dominant views on governance reform priorities for developing countries implicitly draw on a particular view of the role of the state that is based on a view of markets as largely able on their own to allocate resources and draw forth entrepreneurial capabilities that are necessary for sustaining economic development. This view argues that the appropriate governance capabilities to ensure growth and development should be market-supporting governance capabilities to maintain a rule of law, stable property rights, control corruption, and operate political institutions that ensure accountability through democratic processes.

This view, which we describe as the liberal "good governance" or "market-enhancing" approach draws heavily on contemporary advanced capitalist countries as models for the types of governance capabilities developing countries should be trying to achieve. Apart from the weakness of the underlying theoretical models, the empirical support for this view comes from a particular reading of the empirical and historical evidence that is partial and in many respects seriously misleading. The long-run correlation between the emergence of liberal market-enhancing institutions and prosperity is not in question. What is in question is the importance of these institutions as sufficient or even necessary conditions for supporting growth and development in poor countries at early stages of development. Here, the historical evidence on processes of change does not provide strong support for the good governance or market-enhancing view of governance priorities. This alone has important implications for the plausibility of the reform agenda that flows from it.

The good governance or market-enhancing governance approach is part of a much broader tradition within modern liberal economics that develops economic models from a minimal set of "plausible" first principles and then looks to cross-country or historical evidence using regression analysis on relatively large data sets to see if particular hypotheses are rejected or supported. This approach to evidence and proof does not work very well in any branch of economics because, if data have to be available for every country, we are limited to working with variables that have to be "coarsely" defined to give a value in every country. This is particularly problematic if an assessment of long historical processes is involved. If we have a presumption that history worked in a particular way, and if we keep looking at this type of coarse data, we will eventually find some way of working on the data or some bits of history that appear to fit. If enough economists start working with these models and the available data in the same way, soon the hypotheses take on the appearance of truth.

Alternative approaches to social understanding start from historical readings of processes of change and transformation in different countries and then attempt to build plausible theoretical models of historical change. An immediate advantage of the alternative approach is that while processes of social change may be broadly similar across countries, very different combinations and even types of variables may have provided solutions to similar problems in different countries. But this requires a demanding combination of historical, political, social, and economic knowledge. It also draws more heavily on case studies and comparisons of groups of countries using case studies. The plausibility of these theories is based on the plausibility of the historical analysis and comparisons of increasingly large numbers of case studies, but the nature of the data in these theories often precludes tests using cross-country regression analysis. It is important to point out that there is no consensus within economics or other social sciences about the relative merits of different methodologies. Nevertheless, it is important for us to be aware that the use of any particular methodological approach has advantages and disadvantages, particularly if each is likely to give different answers. In the end, it is up to each of us to decide which approach is more plausible and more likely to provide workable policies and approaches for the broader reform process in each country.

Thus, these alternative approaches to governance not only take a different position on theoretical aspects of how markets and states work, but often derive this analysis from different methods of reading the processes of economic transformation in developing countries. For instance, a historical method of looking at the emergence of market-enhancing governance capabilities in contemporary advanced countries soon shows that no country achieved significant "good governance" capabilities *before* they developed. Once persistent historical processes are identified we can begin to look for general theoretical reasons to explain why these patterns exist. It turns out that good governance capabilities are actually capabilities of delivering significantly expensive public goods and it is difficult if not impossible to achieve this to any significant degree in very poor economies with limited fiscal resources. Since some countries nevertheless developed, we have to conclude that good governance as it has been defined cannot plausibly be a precondition for development. Thus, the problem of looking at the cross-country data in an ahistorical way is that the dominant governance models miss more important questions about the *processes* through which market-enhancing governance itself developed. How did successful countries achieve better governance as described by good governance characteristics? Did they conjure up good governance before they developed and develop as a result? Or did they have other governance capabilities that allowed them to grow *and then* sequentially develop aspects of good governance as the growth process generated resources to pay for the public goods that good governance represents?

The case study evidence from the successful developers of the last century, which we have reviewed elsewhere, shows that the growth process is much better described by the second type of process (Khan 2000b, 2002, 2004a, 2005, 2006). Successful countries had critical "growth-promoting" governance capabilities that allowed them to sustain growth but these were very different from the capabilities identified by the dominant liberal good governance consensus. As they grew, characteristics described by the good governance model did indeed emerge, and did indeed assist their economic performance in some ways as they emerged. As a result, if we look at the cross-country data, we can indeed find "proof" that good governance is associated both with higher incomes and to a weaker extent, even with growth. But these correlations do not tell us how the successful countries actually achieved and sustained growth. They miss the critical process questions that would help us identify vital growth-enhancing governance capabilities. But these are the only questions of much interest for developing economies that want to know what they should be doing.

Instead of the broad public goods describing good governance, we find that successful countries instead had a more limited and specific set of capabilities and political arrangements that allowed their states to push accumulation, technology acquisition, resource allocation, and political stabilization in very difficult contexts using an array of pragmatic strategies that differed from country to country. Some of these developers were dramatically successful, others less so. Their governance capabilities and political arrangements also display considerable variation across countries. This variation and the absence of a blueprint has been a disadvantage for the historical approach because policy advisors from advanced countries have tried to protect developing countries from the possibility of making mistakes that come from the absence of hard guidelines. But the attempt to protect developing societies from the dangers of policy autonomy is not only deeply patronizing, it can be deeply damaging as well. Even if some states have made serious and costly mistakes in the past and even if there were such things as "right policies" known to more intelligent policymakers from other countries, societies cannot be put on sustainable growth paths by introducing the "right" policies and limiting the autonomy of their states to make variations.

Growth requires a continuous adaptation to changing economic and political circumstances and this most vital capability can be destroyed or prevented from developing by the assumption that policy autonomy is dangerous and developing countries need to be protected from too much autonomy on the part of their policymakers. Even the most ideological supporters of market economics will concede that within broad limits, sustaining growth requires a significant amount of policy autonomy to respond to crisis and challenge in creative ways. Indeed, crisis and challenge can be created by the operation of markets themselves, a fact that we are temporarily reminded of during deep global crises and then tend to forget very rapidly. More seriously, the historical reality is that the ability to act autonomously may be even more important at earlier stages of development because there is actually a much wider range of variation in successful strategies of social transformation than would be conceded by market-fundamentalist economists.

Sustaining growth and development requires nothing less than the transformation of pre-capitalist and largely agrarian societies into modern productive ones. These processes involve interlinked strategies of accumulation, technology acquisition, and the management of deeply conflictual processes of social and class transformation. Given that societies start with different political, social, and economic histories, it is hardly surprising that there is no blueprint of transformation that we can discern in actual history. The real irony is that in sanitizing the messiness of history, the sequence of reforms identified in the good governance strategy names a series of reform steps that were never actually successfully followed as reform priorities by any real country making the transition from poverty to development. The danger is that by setting the apparently plausible set of good governance capabilities as the priority policy goal for developing countries, policymakers may have set forth a task that they cannot possibly achieve.

The growth-enhancing approach to governance not only draws on a richer historical experience, but also is supported by a wide range of economic theory that shows that the state plays a fundamental transformational role in the transition to development (Stiglitz 1987, 1989a, 1989b, 2007; Khan 2004a, 2007a). This is partly because "market failures" are endemic in all economies, particularly in developing ones. The liberal economics approach assumes that most market failures are caused by bad states intervening in silly ways (and indeed examples of such interventions are easily found). Therefore the solution to market failures in the dominant view is to get the state out of the economy, and to focus on governance capabilities that allow markets to work better. But in reality there are many significant market failures that would still remain, particularly in developing countries where a reasonably effective market is difficult to construct for structural reasons to do with the cost of providing the vital governance-related public goods. In these contexts, successful development requires the identification of significant market failures (which may be different in different countries) and finding solutions that limit the risk of government failure. As the political and social conditions of countries determine the types of likely government failures, successful solutions are likely to vary across countries. The growth-enhancing governance agenda is about identifying significant market failures country by country, and developing the capabilities to respond to them in ways that limit the risk of government failures. Far from reducing the autonomy of states, this approach seeks to create strong capabilities (as much as is possible in each country) to discover and find solutions appropriate to their conditions.

The absence of blueprints is therefore a feature of the historical problem, not a weakness of the historical methodology. As the internal political histories and class structures of countries are different, as well as their economic problems, it is not surprising that there are no blueprints for successful growth-promoting governance. Nevertheless, even if blueprints are not available, the growth-enhancing governance analysis can give political leaders, state officials, emerging entrepreneurs, and representatives of other classes and groups in developing countries alternative sets of questions about the goals of governance in societies going through developmental transformations. Ultimately, societies have to devise their own political compromise and governance institutions that can pragmatically address their growth challenges as best as possible given their specific historical and political constraints. The policy *priority* for poor countries is not to measure themselves against good governance scores and attempt to improve these scores but to identify areas of governance that are most likely to make a difference to the growth challenges they face.

Governance and institutions

Economic development requires an appropriate framework of institutional rules to accelerate and sustain growth and achieve other social objectives. A framework of rules creates the incentives and opportunities that promote growth and social objectives as well as creating sanctions for behavior that is counterproductive. This much is widely recognized by policymakers in both developing and advanced countries. The question for poor developing countries is a more specific one. These countries uniformly suffer from weak governance capabilities, so in principle improvements along a wide variety of fronts could be called for. The specific problem is therefore to identify the most important rules and develop the appropriate governance capabilities for enforcing these rules.

A distinction immediately emerges between institutional rules that may be optimal in terms of economic theory or in terms of observations of how more advanced and successful countries operate and rules that can actually be enforced given the historical and political conditions of particular countries. When Douglass North (1990) defined institutions as rules, he was careful to point out that the existence of a formal rule meant little if it could not be enforced. The significance of this observation is often missed. Most developing countries have many rules that are very good rules on paper. In practice the reality is often very different. The discussion about governance priorities is therefore both about the particular *rules* that a developing country needs to enforce to accelerate growth and development, and also about the *governance capabilities* that need to be developed to enforce particular rules. If very ambitious public goods, such as a comprehensive rule of law, cannot be effectively enforced, then focusing on the enforcement of specific rules that are vital for economic performance, social justice, or political stability may be crucial.

The choice of rules and enforcement capabilities are closely related because if a particular set of rules cannot be enforced, focusing on those rules and governance capabilities may not be appropriate. The desirability of many rules that would work to make markets more efficient or contracts easier to enforce is often not in question. We may even find strong empirical support "proving" the importance of some of these institutions when we compare less developed with more developed countries. We may find that the rules under discussion not only exist in more advanced countries, but also work to make markets more efficient in the way theory suggests. But if it is implausible to enforce some of these rules in any effective way in a particular country, or to make sufficient improvements in governance capabilities that would improve the enforcement of these rules over a reasonable time frame, these rules may be inappropriate as policy priorities in a practical sense.

This may seem obvious but it is frequently ignored in policy discussions. Developing countries have often been criticized for attempting excessively ambitious interventionist programs in the past. Often the very same countries are now regularly urged to embark on massively ambitious programs of improving the rule of law, reducing corruption across the board, improving the accountability of government, and other equally ambitious "good governance" measures. These may all be desirable in their own right but they are unlikely to be achieved in the medium term to an extent that is likely to make a significant impact on the economic performance of the country. This does not mean that these reforms should not be pursued. Precisely because most of these reforms are desirable in their own right, they should indeed be pursued. But they cannot be the core of a growth-promoting strategy with immediate and intermediate objectives. Accelerating growth even in the medium term does require appropriate policies and institutions and these in turn require specific governance requirements if they are to be successfully implemented.

From this practical perspective, the design of a growth-promoting governance strategy must begin with a discussion of an economic growth strategy and its compatibility with the country's political economy, which determines its likelihood of implementation and enforcement. This suggests that the identification of the governance priorities for growth is likely to be an iterative process where the most promising growth strategies and complementary governance capabilities are simultaneously identified. Other things being equal, a growth strategy that is most likely to promote growth is one where the growth strategy has governance requirements that are likely to be delivered. As a practical question, we need to identify the critical governance requirements for particular growth strategies and make the achievement of these governance capabilities the priorities for governance reform.

Governance and growth

The ability to compete in global markets has rightly been identified as an essential condition for sustaining growth. However, it is often wrongly concluded that since competitiveness is critical, it is sufficient to introduce free markets and expose domestic producers to the competitive discipline of global markets. If free markets mean the adoption of policies that prevent domestic producers from getting assistance to achieve competitiveness in global markets, free markets may have very different effects on growth depending on the already pre-existing productive capabilities of the country. If domestic producers are far away from the global frontier of productivity, product quality, and price, free markets could lead to a collapse of domestic productive capacity rather than a rapid improvement in productivity. The possibility that free markets could lead to divergence rather than convergence was most powerfully experienced by many developing countries during their colonial histories when virtual free trade was accompanied in most cases by a growing divergence between themselves and the advanced countries.

For instance, from 1873 to 1947, Indian per capita income declined from around 25 percent of US per capita income to under 10 percent of the US level (Clark and Wolcott 2002). This happened during a period of virtual free trade, as India was only allowed minimal tariff protection, a period when there was relatively strong protection of the rights of foreign (British) investors and virtually no restrictions on the repatriation of capital and profit. The proximate cause of this relative decline was simply that it was not profitable to invest in higher-productivity manufacturing industries in India because of the low productivity of Indian workers, which was so low that even its low wages compared to the home country did not give India a competitive advantage for prospective British investors in most industries. This problem remains today for most sectors in most developing countries. Without any corrective assistance and strategies, the only areas that are likely to grow in a free-market economy are sectors which have already achieved international competitiveness. In most developing countries these are likely to be low technology and low value-added sectors in which the productivity gap with more advanced countries is likely to be low and the wage differential can more than compensate for this, giving the developing country a competitive advantage in these sectors. These are sectors like garment stitching, cut flowers, simple toy and shoe manufacturing, or simple food processing and packaging. In the poorest developing countries technological capabilities may be absent even for the simplest technologies to take off.

In theory, there are two broad types of policy responses to this problem, with different governance requirements. Both are responses to a common underlying problem that we need to first understand. Low productivity levels in a country may explain why investments in many areas are not *immediately* profitable but do not necessarily explain why investment to raise productivity in these sectors does not take place. If productivity can be raised through investment, and if wages are low, high profits are assured over time and this should typically pay for the additional time and risk involved in raising productivity. If this is not happening, we need to look at the *market failures* that may be preventing private investors from raising the underlying productivity at an acceptable level of risk. Many different market failures can prevent optimal levels of investment in late developers (Arrow 1962; Murphy et al. 1989; Stiglitz 1989b; Greenwald and Stiglitz 2006). A market failure that has recently received attention is that involved in financing "discovery" in developing countries (Hausmann and Rodrik 2003). The products in which a country may have competitive advantage are not known *ex ante* and require an investor to make investments to discover the underlying capabilities of the country. In many cases the investor will lose money, but investment can still be sustained if there are high profits for investors who strike it lucky. But if new entrants can easily enter the sectors that have been "discovered" they can bid up wages and raw material costs and wipe out the profits of the pioneers. The market failure is that it is not possible to protect the profits of the Schumpeterian investors in this case and the answer may be to provide carefully designed subsidies for start-up firms in such contexts. This market failure assumes that there are innate competitive advantages that some countries have because they are better at producing some low-technology products rather than others. Such innate advantages are not necessarily convincing for many types of products and processes.

Other market failures may be even more serious in preventing investment in new sectors in developing countries. We know that if it takes time to learn new technologies, even if a country has a *potential* comparative advantage in a product, it will not be immediately profitable (Khan 2000a). As a result, investors (whether private or public) will have to act as principals providing finance to firms, with managers and workers within these firms acting as agents undertaking the *learning*. Initially, the principals will be making a loss, but they expect to make a substantial profit eventually. In other words, learning, like innovation, requires some individuals to earn rents for a period; and like innovation, if these rents are mismanaged the outcome may be poor. The likelihood of success now depends on the effort the agents put in. In a world where contracts were perfectly enforced, investors could ensure that managers and workers receiving temporary rents will put in the optimal effort, and this would enable private investments to take place by making the risk involved acceptable. In reality, if contracts are difficult to enforce, it may be very difficult to enforce compulsions on firm-level agents. In these circumstances, private investors external to the firm may not be willing to take the risk of investing for productivity improvement. This is an example of a market failure that may condemn the developing country to low levels of investment in productivity-enhancing industries.

This brings us to the two types of responses to these problems of market failure constraining growth in developing countries. The first type is to respond to specific market failures with narrowly defined interventions that create incentives or compulsions to move the outcome closer to what a more efficient market may have achieved. For instance, subsidies to investors may help to compensate for the costs of discovery or the higher uncertainty they face as a result of unenforceable contracts. Indeed, this was the type of intervention that was very common in the 1950s and 1960s as developing countries attempted to reverse their performance under colonialism. This strategy was in the end disappointing in many developing countries because the range of market failures that policymakers tried to address were too broadly defined, and in most cases existing governance capabilities were not remotely sufficient to enforce the requirements for success with such a range of interventions. While there were some attempts to improve the governance capabilities required to effectively manage these interventions, these governance requirements were not sufficiently recognized at the time.

In the absence of a sufficient effort to develop these governance capabilities, interventions to correct market failures often resulted in poor outcomes in many countries. Figure 2.1 summarizes the relationship between corrections of market failures, rents, and therefore the possibility of government failures of various types. By definition, any social attempt to correct a market failure creates new income flows and therefore rents. Indeed, the rents are potentially the mechanisms through which new incentives and compulsions are created. But for these rents to have the appropriate effect, governance capabilities are required that can enforce, withdraw, or otherwise respond to the results. This does not mean that all rent-seeking has to be ruled out—an impossible goal in any economy (Khan 2000b). The governance requirement is more modest, namely that the

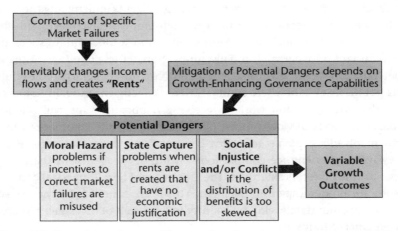

Figure 2.1 Growth requires specific growth-enhancing governance capabilities

rent-seeking does not disrupt the intervention to the extent that the net effect is low or negative. Many developing countries did not achieve this, and many rents that were created in the attempt to correct market failures were often wasted or captured by powerful groups that did not in the end deliver growth, or delivered insufficient growth.

Policies to correct specific market failures can result in a number of types of problems. First, there is a problem of moral hazard when policy creates some new benefits for some market participants but fails to achieve the desired policy goal. For instance, subsidies to assist training or making credit lines available to new start-up companies to overcome capital market failures may simply be wasted without achieving the desired result. For this not to happen, governance capabilities of oversight and policy withdrawal are required so that the rents are not permanent and may be withdrawn if results are not achieved. The more narrowly defined the policy, the more plausible it may be to develop the governance capability to administer the policy reasonably effectively. A second problem is that policymaking agencies of government may get captured by rent-seekers who may engineer solutions to market failures that do not really exist, simply to benefit from the rents created as a result. Limiting these possibilities requires governance capabilities and political arrangements to ensure that state capture cannot reach damaging proportions.

Finally, policy responses to market failures may be politically controversial because the solutions may benefit particular constituencies or groups. One market failure can be addressed by many different policy approaches with different distributions of benefits. For instance, environmental pollution can be addressed by taxing the emitter of pollution, by subsidizing the polluter not to emit, by regulatory limits on emissions, or by creating property rights on emissions so they become tradable. Each solution has different transaction costs and therefore chances of success; but more significantly, each has different distributions of benefits, even if the net social benefit of addressing the externality is the same in all solutions. What this suggests is that if in a particular solution the distribution of net benefits is excessively adverse for powerful or significant groups in society, or if they have significantly adverse welfare implications on marginal groups, then even if the policy enhances growth overall there may be resistance and opposition that in turn will have social costs in the form of conflict. Once again, success in solving specific market failures requires governance capabilities to ensure that the policies that are adopted do not have excessively damaging political consequences in that specific context. The growth outcomes, satisfactory or otherwise, thus depend both on the types of policies that seek to address market failures as well as on the governance capabilities that limit the possibility of government failures.

Instead of responding to this experience with the conclusion that perhaps the range of interventions needed to be scaled back in some of the less dynamic countries to target critical market failures, and that critical governance capabilities

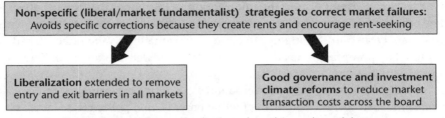

(But the relationship between liberalization and growth is complex partly because significant reductions in transaction costs through market-enhancing governance may not be possible)

Figure 2.2 The liberal/good governance approach

needed to be developed, the response from the late 1970s onwards was to persuade poorly performing developing countries to abandon all attempts to address their market failures through specific interventions. The new strategy was to address market failures by making markets more efficient across the board. The two prongs of the new "market-fundamentalist" strategy were to remove interventions (liberalization) combined with the development of governance capabilities that aimed to reduce market failures by making markets more efficient. This approach is summarized in Figure 2.2.

And so paradoxically liberal policymakers began to incorporate the importance of the state and of governance capabilities into the reform agenda. But it was explicitly understood that the governance capabilities to be developed or strengthened were the ones necessary for the creation of efficient markets, not the capacities required to address market failures. While we agree that the results of intervention in many developing countries in the 1960s were disappointing, we draw a different set of conclusions about policy priorities. Interventionist strategies in the 1960s and 1970s were disappointing in many developing countries because the market failures were not carefully identified, and the interventions were overambitious and not tailored to the feasible governance capabilities of particular countries. Yet these strategies did succeed dramatically in a few countries, which, for historic accidents, had the appropriate governance capabilities to enforce the strategies they had embarked on. The lesson we wish to learn from the history of our experiences with both the interventionist strategies of the 1960s and the more recent history of good governance reforms of the 1990s is that neither address the pressing problems of triggering and sustaining growth and development in poor countries. An alternative growth-promoting governance strategy is to promote sequential and specific governance improvements tailored to effectively implement limited strategies that aim to overcome specific growth constraints in developing countries. Such an incremental growth-promoting governance strategy is most important for the least developed countries, given their limited capacities for making significant progress in the medium term on ambitious generalized governance improvement strategies (Khan 2008a). This does not at all suggest that good governance reforms should be abandoned, but that the acceleration and sustaining of growth requires serious attention to an alternative set of governance goals.

Good governance: the theory

The consensus behind the good governance agenda draws heavily on a large body of theoretical contributions that are part of the New Institutional Economics that emerged in the 1980s (North 1984, 1990, 1995; Matthews 1986; Clague et al. 1997; Olson 1997; Bardhan 2000; Acemoglu et al. 2004). The main theoretical links identified in New Institutional Economics that explain economic stagnation are summarized in Figure 2.3.

The fundamental link in all market-focused approaches is link 1 in Figure 2.3: Economic stagnation and underdevelopment in poor countries is explained primarily by the persistence of inefficient markets. High transaction costs are simply a technical description of inefficient markets that suffer from extensive market failures. These high transaction costs are in turn explained by link 2: Weak and contested property rights and unnecessary state interventions raise the costs of transacting in markets and create uncertainty, which increases transaction costs. Unnecessary state interventions also create damaging rents that can signal lost economic opportunities. But link 3 shows that attempting to enforce property rights or to remove unnecessary government interventions will not work because

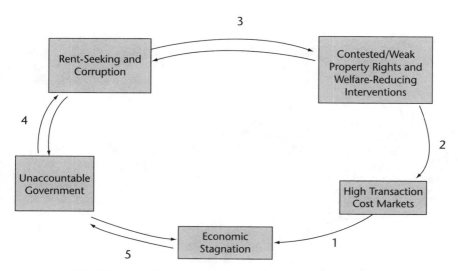

Figure 2.3 Theoretical linkages underpinning the good governance agenda

these in turn are sustained by rent-seeking and corruption, as privileged groups spend resources both legally and illegally to influence the state to distort property rights in their favor or create or distort interventions in their favor. There is a two-way causality here because weak property rights and welfare-reducing interventions also create incentives for rent-seeking and corruption, as individuals and groups try to work their way around these governance failures by bribing or influencing bureaucrats and politicians. Link 4 shows that rent-seeking and corruption in turn are sustained because, although very small groups of people benefit from these processes, the majority is unable to stop the damage these groups do because of the absence of accountable government. So to fight corruption and rent-seeking it is also necessary to reform politics and improve democratic accountability. Again, link 4 shows a two-way causality because rent-seeking and corruption can also be used to subvert democracy in favor of the interests of small groups.

During the time of the structural adjustment policies of the 1980s, the focus of reform was limited to link 2 in Figure 2.3. At that time the belief was that by removing unnecessary state interventions, the efficiency of markets would be enhanced. The expectation was that these reforms would suffice to make markets more efficient through link 1, as well as to reduce rent-seeking and corruption through link 3 in Figure 2.4, as these links operate in both directions. The new governance agenda adds to this the necessity of directly fighting corruption and rent-seeking, as well as pushing forward with accountability reforms. The new belief is that only by attacking all the links in Figure 2.3 simultaneously is it possible to break out of the low-level development trap that many poor countries find themselves in.

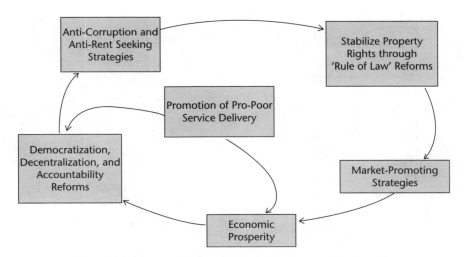

Figure 2.4 The good governance and anti-corruption agenda

The multipronged policy agenda enshrined in the new good governance agenda is summarized in Figure 2.4. The new agenda suggests that unless *all* the links in Figure 2.4 were simultaneously addressed, market efficiency would not improve. The logic was that property rights instability and welfare-reducing interventions could not be attacked unless rent-seeking and corruption were directly addressed, and in turn, these could not be significantly tackled unless the privileges of minorities engaged in rent-seeking and corruption that harmed the majority could be challenged through accountability and democratization. In addition, to promote democratic accountability, donors argued that states in poor countries should be encouraged to deliver services to the poor. Western donors, particularly in Africa, have taken the line that poor countries should prioritize pro-poor spending financed by aid where necessary, and the poor should be mobilized through democratic processes to ensure that the state effectively delivers these goods and services (such as primary education and health care). Though pro-poor service delivery directly tackles poverty, the broader case that is made for these reforms is that by empowering and raising the expectations of the majority (the poor), governments will become more accountable and this will feed into the broader governance reform agenda in the way shown in Figure 2.4.

At the same time, civil society groups in developing countries often support attempts to enforce these rules on the grounds that many are highly desirable goals regardless of their economic efficacy. And finally, the fiduciary responsibility of donor agencies to protect taxpayer-funded aid programs has driven donor concerns about corruption and the diversion of resources in developing countries. This too has provided support for anti-corruption strategies and for accountability reforms. The convergence of support from multiple constituencies who are at loggerheads on most other issues explains why support for this particular reform agenda is so deep-rooted and pervasive. Suggesting an alternative or even complementary governance agenda requires the construction of a new constituency that may be quite difficult to achieve compared to the broad constituency backing the good governance agenda.

A number of closely related measures of governance and approaches to reform have developed out of this framework, including the Doing Business surveys, Business Environment and Economic Performance surveys, and Productivity and Investment Climate surveys that are now produced by the World Bank and other agencies. These measure along different dimensions the degree to which states provide services that are consistent with market strategies. While there are differences between them, all of these measures fit in very well with the overall good governance agenda but look at micro-level indicators like the time it takes to get a telephone connection, the number of times a factory is visited by inspectors (the fewer the visits the better because inspections are assumed to create obstacles and provide opportunities for petty corruption), and business perceptions about the effectiveness of contract enforcement. What is common among all these measures is that there is no attempt to measure the success of a state in addressing market failures because it is assumed that any attempt to do so is itself counterproductive.

The evidence

Support for the market-enhancing approach comes from cross-country regressions using measures of relevant governance capabilities to explain growth, often based on subjective assessments collected in surveys and expert opinions. An extensive academic literature has used this data to establish a positive relationship between market-enhancing governance conditions and economic performance (Knack and Keefer 1995, 1997; Mauro 1995; Barro 1996; Clague et al. 1997; Johnson et al. 1998; Hall and Jones 1999; Kauffman et al. 1999; Lambsdorff 2005). This literature typically finds a positive relationship between the two, supporting the hypothesis that an improvement in market-enhancing governance conditions will promote growth and accelerate convergence with advanced countries. We will summarize some of the problems with approaches using governance indicators, as these are well known and have been extensively discussed elsewhere (Arndt and Oman 2006; Carlin et al. 2006; Khan 2007a; Meisel and Aoudia 2008).

The most important problem is that multiple directions of causality exist and are widely recognized. Even those who believe that market-enhancing governance capabilities have strong effects on growth also recognize that growth itself can provide greater resources for the provision of market-enhancing governance. Much of the econometric effort is in trying to resolve these directions of causality. Econometrics is not very good at determining causality in general, but in this case the data series for different aspects of market-enhancing governance are only available from the 1990s in any extensive form, making credible causality tests even more difficult. As an example, the general problem can be demonstrated with reference to a single indicator, that for the rule of law, shown in Figure 2.5. This is an important component of measures of market-enhancing governance capabilities, and part of the set of World Governance Indicators provided by the World Bank.

Without attempting any causality analysis, a visual examination of the data in Figure 2.5 suggests why sophisticated causality analysis on this type of data may be very misguided. If all the available data on the rule of law score for 1996 (the earliest available year) are plotted against growth rates for the 1990s, we do indeed get the impression that better rule of law will result in higher growth rates. But once we distinguish between advanced and developing countries (to address the possibility of reverse causation since advanced countries are expected to have a better rule of law anyway) the picture becomes muddied. Diverging developing countries (with growth rates lower than the median advanced country growth rate) had virtually the same mean and dispersion of their rule of law indicators

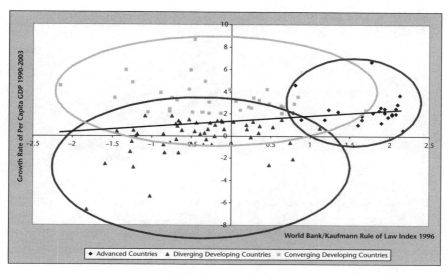

Figure 2.5 An example of the evidence: "rule of law" and growth, 1990–2003

compared to the high-growth converging developing countries (whose growth rates were higher than the median advanced country growth rate). In other words, performance on the rule of law indicator does not appear to distinguish high-growth from low-growth developing countries. The same pattern emerges when we look at corruption indicators, indicators for political accountability, or indeed any indicator of market-enhancing governance (Khan 2004a, 2007a, 2008b). Of course there are many other variables determining growth differences between countries, but the governance indicators are "deep" variables which are supposed to determine for instance the magnitude of investment and the efficiency of investment, so if we fail to see any visual relationship at all it should alert us to some problem with the underlying hypothesis.

Our interpretation of the general problem is summarized in Figure 2.6. The characteristics of advanced economies are not really interesting for developing countries, nor is there any historical *process* evidence that reforms of the type suggested by good governance resulted in countries from group 1 reaching group 3. Our focus should rather be on group 1 and group 2 countries. Some critical governance capabilities allowed some group 1 countries to become high-growth group 2 countries, but in general it was *not* superior scores on good governance indicators. We also know that group 2 economies include many different types of growth stories, some more sustainable than others. Some converging economies have significant growth-enhancing governance capabilities that allow them not only to grow fast for a while, but to sustain this growth and spread it across the economy to make a sustained transition to prosperity. The North East Asian countries were examples of countries with such governance capabilities. Other countries may be in the converging group

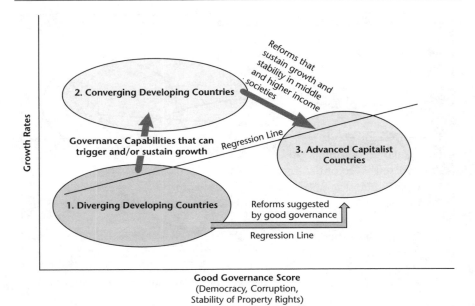

Figure 2.6 Governance characteristics of growth economies
Source: Khan (2007b)

because they have some sectors or regions or minerals that produce globally competitive products, but they may be quite vulnerable unless further growth-enhancing sectors and capabilities are developed.

The only thing that *is* clear is that developing countries do *not* in general solve the market failures that constrain their growth through good governance capabilities. In theory significant improvements in good governance characteristics may have helped to improve the efficiency of markets and thereby contributed to sustaining growth. But in reality such improvements are structurally beyond the reach of developing countries, which are significantly below upper-middle income status. The cross-country empirical evidence strongly supports that conclusion (Khan 2007b, 2008b).

As the problems with supporting the good governance agenda using contemporary governance indicators are well known, attempts have been made to support the argument for good governance using instrumental variables and longer historical data. One of the most influential arguments frequently referred to in support of the good governance agenda comes from Acemoglu, Johnson, and Robinson (Acemoglu et al. 2001, 2002) henceforth AJR. But while their econometrics is impressive, they implicitly present an interpretation of history that is at variance with historical knowledge. The argument they develop is that "bad" colonialism in non-settler colonies created unstable property rights because colonial powers in these countries were only interested in extracting resources. In contrast, they argue, "good" colonialism in settler colonies created stable property rights because settlers wanted to live there and the result was prosperity. This comforting but deeply misleading narrative diverts our attention from the economics and politics of growth-enhancing property rights reform and the governance capabilities required by developing countries to sustain growth during their contemporary transitions.

AJR's innovation was to use exogenous proxy variables (settler mortality or low initial population density) as instruments for locating where white settlers settled and set up settler colonies. It has long been known that settler colonies did significantly better in achieving development than non-settler colonies. The problem that their instruments arguably correct for is that they ensure that the analysis does not pick up the possibility that white settlers settled in areas that had an advantage for some other reason. But in the end, their econometric sophistication says little more than something that is quite uncontroversial: White settler colonies did a lot better than other developing regions. The question is why? Here they make an assertion that has nothing to do with their econometrics. They assert that the reason was that settler colonies set up stable property rights while non-settler colonies set up extractive systems that disrupted property rights, apparently with lasting and persistent consequences. This reassuring version of colonial history, summarized in Figure 2.7, is becoming increasingly accepted as having been *proved* by their econometric exercise.

In fact, nothing of the sort is actually demonstrated in their work. All that their work shows is that settler colonies ended up with significantly higher per capita incomes and higher scores in property rights stability a century or so later. AJR present no conclusive argument that the eventual outcomes were achieved *because* these states *first* established stable property rights and set up limited government. In reality, as Glaeser et al. point out, the same evidence could be used to argue that

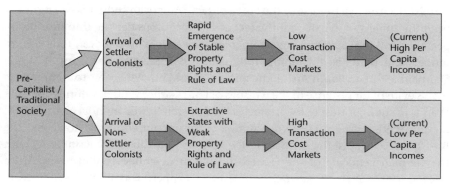

Figure 2.7 The Acemoglu et al. version of colonial history
Source: Khan (2009: Figure 7)

what the settlers brought with them was primarily their human capital (that is themselves) rather than their institutions, which arguably developed much later (Glaeser et al. 2004). What is worse, since the acquisition of human capital is in the long run a policy choice, a sophisticated racist could use the AJR evidence to argue that the superior performance of white settler colonies demonstrates the genetic advantage of whites in acquiring human capital (or indeed in setting up good institutions). AJR's regressions only establish that white settler colonies did better (which no one questioned anyway), and that where white settlers settled probably had little to do with the pre-settler productivity of the region. However, AJR's own work shows that settler colonies were more likely to be set up in areas where indigenous populations were not dense (Acemoglu et al. 2002). But they failed to pick up the significance of this for the historical *processes* through which social transformations were achieved.

If anything, AJR's story of expropriation can be turned on its head for the early period of colonialism in settler and non-settler colonies. The most obvious and striking fact about settler colonialism is the *qualitatively more violent process* that was unleashed on indigenous populations, verging on and in some cases amounting to genocide. The Belgian Congo was a possible exception to the rule that non-settler colonies faced lower levels of violence compared to settler colonies. In the non-settler colonies the colonial power faced dense populations that were relatively well organized and they immediately made complex political compromises with pre-existing and new elites to sustain colonial rule. In contrast, in settler colonies pre-existing populations were thinly spread out and the consequences of this turned out to be devastating for them. It meant that settlers could follow much more aggressive military strategies of land grabbing and destruction of pre-existing rights. Here indigenous populations faced dramatic and rapid expropriation of their lands, were pushed into smaller and smaller pockets of territories, and in many cases suffered precipitous collapses in numbers that in some cases amounted to genocide.

In North America the size of the "pre-contact" American Indian population has been the subject of debate, but the fact of its precipitous decline into near disappearance and the rapid and largely uncompensated loss of American Indian communal land rights is not (Snipp 1989; Sale 1990; Stiffarm and Lane Jr. 1992; Stannard 1993). In South Africa, the militarism and unwillingness to compromise that is evident for instance in the writings of Lord Garnet Wolseley during the Zulu Wars is in stark contrast to the strategies the British followed in India (Gump 1996; Lieven 1999). Indeed, Lieven's description of the uncompromising "total war" the British waged against the Zulus and their economy has elements of similarity with the German genocide of the Herrero people in neighboring south-west Africa (Lieven 1999: 631). In Australia, there is an explicit discourse of genocide to describe what happened to the aboriginal population (Tatz 1999; Moses 2000). Violence against aboriginal peoples in Australia was directly related to settler demand for land and the need to clear the land of the hunter-gatherer aborigines. The simple expedient was to deny any recognition of prior rights. The forceful exclusion of aboriginal peoples from their livelihoods led to precipitous population declines, in some areas by as much as 80 percent (Moses 2000). To describe these processes in terms of the settler states establishing a rule of law and stable property rights clearly does huge injustice to our understanding of history and is at least manifestly economical with the truth.

The inconvenient truth about the settler colonies summarized in Figure 2.8 is that they did indeed make a transition to "stable property rights" but only after the rights inappropriate for the new capitalist economies were thoroughly destroyed. Settlers from already capitalist countries came with ideas of how to organize production but they did not try to work with pre-existing rights, defining them better, creating markets and a rule of law, and then trying to reallocate assets through voluntary contracts in markets. Instead, the transitions here were *not* periods of stable property rights but the absolute reverse. They were periods of systematic, widespread, and violent destruction of almost all pre-existing rights because these rights did not serve the interests of settlers who were setting up capitalist economies in their own interest. Thus, this sophisticated econometric attempt to establish causality fails because its claim that stable property rights *explain* the higher growth of settler colonies does not stand up to the scrutiny of historical process. The social and economic transformation that created the preconditions for growth in settler colonies was carried out entirely outside the framework of a rule of law and a market economy based on contractual transfers of assets. The emergence of stable property rights, contracts, and political accountability emerged in these societies *after* the critical transformations in economic,

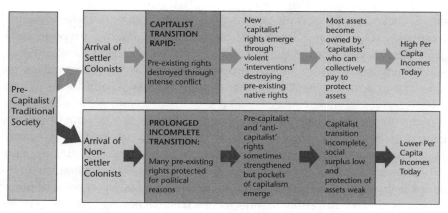

Figure 2.8 Colonial history's inconvenient truths
Source: Khan (2009: Figure 8)

social, and political structures had already been carried out, in these cases through processes of enormous violence.

Paradoxically, pre-existing property rights were much better protected in the non-settler colonies. For instance, Austin argues that in Ghana, the colonial state supported productive African property rights and intervened to moderate monopsonistic behavior by European commodity purchasers (2008: 1011). However, Austin's examples of support for productive African property rights can also be interpreted as a demonstration of the willingness of the colonial power to support conflicting sets of rights out of political expediency. Thus, Austin provides an example where the British colonial power supported the rights of cocoa planters to the trees they had planted under indigenous Akan land law even when the land did not belong to the chief of the planters. At the same time, the traditional rights of the chiefs were left intact.

The complex political constraints driving colonial land property policy is even more obvious in the example of the British West Africa Lands Policy when British policy suddenly changed from supporting individual ownership of land in Lagos in 1861 to a newly discovered preference for "traditional" land tenure in the Nigerian territories acquired between 1892 to 1903 (2008: 1009). The shift to a form of property right that was theoretically inferior for a capitalist transition cannot be explained by the presence of an extractive state of the Acemoglu et al. type since the non-settler colonial power had supported individual property rights in the immediate past and it is not at all clear how traditional land rights would allow more expropriation. A more plausible explanation is that the thinning out of British military power as its territories expanded led colonial administrators to prioritize the avoidance of social conflict and to seek to retain the support of the broadest possible definition of "traditional elites."

Consistent with this interpretation, a growing body of literature has corroborated critical aspects of Mamdani's (1997) analysis of the "bifurcated state." This argued that *traditional* or *customary* forms of tenure in Africa are largely colonial creations that had tenuous roots in pre-colonial history. The colonial power artificially created "customary authorities" as a method of exercising social, political, and administrative control in a context where direct rule was difficult given the military and demographic disadvantage faced by colonial administrators in non-settler colonies. In these cases, colonial powers created new rights for the constituencies they needed, not for expropriating resources but to achieve political control in a context where they had limited roots in indigenous society. This perspective is supported by a considerable body of corroborating evidence (Chimhowu and Woodhouse 2006). Clearly the recognition of traditional rights aimed to draw in different layers of traditional elites located in pre-colonial power structures. It is not surprising that non-settler colonial powers very often created conflicting and incoherent rights that could impede economic transformations.

The analysis of settler versus non-settler colonialism is important for contemporary policy for several reasons. First, a historical understanding of the problems created by colonialism suggests that the challenge facing contemporary developing countries is not to create, through good governance, the stable property rights that settler colonies apparently created. A rapid creation of such rights is precluded once we understand what that would entail in terms of transition costs. Once these are taken into account, the settler colonies should serve as models of what *not* to do, because they solved the problem with a degree of violence that cannot be recommended today and was not justifiable at the time. If developing countries today are not following the example of settler colonies and moving rapidly in the direction of capitalist property rights it is not because they necessarily lack the political will, but more likely because they implicitly understand the issue of transition costs.

Second, the long history of non-settler colonial rule has also left serious problems in the form of social engineering that created a multitude of rights and social entitlements that were inappropriate for asset reallocations and for creating the productivity compulsions necessary for driving growth (Khan 2009). Finally, in the nineteenth century when settler economies were being set up, the technological gap between leader and follower countries was not so great that significant market failures constrained investments particularly in the agricultural sectors of the settler colonies. Nevertheless, even at that early stage, the manufacturing take-off needed tariffs and protection in settler colonies such as the United States (Greenwald and Stiglitz 2006). The refusal of non-settler colonial administrations in places such as India to allow significant tariff protection for domestic manufactures till the early twentieth century resulted in the relative de-industrialization of India and its falling behind that we referred to earlier. In other words, there were significant differences in the growth strategies followed by settler and non-settler colonies but the differences had little to do with the mythology that settler colony growth was driven by their respect for property rights, rule of law, and a minimal state. Yet, stable property rights and a rule of law did develop faster and deeper in the settler colonies as their capitalist sectors grew, became economically viable, and started paying significant taxes that paid for their protection.

Given the ahistorical governance advice that developing countries in Africa and elsewhere have received, it is not surprising that progress has been limited. The contemporary good governance agenda identifies areas of policy *priority* that are hard to justify on the basis of the historical evidence of capabilities and strategies of rapid developers in Asia and elsewhere. It is important to understand that we are talking about sequences and priorities. We are not saying that improving political accountability, fighting corruption, or improving the rule of law is not a set of desirable goals for any society. Even if we all agree that these are desirable objectives, we still have to answer the question: How are we going to implement and achieve these governance capabilities? The answer may be that we need to achieve some intermediate and immediate growth-promoting governance capabilities to sustain growth which will eventually provide the resources to improve some of these market-enhancing governance capabilities as well as achieve other developmental objectives.

Growth-enhancing governance and economic growth

The historical evidence from Asia and elsewhere suggests that transitions to development have required strong state capabilities for dealing with critical market failures. The historical evidence that is available suggests that none of these countries would have passed the good governance test at early stages of their development and transformation. The role of the state in the "statist" transitions in East Asian countries is widely recognized, but liberal economists argue that these experiences cannot be replicated in other countries. If replication means the reproduction of any particular country's blueprint in another, we would agree. But recent attempts to present settler colonies as examples of transitions driven by stable property rights and limited government are historical misrepresentations. In fact transitions in all countries required significant non-market activities by states and what is more, the degree of violence and injustice was significantly greater in the settler colonies compared to the East Asian examples. As strategies of transformation there is little to recommend the settler colonies. While no historical example provides a blueprint for contemporary societies, the growth-enhancing governance approach aims to identify broad structural problems that historical transitions addressed so that contemporary societies can address the problems of social transformation with greater social justice and with fewer costly mistakes.

In understanding the challenges facing Africa, we need to keep in mind the structural features of developing countries that require the development of growth-enhancing governance capabilities (Khan 2004b, 2005). These are capabilities that give states an ability to deal with critical market failures that in broad outline have faced all developing countries. Two areas in particular stand out as requiring close attention and country-specific responses. First, developing countries require governance capabilities to manage property rights over many valuable resources that will remain weakly defined during early stages of development. Historical evidence and theory suggest that contrary to good governance theory, the weakness of property rights in developing countries is structural and not entirely due to the extractive greed of political leaderships or their inadequate political will to enforce the rule of law. It is very expensive to protect property rights and enforce contracts to an extent that would allow most asset reallocations to be organized through markets. The historical examples of successful development demonstrate that in the meantime, significant state capabilities for achieving vital asset allocations through non-market processes were vitally important.

The differences between countries have been in their effectiveness, and in the degree of injustice and violence that was involved. The challenge is to achieve capabilities for allowing industrial and agricultural development through land allocation and other asset allocation strategies that achieve greater efficiency than existing high transaction cost markets together with as much justice as possible through fair levels of compensation and consensus building about social objectives.

Second, market-led development is typically constrained by a variety of market failures that prevent investment in potentially high-value sectors and the absorption, adaptation, and learning of more advanced technologies. In particular, entrepreneurs face a structural problem in acquiring the tacit knowledge and learning required for using modern technologies essential for achieving international competitiveness. Achieving these capabilities requires complementary governance capabilities on the part of the state to manage incentives and opportunities for technological catching up, while creating compulsions for entrepreneurs not to waste resources. Countries differ widely in these capabilities, and therefore in their capacities to absorb new technologies rapidly. The experience of East Asia shows that the relevant state capabilities differed widely because the underlying strategies of technology acquisition were also significantly different between countries depending on their initial conditions of entrepreneurial abilities and technological trajectories.

Technology acquisition strategies and complementary governance capabilities ranged from governments being able to effectively discipline subsidies for technology acquisition as in South Korea, licensing new technologies and providing them to the private sector as in Taiwan, or attracting higher-technology multinationals with appropriate incentives and conditions as in Malaysia (Khan 2000b; Khan and Blankenburg 2009). In each case strategies were more or less successful depending on the governance capabilities of the respective states to implement these strategies effectively. Very similar strategies failed to deliver good results in other developing countries because the appropriate governance capabilities for implementation were missing. Clearly, the initial conditions are more adverse in some African countries in terms of entrepreneurial skills and knowledge of technologies compared to the high-growth Asian countries in the 1960s. Nevertheless, opening up markets and making the relatively small improvements in market-enhancing governance conditions that are feasible are clearly not going to work in terms of attracting the necessary investments in learning and technology adoption. Identifying feasible strategies of building growth-enhancing governance capabilities in Africa based on these types of insights from historical evidence is likely to be more useful than the generalized good governance approaches that developing countries have been following.

References

Acemoglu, D., Johnson, S., and Robinson, J. A. (2001). "The Colonial Origins of Comparative Development: An Empirical Investigation," *American Economic Review*, 91 (5): 1369–401.

—— (2002). "Reversal of Fortune: Geography and Institutions in the Making of the Modern World Income Distribution," *The Quarterly Journal of Economics*, 107 (4): 1231–94.

—— (2004). "Institutions as the Fundamental Cause of Long-Run Growth," Working Paper No. 10481, National Bureau of Economic Research, available at <http://www.nber.org/papers/w10481>.

Arndt, C. and Oman, C. (2006). *Uses and Abuses of Governance Indicators*, Development Centre of the Organisation for Economic Co-operation and Development (OECD). Paris: OECD.

Arrow, K. J. (1962). "The Economic Implications of Learning by Doing," *The Review of Economic Studies*, 29 (3): 155–73.

Austin, G. (2008). "The 'Reversal of Fortune' Thesis and the Compression of History: Perspectives from African and Comparative Economic History," *Journal of International Development*, 20 (8): 996–1027.

Bardhan, P. (2000). "The Nature of Institutional Impediments to Economic Development," in O. Mancur and S. Kähkönen (eds.), *A Not-So-Dismal Science: A Broader View of Economies and Societies*. Oxford: Oxford University Press.

Barro, R. J. (1996). "Democracy and Growth," *Journal of Economic Growth*, 1 (1): 1–27.

Carlin, W., Schaffer, M. E., and Seabright, P. (2006). "Where are the Real Bottlenecks? A Lagrangian Approach to Identifying Constraints on Growth from Subjective Data," Centre for Economic Reform and Transformation Discussion Paper No. 2006/04, available at <http://www.sml.hw.ac.uk/cert>.

Chimhowu, A. and Woodhouse, P. (2006). "Customary vs Private Property Rights? Dynamics and Trajectories of Vernacular Land Markets in Sub-Saharan Africa," *Journal of Agrarian Change*, 6 (3): 346–71.

Clague, C., Keefer, P., Knack, S., and Olson, M. (1997). "Democracy, Autocracy and the Institutions Supportive of Economic Growth," in C. Clague (ed.), *Institutions and Economic Development: Growth and Governance in Less-Developed and Post-Socialist Countries*. Baltimore: The Johns Hopkins University Press.

Clark, G. and Wolcott, S. (2002). "One Polity, Many Countries: Economic Growth in India, 1873–2000," in D. Rodrik (ed.), *Institutions, Integration, and Geography: In Search of the Deep Determinants of Economic Growth*. Princeton, NJ: Princeton University Press, available at <http://ksghome.harvard.edu/~.drodrik.academic.ksg/Growth%20volume/Clark-India.pdf>.

Glaeser, E. L., La Porta, R., Lopez-de-Silanes, F., and Shleifer, A. (2004). "Do Institutions Cause Growth?" *Journal of Economic Growth*, 9 (3): 271–303.

Greenwald, B. and Stiglitz, J. E. (2006). "Helping Infant Economies Grow: Foundations of Trade Policies for Developing Countries," *American Economic Review*, 96 (2): 141–6.

Gump, J. O. (1996). *The Dust Rose Like Smoke: The Subjugation of the Zulu and the Sioux*. Lincoln: University of Nebraska Press.

Hall, R. and Jones, C. (1999). "Why Do Some Countries Produce So Much More Output Per Worker Than Others?" *The Quarterly Journal of Economics*, 114 (1): 83–116.

Hausmann, R. and Rodrik, D. (2003). "Economic Development as Self-Discovery," *Journal of Development Economics*, 72 (2): 603–33, available at <http://ksghome.harvard.edu/~drodrik/selfdisc.pdf>.

Johnson, S., Kaufmann, D., and Zoido-Lobatón, P. (1998). "Regulatory Discretion and the Unofficial Economy," *American Economic Review*, 88 (2): 387–92.

Kauffman, D., Kraay, A., and Zoido-Lobatón, P. (1999). "Governance Matters," World Bank Policy Working Paper No. 2196.

Khan, M. H. (2000a). "Rents, Efficiency and Growth," in M. H. Khan and J. K. Sundaram (eds.), *Rents, Rent-Seeking and Economic Development: Theory and Evidence in Asia*. Cambridge: Cambridge University Press.

—— (2000b). "Rent-seeking as Process," in M. H. Khan and J. K. Sundaram (eds.), *Rents, Rent-Seeking and Economic Development: Theory and Evidence in Asia*. Cambridge: Cambridge University Press.

—— (2002). "Corruption and Governance in Early Capitalism: World Bank Strategies and their Limitations," in J. Pincus and J. Winters (eds.), *Reinventing the World Bank*. Ithaca: Cornell University Press.

—— (2004a). "State Failure in Developing Countries and Strategies of Institutional Reform," in B. Tungodden, N. Stern, and I. Kolstad (eds.), *Annual World Bank Conference on Development Economics Europe (2003): Toward Pro-Poor Policies: Aid Institutions and Globalization, Proceedings of Annual World Bank Conference on Development Economics*. Oxford: Oxford University Press and World Bank, available at <http://www-wds.worldbank.org/servlet/WDS_IBank_Servlet?pcont=details&eid=000160016_20040518162841>.

—— (2004b). "Strategies for State-Led Social Transformation: Rent-Management, Technology Acquisition and Long-Term Growth," in *Which Institutions are Critical to Sustain Long-Term Growth in Viet Nam?* Asian Development Bank, Hanoi.

—— (2005). "The Capitalist Transformation," in K. S. Jomo and E. S. Reinert (eds.), *Development Economics: How Schools of Economic Thought Have Addressed Development*. London and New Delhi: Zed Press and Tulika.

—— (2006). "Determinants of Corruption in Developing Countries: The Limits of Conventional Economic Analysis," in S. Rose-Ackerman (ed.), *International Handbook on the Economics of Corruption*. Cheltenham: Edward Elgar.

—— (2007a). "Governance, Economic Growth and Development since the 1960s," in J. A. Ocampo, K. S. Jomo, and R. Vos (eds.), *Growth Divergences: Explaining Differences in Economic Performance*. Hyderabad, London, and Penang: Orient Longman, Zed Books and Third World Network, available at <http://www.un.org/esa/desa/papers/2007/wp54_2007.pdf>.

—— (2007b). "Governance and Growth: A Preliminary Report," Research Paper supported by DFID grant, SOAS, London, available at <http://mercury.soas.ac.uk/users/mk17/Docs/Preliminary%20Report.pdf.>

—— (2008a). "Building Growth-Promoting Governance Capabilities," background paper for *The Least Developed Countries Report 2008*, UNCTAD, Geneva, available at <http://mercury.soas.ac.uk/users/mk17/Docs/Building%20Growth%20Promoting%20Governance.pdf>.

—— (2008b). "Governance and Development: The Perspective of Growth-Enhancing Governance," in GRIPS Development Forum (ed.), *Diversity and Complementarity in Development*

Aid: East Asian Lessons for African Growth, National Graduate Institute for Policy Studies, Tokyo, available at <http://mercury.soas.ac.uk/users/mk17/Docs/GRIPS.pdf>.

—— (2009). "Governance Capabilities and the Property Rights Transition in Developing Countries," DFID Research Paper Series on Governance for Growth, School of Oriental and African Studies, University of London, London, available at <http://mercury.soas.ac.uk/users/mk17/Docs/Property%20Transitions%20internet.pdf>.

—— and Blankenburg, S. (2009). "The Political Economy of Industrial Policy in Asia and Latin America," in G. Dosi, M. Cimoli, and J. E. Stiglitz (eds.), *Industrial Policy and Development: The Political Economy of Capabilities Accumulation*. Oxford: Oxford University Press.

Knack, S. and Keefer, P. (1995). "Institutions and Economic Performance: Cross-Country Tests Using Alternative Institutional Measures," *Economics and Politics*, 7 (3): 207–27.

—— (1997). "Why Don't Poor Countries Catch Up? A Cross-National Test of an Institutional Explanation," *Economic Inquiry*, 35 (3): 590–602.

Lambsdorff, J. G. (2005). "Consequences and Causes of Corruption: What do We Know from a Cross-Section of Countries?" *Universität Passau Wirtschaftswissenschaftliche Fakultät Diskussionsbeitrag*, Nr. V-34-05. Passau: University of Passau.

Lieven, M. (1999). "'Butchering the Brutes All Over the Place': Total War and Massacre in Zululand 1879," *History*, 84 (276): 614–32.

Mamdani, M. (1997). *Citizen and Subject: Contemporary Africa and the Legacy of Late Colonialism*. Oxford: James Currey.

Matthews, R. C. O. (1986). "The Economics of Institutions and the Sources of Growth," *Economic Journal*, 96 (384): 903–18.

Mauro, P. (1995). "Corruption and Growth," *Quarterly Journal of Economics*, 110 (3): 681–712.

Meisel, N. and Aoudia, J. O. (2008). "Is 'Good Governance' a Good Development Strategy?" Working Paper No. 58, Agence Française de Développement (AFD), Paris, available at <http://www.afd.fr/jahia/webdav/site/afd/users/admirecherche/public/DT/WP_58_GB_pour_mise_en_ligne.pdf>.

Moses, A. D. (2000). "An Antipodean Genocide? The Origins of the Genocidal Moment in the Colonization of Australia," *Journal of Genocide Research*, 2 (1): 89–106.

Murphy, K. M., Shleifer, A., and Vishny, R. W. (1989). "Industrialization and the Big Push," *Journal of Political Economy*, 97 (5): 1003–26.

North, D. C. (1984). "Three Approaches to the Study of Institutions," in D. C. Collander (ed.), *Neoclassical Political Economy: The Analysis of Rent-Seeking and DUP Activities*. Cambridge, MA: Ballinger Publishing.

—— (1990). *Institutions, Institutional Change and Economic Performance*. Cambridge: Cambridge University Press.

—— (1995). "The New Institutional Economics and Development," in J. Harriss, J. Hunter, and C. Lewis (eds.), *The New Institutional Economics and Third World Development*. London: Routledge.

Olson, M. (1997). "The New Institutional Economics: The Collective Choice Approach to Economic Development," in C. Clague (ed.), *Institutions and Economic Development*. Baltimore: Johns Hopkins University Press.

Sale, K. (1990). *The Conquest of Paradise: Christopher Columbus and the Columbine Legacy*. New York: Alfred A. Knopf.

Snipp, C. M. (1989). *American Indians: The First of the Land*. New York: Russell Sage Foundation.

Stannard, D. E. (1993). *American Holocaust: The Conquest of the New World*. New York: Oxford University Press.

Stiffarm, L. A. and Lane Jr., P. (1992). "The Demography of Native North America: A Question of American Indian Survival," in M. A. Jaimes (ed.), *The State of Native America: Genocide, Colonization and Resistance*. Boston: South End Press, 23–53.

Stiglitz, J. E. (1987). "Learning to Learn, Localized Learning and Technological Progress," in P. Dasgupta and P. S. Stoneman (eds.), *Economic Policy and Technological Development*. Cambridge: Cambridge University Press, 125–53.

—— (1989a). "On the Economic Role of the State," in A. Heertje (ed.), *The Economic Role of the State*. Amsterdam: Bank Insinger de Beaufort NV.

—— (1989b). "Markets, Market Failures and Development," *American Economic Review*, 79 (2): 197–203.

—— (2007). *Making Globalization Work*. London: Penguin.

Tatz, C. (1999). "Genocide in Australia," *Journal of Genocide Research*, 1 (3): 315–52.

3

Institutional Monocropping and Monotasking in Africa

Thandika Mkandawire

Introduction

The study of institutions is once again at the center of development thinking on Africa. The excitement about the discovery of the "key" to development has been most pronounced among those working within an essentially neoclassical economics framework. Since its inception, development economics—the intellectual scaffolding for development strategies—identified itself with the task of "government-engineered economic transformation" (Toye 2003). Early development economists were keenly aware of institutions as the framework within which economic decisions and transactions were made. Even when economists did not always pronounce themselves on institutions, there was often the belief that someone else was looking into it. This was because development economics evolved side by side with approaches to development that drew on other disciplines that sought to identify the kind of institutional arrangements that were appropriate to development and lessons that could be learned from the past. Not only were institutions the framework within which markets functioned, they were also motors that would drive markets to perform differently than would be expected by simple extrapolation of the performance of markets in the past. The issue raised then was: What institutions are appropriate for accumulation and structural transformation in the context of catching up? In the linear view of history, latecomers would simply adopt institutions from leading countries so as to bypass the "stages" that the leading countries had already traced (Rowstow 1960). The main task of research was to identify the preconditions for each stage and accelerate the movement from one stage to the next. In contrast, Alexander Gerschenkron, who was skeptical of "preconditions" for growth, put forward a substitution for such prerequisites. Gerschenkron's primary contribution was his suggestion that institutional innovations would circumvent the establishment of market-based relationships by mapping out the boundaries of the firm, type of finance likely to be appropriate for "late industrializers," the role of the state, etc. Institutions would be designed to skip certain stages or telescope certain processes, allowing the latecomers to move at a faster rate than that suggested by the linear theory of history.

This chapter argues that, while the upsurge of interest in institutions is welcome and long overdue, the new focus is marred by the tethering of institutions to a one-size-fits-all policy perspective, which leads to what Peter Evans refers to as "institutional monocropping." This involves an "imposition of blueprints based on idealised versions of Anglo-American institutions whose applicability is presumed to transcend national cultures and circumstances" (Evans 2004). The focus on institutions also suffers from an insistence on institutional "monotasking," whereby institutions are reduced to servicing a standard set of often-imposed policies or tasks, and from the endless institutional experimentation that renders institutions highly unstable and unpredictable. The field's attachment to "rational choice institutionalism" has tended to focus on the restraining role of institutions, while ignoring the developmental and transformative role that historical and sociological forms of institutionalism have highlighted.[1] And finally, by a proliferation of tasks to be performed by highly restrained institutions, the focus on institutions undermines the coherency of national bureaucracies.

From "getting prices right" to "getting institutions right"

To understand the turn toward institutional reforms, it is important to bear in mind the theoretical underpinnings of the new model behind them. Neoliberal policymakers claimed to draw their policy diagnoses and prescriptions from the notions of Adam Smith's "invisible hand," formulated more rigorously by Arrow and Debreu. In its pristine form, the Arrow-Debreu model of decentralized allocation of resources—which assumes a full set of complete and contingent markets extending infinitely into the future with economic actors endowed with perfect information to operate in all these markets—institutions are superfluous and likely to lead only to distortions.[2] The World Bank's initial characterization of the underlying market economy drew straight from the Arrow-Debreu world:

> If the economy is producing efficiently, scarcity values must be equal to opportunity costs, and their common value is the efficiency price...An economy is efficient, as opposed to just production efficient, if it is impossible to make anyone better off without making someone else worse off. In addition to producing efficiently, the final consumers must have exhausted all possibilities of mutually beneficial exchange. This in turn

requires they all face the same market prices and that these are equal to efficiency prices ... The case for removing distortions and moving market prices closer to efficiency prices rests on the argument that prices influence production efficiency and the reform will increase production efficiency (World Bank 1983: 42).

If the concern of the "interventionist era" was "getting investment right" through planning and later through project evaluation, the neoliberal view was initially simply "getting the prices right." There was little concern about institutions that would facilitate the workings of the market. Consequently, adjustment basically involved the liberalization of the market from both the primordial and modern state interventionist institutions associated with market distortions. And of all the institutions, the one identified as most likely to play a negative role was the state.

Failure of adjustment

By the end of the 1980s, there was already the growing realization that neoliberal policies were not working in Sub-Saharan Africa, which had been subjected to more conditionalities per capita than any other region (Killick 1996). This led to a focus on other variables that could account for the failure of the African patient to respond to the nostrums in the way that was expected. This shift was first hinted in the World Bank's *From Crisis to Sustainable Growth* (World Bank 1989), a report on Africa that categorically declared: "Underlying the litany of Africa's development problems is a crisis of governance. By governance is meant the exercise of power to manage a nation's affairs" (World Bank 1989: 60). And since then the issues of "good governance" and "institutional reform" have become part of the Pavlovian punditry regarding Africa's crisis.

There were two interpretations of the crisis underlying the good governance agenda. One view, with strong neo-Weberian underpinnings, suggested that for all its size and ubiquity, the African state was a "lame Leviathan" (Callaghy 1987). The consensus was that African states had been based on patron-client relationships that drew from African culture and the peculiar path that modernity was taking in Africa. The more optimistic view sought to set up institutions that would be shielded from African culture (Hyden 1980). In a Panglosian sense, the current Africa was the best of all possible Africas; the institutions that have emerged in Africa are what one would expect from Africa's historicity. The corruption, kleptocracy, and violence were manifestations of "how Africa works" and evidence of the "political instrumentalization of disorder" (see especially Bayart 1993; Chabal and Daloz 1999). The more "Afropessimistic" view argued that the reforms made in Africa were a mere charade, or so totally out of sync with African culture that they were doomed to fail. The other pessimistic view drew on the neoclassical tradition and its methodological individualism. In this, the institutions that subscribed to the analytical political economy school were treated as instruments to advance sectional interest groups in order to capture rents.[3] Donors had been hoodwinked by the neo-patrimonial elites into believing that any adjustment had actually taken place (Chabal and Daloz 1999; Van de Walle 2001). While both of these pessimistic positions initially counseled for the establishment of institutions that would be insulated from domestic entanglements, it later became clear that the cynical view of politics made the whole aid business pointless if indeed the existing policies represented a self-reinforcing political equilibrium (Toye 1995).

Both these formulations posed problems for donor financial institutions. For a while, economists at the World Bank and other aid agencies treated the "good governance" turn with hesitation, viewing it as a distraction from the key message of getting prices right. In addition, the formulation did not suggest exactly how this would relate to the corpus of neoclassical economics that underpinned the stabilization and structural adjustment programs. In *Adjustment In Africa* (World Bank 1994), the World Bank argued that adjustment was working, but also noted that the response of private investment to adjustment had been "disappointing." Significantly the report did not pay much attention to the governance issue and *getting policies right* remained its core mantra. Overwhelming evidence contradicted this report and suggested that, in fact, adjustment was not working. For a while, the Bretton Woods Institutions (BWIs) maintained their paradigm by moving the goalposts and finding reasons to argue that policymakers had not done as instructed and had been slow to abandon their retrograde ways.[4] However, after some time, the policy failure argument simply ceased to make sense and it could no longer be argued in good faith that developing countries, especially the Latin American ones, had not implemented the putative "right policies." In official circles the failure of adjustment was signaled by calls for post-Washington policies and comprehensive policy framework.

In light of the failure of the get-policies-right injunction, a new question arose: "Why is it that when the recommended policies are put into place (often under the guidance of—and pressure from—the International Monetary Fund and the World Bank), the hoped for results do not materialize quickly" (Clague 1997: 1). The answer was "institutional weakness."[5] New institutional economics provided the answer to this failure and suggested a strikingly obvious point, namely that poor legal systems and inadequate contractual enforcement deter investment and credit. The new interest in institutions was inspired by new institutional economics as formulated in the seminal work of Douglass North. In this approach, institutions were overarching structures shaped by "path dependence" and the unintended consequences of individuals pursuing their own interests. They also provided the kind of constraints that would facilitate transactions and reduce unpredictability of individual choices and behaviors. This new approach provided a formulation of the good governance agenda that could be reconciled with neoclassical economics. It also dovetailed neatly with the new growth theories and attempts to take on a wide range of determinants of and included in cross-country regression equations, proxies of the rule of law, financial institutions, and intellectual property law, which are mainly the outcome of the institutional set-up of a country.

Given the irreversibility of many investment decisions, predictability was important in encouraging private investors. The most important role of institutions was lending credibility to policy. One way of ensuring this was through the reduction of the discretionary space of the state. The theory informing this choice drew from a seminal paper by Nobel Prize winners Finn Kydland and Edward Prescott,[6] who argued that the central problem with policy was its credibility: Fixed rules are preferable to discretionary ones because they increase credibility, while discretion leads to "time inconsistency," which arises as policymakers renege on commitments made during an earlier period. In this approach, rational agents use a uniquely correct economy model and take into account all the available information when forming expectations about the future and making decisions. Correct policy respects the fundamentals of new economic theory. From this model, there arose the need to ensure credibility and alleviate risks caused by the problems of time inconsistency and policy reversals; it was logically necessary to create insulated institutions.[7] Governments were then faced with the problem of making private-sector agents believe that the policy rule they announced in time (t) would actually be carried out in $t +1$. Presumably, the rules were more credible if they were endorsed or even enforced by outside institutions. Governments could delegate authority to an already credible entity (read: the IMF) or deliberately surrender authority and responsibility to the authorities of an independent central banking system. Rule-based policies were strongly recommended to reduce the risk of recidivism, opportunistic behavior, and time inconsistency. Indeed, conditionality "provide[d] the theoretical underpinning for the widespread notion that an IMF agreement is akin to the Good Housekeeping Seal of Approval for government policy, increasing the attractiveness of a country to foreign investors" (Gordon 1993: 112).[8]

The second pillar of this new argument was the need to ensure property rights. It should be recalled that this was seen to include protection of the market-sanctioned returns so that rent control, inflation, or state revenues from seigniorage were tantamount to the violation of such rights.

"Good governance" once again

It was noted how early on, the World Bank's good governance argument was given a lukewarm reception; but this time around, the response was different. In 1998, Wolfensohn declared that the World Bank has "ignored institutional infrastructure, without which a market economy simply cannot work" (Wolfensohn 1998:

11–12). According to Stiglitz, then chief economist at the Bank, "The post-Washington consensus was aimed at the creation of institutions that helped markets (e.g. legal framework and institutions, property rights, competition policies, and contract enforcement)" (Stiglitz 1998). In light of these intellectual and policy shifts, the 1990s was the era of institutional reform. Virtually all donor agencies were now involved in supporting institutional reform and capacity building. Often the new initiatives simply involved relabeling existing activities from say, *Public Administration* to *Governance and Institution-Building*. Remarkably, in many cases there was not even the attempt to cover up the continuity. Thus, although the IMF now took on good governance it also insisted that the many reforms it had been involved in over the years (tax reforms, banking reforms, etc.) were core components of good governance. As stated by Michel Camdessus, then managing director of the IMF, "Our approach is to concentrate on those aspects of good governance that are most closely related to our surveillance over macroeconomic policies—namely, the transparency of government accounts, the effectiveness of public resource management, and the stability and transparency of the economic and regulatory environment for private sector activity" (cited in International Monetary Fund 1997b).

By the end of the 1990s, many countries had adopted aspects of the good governance agenda. Central banks had been made autonomous; parastatals had been privatized; legal reforms had strengthened property rights; stock markets had been set up; bureaucracies had been trimmed down to produce the desirable "lean and mean state." And in a significant number of cases, countries had made significant steps toward democratization. However, accelerated development still remained elusive. The new question became: Why is it that even when countries have adopted good policies and good institutions, economic growth has remained anemic? So a new set of explanations had to be invoked to explain the ineffectiveness of institutional reforms in Africa. Some pointed to the large numbers of ethnic groups that can undermine the national cohesion required for development (Easterly and Levine 1995). For some, religion was important. Others suggested a lack of social capital, while others suggested that there was plenty of the stuff, but that it was of a pathological type. Path dependence was also used to suggest something like "getting your past right," as still others pointed to how different patterns of colonization determined the quality of contemporary institutions (Acemoglu et al. 2001), and that Africa, outside the white settler colonies, had been dealt a bad hand. Others stressed lack of human capital (Glaeser et al. 2004); some argued that geography had trumped institutions and pointed to Africa's unfortunate geographical location—a large number of landlocked countries, unhealthy climates, and the difficulty of governing such thinly populated countries (Herbst 2000; Sachs and Warner 1997; Sachs 1996, 2000, 2003).[9]

What went wrong with institutional reforms?

Weak conceptual underpinnings and measurement problems

It was noted that some of the interest in institutions was driven by new thinking in economics. Following the work of Douglass North, there has been some kind of an econometric cottage industry, with growth on the left hand of the equations and some measure of institutions included among the right-hand determinants of growth. This kind of analysis, which putatively informs the current institutional reform agenda, presents many problems for policymakers and institution builders. First, economic theory does not specify the functional forms for the relationships between institutions and economic growth, so that the link in the econometric specification of the relationship between theory and the estimated regression often involves a leap of faith. There is definitely no robust, long-term causal relationship among political, legal, economic, and financial institutions. There are also doubts regarding the exact channels of their effects on growth, about their relative importance *vis-à-vis* other exogenous and endogenous variables, such as trade policy and geography, and about interpretations of findings that remain unanswered. Thus, the empirical evidence on the relationship between growth and institutions such as stock markets and independent central banks is still highly contested.

Second, as most authors admit, problems of simultaneity are prevalent in such cases so that endogeneity bedevils some of the simplistic derivations of appropriate institutions from econometric analysis. The direction of causation is not clear and may run in both directions. In fact, since institutions are both conditioning factors and responses, this should not be surprising. The simultaneous relationship between growth, investment, and institutions makes it difficult to find out the relative importance of the indirect and direct effects. Under an appropriately worded subtitle—"An Obituary for Growth Regression"—Lindauer and Pritchett (2002: 19) observe that "by now, there are thousands of papers that put economic growth on the left-hand side and other stuff on the right-hand side ... [yet] estimates in the typical growth regressions are unstable over time and across countries."

In addition, the "institution variable" raises enormous problems of measurement. Most of the measures for institutions are dubious empirical proxies for their theoretical counterparts, subject to errors and biases of measurement. Although in most models, institutions are treated as prior or as determinants of behavior, the actual proxies used are derived through the behavior or action of agents. Such proxies suffer from both the "subjective bias" (since the index may be influenced by a country's overall economic condition) and "reputation" (which has a self-fulfilling quality), as well as from an "endogeneity bias," since there is often feedback from growth to institutional quality. And so the fact that people are investing in a particular country (driven essentially by "animal spirits" or "herd behavior") is used to suggest the presence of "good institutions." We should also bear in mind both cultural and racial bias in these measures and the so-called CNN factor. In the case of Africa, this manifests in the many studies that suggest that Africa is systematically rated as more risky than is warranted by the underlying economic characteristics (Collier et al. 1999). However, policy literature usually includes the perfunctory admission that proxies are subject to endogeneity, but the analysis then proceeds as if the problem of direction of causation has been solved. And so the imposition of institutions takes place when "social scientific ignorance persists about the relationship of specific institutions and processes of institutional change to economic development" (Dunning and Pop-Eleches 2005).

Finally, the high correlation between some of the measures of governance and growth suggests that indices instruments measure the economic outcomes of economic development rather than the efficacy of institutional characteristics in promoting growth (Glaeser et al. 2004). As Figure 3.1 shows, there is a high correlation between good governance and GDP per capita. Indeed, in using these measures, we find that many countries are as well governed as their levels of development will permit, with quite a number of African countries being better governed than one would expect given their levels of development.[10] Ha-Joon Chang (Chang 2002, 2007) has stressed in most of his works that, generally

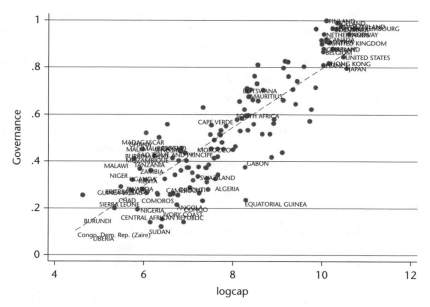

Figure 3.1 Relationship between governance and per capita income. Governance is derived from the normalization of the unweighted sum of the indicators in the World Bank "Governance Matters" database (Kaufmann et al. 2005)

speaking, the poor countries of today have better institutions than today's industrial countries had at similar levels of economic development. This is not to dismiss the importance of good institutions for today's poor countries, but rather to point out that what may matter most is the normative argument that such institutions are of intrinsic value and that their developmental role may be oversold.

Institutional monocropping and monotasking

Monocropping

The assumption was that good policies were known, a highly dubious proposition,[11] and that there was one isomorphic mapping between the policies (or tasks) and institutions—drawn from the notion that in perfect markets there is only one optimum to which all economies must move if they are not to end in non-Pareto optimum situations—led to an "institutional monocropping" through the imposition of what Peter Evans described as "ideal-typical versions of a particular subset of supposed Anglo-American institutions" (Evans 2004). Since this singular truth maps monotonically into one type of institution, the whole idea of context specificity and path dependence is jettisoned as countries simply borrow best practices from Western countries.

In reality, economies are confronted with possibilities of multiple equilibriums that can be reached through different institutional arrangements (Freeman 2000).[12] One consequence is that the relationship between institutions and economic fitness is multi-peaked, and each of these peaks may be associated with entirely different social institutions. The peak a country reaches depends on from whence it came (path dependence) and the context within which choices are being made about institutions.[13] Consequently, the kind of standardized policy advice on institutions is unjustified and "the search for a single institutional 'taproot' of growth is likely to be a misguided exercise" (Haggard 2003: 53), nor will simply mimicking a leader or "best practice" do (Schettkat 2002).

Monotasking

One remarkable aspect of adjustment has been its failure to stimulate investment. Institutions perform many roles, intentional and unintentional, including the task of encouraging or attracting investments, mostly foreign. So, not surprisingly, the elements that institutions have acquired from new institutional economics have been those relating to attracting foreign investment, including: reinforcing property rights, regulating markets to promote competition (leveling the playing field), clamping down on corruption, bolstering political credibility, enhancing the administrative capacity of government agencies, and transparency. Virtually every aspect was to be harnessed to the central task of ensuring private property. This has had serious implications for the design and functioning of institutions in Africa, including the encouragement of monotasking.

Ultimately, good governance has been reduced to serving the market, just as development administration of an earlier era was aimed at serving development plans. Democracy has been defended, on the basis that it is good for property rights, a position buttressed by econometric studies suggesting that property rights are more stable under democracies than autocracies (Clague et al. 1996).[14] However, central liberal and egalitarian (civil) components of democratic governments have been shorn off the governance agenda. Tuozzo's observations with respect to Argentina have resonance within the African situation:

> This rationale has led to the prioritisation of certain normative values above others, making democratic institutions more concerned with elements of 'performance' and 'effectiveness,' whilst elements of representation, fairness and equality have moved into the back burner. The prioritisation of goals produces complex tensions and incomplete institutional initiatives that only partially address governance problems in Argentina. Since the Bank believes that to govern is to manage the economy effectively, it sustains a managerial view of governance processes that may have detrimental implications for the unfolding process of democratic consolidation (Tuozzo 2004: 106).

In such a context even the notion of transparency, so germane to accountability, is subjected to the exigencies of this technocratic vision of policy markets and the perceived needs of the markets. Blyth argues that "promotion of transparency enhancement as a governance solution derives from erroneously viewing information failures as the primary cause of financial market instability" (Blyth 2003). Transparency is thus intended more to ensure the global legibility of local financial practices than to facilitate democratic oversight, which has in many cases been circumscribed by the ringfencing of many economic institutions. Since accountability was important in ensuring "congruence between public policy and actual implementation, and the efficient allocation and use of public resources" (World Bank 1992: 13–14), even institutions of civil society were perceived in this narrow sense: "The Bank's promotion of civil society is linked to its promotion of accountability, legitimacy, transparency and participation as it is these factors which empower civil society and reduce the power of the state" (Williams and Young 1994: 87).

Monotasking has even sought to reduce the functions of such institutions as the judiciary to the task of protecting private property.

It was noted above that, according to the new institutional economics, the reason for the failure of adjustment to attract private investment in Africa has been that institutions protecting property rights and enforcing contracts are weak and transaction costs were generally high, largely due to cumbersome bureaucratic procedures.

Confidence in the enforceability of contracts is also crucial to the reduction of unreasonable delays, high costs, and uncertainty. It is important that an independent and credible judicial system be formed to ensure that private contractual arrangements are respected and court procedures are expedited. According to a World Bank lawyer, judicial reform is part of a larger effort to construct the legal systems in developing countries:

> Concern for rules and institutions is particularly relevant to a financial institution which at present does not only finance projects but is also deeply involved in the process of economic reform carried out by many of its borrowing members. Reform policies cannot be effective in the absence of a system, which translates them into workable rules and makes sure they are complied with. Such a system assumes that: a) there is a set of rules which are known in advance, b) such rules are actually in force, c) mechanisms exist to ensure the proper application of the rules and to allow for departure from them as needed according to established procedures, d) conflicts in the application of the rules can be resolved through binding decisions of an independent judicial or arbitral body and e) there are known procedures for amending the rules when they no longer serve their purpose (Shihata 1991).

It should also be stressed that this understanding of the function of law dovetailed neatly with a political economy analysis that sought to reduce discretionary practices by the state (Tshuma 1999). The Word Bank Report of 1997 clearly spelled out this understanding of the law and development. Its involvement with law reform was confined to governance aspects related to development and so the aspects of the judiciary relating to property rights received better funding from donors.

This focus on formal law downplays other normative or semiautonomous spheres in society that set rules and facilitate enforcement.[15] This form of monotasking also tends to downplay other functions of the judiciary. In addition, as John Ohnesorge argues, "the international financial institutions advocate judicial independence largely in terms of enforcing written rules, and as a check on populist politics" (Ohnesorge 2007). And Shapiro notes the popularity of reforming the judiciary "may have more in common with the popularity of independent banks than with the protection of individual freedoms. They can operate as devices to signal foreign investors and international economic institutions that the capacity of elected officials to engage in redistributive policies or interfere with property rights will be limited" (Shapiro 2003: 21).[16] Finally, the view that legal reforms are apolitical and are confined to neutral technical reform is deceptive. Establishing property rights always has political implications because, in the context of scarcity, property rights are not only about incentives, but also about the exclusion of some from those protected properties. In Africa, such schemes as land entitlement have meant depriving communities of their property rights in favor of individuals. Consequently, "imposing new sets of formal rules without simultaneously reshaping the distribution of power that underlies prior institutional arrangements is a dubious strategy from the perspective of political economy" (Evans 2004).

It is also important to recognize that the reach of institutions goes well beyond the narrow needs of the market. Institutions play many roles in development processes and seemingly identical institutions can take on different roles at different times within the same country and among different countries. The fact that an institution may be necessary for a particular function does not mean that this is the only function that that particular institution can serve. In the apt words of Béteille:

> As I see things, social institutions, for all the limits they impose, are far too important in the lives of human beings to be judged solely by what they contribute to the annual rate of growth. Certainly, one is entitled to turn the question around, and ask what economic growth contributes to the well-being of institutions, for there are many who value the well-being not only of individuals but also of institutions (Béteille 2000).

In addition, even when institutions are designed as single-purpose entities, their actions have multiple effects, not all of which may be intended. There is little consideration of the distributive outcomes of institutional reforms because they are demanded and supplied by the aid establishment and designed to empower groups favored by external actors. Thus the main issues that are covered by the literature on institutional reforms—process, the collective action problems, the relationships and asymmetries of power, the problems of vested interests—are simply sidestepped. This effectively means that a whole range of issues related to institutions—social equity and legitimacy of power—were also avoided (Santiso 2001). Even less emphasis has been placed on the role of institutions in enhancing other things that societies may value.

Consequences of Monocropping and Monotasking

Wrong institutions

Monocropping and monotasking unnecessarily restrict the range of possible institutional arrangements by rendering institutions one-dimensional. In most cases, they also are predicated on institutions that are either unnecessary or insufficient. The World Bank has based most of its initiatives on the Anglo-Saxon model of privatization, presumably on "best practice" assumptions, since the Anglo-American common-law tradition is more conducive to economic development than the civil-law tradition (La Porta et al. 1999).[17] In the case of Africa, the World Bank has published studies claiming that "formal rule-bound governance" (FRBG) was more entrenched in Anglophone countries, "consistent with the emphasis which the British placed on building a foundation of law during the colonial period."[18] However, other researchers have challenged both the accuracy of the portrayal of real Anglo-Saxon economies and the assertion of the superiority of the model because even among Anglo-Saxon countries, the real economies are not similar or even close to the Chicago School model (Brautigam and Knack 2004; Carruthers and Halliday 2007; Ohnesorge 2007). Furthermore, there is no evidence that civil laws have hindered industrialization and indeed, some of the most dramatic cases of industrialization have been inspired by lessons from Germany: Among most of the high-performing developing countries, the so-called Rhine model has been a major object of emulation and adaptation (Ohnesorge 2007). Finally, in Anglo-Saxon countries, informal, out-of-court arrangements have been important in accounting for the flexibility of the system. Carruthers and Halliday argue, "Anglo-American commercial life unfolds outside the law as well as within it. And the variability of 'law in action,' as opposed to 'law on the books,' should never be underestimated. Furthermore, commercial predictability can be achieved outside the law as well as within it"[19] (Carruthers and Halliday 2007: 272). This is the case particularly in developing countries where enforcement of existing laws may be quite weak and consequently, preoccupation with legal forms and structure may be misplaced.

Many of the specific institutions included in econometric studies do not seem to have played the role assigned to them in the new success stories of Taiwan, South Korea or, even more spectacularly, China. Or as Evans puts it, "the star performers in terms of sheer economic growth during the last ten years—e.g., China, Vietnam, and Malaysia—exhibit institutional patterns that are embarrassingly hybrid relative to the monocropping ideal" (Evans 2004: 35). Daya Shanker (2003) argues that in China, most of these institutions, such as "rule of law" financial institutions, independent judiciary, property rights, etc. are underdeveloped or take a form diametrically opposite to the ones presumed in the literature.[20] Indeed the contrast between India and China in this respect compels Bajpai and Sachs to ask, "why can India not match China or even outpace China in attracting foreign direct investment, given India's superior conditions regarding the rule of law, democracy, and the widely spoken English language" (Bajpai and Sachs 2000: 3). Hausmann and Rodrik note:

> China achieved phenomenal growth rates without formally enacting private property rights—something that would have seemed impossible to many economists had the Chinese miracle not taken place. India barely reformed its incredibly cumbersome trade and industrial regime before its economy took off in the 1980s. And even after more ambitious reforms were enacted in the early 1990s, the Indian economy remained among the world's most protected (Hausmann and Rodrick 2002).

In a similar vein, Donald Clarke (2002), considering the property rights hypothesis, notes that, on the one hand, China has attained high growth rates while on the other, the institutions by which rights are enforced, in particular courts, are perceived to be weak, and thus property rights are perceived to be unenforceable.[21] In fact, it turns out that the institutions that have mattered—the Chinese family networks, repressive laws, a highly restricted stock market, and a banking system still tethered to a central-planning view of enterprise success—are not exactly what is being recommended in the new literature (Clarke 2002; Shanker 2003). Many recommended institutions are also based on a misreading of Western practices, which are often drawn from ideal types. The insistence on these ideals, rather than the ones that the developed countries actually had, is something tantamount to what Ha-Joon Chang calls "kicking away the ladder" (Chang 2002).

The standard set of new institutions are tethered to a minimalist economic agenda to facilitate open capital accounts, deregulated labor markets, and arms-length finance—and are hostile to intervention in general and in particular to industrial policies and financial arrangements that clearly facilitated rapid indus-trialization elsewhere. In many ways, the favored institutions were actually de-signed for the wrong types of investments. The literature on foreign investments is consistent in arguing that developing countries need foreign direct investment, which not only brings funding for new greenfield investments (rather than merely acquisitions and mergers) but also technology and access to foreign markets. The incentives and institutions appropriate to these types of investment are not the same as those required by portfolio investments around which much of the institutional building in Africa has evolved. The incentives for foreign direct investments will tend to be sector- and location-specific and may require inter-ventionist states.

Institutional dualism

The literature on institutions underscores the significance of the "match" among formal institutions and local social, political, economic, and cultural settings. It also stresses the importance of complementarities within institutional systems. The implications of dualities (e.g. modern versus tradition, capitalist versus pre-capitalist) surrounding development were a major preoccupation during earlier discussions of institutions and development. In the debates of the 1960s, there were also concerns that national institutions might be "overdeveloped" because they were designed for non-national tasks or were empowered by foreign actors. The concerns regarding the institutional dualities, together with those about nation-building and about specificities of underdeveloped economies, were brought to an abrupt end by a "monoeconomics" that was essentially negative toward analyses suggesting that different economies or sectors within economies would be driven by anything other than neoclassical utility maximization. Instead, the existence of such dualities and segmentations was attributed to such artifacts as policy biases and by the view that the real problem was the state, which had favored or succumbed to urban interests and created market distortions that had blocked agrarian transformation. The long-awaited unification of the modern and traditional could be ensured by relying on the market and a level playing field, the product of state non-intervention.

Consequently, much of the analysis lacks detailed information on existing institutions. Instead, African institutions are often studied not for what they are but for what they are not (Ake 1996). The consequence of this *tabula rasa* approach is that institutional reforms often involve throwing out the baby with the bathwater or grafting institutions onto a body whose rejection mechanisms are poorly understood. This is the feature of the current modular view of institutions, whereby best practices can easily be added to existing practices (Roland 2003). African states set up a range of institutions to address their colonial pasts, their developmental goals, and nation-building needs. Many of these institutions are badly designed, poor copies of the original metropolitan institutions, or have simply outlived their original intention. But they do constitute part of the landscape or initial conditions that serve as the point of departure for serious reform. Failure to take them seriously has produced many surprises engendered by the law of unforeseen consequences. If the result is that the final institutional outcomes differ from those that were prescribed, it is tempting, but wrong, to argue that lack of growth is due to countries not having implemented the recommended policies.

Recent reforms have introduced new dualities, partly as a result of the new institutions being isolated from the broad developmental agenda (monocropping) and partly because of the highly restrictive agenda (monotasking) laid out for these institutions. Such a dichotomy differs from the institutional layering in which the old and new are fused by processes of mutual adjustment and accommodation. The new duality manifests itself in the professionalization and ringfencing of the elements that the state designed around monotasking on the one hand and the informalization of institutions addressing other aspects of the economy on the other. With respect to law, improved protection of property rights for a few is accompanied by increased social security for the many, greater criminalization of their neighbors, and insecurity of property—both individual and collective.[22]

In the political scheme, the new institutional reforms have sought to democratize while seeking to create "authoritarian enclaves" that are excepted from government oversight. Institutions intended to address issues of local development and those designed to facilitate global governance do not necessarily work well together. One consequence has been an institutional dualism within governments—with a visible, modern, and technologically advanced part aimed at donors, and another, poorly equipped, demoralized, and often resentful aspect that often is responsible for the heavy tasks of development—rural clinics, basic administrative services, etc.

In the area of finance, most of the institutions that the World Bank insists upon are overly dimensioned and extremely expensive. One reason for this is that these institutions are set up to attract foreign private investment, which often requires legal, codifiable, and court-verifiable information that may be too rigorous for domestic capital sources. Thus it is doubtful that stock markets that meet the standards of American pension funds are appropriate for providing funding to local capitalists. The needs and perceptions of domestic investors may be quite different from those of the foreigners and the standards set up may be too restrictive for them.[23]

Institutional instability and sclerosis

One essential characteristic of institutions is stability. Indeed, the World Bank argues that its choice of the procedural and institutional version of the rule of law is because it is supposed to guarantee stability and predictability, essential elements of a climate in which business risk may be rationally assessed and the cost of transactions lowered (Tshuma 1999: 84). Stability can create tension between conformity and change and can at times fetter development, though it can also provide predictability, valuable to economic actors. People who work on institutions stress not only coherence and predictability, but also flexibility and adaptability. However, there is a limit to the flexibility and malleability an institution can accommodate before it ceases to be one. Many of the new institutionalists claim to derive their inspiration from Douglass North, who argued that institutions change gradually in response to changes in relative price and transaction costs. One argument for gradualism and the tailoring of changes to pre-existing institutions is that it economizes on institution building. There is a contradiction between the perception that institutions (the establishment of which is inherently gradual) would coexist with what David Ellerman refers to as "Big Bangery," "shock therapies," and "counter-revolutionary" impositions (Ellerman 2005). For Africa, the 1980s and 1990s was a period of what Whitehead aptly describes as a "veritable cannibalization of the state apparatus" (Whitehead 1993: 1381) brought about by untrammeled experimentation with untested ideas about how markets performed. Because institutional reforms are often the result of passing fads and donor institutions, they lacked the kind of anchoring that is key to Schumpeter's "creative destruction." Instead, there is uncreative destruction, as donors move on in the immediate aftermath, without taking time to create new institutions.[24]

In line with rational choice perspectives on what motivates individuals, reforms were made to "incentivize" the civil service by introducing competition into public-service provision (agentization, the tendering of services) through the New Public Management approach (Bangura and Larbi 2006; Harrison 2005). As had been noted, the introduction of New Public Management reforms in Tanzania and Uganda represented a "radical departure from the administrative logics that previously existed within Uganda's and Tanzania's bureaucracies" (Harrison 2005). Furthermore, the reforms have been introduced into emaciated administrations— poorly resourced, or in Uganda's case, all but entirely depleted by a long period of civil war and extreme authoritarianism. First-best reforms (often textbook models) have not only proved costly but often are simply unable to be implemented in the real world and are therefore highly ephemeral. By the end of the 1990s, these experiments were being quietly shelved as their non-workability became clear. The reforms' focus on efficiency also ignored other vital political considerations that have structured civil societies in ethnically diverse countries (Bangura 2006).

To signal to private investors that policy changes were serious, it was also important to shrink the state for budgetary reasons and as a clear indicator that the market would reign supreme in the economic sphere. Significantly, both the IMF and the World Bank produced data suggesting that, after years of retrenchment, Africa was the least governed part of the world with the lowest number public-sector employees per capita. A World Bank study (Schiavo-Campo 1996), which noted that among developing countries, Sub-Saharan Africa has the lowest government employment as a percentage of the population, had the following observations:

> In many countries in sub-Saharan Africa, the civil service has sharply deteriorated in almost every way since the 1970s. (Botswana is one of the few exceptions.) Beginning in the 1980s, a succession of fiscal stabilisation programs has reduced government employment in Africa to the lowest level of any developing region. Thus, although additional downsizing may be necessary in some countries, most do not need to shrink the workforce but to overhaul the entire civil service system.[25]

The United Nations Economic Commission for Africa (2003) observed with respect to Ghana and Egypt:

> Egypt and Ghana demonstrate the predicament. Despite 20 years of institutional reforms in the public sector, there is little to show for it. These reforms, like those in many African countries, focused on quantitative issues—wage and hiring freezes, downsizings, and retrenchments. They paid little attention to more subtle and challenging issues of bureaucratic quality. In Egypt, state capacity needs badly to be reinvigorated to improve export competitiveness and propel the economy to a higher stage of development. But the reform of institutions faces political and administrative constraints. In Ghana the situation has deteriorated so much that the current government now faces a crisis in the public service (UNECA 2003: 11).

The donors themselves have become keenly aware of the incoherence and instability they have rendered to the development policies and a large volume of literature and an outpouring of *mea culpas* has been produced on problems of incoherence of aid and its debilitating effects on the institutions of the recipient country (see, for instance, Forster and Stokke 1999).

Restraining versus transformative institutions

For latecomers, the developmental role of institutions is central. After years of touting the Asian economies as evidence of the efficacy of BWI policies, in 1993 the World Bank finally accepted the overwhelming evidence that the state had played a central role in the developmental experiences of these countries and that credit rationing (the allocation of rents) had been central (World Bank 1993). However, this concession regarding the Asian experience was immediately set aside, at least as far as Africa was concerned. First, it was argued that "the fact that interventions were an element of some Asian economies' success does not mean that they should be attempted everywhere, nor should they be used as an excuse to resist needed market reform" (World Bank 1993: 26). This view was buttressed by a number of academic publications that suggested the impossibility of a developmental state in Africa (Mkandawire 2001). In addition, the Asian financial crisis of 1997 severely tested the robustness of the Asian developmental state and reinforced the view that while institutions matter, only specific sets of institutions were appropriate. It was argued that the Asian crisis was the consequence of bad institutions—relationship banking, weak corporate governance structures, and lack of competition—all excrescences of the developmental state. In such an insider-dominated system, there was no transparency and poor information exacerbated the crisis. In one stroke, institutions that had accounted for the remarkable thirty-year growth were dismissed as dysfunctional "crony capitalism."

Institutions have tended to be presented largely as constraints and not as transformative or developmental instruments, even by those new institutional economists who have contributed significantly to the understanding of the broader role of institutions.[26] One of the unfortunate consequences of this interpretation of both African capacities and the Asian experience was the downplaying of agency in the process of development. In addition, the marriage of the literatures on rent-seeking and institutions has further reinforced the view of institutions as constraining mechanisms. The literature on the former was largely preoccupied with problems of the "capture" of the state by rent-seeking local groups. Much of technical assistance has taken the form of strengthening watchdogs over the "spending ministries" that are crucial for development of human capital and infrastructure. Institutions are also portrayed as "enabling" devices and are constitutive in the sense that they shape agency (e.g. by inculcating certain values) (Chang and Evans 2000). The neoliberal policy seems to be based on an assumption that there is some "welfare function" that is maximized, subject to constraints (including institutions). In real life, what we have is a positive feedback process in which institutions can shape the welfare function and can be used to relax some of the constraints while the pursuit of certain social objectives can lead to the setting up or adjusting of institutions. Andre Beteille suggests that while it might be natural for economists "to treat institutions, along with the standard constraints of economic theory," as merely constraints, institutions are also used instrumentally as means to an end and even as desirable ends (Beteille 2000).

Perhaps even more damaging, these reforms have led to the creation of institutions that undermine development efforts. Indeed students of developmental states argue that many of the institutions currently being promoted by proponents of the good governance framework may not be necessary for development (see for instance Chang 2003). Through monotasking, many institutions that had served a broad development agenda have been rendered impotent as developmental institutions. Institutions that strategically allocate rents, such as development banks and other institutions that make up a nation's innovation systems and extension services, have often been paralyzed or closed down.

The most emblematic case of monotasking has been the reforms in the statutes and mandates of central banks. Under the reform regime, "inflation targeting" has become the operational objective of central banks as monetary policy focuses almost exclusively on keeping inflation low, often at the expense of growth and employment creation. Historically, central banks have played a wide range of functions:

> [V]irtually throughout their history, central banks have financed governments, used allocation methods and subsidies to engage in 'sectoral policy' and have attempted to manage the foreign exchanges, often with capital and exchange controls of various kinds. The current 'best practice recipe,' then, goes against the history and tradition of central banking in the countries now most strongly promoting it ... (Epstein 2006).

Epstein notes that virtually all central banks have engaged in "industrial policy" or "selective targeting." In their credit-allocating functions, central banks have been "most effective in helping to foster development, especially in 'late developers,' where they have been part of the governmental apparatus of industrial policy" (Epstein 2006). In South Korea, the central bank was subservient—"nearly an administrative arm of the Economic Planning Board and the Ministry of Finance" (120). Significantly, Maxfield attributes this to the absence of the need to compete for international creditworthiness and pressures to attract foreign investment due to the high export performance of the economy, ability to borrow cheaply in financial markets, aid, and effective capital controls (Maxfield 1997). In addition, the new practice differs substantially even from current practice in Organization for Economic Co-operation and Development countries. In the US for instance, the Federal Reserve has at least two tasks to ensure low inflation rates and high employment rates. As Ha-Joon Chang observes, this monotasking—exclusive focus on monetary stability—not only deprives these countries of a powerful instrument of resource mobilization and allocation, but also forces the monetarist biases of these institutions on developing countries:

> Given the costs of pursuing a restrictive monetary policy giving independence to the central bank with the sole aim of controlling inflation is the last thing a developing country should do because it will institutionally entrench monetarist macroeconomic policy that is particularly unsuitable for developing countries. This is all the more so when there is actually no clear evidence that greater independence even lowers the rate of inflation in developing countries, let alone helps to achieve other desirable aims like higher growth and lower unemployment (Chang 2007: 154).

Foreign ownership

The initial logic informing institutional reform militated against local ownership. The negative perception of the capacity and cultural foundations of the African states, adhesion to the "negative politics" of rational choice (Harrison 2005; Toye 1995; Williams and Young 1994), and the cavalier dismissal of the defining characteristics of Asian developmental states led to the view that local elites could not be trusted to run, let alone create, developmental institutions. The self-imposed conundrum then became how the criminalized leviathan would be the political instrument for such a property regime. Why would the state, which is presumably dominated by interest groups, create institutions that favored the common good or that curtailed the power of interest groups? Furthermore, there was the "paradox" (for the Public Choice School) that states that were deemed incapable of adopting policies of liberalization in fact did.[27] One other consequence has been an internally inconsistent process of "capacity building," which involves training people to do virtually nothing that is developmental.

One of the most conspicuous institutions in African development is the aid juggernaut, which has added to the already confused state of things. Aid in Africa is no longer focused on providing funds to fill resource gaps, but on ways of doing things, implementation of objectives (some national, some bilateral, and some international), standards-setting, conditionalities. It often comes with an overwhelming foreign presence in African institutions. This is not meant to refer to the recruitment of foreigners by African governments or borrowing from foreign institutional arrangements, but to foreigners assuming key decision-making activities and responsibilities. It would be difficult enough if the foreigners in question came from one institutional culture with one coherent set of practices or norms. However, striking features among aid workers in Africa is the array of institutional idiosyncrasies that recipient countries must live with, the diversity of foreign actors within African institutions, and the parcelization of African institutions among different donors. In some cases, donors are explicitly opposed to the imposition of the Anglo-Saxon model and propose their own ways of doing things. Hence the German government states:

> The German Government is quite explicit about the differences between its agenda on legal reform and that of the Anglo-Saxon model: This specific vision of the rule of law has to do with the *German legal system*, which follows the continental European legal tradition and differs fundamentally from the Anglo-American legal system. These differences are also reflected in our cooperation countries' systems (Federal Ministry for Economic Cooperation and Development 2002: 81).

The German government is adamant that its model makes the most sense in developing countries: "Due to the lack of stable public institutions in many cooperation countries, an approach based on civil law and hence the German codification tradition serves the purpose better" (Federal Ministry for Economic Cooperation and Development 2002). For their part, the Nordics have been pushing for the institution of the ombudsman. Lessons from other areas that chaos ensues when donors insist on their own models and experiences have not affected the current wave of judicial reform, apparently because, as a recent review of a Swedish aid agency observes, "Many actors in the legal arena are unwilling to accept general development co-operation experiences" (Swedish International Development Cooperation Agency 2002). Not surprisingly, some research suggests that higher levels of aid are associated with larger declines in the quality of governance (Brautigam and Knack 2004).[28]

The historical record persuasively suggests that an institution's capability to learn and adapt is a major determinant of its appropriateness and efficacy. "Ownership" of the process of learning and adoption best facilitates this. Berkowitz and colleagues (Berkowitz et al. 2001) illustrate this proposition with the case of law when they argue that the way the law was initially transplanted and received is a more important determinant than the supply of law from a particular legal family (i.e., English, French, German, or Scandinavian).[29] Furthermore recent history clearly suggests that experimentation, "muddling through," deviations from the beaten path, attention to local contexts, and histories have played an important role in the cases of successful development. The literature on institutions is replete with words such as "context specificity," "path dependence," and "history", all of which suggest a "concrete analysis of concrete situations." One argument for a participatory and deliberative process is that a society's collective knowledge can shape the institutions that are appropriate to address the problems that a given society deems important. This is in sharp contrast to the view that good institutions are well known and the process ineluctably guarantees the outcome of the process will be an Anglo-Saxon model.[30] Foreign presence and pre-eminence in institution-building has had considerable effect on the morale and ésprit de corps of local bureaucracies (Mkandawire 2002). The sense of autonomy and national purpose among local technocrats depends to a large extent on the posture of the political leadership. To the extent that national leadership has yielded too much national sovereignty to external forces, it is unrealistic to expect technocrats to be assertive about national objectives and priorities. Time and again, local experts are overruled by foreign experts who can always count on the support of the head of state or ministry. This has not only undermined learning activities but has also wasted institutional memory, contributing to endless reinventions of the wheel in institution-building in Africa, and the sense of déjà vu that characterizes every encounter with foreign expertise.

Although it is argued that the credibility of certain institutions is enhanced when they retain autonomy from societal pressures, in practice their credibility comes from the tutelage of multilateral financial agents or by their managers belonging to an epistemic community that shares a common body of knowledge and understanding of the fundamentals (Grabel 2000: 11–12). Hence the pre-eminence of the peripatetic foreign consultants, the constant retraining of staff by the international financial institutions, the impositions of individuals on national institutions (through secondment or topping up of salaries of selected individuals), etc. Were these autonomous institutions to pursue policies that were in conflict with those of the international financial institutions, their autonomy would cease to signal credibility. In other words the credibility of institutions is endogenous.[31]

What have been ignored are the implications of foreign institutions capturing the key decision-making instruments of the state.[32] Only later did the BWIs begin to recognize the negative results of their presence. The discussion about owner-ship, although couched in populist language—participation, transparency—was really an admission that the alienation of the state from key domestic actors was counterproductive. The single most important argument has been that property rights are to be protected and if institutions matter for the functioning of the markets, then it is important to find local actors—state bureaucrats, capitalists, lawyers, NGOs—to give life to these institutions. The obsequiousness of African policymakers had become so excessive that it became an embarrassment to the donors themselves.

Mismatch between institutions and tasks

One of the great contradictions of the new reform was that the conceptual frame-work—the marriage of the new institutional economics and new growth theories through econometric modeling—that was used to justify both monocropping and monotasking also suggested an endless list of variables as determinants of growth. One effect of the state of disarray in development thinking has been the produc-tion of a laundry list of what needs to be done by states to create the environment conducive to private investment. The eclectic list of determinants of economic growth has increased the tasks that states must accomplish, without the means to carry them out, and led to institutional-reform overload. For aid-dependent econo-mies, "aid creates an incentive to expand operations to include all the initiatives donors want to fund" (Brautigam and Knack 2004: 263). New Public Management has insisted on creating new institutions to manage these tasks or further privatiz-ing parts of the state apparatus or functions. But as Hague (1996) observes:

> The process of privatization itself creates the need for a different set of governmental activities—such as regulation (currency, prices, banking, licensing), administration (law, property rights), enforcement (police, surveillance), distribution (transfers, gifts), extrac-tion (taxation, information gathering), and distribution (transfers, insurance)—that requires a large public sector.[33]

Even as donors insisted on monotasking institutions devoted to the issue of attracting investment, they also insisted on a whole range of other activities to be accomplished. Richard Sandrook captures this mismatch between tasks and capabilities in Africa:

> Initially, structural adjustment involved an effort to remould the economies of develop-
> ing countries in the idealised Western image of self-regulating markets. As this project
> met with political and administrative obstacles, the donor agencies recommended fur-
> ther social engineering. Capacity-building initiatives have sought to restructure Third
> World administrations into Weberian-style bureaucracies. Programmes to promote bet-
> ter governance and the political capacity of reformist regimes have led the agencies even
> further afield. Almost unnoticed, the agencies have taken on responsibilities that surpass
> those assumed even by the original colonial powers (Sandbrook 1996: 69).

The World Bank, which had initially applauded the retrenchment of the civil service that came with structural adjustment programs and the general retreat of the state from active developmental policies, began to realize that its new post-Washington agenda called for a much broader repertoire of skills and capacities. While monotasking fit in well with the agenda of the IMF, the reforms which could be carried out by only a few individuals in one or two institutions (the Ministry of Finance and the Central Bank), the new agenda relied heavily on the "spending ministries" and required a much broader array of institutions for its implementation. The obvious solution should have been the active involvement of planning units in several ministries and some coordinating body at the top. This would, of course, involve revival of the ideologically unpalatable institutions that the new orthodoxy had helped destroy.

And so while the new institutional approaches have placed politicians and bureaucrats at the center of analysis, this has been a time when the resources and relative weight of the state are being drastically reduced and their leverage is at its lowest. Essentially what we are witnessing is the violation of Tinbergen's principle that the number of policy instruments must, at least, be as many as the policy objectives.

Conclusion

After two decades of adjustment and the evisceration of developmentalist argu-
ments for state intervention, the return to institutions must indeed be a major shift. Outside the rarefied world of neoclassical economics, it has always been common knowledge that markets are embedded in complex social relations that govern property relations and many other things. The issue is not whether or not a country has institutions. The unresolved question is about what institutions are appropriate in what context to achieve what and to do what? The answer to this

question has been essentially faith-based. We know the good policies, just give us the institutions, or better still, "accept our package of institutions, which is the only one compatible with our good policies." What we have witnessed in Africa is the dismantling of institutions that might conceivably play a developmental role and the strengthening of institutions which, at best, are good for stabilization and which were not conceived as if development matters. For all the Spartan certainty about what institutions African countries should have and the monocropping that this begets, history and experience elsewhere suggested that institutions do not monotonically map into any one set of policies, nor do certain policies require a specific set of institutions. There is no standard market economy model. Instead, market economies are compatible with a diverse range of institutional arrangements, products of path dependence, serendipity, luck, and the force of unintended consequences of the actions of many agents. This involves layering and adaptation. One costly feature of the lost decades was the reduction in the space for experimentation within Africa and the one-size-fits-all institution-building tradition has produced a size that seems to fit no one. The institutional reform process has denied African countries the challenges and opportunities to experiment with different institutional arrangements.

"Legitimacy" is a useful attribute for any institution. Such legitimacy may accrue from custom and habit, from the legitimacy of the process or other institutions that set them up and from the demonstrated efficacy of institutions. Imposition of new institutions and the excessive restriction of existing institutions can in fact undermine their legitimacy. Institutions that are perceived as merely adjuncts of foreign institutions and whose authority and independence derived from these foreign institutions or whose agenda is narrowly set to meet externally imposed conditionalities, are unlikely to enhance their standing in the eyes of a public that expects every major institution to be involved in the developmental project.

The current focus on institutional design placing a great premium on creating enabling environments of stability and predictability for global investors is not necessarily the most desirable one from a developmental point of view. The single-minded subjugation of institutional reform to one set of policies has denied local institutions the capacity for learning from the wide range of experiences from other parts of the world. The institutions that are being called for are not ones likely to come up with policy options or capacities to meet the specific needs of individual countries. They are definitely not up to the urgent task of edifying stable, developmental, democratic, and socially inclusive social orders that have thus far remained elusive in Africa. It has also led to the marginalization of the many concerns that Africans have sought to address with their own or borrowed institutions. Worse, this practice has blunted the efficacy of institutions by denying them context specificity and flexibility.

Notes

1. For the distinction among the three forms of institutionalisms, see Thelen (1999).
2. The "a-institutional" nature derived from the axiomatic grid of neoclassical economics was one of the questions raised against structural adjustment programs (Stein 1997). In an earlier paper, I pointed how the wrong "stylization" of African economies as immanently competitive had contributed to the marginalization of the question about institutions for rapid accumulation (Mkandawire 1996).
3. This was essentially Bates' interpretation of marketing boards (Bates 1981). The World Bank also adhered to this approach of African policy (Harrison 2005).
4. The "moving goal" aspects of policymaking in Africa has led Joseph Stiglitz to equate it to the manner in which religious beliefs are never falsifiable: "Undermining this particular religion was the disturbing observation that countries that seemed to get the prices right—to follow the visiting preachers of the free market—too often failed to grow. To be sure, like medieval medicine, there was always the allegation that the patient had not followed the doctor's orders precisely, and it was this that accounted for the failure of the remedy" (Stiglitz 1996: 155).
5. It should also be added that the debacle of "shock treatment" in the former Soviet Union provided an important sign of how institutionally embedded markets are. As Dunning and Pop-Eleches note:

> When such replicas failed to materialize in most of the ex-Communist bloc (and, moreover, an unexpectedly sharp decline in output followed liberalization), the 'rediscovery' of institutions by the IFIs led to a veritable explosion of structural conditions in International Monetary Fund (IMF) programs, from an average of four structural conditions per IMF program in 1991 to a peak of sixteen in 1997. The emphasis on structural reforms mirrored a realization that implementation of the 'right' policies required the creation of the 'right' institutions, and thus marks the beginning of a second 'deep' stage of institutional monocropping during the mid 1990s (Dunning and Pop-Eleches 2005).

6. For a non-technical presentation of their argument see The Royal Swedish Academy of Sciences (2004).
7. Note, however, that the insulation and autonomy were only with respect to national institutions and politics as these autonomous institutions were essentially beholden to outside institutions as they are often compelled by structural adjustment programs to adhere to certain operating practices such as refusal to finance government debt or were simply based on operating guidelines of credible Western central banks or by employing central bank staff directly from these institutions.
8. The IMF's own perception of the importance of its conditionalities was couched in this language: "Clearly endorsing IMF conditionality is a means by which borrowing countries establish the credibility and predictability of their policies...Markets want proof not only of the technical merit of policies but also of the authorities' will to sustain them. IMF financing vouches for this will, and conditionality helps countries signal their determination to act predictably, in accordance with prior commitments" (International Monetary Fund 1997a: 82). See also Dhonte (1997). As it turns out, the catalytic effect of

IMF policies proved illusory (Bird 1997; Bird and Rowlands 1997; International Monetary Fund 1997a). Hajivassilou found that between 1970–82, there was a significantly negative correlation between IMF support and new private-sector lending (Hajivassilou 1987).

9. A recent one is the debate on the relative importance of institutions in particular *vis-à-vis* trade and geography. On one side is a group of researchers headed by Dani Rodrik (Rodrik et al. 2002) who stresses the dominant importance of institutions ("trumps everything else") and another centered around Jeffery Sachs (Sachs 2003) for whom geography is the most important factor explaining differences in growth rates.

10. Or as Naím observes: "The difficult paradox, is that any country that is capable of meeting such stringent requirements is already a developed country" (Naím 2000: 9).

11. History and Africa's own recent past suggest that the policies being pursued under the aegis of the BWIs are not the "good policies" associated with economic development and structural change. As Dani Rodrik (2002) notes: "The few instances of success occurred in countries that marched to their own drummers—and that are hardly poster children for neoliberalism. China, Vietnam, India: all three violated virtually every rule in the neoliberal guidebook, even as they moved in a more market-oriented direction."

12. Strictly speaking, the inference drawn from neoclassical theory about the required institutions has much more to do with ideology than the strict logic of neoclassical economics. As Dani Rodrik argues, "first-order economic principles—protection of property rights, contract enforcement, market-based competition, appropriate incentives, sound money, debt sustainability—do not map into unique policy packages. Good institutions are those that deliver these first-order principles effectively. There is no unique correspondence between the functions that good institutions perform and the form that such institutions take. Reformers have substantial room for creatively packaging these principles into institutional designs that are sensitive to local constraints and take advantage of local opportunities. Successful countries are those that have used this room wisely" (Rodrik 2005).

13. Hodgson (1996) notes that this multiplicity of adaptive peaks may lead to the congregation of units around a local rather than global maximum, which may be too costly to reach from any given position.

14. This turn in argumentation is a recent one. Both the historical and conceptual analysis has often suggested that when the propertyless are the majority there is always the danger that numbers can be used against the few propertied classes. As Przeworski and Limongi note "the idea that democracy protects property rights is a recent invention and we think a far-fetched one" (Przeworski and Limongi 1993). The case for democracy is that it ensures the rule of law, which presumably encourages investment. However, it should be noted that what matters for investors is predictability and not accountability "and it is not clear that an authoritarian regime cannot provide a framework for a predictable set of contacts" (Bardhan 1999). This has been the main attractive feature of authoritarianism to business. In more recent cases, Glaeser et al. (Glaeser, La Porta, Lopez-de-Silane, and Shleifer 2004) observe with respect to China:

> With respect to policy, our results do not support the view that, from the perspective of security of property and economic development, democratization and constraints on government must come first. In many poor countries, such security came from

policy choices made by dictators. The economic success of East Asia in the post war era, and of China most recently, has been a consequence of good-for-growth dictators, not of institutions constraining them. Indeed, the Chinese example illustrates this point forcefully: there was nothing pre-destined about Deng, one of the best dictators for growth, succeeding Mao, one of the worst.

15. An often-cited case is the land registration scheme, which failed because the formal law failed to accord attention to traditional norms of land ownership and inheritance.

16. With respect to Africa, Nyamu-Musembi notes that reforms to equip the judicial sector (for example, through provision of new buildings and computerization) have privileged commercial dispute resolution and underinvested in judicial subsectors, such as family courts and legal aid for family proceedings (Nyamu-Musembi 2005).

17. The researchers concluded from their regression analysis that "countries that are poor, close to the equator, ethnolinguistically heterogeneous, use French or socialist laws, or have high proportions of Catholics or Muslims exhibit inferior government performance... the larger governments tend to be the better performing ones" (La Porta et al. 1998).

18. The World Bank has strongly denied that its proposals on corporate governance favor any particular model; however, as Ajit Singh, Alaka Singh, and Bruise Weise argue, the actual recommendations that the Bank have made leave little doubt that the preferred model is the Anglo-Saxon one. Brian Levy, Adviser, Public Sector Governance at the World Bank, cites Ghana, Malawi, Mauritius, South Africa, and Uganda as good examples of countries with "strong credibility and strong FRBG." The shallowness of the intended institutional reforms is suggested by the following observation by the authors: "To be sure, even these five countries did not emerge in the survey as unequivocal paragons of good governance: Ghana and Uganda, for example, both scored worse for corruption than the global median. Nonetheless, in contrast with the other countries surveyed, their institutional task seems to be more one of consolidation—for which a variety of supply-side technocratic reform initiatives can be helpful—than the more fundamental challenge of building a stable governance foundation for economic development" (Levy 2002: 10–11).

19. Ohnesorge argues that "comparative studies of regulatory styles and administrative law suggest that 'rules' are really not the answer—that successful regulatory systems mix rule, discretion and judicial review to varying degrees, and that discretion is both inevitable and desirable.... Rule of Law advocates that forget this fact in the effort to provide the tightly rule-based environment that will maximize predictability and certainty for the private sector are not only out of touch with the realities of regulation and administrative law in actual existing market democracies, but are selling a one-sided and potentially unsustainable vision" (Ohnesorge 2007: 83).

20. And with respect to security market regulations, the necessary institutions are probably better in some Latin American countries than in a number of high-performing countries. This is probably the case with the stock markets in South Africa, Kenya, and Zimbabwe.

21. Note that it is perception, which determines whether persons are willing to invest and make deals, that counts for purposes of the Rights Hypothesis.

22. On increasing violence and informalization in Latin America, see Kruijt et al. (2002) where, as in Brazil "urban social tranquility rests on the permanence of a state of siege" (Gledhill).

23. Thus in the case of China, ethnic Chinese investors have entirely different perspectives and pay much less attention to the variables that enter the stand measures of "high-quality institutions." As Singapore's Minister of Information observed: "Investment and trading conditions are very complicated, with a weak legal system and unsettled frameworks for investments and currency exchange . . . China has never been a civilization with a tradition of the rule of law above the rule of men . . . The overseas Chinese . . . are relatively untroubled by the absence of legal and accounting framework (cited in Pfeffermann 1997).

24. The "slash and burn" approach to institutional reform is evidenced in the closure of development banks even before new regulations to induce the banking system to engage in long-term investment had been made.

25. It should be noted that the "overhauling of the entire system" has been a license to reckless experimentation with African institutions.

26. Thus Douglass North states that "institutions consist of a set of *constraints* on the behaviour in the form of rules and regulations; a set of moral, ethical behavioural norms which define the contours that *constrain* the way in which the rules and regulations are specified and enforcement is carried out" (North 1984).

27. Some of the more resolute members of the school have simply denied that African countries had in fact carried out major reforms since such a behavior was excluded by their theoretical contrasts. Adjustment had not taken place and the "criminalized state" had simply hoodwinked donors into believing that reforms had actually taken place (Van de Walle 1994).

28. The view that law could play an important role in development is, of course, not new. In earlier programs, it was often assumed that the guiding assumption of the law and development movement was that law is central to the development process. A related belief was that law could be used as an instrument to reform society and that lawyers and judges could serve as social engineers. Huge amounts of money were spent by aid donors and foundations in "law and development" programs. After little more than a decade, the program was declared a failure, and support quickly evaporated (Messick 1999).

29. They note: "Countries that have developed legal orders internally, adapted the transplanted law to local conditions, and/or had a population that was already familiar with basic legal principles of the transplanted law have more effective legality than 'transplant effect' countries that received foreign law without any similar pre-dispositions. The strong path dependence between economic development, legality and the transplant effect helps explain why legal technical assistance projects that focus primarily on improving the laws on the books frequently have so little impact. Finally, our statistical methodology produces a legality index based on observed legality proxies that almost fully captures their interaction with the way in which the law was transplanted, the supply of particular legal families and economic development."

30. These insights are not entirely alien to the international financial institutions. Thus, two IMF economists observe that, faced with weak legal institutions, poor governance, and poor-quality economic data, the Chinese have chosen to make reform incrementally and through trial and error and learning by doing (Prasad and Rajan 2006). The IMF authors observe: "The learning-by-doing approach to reform has a number of advantages. In a

second best world with multiple distortions, where the effects of individual policy reforms can be unpredictable, it reduces the costs of policy errors and uncertain outcomes in the reform process. It also gives policymakers a clearer sense of the political and social pressures that could arise in opposition to such reforms, allowing those pressures to be tackled more effectively when the reforms are instituted at a broader level" (Prasad and Rajan 2006: 6).

31. Or as Grabel (2003: 42) states, "These institutions and the policies they implement, are not inherently credible—their credibility results from the response of investors and multilateral agents whose actions provide important ideological and material capital to those who advocate the neoliberal agenda."

32. One reason for the failure to address this issue was what David Green and Ian Shapiro call arbitrary "domain restriction" (on who can be self-interested or not self-interested). By the logic of the rational choice, rent-seeking could also be extended to international bureaucracies. It could thus be argued that the international bureaucracies favor institutional reform, which extends their own interests and their disparagement of their local counterparts is often self-serving.

33. This "paradox" was clearly recognized by Gramco when he argues: "It must be clear that laissez faire too is a form of state regulation introduced and maintained by the legislative and coercive means...[it] is a deliberate policy, conscious of its ends, and not the spontaneous, automatic expression of economic fact. Consequently laissez faire liberalism is a political programme (Gramsci 1971).

References

Acemoglu, D., Johnson, S., and Robinson, J. A. (2001). "The Colonial Origins of Comparative Development," Working Paper 7771, National Bureau of Economic Research, Cambridge, MA.

Ake, C. (1996). *Democracy and Development in Africa*. Washington, DC: The Brookings Institution.

Bajpai, J. N. and Sachs, J. D. (2000). "Foreign Direct Investment in India: Issues and Problems," Development Discussion Paper 759, Harvard Institute for International Development, Harvard University, Cambridge, MA.

Bangura, Y. (2006). *Ethnic Inequalities and Public Sector Governance*. Basingstoke: Palgrave Macmillan/UNRISD.

Bangura, Y. and Larbi, G. (eds.) (2006). *Public Sector Reform in Developing Countries: Capacity Challenges to Improve Services*. Basingstoke: Palgrave Macmillan/UNRISD.

Bardhan, P. (1999). "Democracy and Development: A Complex Relationship," in I. Shapiro and C. Hacker-Cordons (eds.), *Democracy's Values*. Cambridge: Cambridge University Press.

Bates, R. (1981). *Markets and States in Tropical Africa*. Berkeley and Los Angeles: University of California.

Bayart, J. F. (1993). *The State in Africa: The Politics of the Belly*. London: Longman.

Berkowitz, D., Pistor, K., and Richard, J. R. (2001). "Economic Development, Legality, and the Transplant Effect," *European Economic Review*, 47 (1): 165–95.

Beteille, A. (2000). "Economics and Sociology: An Essay on Approach and Method," *Economic and Political Weekly*, 35 (18): 1531–8.

Bird, G. (1997). "Conditionality, Credibility and Catalysis: A Theory Discredited," SCIES Working Paper 97/04, Surrey Center for International Economic Studies, University of Surrey, Guildford.

—— and Rowlands, D. (1997). "The Catalytic Effect of Lending by the International Financial Institutions," SCIES Working Paper Series 97/07, Surrey Center for International Economic Studies, University of Surrey, Guildford.

Blyth, M. (2003). "The Political Power of Financial Ideas: Transparency, Risk, and Distribution," in J. Kirshner (ed.), *Monetary Orders: Ambiguous Economics, Ubiquitous Politics*. Ithaca, NY: Cornell University Press.

Brautigam, D. A. and Knack, S. (2004). "Foreign Aid, Institutions, and Governance in Sub-Saharan Africa," *Economic Development and Cultural Change*, 52 (2): 255.

Callaghy, T. (1987). "The State as Lame Leviathan: The Patrimonial Administrative State in Africa," in E. Zaki (ed.), *The African State in Transition*. London: Macmillan.

Carruthers, B. G. and Halliday, T. C. (2007). "Institutionalizing Creative Destruction: Predictable and Transparent Bankruptcy Law in the Wake of the East Asian Financial Crisis," in M. Jung-En Woo (ed.), *Neoliberalism and Institutional Reform in East Asia: A Comparative Study*. Basingstoke: UNRISD and Palgrave Macmillan.

Chabal, P. and Daloz, J. P. (1999). *Africa Works: Disorder as Political Instrument*. London: James Currey.

Chang, H.-J. (2002). *Kicking Away the Ladder: Development Strategy in Historical Perspective*. London: Anthem.

—— (2003). "The Market, the State and Institutions in Economic Development," in H.-J. Chang (ed.), *Rethinking Development Economics*. London: Anthem Press.

—— (2007). Bad Samaritans: Rich Nations, Poor Policies and the Threat to the Developing World. London: Random House.

Chang, H.-J. and Evans, P. (2000). "The Role of Institutions in Economic Change," Meeting of the "Other Canon" Group, Venice, Italy.

Clague, C. (1997). "Introduction," in C. Clague (ed.), *Institutions and Economic Development: Growth and Governance in Less-Developed and Post-Socialist Countries*. Baltimore: John Hopkins University Press.

Clague, C., Keefer, P., Knack, S., and Olson, M. (1996). "Property and Contract Rights in Autocracies and Democracies," *Journal of Economic Growth*, 1 (2): 243–76.

Clarke, D. C. (2002). "Economic Development and the Rights Hypothesis: The China Problem," Working Paper, University of Washington School of Law, Seattle.

Collier, P., Hoeffler, A., and Pattillo, C. A. (1999). "Flight Capital as Portfolio Choice," IMF Working Paper 99/171, International Monetary Fund, Washington, DC.

Dhonte, P. (1997). "Conditionality as an Instrument of Borrower Credibility," IMF Paper on Policy Analysis and Assessment 97/2, International Monetary Fund, Washington, DC.

Dunning, T. and Pop-Eleches, G. (2005). "From Transplants to Hybrids: Exploring Institutional Pathways to Growth," *Studies in Comparative International Development*, 38 (4): 3–29.

Easterly, W. and Levine, R. (1995). "Africa's Growth Tragedy," Working Paper, World Bank, Washington, DC.

Ellerman, D. (2005). "Can the World Bank Be Fixed," *Post-Autistic Economics Review*, 33 (14): 2–16.

Epstein, G. (2006). "Central Banks as Agents of Economic Development," Research Paper 2006/54, UNU/WIDER, Helsinki.

Evans, P. (2004). "Development as Institutional Change: The Pitfalls of Monocropping and Potentials of Deliberation," *Studies in Comparative International Development*, 38 (4): 30–52.

Federal Ministry for Economic Cooperation and Development (2002). "Legal and Judicial Reform in Development Cooperation," Vol. 2007. Berlin: Federal Ministry for Economic Cooperation and Development.

Forster, J. and Stokke, O. (eds.) (1999). *Policy Coherence in Development Cooperation*. London: Frank Cass.

Freeman, R. (2000). "Single Peaked vs. Diversified Capitalism: The Relation Between Economic Institutions and Outcomes," NBER Working Paper 7556. Cambridge, MA: National Bureau of Economic Research.

Glaeser, E. L., La Porta, R., Lopez-de-Silane, F., and Shleifer, A. (2004). "Do Institutions Cause Growth?" NBER Working Paper w10568. Cambridge, MA: National Bureau of Economic Research.

Gledhill, J. (2005). "The Rights of the Rich versus the Rights of the Poor," Working Paper GPRG-WPS-019, Global Poverty Research Group, available at <http://www.gprg.org>.

Gordon, D. (ed.) (1993). *Debt, Conditionality, and Reform: The International Relations of Economic Structuring in Sub-Saharan Africa*. New York: Columbia University Press.

Grabel, I. (2000). "The Political Economy of Political Credibility: The New-Classical Macro-economics and the Remaking of Emerging Economies," *Cambridge Journal of Economics*, 24 (1): 1–19.

—— (2003). "Ideology, Power, and the Rise of Independent Monetary Institutions in Emerging Economies," in J. Kirshner (ed.), *Monetary Orders: Ambiguous Economics, Ubiquitous Politics*. Ithaca, NY: Cornell University Press.

Gramsci, A. (1971). *Selections from the Prison Notebooks of Antonio Gramsci*. New York: International Publishers.

Haggard, S. (2003). "Institutions and Growth in East Asia," *Studies in Comparative International Development*, 38 (4): 53.

Hague, S. (1996). "Public Service Under Challenge in the Age of Privatization," *Governance*, 9 (2): 186–216.

Hajivassilou, V. A. (1987). "The External Debt Repayments Problems of LDCs: An Econometric Model based on Panet Data," *Journal of Econometrics*, 36: 205–30.

Harrison, G. (2005). "The World Bank, Governance and Theories of Political Action in Africa," *British Journal of Politics and International Relations*, 7 (2): 240–60.

Hausmann, R. and Rodrick, D. (2002). "Economic Development as Self-Discovery," Faculty Research Working Papers Series, RWP02-023, John F. Kennedy School of Government, Harvard University, Cambridge, MA.

Herbst, J. (2000). *States and Power in Africa: Comparative Reasons in Authority and Control*. Princeton, NJ: Princeton University Press.

Hodgson, G. (1996). "Organisation Form and Economic Evolution: A Critique of the Williamson Hypothesis," in U. Pagano and R. Rowthorn (eds.), *Democracy and Efficiency in the Economic Enterprise*. London: Routledge.

Hyden, G. (1980). *Beyond Ujamaa in Tanzania: Underdevelopment and an Uncaptured Peasantry*. Berkeley: University of California Press.

International Monetary Fund (1997a). "IMF Conditionality Can Signal Policy Credibility to Markets," *IMF Survey*: 81–3. Washington, DC: IMF.

—— (1997b). "The Role of the IMF in Governance Issues: Guidance Note," Guidance Note. Washington, DC: IMF.

Kaufmann, D., Kraay, A., and Mastruzzi, M. (2005). "Governance Matters IV: Governance Indicators for 1996–2004," World Bank Policy Research Working Paper Series No. 3630. Washington, DC: World Bank.

Killick, T. (1996). "Principals, Agents and the Limitations of BWI Conditionality," *World Economy*, 19 (2): 211–19.

Kruijt, D., Sojo, C., and Grynspan, R. (2002). *Informal Citizens. Poverty, Informality and Social Exclusion in Latin America*. The Latin America Series. Amsterdam: Rozenberg Publishers.

La Porta, R., Lopez-de-Silanes, F., Shleifer, A., and Vishny, R. W. (1998). "Law and Finance," *Journal of Political Economy*, 106 (6): 1113–55.

—— —— —— —— (1999). "The Quality of Government," *Journal of Law, Economics, and Organization*, 15 (1): 222–79.

Levy, B. (2002). "Patterns of Governance in Africa," African Region Working Paper Series 36. Washington, DC: World Bank.

Lindauer, D. L. and Pritchett, L. (2002). "What's the Big Idea? The Third Generation of Policies for Economic Growth," *Economia*, 3 (1): 1–39.

Maxfield, S. (1997). *Gatekeepers of Growth: The International Political Economy of Central Banking in Developing Countries*. Princeton, NJ: Princeton University Press.

Messick, R. E. (1999). "Judicial Reform and Economic Development: A Survey of the Issues," *World Bank Research Observer*, 14 (1): 117–36.

Mkandawire, T. (1996). "Stylising Accumulation in Africa: The Role of the State," in M. Lundhal and B. Ndulu (eds.), *New Directions in Development Economics: Growth, Environmental Concerns and Governments in the 1990s*. London: Routledge.

—— (2001). "Thinking About Developmental States in Africa," *Cambridge Journal of Economics*, 25 (3): 289–313.

—— (2002). "Incentives, Governance and Capacity Development: What Role for Technical Assistance in Africa?" in S. Fukuda-Parr, C. Lopes, and K. Malik (eds.), *Capacity for Development New Solutions to Old Problems*. London: Earthscan Publications.

Naím, M. (2000). "Washington Consensus or Washington Confusion?" *Foreign Policy*, 118 (Spring): 87–103.

North, D. (1984). "Transaction Costs, Institutions, and Economic History," *Journal of Institutional and Theoretical Economics*, 145 (4): 661–8.

Nyamu-Musembi, C. (2005). "For or Against Gender Equality? Evaluating the Post-Cold War 'Rule of Law' Reforms in Sub-Saharan Africa," Occasional Paper 7. Geneva: UNRISD.

Ohnesorge, J. K. M. (2007). "Asia's Legal Systems in the Wake of the Financial Crisis: Can the Rule of Law Carry any of the Weight?" in M. Jung-En Woo (ed.), *Neoliberalism and Institutional Reform in East Asia: A Comparative Study*. Basingstoke: UNRISD and Palgrave Macmillan.

Pfeffermann, G. P. (1997). "Beyond Macro and Education Policies," in N. Birdsall and F. Jaspersen (eds.), *Pathways to Growth: Comparing East Asia and Latin America*. Washington, DC: Inter-American Development Bank.

Prasad, E. S. and Rajan, R. G. (2006). "Modernizing China's Growth Paradigm," *The American Economic Review*, 96 (2): 331–6.

Przeworski, A. and Limongi, F. (1993). "Political Regimes and Economic Growth," *Journal of Economic Perspectives*, 7 (3): 51–71.

Rodrik, D. (2002). "After Neoliberalism, What?" Project Syndicate, available at <http://www.project-syndicate.org/commentary/rodrik7>.

—— (2005). "Growth Strategies," in P. Aghion and S. Durlauf (eds.), *Handbook of Economic Growth*, 1(1): 967–1014.

Rodrik, D., Subramanian, A., and Trebbi, F. (2002). "Institutions Rule: The Primacy of Institutions over Geography and Integration in Economic Development," NBER Working Papers 9305. Cambridge, MA: National Bureau of Economic Research.

Roland, G. (2003). "Understanding Institutional Change: Fast-Moving and Slow-Moving Institutions," *Studies in Comparative International Development*, 38 (4): 109.

Rowstow, W. W. (1960). *The Stages of Economic Growth: A Non-Communist Manifesto*. Cambridge, MA: Harvard University Press.

The Royal Swedish Academy of Sciences (2004). "Finn Kydland and Edward Prescott's Contribution to Dynamic Macroeconomics: The Time Consistency of Economic Policy and the Driving Forces Behind Business Cycles." Stockholm: The Royal Swedish Academy of Sciences.

Sachs, J. D. (1996). *Sources of Slow Growth in African Economies*. Cambridge, MA: Harvard Institute for International Development.

—— (2000). "Tropical Underdevelopment," Working Paper 57, CID. Cambridge, MA: Harvard University.

—— (2003). "Institutions Don't Rule: Direct Effects of Geography on Per Capita Income," Working Paper, National Bureau of Economic Research, Boston.

Sachs, J. and Warner, A. (1997). "Sources of Slow Growth in African Economies," *Journal of African Economies*, 6 (3): 335–76.

Sandbrook, R. (1996). "Democratisation and the Implementation of Economic Reform in Africa," *Journal of International Development*, 8 (1): 21–8.

Santiso, C. (2001). "International Co-operation for Democracy and Good Governance: Moving Toward a Second Generation?" *European Journal of Development Research*, 13 (1): 154–80.

Schettkat, R. (2002). "Institutions in the Economic Fitness Landscape: What Impact do Welfare State Institutions Have on Economic Performance?" Discussion Paper FS I 02 - 210, Faculty of Social Sciences, Utrecht University, Utrecht.

Schiavo-Campo, S. (1996). "Reforming the Civil Service," *Finance and Development*, 33 (3): 10–13.

Shanker, D. (2003). "Developing Countries, China and Economic Institutions," Working Paper Series. Social Science Research Network, available at <http://papers.ssrn.com/sol3/papers.cfm?abstract_id=277928>.

Shapiro, I. (2003). *The State of Democratic Theory*. Princeton: Princeton University Press.

Shihata, I. F. I. (1991). "The World Bank and 'Governance' Issues in its Borrowing Members," in F. Tschofen and A. R. Parra (eds.), *The World Bank in a Changing World*. Dordrecht: Martinus Nijhoff.

Stein, H. (1997). "Institutional Theories and Structural Adjustment in Africa," in J. Harris, J. Hunter, and C. Lewis (eds.), *The New International Economics and Third World Development*. London: Routledge.

Stiglitz, J. (1996). "International Economic Justice and National Responsibility: Strategies for Economic Development in the Post Cold War World," *Oxford Development Studies*, 24 (2): 101–9.

—— (1998). "Broader Goals and More Instruments: Towards the Post-Washington Consensus," 1998 WIDER Annual Lecture, UNU/WIDER, Helsinki.

Swedish International Development Cooperation Agency (2002). *Swedish Development Cooperation in the Legal Sector*, SIDA, Stockholm.

Thelen, K. (1999). "Historical Institutionalism in Comparative Politics," *Annual Review of Political Science*, 2: 369–404.

Toye, J. (1995). "The New Institutional Economics and its Implications for Development Theory," in J. Harris, J. Hunter, and C. Lewis (eds.), *The New Institutional Economics and Third World Development*. London: Routledge.

—— (2003). "Changing Perspectives in Development Economics," in H.-J. Chang (ed.), *Rethinking Development Economics*. London: Anthem Press.

Tshuma, L. (1999). "The Political Economy of the World Bank's Legal Framework for Economic Development," *Social and Legal Studies*, 8 (1): 75–96.

Tuozzo, M. F. (2004). "World Bank, Governance Reforms and Democracy in Argentina," *Bulletin of Latin American Research*, 23 (1): 100–18.

United Nations Economic Commission for Africa (2003). *Economic Report on Africa 2003*, United Nations Economic Commission for Africa, Addis Ababa.

Van de Walle, N. (1994). "Political Liberalization and Economic Policy Reform in Africa," *World Development*, 22 (4): 483–5.

—— (2001). *African Economies and the Politics of Permanent Crisis, 1979–1999*. New York: Cambridge University Press.

Whitehead, L. (1993). "On 'Reform of the State' and 'Regulation of the State'," *World Development*, 21 (8): 1371–93.

Williams, D. and Young, T. (1994). "Governance, the World Bank and Liberal Theory," *Political Studies*, 42 (1): 84–100.

Wolfensohn, J. (1998). "Foreword," in R. Picciotto and W. Durán (eds.), *Evaluation & Development: The Institutional Dimension*. New Brunswick: Transaction Publishers for the World Bank.

World Bank (1983). *World Development Report 1983*. Washington, DC: World Bank.

—— (1989). *Sub-Saharan Africa: From Crisis to Sustainable Growth: A Long-Term Perspective Study*. Washington, DC: World Bank.

—— (1992). *Governance and Development*. Washington, DC: World Bank.

—— (1993). *The East Asian Miracle: Economic Growth and Public Policy*. Washington, DC: World Bank.

—— (1994). *Adjustment in Africa: Reforms, Results and the Road Ahead*. Washington, DC: World Bank.

4

Governance and Growth Challenges for Africa

Mushtaq H. Khan

The World Bank recognized the role of concerted state strategies in driving growth in a number of successful East Asian countries (World Bank 1993). However, this qualified recognition was attended with the observation that the appropriate state capacities for productive interventions were missing in most other developing countries. In these countries, attempts to replicate East Asian strategies would not only fail, but would make things worse due to static efficiency losses and rent-seeking costs. On one level, the World Bank's argument against growth-promoting strategies of the East Asian type in most developing countries is absolutely accurate. The appropriate governance capabilities are clearly absent in many of the poorest countries that are most in need of growth strategies. Moreover, an attempt to acquire state capabilities on a scale that would enable these countries to attempt the types of interventionist programs seen in East Asian countries in the 1960s and 1970s is probably beyond the feasible capacity of reform in these developing countries.

However, while we recognize the obvious truth in the World Bank's analysis of the problem, their policy conclusion does not necessarily follow. The conclusion was that because the substantial growth-promoting governance capabilities of the East Asian economies did not exist in most other developing countries (and indeed could not be feasibly replicated), their optimal strategy was to abandon *all* growth-promoting strategies and resort to the alternative of seeking to promote market efficiency through market-enhancing governance. This does not follow because a market-enhancing governance strategy is equally overambitious in the demands it makes on state capabilities and focusing on this may not deliver any significant returns. To attempt to make markets in general work so efficiently that market failures are no longer a problem may be just as overambitious as the attempt to correct vast swaths of market failures through extensive interventions. In addition, there are structural reasons which set a ceiling to the development of market-enhancing governance capabilities in developing countries. Focusing purely on market-enhancing governance is therefore likely to yield disappointing results.

To take account of the limited reform capabilities in real contexts, a targeted approach to developing governance capabilities makes sense. The experience of successful developers suggests that growth-promoting governance was important, but many of the political and institutional initial conditions enjoyed by the successful countries of East Asia were indeed very different from those in Africa. Any simplistic attempt to learn the lessons of East Asia is therefore likely to be misleading because the scale of these growth-enhancing governance capabilities cannot be replicated in most contemporary developing countries. Attempts to do so are likely to result in significant government failures and the abandonment of these strategies. A more relevant approach for Africa is to learn from the experience of successful developers, while aiming for sequential and incremental "Hirschmanian" strategies of addressing critical constraints in particular areas where it is likely that the development of specific governance capabilities are feasible and can deliver results.

Good governance and the liberal economic analysis of Africa

Developing countries in Africa, as elsewhere on the planet, do not fit the conditions that the good governance model identifies as necessary for economic development. As most African countries face difficult development problems, it has been easy to build coalitions arguing that governance capabilities, as defined by the market-enhancing governance model, were responsible for African misfortunes. In particular, the analysis that the lack of democratic accountability and the presence of patron-client politics, extensive corruption, and a weak rule of law had a lot to do with Africa's relatively poor performance found many supporters within and outside Africa (Commission for Africa 2005). Indeed, to some extent these arguments are true because it must be the case that less corruption is better than more, for instance. However, these arguments did not establish (a) that these challenges were the most important ones for Africa, or (b) that they could be addressed feasibly even if they were quite important. We discuss these two issues in turn in the context of the African debate and then turn to alternative approaches that African countries need to explore.

The argument that conventional market-enhancing governance was an important, if not the most important, constraint for Africa has been challenged by a number of empirical works. An influential argument coming from Jeffrey Sachs and his associates (Sachs et al. 2004) argues that the specific characteristics of Africa in terms of low population density, vast areas, poor infrastructure, and the prevalence of difficult diseases makes many of the conventional governance arguments irrelevant. What Africa requires, according to this argument is a "big push" in terms of massive investment in infrastructure and disease control before attention to governance can deliver any results. They use a sample of thirty-three Sub-Saharan African countries to show two things. First, that once we adjust for their levels of income, only five of these countries have a governance level in 2002, as measured by the World Bank governance indicators, that is below the level expected for their level of income. Eight have governance scores that are above the level we would expect for their level of income. The rest are average, meaning their scores are about what we would expect at their income levels. But even relatively well-governed African countries failed to significantly improve their living standards. Secondly, they show that even when governance indicators are included in a general regression exercise to explain growth of per capita incomes over 1980–2000, African countries as a group do particularly badly compared to other developing countries. The dummy variable for Africa suggests that African countries grew on average 3 percent points less a year than we would expect for their per capita income and governance indicators.

We have already pointed out (Chapter 2 in this volume) the general problems with establishing causality using regression analysis. In criticizing the results reported by Sachs and associates, Kaufmann et al. make the point that two-way causality undermines the argument made by Sachs (Kaufmann et al. 2005). What they do not say is that the problem of two-way causality also undermines their own attempt to establish causality in the opposite direction, and that historical causality is difficult if not impossible to establish using regression analysis, particularly with data for a limited number of years. While the general argument for a big push in Africa can be supported, Sachs et al. underplay the importance of the governance capabilities that may also be required to implement the big push. Here, an evaluation of the historical experience of successful developers elsewhere is relevant for identifying the specific growth-enhancing governance capabilities that it will be important to develop in particular countries, given the growth strategies they are attempting. Regression analysis is not likely to help much in identifying these strategies.

An influential approach arguing for the minimal state in Africa comes from Paul Collier (2007) drawing on much work done by his research team over the years. This is a sophisticated approach that makes distinctions in governance priorities for resource-rich and resource-poor African countries, further dividing the latter group into coastal and landlocked groups. However, the underlying presumption running through the analysis is that a minimalist state is least likely to do damage, and that a state that can create conditions for markets to work reasonably well will need to do little else. Free trade is the best option for African states (with some minor exceptions that we will discuss later). The role of the state is to use available tax resources to provide security and essential public goods and, in the case of resource-rich countries, to smooth income fluctuations over time. The implicit assumption is that other market failures are not significant and that even in poor African countries, market efficiency can be sufficiently improved through good governance type reforms for most market failures to disappear (see Chapter 2 in this volume for a more complete discussion).

As these are claims about historical processes and not about the logical coherence of models, we argued that they need to be tested against a historical analysis of processes of transition in countries that have developed earlier. Collier does not engage in the bigger debate, but provides another set of regression exercises that purport to show that the underlying argument is valid. This is their analysis of state-created "syndromes" that could explain why African countries did poorly in the 1980s when some other developing countries, particularly in Asia, experienced significant growth takeoffs. Drawing on Collier and O'Connell (2007), a number of "syndromes" are identified which are essentially different aspects of state policies gone wrong. These include the mismanagement of natural resource windfalls (overspending in boom years and then having to cut back seriously in subsequent years); redistributive strategies (particularly those which benefit particular ethnic groups); excessive regulation (which is a malleable definition that can include a variety of policies that are not working); and state breakdown (conflict and civil war). The regression looks at the numbers of years between 1960–2000 when African countries suffered from "syndromes" and the relationship with growth. The unsurprising finding is that the longer the period of syndromes, the poorer the growth performance. As the authors themselves point out, the absence of syndromes did not guarantee growth (no African country was a stellar performer), but syndromes were associated with growth declines. But clearly, these regressions cannot tell us what African states should do to achieve and sustain growth at the levels that successful developers elsewhere were able to, since the absence of syndromes does not help very much in Africa according to the authors themselves.

The problem is that these results are presented as showing that not messing with the market is the best policy option for African countries. In fact, what the results show is that intervening in wrong ways or without the capabilities to do so can be damaging. It does not show that not intervening achieves or sustains the growth rates that would allow any African country to converge toward advanced country standards of living. A historical approach would ask how successful developers achieved and sustained growth over decades. Would China's sustained intervention in exchange rates and interest rates over decades, or South Korea's intervention in its financial sector and in trade policy count as syndromes? The syndrome analysis is also used to argue that the reason why Africa did not benefit from globalization and the relocation of many manufacturing activities in the 1980s is that many African countries were suffering from syndromes just at that time (Collier 2007). However, in the 1990s "when many African countries got rid of many of these syndromes" manufacturing still did not relocate to Africa. Collier pessimistically argues that this shows that Africa had simply "missed the boat" and will have to wait for several decades until its wage gap with Asia is as great as Asia's was with the OECD in the 1980s. Unfortunately, if Africa waits for the market to solve all its problems it may have to wait even longer.

Fosu's application of the syndrome approach to African growth (Chapter 6 in this volume) is subject to the standard problems of attempting to resolve questions of historical transition using regression analysis for a limited set of countries over a limited period. It may well be true that if we look at a set of African countries over a limited period, fewer syndromes were associated with higher growth. Even abstracting from problems of directions of causality and multiple explanations, there is an even more fundamental historical question of *process* that we discussed in an earlier chapter (Chapter 2 in this volume). Is there any example of a country that made the transition from poverty to high standards of living simply by getting rid of "syndromes" as defined by these authors? I do not know of any.

We have to be even more careful about the governance conclusion in Fosu (Chapter 6 in this volume)—that higher degrees of constraints on executives are associated with fewer syndromes. Implicitly, the argument is that since being syndrome-free is good, and since executive freedom is associated with a greater probability of syndromes, constraining executives in developing countries must be good. Deriving principles appropriate for historical processes from these types of correlations should obviously be treated with great care. Since there is no historical evidence that being syndrome-free is sufficient for transforming societies, constraining executives may be the wrong governance priority for developing countries, even if their current or past executives would appear to benefit from constraints. We need to understand why executives in some countries behave differently from others, because it is not the case in any historical comparison that successful developing countries had highly constrained executives.

Reading too much into correlations may have unintended consequences that the authors may not have considered. How might the United States have responded to the financial crisis of 2007–8 if its executive branch had been more constrained in its freedom of action? In comparison to advanced countries, developing countries are in a permanent state of crisis. They may commit a serious mistake by constraining their executives in the absence of strong historical evidence that unconstrained (syndrome-free) markets and constrained executives have been sufficient for taking societies out of civil wars, deep structural crises, and high levels of poverty into developed country status. Again, I do not know of any examples of such transitions. So while all regression exercises can provide useful insights, we should remember that answering big historical questions requires us to look at the historical evidence in addition to any econometric studies that may also be available.

This discussion confirms what we said earlier, namely that different methods of analysis need to be recognized and they give very different answers to big historical questions. At least we can say that the regression analysis does not prove conclusively to anyone not already convinced that liberal markets and the governance capabilities for achieving these will be sufficient to ensure African prosperity. At most they allow us to say that if African states made egregious mistakes in the past, stopping these mistakes will make things a little better. But the first proposition does not follow from the second: Stopping mistakes may not be sufficient for ensuring a developmental transformation of these societies.

We now come to the second question: To what extent is it even possible for African countries to make significant progress in achieving market-enhancing good governance goals that are recommended for them? It is important to recognize the structural factors constraining progress toward good governance capabilities in the medium term. Some of these factors may also be a problem for developing growth-enhancing governance capabilities, except that the latter recognizes that we can only develop limited areas of effective governance capabilities in most developing countries.

Stable property rights are expensive and take a long time to achieve

The achievement of property rights stability in poor countries faces extensive structural constraints. North's analysis of property rights and transaction costs has implications that are often ignored. Reducing transaction costs is itself very costly. In rich countries, almost all assets are productive and their owners pay very significant taxes, which pay for the protection of all property rights as a *public good*. In developing countries the tax base for protecting property rights as a public good simply does not exist in most cases, particularly in the poorest developing countries. Most assets are by definition in non-capitalist and low-productivity sectors, such as peasant agriculture and the informal sector. Typically these generate an insignificant surplus that is not sufficient to pay for the general protection of all assets through taxation. If stable property rights across the board cannot be achieved as a public good, institutional arrangements that protect critical investors are much more important, and these may often be informal institutions. Growth-promoting governance capabilities for managing investor property rights in developing countries can therefore often look very different from the good governance capabilities of establishing and protecting property rights as a public good (Qian 2003). What can look like a set of informal and ad hoc arrangements for protecting specific investments may well be the most effective institutional arrangement in a poor country to promote investments in critical areas.

Similarly, if property rights are not well defined and transaction costs are high, investors may often be unable to purchase the assets they need, in particular land. The strategy of improving market efficiency in these cases may take too long and specific governance capabilities need to be developed to deal with the growth constraints emanating from high transaction cost asset markets. We saw in Khan

(Chapter 2 in this volume) that non-settler colonies left many societies with conflicting and inappropriate property rights structures. For instance, only between 2 and 10 percent of land in contemporary Sub-Saharan Africa is held under freehold title while much of the rest is held in various forms of communal or customary tenures (Deininger 2003: 62). An important growth-enhancing governance capability that many of these countries need to develop is the institutional and political capability to develop industrial parks and other zones where high-productivity agriculture and industry can be set up, with adequate compensation of prior rights holders, and perhaps involving them in new productive activities. It is not an accident that different types of land reform were an important prelude to growth in high-growth economies. But in many countries, it is important to be modest and not attempt too much. A specialized and high-powered agency empowered to set up one or two industrial parks may stretch the reform capabilities of some countries, but it would be a huge achievement to show what can be done on a small scale (Khan 2009).

The fight against corruption is a long-term one

Corruption has multiple drivers and many of these are very difficult to attack in the short term in developing countries (Khan 2006b). A governance strategy that focuses on achieving significant improvements on this front is likely to disappoint in many developing countries. This does not mean that anti-corruption strategies are not desirable. It simply means we should not expect significant growth dividends from anti-corruption strategies delivering significant and *sustained* reductions in corruption. The sustainability of corruption reduction is particularly important. In many developing countries, sharp shocks from new anti-corruption agencies sometimes have a temporary effect on corruption; but over time, the tendency is for corruption to creep back. We will not discuss the reasons for this here, but we have discussed these extensively elsewhere (Khan 2006a, 2006b). What is relevant here is that if corruption cannot be significantly reduced in the medium term, we cannot expect a significant growth dividend from anti-corruption strategies.

A related problem with the good governance agenda is the assumption that *all* rents and rent-seeking are damaging. Stiglitz and others have shown that a vast range of rents are essential for the proper functioning of market economies, even advanced ones (Stiglitz 1996; Khan 2000a). Rents are no less critical in developing countries. Indeed, the catching-up and technology acquisition problems that developing countries face require significant rent-management capabilities on the part of governments if entrenched market failures are to be overcome. This is because assistance for technology acquisition necessarily creates rents. The only question is whether the rent is well-managed, resulting in growth accelerations or poorly managed, resulting in a waste of national resources. Clearly, while many rents are indeed damaging, others are second-best responses to market failures that would have worse effects without the rents. In such a context, targeting rent-seeking in general without a strategy of distinguishing between different types of rents can be misleading. The strategy must be to realize that many rents can be damaging and others are vital for development and to develop governance cap-abilities to manage some of these essential rents. These capabilities are part of the critical growth-promoting governance capabilities that developing countries need to focus on. If growth-enhancing governance capabilities are initially limited, technology policies have to be cut to size, not done away with.

To some extent Collier implicitly recognizes the importance of rents for tech-nology acquisition when he argues for preferential trade policies for Africa (Collier 2007) to give African countries a (temporary) differential advantage over Asia. Such a differential advantage provides temporary rents for African producers. Trade policy is an effective way of providing temporary rents for kick-starting investments in some sectors, but may not be sufficient in very technologically backward economies which face significant disadvantages not only in labor and management skills, but also in physical infrastructure. Other types of temporary rents have of course been used in the past, but each strategy requires specific local governance capabilities if positive results are to be achieved.

Democracy in developing countries is fragile and often works through patron-client networks

Clearly democracy is an end in itself and should be supported on these grounds alone (Khan 2005). But if we support democracy *because* we believe it is a mechanism that reduces rent-seeking and corruption, we are likely to be frequently disap-pointed. Moreover, democracy in the least developed countries remains fragile because conflicts over resources are intense, particularly between competing political factions. Fiscal constraints in developing countries often mean that democracies find it difficult to deliver public goods for everyone and political stability is often depen-dent on the ability of the political system to deliver to powerful factions. In these contexts, programs to increase democratic accountability may or may not directly assist the management of growth and productivity enhancement strategies. Some-times, powerful patron-client factions, among those who are the primary players in the democratic process in these countries, are the very organizations that impede the efficient allocation of public resources, while at other times their competition may enable the introduction of reforms and the efficient allocation of resources (Jenkins 2000; Khan 2005). The only general conclusion that we can draw is that support for democracy in developing countries should not be justified by the assertion that democracy will always improve market efficiency. Rather, democracy deserves sup-port as an end in itself, and should not be confused with the more difficult task of creating governance capabilities for supporting growth.

121

Specific problems attributed to Africa

The difficulty of implementing the good governance agenda in Africa has also had the unfortunate effect of reformers identifying a number of apparently specific African problems that have made progress difficult. In many cases the story of African exceptionalism is too pessimistic, though clearly Africa may have special problems with its size, historically lower population density, and therefore generally less developed states. Nevertheless, where Africa is not exceptional at all is that no developing country has actually succeeded in implementing good governance at levels of per capita income that we see in Africa (Khan, Chapter 2 in this volume). The true African exceptionalism may be that Africa is now expected to do something that no one else has done. We look at a number of areas where specific problems have been identified. These features point not to a significant difference in African challenges compared to general developing country problems but rather perhaps the need to go slower with ambitious reform programs and developing growth-enhancing governance capabilities in more modest ways in countries with poor initial conditions.

Neo-patrimonialism and fragmented polities

The neo-patrimonial argument is that African states are distinctively pre-modern. This analysis goes back to Médard who has written a number of pieces, with the main arguments summarized in Médard (2002). The neo-patrimonial state contrasts with a modern Weberian state that is supposed to be impersonal, formal, accountable, and non-corrupt. The neo-patrimonial state is the precise opposite, with personalized and informal relationships between the boss or patron and his clients. The patron is unaccountable and corrupt, treating the public domain as a private fief, and dispensing benefits to clients to stay in power. While all these characteristics are clearly visible in Africa, a comparative historical analysis shows that these features are common to all developing countries going through the developmental transformation. The scarcity of fiscal resources for providing generalized public goods means that in all developing countries variants of patron-client politics are used as a means of delivering to politically powerful constituencies whose support is vital for the survival of the ruling group (Khan 2005).

Médard argues that the problem in Africa is the absence of accountability that allows leaders to treat the public domain as their private fief. The policy suggested is the support of democratization and accountability as a way of weakening the hold of the personal power of the "big men," thereby helping to make the state become more modern and Weberian. In this respect, the argument is close to the general good governance one summarized earlier in Khan (Chapter 2 in this volume). However, this theoretical argument is not supported by any historical observation from anywhere in the world that shows that democratization has systematically driven (rather than having followed or coevolved in complex ways with) the emergence of a modern capitalist economy and the Weberian state that is associated with it (Khan 2005). In particular, democratization in developing countries does not do away with patron-client politics but does change their organization in ways that are sometimes more developmental and sometimes less. But because gradually building democratic institutions has long-term benefits, democracy should be pragmatically supported for its own sake.

A related issue is the political fragmentation of polities in Africa. For instance, Chabal and Daloz (1999) in an influential argument observed that in African states *disorder was institutionalized*. What they refer to is precisely the disorder that allows the transfer of resources down patron-client networks. The weakness of their argument is that what they refer to as a specifically African problem is actually a general characteristic of all developing countries. Or to put it differently, the institutionalization of order (stable property rights, entrenched democracy, low or negligible corruption, the accountability of leaders, and so on) requires a significant level of development in order to be effectively implemented.

So what is distinctive about Africa? Chabal and Daloz, and many other commentators on Africa, appear to be saying that African leaderships do not have the "political will" to impose order to capture more significant productive surpluses by enhancing production compared to the easy surpluses available through unproductive means. Similar problems exist in many Asian countries and regions and I have argued that this problem is deeper than one of political will. Some societies have very fragmented polities, and the extent and type of political fragmentation in Asia can improve our understanding of the differential performance *within* Asian countries (Khan 1996b, 1999, 2000b). Some of these ideas have been developed in the African context by Lockwood (2005). This work suggests that the focus of attention should be on the institutional and political fragmentation of African states, and not just or even primarily on the political will, integrity, or other characteristics of the leadership, important though these may also be in some contexts.

The performance of political leaderships can change dramatically with the political organizations they can deploy. This is because their capacity to enforce depends on the effectiveness of the political organizations they work with. It is widely recognized that a poor capacity to implement or enforce can result in predatory behavior for a number of reasons. A lack of confidence in their ability to protect their own wealth in the future can induce elites to steal and export their capital. This is a variant of the argument put forward by Olson when he contrasted stationary bandits (a stable state where elites can expect to protect themselves in the future) with roving bandits (where elites are fragmented and short-lived) (Olson 2000). Similarly, poor political and institutional coordination can result in different parts of the state behaving in uncoordinated ways to raise revenue and inadvertently reducing their own incomes (Shleifer and Vishny 1993; Khan 1996a). Of course, building the political organizations and enforcement institutions that may eventually allow African societies to make more rapid transitions to productive economies is also a matter of conscious political activity. But the reference here is to collective political activity, not the political will of a specific leadership. And again, Africa does not face qualitatively different problems here compared to many Asian societies.

African culture

A variant of the neo-patrimonial argument is that the personalized politics observed in Africa is supported by a specific African peasant culture. The "economy of affection" that describes this culture in turn emerges in the fragmented economy of African agriculture where exchange has to be based on personalized relationships. Patrimonial politics results from this economy and the culture that it generates (Hyden and Williams 1994). But again, a comparison with the Asian experience suggests there is nothing unique about the African peasant economy. James Scott made exactly the same observations about the Asian peasantry in his account of the *moral economy* of the Vietnamese peasantry (Scott 1977). These accounts are consistent with our explanation that formal property rights and institutions cannot be sustained in poor economies since the underlying assets do not yet generate enough of a surplus to pay for their protection and the maintenance of a rule-of-law society that allows impersonal private contracting at low transaction cost. However, none of this precluded *transitions* to productive capitalist economies in Asia. It is not clear why peasant culture should be playing a significantly more negative role in Africa.

Ethnic fragmentation

A common perception is that Africa suffers from excessive ethnic fragmentation and that many African states have not resolved fundamental questions about their territorial limits and ethnic compositions. The argument here is that this prevents any dominant group in an African polity from acquiring the legitimacy to enforce rights or even decisions about the allocation of social resources at low cost. Moreover, the attempt by ruling groups to benefit their own tribe or region further exacerbates these underlying problems. There is an element of truth in this argument, but ethnic fragmentation should not be overstated as an explanation of state weakness. The extent of fragmentation varies across African countries. Often conflicts over resources can take an ethnic form, but these conflicts would probably have been just as intense in ethnically homogenous societies where cleavages would have been organized along other lines. It is also worth remembering that many African countries are relatively new, having just emerged from colonial occupation as in Mozambique and Angola. The Asian experience of post-independence development shows that periods of considerable turmoil can follow independence even in ethnically homogenous societies (for example Bangladesh in the 1970s).

It is equally important to remember that national identities even in states that now appear to be ethnically homogenous have always been the product of social engineering. Successful states in Asia and Europe created national identities with differing degrees of success. Asian states that appear to be ethnically homogenous today, such as Thailand, achieved this through very specific state policies of nation-building that were often not very pleasant for minorities (such as the Chinese who were forced to adopt Thai names and stop going to Chinese schools). These are not necessarily examples to emulate, but it is important to remember that ethnicity, like nationhood, is a construct. Then there are Asian states, such as India, that in terms of ethnic, religious, caste, and other cleavages should not even have lasted, but in fact emerged as one of the most effective states in the region. Again, simple answers such as, "India works because of its democracy" are too simplistic. India works because of complex internal bargains that also involve corrupt patron-client politics and often the exercise of significant amounts of state and non-state violence. Examples of states working to create homogenous or at least cohesive national identities are not absent in Africa: The case of Tanzania is particularly interesting because the creation of a composite national identity was one of the primary goals of the Nyerere years, and by all accounts, the results were quite remarkable in the African context. The Tanzanian experience shows that nation-building is a long process in which outsiders can contribute little but can potentially do much damage by suggesting easy options that may not exist.

Africa is a relative newcomer to the long centuries of ethnic wars and conflicts that have marked state-building in Europe and Asia. This included two world wars that had their origins in European national conflicts. The lesson from the European and Asian experiences should not be that Africa has a problem because it is too ethnically fragmented, but rather it should be that Africa has been relatively civilized so far in its several decades of building nation states compared to the human costs in Europe and Asia over the last few centuries. The question could be rephrased to ask how Africa could learn the lessons of state-building from Europe and Asia so that it may progress in a less bloody and socially costly way. This way of asking the question focuses on the historical process: Democratic norms only took deep root in many European countries after centuries of national conflicts. While it is clear that a minimal national consensus is required for a society to embark on any development strategy, the challenge is to identify what needs to be done in terms of reform priorities once a minimal national consensus emerges in countries such as Tanzania.

Africa's resource curse

It is often also argued that in many resource-rich African countries, the descent into predation stems from the easy availability of *natural resource rents*, while Asia was helped by the absence of these natural resource rents. The argument is that warring factions in Africa can sustain conflict by financing themselves using natural resources. Conversely, the leadership of resource-poor Asian countries had to concentrate on how to produce wealth through industrialization. But while the easy availability of resources can sustain conflict, it does not explain why fragmentation exists in the first place since the discovery of windfall incomes in a country with a cohesive state could be a spur to development. Industrialization requires resources for investment, and where states with some enforcement capacity exist, natural resources can be very helpful in generating resources for high rates of investment in industry or high-value services. This strategy was very successfully followed, for instance, by Malaysia and more recently by Dubai.

In themselves, natural-resource rents do not have to be damaging (see for instance Khan 2000a). Indeed, these are necessary rents from an economic perspective, as they help to achieve a rate of extraction of natural resources that is closer to the sustainable or optimal level. As with all rents, the existence of natural-resource rents will induce rent-seeking and in some cases where easy rents are available, this rent-seeking can divert economic and political entrepreneurs into unproductive activities to an excessive extent. While this is theoretically possible, there is no reason to believe that it is inevitable. Even in Africa, there are already plenty of counterexamples. Botswana's success has been based on natural-resource rents but it has not succumbed to civil war. Ghana exports large amounts of gold but is relatively peaceful, and even Angola is moving into a more peaceful era despite being a major oil exporter and Africa's largest diamond exporter.

We can accept the argument that natural resources can sustain conflicts that would otherwise have to be fought using more primitive weapons, but this does not mean that in the absence of these rents the fragmented states would have become cohesive. Fragmented states without natural resources can always discover new ways of generating income to sustain conflict, ranging from drugs to intervening in conflicts in neighboring countries. It is quite plausible to argue that, for instance, Saudi Arabia without the oil may have been more like Afghanistan than South Korea. Thus, without denying the complications (both positive and negative) created by the presence of natural-resource rents, we need to ask why states remain institutionally fragmented and politically weak in some contexts but manage to reform themselves and become developmental in others. The Asian experience suggests that developmental states emerged in both resource-poor countries (South Korea, Taiwan) as well as in resource-rich countries (Malaysia). Equally, non-developmental states have persisted in many Asian countries that are resource-poor, both coastal and otherwise (Nepal, Afghanistan, Myanmar,

Cambodia, Laos to name a few). These observations are particularly relevant for Africa, where large natural resource endowments should be seen as an opportunity rather than a curse. Institutional and governance capacities could develop that allow resource-rich African countries to manage these rents for economic development.

However, some of the proposals coming from the good governance approach are likely to be impossible to implement and have problematic implications for the development of growth-oriented states. For instance, there is a frequent suggestion that hydrocarbon and mineral rents should be in ring-fenced development accounts that are pre-committed to service delivery expenditures, preferably in pro-poor public goods like health and education. These suggestions may appear to be a huge improvement on the corruption and capital flight that is often associated with mineral rents in many African countries, which are real enough problems. But it is hard to imagine how the expenditure of such large chunks of national income can be effectively de-linked from internal power structures for too long. This is likely to be another example of a good idea that on closer inspection turns out to be implausible as an implementable strategy in the long term. Nor is it clear, given the market failures affecting investment in new technologies and sectors in these countries, that ring-fencing all these potential investment resources away from the ruling elites who are potential investors is necessarily a good idea. It may be a better long-term bet in many of these countries to develop effective governance capabilities for managing growth-enhancing strategies, however shaky the progress. Capital flight happens when countries fail to develop profitable investment opportunities for their elites. If mineral and hydrocarbon rents are even moderately efficiently used in investment strategies, the long-run outcome for the country is likely to be satisfactory. This is easier said than done, but an objective of developing indigenous investment capabilities is a very different one from developing ring-fenced accounts that are pre-committed to provide pro-poor public goods. Each requires different incremental steps and the construction of different political coalitions. But one may be more viable than the other.

Growth-promoting governance strategies

A decade of reforms beginning in the 1990s, including a big push on good governance reforms, was associated with spurts of growth in a number of African countries. However, although there are variations across countries, manufacturing remains weak in Africa and agriculture faces serious constraints in terms of infrastructure and investment. Much of the growth in the 1990s, though by no means all, was associated with a commodity boom that included good performance not only for hydrocarbon and mineral producers, but also for producers of some agricultural commodities such as coffee. The challenge is to extend these growth gains into manufacturing and higher-value agriculture and services, and here the market failures discussed earlier (Chapter 2 in this volume) need to be addressed. Since low transaction cost markets cannot be achieved through good governance reforms, specific market failures constraining particular sectors and technologies have to be addressed in a sequential way.

Ambitious growth-promoting strategies

Supporters of growth-promoting governance interventions often refer to the examples of the Asian countries, particularly in East Asia, which used extensive interventions including industrial policy to accelerate technology acquisition and move up the value chain at a more rapid pace than would have been likely without these interventions. These countries, which include South Korea, Taiwan, Malaysia, and others demonstrate the possibility that extensive interventions across a range of sectors can achieve accelerated productivity growth and learning, and sequential moves up the value chain. Moreover, they managed to achieve these results without attempting or succeeding in achieving good governance as defined in the good governance consensus. However, their success was based on a different set of state capabilities and the very scale of their successful interventions suggests that it may not be possible to develop a growth-enhancing governance strategy for poorly performing developing countries simply by looking at and attempting to imitate the governance capabilities of more successful developers. This is so for at least two different sets of reasons.

First, the more successful developers enjoyed more favorable historical endowments of institutions and political conditions to begin with, which amounted to significant governance capabilities in some areas. They also had some pockets of capitalist development, such that entrepreneurs and technological capabilities were present to a greater extent than in many of the poorest countries in contemporary Africa. These initial conditions allowed a range of interventions to be *effectively policed* in the sense that it was difficult for inefficient rent-seekers to capture state-created rents if they failed to produce results (the relevant literature is reviewed in Khan 2004).

But secondly, successful developers had many different strategies of overcoming market failures, backed by different governance capabilities that were appropriate for the strategies they were following. Success in each case depended on the country selecting economic instruments to correct market failures that it could actually enforce given its internal political settlement and institutional capabilities (Khan 2000b, 2006b). This is an important observation for many poorly performing countries, where overall governance capabilities are poorer and where it is therefore much more important to design interventions and governance reforms very carefully to achieve the maximum effect and to avoid failures that can easily happen if limited capacities are overstretched.

These observations suggest that the only viable strategy for most developing countries would be a less ambitious strategy that addressed some of the market failures that the good governance strategy is implicitly trying to address, but without attempting the ambitious implementation strategies of either the good governance agenda or the East Asian developmental states. In this *incremental strategy* the goal would be to address critical market failures, but to focus on a few at a time using instruments and strategies that were most likely to be implementable given feasible improvements in targeted governance capabilities. The distinctive part of the alternative approach suggested here is that interventions to overcome market failures and governance capabilities appropriate for their effective implementation should be simultaneously identified and developed so that the feasibility of the strategy as a whole is addressed (Khan 2008a, 2008c; UNCTAD 2009).

Incremental approaches to governance reform

While Africa is not necessarily exceptional, most African countries, in common with many Asian ones, suffer from fragmented polities, weak political organizations, and elites who lack sufficient legitimacy to be fully confident of the future. These characteristics rule out ambitious growth-enhancing strategies and point to the need to develop careful country-specific strategies for enhancing growth by addressing specific market failures. Enforcement capacities and governance capabilities for addressing these problems are likely to be limited. In these contexts, growth and governance strategies are more likely to succeed if they are narrowly defined and supported by *pragmatic and limited instruments* (Khan 2008a). These may make a big potential impact, provided some very specific and limited governance capabilities are developed to support these instruments.

If the question is put in such a pragmatic way, it is unlikely that we should conclude that in general there are no intermediate steps that a developing country could take to counter the types of market failure that slow down technology upgrading, learning, sectoral diversification, and so on. But even here, the optimal strategy will be different in different countries because of differences in their initial conditions and in particular their governance and enforcement capabilities. We should expect that countries will have to go through a process of experimentation to identify the mix of instruments and strategies that are most likely to deliver results given their initial conditions and in particular their political settlements.

The link with Hirschman's ideas on entrepreneurial development in poor countries is very instructive (Hirschman 1958, 1967). In a series of pioneering works, Albert Hirschman pointed out that the most limiting resource in a developing country was likely to be its supply of entrepreneurs. Trying to do too many things was therefore not a good strategy. Rather, an incremental approach that relied on disequilibria to attract scarce entrepreneurial capacity into the most important sectors would produce the best results. The aim of development strategy would be to identify areas of critical bottlenecks where entrepreneurial effort was likely to have the biggest spillover effects through backward and forward linkages. To a great extent, this approach to the problems of entrepreneurship is just as relevant for thinking about the problems of governance.

The pool of competent and committed personnel and resources that are available to make a dent on the problems of governance is if anything even more limited than the pool of potential entrepreneurs in many developing countries. The best use of this scarce resource is to identify a few agencies where the best "administrative entrepreneurs" can be allocated to address specific market failures, say in technology acquisition for a particular sector or to ease labor training requirements in that sector, or to ease a constraint on industrial or agricultural land availability. And as in Hirschman's original argument, the critical condition for success would be that mistakes must not be allowed to continue for too long, and *if the entrepreneurial capacities to solve problems did not emerge in particular projects, there had to be some process of exit* otherwise the likely social costs were obvious.

Therefore a Hirschmanian incremental approach to governance would have a number of components: We should not stretch existing governance and productive capabilities too much by trying to do everything at once. Rather we should focus on a few areas that appear to be relatively obvious areas where growth could be further promoted (we will discuss what *obvious* means in this context later). The essential Hirschmanian insight is that we should not expect a scientific and conclusive *ex ante* identification of critical bottlenecks or constraints a society faces because success depends on the *ex post* effort put in by stakeholders into the process of discovery and experimentation and so results cannot be "pre-planned." What appears to be a good bet may turn out to be otherwise, and what appears to be an unlikely area *may* provide a challenge that results in the unexpected development of new productive and governance capabilities. Most importantly, therefore, *we need to have good exit strategies for the few things that we do try, and not try to do things where vested interests are likely to be so strong that exit may be precluded.* If we keep in mind these pragmatic pointers, we should be able, through a process that must involve both prior analysis but also some experimentation, to identify a pragmatic set of strategies for developing countries that recognize both the reality of pervasive market failure and the limited capacities for overcoming them.

The argument that governance priorities for developing countries should be modest and should focus on the most important constraints has already been powerfully made by a number of observers, including Rodrik and his team (Hausmann et al. 2007). They have also pointed out that the detailed governance capabilities that have been found to work in different countries can vary widely (Qian 2003). However, Hirschman's perceptive observations of fifty years ago on the indeterminate nature of the feasibility studies that preceded the adoption of projects in developing countries are just as applicable today to the sophisticated "growth diagnostics" methods that are often suggested for identifying binding constraints in developing countries (Hausmann et al. 2007). When the binding constraint approach is actually used in different countries, different economists can come up with very different conclusions about what the binding constraint is. A lot depends on the methodologies different economists may use, their own methodological assumptions and their degree of knowledge about the country (Leipziger and Zagha 2006). The conclusion that the assessment of a binding constraint is a "disciplined art" rather than a "science" would not have surprised Hirschman at all.

Apart from the problem of the many different methodologies that different observers can use to assess binding constraints, the real difficulty, as Hirschman pointed out, is the uncertainty that comes from not being able to foresee *future* problems and opportunities that will open up with *any* strategy chosen. The importance of *exit strategies*, and therefore the importance of choosing areas of intervention where exit is more likely to be feasible if future problems appear can thus emerge as the critical issue. The issues of uncertainty, experimentation, and therefore the necessity of exit strategies are critical issues that the binding constraints approach ignores.

Hirschman's approach suggests a different focus for attention. The focus here is not on how to identify and select in a scientific way the binding constraints that first need to be tackled to support growth. Rather the focus suggested by a Hirschmanian reading of development history is on how to develop *new capabilities* in a pragmatic experimental way *through a process of experimentation and problem solving that could not have been foreseen from the beginning. From this perspective, it makes sense to select a number of reasonably obvious starting points for capacity building that make sense in terms of challenges currently being faced by growth sectors in the country. The critical condition is rather that the priorities for capacity building should be selected in such a way that the political capacity for exit is assured if the results are not satisfactory.*

It is here that we should focus because we believe that in the poorest countries, reform can begin at various points and that typically it will not be possible to find or agree on a single binding constraint. The starting point is likely to depend on specific political possibilities and capabilities, and there are likely to be a number of obvious places where we could begin (Khan 2008a). If success is achieved in one sector, the capabilities and lessons learned can then be transferred to strategies for other sectors. The simplest strategy for a country is to begin with sectors which have already achieved some global market presence or are close to doing so. This is a pragmatic way to begin because to identify market failures in abstract may be beyond the technical and planning capabilities of many least developed countries. However, every country has some sectors in which growth has been higher than in others, and where exports are actually making some progress even if more could be achieved. If we begin with these sectors and ask how capacity expansion, technology upgrading, and increases in value addition could be accelerated, government agencies and governance capabilities could be developed (in a Hirschmanian incremental way) that have broader application to other sectors.

The steps involved in such a strategy are summarized in Figure 4.1, based on Khan (2008a). Step 1 in Figure 4.1 is to identify a few sectors in which growth policy (the investment and technology policy) should focus in terms of addressing constraints on further productivity enhancement and moving up the value chain. In most developing countries, there are a number of sectors in which some growth has been achieved and a pragmatic approach would be to start with these sectors and ask what needs to be done to improve productivity, move up the value chain, and enhance growth in these sectors. Unlike good governance type reforms, here

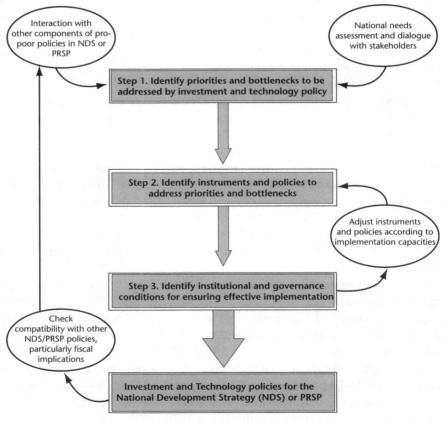

Figure 4.1 Steps in developing a national growth strategy
Source: Khan (2008a: Figure 1)

we recognize that general governance improvements that would in theory impact *all* sectors should not be the *sole* focus of governance or growth policies in poor countries. Once a number of initial sectors and bottlenecks have been identified in Step 1, the critical decisions are in Steps 2 and 3 in Figure 4.1, which are the stages at which a discussion of the requisite governance capabilities for the growth strategy comes into focus.

The identification of "obvious" sectors could be managed through a transparent process of evaluation and dialogue that involves key business organizations in the country. But while there may be debates at the margin about which sectors should be selected as the initial few for policy attention, the sectors that must be included will be less controversial. For instance, in Ethiopia, the leather sector, cotton textiles, and cut flowers immediately attract attention as sectors that have already achieved some success. Or in Tanzania, cotton textiles, tourism, and mining are obvious candidates for initiating the policy investigation. This is not to suggest that identifying the sectors that policymakers should initially focus on is always going to be uncontroversial. There are likely to be intense conflicts in some countries where growing sectors that are not included feel that they have been discriminated against. For the policy process to be inclusive and transparent it is therefore important for as many as possible of the important sectors to be included, without excessively diluting the efficacy of the policy dialogue by including the whole economy (see also Khan 2008a).

By focusing on a few sectors and looking for the constraints that are preventing growth, it is more likely that market failures will be discovered in a pragmatic way that could be the target for specific policy interventions to correct these failures. The focus then shifts to Steps 2 and 3, which describe a process of iteration through which a number of narrowly defined instruments are selected *such that agencies charged with their implementation already have the necessary governance capabilities to implement them effectively or these capabilities can be feasibly developed.*

Even in a limited number of areas, the task of identifying plausible constraints created by market failures is not easy and requires the presence of capable policymakers in key positions. The technical capacities in government agencies are often lacking. Entrepreneurs themselves may have perceptions about the constraints on their expansion that are based very closely on the consensus opinion of international financial institutions, regularly reported in the national press. For instance, Doing Business surveys ask very limited questions of entrepreneurs on things like how long it takes to export and import, their opinions about infrastructure constraints, and so on, but does not ask questions about whether poor labor skills made the business uncompetitive and the constraints preventing firm-level investments in these labor skills. These results are then reported back to the national media as an objective identification of *the* constraints facing business and soon a wide swath of newspaper-reading entrepreneurs in the country are likely to identify exactly the problems of governance and investment climate identified in these surveys as *the* problems constraining them (Khan 2008b).

There is no question that if electricity supply could be improved, if roads and ports appeared, and if the bureaucracy became more efficient, enterprise across the board would benefit. But these are precisely the big-ticket public goods that take a long time to develop and deliver. They should be developed, but in the meantime the trick is to identify areas where there are potentially big returns to relatively small investments but where these investments will not be made by private investors because market failures prevent them from being assured of private returns or the private risk is too high. If policy attention in these areas actually sustained and even accelerated growth, the resources for the big-ticket public goods would be more likely to be forthcoming in the future. Examples follow of the types of market failures that could be addressed.

Market failures affecting investment in new sectors and technologies

In many developing countries, finance for potentially profitable manufacturing investment is simply not available. This could either be because the entrepreneurial base is so underdeveloped that existing entrepreneurs do not have the track record or collateral to borrow from commercial banks. Or it could be because banks have excessive risk premiums for productive investments and prefer to lend to consumers to finance consumer goods purchases. In other developing countries, finance may be available for a few rapidly growing sectors as long as entrepreneurs continue to invest in known technologies where the risk is low, but they may be forced to finance more risky investments on their own because banks or other outside investors do not want to share these risks.

These are all examples of potential market failures. Specific agencies providing relatively small amounts of seed capital for small-scale investments in start-ups can have potentially large social benefits provided the caveats about exit strategies for programs are adhered to. The development of entrepreneurial skills and the development of knowledge and capabilities to use new technologies are vital for most developing countries. It is a very big assumption to assume that the risk-sharing arrangements for these risky investments are likely to emerge through private contracting in contexts where contract enforcement is weak because of structural reasons. With public agencies absorbing some of these risks, some mistakes will inevitably be made, some rent-seeking will take place, and some entrepreneurs will fail for no fault of their own. But clearly these costs can be reduced significantly by limiting the program to manageable proportions for that country and providing well funded and capable individuals in key agencies charged with delivering results. The examples of successful countries show that in the early days their success was typically based on islands of effective agencies operating in unpromising environments. These islands are likely to be even smaller and more modest in developing countries with less promising initial conditions. But it is still important to plan appropriately and develop these approaches.

An incremental growth-promoting governance approach in this context would be to work with existing financial institutions, the government, and the private sector to develop feasible governance capabilities that allow *existing* financial instruments or ones similar to those used by other developing countries to be implemented to allow risk-sharing investments. The critical issue is not just to provide implicit subsidies to financing instruments, or for government to absorb some of the risks involved, but to have well-designed instruments so that the desired results are achieved. In particular, poor countries would be right to start with relatively small experiments with specific financial instruments and scale up if the governance capabilities for these instruments can be developed.

These market failures are of course well recognized in the market-promoting agenda. However, the standard good governance reform strategy is to make markets more efficient by focusing on rule-of-law reforms, anti-corruption strategies, and competition policies. In theory, if a broad-based rule of law could be enforced, contract-enforcement would improve, allowing long-term profit-sharing investments including through stock markets. However, the practical question is whether these market-enhancing governance reforms can be implemented to a sufficient extent and soon enough to have any effect on these pressing market failures. How much further would contract enforcement, rule of law, anti-corruption, and disclosure reforms have to proceed to allow firms with no track record to raise money in efficient capital markets from domestic venture capitalists willing to bet on the learning skills of particular entrepreneurs? The historical evidence suggests this is not likely to happen any time soon.

Labor skills and training

Despite being labor surplus economies, when it comes to manufacturing employment even in relatively low-technology sectors, many poor countries appear to suffer from perennial labor shortages. Some of the shortages are due to a dearth of specific skills, but there is also a shortage of "unskilled" labor. The reason for the latter is that while labor is abundant, workers exposed to factory discipline and conditions of work in a high-pressure export sector are difficult to find. The skills provided by formal school education are socially important but do not necessarily fill this gap. Firms in these countries therefore have to engage in on-the-job training but they systematically invest too little in this. At the same time, private-sector training institutes for skilled workers have been set up in more advanced developing countries with larger manufacturing sectors. But here too there is low uptake and an unwillingness of employers to pay very much for training their workforce. These are clear examples of market failures. Training is available and required, but is not taken up despite employers facing serious shortages of skills. The problem is that the employer financing the training faces a market failure (externality) problem because the worker could leave the firm with the training and bargain for a higher wage elsewhere.

Once again, a number of simple solutions could address the market failures affecting labor skills and training. However, each solution requires specific governance capabilities on the part of the government to deal with that market failure. The possibility of long-term employment contracts with the personnel receiving training is one solution that is ruled out by the implausibility of enforcing such contracts in a developing country environment. This leaves the possibility of subsidizing the provision of training. The training at issue could range from orientation programs for new entrants into the industrial workforce to very specific programs of skill development required for specific technologies.

However, for a training scheme not to waste public funds, it would need to be carefully designed and managed, bringing us back to the issue of developing specific governance capabilities in selected agencies. Depending on the stage of development of the country, training could range from very simple to fairly sophisticated. Government could assist the solution of the market failures in a variety of ways including co-financing training programs set up by industry associations, providing low or zero interest loans to workers attending accredited training programs, and so on. In each case the design of the program would have to respond to industry needs as well as the capabilities of available public officials to monitor and implement the program.

Land allocation and the achievement of scale economies

Market failures in the land market can be a serious constraint for new projects and for expansions in developing countries, particularly in relatively densely populated ones or ones where land rights are particularly poorly defined. Land typically does not have clearly established property rights in most developing countries. It is often difficult to establish clear ownership, there are often multiple claimants for most plots of land, and the plot sizes are typically small. There are structural reasons for this, to do with the limited productivity of most land, and the high cost of establishing clear property rights on assets like land (Khan 2006c, 2009). Potential investors can face long and complex processes for acquiring a piece of uncontested land.

In the conventional good governance approach the solution to these problems is to improve the land market as a whole by improving land records, the court system, and by fighting corruption, so that land market transactions can take place smoothly. The importance of land use regulation is obviously also recognized but by itself this will not solve the problem faced by industry if overall land market efficiency does not also improve. These good governance or market-enhancing governance strategies are clearly only likely to deliver in the very long run. In contrast, an incremental growth-promoting governance approach would be to identify specific land bottlenecks and develop moderately efficient agencies to address land use problems in these priority areas.

The precise configuration of tasks and capabilities for a land agency would obviously vary from country to country, depending on the types of problems and the political and institutional initial conditions. One possibility is to charge it with the acquisition of land for industrial zones and to provide adequate infrastructural amenities. Such agencies exist in many countries but they are often ineffective. The prioritization of growth-enhancing governance capabilities is precisely to focus on vital areas. In developing countries where almost everything could be improved, the absence of prioritization often means that nothing gets done. The essential point is simply that the growth-promoting approach is about focusing on a limited range of things that *can* be done, and then ensuring that the highest quality personnel with clear political support are made available for these agencies. As with the other types of interventions discussed, the ability to change the policy and indeed to exit from strategies that are not working is critical for improving the chances of success.

References

Chabal, P. and Daloz, J.-P. (1999). *Africa Works: Disorder as Political Instrument*. Oxford and Indianapolis: James Currey and Indiana University Press.

Collier, P. (2007). "Growth Strategies for Africa." Paper prepared for the Spence Commission on Economic Growth, University of Oxford, Oxford.

——and O'Connell, S. A. (2007). "African Economic Growth: Opportunities and Choices," in B. J. Ndulu, S. A. O'Connell, R. H. Bates, and P. Collier (eds.), *The Political Economy of African Economic Growth 1960–2000*. Cambridge: Cambridge University Press.

Commission for Africa (2005). *Our Common Interest: Report of the Commission for Africa*. London: Commission for Africa.

Deininger, K. (2003). *Land Policies for Growth and Poverty Reduction*. Washington, DC: The World Bank.

Hausmann, R., Rodrik, D., and Velasco, A. (2007). "Growth Diagnostics." Initiative for Policy Dialogue Working Paper Series. Columbia University: New York. Available at <http://policydialogue.org/files/publications/Ch_15.pdf>

Hirschman, A. O. (1958). *The Strategy of Economic Development*. New Haven: Yale University Press.

——(1967). *Development Projects Observed*. Washington, DC: The Brookings Institution.

Hyden, G. and Williams, D. C. (1994). "A Community Model of African Politics: Illustrations from Nigeria and Tanzania." *Comparative Studies in Society and History*, 36 (1): 68–96.

Jenkins, R. (2000). *Democratic Politics and Economic Reform in India*. Cambridge: Cambridge University Press.

Kaufmann, D., Kraay, A., and Mastruzzi, M. (2005). "Governance Matters IV: Governance Indicators for 1996–2004." World Bank Policy Research Working Paper No. 3630, available at <http://www.worldbank.org/wbi/governance/pubs/govmatters4.html>.

Khan, M. H. (1996a). "The Efficiency Implications of Corruption," *Journal of International Development*, 8 (5): 683–96.

——(1996b). "A Typology of Corrupt Transactions in Developing Countries," *IDS Bulletin (Liberalization and the New Corruption)*, 27 (2): 12–21.

——(1999). "The Political Economy of Industrial Policy in Pakistan 1947–1971." SOAS Department of Economics Working Paper No. 98, School of Oriental and African Studies, University of London, London.

——(2000a). "Rents, Efficiency and Growth," in M. H. Khan and Jomo K. S. (eds.), *Rents, Rent-Seeking and Economic Development: Theory and Evidence in Asia*. Cambridge: Cambridge University Press.

——(2000b). "Rent-seeking as Process," in M. H. Khan and Jomo K. S. (eds.), *Rents, Rent-Seeking and Economic Development: Theory and Evidence in Asia*, Cambridge: Cambridge University Press.

——(2004). "State Failure in Developing Countries and Strategies of Institutional Reform," in B. Tungodden, N. Stern, and I. Kolstad (eds.), *Annual World Bank Conference on Development Economics Europe (2003): Toward Pro-Poor Policies: Aid Institutions and Globalization, Proceedings of Annual World Bank Conference on Development Economics*. Oxford: Oxford University Press and World Bank, available at <http://www-wds.worldbank.org/servlet/WDS_IBank_Servlet?pcont=details&eid=000160016_20040518162841>.

——(2005). "Markets, States and Democracy: Patron-Client Networks and the Case for Democracy in Developing Countries," *Democratization*, 12 (5): 705–25.

——(2006a). "Corruption and Governance," in Jomo K. S. and B. Fine (eds.), *The New Development Economics*. London/New Delhi: Zed Press/Tulika.

——(2006b). "Determinants of Corruption in Developing Countries: The Limits of Conventional Economic Analysis," in S. Rose-Ackerman (ed.), *International Handbook on the Economics of Corruption*. Cheltenham: Edward Elgar.

——(2006c). "Governance and Anti-Corruption Reforms in Developing Countries: Policies, Evidence and Ways Forward." G-24 Discussion Paper Series: Research Papers for the Intergovernmental Group of Twenty-Four on International Monetary Affairs and Development No. 42, United Nations Conference on Trade and Development, New York and Geneva, available at <http://www.unctad.org/en/docs/gdsmdpbg2420064_en.pdf>.

——(2008a). "Investment and Technology Policies," in Department of Economic and social Affairs (DESA) (ed.), *National Development Strategies: Policy Notes*, New York: United Nations.

——(2008b). "Technological Upgrading in Bangladeshi Manufacturing: Constraints and Policy Responses Identified in a Study of the Ready-Made Garments Industry." *Unpublished UNDP Report*. UNDP: Dhaka. Available at <http://eprints.soas.ac.uk/9961/1/Technological Upgrading.pdf>.

——(2008c). "Building Growth-Promoting Governance Capabilities." *Background paper for The Least Developed Countries Report 2008*, UNCTAD, Geneva, available at <http://mercury.soas.ac.uk/users/mk17/Docs/Building%20Growth%20Promoting%20Governance.pdf>.

——(2009). "Governance Capabilities and the Property Rights Transition in Developing Countries." DFID Research Paper Series on Governance for Growth, School of Oriental and African Studies, University of London, London, available at <http://mercury.soas.ac. uk/users/mk17/Docs/Property%20Transitions%20internet.pdf>.

Leipziger, D. M. and Zagha, R. (2006). "Getting Out of the Rut: Applying Growth Diagnostics at the World Bank," *Finance and Development*, 43 (1): 16–17, available at <http://www.imf. org/external/pubs/ft/fandd/2006/03/leipzige.htm>.

Lockwood, M. (2005). *The State They're In: An Agenda for International Action on Poverty in Africa*. Bourton-on-Dunsmore: ITDG Publishing.

Médard, J.-F. (2002). "Corruption in the Neo-Patrimonial States of Sub-Saharan Africa," in A. J. Heidenheimer and M. Johnston (eds.), *Political Corruption: Concepts and Contexts*, 3rd edn. New Brunswick: Transaction Publishers.

Olson, M. (2000). "Dictatorship, Democracy and Development," in M. Olson and S. Kähkönen (eds.), *A Not-so-Dismal Science: A Broader View of Economies and Societies*. Oxford: Oxford University Press.

Qian, Y. (2003). "How Reform Worked in China," in D. Rodrik (ed.), *In Search of Prosperity: Analytical Narratives on Economic Growth*. Princeton, NJ: Princeton University Press, available at <http://ksghome.harvard.edu/~.drodrik.academic.ksg/Growth%20volume/Qian-China. pdf>.

Sachs, J. D., McArthur, J. W., Schmidt-Traub, G., Kruk, M., Bahadur, C., Faye, M., and McCord, G. (2004). Ending Africa's Poverty Trap, *Brookings Papers on Economic Activity*, 1: 117–240.

Scott, J. C. (1977). *The Moral Economy of the Peasant: Rebellion and Subsistence in Southeast Asia*. New Haven: Yale University Press.

Shleifer, A. and Vishny, R. W. (1993). "Corruption," *Quarterly Journal of Economics*, 108 (3): 599–617.

Stiglitz, J. E. (1996). *Whither Socialism?* Cambridge, MA: MIT Press.

UNCTAD (2009). *The Least Developed Countries Report 2009: The State and Development Governance*. New York and Geneva: United Nations Conference on Trade and Development, available at <http://www.unctad.org/en/docs/ldc2009_en.pdf>.

World Bank (1993). *The East Asian Miracle: Economic Growth and Public Policy*. Oxford: Oxford University Press.

5

States and Markets: Neoliberal Limitations and the Case for a Developmental State

Meles Zenawi[1]

The political and economic renaissance of Africa is an issue that continues to preoccupy Africans and non-Africans alike. Various methods of achieving such a renaissance have been proposed, mostly variations of the dominant neoliberal paradigm of development. My argument elaborated elsewhere[2] is that the neoliberal paradigm is a dead end incapable of bringing about the African renaissance, and that a fundamental shift in paradigm is required to effect a revival. In this paper, the focus is on the theoretical or conceptual limitations of the neoliberal paradigm and the need for African states to move toward becoming developmental.

The neoliberal political economy

A central premise of the neoliberal paradigm is that the role of government in the economy should be limited largely to the protection of individual and property rights, the enforcement of contracts that have been entered into voluntarily, and safeguarding competition among economic actors. It is believed that the smaller the role of the state, the better. The neoliberal paradigm's ideal state is the night-watchman state.

The neoliberal paradigm's prescriptions on the role of the state in the economy have two pillars. It stands on two legs, as it were. The first leg is the neoliberal political economy based on the theory of rent-seeking and rational choice theory; the second is the conviction of the efficiency and pervasiveness of competitive markets.

The political economy leg of the neoliberal paradigm has a distinguished parentage in the form of the classical economists starting with Adam Smith, who recognized that if left to themselves, businessmen would collude to undermine competition. He nevertheless advocated a very limited role for the state. The advocacy of a nightwatchman role for the state by the classical economists did not directly follow from their theoretical analysis. They did not provide a theoretical basis for the role they prescribed to the state. Their view on the role of the state was based on their imperial judgment of how the state functions. They were convinced that government was about creating monopolies to favor their officials and clients and hence about hindering competition and efficient resource allocation.[3]

The empirical judgment of the classical economists of the governments of the day was accurate. Public administration that is largely free of patronage, and that institutionalizes the values of economy, honesty, and neutrality, was a nineteenth-century phenomena. Even in Britain, which was a pioneer in developing such an administration, the process was not completed until the 1870s, well after the flourishing of classical economics.[4] In eighteenth- and early nineteenth-century Europe, patronage was widespread. Outright selling of government offices, including military ranks, was not unheard of in Britain. In France, the sale of government offices was the norm.[5]

Emerging as it did, in an environment of pervasive patronage, clientelism, and state predation, classical economics could not avoid making the empirical judgment that state intervention in the economy is detrimental, and that a smaller role for the state in the economy was better. But this judgment did not of itself constitute a theory of the role of the state in the economy.

It is the neoliberal paradigm that has attempted to provide a theoretical, as opposed to empirical, basis for the nightwatchman state.[6] Two interrelated concepts—the concepts of rent-seeking and the solely self-interested behavior on the part of citizens, politicians, public officials, and states—are central to the theory.

The concept of rent-seeking is one that has been a source of some confusion. Rent in economics is payment above and over the opportunity cost of an asset. Entrepreneurs are always on the lookout for such rent. They can get such rent by discovering new ways and means of producing some good or service more cheaply or with better quality. In doing so, they initially get profits above and beyond the marginal cost. Once discovered, however, others follow in their footsteps and the rent is dissipated through the competitive process, until a new method of doing things better or more cheaply is discovered. Such a process is repeated over and over again promoting more efficient resource allocation and accelerated growth.

Rent that is the result of innovation is called rent creation, as opposed to rent-seeking, in neoliberal political economy. Rent creation is dissipated by the competitive process. It is created by innovation and is not perpetuated indefinitely because it is dissipated by competition. Rent creation can be both positive and negative: An asset can get both more and less than its opportunity cost, and hence resources can flow out of areas of negative rent creation and into areas of positive rent creation, improving efficiency and resource allocation.

Rent-seeking is defined as a process of wealth transference through the aegis of government. It is not about creating new value, but about transfer of already produced value through the state. As rent-seeking is an act of the state to transfer value to preferred clients, it is perpetuated indefinitely by that act of the state and is incapable of being dissipated through competition as in rent creation. From the point of view of the recipient of the transfer, rent-seeking is always positive in that his or her wealth is increased. Hence rent-seeking activity does not result in efficient resource allocation; on the contrary, it is socially wasteful as people are encouraged to spend resources and time in socially wasteful lobbying to benefit from such rent-seeking activity.[7]

It is argued in the neoliberal political economy literature that so long as the state limits its activity to its nightwatchman role, the economic process dominates and there will not be rent-seeking, only rent creation. When the state intervenes beyond such confines the opportunities for rent-seeking are created. Rent-seeking activity is thus a phenomenon that is created by state intervention and is directly related to the scope and range of governmental activity in the economy: To the relative size of the public sector.[8]

The second aspect of neoliberal political economy has to do with the motive of economic actors with the rational choice that they are supposed to make. It is assumed that everyone is motivated solely by maximizing self-interest. Politicians want to maximize and maintain power. Citizens want to maximize wealth. Citizens lobby politicians to maximize self-interest through rent-seeking activity. Politicians maximize and maintain power by providing rent-seeking opportunities to clients in return for votes and political support. Civil servants want to use their position to maximize self-interest through corruption and the establishment of protected businesses on the side in return for providing rent-seeking opportunities for their clients.[9]

In the presence of such pervasive self-interest-maximizing behavior, it is argued that expansion of state activity above and beyond protection of personal and property rights and enforcement of contracts creates opportunities for wasteful rent-seeking activity, results in inefficient resource allocation, and retards economic growth. It is asserted that the further the state goes in intervening in the economy, the higher the scope for rent-seeking activity. Hence, the way to ensure efficient resource allocation and accelerate economic growth is to confine the state to a nightwatchman role as much as possible.

The distinction between growth-enhancing rent creation and socially wasteful and state-created rent-seeking arises largely because rent-seeking is considered to be exogenous to the firm, i.e. resource transfer that is unrelated to what the firm does internally. There is no reason why state-created rent should necessarily be external to the firm. It is possible for state-created rents to be directly related to activities within the firm and related to its performance. Firms that perform in a certain manner would be given access to the rent, and those that perform differently would have no such access. In an environment of imperfect competition and market failures, endogenizing rent-seeking activity and linking it with growth-enhancing performance of firms would result in accelerated growth.[10]

Such rent-seeking would be very similar to rent creation. The rent would be dissipated over time, not necessarily because of competition but also because the state would reduce and finally eliminate the rent as its necessity for growth diminishes. It would result in efficient resource allocation as firms respond to the higher profits and invest in areas where the rent has been created by the state with the view to accelerating growth. There would be limited wasteful lobbying as the rent is provided on the basis of performance. Rents would be both positive and negative as the state provides rewards (positive rent) for good performances and penalties (negative rent) for bad performers. Endogenizing rent-seeking and basing it on growth-enhancing performance would essentially remove the distinction between rent creation and rent-seeking and thus undermine a key basis of neoliberal political economy. But such endogenization would be challenged by the neoliberal school on two counts. First, they would challenge the assumption that state intervention can result in more efficient resource allocation. They would insist that competitive markets are both pervasive and Pareto-efficient, hence state action cannot result in more efficient resource allocation. They would also argue that state actors make choices based on maximizing their self-interests and hence would not create rent on the basis of performance as opposed to lobbying-based rent. In other words, the arguments of the neoliberal political economy can be reduced to the rational choice theory.

While self-interested behavior as an important source of motivation of economic actors is self-evident, motivation that is solely based on self-interest maximization, which is the cornerstone of the rational choice theory, is difficult to relate to how economies and states behave. Assuming that all actors within the state are motivated solely by self-interest maximization, everyone would act to maximize his or her self-interest and the state will be unable to act as a coherent corporate entity. It would be transformed into an arena of warring individuals with nothing to hold them together. Even if such chaos within the state were to be somehow overcome, it is very difficult to see why the state with its monopoly of coercion would limit itself to being the trustworthy nightwatchman. The solely self-interested individuals who populate the state would use their monopoly of coercion not to protect private property but to loot it to their benefit, not to impartially enforce contracts but to steal the property of others. As the sole motivation would be maximizing self-interest, the state would do whatever it takes to maximize its benefit and not limit itself solely as a nightwatchman. A nightwatchman state that is based on the motivation of maximizing self-interest is almost a theoretical impossibility.[11]

The logic of the rational choice theory thus leads to logical absurdity. If the sole motivation for the state and state actors is maximizing self-interest, it is difficult if not impossible to imagine a stable and coherent state. The state actors would all behave like interest-maximizing individuals and there would be nothing to hold them together. Even if there were to be stability within the state, the state actors would use the state to maximize their own interests. They would use their monopoly of coercion not to act like a well-behaved nightwatchman protecting the property of others and impartially enforcing contracts, but to act like a predator to loot and rob so as to increase the wealth of its officials.

A well-behaved nightwatchman state can exist only if state actors are not solely interest-maximizing. Such a state can exist only if the state actors have motives that can keep their self-interest-maximizing behavior in check. If people are not only self-interest maximizing, such behavior can be kept in check whether the state intervenes in the economy extensively or keeps to its nightwatchman role.

In other words, if rational choice theory is correct and all people are solely self-interest maximizing to the extent that states can exist for any length of time and act as coherent entities, they would necessarily be predatory states. To the extent that a nightwatchman state is possible, state actors cannot be solely self-interest maximizers and rational choice theory must be wrong. If rational choice theory is wrong and people are not solely self-interest maximizers, the question of whether the state should be a nightwatchman state or not would become an empirical rather than a theoretical question.

The institutional underpinning of a market economy

While rational choice theory fails to adequately explain the motivations of economic actors including state actors, it does pose the fundamental economic question of what motivates economic actors. Human beings are social animals and hence a sociobiological explanation of their motives would be appropriate. Such a motivation would be one of maximizing survival potential. Such motivation would sometimes, but not always, be wealth maximizing. Wealth maximization by the individual at the expense of everything else would not necessarily be maximizing survival potential.[12]

Maximizing survival potential, which has been a valid biological explanatory variable for living things other than human beings, applies to human behavior when combined with the social nature of human beings and becomes a sociobiological explanatory variable. The fact that human beings are social animals means that the survival potential of human beings as individuals and groups is maximized within the context of the appropriate social environment. Such an environment would have to be one that reduces the impediments to complex economic interactions of individual economic actors. Only such a social context would create an environment that would sustain wealth maximization by individuals, just as any wealth maximization by individuals that does not undermine the necessary social context can be sustained.

An economy such as capitalism that is based on complex economic interactions requires motivation that is not solely based on maximization of self-interest. It requires a peculiar combination of self-interested behavior—enough to induce individuals to be on a continuous lookout for profitable opportunities and to seize such opportunities, and non-self-interested behavior where one's word is one's honor, where social rather than economic sanctions suffice to enforce contracts.[13]

A market is not merely about supply and demand, buying and selling. It is a social institution that is based on complex human interaction. Like all human interactions economic interactions in the market are plagued by uncertainties. These uncertainties arise both from the environment and from the computational limitations of the person.

The uncertainties that arise from the environment are related to incomplete information about the goods and services to be exchanged and incomplete information as to behavior of individuals—whether they will shirk and defect or cooperate and fulfill their obligations.

All people have limited computational capabilities. They cannot take in and compute all the information they get from the environment within a reasonable amount of time to come up with a perfect understanding of the environment. Therefore, people have to supplement their computational capabilities with subjective perceptions of reality to make sense of it. The subjective perception of reality, of the environment, that characterizes human understanding is another source of uncertainty in human interaction. These subjective perceptions, including their perceptions of the fairness or injustice of the institutional environment, constitute the ideologies of individuals.[14]

Institutions, rules, norms, ideologies are required to reduce such environmental and computational uncertainties. Such institutions perform three essential functions: They transmit information, enforce property rights and contracts, and manage competition. Enforcement of property rights and contracts, which is central to the effective and efficient performance of a market economy, in turn require that individuals fulfill their obligations under the contracts. There are three reasons why individuals do so.[15] The first reason is an internalized norm, such as a shared belief system, or sense of obligation to peers. People are convinced that it is the right thing to do (their subjective perception of reality or their ideology tells them so) and they voluntarily fulfill their obligations. The second reason is social sanctions. Behavior that is opportunistic and results in defection is considered socially deviant and is sanctioned accordingly. People thus fulfill their obligations to avoid such social sanctions. The third reason is economic sanctions. People who do not fulfill their obligations are economically penalized.[16]

145

Individual norms and social sanctions play a critical role in reducing uncertainty and transaction cost. Imagine everyone having to take everyone else to court in order to enforce a contract. Even if it were possible to completely specify a contract and verify exactly whether it has been fulfilled, it would be very expensive and time-consuming to go to court in order to enforce every contract. Where a credit culture that ensures that loans are generally repaid is lacking, very high uncertainty about loan repayments would inhibit extensive economic interaction.[17] The development of individual and social norms that combine self-interested behavior with socially responsible behavior is central to reduce uncertainty and transaction costs and to facilitate complex economic interaction among individuals.

However, in a modern setting, self-enforcement and trust is not enough. In such a setting, the returns to opportunism, cheating, and shirking are too high to be eliminated or reduced by self-enforcement and trust alone. Third-party enforcement mechanisms above and beyond the norms of the individual and social sanctions are required. Such third-party enforcement can only be state enforcement mechanisms, and is most effective when it creates the environment for the other two to be effective.[18]

Recognition of both the centrality and limitations of individual norms and values, and social norms and sanctions in reducing uncertainty and transaction costs, leads us to try to understand the complex interaction between them and state enforcement. In an environment where individual norms and values are solely self-interested, it would be difficult to imagine the development and effectiveness of social norms and sanctions. Likewise in an environment where the required social norms and sanctions are lacking, it will be difficult to entrench and sustain individual norms and values that reduce transaction costs. State enforcement in an environment of pervasive pure self-interest maximization would result in predation and enormously increase uncertainty and transaction costs. The presence of appropriate individual and social norms, values, and sanctions is therefore the bedrock of effective third-party state enforcement. Likewise state enforcement is central to sustaining self- and social enforcement.

It is the presence and interaction of all three enforcement mechanisms that generates the peculiar combination of self-interested and non-self-interested behavior that is essential for the flourishing of complex and extensive economic interaction without which accelerated economic growth cannot be imagined. Indeed, some studies indicate that it is the inability of societies to develop effective institutions for low-cost enforcement of contracts, as well as to develop institutions, norms, and values to reduce uncertainty, and transaction costs, and hence the inability to facilitate extensive and complex economic interactions that constitute one of the most important sources of both historical stagnation of societies and contemporary underdevelopment.[19]

Understanding that the market is above all a social institution for the facilitation of complex human interaction leads to a better understanding of the motivation of economic actors in a market economy and its institutional basis. The motivation of economic actors in the complex interaction of a market economy is a combination of self-interested and non-self-interested behavior that maximizes survival potential in the appropriate social context. It is such a combination that reduces uncertainty related to incomplete information and transaction costs and also facilitates the development of an economic system that is based on complex economic interaction such as the capitalist system. Indeed, just as it is impossible to imagine a developed capitalist economy without such norms, values, and institutions, the limited development of such norms, values, and institutions can be a critical part of the explanation for the economic stagnation or underdevelopment of countries.

Where rational choice theory leads to logical absurdities, a sociobiological approach to the motivation of economic actors and the study of institutional economics can lead to a clearer understanding of the institutional underpinnings of a market economy and the motivation of its economic actors. It helps us understand the peculiar combination of economic actors' self-interested and non-self-interested behaviors and the norms, values, and rules—which have sometimes been called social capital—that underpin them. Likewise, the development of social capital has been called social development, which constitutes one of the key instruments for overcoming economic stagnation and underdevelopment, a key instrument in reducing transaction cost and accelerating economic growth.

There are two characteristics of social capital that distinguish it from other forms of capital: It is a public good and it has increasing returns to scale. Once the norms, values, and networks comprising social capital have been created, the benefit derived by individuals utilizing such capital is not diminished when others use the same social capital. In other words, the consumption of social capital is non-rivalrous and non-excludable. Once social capital has been created and made available to one individual, it will be difficult or impossible to exclude others from benefiting from it as well. Social capital has the basic characteristics of a public good and like all public goods it is undersupplied by the market and by individual economic actors.[20]

Social capital is the result of complex interactions among internalized individual values, social norms, sanctions, and state enforcement. The nature of the interaction among these three elements would suggest that social activity plays a critical role in its creation. As a public good, social capital would be expected to be the by-product of social activity.[21] The state would also be expected to play an important role in its creation and supply as would be the case for other public goods.

Creating the proper blend of norms, values, and rules to reduce uncertainty and transaction costs is a critical factor in accelerated growth and development.

Social development is thus not only an essential element of development but also a critical instrument of accelerated economic growth.

Social development, which plays such a critical role in accelerating economic growth, is a public good that has increasing returns to scale. It is undersupplied by the market and is subject to a vicious and virtuous circle phenomenon. It is created by social activity, by civic engagement in the context of horizontal and dense networks, and inculcated and sustained through modeling, socialization, and sanctions. The state plays a critical role in social capital accumulation through undermining patronage networks and promoting fairness and equity, through the promotion of participation and democracy, and through appropriate sanctions and efforts at socialization.

Conclusions so far

The neoliberal paradigm that suggests a nightwatchman state is conducive to economic growth bases such conclusions on two pillars: The assertion that competitive markets are both pervasive and Pareto-efficient and the neoliberal political economy based on the theory of socially wasteful rent-seeking activities and the rational choice theory of solely self-interest-maximizing individuals.

Government-created rent does not necessarily have to be socially wasteful. It becomes wasteful only if solely self-interest-maximizing individuals use it to create wealth at the expense of society and only if the state is incapable of improving on the market—if there are no market failures.

The theory of solely self-interest-maximizing individuals does not hold water. History, everyday observation, and theoretical analysis based on the two suggests that an economy based on complex economic interaction, such as a market economy, requires a blend of self-interested and non-self-interested behavior. In the absence of such norms, the state, if it can exist as a coherent corporate entity for any period of time, becomes predatory. A properly regulated nightwatchman state populated by solely self-interest-maximizing individuals is thus a practical and theoretical impossibility. Only individuals with a blend of self-interested and non-self-interested behavior can create a nightwatchman state, and such people are equally capable of creating a state that intervenes in the economy.

Creating the proper blend of norms, values, and rules to reduce uncertainty and transaction costs—social development or social capital accumulation—is a critical factor in accelerated growth and development. Social development is thus not only an essential element of development, but also a critical instrument of accelerated economic growth.

The black box of development

The neoclassical model of growth

The basic neoliberal model of growth is the Solow model. Like all neoliberal thinking, the Solow model is based on the assumption of pervasiveness and efficiency of markets. In addition, the model assumes that knowledge, which it defines very broadly to include all the abilities and skills that are needed to assimilate technology into the local market, is acquired costlessly and instantaneously. The local environment is distinguished from others solely by its set of relative prices.[22]

Change in output is the result of the contribution of labor, capital, and technology (which is also referred to as total factor productivity). Capital has diminishing returns: As more and more capital per worker is used, it reaches a stage where it becomes less and less productive. Labor too has diminishing returns: As more and more labor is used in combination with a given capital, it becomes less and less productive. It is therefore not possible to continuously increase production per worker by simply increasing capital or labor. Such continued growth in per capita income and production can only come from increase in total factor productivity—from changes in technology.[23] The conclusion that technological change is the only source of continued increase in per capita income is one of the most important insights of the Solow model and the neoliberal paradigm in general.

The Solow model has clear implications for developing countries. The difference between developing and developed countries would be essentially that of a differing set of relative prices. This differing set of relative prices would result in the flow of scarce resources from where they are abundant to where they are scarce and eventually there would be convergence. The scarcity of highly skilled personnel in developing countries would therefore result in the flow of skilled labor from developed to developing countries. The same thing would happen to capital.

These predictions based on the Solow model have failed to materialize. There is no necessary trend of convergence between developing and developed countries. On the contrary, they have continued to diverge. The flow of skilled labor is in the opposite direction to that of the predictions of the neoclassical model. Much of the flow of capital has been between developed countries, and net flow of capital to developing countries has not been consistent with the predictions of the model.[24] The predictions made through logical deduction on the basis of the neoclassical model are thus almost the exact opposite of the reality. Clearly such a model must be deeply flawed.

The Solow model treats technological change as something external to the economic process, as an exogenous factor, as a sort of black box of development. It does not try to explain it in the context of the economic process. The treatment of the key to economic growth as something external to the economic process, the failure to analyze the vital source of economic growth by the economic process itself, has been identified as another flaw of the Solow model and the neoclassical theory of growth.

An attempt to make technological change internal to the economy to explain it in economic terms has resulted in a field of economic theory that has been called the endogenous growth theory. The development of the endogenous growth theory has shed some light on the process of technological change and served to explain the failure of the predictions of the Solow model to materialize.

The endogenous growth theory makes three basic assumptions. First, consistent with the Solow model, it assumes that technological growth is at the heart of economic growth. Second, technological growth takes place as a result of intentional actions of people responding to incentives and hence can be treated like any other economic activity. Third, developing new technologies is like incurring fixed costs and its consumption is non-rivalrous.[25]

The fact that technology is non-rivalous, that is the use of one economic actor of a technology does not diminish its use by another economic actor, suggests that it has characteristics of a public good. Technology is inherently not excludable. Legal protection through patenting and definition of property rights in technology provides a means of excluding non-owners from using it without the permission of the owner. But such exclusion is not leakage-free, even in countries where the enforcement and protection of property rights is good. More importantly, the patent does not prevent any one from basing his research on it, and using it to discover new technology. There is at best an incomplete appropriability, an incomplete excludability.[26] The non-rivalous and incomplete excludability nature of technology suggests that it has the characteristics of a public good and that there is market failure; the market will undersupply new technology if it is left to its own devices.

The endogenous growth theory recognizes that technology has certain characteristics of a public good and accepts the need for government intervention to address the market failures in skilled manpower training, and in patenting and intellectual property rights (to being about at least partial excludability) protection. But it limits its analysis of market failure in the technology market to the above and disregards other and related market failures and can to that extent be considered as a variant of the neoliberal model.[27] A full analysis of the market failures and institutional factors in technological change can start with the insights of the endogenous growth model but must go well beyond the confines put on such analysis by the neoliberal paradigm.

Market failures in technological change

The public-good nature of technology is a market failure in that technological change is recognized by even the neoliberal school, particularly its endogenous growth variant. This suggests that the market cannot ensure efficient outcome in the technology market and non-market intervention can bring about more efficient outcomes. Public interventions in patenting and property rights protection, in human resource development, and public research have been advocated by many neoliberal economists.

Another related market failure involves increasing returns to technological capability. Technological change is brought about by two sets of persons: The inventors who come up with new ideas and the innovators who make use of the inventions to produce new products or improve the quality or reduce the cost of old products. The more innovators there are in a society, the more it pays to be an inventor, because there will be innovators that will pay for and make use of the inventions and vice versa.[28] The more inventors and innovators, the higher the return on technological change.

There is another aspect to this phenomenon of increasing returns to scale in technological development. New knowledge makes existing knowledge more productive if there is leakage and incomplete appropriability of technological change (as is indeed the case). Likewise, the rate of return on new knowledge depends upon how much knowledge already exists. If there is much, it will be possible to exploit the opportunities created by the new knowledge to the maximum extent possible. If available knowledge levels are low, the opportunities created by the new knowledge will not be fully exploited, if at all, and hence the returns on that new knowledge will be limited.[29] The availability of more knowledge not only increases the rate of return on new knowledge but increases the possibility of creating it.

If pre-existing knowledge in a society is high, the means of creating new knowledge and the returns on doing so will also be high, creating a virtuous circle. The presence of virtuous and vicious circles suggests that there is a threshold where one is transformed to the other. Below the threshold the vicious circle keeps a country in a low-technological development trap, which the market would be unable to overcome. It requires a coordinated and persistent push involving action by non-market means to cross the threshold.[30]

Technological development involves externalities. The creation of new knowledge by one actor is not only diffused to others, but also becomes the basis for additional knowledge. Such externalities cannot be adequately captured by the market.[31] Appropriate institutional mechanisms, such as clustering, will have to be created to fully capture the externalities.

Clustering by providing such a platform for smooth and extensive communication enables the economic actors and the country as a whole to capture the externalities.[32] When suppliers and related industries cluster in a given geographic area, suppliers will provide customers with new information on new technologies and methods; the customers will direct the effort of suppliers to addressing their specific technological problems; and the suppliers will disseminate information among their customers. A two-way and extensive transfer of technology and information of technology, facilitated by geographic and cultural proximity, will take place. The presence of related and identical industries will also facilitate the same type of flow of information and technology.

The clustering of supplier and customer and related industries helps to draw common inputs into the cluster. Skilled personnel with specialized skills in the industry in question congregate in the area. Research and specialized training and support institutions are established as the congregation of establishments makes it both necessary and possible to establish special support institutions and infra-structures serving the industry. By attracting and facilitating the development of specialized infrastructures and support institutions, clustering enables the actors to capture the externalities.

Specialization and extensive division is also facilitated by clustering. As more and more suppliers and related industries cluster in a given area, it becomes possible and worthwhile for businesses to specialize and outsource much of their activity. Such extensive specialization and division of labor facilitates technologi-cal change and capturing of externalities.[33]

It is because clustering is one of the most important means of capturing extern-alities that clusters have emerged in many areas of production and in many developed countries. Silicon Valley with its information technology is only one and perhaps the most famous example. Such clusters ranging from textiles to steel products, from chemical to electrical engineering are very common. Such cluster-ing is facilitated by the availability of specialized infrastructures and institutions, the absence of which makes it difficult to capture externalities. Clustering is not only an institutional mechanism for capturing externalities, but also a practical manifestation of the presence of such externalities and market failure in techno-logical development.

Risk of entry is another source of market failure. Introducing new products or new processes is a very risky exercise: The product or the process may not be received by the market. But once someone tries it and proves that introduction of such new products or processes works, the risk is drastically reduced and there will be many followers, with enormous benefits to the followers and the economy as a whole.[34] In such a circumstance it pays more to be the risk-free follower than the risk-shouldering leader. The market undersupplies such risk-taking leaders and fails to bring about the most efficient outcome in terms of technological change.

Trained labor is central to technological change and development. As already indicated, human resource development has its externalities—the training of a person making other trained persons more productive. But the highly skilled labor required for technological development cannot be created by educational and training institutions alone. The required specialized skills can only be created through the acts of production and marketing, and through an increased effort to gain competitive advantage.[35]

Studies have shown that education and training that is not explicitly linked to the rate of innovation and the speed of technological catch-up will have no significant impact on productivity and hence on accelerated economic growth. Thus policies which affect rates of innovation and investment will affect the relative demand for skilled people and the aggregate skill distribution within the economy.[36] In addition to the known externalities in the training of the workforce, there is an additional market failure related to coordination failure between production and skill formation. In the absence of the appropriate production facilities and environment, skill formation will not take place adequately. In the absence of the appropriate and adequate skills, production will not take place.

The assumption of neoliberal theory includes the assumption of homogenous goods. Goods of sufficient quantity and identical attributes (so as to make them homogenous) have to be available for the market to operate efficiently. If every good is fundamentally different from every other good, then there cannot be a competitive market. Every good would be a stand-alone good, obviating the potential for a perfectly competitive market. The market for technology and ideas is a market where the assumption of homogenous products does not hold. Every new idea is different from every other idea or else it would not be a new idea. There could not possibly be a perfectly competitive market for new ideas or new technologies.[37]

The heterogeneous nature of new technology and the associated extreme form of information asymmetry is an additional source of market failure in the technology market[38] because the market for new ideas and technologies is marred by extreme forms of information asymmetry. The inventor of an idea will obviously have much more information about it than the prospective buyer. Perhaps more importantly, if the inventor reveals everything about his new idea before selling to the buyer, the buyer could say, "there is nothing new in it, I am not buying" and move on and make use of the idea in some fashion without paying. Institutional mechanisms for reducing this problem have evolved over time, but the underlying extreme form of information asymmetry is always there. A competitive market can result in efficient outcomes where there is perfect information, or at least approaching perfect information. In the case of markets for ideas, the information failure is extreme; there is nothing remotely resembling perfect information.

Clearly the neoliberal paradigm in the form of the Solow model not only fails to provide insight into technological development, treating it as a sort of black box, but all the main predictions about development made on the basis of that theory have been proved wrong. The endogenous growth theory does address some of these limitations. It has, as it were, opened up the black box and explained why the predictions of the Solow model have not come to pass. But much of the thinking in the endogenous growth theory is confined within the neoliberal paradigm of the pervasiveness of markets that operate relatively efficiently. While recognizing some market failures in the technology market, it does not recognize their pervasiveness. As described previously however, market failures are pervasive in the technology market and dominate it. A paradigm based on competitive markets in technological development cannot explain it in any meaningful way, nor can it explain the most important source of sustained and accelerated economic growth.

The problem with the neoliberal theory is not limited to its inability to explain the issue that is at the heart of economic growth—technological change. The problem is that technological development is fundamentally inconsistent with perfectly competitive markets. The fact that technology is non-rivalrous and has clear characteristics of non-convexities means that price is not equal to marginal cost and has no necessary tendency to be equal to it.[39] Prices have to be higher than marginal cost if there is to be continued technological development. Where prices have to be higher than marginal cost, there cannot be efficient markets.

National innovation systems

The pervasiveness of market failures in the technology market means that, contrary to the neoliberal theory, countries have not left technological development to the tender mercies of the market. The countries that have successfully achieved development have over time developed various institutions that address the pervasive market failures. Such systems that have evolved in the historical process of development are sometimes called the national innovation systems.

Innovation cannot exist without learning, which is an interactive exercise and cannot but be rooted in the institutional setting in which it takes place. It is not possible to envisage innovation and learning outside the institutional context of the economy. Learning and innovation partly emanate from routine activities in production. This means that there are more learning opportunities; learning is much easier in certain periods, with certain linkages among industries and certain elasticity and technological opportunities. In other words, learning and hence innovation is dependent on the structure of the economy. These institutional and structural determinants suggest that innovation is based on the history of the economy.[40]

Much the same can be said from the point of view of a single firm, the technological capabilities of which reside not only in its machinery and in its individual employees, but also and most importantly in its overall system of transforming inputs into outputs and its organizing capabilities to carry out the transformation. This in turn depends on the institutional relationships with customers, suppliers, public agencies, research institutions, and on the national institutional set-up as a whole.[41]

A national system of innovation can be defined to include all interrelated, institutional, and structural factors in a nation that generates, selects, and diffuses innovation.[42] Such a system requires a system of education and training for supplying the skills and technology, a legal system for defining and enforcing property rights, and processes, such as standardization, to reduce transaction costs.[43] A central element of any national innovation system is the technological infrastructure, which includes the system of education and training, the public and private research laboratories and facilities, the network of scientific and technological associations, and similar support institutions.[44]

Two distinct national innovation systems related to two different histories and structures of the economies of developed countries have evolved. The system that has been called the mission-oriented system is found in countries such as the US, UK, and France, but the archetypical case would be the national innovation system that has evolved in the US. The second system, which is also called the diffusion system, has evolved in countries such as Germany, Sweden, and Switzerland, but the archetypical case is the national innovation system in Germany.[45] Other countries, particularly the late developing countries such as Japan, Korea, and Taiwan, have adapted one or the other of the two systems, but for reasons that will be made clear, have opted to model their national innovation system mostly on the diffusion system.

The mission-oriented system in the United States evolved in an environment of large unified national market, abundant unskilled labor, no adequate system of training skilled craftsmen, and the related low differentials in pay between unskilled workers and craftsmen and abundant highly skilled labor. An economic structure with highly skilled labor at one end and unskilled labor at the other, with very little in-between and a large market, has led firms to pioneer mass production methods to economize on craftsmen and maximize the use of the abundant unskilled labor to develop organizational innovations intensive in managerial and supervisory staff, both in order to compensate for lack of craftsmen and to maximize the use of the available highly skilled labor.

For such a system to generate continued growth, the continuous generation of new ideas and technologies is required. The lack of craftsmen means that productivity improvements generated continuously on the shop floor cannot be relied upon. Minor but continued improvement of this nature cannot be an important source of continued technological change. A large public and private research infrastructure that makes full use of abundant, highly skilled workforce and that continuously creates new technologies is the only option for such a system to continuously grow. Moreover, as and when such technologies emerge, the firms will have to quickly exploit the new opportunities and move away from mature technologies. Exploitation of mature technologies through shop floor excellence is not the forte of the system. Continuously shifting from mature to new technologies in typical technological life cycle fashion is the way out for such a system.

The US has developed such a system of first-rate universities, initially public but with more and more private-sector involvement, engaged not only in the training of highly skilled workers, but also in research. Its school system leaves much to be desired and one cannot even talk of a system of vocational training for craftsmen.

There is very high mobility of labor, particularly of highly skilled labor. Finance is very mobile and specialized mechanisms, such as venture capital firms to finance innovative technologies, have been firmly established. An effective patenting and intellectual property right system has also evolved. A research system that continuously generates new ideas, highly mobile labor, and capital that can quickly shift from mature to new technologies has evolved in the US, enabling it to continuously be on the frontier of new technology and to generate growth.[46]

The US has succeeded in evolving a national innovation system that is consistent with the structure of its economy and the history of its economic development. The success of the US economy can, to a large extent, be attributed to the development of such institutions, technological infrastructure, and an internally consistent system of innovation.

The diffusion system in Germany evolved from completely different circumstances: The industrialization push and its related innovation in higher education, training of engineers and craftsmen, and early specialization in chemical, electrical, and mechanical engineering industries. Chemical and electrical engineering industries needed a high-quality university system to train scientists, provide support for research laboratories, and monitor developments of new technologies in the fields concerned. The mechanical engineering industries needed comprehensive vocational education, product standardization, and cooperative research.[47]

The central feature of the innovation system as it has evolved in Germany is the depth and breadth of investment in human capital. A dual system based on excellent comprehensive secondary education streaming to high-quality university education on the one hand, and a parallel and extensive vocational education on the other hand has been established. This creates top-level scientists who are able to remain in touch with the frontiers of new technology, if not expand its frontiers, and a highly skilled workforce. Systems of standardized examinations and of continuous certification of craftsmen eases information problems and facilitates labor mobility, which in turn facilitates technology diffusion among firms.[48] Employers are assured that the people they employ are indeed highly skilled and able to do their jobs adequately.

A system of industrial standardization where standards for products and parts are set and continuously upgraded has been put in place. Such standardization reduces transaction costs dramatically and facilitates specialization and division of labor. Moreover the continuous upgrading of standards involving all the stakeholders exerts pressure on firms to innovate and upgrade their technology at the same time that it provides them with the information that facilitates such upgrading.

A related system of cooperative research involving universities, industry associations, and firms has also evolved. Such cooperative research increases the cost-effectiveness of research and development and reduces the burden of technological development on firms, and helps to generalize the experience of related firms and in transmitting such information to the industry as a whole, facilitating the diffusion of technology. The process of identifying research programs in such a system of cooperative research helps focus the attention of all the participants on emerging technological opportunities and threats.[49]

The key problem of technology policy is less about generating new ideas than in ensuring their effective utilization. Long-term growth of an economy depends on using technological capabilities across a range of economic activities. The two systems of innovations achieve that in their own ways and with varying degrees of effectiveness.

In the mission-oriented system of the US, diffusion is achieved through factor mobility in the context of continuously shifting production. The continuous supply of technology provided by the national innovation system is used with high-mobility capital and labor to shift resources away from mature technologies to emerging ones. The high mobility facilitates the diffusion of the new technologies across the economy and speedy exit of mature technologies. Market factors are combined with the largely non-market system to ensure speedy diffusion.

In the diffusion-oriented system of Germany, diffusion is facilitated mainly by social mechanisms such as standardization of products, cooperative research, and the apprenticeship system of training craftsmen.[50]

The US system is good at continuously expanding the frontiers of technology, but is not effective at exploiting fully technologies that have emerged through minor but continuous improvements at the shop-floor level. The skills of the workers at the shop floor and the organizational system are such that this cannot be a major source of innovation. The success of the system depends on its ability to come up with new technologies rather than on full and continued exploitation of existing ones. This, among other things, means that US firms are more willing to transfer technology than their German counterparts, as they are likely to move out of established technologies.

The diffusion-oriented system of Germany is very good at fully exploiting existing technologies. The high skill levels in the firms mean that a continuous stream of minor improvements can come from the shop floor. The continuous upgrading of standards also suggests continued innovation along the trajectories of already-existing technology. Such a stream of continuous small improvements thus becomes a major source of technological change in such a system. The skill level also means that by scanning the technological frontier, quickly acquiring and improving it, the system can remain on the frontiers of new technology. While it is also able to generate new and novel technology, the pressure to do so is not as overwhelming as it is in the mission-oriented system. The system is thus much better at exploiting and mastering existing technologies, than generating new ones. It is therefore not surprising that many late developing countries have tried to emulate this system.

The historical evolution of the two systems of innovation suggests that techno-logical development is dependent on the structure and histories of specific econo-mies, and that those countries that have evolved systems that are consistent both internally and with the structure of the economy and its institutional underpin-nings succeed in bringing about continued technological change. It also suggests that radically different systems that are adequate for the purpose can evolve from differing environments. Technological development has more to do with his-tories, structures of economies, and their institutional environment than with anything resembling the perfectly competitive markets of neoliberal theory.

The evolution of the two systems also suggests that differing localities are not solely defined by differing relative prices that then determine the pace and trajec-tory of their technological environments. The main differences between Germany and the US at the time that their differing innovation systems emerged were not differing relative prices but differing institutions, differing skills, and skill mixes. It is these factors, rather than the differing relative prices that have determined the pace and trajectory of their technological development.

Easterly makes the same point from a different angle. He argues that compara-tive advantage has to do more with skills and technological capabilities than with factor endowments. He suggests that countries with low levels of skills will have to focus on low-value-added primary production and processing. Giving high-value semi-processed material to unskilled people in firms with low technological cap-abilities would mean that substandard product would likely be produced. The cost of such results to the firm would be very high. But if the value of the material on which unskilled workers and low-technological capability firms work is low, even if there is high wastage, the cost to the firm will be lower.[51]

From a dynamic point of view, it is the evolution of the imitative and innovative capabilities of a country rather than factor endowments that shape the trend in relative and absolute growth of tradeables of each economy.[52] Thus having cheap and abundant labor does not necessarily make a country competitive in labor-intensive industries. Indeed, studies have shown that China and India, which had (and have) much more abundant and cheap labor than Japan, had their textile industries—a quintessential labor-intensive industry—devastated by Japan between the two World Wars. These studies of relative productivities of labor of Japan on the one hand and China and India on the other hand have shown that labor costs in India and China would have had to be negative for them to compete with Japan in textiles.[53]

Having the same or even better machinery does not mean having the same or better productivity and technology. The technological capability of a firm is not primarily its machinery or its employees; it is primarily its organizing abilities, which in turn are dependent on the institutional set-up of the economy. Studies carried out to compare productivity of firms in Japan, Thailand, and Malaysia have been revealing in this sense. Cement factories in the three countries were studied.

The Malaysian factory had the most up-to-date machinery, whereas the Japanese factory had the oldest machinery of the three. Nevertheless, labor productivity in the Japanese factory was found to be at least three times higher than that of the Malaysian factory.[54]

Comparative advantage does not automatically follow from factor endowments, and simply buying up the latest machinery does not mean enhancing competitiveness. Ultimately the competitiveness of a country's firms depends on skills and technological capabilities.

The generation of new technology and the pervasive market failures for new technology apply whether a country is developed or developing. But at least initially, developing countries advance by adopting and adapting existing technology rather than generating new technology; hence the market failures we have identified above could be said to be irrelevant to the processes of economic growth in developing countries. But as we shall see, transfer of technology is itself plagued by market failures.

The accumulation of technological capability

Technological capability is best understood by looking at its three separate parts: Production capability, investment capability, and innovation capability. Production capability refers to operating production facilities and includes production management, production engineering, repair and maintenance, and marketing. Investment capability refers to expanding capacity and establishing new ones and includes labor training, pre-investment feasibility studies, project execution, and start-up operations. Innovative capacity refers to developing new technology.[55] For a developing country, accumulation of technological capability involves two processes: Absorption and diffusion. Absorption is an active process of acquiring, utilizing, and improving upon foreign technology by a domestic firm. Diffusion is to further adapt and develop a particular technological and organizational innovation and the extension of technological learning beyond the firm into the economy in general and the national innovation system.[56]

Almost by definition, developing countries are not at the frontier of global technology. For them, accumulation of technological capability means the importation, assimilation, and adoption of foreign technology and building up effective national innovation systems. Seven steps have been identified in the process: (1) determining the need; (2) surveying the alternative technologies and the alternative suppliers; (3) choosing a particular combination of technology and supplier; (4) absorbing the techniques in their first application in the importing country; (5) disseminating the techniques throughout the economy; (6) improving upon them; and (7) developing new and superior techniques through research and development in the country.[57]

Every step in the process is plagued by pervasive market failures. The last step, that of developing new technology, has already been dealt with and shown to be replete with market failure. The same principles apply whether the technology is developed in an advanced country or a developing one.

Steps 1–3 are the critical initial steps in the process. They determine whether the most appropriate technology for the firm and the country has been identified and selected, whether the least possible cost has been paid, and whether the procurement has been made in a manner that facilitates the assimilation of the technology. The firm carrying out the exercise must have adequate prior knowledge of the technology it needs, sufficient information on alternative technologies and suppliers, and good negotiating skills and strength. If mistakes are made in this process, the wrong technology at the wrong price and wrong conditions for transfer may be bought. In such circumstances the firm may be plagued by difficulties from the very start, collapse in the process of operating the technology, and technology transfer may not take place.

The exercise is risky and expensive. The firm will have to hire experts, scan the technologies available, and select the best alternative for them, which requires hiring people with the necessary knowledge, carrying out a global scan of alternatives, and collecting as much information as possible. It could require foreign visits to have a look at the technology in operating plants. It would require hiring people with the necessary negotiation skills. All of these involve high costs for a firm from a developing country.

The risks and costs involved in the initial process of acquiring new technology are further complicated by the inappropriability of the information gathered in the process. Once a firm has shouldered all the risks and costs and imported the technology and proved that it works, it will not be able to keep it a secret or patent it. Others will quickly follow and import the same technology from the same source, with none of the risk and a negligible part of the cost. If the initiator firm makes a mistake and selects the wrong technology, it bears all the consequences; if it makes the correct decision, it is faced with competition from others who have not paid the same initial costs. Heads it loses, tails the others win. So it would not be a surprise if there is an acute undersupply by the market of firms that are prepared to carry out the initial steps of technology acquisition. This market failure is exacerbated by information failures in the technology market. Information about alternative technologies and suppliers is never perfect and that increases the market failure in the initial process of technology acquisition.

The process of absorbing technology—the fourth step—is mainly one of learning by doing. Sometimes this is understood to be a mechanical process in which the firm erects the machinery and starts producing; the more it produces, the more it assimilates the technology. That is very far from the process of real learning, an interactive process that takes place within institutions. The firm will need in-house capacity to understand the processes involved so as to be able to make the acquired technology fully operational and to adapt it to local circumstances. If people with the right skills and attitudes are not made available to the firm, there will not be much learning.[58]

In the process of procuring and quickly assimilating the technology, the firm learns not only to master the technology concerned but also learns to learn. The experience gained by the firm involving all the steps of the process will enable it to acquire knowledge for carrying out both the procurement and assimilation of the technology quicker and cheaper in its future investment activities.[59] For this to happen, the firm must be involved in repeated investments and have the institutional capacity and memory to learn how to learn.

The internal requirements of the firm in absorbing new technology are thus quite stringent, but the requirements of the external environment are even more stringent: Trained labor that can easily assimilate the technology and the entrepreneurial and managerial skills to organize the process must be available, as well as support institutions. Research and development facilities and other technological support institutions that help the firm to assimilate technology and to address production and other bottlenecks that inevitably occur in the process of assimilation need to be available.[60]

A firm masters the technology if it is continuously trying to improve productivity and quality of products. Where a firm does not need to or does not feel compelled to improve productivity and quality of products, there is no urge to quickly master the technology. The firm must therefore work in an environment that exerts continuous pressure to improve productivity and quality of products if it is to accumulate technological capability. But pressure alone is not enough; if a firm does not have a reasonable chance of making profit by assimilating the technology, it won't even try. Hence the environment must balance the pressure to improve productivity and quality of products with the assurance that such an effort has a reasonable chance of success.[61]

Technological capability accumulation in developing countries is about learning by doing, and learning to learn by doing. A process of production and repeated investments in an environment where firms are pushed to master the technology and are assured that they can do so with profit if they make the effort is required to enable such accumulation. An environment of increasing demand and investment is thus critical for the success of the process.[62]

In the end, entrepreneurs will have to make the decision to devote their energy and their money in productive investments, to go through the difficult and risky process of assimilation of new technology, and make profits. They will do so only if there are no other less risky and less difficult ways of making profits, such as through rent-seeking opportunities. Technological capability accumulation in a developing country can thus take place only where rent-seeking opportunities are eliminated or severely curtailed and where the available capital is directed toward socially productive investments.[63]

The pattern of technological capability accumulation in developing countries has to start at the low end of the market, by producing commodity type products. Such products can be produced with low levels of skill and technological capability and it is only logical that countries use such products as the entry point. But unless countries move to the next step in the technological ladder, they will be trapped in a low-value, low-wage, low-growth trap.[64] They have to move to the next step which is producing complex products with high potential for learning by using technologies that are one step away from the technological frontier and low-wage but high-skill labor. This is an even more perilous step. The environment must guide investment to continuously scale the ladder of technological change. The experience the firms gain in the process of producing commodity type products and the production and investment capabilities they build up during this stage must be used to move up to making adaptations and minor improvements in the technology acquired and to assimilate more complex technology.

The absorption of new technology by a firm in a developing country requires not only in-house capabilities with regards to skilled labor, and entrepreneurial and managerial flair, but also the appropriate external environment that provides adequate skilled labor and effective technological support institutions. It requires an external environment that delicately balances a reasonable chance of making profits with adequate pressure to improve productivity and quality of products, as well as expanding demand and investment opportunities that adequately curtails socially wasteful rent-seeking and directs the investible resources of a country toward socially productive investments.

Assuming that all of the environmental and internal factors needed for a firm to assimilate the technology acquired are fulfilled, the firm still faces another problem. As soon as it has mastered the technology, having had to pay all the costs, take all the risks, and manage all the hustle involved in the process, copycats arrive and begin to compete with it and undermine its profits. As the firm has no proprietary rights to the technology, it can do nothing about it but try to keep its skills a secret. But its employees will leak it either though labor mobility or establishing their own firms, and by word of mouth.

The leakage of such information and the diffusion of technology associated with it are perfectly rational from the point of view of the economy. Indeed, it is such diffusion, which enhances the national innovation system of a country, and accelerates its growth. But from the point of view of the firm, it is unable to capture these externalities and the rational behavior would be not to be the initiator of the process or to retard the diffusion of the technology to the maximum extent. Both rational responses are damaging to the country's accumulation of technological capability and to its accelerated development. The market is powerless to resolve this fundamental problem.

Conclusions

The neoliberal paradigm correctly identifies technological change as the heart of the development process and as the only source of continuous increase in per capita income. The main stream of neoliberal theory treats the heart of the development process as an exogenous factor and does not even attempt to explain it in economic terms. Endogenous growth theory, which in many respects is a variant of neoliberal theory, does begin to open up the black box and see the market failures involved, but fails to provide a comprehensive understanding of the process as it is tied to the most basic neoliberal assumption of the pervasiveness and efficiency of markets.

Developing countries cannot compete simply on the basis of factor endowment or by buying up the latest machinery. They need to assimilate technology developed elsewhere, and they need to continuously move up the technology ladder if they are to achieve continued growth and development. In other words, technological capability accumulation is as central to developing countries as it is to developed countries. The difference is that in developing countries, such accumulation takes place primarily through the assimilation of foreign technology rather than through the development of new technology.

Firms take a lot of risks and incur heavy expenses to identify and assimilate foreign technology but are unable to fully appropriate the benefits of their efforts. Indeed, national development would be hindered if they were to fully appropriate the benefit of their effort as the newly introduced technology would not be diffused. Moreover, the required external environment is such that it would not be possible to create it through the market mechanism alone.

A deeper analysis of technological change shows that it is plagued by information failures and extreme forms of information asymmetry, of increasing returns, of extensive externalities, and coordination failures. It shows that technology has the essential characteristics of a public good. In other words, a deeper analysis of technological change shows that in both developed and developing countries, technological change takes place in an environment of pervasive market failures.

A historical analysis of technological development shows that successful societies have developed national innovation systems that address market failures, and that such systems are based more on the structures and histories of the economies than on relative factor prices. It shows that there are differing national systems of innovation reflecting the differing histories and structures of the economies that can do the job, and that it would be impossible to envisage successful technological development outside of such institutional environment in any country, developed or developing.

When it comes to the heart of accelerated economic growth and technological development, the neoliberal assumption of efficient competitive markets has no basis in fact or theory. Its assumption of a nightwatchman state as an instrument that facilitates technological development by letting the markets do the job while it stands guard protecting property rights and enforcing contracts does not hold up. The neoliberal paradigm cannot explain or guide technological growth.

Stiglitz goes even further and plausibly argues that the neoliberal theory is fundamentally inconsistent with technological change. Where there are competitive markets, where prices are equal to marginal costs, there is no room for technological change; where there is room for technological change, there are no competitive markets.

The developmental state

The historical evolution of the concept

It has been shown that developing countries are plagued by deep-rooted and pervasive market failures that create poverty traps and vicious circles that cannot be overcome by the market. We have indicated that only concerted and persistent political action can overcome the poverty traps. We have shown that development requires the accumulation of social capital, which cannot be adequately supplied by the market. We have briefly shown that the nightwatchman state of the neoliberal paradigm is inadequate to overcoming such bottlenecks and accelerating development. We have argued that rent-seeking has less to do with the size of the state than with the nature of the state. But we have not identified the nature of the state that would be active in overcoming the market failures and poverty traps without succumbing to the rent-seeking trap.

In his seminal study of the history of industrialization in Europe, Alexander Gerschenkron came up with a number of fundamental conclusions that can be summarized as follows: (1) The more delayed industrialization, the more explosive the great spurt of industrialization if and when it comes; (2) the higher the degree of backwardness of the country at the outset, the greater the tendency toward monopolization; (3) the more backward the country at the outset, the more likely it is that the process will be carried out under central direction, although the institutional characteristics of such central direction will vary from country to country; and (4) the process of European industrialization is thus not a process of countries repeating the first industrialization but one of graduated deviation from it.[65]

The first point he makes is plausible. A country in a poverty trap will either fail to create the institutional environment necessary to overcome it or it will succeed in creating such an environment, in which case it will be in a position to bring about accelerated development. When a country starts the process of development, it does not have to reinvent the wheel because much of the technology needed for such growth will be available. While the assimilation of already-existing technology is an arduous task that requires time and money, it cannot necessarily be as slow as creating it in the first place. Hence, if and when late industrialization takes place, it is likely to happen at a more accelerated pace than early industrialization. History appears to bear that out.

Gerschenkron's second point has also largely but not fully been borne out by experience elsewhere. Various explanations have been sought for this phenomenon to the extent that it is accepted as a pattern of late development. One such explanation has to do with the ability to quickly build up technological capabilities and continuously upgrade them. It is suggested that such efforts require or at least are facilitated by the emergence of massive conglomerates such as the Korean Cheabols.[66]

Gerschenkron's third point has also been borne out by evidence, particularly in East Asia. Not only has such development been centrally directed, and directed by the state, but state direction has been much more intrusive and comprehensive than was the case in Europe. A more subtle point is worth noticing: The later the process starts, the greater the need for central direction, which implies that the early industrializers recommend more central direction of the process of the late ones.

It is only natural that there is interaction between early and late industrializers and that such interaction affects both the pace and direction of late industrialization. The availability of developed technology and learning in order to avoid mistakes and replicate successful experiences are factors that can speed up the pace of late industrialization. At the same time, late industrializers may find it difficult to compete successfully with the early industrializers on a level playing field. This could be one reason for more state intervention in the context of late industrialization.

Tariffs are the quintessential rent-seeking instruments adamantly opposed by neoliberalism. Indeed the whole concept of rent-seeking behavior originates with the analysis and criticism of trade tariffs and barriers. But historically no country except England, the first country to industrialize, has succeeded in industrializing without tariffs and trade barriers. The trade tariffs could be very high as was the case in the industrialization process of Germany and to a certain extent the US, or they could be relatively low as was the case in Japan. Interestingly, the same historical study also shows that not all those with trade tariffs have had sustained and accelerated industrialization, as the experience of Russia in the first decade of the twentieth century attests.[67]

This seems to suggest that the impact of the early industrializers on the late ones involves disadvantages in competing on a level field that requires some corrections through trade tariffs. Perhaps more importantly, it suggests that various levels and forms of policy intervention can result in required outcomes and that the same policies can have different outcomes depending on other circumstances. In the case of tariffs, the same policy has resulted in very different outcomes in Germany and Russia.

Other studies have shown that effective implementation, rather than policy, makes the difference. The same policy can create a haven for rent-seeking activity or inhibit such activity, depending on the nature of the state. These studies suggest that only correct policy implemented by an autonomous state with the capacity to discipline private economic agents can create a stable policy environment and have the desired impact.[68] The differing outcomes of the same policy interventions are thus explained by the differing natures of the states implementing the policies, as reflected in their differing capabilities.

It has also been argued that the key issue in development is the economic issue of improving agricultural productivity and directing the surplus generated as a result of industrialization. Behind the economic process lies a fundamentally political one: That of the coming to power of a class that has both the will and ability to bring about the economic process mentioned above.[69] In the end, development is a political process first and a socioeconomic process second.

Studies of such political transformation have shown that they can be brought about by various means—by revolutions from below or revolutions from above (or some combination of the two). In Japan and Germany, successful industrialization has taken place after revolutions from above succeeded in bringing about the required political changes in the form of semi-parliamentary regimes. Similar process in Italy have also been quite successful, while that of Spain has been significantly less so. Revolutions from above are thought to need to fulfill certain requirements if they are to be successful in carrying out accelerated development. They must possess: (1) a very able leadership that recognizes the need for such a revolution and that perseveres in the pursuit of its objectives, dragging along society and most particularly the old elite from which the faction that leads the revolution emerges; (2) a powerful bureaucratic apparatus, including powerful police and army to free itself from pressures both from the elite and the population at large.[70]

The process of revolution from above as articulated by Barrington Moore is a peculiar process of political transformation that comes about not because the population has risen up in revolt, swept aside the old elite, and replaced it with a new one that starts the process of socioeconomic development, but one that emerges as a result of the action of members of the old elite who recognize the need for political transformation and who bring it about through direction and guidance from above.

A group that brings about such change must be very able and dedicated indeed to go beyond its narrow interests and recognize that society as a whole will be better off through such change. It also must walk a very tight rope because the old elite will inevitably feel betrayed and threatened. The people will inevitably feel that such changes are too little too late and designed to perpetuate the privileges of the elite by other means. Such a group will need more than ability and dedication to maintain its effort. It needs a powerful state apparatus to shield it both from the left and the right. It needs to be autonomous from society at large and tower over it like a colossus. It can be semi-democratic, semi-parliamentarian at best.

The recognition of the fact that the state has played a crucial role in development and the tentative conclusions on the nature of the state that brings about such change have evolved over time into a well-articulated theory. The spectacular development success in East Asia—most particularly in Japan, Korea, and Taiwan—and the active role of the state in these countries has facilitated the articulation of the theory. The nature of the state that can build such development has been analyzed in depth and such a state has been given a specific name: The developmental state.

The nature of the developmental state

It is argued that the developmental state has two components, ideological and structural, and that it is the nexus between these two components that defines and distinguishes it from other states. At the ideological level, accelerated development is the mission, its source of legitimacy. Moreover, the development project is a hegemonic project in the Gramscian sense—the key actors voluntarily adhere to its objectives and principles. Structurally it has the capacity to implement policy effectively, which is the result of various political, institutional, and technical factors, which in turn are based on the autonomy of the state. This autonomy enables the state to pursue its development project without succumbing to myopic interests.[71]

The definition of the state based on the nexus of characteristics that include the single-minded pursuit of accelerated development, the autonomy of the state, and the "hegemonic character of the development project" appears to have gained wide acceptance. The same points have been made by another study.[72] While the single-minded pursuit of accelerated development by the developmental state appears to be self-evident, the concepts of state autonomy, the widespread support for the development process, and the need for a national consensus on the matter need to be elaborated.

Analysts have plausibly argued that all states in market economies need to and have certain autonomy. They need such autonomy to maintain corporate coherence and serve the systemic interests of a market economy. If they were to simply reflect society with its conflicting interests and demands, the state would lose all semblance of corporate coherence and cease to serve any interests adequately. It is suggested that such a level of autonomy is the normal characteristic of the run-of-the-mill state in a market economy.[73]

If indeed state autonomy is one characteristic that distinguishes the developmental state from others, how different is the autonomy of a developmental state from the autonomy of the run-of-the-mill state in a market economy? The answer to this crucial issue has been provided by Dani Rodrik, who has defined the autonomous state by comparing it to what has been called the subordinate state.

The distinction between an autonomous state and subordinate state has to do with implementation of policy decisions. On one end we have a state in which decisions are made autonomously based on its development agenda; the private sector lacks the means to reshape them or avoid compliance as they are implemented. On the other end, we have a state in which decisions and their outcomes are the result of the interplay between private-sector pressure and government motives and are rarely final.[74]

Obviously these examples represent polar opposites and many states are likely to have shades of both, but defining the limits helps to clarify the essence of the autonomy of the developmental state. In this regard, two very critical points have been made. First the autonomy of a developmental state is reflected and described by its ability to make and effectively implement policy regardless of the views of the private sector on the issue. The subordinate state cannot do that because it makes and implements decisions through a process of juggling interests among various sections of the private sector. In this sense it is directly accountable to these interests. It may have enough autonomy to enable it to maintain some corporate coherence and to pursue the interests of the system as a whole, but not enough to make and implement decisions independent of the views of the private sector. From this perspective, our run-of-the-mill state in the market economy would be a subordinate state.

The second and related point has to do with identifying that the developmental state ought to be autonomous from the private sector. In the absence of state direction of the economy, it would be the private sector that would provide overall economic guidance to the economy. If the state is not autonomous from the private sector, it cannot provide guidance to the economy. Moreover, day-to-day economic decisions in a market economy are made essentially by the private sector. The developmental state tries to guide the private sector to make its decisions in a manner that accelerates growth by using a set of incentives and disincentives. If the state is not autonomous from the private sector, it will not be able to discipline, encourage, and cajole it to act in a manner designed by the state.

One of the identified characteristics of a developmental state is that it must achieve broad support for its development agenda. Development is an exercise that requires appropriate behavior on the part of millions of individuals. It is based on the development of social capital through civic engagement in mutually beneficial horizontal networks. None of these can be created and sustained by coercion alone. The development agenda must be hegemonic if successful development is to take place and if a developmental state is to be established.

As clear as the need for a developmental state based on national consensus is, it appears to be contradicted by historical experience. Most, if not all, of the well-known developmental states have not been democratic; they have at best been "semi-parliamentarian," to use Barrington Moore's words. The insistence on the part of theorists for the need of broad support for the development agenda, while at the same time recognizing that developmental states have in general been undemocratic, suggests that a distinction between national consensus on the development agenda and democratic governance is being made.

Some analysts have gone even further and made explicit the distinction and the relationship between democracy and developmental state. They argue that the difference between autonomous and subordinate states is not that one is undemocratic while the other is democratic. Both the autonomous and the subordinate state can be democratic and both can also be undemocratic.[75] An autonomous state, whether it is democratic or not, will have to build some sort of consensus on its development agenda if it is to be a developmental state. Whether it builds such a consensus in the context of a fully democratic order or not does not determine its characteristics as a developmental state.

Government actions can lead to socially wasteful rent-seeking activity. The difference between the neoliberal school and the theorists of the developmental state is not whether government intervention in the economy can result in socially wasteful rent-seeking activity, because both agree that this is indeed the case. The difference is whether the government can be activist and avoid socially wasteful rent-seeking activity or not. The neoliberals say "no" and the theorists of the developmental state say "yes". The developmental state needs to have both the incentive and the means to do so. The subordinate state does not have the incentive because it exists via juggling private-sector interests; it does not have the means because it does not have the ability to reward and punish the private sector depending on whether their behavior is rent-seeking or growth-enhancing.[76] The developmental state, however, has the motivation because its purpose is to accelerate growth and it can do so—and maintain its legitimacy—only by rewarding growth-enhancing activities and restricting and penalizing socially wasteful activities. Its autonomy from the private sector gives it the means and the will to discipline the private sector through rewards and penalties.

The various historical examples of the emergence of developmental states have shown that they are the results of political and social processes and created by social and political action. They are not given characteristics of a given set of countries. They are states created by "social and political engineering."[77] As social constructs of historical process, they come in different sizes and shapes, reflecting the context of their creation. But whatever the variations among developmental states might be, we can identify certain basic characteristics that are common to all and which can be summarized as follows: (1) The motive and source of legitimacy of developmental states is the single-minded pursuit of accelerated development. (2) The development project is broadly shared in the country. (3) They are autonomous from the private sector; they make and implement decisions regardless of the views of the private sector; and they have the motive, the incentive, and the means to reward and punish the private sector in order to promote desired behavior and activity. (4) They can be either democratic or undemocratic, and this does not determine whether they are developmental states or not.

Conclusions

It has been argued that inhibiting rent-seeking behavior does not depend on the size of the state or on the degree of its activism in economic matters, but on the nature of the state, which can be an activist state at the same time as inhibiting socially wasteful rent-seeking activity. Similarly it has been argued that developing countries face formidable market failures and institutional inadequacies that create vicious circles and poverty traps, which can adequately be addressed only by an activist state. It has been shown that the historical practice bears this out. However, we had not defined what sort of activist state is required. The analysis of the developmental state in this chapter is intended to fill this gap.

We can conclude that development is a political process first and economic and social process second. It is the creation of a political set-up that is conducive to accelerated development that sets the ball of development rolling. Only when there is a state that has the characteristics of a developmental state can one meaningfully discuss the elimination of rent-seeking behavior. In its absence, rent-seeking will be rampant no matter what the size of the state might be. Only in the context of such a political environment can one debate about development policy in a meaningful manner. In its absence, all government policy and action—however limited and timid it might be—will be riddled with rent-seeking behavior and this is particularly so in developing countries, which will be emerging from a social and political environment in which vertical, patron-client networks are pervasive.

The neoliberal paradigm states that socially wasteful rent-seeking is the result of government activity and of the size of government activism. It does not distinguish between state activism. This leads it to the conclusion that most if not all government intervention in the economy is detrimental to growth and to the suggestion that the nightwatchman state is the best state from the point of view of accelerated growth. Historical practice has shown that state intervention has been critical in the development process. Economic theory has shown that developing countries are riddled with vicious circles and poverty traps that can only be removed by state action. The theory of the developmental state completes the alternative paradigm by showing what type of state can intervene in the economy to accelerate growth while at the same time limiting socially wasteful rent-seeking activities.

Notes

1. The author is Prime Minister of Ethiopia but the views expressed here are personal and do not necessarily reflect the official position of the Government of Ethiopia.
2. Zenawi (2006). Extracts from the draft are posted on IPD website in the section on the Africa Task Force.
3. Colander (1984).
4. World Bank (1997).

5. Moore (1966).
6. Colander (1984).
7. Buchanan (1980).
8. Ibid.
9. Todaro (1996).
10. Mkandawire (2001).
11. Evans (1992).
12. North (1990).
13. Stiglitz (1994).
14. North (1990).
15. World Bank (2002).
16. Ibid.
17. Stiglitz (2002).
18. North (1990).
19. Ibid.
20. Putnam, Leonardi, and Nanetti (1993).
21. Ibid.
22. Enos and Park (1985).
23. Mankiw (2002).
24. Easterly (2002).
25. Romer (1990).
26. Ibid.
27. Todaro (1996).
28. Stiglitz (1989).
29. Easterly (2002).
30. Ibid.
31. Stiglitz (1989).
32. Porter (1985).
33. Ibid.
34. Stiglitz (1989).
35. Porter (1985).
36. Aghion and Howitt (1998).
37. Stiglitz (1994).
38. Ibid.
39. Ibid.
40. Johnson (1992).
41. Dalum, Johnson, and Lundvall (1992).
42. Johnson (1992).
43. Ergas (1987).
44. Ibid.
45. Ibid.
46. Ibid.
47. Ibid.
48. Ibid.
49. Ibid.

50. Ibid.
51. Easterly (2002).
52. Dosi and Soete (1998).
53. Amsden (2001).
54. Koike (1990).
55. Westphal, Kim, and Dahlman (1985).
56. Ernest, Ganiatsos, and Mytelka (1998).
57. Enos and Park (1985).
58. Mytelka (1985).
59. Enos and Park (1985).
60. Mytelka (1985).
61. Park (1991).
62. Enos and Park (1985).
63. Ibid.
64. Porter (1985).
65. Kron (1962).
66. Amsden (1992).
67. Morris and Adelman (1989).
68. Rodrik (1995).
69. Moore (1966).
70. Ibid.
71. Mkandawire (2001).
72. Lall and Stewart (1996).
73. Rueschemeyer and Evans (1985).
74. Rodrik (1992).
75. Ibid.
76. Ibid.
77. Mkandawire (2001).

References

Aghion, P. and Howitt, P. (1998). *Endogenous Growth Theory*. Cambridge, MA: MIT Press.

Amsden, A. H. (1992). *Asia's Next Giant, South Korea and Late Industrialization*. Oxford: Oxford University Press.

—— (2001). *The Rise of the "Rest": Challenges to the West from Late-Industrializing Economies*. Oxford: Oxford University Press.

Buchanan, J. N. (1980). "Rent seeking and Profit Seeking," in J. M. Buchanan, R. D. Tollison, and G. Tullock (eds.), *Toward a Theory of the Rent-seeking Society*. College Station: Texas A&M University Press.

Colander, D. C. (1984). "Introduction," in D. C. Colander (ed.), *Neoclassical Political Economy: The Analysis of Rent seeking and DUP Activities*. Cambridge: Ballinger.

Dalum, B., Johnson, B., and Lundvall, B.-A. (1992). "Public Policy in the Learning Society," in B.-A. Lundvall (ed.), *National Systems of Innovation: Toward a Theory of Innovation and Interactive Learning*. London: Pinter.

Dosi, G. and Soete, L. (1998). *Technical Change and International Trade*. London: Pinter.

Easterly, W. (2002). *The Elusive Quest for Growth: Economists' Adventures and Misadventures in the Tropics*. Cambridge, MA: MIT Press.

Enos, J. L. and Park, W. H. (1985). *The Adoption and Diffusion of Imported Technology: The Case of Korea*. London: Croom Helm.

Ergas, H. (1987). "The Importance of Technology Policy," in P. Dasgupta and P. Stoneman (eds.), *Economic Policy and Technological Performance*. Cambridge: Cambridge University Press.

Ernest, D., Ganiatsos, T., and Mytelka, L. (1998). "Technological Capabilities in the Context of Export-Led Growth: A Conceptual Framework," in D. Ernest, T. Ganiatsos, and L. Mytelka (eds.), *Technological Capabilities and Export Success in Asia*. London: Routledge.

Evans, P. (1992). "The State as Problem and Solution: Predation, Embedded Autonomy and Structural Change," in S. Haggard and R. R. Kaufman (eds.), *The Politics of Economic Adjustment: International Constraints, Distributive Conflicts, and the State*. Princeton, NJ: Princeton University Press.

Johnson, B. (1992). "Institutional Learning," in B. A. Lundvall (ed.), *National Systems of Innovation: Toward a Theory of Innovation and Interactive Learning*. London: Pinter.

Koike, K. (1990). "Theory of Skill Formation Systems," in K. Koike and T. Inoki (eds.), *Skill Formation in Japan and Southeast Asia*. Tokyo: University of Tokyo Press.

Kron, A. G. (1962). *Economic Backwardness in Historical Perspective: A Book of Essays*. Cambridge, MA: Belknap Press of Harvard University Press.

Lall, S. and Stewart, F. (1996). "Trade and Industrial Policy in Africa," in B. Ndulu and N. van de Walle (eds.), *Agenda for Africa's Economic Renewal*. New Brunswick, NJ: Transaction Publications.

Mankiw, N. G. (2002). *Macroeconomics*. New York: Worth Publishers.

Mkandawire, T. (2001). "Thinking About Developmental State in Africa," *Cambridge Journal of Economics*, 25 (3): 289–313.

Moore, B. (1966). *Social Origins of Dictatorship and Democracy: Lord and Peasant in the Making of the Modern World*. Boston: Beacon Press.

Morris, C. T. and Adelman, I. (1989). "Nineteenth Century Development Experience and Lessons for Today," *World Development*, 17 (9): 1417–32.

Mytelka, L. K. (1985). "Stimulating Effective Technology Transfer: The Case of Textile in Africa," in N. Rosenberg and C. Frischtak (eds.), *International Technology Transfer: Concepts, Measures and Comparisons*. New York: Praeger.

North, D. C. (1990). *Institutions, Institutional Change and Economic Performance*. Cambridge: Cambridge University Press.

Park, E. (1991). "Foreign Trade, Direct Investment and Industrialization Strategy of Korea," Center for International Development, Korea Development Institute. Available at http://cid.kdi.re.kr/cid_eng/public/report_read05.jsp?1=1&pub_no=3758.

Porter, M. E. (1985). *The Competitive Advantage of Nations*. New York: The Free Press.

Putnam, R., Leonardi, R., and Nanetti, R. Y. (1993). *Making Democracy Work: Civic Traditions in Modern Italy*. Princeton, NJ: Princeton University Press.

Rodrik, D. (1992). "Political Economy and Development Policy," *European Economic Review*, 36 (2–3): 329–36.

—— (1995). "Trade and Industrial Policy Reform," in J. Behrman and T. N. Srinivasan (eds.), *Handbook of Development Economics*, Vol. 3B. Amsterdam: Elsevier Science Publishers.

Romer, P. M. (1990). "Endogenous Technological Change," *The Journal of Political Economy*, 98 (5): S71–S102.

Rueschemeyer, D. and Evans, P. B. (1985). "The State And Economic Transformation: Toward an Analysis of the Conditions Underlying Effective Intervention," in P. B. Evans, D. Rueschemeyer, and T. Skocpol (eds.), *Bringing the State Back*. Cambridge: Cambridge University Press.

Stiglitz, J. E. (1989). "Markets, Market Failures and Development," *The American Economic Review*, 79 (2): 197–203.

—— (1994). *Whither Socialism?* Cambridge, MA: MIT Press.

—— (2002). "Participation and Development, Perspectives from the Comprehensive Development Paradigm," *Review of Development Economics*, 6 (2): 163–82.

Todaro, M. P. (1996). *Economic Development*, 6th edn. London: Longman.

Westphal, L. E., Kim, L., and Dahlman, C. S. (1985). "Reflections on the Republic of Korea's Acquisition of Technology," in N. Rosenberg and C. Frischtak (eds.), *International Technology Transfer*. New York: Praeger.

World Bank (1997). *The State in a Changing World: World Development Report 1997*. New York: Oxford University Press.

—— (2002). *Building Institutions for Markets: World Development Report 2002*. New York: Oxford University Press.

Zenawi, M. (2006). "African Development: Dead Ends and New Beginning," Monograph. Available at http://cgt.columbia.edu/files/conferences/Zenawi_Dead_Ends_and_New_Beginnings.pdf.

6

The African Economic Growth Record, and the Roles of Policy Syndromes and Governance[1]

Augustin Kwasi Fosu[2]

Introduction

Most countries in Sub-Saharan Africa (SSA) had attained political independence from colonial rule by the mid 1960s.[3] The evidence shows that the region's economic performance, on average, has substantially lagged behind that of other regions of the world. Nonetheless, the performance has been rather episodic, with African[4] countries growing fairly strongly until roughly the mid-to-late 1970s, when the region's GDP growth began to decline substantially, falling short of population growth. Since the mid 1990s, however, Africa has once again experienced strong growth generally, with some signs of growth acceleration at the beginning of the twenty-first century.

In 2007, for instance, the GDP growth of SSA economies averaged 6.2 percent, nearly double the rate in 2002 (World Bank 2009) and comparable to GDP growth in other regions of the world (Arbache et al. 2008). Some twenty-six African countries, representing 70 percent of the SSA population and 78 percent of the GDP, grew by at least 4 percent per year on average (ibid., table 1). Indeed, since 1995, the annual growth rates of these countries have averaged 6.9 percent (ibid.), a rate that is comparable to the 6.7 percent average growth rate over the same period for India, for instance, the recent growth record of which is oft-cited.[5]

The poverty picture

The weak growth since the late 1970s until recently is reflected in the dismal poverty picture in SSA over the last two-and-a-half decades. Based on World Bank (2007) data, the proportion of the population earning less than $1 decreased only slightly, from 42 percent in 1981 to 41 percent in 2004 (Fosu 2009: table 1).

Over the same period, this measure of poverty fell substantially for South Asia (SAS), as a reference region, from 50 percent in 1981 to 31 percent in 2004, so that the relative SSA/SAS poverty rate gap increased steadily by nearly 50 percentage points (ibid.).[6]

The resurgence in growth in Africa has brightened the poverty picture somewhat during the last decade or so. Indeed, the rates of poverty reduction in SSA and SAS have been comparable since the mid 1990s, falling by 4.4 and 6.1 percentage points, respectively, between 1993 and 2004 (ibid.). Similarly, the poverty rate measured at the $2 standard fell by 4.1 percentage points and 5.1 percentage points for SSA and SAS, respectively. There appears, then, to have been a reversal in course for the poverty rate in SSA since the mid 1990s, mirroring the growth pattern.[7] Thus, understanding the growth record should be useful not only in its own right, but also in terms of charting the course of human development as reflected by changes in the poverty rate for instance.[8]

The current chapter first discusses the African growth record. Second, it presents evidence on the historical sources of growth. Third, reflecting the main premise underlying a recent research project on growth, the chapter employs the taxonomy of "policy syndromes" to explain the observed growth patterns.[9] Fourth, it extends the analysis to include the role of governance by exploring its direct impact on growth as well as its indirect effect via policy syndromes.

The African growth record

GDP of the SSA region grew fairly strongly at an average yearly rate of approximately 5 percent (per capita rate of nearly 2 percent) for about a decade and a half from 1960, with significant positive contributions from a substantial number of countries (see Tables 6.1 and 6.2).[10] This record of growth could not be sustained in subsequent years, however, as the growth rate fell to as low as 1.2 percent per annum during 1981–5, a rate that was much smaller than population growth of roughly 2.9 percent. Hence, per capita GDP deteriorated by an average of nearly 2 percent annually during this period. It was not until the latter part of the 1990s that SSA began to grow sufficiently to overcome population increases. Thus, the issue of the overall African growth record is not necessarily a case of consistently dismal performance, but rather one of episodic growth.

As Tables 6.1 and 6.2 further indicate, the aggregate evidence masks the considerable disparities in growth among SSA countries. During 1981–5, for example, when growth was at its nadir in SSA as a whole, a number of African countries actually registered growth rates of at least 4 percent (about 1 percentage point above population growth), including Benin at 4.7 percent, Botswana at 10 percent, Burkina Faso at 4.2 percent, Burundi at 5.4 percent, Cameroon at 9.4 percent, Chad at 9.2 percent, and Republic of Congo at 10.6 percent.

Table 6.1 GDP growth (annual %), five-year averages

Country Name	Code	61-65	66-70	71-75	76-80	81-85	86-90	91-95	96-00	01-05	2006	Avg
Angola	AGO						3.28	-3.78	6.43	10.55	18.56	4.81
Benin	BEN	3.28	2.69	1.42	4.09	4.66	0.89	4.25	5.35	3.88	4.10	3.40
Botswana	BWA	6.32	11.02	18.15	12.23	10.01	11.87	4.06	8.35	5.43	2.15	9.55
Burkina Faso	BFA	2.99	2.91	3.09	3.59	4.18	3.01	3.96	6.78	6.22	6.39	4.13
Burundi	BDI	1.94	7.60	0.64	4.23	5.35	3.73	-2.40	-1.34	2.20	5.13	2.50
Cameroon	CMR	2.71	1.61	6.70	6.86	9.40	-2.22	-1.86	4.75	3.66	3.76	3.52
Cape Verde	CPV					8.62	3.50	5.23	6.40	5.16	6.09	5.79
Central African Rep.	CAF	0.71	3.23	1.95	0.70	2.29	0.04	1.09	2.38	-0.88	4.10	1.34
Chad	TCD	0.65	1.45	0.90	-4.55	9.18	1.94	2.44	2.65	15.29	0.47	3.27
Comoros	COM					4.29	1.62	0.89	1.47	2.79	0.50	2.15
Congo, Dem. Rep.	ZAR	2.82	3.84	2.49	-1.45	1.86	0.01	-7.12	-3.89	4.05	5.08	0.39
Congo, Rep.	COG	3.40	5.00	8.04	5.15	10.57	-0.26	0.50	2.48	4.32	6.40	4.40
Côte d'Ivoire	CIV	8.03	9.73	6.44	4.52	0.32	1.18	1.51	3.22	-0.01	0.85	3.82
Equatorial Guinea	GNQ						1.36	7.05	35.43	27.00	-5.56	16.60
Eritrea	ERI							12.51	1.17	3.67	-0.98	5.36
Ethiopia	ETH							1.34	4.92	5.75	8.99	3.44
Gabon	GAB	8.24	5.58	18.09	0.40	-1.21	5.27	3.13	0.41	1.74	1.18	4.58
Gambia, The	GMB		4.54	5.54	4.41	2.56	1.73	2.11	4.50	3.92	4.50	4.06
Ghana	GHA	3.10	2.98	0.01	1.04	-0.25	4.81	4.28	4.32	5.04	6.20	2.89
Guinea	GIN				2.60	2.02	4.21	3.90	4.25	3.08	2.82	3.33
Guinea-Bissau	GNB			3.20	-0.61	6.45	3.78	3.18	1.06	-0.12	4.20	2.47
Kenya	KEN	3.49	5.88	10.02	6.35	2.53	5.64	1.61	2.16	3.61	6.11	4.62
Lesotho	LSO	7.64	2.77	5.76	10.26	3.09	5.86	4.00	3.24	2.86	7.17	5.10
Liberia	LBR	3.20	6.63	1.61	2.18	-1.88	-16.48	-21.66	39.34	-3.36	7.80	1.21
Madagascar	MDG	1.38	4.68	0.66	1.46	-1.55	2.75	-0.28	3.84	2.60	4.89	1.80
Malawi	MWI	4.64	4.99	7.60	4.89	2.17	2.32	3.52	3.92	1.06	7.42	3.98
Mali	MLI		3.36	3.41	4.92	-2.25	3.86	2.99	5.19	6.39	5.30	3.53
Mauritania	MRT					0.92	2.47	3.26	2.61	4.04	11.70	3.94
Mauritius	MUS	11.62	5.45	0.71	2.86	4.33	7.39	5.13	5.38	4.15	3.54	5.27
Mozambique	MOZ					-4.62	5.62	2.68	7.52	8.60	7.97	4.11

(continued)

Table 6.1 Continued

Country Name	Code	61–65	66–70	71–75	76–80	81–85	86–90	91–95	96–00	01–05	2006	Avg
Namibia	NAM					-0.19	2.68	4.96	3.51	4.78	2.90	3.14
Niger	NER	6.26	-0.46	-2.11	5.37	-2.32	2.60	0.81	2.92	4.22	4.80	1.98
Nigeria	NGA	4.54	5.59	5.79	4.05	-2.75	5.42	2.49	3.08	5.71	5.20	3.80
Rwanda	RWA	-1.65	7.59	0.84	10.29	2.68	1.50	-3.95	9.80	5.40	5.30	3.65
Senegal	SEN	1.99	1.99	2.48	1.19	2.92	2.38	2.09	4.12	4.68	2.30	2.64
Seychelles	SYC	3.70	3.81	7.14	8.56	0.92	5.56	2.90	6.28	-1.72	5.30	4.15
Sierra Leone	SLE	4.38	4.18	2.36	2.27	0.87	1.09	-5.05	-3.55	13.91	7.37	2.39
Somalia	SOM	-1.09	3.99	4.52	3.88	2.54	1.25					2.43
South Africa	ZAF	6.81	5.15	3.66	3.12	1.40	1.68	0.89	2.80	3.89	4.99	3.30
Sudan	SDN	1.95	1.43	4.99	2.69	0.83	4.55	5.13	6.46	6.48	11.80	4.01
Swaziland	SWZ			9.57	3.15	2.61	10.26	2.88	3.31	2.38	2.08	4.80
Tanzania	TZA						5.40	1.80	4.08	6.54	5.94	4.53
Togo	TGO	10.14	6.66	3.75	5.07	-0.24	2.51	0.61	4.52	2.18	4.10	3.91
Uganda	UGA					0.70	5.09	7.05	6.55	5.64	5.44	5.02
Zambia	ZMB	6.20	1.59	2.46	0.44	0.53	1.64	-1.28	2.84	4.78	6.20	2.22
Zimbabwe	ZWE	3.56	9.37	4.91	1.72	4.36	4.60	1.39	0.89	-5.32		2.77
n = 46												
SSA simple average		4.10	4.59	4.61	3.66	2.41	2.92	1.56	5.15	4.58	5.01	3.76
WB SSA weighted average		5.19	4.70	4.30	3.11	1.13	2.61	1.17	3.43	4.55	5.60	3.40

Source: World Bank (2008).

Table 6.2 GDP per capita growth (annual %), five-year averages

Country Name	Code	61–65	66–70	71–75	76–80	81–85	86–90	91–95	96–00	01–05	2006	Avg
Angola	AGO						0.69	-6.73	3.84	7.40	15.26	1.96
Benin	BEN	1.44	0.46	-1.13	1.13	1.17	-2.38	0.53	2.19	0.59	0.90	0.46
Botswana	BWA	3.64	7.75	14.33	8.12	6.45	8.51	1.27	6.23	4.17	0.93	6.59
Burkina Faso	BFA	1.40	0.89	0.80	1.28	1.68	0.16	0.96	3.71	2.89	3.24	1.57
Burundi	BDI	0.15	5.70	-0.29	1.87	1.88	0.60	-4.20	-2.63	-1.10	1.08	0.24
Cameroon	CMR	0.44	-0.86	3.86	3.73	6.23	-5.15	-4.54	2.25	1.30	1.59	0.82
Cape Verde	CPV					6.40	1.30	2.71	3.95	2.71	3.69	3.43
Central African Rep.	CAF	-1.21	1.08	0.02	-1.74	-0.53	-2.26	-1.64	0.09	-2.49	2.30	-0.89
Chad	TCD	-1.51	-0.71	-1.50	-6.52	6.47	-1.20	-0.72	-0.75	11.19	-2.62	0.46
Comoros	COM					1.60	-1.00	-1.31	-0.65	0.64	-1.64	-0.20
Congo, Dem. Rep.	ZAR	0.11	0.70	-0.58	-4.51	-1.04	-3.07	-10.35	-6.01	1.02	1.79	-2.54
Congo, Rep.	COG	0.74	1.99	4.76	1.95	7.28	-3.10	-2.33	-0.29	1.86	4.11	1.49
Côte d'Ivoire	CIV	4.06	5.15	1.94	-0.29	-4.20	-2.71	-1.67	0.58	-1.72	-0.91	0.10
Equatorial Guinea	GNQ							4.56	32.23	24.06	-7.76	13.91
Eritrea	ERI							12.19	-1.51	-0.51	-4.47	2.90
Ethiopia	ETH						1.84	-0.50	1.81	2.98	6.19	0.66
Gabon	GAB	7.54	4.45	15.27	-2.23	-3.93	-1.34	0.28	-1.84	-0.03	-0.37	2.35
Gambia, The	GMB		1.55	2.04	1.06	-0.35	0.19	-1.62	0.87	0.74	1.61	0.60
Ghana	GHA	0.28	0.92	-2.57	-0.93	-3.56	1.82	1.44	1.87	2.71	4.01	0.30
Guinea	GIN				-0.19	-0.50	1.10	-0.05	1.91	1.18	0.82	0.58
Guinea-Bissau	GNB			0.96	-4.48	3.95	1.10	-0.04	-1.74	-3.13	1.12	-0.44
Kenya	KEN	0.22	2.37	6.11	2.45	-1.28	2.00	-1.49	-0.51	0.95	3.34	1.25
Lesotho	LSO	5.68	0.71	3.52	7.66	0.49	4.10	2.49	1.38	1.85	6.42	3.17
Liberia	LBR	0.47	3.65	-1.32	-0.88	-4.78	-16.32	-21.86	29.50	-5.60	3.67	-1.78
Madagascar	MDG	-1.14	2.02	-1.96	-1.27	-4.30	-0.13	-3.18	0.79	-0.26	2.06	-0.98
Malawi	MWI	2.18	2.34	4.32	1.51	-0.98	-2.90	2.14	1.03	-1.52	4.69	0.99
Mali	MLI		1.29	1.10	2.67	-4.43	1.38	0.34	2.38	3.27	2.16	1.03
Mauritania	MRT	8.85	2.76	-1.94	0.15	-1.71	-0.08	0.52	-0.27	1.09	8.74	1.21
Mauritius	MUS					3.29	6.55	3.87	4.21	3.18	2.70	4.16
Mozambique	MOZ					-6.38	5.30	-0.62	4.71	6.01	5.71	1.95
Namibia	NAM					-2.75	-1.85	1.73	0.94	3.28	1.55	0.32

(continued)

Table 6.2 Continued

Country Name	Code	61–65	66–70	71–75	76–80	81–85	86–90	91–95	96–00	01–05	2006	Avg
Niger	NER	2.88	-3.62	-5.17	2.10	-5.18	-0.50	-2.59	-0.73	0.62	1.20	-1.30
Nigeria	NGA	2.12	3.05	3.10	0.98	-5.41	2.38	-0.40	0.33	3.10	2.75	1.07
Rwanda	RWA	-3.67	4.10	-2.24	6.73	-0.68	-1.96	0.75	2.00	2.85	2.74	0.92
Senegal	SEN	-0.87	-1.09	-0.56	-1.54	-0.04	-0.64	-0.67	1.40	1.99	-0.26	-0.23
Seychelles	SYC	1.04	1.33	4.88	6.88	0.01	4.77	1.41	4.71	-2.16	3.18	2.56
Sierra Leone	SLE	2.60	2.27	0.58	0.36	-1.16	-1.53	-5.30	-5.23	9.19	4.45	0.29
Somalia	SOM	-3.38	1.38	1.55	-5.17	2.57	0.49					-0.41
South Africa	ZAF	4.05	2.91	1.35	0.89	-1.14	-0.68	-1.22	0.41	2.58	3.88	1.08
Sudan	SDN	-0.36	-1.02	1.96	-0.49	-2.36	2.12	2.46	3.88	4.35	9.41	1.35
Swaziland	SWZ			6.54	-0.07	-0.50	6.88	-0.28	0.27	0.77	1.46	1.93
Tanzania	TZA						2.13	-1.39	1.53	3.84	3.31	1.61
Togo	TGO	8.16	2.10	1.00	2.38	-3.89	-0.84	-2.01	0.84	-0.72	1.31	0.79
Uganda	UGA					-2.48	1.24	3.38	3.39	2.33	2.08	1.59
Zambia	ZMB	3.06	-1.55	-0.93	-2.79	-2.65	-1.39	-3.84	0.38	2.83	4.22	-0.66
Zimbabwe	ZWE	0.22	5.86	1.40	-1.62	0.37	1.11	-0.95	-0.55	-6.00		-0.02
n = 46												
SSA simple average		1.64	1.87	1.80	0.55	-0.39	0.13	-0.86	2.29	2.10	2.54	1.05
WB SSA weighted average		2.63	2.02	1.52	0.07	-1.76	-0.34	-1.45	0.70	1.97	3.04	0.65

Source: World Bank (2008).

Tables 6.1 and 6.2 also show that while the biggest economy, South Africa, led growth in the early periods, it actually began to pull down the SSA average beginning in the early 1970s. That situation has persisted, though less so in the most recent half-decade. Because the overall SSA average is weighted heavily toward South Africa, which has a large relative weight due to its substantially higher GDP than the rest of SSA, Table 6.1 reports the simple mean together with the usual weighted average of the growth rates. However, there are extreme values, especially for small economies, which appear to exaggerate the simple average as well. To avoid statistical dominance by South Africa and the potential distortion from extreme values, the subsequent discussion will be based on the SSA weighted average that excludes South Africa (see Table 6.3 and Figure 6.1).

Another observation about the African growth record is the heterogeneity in pattern across countries. Many economies that started as growth leaders in the 1960s had by 2000 become growth laggards (e.g., Côte d'Ivoire, Gabon, Kenya, South Africa, Togo, and Zambia) (see Tables 6.1 and 6.2). Conversely, several laggards in the earlier period became growth leaders as of the 1990s (e.g., Benin, Burkina Faso, Ghana, Senegal, and Sudan). In contrast, one African country that has exhibited consistently high economic growth is Botswana. Its GDP growth averaged about 10 percent annually over the entire period, and at least 5 percent in every decadal period. The record since the 1990s has been less than spectacular,

Table 6.3 Half-decadal mean annual SSA GDP growth rates (%), 1961–2005 (2nd row excludes South Africa)

1961–65	1966–70	1971–75	1976–80	1981–85	1986–90	1990–95	1996–2000	2001–2005
5.4	5.1	4.6	2.7	1.0	2.5	1.1	3.3	4.1
3.5	4.1	4.9	3.2	1.7	3.1	2.0	3.9	4.5

Source: A. Fosu and E. Aryeetey (2009), "Explaining Four Decades of Growth in Sub-Saharan Africa," in G. McMahon, E. Salehi, and L. Squire (eds.), *Diversity in Economic Growth: Global Insights and Explanations*, Edward Elgar Publishing Ltd.

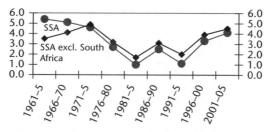

Figure 6.1 Half-decadal mean annual SSA GDP growth rates (%), 1961–2005
Source: See Table 6.3.

though. This result might be attributable to a combination of poor terms-of-trade performance and the high incidence of HIV/AIDS in the country during the more recent period.[11]

Furthermore, African countries have exhibited highly variable growth rates over the last four decades. The standard deviation of the per-worker GDP growth for a sample of nineteen SSA countries with consistent data averaged 3.2 percent from 1960–2000, which was the highest among all regions of the world (see Table 6.4).[12] Indeed, SSA's coefficient of variation (CV) is nearly four times the world average, so that the region exhibited a lower mean growth with higher variance as compared to the rest of the world.

On the basis of primarily cross-country studies, numerous explanations have been offered for the above growth record. These include: governance, geography, ethno-linguistic fractionalization, neighbors, debt, domestic policies, the global setting, political instability, resource endowment, and colonial heritage.[13] The Growth Project of the African Economic Research Consortium (AERC) provides a most recent comprehensive study on the subject. That study combines both cross-sectional analysis and twenty-six country cases to explain the African growth record since 1960.[14] Using data generated from the Growth Project, the present study re-explores the implications of adverse policies for growth, based on the policy syndromes taxonomy adopted therein. In particular, I employ here the production function approach to examine how the "syndrome-free" (SF)[15] regime influences growth via its effects on investment levels versus total factor productivity (TFP). Additionally explored is the role of governance in growth, both directly and via the SF regime. Finally, relying on the country-case evidence generated from the Growth Project, the present paper provides a synthesis of likely factors underlying policy choice by African governments. Presented first, however, is the historical evidence on the sources of growth.

Table 6.4 Annual growth of real GDP per worker, SSA versus other regions: mean and variability measures, 1960–2000 (percent)

	SSA	LAC	SAS	EAP	MENA	IC	Total
Mean (m)	0.51	0.76	2.18	3.89	2.37	2.23	1.63
S. Dev (s)	3.24	2.79	1.47	2.46	3.13	1.77	2.87
CV (s/m)	635	367	67	63	132	79	176

Notes: SSA=Sub-Saharan Africa (19), LAC=Latin America and Caribbean (22), SAS=South Asia (4), EAP=East Asia and Pacific (8), MENA=Middle-East & North Africa (11), IC=Industrial Countries (20); figures in parentheses are the respective numbers of countries with consistent data over the period. These countries are selected because they have consistent data over 1960–2000 and seem sufficiently representative of the respective regions. The 19 SSA countries are: Cameroon, Côte d'Ivoire, Ethiopia, Ghana, Kenya, Madagascar, Malawi, Mali, Mauritius, Mozambique, Nigeria, Rwanda, Senegal, Sierra Leone, South Africa, Tanzania, Uganda, Zambia, and Zimbabwe.

Source: A. Fosu and E. Aryeetey (2009), "Explaining Four Decades of Growth in Sub-Saharan Africa," in G. McMahon, E. Salehi, and L. Squire (eds.), *Diversity in Economic Growth: Global Insights and Explanations*, Edward Elgar Publishing Ltd.

Sources of growth in Africa

Table 6.5 reports data on the sources of GDP growth for SSA over 1960–2000, based on the Collins-Bosworth decomposition.[16] These statistics show that when SSA grew fairly strongly from the 1960s through the mid 1970s, growth was supported about equally by both investment and growth of TFP. However, when economic growth fell substantially in the early 1980s and again in the early 1990s, there was also a large decline in TFP each time. Furthermore, the primary source of the growth recovery in the late 1990s was TFP improvement.

As Table 6.5 further shows, the overall per-worker growth in SSA during the forty-year period was positive but modest. Moreover, both physical capital and human capital (education) contributed favorably to this growth. In contrast, TFP's contribution was negative, though small. There are also subperiod differences in the overall performance of African countries, in terms of growth as well as its sources, a subject to which I now turn.

African growth experience, 1960 to mid 1970s

The period from 1960 to the mid 1970s was an era of newly politically independent African states. The subperiod is also characterized by relatively high growth performance (see Tables 6.1–6.3). This high annual per capita growth of about 2 percent is primarily associated with physical capital accumulation and TFP growth at approximately 45 percent shares each (Table 6.5). Growth performance was, however, uneven across countries (Tables 6.1 and 6.2).

Table 6.5 Growth decomposition for Sub-Saharan Africa

Year	Growth of Real GDP per Worker	Contribution of Growth in		Estimated Residual*
		Physical Capital per Worker	Education per Worker	
1960–4	1.33	0.53	0.12	0.68
1965–9	1.74	0.80	0.20	0.75
1970–4	2.33	1.05	0.22	1.06
1975–9	0.19	0.74	0.24	−0.79
1980–4	−1.70	0.16	0.29	−2.16
1985–9	0.45	−0.22	0.34	0.33
1990–4	−1.74	−0.08	0.30	−1.95
1995–00	1.51	−0.12	0.26	1.37
Total	0.51	0.36	0.25	−0.09

*Used as a measure of growth of total factor productivity (TFP)

Notes: These results are based on 19 SSA countries with consistent data over 1960–2000: Cameroon, Côte d'Ivoire, Ethiopia, Ghana, Kenya, Madagascar, Malawi, Mali, Mauritius, Mozambique, Nigeria, Rwanda, Senegal, Sierra Leone, South Africa, Tanzania, Uganda, Zambia, and Zimbabwe.

Source: A. Fosu and E. Aryeetey (2009), "Explaining Four Decades of Growth in Sub-Saharan Africa," in G. McMahon, E. Salehi, and L. Squire (eds.), Diversity in Economic Growth: Global Insights and Explanations, Edward Elgar Publishing Ltd.

Country-specific conditions obviously explain some of the differences in country performance during this early period. However, one common factor recognized in the country studies is the dichotomy of political institutions (Fosu 2008a). Nearly all the high-growth countries during this subperiod had relatively liberal economic regimes nurtured by conservative political governments, while the reverse was the case for most of the low-performing countries. For example, during this period, Botswana, Côte d'Ivoire, Ethiopia, Kenya, Lesotho, and Malawi were countries with both high growth and market-oriented policies supported by politically conservative governments. In contrast, weak-growth performers such as Benin, Burkina Faso, Cameroon, CAR, Chad, Ghana, Guinea, Senegal, and Zambia had market-interventionist policies.[17]

Beyond the control nature of the regime, the relatively weak economic performance in several countries, despite the overall good SSA record, could also be attributed to external factors, political instability, weak institutions, and low capacity. For example, Burundi's dismal performance during the early to mid 1960s (see Tables 6.1 and 6.2) may largely be explained by the large trade deficit resulting from the loss of half of its Eastern Congolese export market (Nkurunziza and Ngaruko 2003). Another culprit was the lack of qualified manpower resulting from decolonization, which gave rise to a substantial drop in capacity utilization of the economy (ibid.).[18] Perhaps the most important factor was the legacy of high ethnic tensions from colonial rule, mainly between the minority Tutsis and majority Hutus, which paralyzed institutions and culminated in the first violent political conflict in 1965, followed by a series of destabilizing coups (ibid.).

Ethnic tensions were similarly taking place in Rwanda, with an outbreak of violence in 1964, contributing to the huge drop in TFP of 6.8 percent per year and an equivalent decrease in GDP during 1960–4 (Appendix Table A). Similarly, the weak institutional structure and an outright civil war in Sudan were the main factors behind the country's poor growth performance in the 1960s, with annual GDP growth averaging less than 3 percent (Table 1; Ali and Elbadawi 2003). Even in the case of Mauritius, where growth has been strong overall during the entire period, the mid 1960s saw the eruption of ethnic tensions, leading to negative per capita growth in 1965–9, exemplified primarily by TFP deterioration (Appendix Table A; Nath and Madhoo 2005). Thus, the periods of political instability also coincided generally with negative growths of TFP in these countries during the subperiod.

Growth performance, mid 1970s to early 1990s

The late 1970s, and particularly the early 1980s, as well as the beginning of the 1990s, registered sharp deterioration in the socioeconomic conditions of most African countries, with a fall in the average annual per capita income of approximately 1 percent (Fosu 2001a). Indeed, the 1980s can be referred to as "Africa's lost decade" since per capita income of Africans at the end of the 1980s had fallen below the level prevailing at the beginning of the decade. The source of the contraction during 1975–94 is primarily the deterioration in TFP (Table 6.5). A major culprit here is very likely the idle capacity, which may have resulted from overinvestment by the state, the dominant investor in most African economies, some of it real and some due to possible overvaluation of new investment at cost rather than based on market value; or from the lack of resources for inputs or upkeep due to the negative supply shocks of the 1970s for several countries, as well as the more widespread terms of trade shocks of the 1980s. In any case, it appears that idle capacity was a major impediment to the industrialization process of African economies (Mytelka 1989).

The relevant question, though, is why did most African economies perform so poorly during this period? A synthesis of the case studies from the Growth Project reveals that much of this state of economic affairs may be attributable to supply shocks and policy syndromes (Fosu 2008a). The mid 1970s constituted a period of supply shocks, both negative and positive. The negative shocks derived primarily from higher petroleum prices and droughts, which resulted in shortages in price control regimes in a number of African countries. The tendency was for governments to tighten existing controls, or to initiate additional ones. Indeed, not only did the frequency of controls rise in the 1970s and into the 1980s, but so did the proportion of controls that were considered "hard" (ibid.).

Meanwhile, the use of price controls as a rationing mechanism provided rent-seeking opportunities that proved detrimental to growth. The global negative shocks from petroleum also decimated embryonic Africa-based firms, most of which enjoyed protection from foreign competition through tariffs and subsidies. Indeed, the shocks contributed to the fiscal difficulties of most African governments, which could no longer afford to continue subsidizing domestic firms.

While many African countries experienced negative supply shocks, several others actually enjoyed commodity booms, especially in the latter part of the 1970s. Indeed, for SSA generally, terms of trade rose substantially in the mid 1970s, following a dip in the early 1970s, before turning sharply down in the early 1980s (UNCTAD 2008: 63, figure 22). Unfortunately, such positive shocks tended to lead to exuberant government spending that would often result in suboptimal intertemporal allocation of resources. When the boom invariably ended, governments became cash-strapped and were forced to borrow in order to continue the often-bloated projects, or would simply abandon the uncompleted projects. In either case, there would be efficiency losses. Such myopic boom-bust phenomena tended to reduce growth overall (ibid.; Fosu and O'Connell 2006; Collier and O'Connell 2008).

In response to revenue windfalls from commodity booms, there was also the tendency for many African governments to engage in adverse redistribution. Such redistributive efforts tended to favor the respective constituencies of the authorities, usually regional in nature and impregnated with ethnic undertones. In turn, when revenues subsequently declined, the resulting pain was seldom shared equally, with the non-favored constituencies having to bear the burden of the cutbacks disproportionately. The strategy would often contribute to political instability in the form of military *coups d'état*, which have become a means for settling scores or misappropriating authority for economic gains (Kimenyi and Mbaku 1993). Furthermore, the resulting "elite political instability," which has been quite rampant in SSA, has tended to be growth-inhibiting (Fosu 1992, 2001b, 2002, 2003). Adverse redistribution might also sow the seeds for actual open rebellions that could lead to even stronger growth reductions.[19]

Although SSA countries generally experienced poor economic growth during this subperiod, there were notable exceptions. For instance, as observed above, when GDP growth reached its historically low point in 1981–5, with a negative mean annual per capita GDP growth rate, a number of countries achieved average GDP growth rates of at least 4 percent annually (about 1 percentage point above the population growth rate). These were Benin, Botswana, Burkina Faso, Burundi, Cameroon, Cape Verde, Chad, Comoros, Congo Republic, Guinea Bissau, Mauritius, and Zimbabwe (Table 6.1). Furthermore, in most of these countries, it was a continuation of the fairly strong growth of the 1970s. While the explanation of such relatively high growth is likely to differ across countries, one common feature was that nearly all these countries experienced considerable appreciations in their terms of trade during this period. Among the previously mentioned countries, for instance, only Benin, Botswana, Comoros, and Mauritius had their net barter terms of trade growing by less than the 1.5 percent SSA annual average for 1980–5.[20]

Nonetheless, most African countries grew dismally during 1981–5, with a number of them actually experiencing negative GDP growth, including Ethiopia, Ghana, Liberia, Madagascar, Mali, Mozambique, Namibia, Niger, Nigeria, and Togo (Table 6.1). Moreover, in all those countries for which the data exist (Ethiopia, Ghana, Madagascar, Mali, Nigeria, and Togo), this negative growth was associated with TFP deterioration (Appendix Table A). Terms of trade explain only a part of this dismal growth performance, though. For example, Ghana, Mozambique, Niger, Namibia, and Nigeria experienced substantial losses in terms of trade, while Togo, Mali, and Madagascar did not. What appears to be a relatively common feature is that most of these poor-performing economies, such as Ethiopia, Ghana, Madagascar, Mozambique, Niger, Nigeria, and Togo, were saddled with control regimes inherent in the socialistic strategy of development.[21] In the case of Liberia, no considerable state controls were apparent; however, there was state failure in the 1980s. Nor were there any significant controls for Mali at the time; nonetheless, political leaders are believed to have looted the country beginning in the late 1960s until circa 1991 (Collier and O'Connell 2008).

In spite of the slight growth recovery for SSA generally in the latter part of the 1980s, the early 1990s were simply calamitous, with abysmal growth similar to the early 1980s. Much of this underperformance could be attributed to severe political instabilities, as in Angola, Burundi, Democratic Republic of Congo, Liberia, Rwanda, and Sierra Leone, all of which experienced negative GDP growth (Table 6.1). In addition, the net barter terms of trade for SSA as a whole deteriorated substantially in the late 1980s and the early 1990s, falling by an average of about 2.5 percent per year during 1989–93.

Indeed, South Africa, the largest economy of SSA, experienced a disappointing mean annual GDP growth rate of less than 1 percent during 1991–5 (Table 6.1), thanks in great part to both political uncertainty and deterioration in its terms of trade. The uncertainty generated by the transition from apartheid to majority rule may have triggered both physical and human capital flight, resulting in overcapacity and a large decline in TFP (see Appendix Table A). At the same time, South Africa's net barter terms of trade declined by an average of 3.3 percent annually during 1988–92. Thus, the abysmal growth performance of African economies in the early 1990s may be attributable, at least in great part, to a combination of severe political instabilities and negative terms of trade shocks.[22]

Even the growth star performer, Botswana, managed only a mean annual GDP growth rate of 4.1 percent during 1991–5, considerably below its historical trend, though still more than twice the SSA (weighted) average. Such below-trend performance may be attributable to the substantial fall in the country's terms of trade resulting from a decline in the price of diamonds.[23]

Despite the overall dismal growth performance of SSA in the early 1990s, there were a number of exceptions. The following countries registered decent GDP growth (at least 4 percent during 1991–5): Benin, Botswana, Burkina Faso, Cape Verde, Equatorial Guinea, Eritrea, Ghana, Lesotho, Mauritius, Namibia, Sudan, and Uganda (Table 6.1). What is interesting about this list of countries is that none of them experienced large terms of trade appreciation during the late 1980s or early 1990s. Hence, it would be difficult to explain their relatively strong growth performance on the basis of terms of trade. Instead, many of these countries, such as Benin, Burkina Faso, Ghana, Namibia and Uganda, had undergone structural adjustment, suggesting that for such countries, structural adjustment programs (SAPs) may have aided growth. In the case of at least two of the decent growth performers, Sudan (see Ali and Elbadawi 2003) and Eritrea, though, post-war rebound might constitute the most plausible explanation.

Growth since mid 1990s

Considerable recovery of African economies generally has occurred since the mid 1990s (Tables 6.1 and 6.2). Annual GDP growth has averaged approximately 4 percent (3.6 percent when South Africa is included and 4.1 percent when it is excluded). Indeed, growth has accelerated to 4.5 percent for non-South African SSA economies since the beginning of the millennium, while South Africa's GDP growth has averaged slightly less at 4.1 percent (Table 6.3). This growth can be accounted for by improvements in TFP (Table 6.5).[24] Bucking the trend during this period are mostly countries experiencing severe political instability, such as Burundi, CAR, DR Congo, Côte d'Ivoire, Guinea Bissau, Seychelles, Togo, and Zimbabwe.

One plausible explanation of the post-1995 growth recovery is the set of SAPs undertaken by most of these countries following the dismal performance in the 1980s.[25] Countries such as Benin, Burkina Faso, Cameroon, Chad, Ethiopia, Ghana, Mali, Rwanda, and Sudan undertook credible SAPs, which led to improvements in their respective macroeconomic environments for growth. Furthermore, a number of the strong-performing countries have experienced booms in their respective exports, especially in oil but also in other commodities such as coffee, cocoa, gold, and other metals. Indeed, the terms of trade of SSA as a whole have improved considerably, particularly since the late 1990s.[26] Coupled with better macroeconomic environments, these improvements have apparently been translated to sustained economic growth so far.

Not all countries undertook significant policy adjustments during this period, however. It is generally agreed that the most populous African country, Nigeria, failed to undergo sufficiently credible reform before the millennium (Iyoha and Oriakhi 2004). The country actually experienced negative per capita growth from the mid 1990s until 2002 (Table 6.2), despite a substantial improvement in its terms of trade in the latter part of the 1990s.[27] The Nigeria case suggests that without a more conducive economic environment, improvements in terms of trade alone may not suffice for generating solid growth. Furthermore, a number of countries—Benin, Botswana, Burkina Faso, Ethiopia, Mali, and Mauritius—have actually grown well since the mid 1990s despite weak performance in their terms of trade. With the exception of Botswana, which apparently did not need SAP, all these countries had undertaken credible SAPs, or were considered syndrome-free during the relevant period.[28]

Most of the growth since the mid-1990s is associated with productivity increases, which could have been made possible by the SAP reforms. Nearly all countries with relatively high economic growth rates during 1995–2000 also experienced large TFP growth (Appendix Table A). With a few exceptions (Ethiopia, Ghana, Mozambique, and Uganda), capital accumulation does not seem to be behind the growth recovery. Indeed, for several countries (Cameroon, Côte d'Ivoire, Madagascar, Malawi, Mali, and Zambia), the contribution by capital was negative, even though per-worker growth was positive (Appendix Table A). It is quite possible, though, that physical capital's contribution may have been delayed as in the case of Ghana and Uganda where capital contributions lagged behind TFP improvements. A considerable portion of the improvements in TFP is likely attributable to reductions in idle capacity following reforms, with increases in capital accumulation lagging behind. With gross domestic capital formation as share of GDP in SSA having risen from 16.8 percent in 2000 to 19.5 percent in 2006 (World Bank 2007), perhaps significant capital's contribution will be realizable in future growth.

As early reformers among SSA economies, Ghana and Uganda stand out as possibly shining examples of how reforms may have worked. Until the latter part of the 1980s when reforms were undertaken, Ghana's growth performance was rather poor (Tables 6.1 and 6.2), registering negative per-worker GDP growth rates in three out of the five half-decadal periods. With the exception of the early 1970s, when short-lived reforms were undertaken, growth was anemic even when positive, and productivity deterioration accompanied much of the dismal performance (Appendix Table A). Following the World Bank-led reforms in the mid 1980s, however, growth has been both considerably high and stable (Aryeetey and Fosu 2003), which can be explained mainly by productivity improvements until the late 1990s, when capital formation kicked in as the primary contributor to growth (Appendix Table A). Although part of this progress since the mid 1980s could be attributable to the "bounce-back" effect as more resources were injected into the Ghanaian economy, it would be implausible to attribute the progress primarily to this effect for two main reasons. First, the progress was not short-lived but continued and remained quite stable; there has even been some acceleration of growth in the beginning of the twenty-first century, though some of this progress might be attributable to improvements in the terms of trade, which increased by 4.4 percent per year during 2001–5. Second, as alluded to above, countries experiencing large improvements in their terms of trade did not necessarily exhibit positive growth (e.g., Nigeria in the early 1990s), and several countries have grown well since the mid 1990s despite deteriorations in their barter terms of trade (Benin, Botswana, Burkina Faso, Ethiopia, Mali, and Mauritius). With the exception of Botswana, which apparently did not need SAP, all these countries had undertaken credible SAPs, or were considered syndrome-free during the relevant period.

The Uganda experience is somewhat similar to Ghana's. Except for the early 1960s, Uganda's growth was quite weak throughout the 1970s, but then picked up in the early 1980s after the overthrow of the Idi Amin regime. Subsequent to the World Bank-led reform in the mid 1980s, however, the country began to record considerable growth, some of which could be attributable to the bounce-back effect. The growth actually intensified in the early 1990s, when such an effect should have worn off, with solid growth continuing through 2006, despite a large deterioration in Uganda's barter terms of trade during 1996–2000, by an average of 12.5 percent annually. Furthermore, the strong growth was associated with substantial improvements in TFP, until the latter 1990s when capital formation began to contribute significantly, though productivity increases continued to be the dominant contributor to growth.[29]

Explaining the African economic growth record

The growth-accounting decompositions that have been discussed have revealed the relative roles of human capital (education), physical capital accumulation, and TFP in the growth of African economies during the post-independence period. The growth or its sources may in turn be accounted for by a number of factors such as: colonial origins (Acemoglu et al. 2001), geography (Bloom and Sachs 1998), demography (ibid.), natural resource endowment (Sachs and Warner 2001), economic instabilities (Fosu 2001c), political instability (Fosu 1992, 2001b, 2002, 2003; Gyimah-Brempong and Traynor 1999),[30] open conflicts (Collier 1999; Collier and Hoeffler 1998; Gyimah-Brempong and Corley 2005), ethnic polarization (Easterly and Levine 1997), governance (Alence 2004; Fosu 2008b; Gyimah-Brempong and de Camacho 2006; Ndulu and O'Connell 1999), and the global (external) environment (Fosu 1990, 2001a; Sachs and Warner 1997). Although many of these factors are related to initial conditions that put Africa at a disadvantage, these impediments need not be destiny and should be overcome by an appropriate set of policies.

Indeed, the main thesis of the Growth Project is that policies matter for growth in Africa, despite the initial conditions. As presented above, the project defines several categories of factors that might be adverse to growth as policy syndromes: "state controls," "adverse redistribution," "suboptimal intertemporal resource allocation," and "state breakdown," with the absence of all of the above syndromes referred to as "syndrome-free."[31] Table 6.6 shows the evolution of these regimes during 1960–2000, a subject that is taken up next.

Table 6.6 Evolution of policy syndromes in Sub-Saharan Africa (half-decadal relative frequencies)

Period	Syndrome-free	Controls	Redistribution	Inter-temporal	State Breakdown	Soft Control	Hard Control
1960–5	0.465	0.334	0.128	0.000	0.073	0.775	0.225
1966–70	0.373	0.323	0.194	0.009	0.100	0.707	0.293
1971–5	0.193	0.408	0.237	0.120	0.042	0.730	0.270
1976–80	0.106	0.432	0.245	0.149	0.068	0.633	0.367
1981–5	0.097	0.442	0.255	0.145	0.061	0.630	0.370
1986–90	0.149	0.381	0.276	0.118	0.076	0.708	0.292
1991–5	0.357	0.216	0.191	0.056	0.181	0.935	0.065
1996–00	0.435	0.147	0.176	0.039	0.203	0.956	0.044
1960–00	0.272	0.335	0.213	0.080	0.101	0.759	0.241

Notes: These figures are for 47 countries. All syndrome/syndrome-free classifications are defined in the text. The frequencies in the first five columns have been adjusted here to sum to 1.0 for each period, as multiple syndromes for a given country-year could occur. The frequencies of the last two columns have also been adjusted here to sum to 1.0.

Source: A. Fosu and E. Aryeetey (2009), "Explaining Four Decades of Growth in Sub-Saharan Africa," in G. McMahon, E. Salehi, and L. Squire (eds.), *Diversity in Economic Growth: Global Insights and Explanations*, Edward Elgar Publishing Ltd.

State controls

In any given year, a country was classified as having state controls if the government was judged to have "heavily distorted major economic markets (labor, finance, domestic and international trade, and production) in service of state-led and inward-looking development strategies" (Fosu and O'Connell 2006: 38).[32] In the 1950s and 1960s, the reigning development paradigm entailed strong reliance on government as the leader of the development efforts, especially in the light of limited markets and private capital. Many African countries had also relied externally on their colonial "masters" for manufactures in exchange for primary products. Leaders of the newly created African countries were determined to free their respective economies from this colonial arrangement, which the leaders viewed as economically disadvantageous. Thus, many African governments opted for inward-looking, import-substitution, state-led development strategies.

As the role of government became more pervasive in the economy and bottlenecks developed, resource rationing became necessary. This situation was particularly characteristic of the external sector, where overvaluation of the domestic currency required that foreign exchange be rationed through quotas, with a proliferation of foreign exchange controls in most African countries by the 1970s. State controls were not limited to the external sector; they were pervasive as well in other markets, including the banking, finance, labor, and consumer-product sectors.

The quest for greater equity in development, especially in socialist-oriented governments, further compelled many of these governments to redistribute resources that proved distortionary. Such redistribution was usually via an implicit tax in the form of a substantial wedge between the world price and the government-mandated producer price of the exportable, administered by the state marketing boards. Meanwhile, the concomitant overvaluation of the domestic convency tended to favor urban consumers. It is often argued that this urban-biased distortion has been deleterious to growth (Bates 1981). In fairness, however, given the difficulties associated with direct revenue collection, many African governments saw indirect taxation as a more efficient source for funding the various development projects, including infrastructure development (schools, roads, communications, etc.), which were so lacking at the time of independence. The real issue is not whether the indirect taxation was warranted, but the degree to which it was distortionary in terms of attenuating production incentives, as well as creating rent-seeking opportunities.

The inward-looking strategy entailed the use of import tariffs and quotas, as well as other trade restrictions, such as import licensing, to protect infant manufacturing firms. In particular, agricultural policies often involved government direct investment and establishment of extension services. Meanwhile, a hallmark of monetary policy in most African countries was fixing nominal interest rates amidst a high inflationary environment. This policy tended to limit financial development. The government also became the main employer in the formal labor sector through the establishment of state-owned enterprises.

The key feature of macroeconomic policies during the period was the fixed exchange rate regime. This policy often resulted in overvaluation of the domestic currency, which afflicted most African economies.[33] The case of the CFA (African Financial Community) countries is especially noteworthy. Designed to achieve total convertibility, the CFA currency was tied to the French franc. While this arrangement fostered monetary and price stability, it also led to overvaluation of the CFA franc, which stymied growth in the CFA zone. It was not until 1994 that the CFA franc was appropriately devalued to remove the overvaluation drag.[34]

Although many of the government programs were well intentioned, they ended up creating state controls. Such a regulatory regime was often highly inefficient, as it tended to breed rent-seeking behaviors in addition to the usual high transaction costs associated with the monitoring of controls.

When negative supply shocks hit in the mid-to-late 1970s, thanks to the unanticipated rise in global petroleum price, as well as drought in many African countries, the state controls became even more binding and widespread.[35] Countries with soft controls tended to upgrade to hard controls (e.g., Benin, Ghana, Madagascar, and Mozambique), while those without controls adopted them as a rationing mechanism (e.g., Kenya, Mauritius, Nigeria, Sierra Leone, Tanzania, Togo, and Zambia).[36]

The prevalence of controls rose generally in the 1970s, while the incidence of hard controls increased even faster; however, the frequencies of both soft and hard controls waned considerably beginning in the mid-to-late 1980s (Fosu 2008a: figures 3.1 and 3.2; Table 6.6 this chapter). During 1960–2000, the regulatory syndrome constituted one third of the country-years; its frequency increased in the 1970s and early 1980s but declined substantially thereafter.

The incidence of state controls is estimated to have reduced per capita annual GDP growth by approximately 1 percentage point, *ceteris paribus* (Fosu and O'Connell 2006: table 7). This estimate is not inconsequential, especially given that SSA's per-worker growth deficit with the rest of the world during 1960–2000 averaged slightly above 1.0 percentage point per year (Table 6.4).

Adverse redistribution

Adverse redistribution is said to occur when redistributive policies favoring the constituencies of respective government leaders lead to polarization, usually regional in nature and with ethnic undertones (Fosu and O'Connell 2006). Regional redistribution need not be adverse, though, if it promotes harmony (Azam 1995). Actually, governments could use redistribution to buy peace. In many West African countries (Chad, Côte d'Ivoire, Ghana, and Nigeria), the south tends to be agricultural and enjoys more financial resources than the north. On the other hand, the north often enjoys greater command over military resources and may use violence, at least potentially, to extract rent from the south. A Pareto-optimal solution would require redistribution from the south to the north, just enough to preclude the latter from taking up arms. The resulting peace would be growth-enhancing (ibid.).

Redistribution could, however, be adverse to growth if it led to (ethnic) polarization. Such redistribution might also undermine efficient resource mobilization, as it tends to attenuate the propensity to pay taxes (Kimenyi 2006). African political history is replete with examples of redistributive policies partial toward certain ethnic groups. Examples include favoring the Tutsis in Burundi during 1975–87 (Nkurunziza and Ngaruko 2004); the Kalenjins in Kenya under President Arap Moi (Mwega and Ndugu 2004); the Temnes in Sierra Leone by the All People's Congress during 1969–90 (Davies 2004); and the Kabeyes in Togo by President Eyadema in 1976–90 (Gogue and Evlo 2004). Also classified under adverse redistributive policies is the case of downright looting, such as the regimes of Mobutu in the Democratic Republic of the Congo (1973–97), Idi Amin in Uganda (1971–9), and Sani Abacha in Nigeria (1993–8) (Collier and O'Connell 2008: table 2.A.2).

The frequency of this redistributive syndrome increased steadily from the time of independence, and it was not until about the early 1990s that it began to reverse course (Fosu 2008a: figures 3.1 and 3.2; Table 6.6 in this paper), perhaps in response to the reforms undertaken in many African countries. During 1960–2000, this redistributive syndrome constituted about 21 percent of the country-years (Table 6.6).

Suboptimal intertemporal resource allocation

Suboptimal intertemporal resource allocation refers to the syndrome of revenue misallocation over time, with overspending during commodity booms and insufficient expenditure allocation during the subsequent busts (Collier and O'Connell 2008; Fosu 2008a; Fosu and O'Connell 2006). While many of the projects undertaken in a number of African countries during booms were probably ex-ante economically justifiable, it is also true that numerous projects were either ill-advised or overallocated resources relative to their absorptive capacities. When the booms invariably ended, many of the projects were simply abandoned so that their potential values of marginal product could not be realized. Instead, bust periods were often characterized by much larger output declines than would have been the case with more prudent intertemporal revenue management. This was the case in countries such as Burundi, 1972–88; Cameroon, 1978–93; Guinea, 1973–84; Niger, 1974–89; Nigeria, 1970–87; Senegal, 1974–8; Togo, 1974–89; and Zambia, 1973–89 (ibid.). In effect, the cumulative impact on growth over the cycle was likely to be negative.[37]

The incidence of this syndrome rose dramatically starting in the early 1970s, maintaining a plateau from the mid 1970s, before finally falling in the latter part of the 1980s (Fosu 2008a: figures 3.1 and 3.2; Table 6.6 in this chapter). Over the entire 1960–2000 period, the syndrome accounted for about 9 percent of the country-years (Table 6.6). It also had the tendency to reduce Africa's overall per capita growth by about 1 percentage point annually (Fosu and O'Connell 2006: table 7).

State breakdown/failure

State breakdown (or state failure) refers primarily to open warfare, such as civil wars, but also to acute elite political instability involving, for instance, *coups d'état* resulting in a breakdown of law and order (Fosu and O'Connell 2006). Such a state is likely to substantially impede efficient resource allocation and inhibit growth. In addition to causing tolls in human suffering, state failure tends to result in major interruptions in production and distribution, as well as in inefficient reallocation of resources from the productive and social sectors into the non-productive military sector.

Over 1960–2000, state breakdown constituted about 10 percent of the country-years, which is considerably lower than that of state controls (33 percent) or adverse redistribution (21 percent) (see Table 6.6). Furthermore, despite popular belief, the incidence of state breakdown was historically rare in Africa until more recently in the 1990s, when its relative frequency quadrupled to 20 percent of the country-years from 5 percent in the 1970s (Table 6.6). Despite its historically low frequency, however state breakdown is estimated to have exerted a rather substantial negative impact on growth. Its reduction of Africa's per capita annual growth of GDP is estimated to be as much as 2.6 percentage points (Fosu and O'Connell 2006: table 7). This estimate is only slightly larger than the 2.2 percentage points obtained for civil wars by Collier (1999).

The syndrome-free regime

The syndrome-free (SF) state constitutes the absence of any of the above syndromes; that is, a regime with a combination of political stability and reasonably market-friendly policies (Fosu and O'Connell 2006). Interestingly, this regime represented more than one-quarter of the country-years during the entire 1960–2000, higher than any of the above syndromes, with the exception of the regulatory syndrome (see Table 6.6). It is noteworthy that in the early period of 1960–5, the relative frequency of SF was about 50 percent, higher than any of the syndromes (Table 6.6). The prevalence of SF began to wane starting in the later 1960s, with the downtrend accelerating in the 1970s when state controls and other syndromes became dominant. The downward trend continued until roughly the mid 1980s when it reversed course; the upward trend actually accelerated in the 1990s, likely as a result of the World Bank and IMF-championed market-oriented reforms (Fosu 2008a).

By the early 1990s, most African countries had undergone substantial economic and political reforms. For instance, the relative frequency of state controls has declined from its peak of more than 50 percent in the early 1980s to just 15 percent by the dawn of the millennium. Though the incidence of adverse redistribution, mainly regional, has remained relatively high at nearly 20 percent by 2000, this prevalence is low compared to the peak of approximately 30 percent in the late 1980s. A notable exception, as observed above, is state breakdown, the relative frequency of which quadrupled from 5 percent in the 1970s to 20 percent in the 1990s. Meanwhile, the relative frequency of SF has skyrocketed to 45 percent by 2000, from its nadir of about 10 percent in the early 1980s.[38]

Over the 1960–2000 sample period, being SF was a necessary condition for sustainable growth and a near-sufficient condition for preventing a growth collapse (Fosu and O'Connell 2006). Indeed, such a regime is estimated to have contributed as much as 2 percentage points to per capita annual growth in Africa (ibid.: table 6). This estimate constitutes nearly twice Africa's growth gap with the rest of the world during 1960–2000, about a third of its gap with East Asia and Pacific, and more than the gap with South Asia (see Table 6.4).

Empirical exploration: roles of the syndrome-free regime and governance

This section takes advantage of the data generated by the Growth Project to further explore the role of the SF regime in explaining the economic growth of African economies. In contrast with Fosu and O'Connell (2006), for instance, which employs a reduced-form model that controls for shocks and geographical endowment,[39] a production-function approach is used here in order to further investigate the channels by which SF may have influenced growth via production factor inputs versus TFP.[40] Moreover, a five-year, rather than annual, panel is employed in an attempt to capture the extended impact of SF beyond one year. Also examined is the role of governance in the growth equation.

To explore the channel by which SF affects growth, a simple Cobb-Douglas production function is postulated:

$$Q = AL^b K^C \tag{1}$$

where Q is output, L labor, and K capital; A, b, and c are the respective parameters. The growth version of equation (1) is:

$$q = a + bl + ck \qquad (2)$$

where q, l, and k are the growth rates of output, labor, and capital, respectively, and a, b, and c are the respective estimable parameters. Equation (2) is the classical production function, an augmented version of which has been estimated in many studies.[41] However, in order to more appropriately compare the current results with those of Fosu and O'Connell (2006), equation (2) is converted to per capita growth as:

$$y = a + (b - n)l + ck \qquad (3)$$

where y is per capita growth; population is assumed to grow at the rate of nl, with n, the ratio of population to labor growth, greater (less) than unity if population grows faster (slower) than labor.

As the Hicks-neutral technological change measuring growth in TFP, the parameter a may be especially susceptible to the syndrome-nature of the economy. Furthermore, TFP has been found to be crucial in explaining the generally low growth of African economies since the 1960s (Bosworth and Collins 2003). Hypothesizing that SF and governance would affect economic growth via their impacts on TFP, a may be expressed as:

$$a = a_1 + a_2 f + a_3 g + a_4 x \qquad (4)$$

where f and g are the SF and governance variables, respectively, x the vector of other variables, such as terms of trade as well as country and time fixed effects, that might affect TFP; a_1, a_2, a_3, and a_4 are the respective coefficients. Combining equations (3) and (4), the model to be estimated may be specified as:

$$y_{it} = a_1 + a_2 f_{it} + a_3 g_{it} + a_4 x_{it} + a_5 l_{it} + a_6 k_{it} + u_i + v_t + e_{it} \qquad (5)$$

where the subscripts i and t are the respective country and time indexes; f and g are the measures of the syndrome-free regime and governance, respectively, l and k are the respective growth rates of labor and capital, and x is a vector of other control variables that might influence y; the respective coefficients of the above variables are to be estimated; u and v are the country and time fixed effects, respectively; and e is the random perturbation.

Equation (5) is first estimated with unbalanced five-year panel data for 1960–2000 for up to 47 SSA countries, and then also for 1981–2000 in order to account for the effect of terms of trade for which consistent data are available for the latter period but not for the entire sample period. To avoid potential problems of endogeneity, both country and time fixed effects are controlled for. The regression results are reported in Tables 6.7 and 6.8 for the above sample periods, respectively; definitions of the regression variables and data sources are provided in Table 6.7.

First discussed are the results for 1960–2000 in Table 6.7, which are generally as expected. The effect of capital formation, measured by the investment share of GDP, is strongly positive and significant in all equations. In contrast, the estimated

Table 6.7 Five-year panel estimation with country and time fixed effects (sample period = 1960–2000). Dependent variable: gdppcga

Regr./Spec.	(1)	(2)	(3)	(4)	(5)	(6)	(7)	(8)
Investment	0.214[a]	0.210[a]	0.235[a]	0.222[a]	0.230[a]	0.218[a]	–	0.216[a]
	(2.75)	(2.64)	(2.92)	(2.79)	(2.80)	(2.67)		(2.73)
Labor	0.313	0.232	0.311	0.310	0.232	0.236	–	0.257
	(1.14)	(0.92)	(1.14)	(1.18)	(0.93)	(0.98)		(1.01)
Xconst	–	–	0.290	2.323[c]	0.190	2.147[c]	–	–
			(0.91)	(1.82)	(0.63)	(1.74)		
Xconst^2	–	–	–	−0.307[c]	–	−0.295[c]	–	–
				(−1.85)		(−1.75)		
Sfree	–	1.909[c]	–	–	2.028[c]	1.912[c]	1.818[c]	2.682[b]
		(1.80)			(1.91)	(1.83)	(1.72)	(2.12)
SF8100	–	–	–	–	–	–	–	−1.389
								(−1.45)
Adj.R^2	0.247	0.261	0.246	0.268	0.260	0.280	0.204	0.261
SEE	3.900	3.864	3.963	3.906	3.925	3.873	3.954	3.862
# of obs	n=282	n=282	n=267	n=267	n=267	n=267	n=308	n=282

[a] significant at 1% level
[b] significant at 5% level
[c] significant at 10% level

Notes: **gdppcga** = per capita GDP annual growth (%) (source: World Bank 2008); **invest** = investment share of GDP (%) (source: Center for International Comparisons 2004 (CIC), University of Pennsylvania); **labor** = annual growth average of total labor force (source: World Bank 2004); **xconst** = degree of executive constraints (range [1, 7]; 7 for "strict rules for governance," 1 for "no one regulates the authority," and 0 for "perfect incoherence"; source: Polity IV Dataset); **sfree**= syndrome-free dummy variable, which equals 1 if the five-year period is syndrome-free, 0 otherwise (source: AERC Growth Project); **SF8100** = SFREE*D8100, where D8100 equals 1 if 1981–2000, 0 otherwise; t statistics are in parentheses. Maximum number of countries equals 47.

impact of the labor variable, though positive, is generally insignificant. This is not surprising, since the coefficient of the labor variable is *(b-n)*, the difference between the labor growth coefficient in the original production function, *b*, and the ratio of population growth to labor growth, *n*. Indeed, this coefficient cannot be signed; it is more likely to be negative the slower the growth of the labor force is relative to the population.

Effect of the syndrome-free regime

The coefficient of the SF variable, SFREE, is significantly positive. Indeed, it is striking that the estimated impact of about 2.0 percentage points here (equations (2), (5), (6), and (7) of Table 6.7) is nearly identical to that obtained by Fosu and O'Connell (2006), despite the difference in models.[42] Furthermore, that the coefficient of SFREE appears invariant to the exclusion of *l* and *k* from the regression (compare for instance equations (2) and (7) of Table 6.7) suggests that the effect of SFREE is primarily via TFP, rather than indirectly through the factors of production. Such a finding was not possible under the Fosu-O'Connell reduced-form model.[43] Concentrating on the investment variable, further support for this TFP channel hypothesis is provided by the observation that the zero-order correlation

Table 6.8 Five-year panel estimation with country and time fixed effects (sample period = 1981–2000). Dependent variable: gdppcga

Regr./Spec.	(1)	(2)	(3)	(4)	(5)	(6)	(7)	(8)	(9)
investment	0.458^a	0.459^a	0.457^a	0.446^a	0.448^a	0.459^a	0.450^a	–	0.441^a
	(5.84)	(5.50)	(5.21)	(5.31)	(5.08)	(5.48)	(5.31)		(4.75)
Labor	0.820^b	0.659^c	0.666^c	0.752^b	0.613	0.665^c	0.880^b	–	0.227
	(2.30)	(1.79)	(1.79)	(2.03)	(1.63)	(1.78)	(2.32)		(0.51)
Totg	0.081^b	0.092^b	0.087^b	0.072^c	0.083^b	0.093^b	0.143	0.104^c	–
	(2.05)	(2.38)	(2.16)	(1.73)	(2.02)	(2.35)	(1.41)	(1.66)	
totg*sfree	–	–	–	–	–	-0.086	–	–	–
						(-0.06)			
totg*xconst	–	–	–	–	–	–	-0.023	–	–
							(-0.74)		
Xconst	–	–	0.218	1.948^b	1.875^b	–	0.259	–	–
			(0.61)	(2.30)	(2.23)		(0.74)		
Xconst^2	–	–	–	-0.263^b	-0.260^b	–	–	–	–
				(-2.04)	(-2.04)				
Sfree	–	2.781^a	2.722^a	–	2.710^a	2.770^a	–	2.997^a	1.652
		(3.70)	(3.37)		(3.32)	(3.59)		(3.19)	(1.43)
Adj.R^2	0.480	0.508	0.495	0.480	0.504	0.504	0.468	0.266	0.213
SEE	3.018	2.935	2.991	3.035	2.963	2.950	3.069	3.614	4.440
# of obs	n=156	n=156	n=150	n=150	n=150	n=156	n=150	n=161	n=172

^{a} significant at 1% level
^{b} significant at 5% level
^{c} significant at 10% level

Notes: See Table 6.7; **totg** is net barter terms of trade annual change (%) (source: World Bank 2007); t statistics in parentheses.

coefficient between SFREE and the investment variable is only 0.08, which is insignificant; this compares with the correlation coefficient between SF and growth of 0.26, which is significant at the 0.01 level (Appendix Table C1). Thus, it appears that the apparent dominant impact of TFP observed in the above sources-of-growth analysis (see Table 6.5) could be attributed primarily to the prevalence, or lack thereof, of the policy syndromes.

The 1981–2000 results in Table 6.8 involving the net barter terms of trade (TOT) are now discussed. They are qualitatively quite similar to those for the entire period shown in Table 6.7, with the investment impact quite strong, and the significance of the (positive) labor coefficient mixed, though greater than that for the entire sample period. Indeed, the respective goodness of fit for the models in Table 6.8 appears much higher than that in Table 6.7.

Most importantly, the estimated coefficient of SFREE is positive and significant in all the relevant equations in Table 6.8. Moreover, the SFREE impact is about 30 percent higher in Table 6.8 than in Table 6.7 (see all the corresponding specifications of Table 6.8, except equation (9)). The results also suggest that the growth in TOT, measured by TOTG, constitutes a critical variable in the growth equation, especially in assessing the effect of SFREE. When TOTG is omitted from the regression, the coefficient of SFREE declines rather substantially and becomes insignificant, while the goodness of fit of the model falls precipitously (equation (2) versus equation (9)). Coupled with the result of equation (8) of Table 6.7, which suggests that a larger SFREE coefficient may actually hold for the earlier period, this finding implies that the resulting higher coefficient when the model is restricted to the 1981–2000 sample period is not attributable to a temporal factor. Instead, accounting for TOT provides a more accurate estimate of the SFREE impact, which is apparently larger than that implied by Fosu and O'Connell (2006).

Why then might the Fosu and O'Connell estimate be on the low side? The most plausible explanation is that an *annual* panel was used in that study. It seems quite likely that the effect of SFREE is felt beyond one year, however. Furthermore, defining SFREE as equal to unity when a given country has been syndrome-free for the entire five-year period (zero otherwise—see Table 6.7), as is done currently, is a more stringent test than that based on a single year. The current definition yields about 30 percent and 25 percent of the sample as SFREE for 1960–2000 and 1981–2000, respectively. These figures are, furthermore, remarkably similar to the respective annual relative frequencies of 27 percent and 26 percent (Table 6.6), suggesting that the five-year aggregation does not lose much information.

Effect of governance

The results in Tables 6.7 and 6.8 show that the impact of governance, as measured by XCONST, the degree of constraints on the government executive,[44] is non-linear: positive initially but negative beyond a threshold. This finding suggests

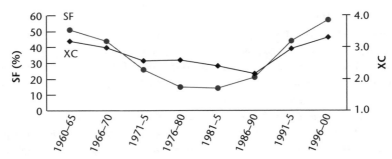

Figure 6.2 Evolutions of syndrome-free (SF) and executive constraints (XC), 1960–2004

Source: See Tables 6.6 and 6.7.

Note: XC = XCONST.

that there could be too much executive constraint. Using equation (5) of Table 6.8, which appears to provide the best fit among the equations where XCONST is included in the model, a threshold value of 3.60 is estimated.[45] While this threshold seems rather low, especially for a variable that ranges from 0 to 7, it exceeds the sample mean of 2.64 (Appendix Tables B.1 and B.2), as to be expected. Of course, this estimate can only be viewed as preliminary. Perhaps the best interpretation is a qualitative one; that is, too much executive constraint can be bad for growth.

Equally important is the observation that SFREE and XCONST might be positively correlated, at least intertemporally. As Figure 6.2 depicts, these two variables tend to move together over time. Indeed, XCONST appears to be more (positively) correlated with SFREE than with per capita GDP growth. For the entire 1960–2000 sample period, the respective zero-order correlation coefficients are 0.15 versus 0.26 (Appendix Table C.1), and for 1981–2000, they are 0.20 versus 0.33 (Appendix Table C.2). Although part of the relatively low XCONST correlation with per capita growth may be due to the non-linear nature of the relationship, the above results suggest that the effect of XCONST transcends its direct impact on growth. It could also augment growth through its positive impact on SFREE.

Explaining the anti-growth policy syndromes

Conditions of the African environment likely influenced policies undertaken by African policymakers. Therefore, anti-growth syndromes could be viewed as endogenous with respect to such conditions. If so, then appropriately altering the environment should aid the pursuit of relatively sound policies for growth.[46] The Growth Project discusses, from a historical perspective, the nature of such endogeneity.[47] A synthesis of the case studies provides a number of explanations for why the anti-growth policy syndromes may have been adopted, including initial conditions, resource opportunity set and supply shocks, political institutions, and economically driven political expediency (Fosu 2008a).[48] These factors are briefly discussed next.

Initial conditions

The initial conditions at the time of independence heavily influenced the policies adopted by many African countries. These conditions included the reigning international paradigms, experiences of the initial leaders, and group identity rivalry.

Reigning international paradigms

A major competing development paradigm in the late 1950s and the 1960s, when most African countries attained independence, was that socialism, with government as the primary agent for development, was more likely than capitalism to attain development objectives.[49] This school of thought rendered the socialist means of development particularly appealing to many African leaders, especially in settings where the vast majority of people lacked investment resources and markets were rudimentary.

The leaders opting for socialistic policies tended to resort to various forms of state controls, which in turn generated rent-seeking opportunities as well as adverse redistribution in favor of political constituencies. Meanwhile, the socialistic ideology of government constituting the best agent for development cemented the dominant role of the central authority, with state controls as a primary mechanism for resource allocation.

Experiences of the initial leaders

The early politically conservative African leaders tended to adopt relatively liberal economic policies, in contrast with their socialist-leaning counterparts. Such conservatism was often based on the background of the leadership, internally or externally. Thus, leaders like Jomo Kenyatta of Kenya, Felix Houphouet-Boigny of Côte d'Ivoire, Sir Khama of Botswana, and Sylvanus Olympio of Togo favored only minimal controls given their rural or business backgrounds. In contrast, leaders such as Kwame Nkrumah of Ghana, Sekou Toure of Guinea, Julius Nyerere of Tanzania, and Modibo Keita of Mali resorted to hard controls, thanks at least in part to their exposure to Fabian socialism.

Actually, the adoption of controls was not dominant among African countries in the immediate post-independence period. For example, less than 40 percent of the country-years could be classified as control regimes in the early 1960s, compared with 50 percent for syndrome-free regimes (Fosu 2008a: figure 3.1; also Table 6.6 this chapter).

Group identity rivalry

The physical and political boundaries of many African countries resulted from colonial partitioning that had no regard for relatively defined (ethnic) groups. Many early African leaders sought to tame (ethnically) group-based centrifugal political forces. The major mechanism for this purpose was often the adoption of strong central governments accompanied by state controls.

Resource opportunity set and supply shocks

The resource opportunity set available to countries played an important role in the prevalence of syndromes.[50] For instance, as net importers of oil, most African countries experienced the negative petroleum supply shocks of the 1970s. A number of countries were also victims of drought in the 1970s that led to diminished supplies of food. Many African governments chose to fix prices in the face of such shocks in order to make goods and services more affordable to the citizenry at large, particularly to the urban elites who seemed to form the political support base for these governments (Bates 1981). Such a policy, however, led to more and stricter state controls.

Yet, there were also a number of African countries that experienced positive supply shocks, especially involving commodity booms in natural-resource economies during the 1970s. These shocks tended to give rise to the *suboptimal intertemporal resource allocation* syndrome involving exuberant spending during the boom and subsequent underspending due to fiscal difficulties: phosphate in Togo, 1974–89 (Gogue and Evlo 2004); oil in Cameroon, 1982–93 (Kobou and Njinkeu 2004); phosphates and groundnuts in Senegal, 1974–9 (Ndiaye 2004); bauxite in Guinea, 1973–84 (Doumbouya and Camara 2003); coffee in Burundi, 1975–85 (Nkurunziza and Ngaruko 2003); uranium in Niger, 1974–85 (Mamadou and Yakoubou 2006); and oil in Nigeria, 1974–86 (Iyoha and Oriakhi 2004). In certain cases, the revenue booms engendered outright looting: e.g., oil in Nigeria over 1974–86 by several governments and during 1993–8 by Sani Abacha (ibid.), and coffee in Uganda during the 1971–8 reign of Idi Amin (Kasekende and Atingi-Ego 2004).

Governments saw the opportunity to use revenue windfalls during booms to reward their cronies and ethnic constituencies, usually regionally based, who would in turn support the leaders' political entrenchment. Conversely, during subsequent bust periods, the tendency was to maintain such redistribution at the expense of the rest of the population.[51] Or, political leaders could just loot (Collier and O'Connell 2008). This is the case of *adverse redistribution*. Furthermore, by generating polarization, the above redistributive syndrome could also lead to *state breakdown*, as in the case of, for instance: Angola (1973–2002), Burundi

(1988–2000), Chad (1979–84), DRC (1996–2005), Sierra Leone (1991–2000), Togo (1991–3), and Uganda (1979–86) (Collier and O'Connell 2008; Fosu 2008a).

Political institutions

Following independence, colonial institutions tended to supplant traditional chieftaincies as governing entities in many African countries. Yet, the resulting political practices were only a shadow of these inherited colonial institutions. For example, the new African leaders often stripped any inherent checks and balances in order to maintain the centrality of the executive branch of government. This meant that the activities of the executive were subject to little control, allowing it to act in its own self-interest. Unfortunately, such interest seldom coincided with that of the populace at large, but instead with those of the urban and other coalitions able or likely to support the political authority at the time (e.g., Bates 1981).

Meanwhile, the Fabian socialism adopted in many African countries contributed to the high frequency of state controls. The executive branch of government became dominant in these countries, usually through the diminution of political checks and balances. Over time, as the executive became entrenched in power, the military was by default the only real institution capable of removing it.

The critical role of the military, coupled with the competition for rent made available by the various controls or high revenues from natural resources, con- tributed to the "elite" political instability involving high frequencies of *coups d'état* (Kimenyi and Mbaku 1993). Meanwhile, where adverse redistribution was severe, polarization was accentuated, eventually resulting in open warfare and state breakdown in many instances.

Economically driven political expediency

As apparent in Figure 6.2, there appears to be a U-shape evolution of SF frequencies over 1960–2000. SF and non-SF events were split about equally during the early post-independence period (Table 6.6). SF then diminished in importance until more recently when it began to rise again beginning in the late 1980s. The relatively high frequency of SF in the early period was likely due to chance, as the early leaders were divided roughly equally between socialistic (interventionist) and capitalistic (free-market) tendencies. In contrast, the most recent upward trend is attributable to reforms necessitated by economically driven political expediency. The socialistic experiments often ran into fiscal difficulties, which, especially with the ending of the Cold War, required the assistance of the Bretton Woods institutions in exchange for reforms.[52]

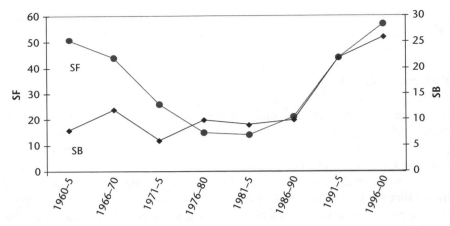

Figure 6.3 Evolutions of syndrome-free (SF) and state breakdown (SB) regimes, 1960–2000 (%)

Source: See Table 6.6.

Unfortunately, many African countries also degenerated into political disorder and open conflicts, perhaps in part as a result of the political reforms that ensued in support of economic reforms. Previously authoritarian governments began to lose their grip on power, creating a power vacuum that tended to undermine the cohesion of the state. In other cases, distributive politics replaced authoritarian rule that had previously succeeded in preserving the nation state, opening up wounds of divisionism and accentuating polarization with ethnic undertones. By the 1990s, countries like Burundi, CAR, Comoros, DRC, Djibouti, Liberia, Niger, Rwanda, Sierra Leone, Sudan, and Togo had all descended into severe political instability, mostly in the form of open conflicts.

While political reforms may be blamed as responsible for many of these outcomes, it is also true that the new international political order that saw the diminution of the Cold War facilitated the overthrow of authoritarian regimes. Thus, as the frequency of the SF cases increased in the 1990s, so did the incidence of state breakdown. Indeed, the increase in the incidence of SF in the 1990s is accompanied by resurgence in the prevalence of state breakdown (Figure 6.3).

Conclusions and Implications for Policy

This chapter first presented the growth record of African economies. It observed that the overall post-independence GDP growth of Sub-Saharan African countries has been quite paltry, especially when compared with the rest of the world. On average, output growth was barely enough to cover population increases. The growth record has, however, been quite episodic. From 1960 until the mid

1970s, African countries generally grew reasonably well, with GDP growth rates of nearly 2 percentage points annually above population growth, though this performance was still below that of other regions. GDP growth declined substantially in the 1980s and early 1990s, however, resulting in decreases in per capita income. Fortunately, there has been growth resurgence in many African economies since the mid 1990s, with per capita growth averaging about 2 percent once again.

The aggregate picture fails to properly reflect the heterogeneity in African country performance, though, at a point in time or across time. For example, Botswana and Mauritius have performed spectacularly well during the overall period. Moreover, even when growth declined substantially in the early 1980s and early 1990s, a number of African countries bucked the trend. Unfortunately, however, the growth of most of the countries has also been episodic, with many of those starting out with relatively strong growth faltering subsequently, and conversely.

Second, this chapter has presented evidence on the decomposition of economic growth. Despite some individual country exceptions, it finds that changes in total factor productivity were strongly associated with economic growth performance in Africa generally. When growth was relatively strong in the 1960s and 1970s, TFP was a major contributing factor, which also explained the substantial deterioration in growth in the early 1980s and early 1990s. Similarly, the recent resurgence in growth has been associated with major TFP improvements.

Third, this chapter has explained the above growth record using the policy syndrome taxonomy adopted by a recent project by the African Economic Research Consortium—the Growth Project. Despite country heterogeneity, reviewing the country studies of the Growth Project has revealed a number of commonalities. These have been categorized into a set of anti-growth policy syndromes: state controls, adverse redistribution, suboptimal intertemporal allocation, and state breakdown.

The chapter finds that the absence of syndromes could have increased annual per capita GDP growth by nearly 3 percentage points, which is rather large, especially when compared with the rather modicum growth of less than 1 percent during the post-independence period. Much of this positive effect of the syndrome-free (SF) regime is attributed to its positive influence on TFP. Improvements in the terms of trade would also tend to raise growth, and accounting for them actually increases the importance of SF for growth.

Fourth, this chapter argues, as in the Growth Project, that the syndromes can be explained by the policy environment within which African leaders operated. This observation has the crucial implication that removing the syndromes in order to raise growth would require that the environment be appropriately altered. Fortunately, the evidence suggests that the frequency of SF has been increasing steadily in recent years. The bad news, though, is that this improvement were accompanied by increasing incidence of failing states in the 1990s. Finding a solution to such state failure problems, then, is critical, if the present momentum toward growth is to be accelerated or at least sustained.

Meanwhile, the role of governance, as measured by the degree of constraints on the executive (XCONST), has not been inconsequential. Its direct impact on per capita GDP growth was found to be positive up to a point, beyond which additional level of constraint could be counterproductive. Moreover, XCONST tends to be more correlated with SF than with GDP growth. From a policy perspective, therefore, improving this measure of good governance appears to be a promising way to accelerate growth directly as well as indirectly via accentuating SF. Finally, with the additional evidence suggesting that increasing electoral competitiveness can enhance growth in relatively advanced-level democracies in Africa (Fosu 2008b),[53] it would be interesting to explore in future research how this form of democracy may be capable of augmenting SF as well as attenuating state breakdown.

Appendix

Appendix Table A Growth-accounting decomposition, African economies, 1960–2000

		1960–4	1965–9	1970–4	1975–9	1980–4	1985–9	1990–4	1995–2000	Total
Cameroon	Growth in Real GDP per Worker	1.39	-0.49	3.15	6.70	4.63	-2.04	-6.60	1.95	1.10
	Contribution of Physical Capital per Worker	-0.19	0.75	1.43	2.25	3.52	1.78	-0.79	-0.79	0.98
	Contribution of Education per Worker	0.12	0.17	0.30	0.35	0.36	0.38	0.28	0.21	0.27
	Residual*	1.46	-1.40	1.42	4.11	0.76	-4.20	-6.09	2.54	-0.15
Côte d'Ivoire	Growth in Real GDP per Worker	6.99	3.20	3.02	4.56	-6.16	-0.77	-3.75	0.72	0.82
	Contribution of Physical Capital per Worker	1.40	1.65	1.52	2.47	0.69	-1.21	-1.88	-0.81	0.43
	Contribution of Education per Worker	0.13	0.13	0.34	0.39	0.42	0.43	0.32	0.29	0.31
	Residual*	5.45	1.42	1.17	1.70	-7.27	0.01	-2.20	1.24	0.08
Ethiopia	Growth in Real GDP per Worker	2.72	1.68	1.71	-0.20	-0.55	-2.35	-0.14	2.96	0.73
	Contribution of Physical Capital per Worker	3.23	2.32	0.88	-0.29	1.42	0.93	0.25	1.13	1.18
	Contribution of Education per Worker	0.05	0.05	0.11	0.13	0.27	0.31	0.28	0.28	0.19
	Residual*	-0.55	-0.68	0.73	-0.04	-2.25	-3.58	-0.67	1.55	-0.63
Ghana	Growth in Real GDP per Worker	0.62	-0.26	1.54	-3.74	-4.17	1.52	1.05	1.77	-0.18
	Contribution of Physical Capital per Worker	1.90	0.65	-0.28	-0.06	-1.19	-1.28	0.05	1.17	0.10
	Contribution of Education per Worker	0.37	1.06	0.43	0.25	0.18	0.15	0.15	0.15	0.34
	Residual*	-1.64	-1.97	1.39	-3.92	-3.17	2.65	0.85	0.44	-0.62
Kenya	Growth in Real GDP per Worker	0.94	4.14	5.02	1.83	-1.05	2.02	-1.91	-0.94	1.21
	Contribution of Physical Capital per Worker	-0.25	0.49	1.72	0.49	-0.52	-0.79	-0.66	-0.28	0.03
	Contribution of Education per Worker	0.26	0.38	0.30	0.69	0.33	0.35	0.36	0.29	0.37
	Residual*	0.93	3.26	2.99	0.64	-0.86	2.46	-1.60	-0.96	0.81
Madagascar	Growth in Real GDP per Worker	-0.51	1.34	-0.90	-0.84	-3.97	-0.06	-2.56	0.21	-0.89
	Contribution of Physical Capital per Worker	-0.20	0.23	0.29	-0.19	-0.28	-0.29	-0.16	-0.57	-0.16
	Contribution of Education per Worker	0.05	0.05	0.19	0.23	0.35	0.38	0.31	0.30	0.24
	Residual*	-0.36	1.06	-1.38	-0.87	-4.04	-0.14	-2.71	0.48	-0.97
Malawi	Growth in Real GDP per Worker	0.33	5.11	3.59	2.96	-1.65	-0.97	-0.65	3.90	1.67
	Contribution of Physical Capital per Worker	4.46	4.45	4.25	2.52	0.07	-0.90	-0.11	-1.29	1.54
	Contribution of Education per Worker	0.06	-0.02	0.24	0.13	0.24	0.18	0.20	0.39	0.19
	Residual*	-4.19	0.67	-0.90	0.30	-1.96	-0.25	-0.74	4.80	-0.06
Mali	Growth in Real GDP per Worker	1.40	0.67	0.40	5.78	-2.94	-0.77	-0.96	2.74	0.82
	Contribution of Physical Capital per Worker	0.71	0.68	0.31	0.26	0.01	0.02	0.27	-0.20	0.24
	Contribution of Education per Worker	0.02	0.05	0.11	0.13	0.09	0.08	0.08	0.10	0.08
	Residual*	0.67	-0.05	-0.02	5.39	-3.04	-0.87	-1.31	2.84	0.50
Mauritius	Growth in Real GDP per Worker	3.86	-1.88	3.42	4.04	-1.55	4.95	3.37	3.83	2.50
	Contribution of Physical Capital per Worker	0.39	-0.40	-0.08	1.02	-0.27	0.63	1.02	0.95	0.42
	Contribution of Education per Worker	0.41	0.53	0.36	0.65	0.41	0.32	0.26	0.24	0.39
	Residual*	3.06	-2.01	3.14	2.37	-1.69	4.01	2.09	2.64	1.69

(continued)

Appendix Table A Continued

		1960–4	1965–9	1970–4	1975–9	1980–4	1985–9	1990–4	1995–2000	Total
Mozambique	Growth in Real GDP per Worker	0.63	4.75	0.49	-6.56	-6.84	4.71	1.05	4.88	0.50
	Contribution of Physical Capital per Worker	-0.44	0.19	1.04	-0.88	-0.69	0.05	0.14	1.06	0.10
	Contribution of Education per Worker	0.11	0.09	0.07	0.10	0.20	0.25	0.15	0.12	0.14
	Residual*	0.97	4.46	-0.63	-5.78	-6.35	4.41	0.76	3.70	0.26
Nigeria	Growth in Real GDP per Worker	1.95	-1.72	8.34	-0.87	-6.93	2.92	0.90	-0.02	0.52
	Contribution of Physical Capital per Worker	1.25	1.36	3.18	3.94	0.62	-1.18	0.13	0.41	1.19
	Contribution of Education per Worker	0.10	0.10	0.08	0.07	0.43	0.52	0.53	0.53	0.31
	Residual*	0.59	-3.19	5.08	-4.87	-7.98	3.58	0.23	-0.96	-0.98
Rwanda	Growth in Real GDP per Worker	-6.76	4.89	-0.43	4.60	0.16	-0.37	-14.03	7.10	-0.26
	Contribution of Physical Capital per Worker	-0.08	-0.01	0.83	1.95	2.13	2.04	1.53	-1.50	0.82
	Contribution of Education per Worker	0.10	0.12	0.28	0.25	0.13	0.19	0.23	0.18	0.19
	Residual*	-6.79	4.78	-1.54	2.40	-2.10	-2.60	-15.79	8.41	-1.27
Senegal	Growth in Real GDP per Worker	-0.24	-2.04	-0.03	0.67	-0.96	0.61	-1.18	2.38	-0.03
	Contribution of Physical Capital per Worker	-0.46	-0.79	-0.26	-0.21	-0.25	-0.01	0.06	0.17	-0.20
	Contribution of Education per Worker	0.00	0.04	0.33	0.16	0.14	0.17	0.19	0.20	0.16
	Residual*	0.22	-1.29	-0.10	0.73	-0.84	0.44	-1.43	2.00	0.01
Sierra Leone	Growth in Real GDP per Worker	2.71	2.75	2.17	0.03	0.49	-0.36	-3.69	-7.37	-0.66
	Contribution of Physical Capital per Worker	-0.09	1.02	0.39	-0.18	-0.07	-0.85	-0.33	-1.08	-0.17
	Contribution of Education per Worker	0.09	0.12	0.40	0.28	0.28	0.30	0.24	0.22	0.24
	Residual*	2.71	1.60	1.38	-0.07	0.27	0.19	-3.60	-6.51	-0.73
South Africa	Growth in Real GDP per Worker	3.46	3.75	3.32	-1.32	0.61	-1.72	-2.15	0.38	0.71
	Contribution of Physical Capital per Worker	-0.09	0.84	1.31	1.02	0.61	-0.39	-0.51	-0.14	0.33
	Contribution of Education per Worker	-0.08	0.31	0.12	-0.18	0.58	0.28	0.52	0.43	0.26
	Residual*	3.63	2.60	1.89	-216	-0.58	-1.61	-2.17	0.09	0.12
Tanzania	Growth in Real GDP per Worker	2.20	3.31	2.57	-0.30	-2.16	0.92	-0.59	1.29	0.88
	Contribution of Physical Capital per Worker	-0.85	-0.02	0.92	0.66	-0.02	-0.04	0.45	-0.26	0.12
	Contribution of Education per Worker	-0.19	-0.13	-0.08	0.02	0.21	0.16	0.10	0.14	0.04
	Residual*	3.25	3.46	1.72	-0.97	-2.34	0.80	-1.14	1.41	0.73
Uganda	Growth in Real GDP per Worker	2.18	0.09	-0.58	-5.84	1.16	0.56	2.82	4.22	0.63
	Contribution of Physical Capital per Worker	1.10	1.63	1.08	-0.02	0.08	0.09	0.18	1.29	0.68
	Contribution of Education per Worker	0.13	0.21	0.11	0.20	0.16	0.59	0.30	0.21	0.24
	Residual*	0.95	-1.75	-1.77	-6.02	0.92	-0.12	2.34	2.71	-0.30
Zambia	Growth in Real GDP per Worker	0.96	0.97	1.59	-3.23	-2.07	-0.76	-4.05	-1.09	-1.01
	Contribution of Physical Capital per Worker	-0.63	0.75	0.94	-0.61	-1.66	-2.03	-2.02	-1.55	-0.88
	Contribution of Education per Worker	0.26	0.23	0.32	0.55	0.24	0.14	0.59	0.28	0.33
	Residual*	1.33	-0.01	0.33	-3.17	-0.65	1.13	-2.63	0.18	-0.46
Zimbabwe	Growth in Real GDP per Worker	0.39	2.83	5.98	-4.60	1.56	0.53	0.02	-0.25	0.79
	Contribution of Physical Capital per Worker	-1.06	-0.68	0.42	-0.07	-1.08	-0.73	0.78	0.06	-0.27
	Contribution of Education per Worker	0.25	0.23	0.25	0.23	0.56	1.25	0.53	0.31	0.45
	Residual*	1.20	3.29	5.31	-4.76	2.07	0.01	-1.29	-0.61	0.61

Appendix Table B.1 Summary statistics (sample period = 1960–2000)

	Average	Std. Dev.	Min	Max
gdppcga	0.771	4.431	−30.453	28.781
Investment	10.296	7.361	1.175	48.779
Labor	2.383	1.037	−4.325	9.247
Xconst	2.639	1.775	0	7
Sfree	0.293	0.455	0	1
SF8100	0.128	0.334	0	1

Notes: See Table 6.7 for definitions of variables and data sources.

Appendix Table B.2 Summary statistics (sample period = 1981–2000)

	Average	Std. Dev.	Min	Max
gdppcga	0.174	5.000	−30.453	28.781
Investment	9.930	6.455	2.384	46.979
Labor	2.613	0.913	−3.609	7.326
Xconst	2.645	1.750	0	7
Sfree	0.255	0.437	0	1
Totg	0.219	7.012	−17.688	34.617

Notes: See Tables 6.7 and 6.8 for definitions of variables and data sources.

Appendix Table C.1 Correlogram of variables (sample period = 1960–2000)

	gdppcga	Investment	Labor	Xconst	Sfree	SF8100
gdppcga	1.000					
Investment	0.316	1.000				
Labor	0.026	0.019	1.000			
Xconst	0.154	0.093	0.083	1.000		
Sfree	0.259	0.077	0.076	0.263	1.000	
SF8100	0.140	0.048	0.125	0.273	0.726	1.000

Notes: See Table 6.7 for definitions of variables and data sources.

Appendix Table C.2 Correlogram of variables (sample period = 1981–2000)

	gdppcga	Investment	Labor	Xconst	Sfree	Totg
gdppcga	1.000					
Investment	0.462	1.000				
Labor	0.099	−0.003	1.000			
Xconst	0.198	0.125	0.063	1.000		
Sfree	0.286	0.134	0.079	0.335	1.000	
Totg	0.219	0.124	−0.176	−0.034	−0.091	1.000

Notes: See Tables 6.7 and 6.8 for definitions of variables and data sources.

Notes

1. An earlier version of this paper was presented at the meeting of the Africa Task Force of Nobel Laureate Stiglitz's Initiative for Policy Dialogue (IPD), Addis Ababa, Ethiopia, July 10–11, 2008. I am grateful to the meeting participants and an anonymous reviewer for helpful comments on earlier drafts of the paper.
2. E-mail Fosu@wider.unu.edu. Views expressed herein are not necessarily attributable to any institution of affiliation.
3. Although the majority of SSA countries had not yet achieved independence by 1960, it is the conventional starting date for the post-independence period. By 1965, however, most of the countries had. Those attaining independence after 1965 are Botswana, Lesotho, Equatorial Guinea, Mauritius, Swaziland, Guinea Bissau, Angola, Cape Verde, Comoros, Mozambique, Sao Tome, Seychelles, Djibouti, Zimbabwe, Namibia, and South Africa, in chronological order.
4. "Africa" and "SSA" will be used interchangeably in the rest of the paper.
5. The latter figure is computed by the author using data from World Bank (2008). During the same period, though, about one third of African countries' growth rates averaged only 2.1 percent (Arbache et al. 2008: table 1).
6. However, the differences in performance between SSA and SAS at the $2 poverty standard since 1981 have been less dramatic. The SSA rate decreased slightly from 74 percent in 1981 to 72 percent in 2004, while the SAS rate fell to 77 percent in 2004 from 88 percent in 1981. Hence, the SSA/SAS difference in the poverty rate increased by less than 10 percentage points, as compared with nearly 50 percentage points in the case of the $1 standard (Fosu 2009).
7. It is not growth alone that affects poverty; income distribution matters as well. The current literature suggests that higher levels of inequality could significantly reduce the rate at which growth might be transformed to poverty reduction. For the most recent African evidence, see for instance Fosu (2009).
8. The lack of poverty data for the earlier periods prevents extending the analysis back to the 1970s or 1960s. However, Sender (1999) argues that there were major improvements in measures of human development in SSA, such as reductions in child mortality rates, presumably before the structural adjustment programs (SAPs) that were shepherded by the World Bank and IMF, most of which took place in the 1980s and 1990s. The relatively strong growth of African economies prior to the mid 1970s should, of course, be credited with such improvements, along with worldwide trends. Sender also argues against these SAPs, which were based on the "Washington Consensus" or "Post-Washington Consensus" prescribing the use of markets as the primary mechanism for resource allocation. As I argue later in the present chapter, however, these SAPs can be credited with improved policies that seem to have so far minimized the anti-growth policies of the past in SSA generally, notwithstanding their oft-cited defects.
9. By "policy syndromes" it is meant ex-ante anti-growth policies, classified as: "state controls," "adverse redistribution," "suboptimal intertemporal resource allocation," and "state breakdown." Details of this taxonomy are presented subsequently.
10. These numbers are the GDP-weighted growth rates presented in the tables, consistent with the usual World Bank statistics.

11. Based on data from World Bank (2007), which constitutes the source for all subsequent statistics on terms of trade cited herein, the net barter terms of trade for Botswana deteriorated in 1991–5 with a yearly average of -1.7 percent, recovered somewhat during 1996–2000 (2.3 percent annual average), but then deteriorated slightly more recently (-0.06 percent during 2001–5). Meanwhile, the HIV/AIDS prevalence rate for the country has been estimated to be high since the 1990s. Revised data show the rate to be 38 percent during 2000–4, as compared with an overall SSA rate of 8 percent (UNAIDS 2006).

12. See the notes of Table 6.4 for details. The 19 countries represent all sub-regions of SSA and constitute 72 percent of the SSA population, as well as the lion's share of the region's GDP. Nonetheless, they still represent less than one half of the number of SSA countries, and this caveat should be noted in interpreting the present results.

13. See, for instance, Acemoglu, Johnson, and Robinson (2001); Collier (2000); Collier and Gunning (1999); Collier and O'Connell (2008); Easterly and Levine (1997, 1998); Fosu (1992, 1996, 2001a); Ndulu and O'Connell (1999); and Sachs and Warner (1997).

14. The "Growth Project" is the AERC Collaborative Research Project, "Explaining African Economic Growth Performance." The project output appears in two volumes: Ndulu et al. (2008a, 2008b). An epitomized version of the study is provided in Fosu and O'Connell (2006).

15. By a "syndrome-free" regime, it is meant a country-year bereft of any of the identified policy syndromes as mentioned above; these are discussed in greater detail later.

16. The decomposition is based on the production function: $q=Ak^{.35}h^{.65}$, where q, k, and h are GDP per worker, physical capital per worker and human capital (average years of schooling) per worker, respectively, with assumed respective capital and labor shares of 0.35 and 0.65. The exercise is conducted on per-country basis, and then aggregated to arrive at the SSA figures for the 19 SSA countries that had consistent data over the sample period (Ndulu and O'Connell 2003).

17. For regime classification, see Collier and O'Connell (2008: table 2.A2). Politically conservative governments tended to have liberal market-oriented economic policies, while the socialist-leaning ones would generally resort to (soft or hard) controls on economic activities. As "policy syndromes," control regimes are expected to inhibit growth. However, as the classifications were conducted independently of growth outcomes, as they should be, a number of cases do not conform to these expectations. For instance, Gabon and the Republic of Congo were classified as control regimes but experienced relatively high growth during this period, while countries like Madagascar, Mauritania, and Rwanda were viewed as syndrome-free regimes for most of the subperiod but experienced low growth. Similarly, Malawi was classified as syndrome-free throughout despite its growth record being checkered. Obviously, factors other than regime classification contributed to growth performance as well.

18. The drop in capacity use would show up in growth accounting exercises as TFP deterioration, for a given level of capital stock.

19. Collier (1999), for instance, finds that a civil war could reduce per capita GDP growth by as much as 2.2 percentage points per year, while Fosu (1992) estimates that African countries classified as high-PI would suffer a reduction in their annual GDP growth rates by an average of 1.2 percentage points.

20. All SSA terms-of-trade statistics are the simple averages based on countries with available data. Note that due to missing data, out of the 48 SSA countries, growth rates could not be computed for eleven, six, five, five, and four countries, respectively, for the periods 1981–5, 1986–90, 1991–5, 1996–2000, and 2001–5.

21. See Collier and O'Connell (2008: table 2.A2) for the classification of a "control regime," which is further elaborated on herein.

22. As observed above, for 1989–93, SSA net barter terms of trade declined at an average of 2.5 percent per year, though they grew strongly in 1994 and 1995 at rates of 2.9 percent and 6.9 percent, respectively.

23. Botswana's net barter terms of trade fell by 4 percent, 6.4 percent and 8.3 percent, respectively, in 1990, 1991, and 1992, and at an average of 1.7 percent annually over 1991–5, compared with a mean appreciation rate of 0.6 percent for SSA. The generally lower growth performance since the 1990s, though, might be attributable in part to the relatively high prevalence of HIV/AIDS affecting approximately a quarter of the population (UNAIDS 2006).

24. Note that Table 6.5 provides no evidence for the more recent post-2000 period.

25. A number of studies have argued that SAPs have been detrimental to African development, including de-industrialization and diminution of the social sector (e.g., Cogan 2002; Lall 1995; Mkandawire and Soludo 1999; Mytelka 1989; Sender 1999). While such arguments have some merit, they tend to ignore the fact that the de-industrialization process had already begun in many African countries before SAPs, resulting from such factors as industrial operation inefficiency and adverse terms of trade shocks. Regarding the social sector, Fosu (2007, 2008c) finds that, on average, public spending on health and education in SSA actually trended upward in the latter 1980s and early 1990s, despite SAPs, an observation that corroborates an earlier finding by Sahn 1992.

26. The growth rates of the net barter terms of trade for SSA countries averaged 0.6 percent and 1.5 percent annually in 1996–2000 and 2001–5, respectively, for a yearly mean of 1 percent since 1996.

27. Nigeria's net barter terms of trade actually grew at the astonishing annual average of 20.5 percent in 1996–2000.

28. There were also countries, such as Malawi, which undertook credible SAPs but did not fare as well due in great part to terms-of-trade deterioration. However, even Malawi's GDP growth rebounded strongly in 2006 to more than 7 percent following a mean annual growth rate of 2.5 percent during 1996–2005 (Table 6.1).

29. This account is not meant to imply that the SAP was successful all over in SSA. Mkandawire and Soludo (1999), for instance, argue that SAP has been deleterious to socioeconomic conditions in SSA.

30. For the role of instabilities generally see also Guillaumont et al. (1999).

31. Much of the present section derives from Fosu (2008a), which presents a number of case studies to illustrate each syndrome or SF regime. The definitions of the regimes, provided below, form the basis for the judgmental classification of each country-year into one or more of the categories by the editorial committee of the Growth Project based initially on the initial 27 case studies, and later extended to all SSA countries (for details see Collier and O'Connell 2008; Fosu 2008a; Fosu and O'Connell 2006). Note that "classification is based on policies, not growth outcomes" (Fosu and O'Connell 2006: 37). For example,

though Sudan grew rather rapidly in the late 1990s it was not categorized during this period as "syndrome-free" but instead as "state breakdown." Conversely, Malawi was designated "syndrome-free" throughout the post-independence period, yet it stagnated in the 1980s, and so did Côte d'Ivoire in the early 1980s despite its syndrome-free classification during that period.

32. Unfortunately, as already discussed above, the relatively weak-growth performers during the early period were generally these state led development countries rather than the more market-oriented countries.

33. Currency overvaluation has been found to be a major deterrent to growth in African economies. See, for instance, Ghura and Grennes (1993).

34. The persistence of the CFA overvaluation, just as in the case of other non-CFA currencies, might be explained in part by the tendency of elite coalitions to form around the relatively cheap imports availed by domestic currency overvaluation, as well as the rent-seeking opportunities that such an arrangement provided.

35. While a number of African countries enjoyed revenue boosts from commodity booms in the 1970s, contributing to the improvements in the overall SSA terms of trade, most SSA countries actually experienced adverse terms-of-trade shocks when the early 1980s are included in the analysis. For example, of the 33 SSA countries examined by Svedberg (1991: 559), "nineteen countries saw their barter terms of trade deteriorate significantly between 1970 and 1985."

36. For classification of these episodes, see Collier and O'Connell (2008: table 2.A2). Different factors other than just terms of trade, including government changes (as in the case of Ghana, for example), may have also contributed to the adoption or hardening of state controls. The case studies, however, suggest that governments tended to adopt more stringent controls in the face of a negative and inflationary supply shock (see Fosu 2008a). In the case of Nigeria, for example, hard controls began about 1983 when the country suffered a major terms-of-trade deterioration due to tumbling oil prices in the wake of oil revenue booms in the 1970s.

37. The misallocation would usually show up as a decline in TFP, as was the case of Nigeria in the late1970s to early 1980s, Cameroon in the 1980s and early 1990s, and Zambia in the 1970s and 1980s (see Appendix Table A).

38. These statistics are based on the annual data that form the basis of Table 6.6. See Fosu (2008a: figure 3.1), for example, for a graphical depiction.

39. Specifically, the controls in the Fosu–O'Connell model are: "partner growth," "rainfall," "coastal," and "resource-rich." However, accounting for these variables does not seem to appreciably affect the impact of the SF variable (see Fosu and O'Connell 2006: table 6).

40. In the present analysis, I focus on SF rather than the individual policy syndromes. The important objective for policy purposes is how to achieve SF, regardless of the relative impacts of the respective syndromes, which actually overlap in many instances. For attempts at separating out the effects of the various syndromes see Collier and O'Connell (2008) and Fosu and O'Connell (2006).

41. The production-function model has traditionally been estimated, alternatively to the Barro-type model, for example, in numerous studies to assess the effectiveness of production factors *vis-à-vis* the role of productivity on growth. See, for instance, Bosworth and Collins (2003) and also Fosu (2001b, 2008c).

42. As indicated above, the Fosu–O'Connell model is in reduced form with the following controls: "partner growth," "rainfall," "coastal," and "resource-rich," while the current model is the augmented-production function.
43. Note that the model estimated in Fosu and O'Connell (2006) does not include investment or labor.
44. This governance variable is used in the regression analysis because as the subsequent discussion shows, the lack of checks on executive power was a major contributing factor toward the creation of the syndromes. An additional justification is that data are available for this variable for the entire sample period, unlike the case of the other measures of governance.
45. That is, $1.875/2(0.26) = 3.60$.
46. Indeed, this assumption underlies the Growth Project. For further exposition see, for example, Fosu and O'Connell (2006).
47. Although this assumption does not imply that SFREE is endogenous with respect to growth, which might result in an endogeneity bias in estimating the effect of SFREE on growth, note that both country and time fixed effects have been controlled for in the estimation in order to mitigate such a possibility.
48. This section borrows generously from Fosu (2008a), which synthesizes the case studies. Thus, the account provided herein is based on the case-study evidence.
49. For details see, for example, Ndulu (2008).
50. See particularly Collier and O'Connell (2008) for a detailed discussion of the relationship between resource opportunity and syndromes.
51. A case highlighted in Fosu (2008a) is one of Togo where President Eyadema redistributed revenues in favor of his Kabeyes ethnic group. As Fosu (2008a: 147) writes: "Even in response to the structural adjustment program (SAP) begun in the mid-1980s when retrenching of the public sector was in effect, the Kabyes are believed to have retained the lion's share of desirable employment."
52. To be fair, other (non-socialistic) countries ran into economic difficulties as well. For example, Gambia (1981–5), Liberia (1971–5), and Malawi (1981–5) all experienced negative per capita GDP growth even though they had been market-oriented and had experienced none of the syndromes by the time of the negative growth.
53. Fosu (2008b) finds that democratization beyond the threshold of approximately 4.4 for the indexes of electoral competiveness (on a 1–7 scale, with 7 as the highest level of democracy) would raise GDP growth among African countries. It is noteworthy that currently, SSA as a whole has transcended this threshold (ibid.).

References

Acemoglu, D., Johnson, S., and Robinson, J. (2001). "Colonial Origins of Comparative Development: An Empirical Investigation," *American Economic Review*, December, 91 (5): 1369–401.

Alence, R. (2004). "Political Institutions and Developmental Governance in Sub-Saharan Africa," *Journal of Modern African Studies*, 42 (2): 163–87.

Ali, A.G. and Elbadawi, I. (2003). "Explaining Sudan's Economic Growth Performance," AERC Growth Project.

Arbache, J., Go, D., and Page, J. (2008). "Is Africa's Economy at a Turning Point?" Policy Research Working Paper 4519, Africa Region. Washington, DC: World Bank.

Aryeetey, E. and Fosu, A. (2003). "Explaining African Growth Performance: The Case of Ghana," AERC Growth Project.

Azam, J. P. (1995). "How to Pay for the Peace? A Theoretical Framework with Reference to African Countries," *Public Choice*, 83: 173–84.

Bates, R. (1981). *Markets and States in Tropical Africa: The Political Basis of Agricultural Policies.* Berkeley: University of California Press.

Bloom, D. and Sachs, J. (1998). "Geography, Demography and Economic Growth in Africa," *Brookings Papers in Economic Activity*, 2: 207–73.

Bosworth, B. P. and Collins, S. M. (2003). "The Empirics of Growth: An Update," *Brookings Papers on Economic Activity*, 2: 113–79.

Cogan, A. L. (2002). "Hazardous to Health: The World Bank and IMF in Africa," Africa Action Position Paper, April.

Collier, P. (1999). "On the Economics of the Consequences of Civil War," *Oxford Economic Papers*, 51: 168–83.

—— (2000). "Ethnicity, Politics and Economic Performance," *Economics and Politics*, 12(3): 229–72.

—— and Gunning, J. (1999). "Explaining African Economic Performance," *Journal of Economic Literature*, 37: 64–111.

—— and Hoeffler, A. (1998). "On Economic Causes of Civil War," *Oxford Economic Papers*, 50 (4): 563–75.

—— and O'Connell, S. (2008). "Opportunities and Choices," in B. Ndulu, S. O'Connell, R. Bates, P. Collier, and C. Soludo (eds.), *The Political Economy of Economic Growth in Africa 1960–2000, Vol. I.* Cambridge: Cambridge University Press.

Collins, S. and Bosworth, B. P. (1996). "Economic Growth in East Asia: Accumulation versus Assimilation," *Brookings Papers on Economic Activity*, 2: 135–203.

Davies, V. A. B. (2004). "Sierra Leone's Growth Performance: 1961–2000," AERC Growth Project.

Doumbouya, S. and Camara, F. (2003). "Explication de la Performance de Croissance Economique en Afrique: le Cas de la Guinee," AERC Growth Project.

Easterly, W. and Levine, R. (1997). "Africa's Growth Tragedy: Policies and Ethnic Divisions," *Quarterly Journal of Economics*, 112: 1203–50.

—— —— (1998). "Trouble with the Neighbors: Africa's Problem, Africa's Opportunity," *Journal of African Economies*, 7 (1): 120–42.

Fosu, A. K. (1990). "Exports and Economic Growth: The African Case," *World Development*, 18 (6): 831–5.

—— (1992). "Political Instability and Economic Growth: Evidence from Sub-Saharan Africa," *Economic Development and Cultural Change*, 40 (4): 829–41.

—— (1996). "The Impact of External Debt on Economic Growth in Sub-Saharan Africa," *Journal of Economic Development*, 21 (1): 93–118.

—— (2001a). "The Global Setting and African Economic Growth," *Journal of African Economies*, 10 (3): 282–310.

—— (2001b). "Political Instability and Economic Growth in Developing Economies: Some Specification Empirics," *Economics Letters*, 70 (2): 289–94.

—— (2001c). "Economic Fluctuations and Growth in Sub-Saharan Africa: The Importance of Import Instability," *Journal of Development Studies*, 37 (3): 1–84.

—— (2002). "Political Instability and Economic Growth: Implications of Coup Events in Sub-Saharan Africa," *American Journal of Economics and Sociology*, 61 (1): 329–48.

—— (2003). "Political Instability and Export Performance in Sub-Saharan Africa," *Journal of Development Studies*, 39 (4): 68–82.

—— (2007). "Fiscal Allocation for Education in Sub-Saharan Africa: Implications of the External Debt Service Constraint," *World Development*, 35 (4): 702–13.

—— (2008a). "Anti-Growth Syndromes in Africa: A Synthesis of the Case Studies," in B. Ndulu, S. O'Connell, R. Bates, P. Collier, and C. Soludo (eds.), *The Political Economy of Economic Growth in Africa 1960–2000, Vol. I*. Cambridge: Cambridge University Press.

—— (2008b). "Democracy and Growth in Africa: Implications of Increasing Electoral Competitiveness," *Economics Letters*, September, 100 (3): 442–4.

—— (2008c). "Implications of External Debt-Servicing Constraint for Public Health Expenditure in Sub-Saharan Africa," *Oxford Development Studies*, 36 (4): 363–77.

—— (2009). "Inequality and the Impact of Growth on Poverty: Comparative Evidence for Sub-Saharan Africa," *Journal of Development Studies*, 45 (5): 726–45.

Fosu, A. K. and Aryeetey, E (2009). "Explaining Four Decades of Growth in Sub-Saharan Africa," in G. McMahon, E. Salehi, and L. Squire (eds.), *Diversity in Economic Growth: Global Insights and Explanations*. Edward Elgar Publishing Ltd.

Fosu, A. K. and Collier, P. (eds.) (2005). *Post-Conflict Economies in Africa*, International Economic Association Conference, Vol. 140. New York: Palgrave/Macmillan, i–272.

Fosu, A. K. and O'Connell, S. A. (2006). "Explaining African Economic Growth: The Role of Anti-Growth Syndromes," in F. Bourguignon and B. Pleskovic (eds.), *Annual Bank Conference on Development Economics (ABCDE)*. Washington, DC: World Bank.

Ghura, D. and Grennes, T. J. (1993). "The Real Exchange Rate and Macroeconomic Performance in Sub-Saharan Africa," *Journal of Development Economics*, 42 (1): 155–74.

Gogue, T. A. and Evlo, K. (2004). "Togo: Lost Opportunities for Growth," AERC Growth Project.

Guillaumont, P., Jeanneney-Guillaumont, S., and Brun, J.-F. (1999). "How Instability Lowers African Growth," *Journal of African Economies*, 8 (1): 87–107.

Gyimah-Brempong, K. and de Camacho, S. M. (2006). "Corruption, Growth, and Income Distribution: Are There Regional Differences?" *Economics of Governance*, 7 (3): 245–69.

—— and Corley, M. E. (2005). "Civil Wars and Economic Growth in Sub-Saharan Africa," *Journal of African Economies*, 14 (2): 270–311.

—— and Traynor, T. (1999). "Political Instability, Investment and Economic Growth in Sub-Saharan Africa," *Journal of African Economies*, 8 (1): 52–86.

Iyoha, M. and Oriakhi, D. (2004). "Explaining African Economic Growth Performance: The case of Nigeria," AERC Growth Project.

Kasekende, L. and Atingi-Ego, M. (2004). "The Uganda Case Study," AERC Growth Project.

Kimenyi, M. S. (2006). "Ethnicity, Governance and the Provision of Public Goods," *Journal of African Economies, Supplement 1*, 15: 62–99.

—— and Mbaku, J. M. (1993). "Rent-Seeking and Institutional Stability in Developing Countries," *Public Choice*, 77 (2): 385–405.

Kobou, G. and Njinkeu, D. (2004). "Political Economy of Cameroon Post-Independence Growth Experiences," AERC Growth Project.

Lall, S. (1995). "Structural Adjustment and African Industries," *World Development*, 23 (12): 2019–31.

Lewis, W. A. (1954). "Economic Development with Unlimited Supplies of Labour," *The Manchester School*, 22 (2): 139–91.

Limao, N. and Venables, A. J. (2002). "Transport Costs, Infrastructure and Growth," *World Bank Economic Review* 15 (3): 451–79.

Maipose, G. S. and Matsheka, T. C. (2004). "Explaining the African Growth Performance: The Case of Botswana," AERC Growth Project.

Mamadou, O. S. and Yakoubou, M. S. (2006). "Climate Vulnerability, Political Instability, Investment and Growth in a Landlocked Sahelian Economy: The Niger Case Study (1960–2000)," AERC Growth Project.

Maundeni, Z. (2001). "State Culture and Development in Botswana and Zimbabwe," *Journal of Modern African Studies*, 40 (1): 105–32.

Mkandawire, T. and Soludo, C. (1999). *Our Continent Our Future: African Perspectives on Structural Adjustment*. Trenton, NJ: CODESRIA/Africa World Press.

Mwase, N. and Ndulu, B. (2005). "Tanzania: Explaining Four Decades of Episodic Growth," AERC Growth Project.

Mwega, F. M. and Ndugu, N. S. (2004). "Explaining African Economic Growth Performance: The Case of Kenya," AERC Growth Project.

Mytelka, L. (1989). "The Unfulfilled Promise of African Industrialization," *African Studies Review*, 32 (3): 77–137.

Nath, S. and Madhoo, Y. (2005). "Revisiting the Economic Success Story of Mauritius," AERC Growth Project.

Ndiaye, M. (2004). "Senegal: State Control and Lost Opportunities," AERC Growth Project.

Ndulu, B. (2008). "The Evolution of Global Development Paradigms and their Influence on African Economic Growth," in B. Ndulu, S. O'Connell, R. Bates, P. Collier, and C. Soludo (eds.), *The Political Economy of Economic Growth in Africa 1960–2000, Vol. I*. Cambridge: Cambridge University Press.

Ndulu, B. and O'Connell, S. (1999). "Governance and Growth in Sub-Saharan Africa," *Journal of Economic Perspective*, 13 (3): 41–66.

—— —— (2000). "Background Information on Economic Growth," AERC Growth Project.

—— —— (2003). "Revised Collins/Bosworth Growth Accounting Decompositions," March, AERC Growth Project.

—— O'Connell, S., Azam, J.-P., Bates, R. H., Fosu, A. K., Gunning, J. W., and Njinkeu, D. (2008a). *The Political Economy of Economic Growth in Africa 1960–2000, Vol. 2, Country Case Studies*. Cambridge: Cambridge University Press.

—— —— Bates, R., Collier, P., and Soludo, C. (2008b). *The Political Economy of Economic Growth in Africa 1960–2000, Vol. 1*. Cambridge: Cambridge University Press.

Nkurunziza, J. D. and Ngaruko, F. (2003). "Economic Growth in Burundi from 1960–2000," AERC Growth Project.

O'Connell, S. and Ndulu, B. (2000). "Africa's Growth Experience: A Focus on Sources of Growth," AERC Growth Project.

Oyejide, A. (2000). "Markets and Economic Growth in Africa," Framework Paper, AERC Growth Project.

Rodrik, D. (1999). "Institutions for High Quality Growth: What They Are and How to Acquire Them," IMF Conference on Second Generation Reform, Washington, DC.

Sachs, J. and Warner, A. (1997). "Sources of Slow Growth in African Economies," *Journal of African Economies*, 6 (3): 335–76.

—— (2001). "The Curse of Natural Resources," *European Economic Review*, 45 (4–6): 827–38.

Sahn, D. E. (1992). "Public Expenditures in Sub-Saharan Africa during a Period of Economic Reform," *World Development*, 20 (5): 673–93.

Sala-i-Martin, X. (2006). "The World Distribution of Income: Falling Poverty and . . . Convergence, Period," *Quarterly Journal of Economies*, 121 (2): 351–97.

Savvides, A. (1995). "Economic Growth in Africa," *World Development*, 23 (3): 449–58.

Sender, J. (1999). "Africa's Economic Performance: Limitations of the Current Consensus," *Journal of Economic Perspectives*, 13 (3): 89–114.

Svedberg, P. (1991). "The Export Performance of Sub-Saharan Africa," *Economic Development and Cultural Change*, 39 (3): 549–66.

UNAIDS (2006). *2006 Report on the Global AIDS Epidemic*, Joint United Nations Programme on HIV/AIDS.

UNCTAD (2008). "Export Performance Following Trade Liberalization: Some Patterns and Policy Perspectives," *Economic Development in Africa 2008*. New York and Geneva: United Nations.

World Bank (1981). "Accelerated Development in Sub-Saharan Africa: An Agenda for Action." Washington, DC: World Bank.

—— (1987). "Ghana: Policy Framework Paper." Washington, DC: World Bank.

—— (2004). *World Development Indicators CDROM*.

—— (2007). *World Development Indicators Online 2007*. Available at <http://data.worldbank.org/data-catalog/world-development-indicators>.

—— (2008). *World Development Indicators Online 2008*. Available at <http://data.worldbank.org/data-catalog/world-development-indicators>.

—— (2009). *World Development Indicators Online 2009*. Available at <http://data.worldbank.org/data-catalog/world-development-indicators>.

Part III
Technology, Industrial, and Trade Policies

7

Dynamic Capacity Development: What Africa Can Learn from Industrial Policy Formulation in East Asia

Izumi Ohno and Kenichi Ohno

Introduction

The transferability of the East Asian experience to Sub-Saharan Africa is becoming a popular topic in development economics; but investigation into this matter needs to go deep to be useful for policymakers. An ad hoc introduction of what an East Asian country did in the past, without analyzing its social context or transferability to other societies, is hardly helpful. Similarly, general assertions that Africa is different from East Asia in such ways that it cannot adopt what the latter did is neither accurate nor useful.

Diversity of ecology, history, and social and economic structure is common to any region including East Asia and Sub-Saharan Africa. In view of this intraregional diversity, it is futile to come up with one or a few concrete policy lessons from East Asia or to offer one or a few concrete policy recommendations to all economies in Sub-Saharan Africa. The lessons from East Asia should not take the form of a small number of generally applicable policy packages. At the minimum, various policy experiences in East Asia should be interpreted as raw materials from which a development strategy unique to each country is built with selectivity and modification.

However, the East Asian experience should not be reduced to merely a list of policies adopted. In terms of specific policy measures, references should be sought throughout the world as there is no reason to confine the search to East Asia. What is striking about East Asian success is not the similarity of development policies within the region—which does not really exist as such—but the *methodology* by which individually unique, but equally effective, policies were designed and implemented. This methodology, in a broad sense, includes not only technicalities of policymaking procedure and organization but also the way non-economic factors, such as social and national concerns and senses of pride and humiliation, are strategically mobilized under strong leadership to serve as driving forces of catch-up industrialization. This approach, more than anything else, is the aspect of successful East Asian policy formulation that is highly distinct from the mainstream development thinking dominated by European donors and international organizations.

This paper aims to extract the methodological essence of East Asian policy formulation in its ideal form for policy practitioners in the rest of the world who are seriously interested in learning lessons from East Asia. The next section stresses the diversity of East Asian experiences, which include both "miracles" and "disasters," as well as impressive but not-so-miraculous "high-performing economies," with significantly different speeds of catching up. The following section makes a general point that the lack of consideration of interaction between politics and economics has been a major cause of development policy failure. Next, we present the key ingredients of industrial policy formulation in East Asia, with some examples of such policymaking from the past and present. Finally, we address the question of how Japan, a donor with rich experience in assisting East Asian countries into graduation from aid, can make a meaningful contribution to African development. Four entry points are suggested.

Diversity of East Asian experiences

The East Asian experience has long been touted as a miracle by those interested in development. The region works as if it were a big factory with individual economies competing to become more effective machines in it. One by one, countries in different stages of development initiate economic growth by participating in the production network spanned by private firms. Linked by trade and investment, an international division of labor with clear order and structure has emerged. Industrialization has proceeded through geographic spreading on the one hand and structural deepening within each country on the other. The term *flying geese* refers to these systematic supply-side developments. Other developing regions have not established such an organic intraregional dynamism as East Asia (Ohno 2008a).

Despite its success *on average*, the most striking feature of East Asia is diversity. It has been noted that each region is diverse. In terms of country characteristics such as size, per capita income, economic structure, religion, and political regimes, East Asia arguably exhibits greater diversity than Sub-Saharan Africa, Latin America, the Middle East, South Asia, or Central Asia. It contains countries which are advanced democracies, boasting incomes that are among the world's highest, as well as countries which number among the world's most oppressive regimes and suffer from horrendous economic mismanagement. The population size also ranges from China (over 1.3 billion) to Brunei (0.4 million). All three major religions of the world are strongly represented in the region. Because of this diversity, to speak of any *average* facet of East Asia is highly misleading.

In this regard, the fact that not all East Asian countries are paragons of high economic performance deserves special mention. The region contains both economic miracles and disasters. There are both participants and non-participants in the East Asian production network. When researchers extract lessons from East Asia, they almost invariably look at experiences in a subset of economies with relatively good performance. But meaningful research can also be conducted by explaining the gap and its causes between the winners and the losers in East Asia.

Even among the so-called high-performing economies of East Asia (World Bank 1993), degrees of success vary considerably. In this regard, there should be a clear distinction among super-high achievers such as Taiwan and South Korea, middle-to-high achievers such as Malaysia and Thailand, and middle-to-low achievers such as Indonesia and the Philippines. The first group is far ahead of the second or the third in terms of income and industrial capability. Figure 7.1 shows

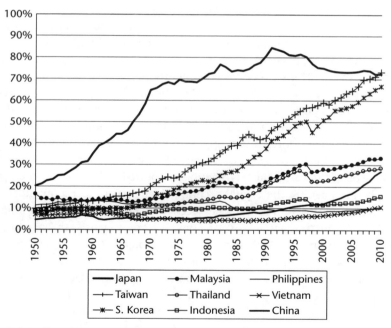

Figure 7.1 Different speeds of catching-up

(Percent of US real income.)

Note: Per capita real income relative to the United States as measured by the 1990 international Geary-Khamis dollars.

Sources: Angus Maddison, *The World Economy: Historical Statistics*, OECD Development Centre, 2003; the Central Bank of the Republic of China; and IMF, *World Outlook Database* (for updating 2002–10).

per capita real income of selected East Asian economies relative to the United States level. Until the mid 1960s, these economies (except Japan) showed no clear sign of catching up. However, Taiwan and Korea, which started from equally low levels, took off in the late 1960s and have raised incomes dramatically. In comparison, the catching up of Malaysia and Thailand looks less impressive, and Indonesia and the Philippines have failed to significantly improve their positions *vis-à-vis* the United States. Divergent performance comes from different speeds of catching up rather than delayed starts (except in the case of Vietnam, where wars and central planning prevented economic takeoff until the early 1990s but which has been growing very rapidly since then). ASEAN4[1] are taking much longer to reach the industrial capability that Taiwan and Korea had achieved by the 1980s and 1990s. The image of flying geese in perfect formation with all birds flying at the same speed is not quite right. In addition, there are economies that are not even on our radar screen—those such as Cambodia, Laos, Myanmar, North Korea, and East Timor that continue to struggle at the bottom of the income ladder.

Different income performance closely reflects different industrial capability. Income rises greatly only when difficult processes in the value chain are internalized.

Another important fact is that policy content and industrial outcome have differed significantly among economies that have reached middle to high stages. With respect to government intervention, Korea and Singapore have had very strong states while Hong Kong has consistently pursued laissez-faire policy. Taiwan, Malaysia, and Thailand have stayed in the middle of this scale. The relative importance of foreign direct investment (FDI) as an instrument for industrial catch-up has increased over time, along with the acceleration of economic globalization. In mobilizing foreign savings, during the 1950–60s, Japan did not avail itself of FDI or foreign loans; Korea accepted foreign loans but not FDI; but from the 1980s on, China and ASEAN4 vigorously courted FDI as the main engine of growth before opening the capital account. With respect to the manufacturing sector, heavy industry promotion was successful in Japan and Korea but much less so in Malaysia and Indonesia. Most latecomers have specialized in labor-intensive manufacturing industries such as electronics, garments, footwear, and food processing, but the city economies of Hong Kong and Singapore achieved high income through finance, commerce, and other high-value services. It is impossible to extract one simple development model from such diverse experiences.

The final point about East Asia is that, like a typical low-income country today, most countries initially had low capabilities. Competitiveness was weak in the private sector and governance was wanting in the public sector. In the early twentieth century, an official report found that Japanese workers were lazy, unskilled, only half as productive as American workers, and that they never saved and hardly remained in one factory long enough to accumulate skills and experience (Ministry of Agriculture and Industry 1903). Until 1960, South Korea was considered a basket case with inept and corrupt officials, heavy dependence on US aid for survival, and no prospect for profitable investment in comparison with the resource-rich North (World Bank 1993; Kim and Leipziger 1993). In 1959, the World Bank report on Thailand pointed to the severe shortage of trained manpower, managers, and administrators as well as the sheer absence of planning in public investment (World Bank 1959). These are familiar scenes in developing countries, but many East Asian economies have by now largely overcome these problems. Clearly, capabilities were built in the process of industrialization; they were not prepared *ex ante* as the precondition for growth.

Interaction of politics and economics

Development is a political as well as an economic process. It succeeds only when both aspects are fully taken into consideration, especially the complex interaction between the two, and appropriate visions, strategies, and action plans are fleshed out and executed. Here, the politics of development refers broadly to *what can be done* under the political landscape of the country as well as the administrative capacity of the government, whereas the economics of development refers to *what should be done* in terms of policy content to move the economy to a higher level given its initial conditions. The former is about the feasibility of development policy and the latter is about its desirability.

Not all feasible policies are desirable and not all desirable policies are feasible. To be effective, a policymaker at any level or in any organization must rack his or her brains for a narrow and delicate set of actions that satisfy both feasibility and desirability. Because all countries are different in both aspects, no one-size-fits-all solution can apply. Since the first best from the viewpoint of economics is often impossible from the viewpoint of politics, compromises must be made and a detour may have to be taken. Policymaking is a very complex game, and any advice that looks only at one aspect is easy to formulate but certain to fail. While this general point may seem obvious, it must be stressed that the lack of consideration of this obvious fact constitutes a major cause of failure in development policy advice.

While the government is directly responsible for designing and implementing development policies, the weight of foreign advice cannot be ignored in latecomer countries. Foreign advisors from aid organizations or academic institutions can contribute significantly to the country's welfare or, conversely, can become part of the problem and contribute to economic stagnation and persistent poverty. This is why we emphasize the importance of the methodology by which foreign advisors or donors assist in the policy formulation of a developing country. Although there may be no need to explicitly state the political and administrative constraints of a developing country, foreign advisors are well advised to take them fully into consideration when they draft any report. Some advisors seem to believe that their job is to find an economically sound solution and that implementation is the problem of the host government. But if the advice is meant to be practical rather than academic, the fact is that policy advice not based on (implicit) feasibility analysis can hardly be implemented regardless of whether proposed actions are few or many, or whether they are globally common or tailored to a particular country.

From this perspective, the shortcomings of the traditional IMF conditionalities and World Bank policy matrices are clear enough and need no further elaboration. By now, few economists defend an international organization that imposes a long list of common policies on countries struggling with macroeconomic crisis or popular discontent.

The argument for good governance suffers from the same problem. The advocates of this view regard the inadequacy of governing institutions as the main source of poor policies. They extract desirable attributes of growth-friendly governments from the advanced West and evaluate and rank developing countries by these criteria. For instance, the World Bank's Worldwide Governance Indicators (WGI) consist of six scales: voice and accountability, political stability, government effectiveness, regulatory quality, rule of law, and control of corruption. Member countries are given grade points ranging from 0 to 100 on each of these scales. This approach has been criticized on a number of levels, including the confusion of causality between growth and governance, and the need for a smaller or different set of institutional targets to start with. Another critique stems from the impossibility—and even non-necessity—of attaining good governance in low-income countries, and the absence of empirical evidence that good governance is necessary for growth (Grindle 2004; Khan 2008; Shimomura 2005). On the last point, it should be recalled that high-performing economies in East Asia generally had poor records in public-sector efficiency, transparency, or corruption at the beginning and even during their high-growth periods. From the viewpoint of interaction of politics and economics, however, the most fundamental shortfall of the good governance drive is the total lack of analysis on the political and administrative feasibility of Western-style governing principles in the sociopolitical context of the country in question.

Growth diagnostics, which is supposed to overcome the problems associated with the long and universal policy menu of the Washington Consensus, is subject to similar criticism. This research program was proposed by three economists associated with Harvard University (Hausmann, Rodrik, and Velasco) to discover a small number of most binding constraints to growth in each country. It proposes a logic tree (the HRV tree) that instructs researchers to look systematically for such binding constraints and also serves as a checklist—albeit a rather simple one (Rodrik 2007). The HRV tree assumes that boosting private investment is the key to growth, which can be thwarted by either low return or high financing cost. For each case, the inquiry continues by asking the reason why it occurs. The idea that policy advice should be simple and geared to the situation of each country is commendable. This research program has already produced a large number of country growth diagnostics at Harvard University, the World Bank, the Inter-American Development Bank, the Asian Development Bank, and the British Department for International Development. However, it must be pointed out that growth diagnostics writes prescriptions only from the economic side. When political and administrative constraints are added, it is highly doubtful that a small number of economic problems identified to be most binding in a particular country are the correct entry point for reform. Sometimes it is more effective not to tackle the greatest constraint head on, and instead work on peripheral issues first to gain political support and administrative competence for a bolder action later. There may also be other sophisticated scenarios for improving the chance of success. It must therefore be concluded that the analytical scope of growth diagnostics is too narrow. Policy sequence which works in the real world requires far deeper thinking than just following down the HRV tree.

How should we cope with the nexus of politics and economics in development with the understanding that the two are inseparable? One obvious suggestion, at least for academicians, is to conduct interdisciplinary research. However, just producing a book with economists and political scientists analyzing development independently and without intellectual cross-fertilization hardly helps. Each discipline is deeply entrenched in its methodology. Operationally meaningful results cannot be had simply by inviting them into the same conference room.

The World Bank's *World Development Report* in 1997 proposed a strategy that may be dubbed as *policy-capability matching* (World Bank 1997).[2] It acknowledged that some policies, such as selective industrial policy, were inherently more difficult and required far more information and policy skill than others, such as providing universal primary education or a level playing field for all businesses. It argued that countries with already advanced institutions might attempt difficult policies but those without them should first build institutional capabilities in three areas: (a) effective rules and restraints, (b) greater competitive pressure, and (c) increased citizen voice and partnership. The latter group should content themselves with easy policies (or "fundamentals") for now and leave difficult ones for later when their institutions are upgraded. This advice can be useful in preventing developing countries from overreaching themselves, but it shares the same weakness as the good governance approach: it is based on the belief that institutions and capabilities can be enhanced generally and more or less independently from the particular development path that the country has chosen to tread. But such unfocused effort at capacity development is difficult to rally politically and too broad to implement administratively. There should be an alternative and more concentrated way to strengthen capability that appeals to the political constituencies as well as to the hearts of the general public.

What East Asia's successful economies practiced was quite different from any of the above. Starting from an incompetent and often corrupt government, a leader rose to take over power, either legally or illegally, to establish a new government with the sole purpose of achieving rapid economic development to maintain national unity or defend the nation from external threats. Such a leader often launched the political regime of authoritarian developmentalism in which he himself became the prime driving force of development. He was backed by a technocrat team to concretize his vision, national ideology that glorified material advancement, unwavering belief in upgrading technology and competitiveness, popular support for rising living standards, and political legitimacy based on industrial results rather than democratic procedure (Ohno 2008a; Watanabe 1995). Military-like discipline ruled to largely wipe out corruption and nepotism. In this process, politics and economics were deeply intertwined. Leaders had no illusion that politics and economics could be practiced separately or solved independently from each other. Social scientists must analyze what these policy practitioners actually did (we sketch some case studies later that could be instructive for further research). We do not mean to blindly justify the "authoritarian" rule, which often leads to human rights violations and political oppression. Nevertheless, it is necessary to recognize that in East Asia's successful economies, economic development preceded political development and that their leaders played a decisive role in pursuing developmental policies in a pragmatic way.[3]

East Asian economies raised policy capability through hands-on efforts to attain concrete goals rather than trying to improve governance generally and aimlessly. Organizations were created or restructured, and officials and advisors were mobilized or reassigned, to execute specific tasks required by the five-year plan, the master plan for a priority industry, or the blueprint for a new industrial zone. This approach had several advantages such as concentrating limited human and financial resources on truly needed areas, clear criteria for monitoring and assessing performance, flexible reshuffling of resources in response to initial results or changing circumstances, and the cumulative pride and sense of achievement that emerge as specific targets were realized one by one. We shall call this approach *dynamic capacity development*. The next section will explain it more in detail with some concrete examples.

Industrial policy formulation in East Asia

There are three interrelated features (explained below) of industrial policy formulation in East Asia that are quite distinct from the dominant development thinking. Dynamic capacity development takes place in the process of designing and implementing policies that satisfy these conditions: (1) real-sector orientation; (2) goal orientation under the multiple policy layers of visions, strategies, and action plans; and (3) enhancement of unique strengths instead of removing general negatives.

Real-sector pragmatism

Yanagihara (1992) distinguishes the "framework approach" practiced by Western aid donors and the "ingredients approach" adopted by the Japanese government in its development aid strategy. The framework approach emphasizes the rules of the game according to which the private sector acts and policymakers make decisions, while leaving the actual outcome of the game to individual matches and players. In this approach, the functioning of markets, the principle of official intervention, budgets and public investment frameworks, empowerment and participation, monitoring mechanisms, administrative efficiency and accountability, and the like, receive great attention. Aid harmonization and general budget support are clearly couched in this tradition. In contrast, the ingredients approach takes deep interest in how individual players are doing in the field and the outcome of each game. It examines the state of technology, factors of production, demand trends, product mixes, industrial structure, marketing and logistic efficiency, and the like in the concrete context of individual sectors and regions of the country in question. Matching crop species with particular soil or training factory inspectors for *kaizen* (the Japanese strategy for continuous improvement at the factory-floor level) and efficient use of equipment are considered to be crucial for successful development.[4] Similarly, the technical specification of roads and bridges to be built, the lot size and administrative supports in an industrial zone, and other details that are normally left to consultants and contractors are the proper concern of Japanese aid officials.

Both approaches are indispensable and should be highly complementary since general frameworks need to be filled with concrete contents. Yet, the two approaches are not well integrated in reality. Japanese aid officials tend to feel uncomfortable with the explosion of new aid rules, tools, and meetings set up by European donors. Conversely, the latter do not look kindly on "selfish" donors who refuse to participate in aid harmonization or do so unwillingly. Europeans should broaden the scope of aid to embrace more concrete ingredients while the Japanese side needs to effectively communicate what it has been doing and become part of the broader aid framework.

Goal orientation

In high-performing economies in East Asia, industrial policy has usually taken a goal-targeting form. The top government leader proclaims a long-term national vision that shows a direction without specifying details. To realize this, appropriate government organizations are created or designated to draft ambitious but feasible strategies and execute concrete action plans. Strategies and action plans may be revised as circumstances change, but the long-term vision remains intact. Working backward from broad goals to phased strategies and concrete action plans, while making necessary adjustments and accumulating experience and confidence along the way, has been the hallmark of East Asian development planning. This is in sharp contrast to the call for wide-ranging reforms without specific real-sector targets such as those of IMF conditionalities, World Bank policy matrices, good governance drive, and other institutional reform agendas.

Japan in the 1960s had the goal of doubling income within the decade as well as competing effectively with Western multinationals as trade barriers were lifted under the GATT Kennedy Round commitments. The Ministry of International Trade and Industry (MITI) together with the Japan Development Bank coordinated and assisted private efforts in improving productivity. Taiwan in the 1980s launched high-tech industry promotion to replace the heavy industry drive of the 1970s. Priority areas were designated, a science and technology industrial park was created in Hsinchu, FDI marketing was conducted, and measures were introduced to support R&D and financing of eligible companies. More examples are given below.

Enhancing unique strengths rather than removing general negatives

Instead of comparing countries across the board to rank them or find faults with individual countries relative to the global norm, the East Asian approach is to identify the future potential (dynamic comparative advantage) unique to each country. Rather than scattering limited resources across many unrelated programs, once an area of future potential is identified, resources are poured into this area to realize that potential. Of course, the development strategy of a landlocked country with rich mineral resources should be entirely different from that of a country with long coastal lines and excellent seaports. A society with a nomad population cannot tread the same path as a densely populated agricultural society. Unique potential for each country should be identified, and the main policy effort must be directed to removing barriers to attain that potential (Secretariat of the Stocktaking Work 2008).

The domestic capability of a latecomer country is often initially very weak. Corruption and rent-seeking are rampant. However, Khan (2008) contends that it is not only difficult but even *undesirable* to eradicate these "evils" in an economy where market-enhancing rules and institutions are severely underdeveloped. In such an economy, commerce, production, and investment are carried out with the help of these non-market activities and their sudden removal (by strict policing and punishment, for example) would bring the economy to a halt. According to Khan, designing policies and incentives so that these non-market activities are channeled toward learning, productive investment, and political and social stability is a better approach. Khan calls this capability *growth-enhancing governance*.

Foreign investors do not expect a latecomer country to become an investors' paradise overnight. They know that inefficiencies and irregularities are part and parcel of a developing country. What they really need is a few specific guarantees that are crucial to their investments—not overall reform. For example, Masaki Miyaji, a Japan International Cooperation Agency (JICA) expert with extensive business experience in Africa, asks each African country to declare its "charm point," an (untapped) advantage unique to that country that would attract investors. Then the government defends that advantage by all means to realize the promised returns. After all, there is no need for a country to improve on all fronts before launching a growth strategy.

When a country clearly understands its real-sector potential and is equipped with a policy system of vision, strategies, and action plans to attain it, it is not difficult to know where to start building capability. Action plans must be implemented, and specific problems arising in this process must be solved as a matter of highest priority. Weak coordination among concerned ministries, gaps in budgeting and execution, delays in land procurement and resettlement, training of officers in charge, and brain drain are some of the issues that may be encountered. Capacity is created where it is needed through solving such problems one by one, rather than by a general campaign to eradicate corruption or promote administrative efficiency. Dynamic capacity development is a natural consequence of the East Asian policymaking, characterized by real-sector pragmatism, goal orientation, and the pursuit of unique strengths.

More examples

East Asian countries include proven good practitioners of development, but they have not been keen to promote their achievements or articulate their differences from the Western approach. There are numerous development policies worthy of study in the region, but few are studied with the rigor they deserve. Four stories from Japan, China, Malaysia, and Thailand are added below to illustrate how East Asian approaches work in policy formulation and implementation for industrial catch-up; these are the stories that should be focused on when considering successful development strategies. The four stories are different yet share the three common features stated above—real-sector pragmatism, goal orientation, and focus on country-specific strengths.

JAPAN

Japan in the late nineteenth century was a backward agricultural country just out of the feudal system. Trade with the West was resumed in 1859 and imports of British cotton products surged. Under the strong competitive pressure from the Western powers, the Meiji government promoted industrialization for *yunyu boatsu* (import substitution). One of the key policy targets was to establish a cotton-spinning industry to replace imported cotton yarn with domestic production. State-owned enterprises (SOEs) were set up in the 1870s but they did not succeed economically. The reasons for the failure included the lack of capital, small capacity, use of water power that was constrained by location and operation hours, and the general lack of expertise. The turning point came when the private Osaka Spinning Company was established in 1883 by Eiichi Shibusawa, a superb business coordinator and former MOF official.[5] Shibusawa was determined to build a factory that overcame the defects of the previous SOEs. Innovations were made in production scale (10,500 spindles instead of 2,000), the use of steam engines for twenty-four-hour operation, adoption of the Ring spinning machine rather than the traditional Mule, and the use of low-cost Chinese cotton instead of domestic. Osaka Spinning was a joint stock company subscribed to by big merchants and former samurai lords who were personally persuaded by Shibusawa to invest. Loans from the First National Bank, where Shibusawa was the president, provided working capital. But what contributed most to Osaka Spinning's performance was the recruitment of Takeo Yamanobe, a young engineer who was persuaded and then financially supported by Shibusawa to study the cotton industry in the United Kingdom. Equipped with the latest technology and pragmatic knowledge, Yamanobe could lead the company into instant success in the first year of operation. This had a powerful demonstration effect. Soon, several spinning factories modeled after Osaka Spinning were established. By the early twentieth century, Japan overtook the United Kingdom to become the top textile exporter in the world and the City of Osaka, where many textile mills were located, was called the Manchester of the Orient. Without Shibusawa's passion and meticulous attention to details, this feat could not have been achieved (Ohno 2006b).

CHINA

Deng Xiaoping, who held power in China during 1978–97, was a pragmatic leader with a penchant for material progress, in sharp contrast to Mao Tsetung who ruled during 1949–76 with political ideology and radicalism. This leadership switch completely changed the economic landscape of China. Under Deng, agricultural liberalization and gradual international integration became the two pillars of "reform and opening" policy.[6] His method was to try everything, even capitalist mechanisms and foreign elements, to increase production, then continue if it worked and adjust or abandon if it did not. Many of his dictums exemplify his unwavering pragmatism: "It does not matter whether the cat is white [SOEs] or black [FDI or private] as long as it catches mice [increases output]"; "My invention is staying away from debates"; "Poverty is not socialism"; and "Even try the stock market and see." The greatest engine of the Chinese economy that Deng introduced was the attraction of FDI into special economic zones and economic development zones along the eastern and southern coasts. FDI flows, initially timid and cautious, by the 1990s had turned into a tsunami, precipitated by a series of pep talks Deng gave in Shanghai and Southern China in early 1992. Strong reaffirmation of "reform and opening" policy by the supreme leader reinvigorated investors and China has grown by double digits ever since. Deng also denied egalitarianism, the hallmark of socialism, and encouraged the pursuit of wealth by those who were able, letting others follow later. This idea was effective in removing the stigma of materialism and accelerating growth, but it also created a huge gap in income and wealth by the early twenty-first century.

MALAYSIA

In Malaysia, *Vision 2020*, an aspiration to become a "fully developed country" by 2020, set by former Prime Minister Dr Mahathir in 1991, remains the overarching goal. The Economic Planning Unit (EPU) of the Department of the Prime Minister directs national efforts to concretize this vision under a system of overlapping policy documents and cascading organizations (Figure 7.2). Dr Mahathir mentioned nine general challenges without further elaboration: national unity, confidence, democracy, morals and ethics, tolerance, science and technology, caring culture, economic justice, and prosperity. To achieve this, Malaysia drafts multiple layers of policy documents such as industrial master plans (Ministry of International Trade and Industry, or MITI), Outline Perspective Plans (EPU), and Malaysia Plans (i.e., five-year plans, EPU). Under MITI, special agencies such as MIDA (FDI policy), SME Corporation (SME promotion), MATRADE (trade), and MPC (productivity) have been established. Although this policy structure may sound quite complex, the Malaysian government manages it surprisingly well, without being bogged down in bureaucracy. In terms of industrial policy framework, Malaysia has reached a level where the focus is no longer how to make policy improvements.[7] Time will tell if Malaysian industries are able to flourish under this approach, but if they fail to emerge strongly, the blame should be on the dearth of local private dynamism rather than the shortage of policy sophistication (Ohno 2006a).

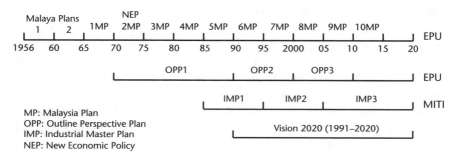

Figure 7.2 Malaysia: overlapping policy structure

233

THAILAND

The entire working of the government of Thailand changed in 2001 when Thaksin Shinawatra came to power. Previously, most Thai governments were weak and uncoordinated; but Prime Minister Thaksin wanted to run the country as if it were a private company. He determined general directions and ordered related ministries and organizations to work out the details and implement actions. This top-down decision-making affected the entire scope of policymaking. The role of economic ministries changed from building policies from bottom up to concretizing predetermined policy orientation. Many officials positively evaluated this change. Previously, Thai ministries did not talk to each other and their policies were often at cross-purposes. Under Thaksin, policies became more integrated, decision-making became faster, and dialogue among concerned ministries, domestic and foreign firms, and international partners was activated. Policy directions were also clearer. The Thaksin government wanted to promote industries that had high domestic value-added and created many jobs regardless of the nationality of the firm. Targeted industries included automobiles, agro-industry, fashion goods, high-value services, electronics and ITC, and energy and renewable energy. For the automobile industry, Thaksin declared the vision of Thailand becoming the "Detroit of Asia," while leaving the Ministry of Industry (MOI) to define what that meant. For this purpose, the master plan of the automobile industry 2002–6 upheld the following numerical targets: (1) produce one million cars per year; (2) export 40 percent of the cars; (3) produce two million motorcycles; (4) export 20 percent of the motorcycles; (5) export 200 billion baht of high quality parts; and (6) achieve localization of over 60 percent. These targets were fulfilled in 2005, one year ahead of schedule, by close cooperation among producers, MOI, and the Thai Automotive Institute, a body set up by the Thaksin government to promote the industry. While Thaksin was ousted for corruption charges in 2006 and the overall effectiveness of his rule remains an open question, his leadership style in industrial promotion has attributes that are well worth investigating (Ohno 2006a).[8]

Entry points for African industrialization

It was argued earlier that policymaking in latecomer countries is a complex game due to the interaction of politics and economics. It was also shown that East Asia's successful economies overcame their weak policy capability by setting clear goals, concretizing implementation plans, and making focused efforts. At least in East Asia, this approach—dynamic capacity development—has proven to be effective in building industrial policy capability, through a joint process of tackling the political and economic factors. The core problem in the reality of developing countries may not be informational but operational in the following sense. Senior officials are usually well informed about the barriers to growth in their countries.

They need to know more than the necessity of investment, productivity, and political stability, or a decision tree that helps them discover bad infrastructure, low human capital, or the lack of domestic saving. In this regard, the Western framework approach may remain too general to be implemented even if it serves as a useful guide for overall diagnosis.

If these frameworks are inadequate, how can outsiders such as donors and foreign advisors help the process by bringing new insights that fit the economic reality, political configuration, and administrative capacity of the country? To give a clue to such a fundamental problem, this section explores the role of Japan in assisting policy capability building for industrial catch-up of Sub-Saharan Africa. More specifically, four suggestions are made so that Japan, a donor with rich experience in assisting East Asian developing countries, may begin to make a meaningful contribution to the development of Sub-Saharan Africa (GRIPS Development Forum 2008b). All of the four entry points for engagement proposed here are the ones that are commonly practiced in East Asia, but their application to a new region requires care and sufficient lead time since the East Asian way is unfamiliar and initial conditions, including the state of intraregional manufacturing dynamism, are not the same.

In considering any approach to aid by a foreign government, it is also important to make plain the political constraints of the donor governments, which we do later in this section. It is important to note that aligning foreign aid with domestic interests does not necessarily mean that the aid has ulterior motives. As we will show, the aid strategy can be methodologically sound in terms of following successful experiences of aid and investment in other parts of the world, as well as satisfying domestic political constraints.

Align assistance to existing policy vision and strategies

If the country already has a valid vision and strategies for development, donors and foreign advisors should provide support for their realization. The vision and strategies must be clear, mutually consistent, and have the quality of being ambitious yet attainable with concentrated effort among all stakeholders. They must be strongly owned by the country's top leaders and shared by all policymakers. However, latecomers that satisfy these conditions are not many.[9] Five-year plans, industrial master plans, and vision papers are produced in abundance, but few are operational.

If the vision and strategies are reasonably good, there is no need to start by debating a national vision. Existing strategies may be revised over time but should be accepted in principle. However, even in a country with a well-formulated vision and strategies, implementation is usually weak and conditions that facilitate implementation are missing—including human and financial resources, institutional mechanisms, public-private partnership, and coordination among programs. Thus, enhancing the ability to design and execute concrete action plans becomes crucial.

In East Asia, there is a standard set of policy measures for industrial promotion. Table 7.1 shows such measures contained in recent support programs of the Japanese government. In light of the fact that both FDI and local firms must play important roles in industrialization, some of these measures assist local firms, others are aimed at inviting a sufficient volume of targeted FDI firms, and others provide links between the two groups of firms and a business-friendly policy framework for all. Careful assessment must be made—jointly with countries—to identify which measures are most needed and how they should be adapted to the reality of individual countries.

In North Africa, JICA has recently provided technical cooperation to assist the formulation of a master plan for quality and productivity improvement in Tunisia,

Table 7.1 Japan: policy menu for enhancing industrial capability in East Asia

Policy area	Measures
1. Capacity-building (for specific firms)	- *Shindanshi* (enterprise evaluation) system - TA for management and technology - Mobilization of current or retired Japanese engineers - Intensive support for limited sectors (e.g., die & mold) - Awards, PR, and intense support for excellent local companies
2. Human resource (general or institutional)	- Management/technical centers and programs - Mobilization of current or retired Japanese engineers - Alliance between FDI firms and local universities/centers - *Monozukuri* school (to be upgraded to university) - Meister certification system
3. Finance	- Credit guarantee - SME finance institutions - Two-step loans
4. Incentives	- Exemption or reduction of taxes and custom duties - Grants or loans for specified actions
5. FDI-local linkage	- Database and matching service - FDI-vendor linkage program - Parts Industry Association and Business Study Meetings - Trade fairs and reverse trade fairs - Improving logistics
6. FDI marketing	- Creation of strategic industrial clusters - Industrial parks and rental factories - Efficient logistics and infrastructure - FDI marketing targeted to specific sectors or companies
7. Policy framework	- Supporting industry master plan - SME law - SME ministry or agency - Business associations and industry-specific institutes - Quality standards and testing centers

Note: This table summarizes Japan's assistance measures to East Asian countries contained in the New Aid Plan for ASEAN (late 1980s to early 1990s), the Mizutani Report for Thailand (1999), the Urata Report for Indonesia (2000), and ongoing discussion for strengthening Vietnam's supporting industries (Ohno 2008b).

where concrete measures were introduced at individual pilot firms in the electronics and electrical industry and the food-processing industry (Kikuchi 2008). This JICA project aimed at strengthening the international competitiveness of Tunisian firms, a key element of the country's existing industrial policies. As such, it is a good example of Japan's concrete assistance in alignment with the country's existing policy vision and strategies. More recently, the Ethiopian government has shown strong interest in this project as an attempt to transfer Japan's factory-level quality and productivity improvement techniques and as one of the key instruments to implement the Ethiopian Industrial Development Strategies. Japan conducted a pilot improvement project in Ethiopia from 2008 to 2010 and further cooperation is expected in coming years.

Policy dialogue with a view to future actions

If the country does not yet have a feasible vision and strategy, the Japanese approach usually starts with a bilateral policy dialogue that leads either immediately or eventually to concrete actions. This may take government-to-government form or public-private partnership depending on the agenda. Each project usually lasts for two to three years, but policy dialogue often continues in multiple phases or overlapping projects with slightly different objectives.

In a country with little knowledge of East Asian experiences of policy formulation, or in a transition country unfamiliar with the market mechanisms or global competition, a general research project that assesses the country's current status and introduces relevant international experiences may be initiated (the Okita Project for Argentina, the Ishikawa Project for Vietnam, the Hara Project for Laos, the Shiraishi and Asanuma Project for Indonesia, and the Odaka Project for Myanmar[10]). If the target area for policy action is already identified, the dialogue may take an appropriate style for that purpose, such as the business forum for improving investment climate and the producer-government dialogue for drafting an automobile master plan. Table 7.2 lists past and current action-oriented policy dialogues between Japan and Vietnam. Similar bilateral dialogues are also conducted in other ASEAN countries.

The Ishikawa Project, formally the "Study on the Economic Development Policy in the Transition toward a Market-Oriented Economy in the Socialist Republic of Vietnam," was the first large-scale bilateral research project for Vietnam after diplomatic relations with the West were restored in the early 1990s. The project was officially agreed upon by the two governments when the Communist Party General Secretary Do Muoi visited Tokyo in April 1995. Shigeru Ishikawa, professor emeritus of Hitotsubashi University, was appointed by the General Secretary as the leader on the Japanese side. The Ishikawa Project was implemented jointly by Vietnamese and Japanese teams over six years as part of JICA technical cooperation. The research examined issues related to the formulation and implementation

Table 7.2 Japan–Vietnam Bilateral Policy Dialogue for Industrial Competitiveness

Program	Period	Principal actor(s)	Content
Ishikawa Project (Study on the Economic Development Policy in the Transition toward a Market-Oriented Economy in Vietnam)	1995–2001 (3.5 phases)	MPI-JICA	Joint research on macroeconomics, finance, agriculture, industry, integration, currency crisis, SOE reform, private-sector development (PSD); based on the principle of country ownership and mutual respect, with emphasis on long-term real-sector issues.
New Miyazawa Initiative (Economic Reform Support Loan)	1999–2000	JBIC	Quick disbursing loan (20 billion yen) with conditionalities in PSD, SOE auditing, and tariffication of non-tariff barriers. Action plans in PSD were monitored and evaluated.
Vietnam-Japan Joint Initiative to Improve Business Environment with a View to Strengthen Vietnam's Competitiveness	2003 4 phases, ongoing)	MPI-4J	Bilateral agreement and implementation of concrete action plans which were monitored and reported to high level, with focus on removal of FDI/business impediments, strengthening of local capabilities, and drafting of missing industrial strategies.
Joint work between Vietnam and Japan to strengthen the competitiveness of Vietnamese industries	2004	MPI-4J	Analyses by Vietnamese and Japanese experts as inputs to the drafting of the Five-Year Plan 2006–10, with attention on industrial policy formulation and competitiveness issues of individual industries (automobile, electronics, supporting industries, etc.).
Joint drafting of Motorcycle Master Plan under MOI and VJJI2	2006–7	Joint Working Group (MOI, VDF, producers, experts)	Drafting of master plan following new content and method, with active participation of large motorcycle assemblers and interaction with other stakeholders; VDF serving as facilitator. Master plan approved in August 2007.
Vietnam-Japan cooperation for promotion of supporting industries	2008–10	MPI, MOIT, 4J	Build strategic partnership for *monozukuri* (high-skill manufacturing) with Japan transferring its know-how to Vietnam. Action plans for supporting industry promotion to be implemented with joint effort.

Abbreviations: 4J (Japanese Embassy, JICA, JBIC, JETRO), JICA (Japan International Cooperation Agency), JBIC (Japan Bank for International Cooperation), JETRO (Japan External Trade Organization), MPI (Ministry of Planning and Investment), MOI (Ministry of Industry), MOIT (Ministry of Industry and Trade), VJJI2 (Vietnam-Japan Joint Initiative Phase 2), GRIPS (National Graduate Institute for Policy Studies), NEU (National Economics University), VDF (Vietnam Development Forum), PSD (private-sector development), SOE (state-owned enterprise).

of Vietnam's long-term development plans and made policy proposals to address them.

An increasingly popular format is the one adopted by the Vietnam-Japan Joint Initiative. Several issue areas, such as law and regulations, industrial policy, labor issues, and others, are identified and a working team is set up for each. Representatives from relevant ministries are appointed on the Vietnamese side and general directors of Japanese firms operating in Vietnam and industrial experts are appointed on the Japanese side. In each working team, concrete targets are proposed, agreed upon, implemented, monitored, and followed up on if not properly executed. Each phase lasts for two years and the Initiative is currently in its fourth phase. In each phase, a total of about forty of the identified issues are addressed with a high completion rate of 80–90 percent.[11]

In Africa, JICA is conducting the "Triangle of Hope" project in Zambia, mobilizing a Malaysian consultant to provide policy advice to improve the investment climate as an example of South-South cooperation. The working format is somewhat similar to the Vietnam-Japan Joint Initiative in that concrete tasks to be completed are reported in matrix form with vivid colors showing the degree of progress made for each task. Based on this work, FDI marketing is underway, targeting Indian and Malaysian firms that might be interested in coming to Zambia. Also, a master plan and a feasibility study for the establishment of Multi-Facility Economic Zones (MFEZ), as a receiver of FDI firms, have been conducted.

Regional development around a core infrastructure

A large part of Japanese ODA regularly goes to building large-scale infrastructure, especially in the transport and power sectors. When such infrastructure is built, it is customary that supporting programs that take advantage of the infrastructure or complement it are also provided for effectiveness and synergy. This includes the formulation of master plans for regional or industrial development, operation and maintenance programs, human resource development, safety and environment programs, local SME development, the "one village one product" program,[12] and the installation of one-stop border posts.

In East Asia, there are a large number of core infrastructure projects accompanied by satellite programs. Examples include the Eastern Seaboard Development Program in Thailand, which created huge industrial zones around a port infrastructure; the development of the Hanoi-Haiphong transport corridor along National Highway No. 5 in conjunction with Haiphong Port improvement, FDI attraction, and traffic safety programs in Vietnam; and the development of Sihanoukville Port and power and telecommunication networks combined with the construction of a special economic zone and FDI marketing in Cambodia. On even a larger scale, the development of the Greater Mekong Region encompassing six countries (China,

Thailand, Vietnam, Laos, Cambodia, and Myanmar) is promoted under the leadership of Japan and the Asian Development Bank where the East-West and the North-South corridors serve as the core infrastructure.

In El Salvador, Japan supports the development of La Union Port situated in the Eastern Region of this small country. By international standards, the quality of El Salvador's transport infrastructure—seaports, airports, and the road network—is above average and even considered the best in Central America. For this reason, infrastructure was not identified as the "binding constraint" in the growth diagnostics conducted for this country by Hausmann and Rodrik (2005). However, the government of El Salvador hoped to upgrade the existing port to augment the country's position as the regional transport hub. This could also contribute to the development of the Eastern Region, which was the poorest region of this country. The Japanese government assisted the drafting of the Master Plan for the Development of the Eastern Region, provided an ODA loan to expand La Union Port as the core infrastructure, and aligned other aid programs to it. For example, an old bridge on the Honduras border was rebuilt, digital map technology was introduced, and the development planning of La Union City was conducted. In addition, Japan provided training for port workers and implemented social-sector programs such as education, clean water, and rural electrification as well as productive-sector programs for SME promotion, aquaculture, agriculture, irrigation, and livestock (Figure 7.3). Although this assistance took place outside East Asia, it had all the features of East Asian policy formulation, such as real-sector pragmatism and boosting the country's strength rather than working generally on its weaknesses.

In Africa, Japan is interested in a multifaceted project along Mozambique's Nacala corridor that will be coupled with industrial development in the Nacala port area—with more programs to follow. The Nacala corridor will become international when it is extended into Malawi and Zambia, with a possibility of even greater impact on the regional development across national borders.

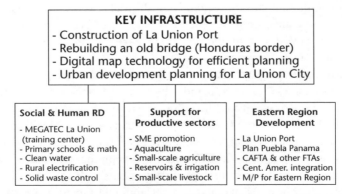

Figure 7.3 El Salvador: the Japanese aid package around La Union Port

Providing conditions for concrete foreign investment

Finally, Japanese ODA may be mobilized in conjunction with the planned investment by a large-scale foreign (especially Japanese) firm. In a low-income country, FDI with a large sunk cost (requiring large capital equipment or geological exploration, for example) will not occur unless sufficient infrastructure and an investor-friendly policy environment are in place. Moreover, Japanese manufacturing enterprises are extremely cautious investors and Africa is a destination largely unknown to them. Part of the Japanese ODA strategy, then, is to make investments that are complementary to the private-sector investments in order to reduce the cost and uncertainty. The Japanese government may build the necessary infrastructure and engage in a policy dialogue with the host government to improve the business environment surrounding the project. The private decision to invest and the official decision to build infrastructure must be made in tandem and in close consultation to overcome the coordination problem. Without such cooperation, the investment will not happen and the ODA project will be underused. In this way, ODA can catalyze private investment in a new region.

For a long time, the Japanese government has been cautious about using public money to assist only one firm (or a very few firms). However, such stigma is gradually melting away and active support for Japanese firms with concrete investment projects abroad is becoming more acceptable—and even desirable in the name of public-private partnership. Although there is no theoretical reason to exclude non-Japanese firms from participating in this strategy, the political reality is such that the core investment will most likely come from a Japanese firm. There are some Japanese constituencies that insist that ODA should be used mainly or even exclusively for pursuing (narrow) national interests.

In reality, Japan has often built large-scale infrastructures in developing countries with the implicit understanding that FDI firms will surely come after its completion (or even before). The two examples mentioned above, the Eastern Seaboard Development Program in Thailand and the Hanoi-Haiphong transport corridor along National Highway No. 5 in northern Vietnam, attracted a large number of Japanese manufacturers in the automobile industry in the former and the motorcycle and printer industries in the latter.

In Sub-Saharan Africa, initial large-scale investors from Japan may be in the extractive or energy-intensive sectors rather than in manufacturing. In such scenarios, the interest of the host country and the interest of Japan may have to be properly adjusted and aligned. Although ODA may be used to build transportation or power capacity to execute a particular investment for the benefit of a Japanese private firm, the core infrastructure should be accompanied by a range of other programs, such as regional development, SME promotion, and human resource development in the way that was discussed previously. Corporate social responsibility of the investing firm may also be evoked to generate the spillover effect to the host society.

Conclusion

The problem of weak policy capability was common in today's successful East Asian countries; but they overcame the problem through focused hands-on endeavors to achieve concrete objectives, which we call dynamic capacity development. This paper analyzed the key ingredients of dynamic capacity development, showing how the East Asian approach works to build policy capability and how it differs from and complements the Western approach. It also discussed how outsiders such as donors and foreign advisors can assist dynamic capacity development of latecomer countries and suggested that Japan make a meaningful contribution to African development by sharing the East Asian approach in which Japan itself has been involved through its own development experience as well as its aid and related assistance in East Asia.

East Asia approaches development as a joint process of political and economic factors where leadership and nation-building matter as much as technicalities. This approach is characterized by real-sector pragmatism, goal orientation, and aspiration for building the country's unique strengths rather than removing general negatives with limited consideration regarding their feasibility. The East Asian approach is also distinct from the Western approach, which emphasizes the functional framework, good governance, and an early adoption of policies and institutions that copy international best practices. Thus, the essence of East Asian development experiences should be sought in the methodology of policy formulation rather than individual policy measures, the applicability of which differs greatly across countries. While East Asia and Sub-Saharan Africa are different, and issues and solutions may differ considerably between the two regions, the methodology of organizing policy formulation transcends the differences and provides valuable lessons.

Notes

1. The Association of South East Asian Nations (ASEAN). The ASEAN4 refers to Indonesia, Malaysia, Thailand, and the Philippines.
2. The exact phrase used in the report was the two-part strategy of "matching the state's role to its capability" and "raising state capability by reinvigorating public institutions." The latter included the five "fundamental tasks" of (1) establishing the foundation of law; (2) non-distortionary policy environment including macroeconomic stability; (3) social services and infrastructure; (4) protecting the vulnerable; and (5) protecting the environment (World Bank 1997: 3–4).
3. For a fuller discussion on "authoritarian developmentalism" and "democratic developmentalism," see Ohno (2008a: 47–60). It argues that the existence of democracy is not an all-or-nothing choice, but a matter of degrees. Since both markets and democracy grow slowly and in steps, low-income developing countries should be able to choose from a broad spectrum of political regimes instead of between full democracy and no democracy.

4. Kikuchi (2008) reports that Tunisia approached the same goal of boosting the competitiveness of its industries in two different ways. The EU's Industrial Modernization Project aimed to assist acquisition of ISO certification, while Japan's Study on the Master Plan for Quality and Productivity Improvement tried to level up the operation of 30 companies in electronic assembly and food processing by dispatching experts with experience in factory management and training the Tunisian trainers. A senior manager of the EU project described this difference as ready-made versus order-made.

5. Shibusawa mobilized capital, technology, and human resources for setting up companies but never assumed general directorship. He delegated the running of the company to others and went on to establish over 500 companies, numerous economic institutions such as the stock exchange and the chamber of commerce, and non-economic organizations such as hospitals and universities. Unlike Yataro Iwasaki who founded the Mitsubishi group, Shibusawa did not form his own zaibatsu.

6. Though SOE reform was also attempted, it met with limited success. Township and village enterprises became another source of Chinese dynamism in much of the 1980s and 1990s, but they emerged more or less spontaneously and cannot be regarded as the direct outcome of Deng's industrial drive.

7. In 2006, a policy research mission from Vietnam asked the representative of the Japan External Trade Organization (JETRO) in Kuala Lumpur to list main constraints for foreign investors in Malaysia. He paused, and replied that he could think of none as far as policies and institutions were concerned.

8. Another policy that Thaksin introduced was subsidies and support for the rural poor who had long been neglected by Thai politics. This made him unpopular with urban voters and partly contributed to his downfall.

9. Ethiopia, which has a core vision of Agricultural Development Led Industrialization (ADLI, formulated in 1991) backed by the Ethiopian Industrial Development Strategy (2003), the Rural Development Policies, Strategies and Instruments (2002), the Growth an Transformation Plan (five-year plan), and other strategic and sectoral documents, MTEF and annual plans, may be an exception.

10. The names of the projects refer to the professors who led the research group.

11. In the first phase (2003–5), 37 out of 44 proposed actions were successfully completed. In the second phase (2006–7), 43 out of 46 proposed actions were implemented. In the third phase (2008–10), 37 actions were proposed. Examples of actions include clarification, revision, or abolishment of certain laws and regulations, privatization of the power sector, drafting of master plans for certain industries, and so on.

12. This program identifies one product for each village to specialize in.

References

Fujimoto, T. (2004). *Nihon no Monozukuri Tetsugaku* (Japan's Monozukuri Philosophy). Tokyo: Nihon Keizai Shimbunsha.

—— (2006). "Architecture-Based Comparative Advantage in Japan and Asia," in K. Ohno and T. Fujimoto (eds.), *Industrialization of Developing Countries: Analyses by Japanese Economists*, 21st Century COE Program. Tokyo: National Graduate Institute for Policy Studies.

—— and Shintaku, J. (2005). *Architecture-Based Analysis of Chinese Manufacturing Industries.* Tokyo: Toyo Keizai Shimposha.

Grindle, M. (2004). "Good Enough Governance: Poverty Reduction and Reform in Developing Countries," *International Journal of Policy, Administration and Institutions,* 17 (4): 525–48.

GRIPS Development Forum (ed.) (2002). *Japan's Development Cooperation in Vietnam: Supporting Broad-Based Growth with Poverty Reduction,* May (English, Japanese, and Vietnamese). Tokyo: GRIPS Development Forum.

—— (2008a). *Diversity and Complementarity in Development Aid: East Asian Lessons for African Growth* (English and Japanese). Tokyo: GRIPS Development Forum.

—— (2008b). *Proposal for a New African Growth Support Initiative,* August.

Hausmann, R. and Rodrik, D. (2005). "Self-Discovery in a Development Strategy for El Salvador," *Economia,* 6 (1): 43–101, Brookings Institution Press.

Khan, M. H. (2008). "Governance and Development: The Perspective of Growth-Enhancing Governance," in GRIPS Development Forum (ed.), *Diversity and Complementarity in Development Aid: East Asian Lessons for African Growth.* Tokyo: GRIPS Development Forum, National Graduate Institute for Policy Studies.

Kikuchi, T. (2008). "The Quality and Productivity Improvement Project in Tunisia: A Comparison of Japanese and EU Approaches," in GRIPS Development Forum (ed.), *Diversity and Complementarity in Development Aid: East Asian Lessons for African Growth.* Tokyo: GRIPS Development Forum, National Graduate Institute for Policy Studies.

Kim, K. and Leipziger, D. M. (1993). "The Lessons of East Asia: Korea, A Case of Government-Led Development." Washington, DC: World Bank.

Ministry of Agriculture and Industry (1903). *Shokko Jijo* (Survey of Industrial Workers), in Japanese. Reprinted 1998 in Giichi Inumaru (ed.), *Shokko Jijo,* 3 vols. Tokyo: Iwanami Bunko.

Motorbike Joint Working Group (2007). *For Sound Development of the Motorbike Industry in Vietnam* (English and Vietnamese). Hanoi: Publishing House of Social Labor.

Nguyen Thi Xuan Thuy (2007). "Supporting Industries: A Review of Concepts and Development," in K. Ohno (ed.), *Building Supporting Industries in Vietnam, Vol. 1.* Hanoi: Vietnam Development Forum.

Ohno, I. (ed.) (2005). *True Ownership and Policy Autonomy: Managing Donors and Owning Policies:* Tokyo: GRIPS Development Forum, National Graduate Institute for Policy Studies.

Ohno, I. and Shimamura, M. (2007). *Managing the Development Process and Aid: East Asian Experiences in Building Central Economic Agencies.* Tokyo: GRIPS Development Forum.

Ohno, K. (ed.) (2006a). *Industrial Policy Formulation in Thailand, Malaysia and Japan: Lessons for Vietnamese Policy Makers* (English and Vietnamese). Hanoi: Vietnam Development Forum.

—— (2006b). *The Economic Development of Japan: The Path Traveled by Japan as a Developing Country.* Tokyo: GRIPS Development Forum.

—— (2007). *Building Supporting Industries in Vietnam, Vol. 1.* Hanoi: Vietnam Development Forum.

Ohno, K. (2008a). "The East Asian Growth Regime and Political Development," in GRIPS Development Forum (ed.), *Diversity and Complementarity in Development Aid: East Asian Lessons for African Growth.* Tokyo: GRIPS Development Forum, National Graduate Institute for Policy Studies.

—— (2008b). "Vietnam-Japan Monozukuri Partnership for Supporting Industries: For Leveling Up Vietnam's Competitiveness in the Age of Deepening Integration." Hanoi: Vietnam Development Forum.

Ohno, K. and Fujimoto, T. (eds.) (2006). *Industrialization of Developing Countries: Analyses by Japanese Economists*, 21st Century COE Program. Tokyo: National Graduate Institute for Policy Studies.

—— and Ohno, I. (eds.) (1998). *Japanese Views on Economic Development: Diverse Paths to the Market*. London and New York: Routledge.

Rodrik, D. (2007). *One Economics, Many Recipes: Globalization, Institutions, and Economic Growth*. Princeton University Press.

Secretariat of the Stocktaking Work (2008). *Report on the Stocktaking Work on the Economic Development in Africa and the Asian Growth Experience*. Tokyo: Japan International Cooperation Agency and the Japan Bank for International Cooperation.

Shimomura, Y. (2005). "The Role of Governance in Development Revisited: A Proposal of an Alternative View," FASID Discussion Paper on Development Assistance, No. 5, March.

Tsai, M.-H. (2006). "The Myth of Monozukuri: Manufactured Manufacturing Ideology," ITEC Working Paper Series 06-04, Doshisha University, Kyoto.

Vietnam Development Forum (2007). "Supporting Industries in Vietnam from the Perspective of Japanese Manufacturing Firms," in K. Ohno (ed.), *Building Supporting Industries in Vietnam, Vol. 1*. Hanoi: Vietnam Development Forum.

Watanabe, T. (1995). *Shinseiki Asia no Koso* (Designing Asia for the New Century). Tokyo: Chikuma Shinsho. (Partly translated and published as Chapter 11 in Ohno and Ohno 1998.)

World Bank (1959). *A Public Development Program for Thailand, Report of a Mission Organized by the IBRD at the Request of the Government of Thailand*. Baltimore: Johns Hopkins University Press.

—— (1993). *The East Asian Miracle: Economic Growth and Public Policy*. Oxford: Oxford University Press.

—— (1997). *World Development Report 1997: The State in a Changing World*. Oxford: Oxford University Press.

Yanagihara, T. (1992). "Development and Dynamic Efficiency: 'Framework Approach' versus 'Ingredients Approach'," in K. Ohno and I. Ohno (eds.), *Japanese Views on Economic Development: Diverse Paths to the Market*. London and New York: Routledge.

8

How can Low-Income Countries Accelerate their Catch-Up with High-Income Countries? The Case for Open-Economy Industrial Policy

Robert H. Wade

The problem of "catch-up" comes to exist when a differential in "productivity" or "competence" opens up between two or more economies that trade freely with each other. The danger for the less productive economy is that firms in the more productive economy can out-compete firms in the less productive one across many sectors. Of course, champions of a "liberal"[1] or strongly free-market philosophy would say that competition among firms in the two open economies leads to changes in relative prices, which in turn releases resources—including people and capital—from less efficient uses to more efficient uses, in line with comparative advantage, leading to output and incomes gains in both. Schumpeterian champions, however, would expect that the less productive economy may be restructured by free-market forces into an appendage or exclave of the more productive economy, specializing in raw materials or agricultural commodities or routine assembly operations, its growth a reflex of growth in the more productive economy because it lacks "endogenous" sources of growth and because its employment growth is concentrated in less skilled activities.

Contrary to the widely held belief that "globalization works," few developing countries have experienced sustained growth since the 1980s quickly enough to reduce income gaps with developed countries, with the exception of a few years in the 2000s. Income gaps have tended to diverge rather than converge. This proposition holds for developing countries as a group when they are not population-weighted, whether incomes are converted at market exchange rates or at purchasing power parity (PPP) rates. It also holds when developing countries are weighted by population and incomes are converted at market exchange rates (both when China is included and when China is excluded). It also holds when population-weighted incomes are converted into PPP dollars and China is excluded. Only when incomes are converted into PPP dollars and China is included is there a trend toward convergence; that is, a rise in the average income of developing countries relative to the average of the North (Western Europe, North America, and Japan).[2] If convergence depends entirely on the inclusion of one giant case and on the use of PPP exchange rates (which are as questionable, though for different reasons, as market exchange rates), it is misleading to say that "developing countries" are catching up with the North, thanks to globalization; ergo we need more globalization.[3] Most of the caravan of countries has been falling further behind the leaders—especially in Latin America and Sub-Saharan Africa.

Here is another way to see the trend to global income divergence. Classify countries into four income categories (in PPP dollars): Rich (average PPP incomes equal or higher than that of the bottom country of the North, which in 1978 was Portugal); Contender (average income two thirds or more that of the bottom of the Rich countries); Third World (average income between one third and two thirds that of the bottom of the Rich countries); and Fourth World (less than one third). Of the Rich countries in 1978, 82 percent remained rich in 2000 (now with Greece as the bottom of the Rich countries). Of the Contender countries in 1978, only 13 percent ascended to the Rich category by 2000, only 5 percent remained as Contenders, and 82 percent descended to the Third or Fourth Worlds. Of the Third World countries in 1978, only 9 percent moved up by 2000 (including South Korea to Rich and Chile and Malaysia to Contender), 27 percent remained constant, and 64 percent descended to the Fourth World. Of the Fourth World countries in 1978, 95 percent remained Fourth World in 2000. The few that escaped the Fourth World sump got only as far as the Third World.[4]

Perhaps there are forces at work in the world economy analogous to gravity that make it very difficult for the majority of developing countries to sustain catch-up growth. There may also be forces analogous to magnetic levitation holding up the now rich countries and making it unlikely that they will experience significant downward mobility anytime soon.[5]

The picture is even bleaker when one considers distribution trends within developing countries. Virtually all developing countries are more unequal than the high-income countries (despite the dictum, "Show me an equal country and I will show you a poor country"). And within-country distributions have generally widened over the past twenty-five years (as measured by the average income of the top decile relative to that of the bottom decile, for example, or the average income of the top 1 percent against that of the median, or the average income against the median). If we were to compare median income in the North with that in southern regions, the trend toward divergence would be even stronger than the above figures (which are averages) suggest.[6] China's vertical as well as horizontal (regional) income inequality has become far more unequal than before the Communist Revolution, to take only one egregious case.

What should be done? In this essay I make the case for a proactive role of government in accelerating industrialization in low-income developing countries—the case for "industrial policies" or "policies for industrialization" (if the former phrase is still considered too toxic). And I discuss the neglected issue of how to organize such a proactive role. The first section challenges the commonly heard claim that no one really believes the Washington Consensus anymore. It argues that, on the contrary, when Western development experts identify "the fundamentals," they endorse the Washington Consensus. The second section provides prima facie evidence that a more proactive role of the state than sanctioned by the Washington Consensus was important in past trajectories of catch-up. The third section summarizes some recent developments in the literature on industrialization and trade, and suggests that they question the theory behind the Washington Consensus. The fourth section discusses the debate about the state's role in managing foreign direct investment, qualifying the recent argument of Theodore Moran. The fifth section deals head-on with the question of how to establish a developmental state, beginning with the misconceptions embodied in the standard "good governance" agenda, which over the 1990s and 2000s has been added to the Washington Consensus. The sixth section concludes.

Reports of the death of the Washington Consensus are exaggerated

Some academic economists have declared the Washington Consensus dead, replaced by a "Washington Confusion."[7] I argue, however, that a kind of schizophrenia has developed in development policy, at least as conceived in the North and advocated for the South. The Washington Consensus remains the consensus when people identify the fundamentals and it remains the consensus encoded in operating procedures of the international development organizations.[8] It is given full-blooded support in mainstream publications such as *The Economist*, which calls anything else "bone-headed," and by academic economists speaking to a lay audience.

A *New York Times* reporter covering the World Economic Forum meeting in 2002 reported that among business executives and government leaders attending the forum, the prevailing view was that, "A nation that opens its economy and keeps government's role to a minimum invariably experiences more rapid economic growth and rising incomes."[9]

The Economist published a survey of the world economy called "The New Titans" in 2006. The New Titans are the developing countries, or some of them. The theme of the survey was that "As these newcomers become more integrated into the global economy and their incomes catch up with the rich countries, they will provide the biggest boost to the world economy since the industrial revolution."[10]

The argument was that their incomes are catching up with the rich countries' because they are becoming more integrated into the global economy. Developing countries as a group, the survey said, have enjoyed growth of GDP per head at 5.6 percent a year over 2001–6, the fastest rate of growth of any large set of people in recorded history, well above the 1.9 percent growth in average incomes in the rich countries, and well above the 2.5 percent growth of average incomes of developing countries over the preceding twenty years. Looking ahead, *The Economist* said that the long-run growth prospects of developing countries

> look excellent, so long as they continue to move towards free and open markets, sound fiscal and monetary policies and better education. Because they start with much less capital per worker than developed economies, they have huge scope for boosting productivity by importing Western machinery and know-how. Catching up is easier than being a leader." (4)

In case a bone-headed reader did not understand, the survey repeats the point again and again in headmistressy tones, as in, "governments [must] do more to free up markets and reduce their own meddling" (12).

Starting in the 1990s the World Bank adopted a Country Policy and Institutional Assessment (CPIA) formula by which borrowing countries were scored—by Bank staff and other experts—according to the "pro-developmental" impact of their policies and institutions. The score counted heavily in the allocation of International Development Association (IDA) loans for the Bank's low-income borrowing countries, and also affected Bank lending to middle-income countries. The scoring criteria for the economic dimensions reflect the Washington Consensus. For example, a country could get the top score on its trade regime only if it had a virtually free-trade regime—with maximum tariff under 15 percent, very low average tariff, and no export subsidies or taxes. A country that established a managed trade regime modelled on East Asian trade regimes of the 1950s to the 1980s would get a low score, carrying tangible costs in terms of foreign assistance.

On the other hand, the operational consensus on development policy continues to ignore industrialization and technology, and to dismiss the very idea of "industrial policy" with jeers like "bureaucrats can't pick winners."

More implicitly than explicitly, the premise is that development and catch-up growth are a function of what happens in the domain of "exchange," as distinct from what happens in the domain of "production." The bigger the market, the bigger the potential for trade and specialization, and the bigger the potential for economic growth.

The World Bank published *Economic Growth in the 1990s: Learning from a Decade of Reform*, in 2005. The preface says that the central lesson of the 1990s is

> that there is no unique universal set of rules. Sustained growth depends on key functions that need to be fulfilled over time: accumulation of physical and human capital,

> efficiency in the allocation of resources, adoption of technology, and the sharing of the benefits of growth. Which of these functions is the most critical at any given point in time, and hence which policies will need to be introduced, which institutions will need to be created for these functions to be fulfilled, and in which sequences, varies depending on initial conditions and the legacy of history. Thus we need to get away from formulae and the search for elusive 'best practices,' and rely on deeper economic analysis to identify the binding constraints on growth (xii).

On the face of it, this is a significant change from the "we know what you should be doing before we get off the plane" spirit of the Washington Consensus. But the report was a one-off, and it is quite possible that most operational staff have never read even the preface. The 360-page report continues the Bank's long-standing neglect of "industrialization" and "technology" (it makes just one reference to "industrial performance," one reference to "industrialization," no reference to "industrial policy," and passing mention of technology over five pages). Apparently, the lessons from the 1990s do not include lessons about industrialization, industrial policy, or technology policy—which from a Schumpeterian perspective should be central. The lessons are about making markets and governance institutions work better.

So antagonistic has the Bank been to the idea of deliberate policy to foster technological learning that a few determined World Bank staff had to struggle for years to persuade senior management to allow a World Development Report focused on technological development (which eventually appeared under the title *Knowledge for Development, World Development Report 1998/99*). At the operational level the Bank has allowed hardly any projects or country work focused on technological development since the early 1980s, when liberal ideas, with their focus on expanding exchange as the engine of development, came to constitute "global development policy."

However, at the other end of the western development community, some academics writing mainly for each other and mostly ignored by the policy-oriented mainstream, have come up with all kinds of empirical and theoretical objections to Washington Consensus ideas, using theoretical arguments already made—but not formalized—fifty years ago about the pervasiveness of market failure in developing countries. These analysts do give attention to industrialization, technological learning, product diversification, and the like.

The problem is that they have been rather reticent when it comes to suggesting alternative policies or strategies. And so the two ends of development thinking tend to talk past each other—even when the two ends are in the same head. Gregory Mankiw, professor of economics at Harvard and former chairman of the President's Council of Economic Advisors, is well aware of the theoretical and empirical literatures that question the Washington Consensus, but when writing for a lay audience he removes the complexities and just gives the "fundamentals": "Adam Smith was right when he said that 'Little else is required to carry a state to the highest degree of opulence from the lowest barbarism but peace, easy taxes and a tolerable administration of justice.'"[11] An unsurprising statement from a Manchester industrialist in 1906 or a British Treasury official. But a professor of economics in 2006?

With little feedback from the thinking on the frontiers to the domain of operational practice, it remains "common sense" to say, with *The Financial Times* (talking about the benefits to Latin America of specializing more in commodities and importing more of its manufactured goods from China),

> The China connection could even pave the way for Latin America to capitalise on its strengths as a low-cost producer of raw materials. If that happened it could open the way to the re-emergence of a development model based on the classical economic concept of comparative advantage rather than on more recent ideas such as import substitution. . . . 'China gives a new hope to Latin America to be a viable part of the world.'[12]

Equally it remains common sense for the World Bank to tell the government of Mongolia that it should stick to free trade, and not impose an export tax on unprocessed wool, as a way to revive the shuttered woollen mills (shuttered after the country's big bang liberalization in the early 1990s).[13]

It remains common sense for the World Bank to tell Mali, the landlocked country in western Africa (population: 14 million), to stick to free trade. The Bank prescribed a structural adjustment program (SAP) in the late 1990s for Mali, with trade liberalization as its centerpiece.[14] Tariffs were brought down to below the EU average. The result? Most of the larger manufacturing plants in Mali closed, including canned goods production, phosphate fertilizer, and cement. Chinese imports flooded in. Carpenters in the capital city, who used to make doors for houses and offices, were out-competed by the makers of light plywood doors in China, who shipped them across the ocean, transported them via rail 1,200 km from the nearest port, and sold them for half the price that local carpenters used to sell solid doors. The latter now cannot invest in new machinery. Almost the only industries to survive after trade liberalization are beverages and bakeries—thanks to transport costs of sending liquids by sea and fresh bread by air. Their survival reflects obstacles to trade, rather than a "good investment climate" and the other governance reforms of the SAP. Similarly, almost the only new industry to have come up in the new liberal trade regime owes its rise to trade restrictions, in form of preferential trade agreements. It is a factory spinning cotton yarn, owned by French and Mauritian investors. It was established in Mali, only because there the investors get access to the US market via the Africa Growth and Opportunity Agreement (AGOA), while Mauritius (where the factory moved from) is excluded.

All this has been intended to substantiate that the core ideas of the Washington Consensus—above all, the liberal assumption that markets are natural and generally benign, while governments are artificial and likely to be malign—are alive and well, and justify a hostile predisposition for government action designed to do more than make markets more competitive (and protect property rights, intellectual property rights, and provide certain public goods that cannot be provided by competitive profit-seeking).[15]

Learning from past growth trajectories

The Economist and other organs of the Washington Consensus would claim that the reason that the opportunities opened by globalization are not seized upon is insufficient "reforms"—where "reform" means policy change that moves toward the ideal world economy in which any economic actor is able to invest, work, and sell anywhere in the world, in any sector, with national borders having no more economic significance than the borders of US states.[16] Insistence on separate regulation within state frontiers is "protectionism," an automatic negative. As markets become more liberalized, more entrepreneurs and investors will come forward—from home and abroad—to exploit the new opportunities for profit. This line of argument puts the "blame" for slow growth on developing country governments: they do not undertake sufficient reforms. It deflects attention from the policies of dominant states and from the rules of the international economy.

Is this line of argument well supported by the empirical evidence of growth trajectories? The short answer is: no better than the broader argument that globalization drives catch-up growth, as seen above.

Development policies of the now-developed countries

Hardly any of today's developed countries, with the partial exception of Britain, the first industrializer, developed on the basis of free trade. Most countries protected and promoted their infant industries on a substantial scale. The United States was "the mother country and bastion of modern protectionism" during the nineteenth and first half of the twentieth centuries, in the words of economic historian Paul Bairoch.[17] At the end of the nineteenth century, when US per capita income (measured in PPP dollars) was about equal to that of the average of developing countries today, its industrial tariffs averaged close to 50 percent, compared to around 10 percent in developing countries today.

Development policies of the East Asian tigers

The East Asian capitalist economies in the period running from the 1950s to the 1980s—the phase of rapid industrialization—experienced intensive government intervention in markets, including high rates of effective protection (though not in the city-states of Hong Kong or Singapore) and active technology-upgrading policies. Further, these interventions were not focused mainly on the market as the unit (as in "making the market work better") but on the production capacity of firms or industries, aiming to accelerate the diversification and upgrading of production.[18] They relied heavily on price-distorting incentive policies, including managed trade and managed foreign direct investment (FDI), and an array of sectorally specific incentives for exports. Taiwan also had a large public enterprise sector covering the commanding heights of the economy.

The fact that East Asian capitalist governments practiced intensive "intervention" does not necessarily mean that the intervention was important to subsequent growth, of course. Disentangling the impact of industrial policies from other things—including heavy investment in education, as well as Cold War-facilitated aid and entry to the American market for manufactured exports—is difficult. But we now have detailed studies of how these industrial policies worked, and these detailed studies make it plausible that the policies had their intended effects.

For example, Alice Amsden argues in *The Rise of the Rest* (2001) that East Asia's success in manufactured exports—and leveraging exporting success into product diversification and upgrading—was related to the governments' use of "reciprocal control mechanisms." Firms had to meet performance targets in exchange for special favors—such as targets for exporting, or local content, or product specifications.

My own work on East Asia provides lots of evidence about the nitty-gritty operation of industrial policies and the various kinds of links between policy support and outcomes. I argue that East Asian industrial policy comprised two kinds—"leading the market" and "following the market"—where "leading" refers to the government making an investment decision that private actors would not make, and "following" refers to the government supporting some of the bets of private firms or supporting a marginal extension of the production frontier in a given product.

The classic example of industrial policy of the "leadership" kind was Posco, the Korean integrated steel firm, which no private firm wanted to undertake and which the World Bank in the early 1970s advised the Korean government not to undertake on the grounds that Korea had no comparative advantage in steel (and should stick to its comparative advantage in . . . radios). By 1987 the World Bank itself swallowed hard and described Posco as "arguably the world's most efficient producer of steel," without, of course, revisiting its earlier advice.[19]

However, a lot of East Asian industrial policy was not the leadership kind. The other kind was aimed at accelerating movement in some of the directions that private entrepreneurs wanted to move in. For example, the Taiwan government used a fiscal incentive scheme that gave incentives to firms for that part of their production comprising specified frontier products. Firms producing products that met the specifications were eligible for tax holidays or accelerated depreciation or both. In 1982 the list of eligible products included "high-efficiency fluorescent tubes, limited to those which have an intensity of 80 lumen or above." Later the threshold standard of fluorescent tube eligibility for fiscal incentives was raised as the volume of production of 80 lumen tubes increased.[20]

The basic point is that the development strategy combined import replacement with export orientation—notwithstanding that these are conventionally understood as mutually exclusive. Firms were given a range of incentives to replace imports but were not thereby insulated from international competitive pressures. Industrial policy officials monitored the price and quality of domestic replacements against international comparators, and judged the assistance in relation to the trajectory of the gap. Firms understood that assistance was given on the condition that they either reduce the gap or show good export performance.

East Asia versus Latin America

In the stylized comparison between Latin America and East and South Asia we find that Washington Consensus policies have not been reliably associated with better economic performance. Latin American countries have, for the most part, been good pupils of the Washington Consensus; yet they have been steadily falling behind the North in terms of income and productive capacity. The first-generation "newly industrialized countries" (Taiwan, South Korea, Hong Kong, and Singapore) had the same aggregate GDP per capita as the big five Latin American countries in 1970. Since then, the first two have scored rather badly by Washington Consensus criteria, yet as a group they have grown faster than the G7 and opened up a wide gap with the Latin American average. India and China, too, have been star growers over the past fifteen to twenty years (though coming from average income levels in 1970 far below South East Asia and Sub-Saharan Africa); yet they would both score quite low by Washington Consensus policy criteria. Something is wrong with what is being taught when the good pupils score the low grades and the bad pupils score the high grades.

To clinch the point, consider two countries, A and B.[21] A is a member of the WTO; it undertook comprehensive trade liberalization in 1994–5 (cutting tariffs to a maximum of 15 percent and removing all quantitative restrictions, in line with the World Bank's Country Policy and Institutional Assessment formula); and has implemented far-reaching liberalization within the domestic economy, including privatization, foreign ownership of national companies, full repatriation of profits, and the like. It made itself into a model pupil of the Washington Consensus, and is also located a few hundred miles by sea from the world's biggest market. B is not a member of the WTO; it has maintained quantitative restrictions and tariffs of 30–50 percent; it conducts much of its trade through state firms and import monopolies; it restricts foreign ownership of national companies; and it is located 4,000 miles from the world's biggest market.

Liberal thinking would identify A as the likely success story. In fact, A is Haiti, the economic performance of which has been dismal, and B is Vietnam, which has grown at more than 8 percent a year since the mid 1980s, has sharply reduced poverty, and rapidly integrated with the world economy—notwithstanding those high trade barriers and restrictions on foreign ownership.

The A/B comparison makes the point that coherent state-led growth strategy to build on increasing returns and the proximity-productivity mechanism (see below) can count for more than trade liberalization; and policy integration with the world economy (such as a free-trade regime) is not a prerequisite of a successful growth strategy. On the other hand, rising trade/GDP and foreign investment/GDP are indeed likely outcomes of a successful growth strategy, and if these ratios are prevented from rising, the strategy may not remain successful. But that is not the way the matter is conceived in the Washington Consensus.

We have a substantial body of historical evidence suggesting that most countries with superior economic growth performance have also experienced active government promotion policies, including protection; even though it is also true that many countries that tried protection and import substitution had poor performance. What about theoretical mechanisms that might suggest causality from active promotion policies to superior economic performance?

New literature on industrialization and trade

Though most students of economics today have never heard of Nicolas Kaldor and his three growth laws (which were much discussed in the dim and distant 1960s), the growth laws are important for understanding economic growth and for making the case for industrial policy. Empirical generalizations rather than theory, they state that there is a strong positive correlation between the growth of manufacturing output and (1) the growth of GDP; (2) the growth of productivity in manufacturing (this one is also known as Verdoorn's law); and (3) the growth of productivity outside of manufacturing (agriculture, services, etc.).

They imply that manufacturing, or industry more generally, is a relatively more powerful engine of growth than other sectors, because of stronger input-output linkages; and that special promotion of manufacturing may be justified for its spillover benefits on (a) growth of output and (b) growth of productivity in non-manufacturing. Test-derived hypotheses across twenty-eight regions of China for the period 1965–91, and for forty-five African countries for 1980–96, are consistent with the argument that industrial activity is the "engine of growth."[22]

While Kaldor's growth laws continue to be neglected, the 1990s and 2000s have seen a burgeoning theoretical literature that has as its central theme the prevalence and multiple sources of market failure. This literature helps to give theoretical content to Kaldor's growth laws. The irony should be noted: many of the arguments about market failure that animated development economics of the 1950s and 1960s, and which were subsequently rejected as irrelevant in the 1980s and 1990s (on the grounds that however bad was market failure, government failure was surely worse), have made a comeback in development economics over the 1990s and 2000s.[23]

For example, the Big Push argument made by Rosenstein-Rodan, Nurkse, and Scitovsky more than fifty years ago has been repackaged into formal models. The core idea is the virtues of government-coordinated investment: that in the presence of increasing returns, industrialization in one sector raises demand for other sectors and raises the profitability of investment in those other sectors; but in the absence of government coordination these complementarities may not be realized.

Also making a comeback is the idea that countries can be stuck in a low-level equilibrium trap, with its implication that more than a market signal, more than market competition, is required to displace the previous equilibrium in order to make new investment projects attractive.[24] Ralph Gomery and William Baumol, and Paul Krugman and Anthony Venables, are leading theorists in this vein.[25]

The empirical starting point is the finding that the location of a given industry in one country or another is often not a matter of comparative advantage but of accident and path dependence. There is no comparative advantage reason why Switzerland has long dominated the watch industry, why Taiwan now dominates the production (but not branding) of laptops, or why Pakistan specializes in soccer balls and Bangladesh specializes in hats (rather than the other way around). It turns out that industries have different "retainability" scores, in the sense that some industries, once established, are sheltered from the blast of full competition and can earn "super-normal" returns, because would-be competitors have difficulty breaking in.

One of the key analytical mechanisms is the increasing returns link from spatial proximity to productivity ("proximity promotes productivity"). Denser clusters of economic activity—in both product markets and labour markets—promote productivity more than looser ones, up to some point of diminishing returns resulting from rising congestion and other costs. This kind of market "externality" explains why spatially clustered networks of supporting industries are often important for the growth of any one industry. Think of Silicon Valley. Boeing's switch of component suppliers to China illustrates the opposite process: US-based component suppliers stop producing in the US, US supply networks fragment, causing knock-on costs to other industries, and Chinese firms buy US component-making technology, the better to supply companies like Boeing from China.

In a world of increasing returns rather than constant or diminishing, as in standard models, the existing market equilibrium may not be optimal. Equilibrium allocations of industries across countries are (a) often fragile and (b) not necessarily "globally" optimal (globally in the sense of better than any feasible alternative, not in the geographical sense). But the market lacks a mechanism for getting to that optimum. The theory suggests that trade liberalization would not necessarily shunt the economy into a more desirable position than it could have reached with more activist trade and industrial policy, contrary to standard comparative advantage theory.[26]

This line of argument highlights that the theory of comparative advantage is essentially short-term, being about how an economy can best exploit its present stock of resources. It cannot tackle the trade-off between acting today to maximize short-term efficiency and acting today to accelerate the economy's shift of tomorrow's comparative advantage into higher value-added, higher return products.

The multiple equilibria theory suggests a new rationale for "infant industry protection," a long but grudgingly accepted partial exception to the general prescription of free trade. In conventional trade theory, the infant industry exception is presumed to apply—if at all—only to newly industrializing countries trying to lay down basic industries that already exist elsewhere. Multiple equilibria theory suggests that the continuous technological evolution of the world economy means that parts of many industries are always "infants," even in the most technologically advanced economies. Governments, even in advanced economies, should take up the task of capturing "high retainability" industries for their jurisdiction, using trade and other industrial policy instruments—even at the cost of short-term inefficiency. The new thinking suggests how strategic industrial policy (including trade as well as technology and education policy) can help in securing the economy's place in higher-potential industries with higher "retainability" scores. But it is critical that the intervention be temporary so that the market then supports the better equilibrium unaided.[27]

Of course, each government tries to disguise what it is doing and to get others to embrace free trade. This is the mercantilist strategy of "optimal obfuscation of national interests."

In these terms we can make sense of the observed intense rivalry between nations as they jockey for industrial advantage—a far cry from the harmonious world of comparative advantage theory (one of its strongest selling points for the international development community, which constitutionally must promote the rhetoric of "mutual benefit" and de-emphasize "conflicting interests"). The rivalry among developed nations is implemented not mainly with trade instruments like tariffs, but with more subtle, less noticeable behind-the-border instruments like anti-dumping legislation, anti-trust, rules of origin, health standards, and government procurement. The rivalry helps to explain why the business school myth of multinational corporations as free-floating, cosmopolitan entities owing allegiance to nowhere, is just that, a myth. State support tends to be geared toward high-tech firms regarded as "nationals" of the same state: the US state channels its support more toward American firms than to foreign firms operating in America, as do states of the other two core zones of the world economy.

In these terms we can also make sense of the difficult-to-deny motive behind the Doha trade agenda (devised almost entirely by the US and the EU)—to hold back developing countries from advancing into industrial and service areas now dominated by the developed countries.[28] The theory shows that productivity growth in the less-productive trading partners of an advanced country (e.g. productivity growth in China and Vietnam *vis-à-vis* the US) is not necessarily in the interests of the advanced country. None other than Paul Samuelson recently developed an argument along these lines, showing that as China catches up in the production of goods that had been produced in the US (whether through outsourcing or domestic innovation), US export prices fall, worsening the US terms of trade. The US still benefits from trade as compared to the alternative of no trade, but less than before.[29]

This body of theory shows how, in contrast to models of comparative advantage which focus on the link between an economy's efficiency of resource use and the openness of markets, a country's rate of growth is much affected by its production structure—its pattern of specialization (a point also made by Kaldor's growth laws as well as by Wassily Leontief's analysis of input-output structures). An economy with more activity in sectors with increasing returns tends to have a higher return on capital and a higher investment rate. Governments that implement coordinated investment programs can achieve industrialization across several sectors at lower explicit cost in terms of industrial policy support than a country that industrializes piecemeal via investment decisions coordinated only through the market or within individual firms.

Another strand of this theoretical literature focuses on firms, as distinct from macro policy regimes, and on knowledge or technology as distinct from factor accumulation. Here technology is treated not (as it was in the 1950s–1980s) as a missing input, akin to capital or labor, but as a learning process. As Sanjay Lall put it, "industrial success in developing countries depends essentially on how enterprises manage the process of mastering, adapting and improving upon existing technologies. The process is difficult and prone to widespread and diffuse market failures."[30] Public support, he says, is often crucial to help build their technological capabilities.

Public support may entail creating "rents" for first-mover firms, via market barriers to entry of one kind or another or via additional public returns to selected activities or products, in contrast to the passive price-taking firms of comparative statics. From this more Schumpeterian perspective, rents, or super-normal profits, are seen as a necessary but not sufficient condition for rapid technological advance, quite contrary to the prevailing view in development economics since Ann Krueger's classic 1974 article that portrayed rents as undermining efficiency and the trump card against selective state interventions.[31] From the Schumpeterian perspective the main qualification to the need for rents is whether governments can discipline the rent-receivers into not growing fat and lazy on their rents, but use the rents for productive reinvestment. Taiwan's fiscal incentive scheme (described above) can be seen as one way to do this disciplining automatically. Later, this chapter extends the discussion about how to discipline rents.

The policy implications of this upheaval in trade theory, and in growth theory more generally, have hardly begun to be developed, but it is clear that they seriously complicate the old verities about free trade and market liberalization. However, even those who have done most to develop the new theories—and to show theoretical mechanisms by which countries might gain from selective interventions—tend to row back toward free trade as the best practical policy. Paul Krugman, for example, developed an elaborate theoretical explanation of why free trade is not optimal for national economies or the world, and then declared at the end, "Free trade rules are best for a world whose politics are as imperfect as its markets."[32] Krugman and the others justify the divorce of theory from policy by appealing to the danger that any more strategic policy would be hijacked by special interests. Yet they make no analysis of this claim, in contrast to their sophisticated arguments against free trade. The row-back to free trade via unanalyzed politics sustains their honorable membership of the neoclassical sect.

Managing foreign direct investment

The new theoretical literature that shows the desirability of coordinating investment and protecting firms until they generate adequate returns tends to ignore ownership, treating firms as nationally owned. But today any catch-up growth strategy must address the question of how to deal with transnational companies and their global strategies. For example, how much should policy aim to encourage firms to integrate into production hierarchies controlled by transnationals and how much to emphasize national research and development (R&D) and purchase of foreign technologies without foreign ownership. (Because classical liberal economics never had to deal with these questions, we should perhaps use the phrase "new liberal" economics rather than just "liberal" economics.)

The new liberal Washington Consensus says that foreign direct investment is good for development and that more is better. In yet another demonstration that the Washington Consensus is still alive and well, the finance ministers of the Group of Eight industrial countries decried what they called the "new investment protectionism" in their draft communiqué for the G8 meeting in June 2007. They declared, "restrictions to market access for foreign investment should only apply to exceptional cases where national security is at stake."[33] Foreign takeovers of domestic firms should be unrestricted.

Theodore Moran's recent study, called "Harnessing Foreign Direct Investment for Development,"[34] takes a more nuanced view. It makes a sharp distinction between FDI that is not integrated into the parent firm's global production chain and oriented to selling on a protected domestic market, on the one hand, and FDI that is integrated into the parent firm's global production chain and oriented to exporting, on the other. The former generates net costs for the host economy, the latter net benefits, says Moran. He is critical of any attempt to impose domestic content requirements or limits on foreign ownership (such as a maximum of 49 percent of equity in the hands of the foreign company), on grounds that such requirements lead the foreign parent to use production technologies and business operations far back from the industry frontier and to produce high-cost, inferior products. On the other hand, "Plants built as part of the parent corporation's strategy to compete in international markets invariably incorporate full economies of scale and operate with cutting-edge technologies, production techniques, and quality-control procedures" (10). But the condition for the host to reap these benefits is to avoid domestic content and joint venture requirements, says Moran.

As for the balance between relying on FDI and emphasizing national R&D and purchase of technology licenses for national firms, Moran argues that the latter is potentially viable only in industries where technology is stable and can be replicated with a combination of licenses and imported technical training. Korea's entry into ships and steel in the 1970s through this "national champion" route was accomplished in these conditions of stable and purchasable technology. But even Korea, which is often held up as a model of an alternative route to technological learning without relying on FDI, did rely on FDI in electronics, where foreign investors laid the base for an internationally competitive electronics industry in Korea from the mid 1960s to the mid 1970s. More generally, Moran argues that in most sectors the only sensible strategy for developing countries is to attract in export-oriented FDI as the prime channel for technological learning: "[F]oreign investors not only introduce new activities into the host economy but also continuously upgrade the technologies, management techniques, and quality-control procedures of their affiliates to keep their sourcing networks at the competitive frontier in the international industry" (21).

Moran's argument is more nuanced than the Washington Consensus's "the more FDI the better," but it is misleading in several ways.[35] First, by suggesting that FDI can play a major role in the development of developing countries in general, it downplays the fact that FDI to developing countries is highly concentrated in a very small number of developing countries: roughly 80 percent goes to only ten countries. The vast majority receives very little. In 1980 the concentration was more or less the same as today—indicating that the evolutionary hope that FDI would spread out across more and more developing countries has not been realized.

Second, the distinction between import-substituting FDI that receives protection but is also under domestic content and joint venture requirements, on the one hand, and on the other, export-oriented FDI that receives no protection and has no domestic content or joint venture requirements, is too sharp and too static.

Moran himself cites approvingly an example that shows how important it is in practical terms not to make the distinction: the case of Singapore's Economic Development Board, which subsidized the salary of an engineer or manager in foreign affiliates whose job it was to hunt out and assist indigenous firms to become suppliers. *Governing the Market* (1990) describes how Taiwan's Industrial Development Bureau (IDB) performed the same function itself, its engineers seeking to marry (export-oriented) foreign affiliates with domestic suppliers, using a variety of more or less subtle means to pressure the foreign affiliates into the marriage—thereby replacing imports, but always with an eye on maintaining the international competitiveness of the foreign affiliate's products. Local content requirements and joint venture requirements were part of the bargaining tools. In motorcycles, for example, two Taiwan firms became major global producers thanks to the combination of joint ventures with Japanese firms, trade protection, and rising local content requirements.

In other words, Moran's two types are not necessarily alternatives; they can be complementary. It is possible to have gradations of both, and to begin with the former and move toward the latter.

Third, Moran's argument ignores evidence on the harmful effects of FDI in Latin America, where foreign firms have dominated the most dynamic manufacturing sectors since their inception, their share of sales relative to national firms increasing with trade liberalization over the 1990s. Without a strong push from government to build up domestic suppliers, transnationals' global strategies have led them to source many of their specialized inputs from abroad, and even to disintegrate existing vertical supplier links within the national economy. The effect has been to shrink intermediate and supplier industries. Yet much evidence suggests that the growth of intermediate inputs and producer services within the national economy is an essential part of industrialization, for these are typically rich sites of innovation.[36]

In the case of Argentina, for example, Kosacoff says, "the data show that the manufacturing sector has itself utilized trade openness and economic deregulation to increase its imports not only of parts and components but of finished production too. This is indicative of a trend toward the vertical de-integration of activities that affects both manufacturing activities . . . and commercialization activities."[37]

The upshot is that reliance on transnational corporations (TNC) can produce an import-intensive or deficit-prone industrialization process. We see this deficit-prone industrialization throughout Latin America, where exports of natural resource processing industries, foodstuffs, and primary commodities have grown quickly, while imports of capital goods and intermediate goods have grown even faster. Also, this pattern of TNC-led growth has caused a rapid increase in economic concentration, as small and medium enterprises, which earlier had supplied big national firms, were marginalized by imports. Mexico's income elasticity of import demand has doubled over the past 15–20 years. All these negative effects are seen even where the growth of output and exports from TNC activities is high, because the multiplier effects and technological spillovers from them to the rest of the economy turn out to be typically low.

The case of FDI illustrates a more general point: FDI can bring large benefits to a developing country host economy, but it can also—individually and in aggregate—bring large costs. The government must build up capacity to be able to manage FDI strategically so as to raise the benefits and reduce the costs. But in the majority of developing countries, FDI will continue to remain marginal, which puts more onus on building up the capacity of national firms to respond to international competition.

Establishing a developmental state

It is one thing to make a case for a more proactive role of the state than the Washington Consensus allows; it is another to identify how to do it. The Washington Consensus came to be extended over the 1990s to include a good governance agenda for strengthening the capacity of the state to provide certain kinds of public goods. The content of the agenda was derived from the proposition that developing countries should undertake institutional reforms aimed at moving toward the degree of formalization and depersonalization of economic rules as found in developed countries. That meant formalizing and enforcing property rights, reducing corruption, improving the effectiveness of the bureaucracy, the judiciary, and the police, and strengthening transparency and political account-ability. The argument was that as rules became more formalized, more impersonal, actors would become more confident in undertaking economic transactions. This would promote investment, which would raise growth rates—out of which the institutions that improved the security of transactions could be further strength-ened, in a virtuous circle.

Indeed, when developing and transitional countries as a group are compared to developed countries, they show markedly less formalization of rules. But this does not mean that the Washington Consensus good governance agenda is correct in urging the former to give high priority to establishing a system of formalized and impersonal rules. If we use a weaker criterion of catch-up than in the earlier discussion—average growth between 1990 and 2004 greater than or less than that of the developed-country average—we find that roughly a third of a sample of seventy developing and transitional countries experienced catch-up growth.[38] The key institutional features differentiating the catch-up countries from the falling-behind countries are not those of the good governance agenda. Many catch-up countries have low scores in terms of the formalization of their rules, yet have grown relatively fast over a sustained period. Countries with equivalent levels of governance show very different economic performance.

The key discriminating institutional features between the catch-up countries and the falling-behind countries are related to the state's capacity to coordinate agents, stabilize their confidence in the state's behavior, and establish national development as an urgent overarching project.[39] These seem to substitute for across-the-board formalization of rules (to which the extended Washington Consensus attaches high priority). On the face of it, raising the state's capacity to coordinate a selected set of economic agents is a more feasible task than across-the-board formalization and enforcement of rules—a task which requires high fixed costs and many decades, and which often provokes fierce resistance, especially from those already in the elite.

Developing countries tend to be regulated by what Douglas North calls "limited access social orders" (as distinct from "open social orders" more characteristic of developed countries), or what could also be called "insider systems."[40] They include the celebrated East Asian catch-up cases, such as South Korea and Taiwan, which all through their high-growth decades operated with strikingly informal, personalized rules of the game and with well-developed insider systems, oiled by plenty of corruption—which nevertheless generated high and sustained economic growth and carried out a subsequent transformation toward a formal and depersonalized mode of regulation.

To oversimplify, many of the catch-up countries created a system of coordination for the insider groups, which constituted the "developmental state." The groups whose specific interests counted most in shaping the content of the "national good" were incorporated in the coordination system, and their sustained interaction and negotiation in one or more focal points encouraged them to mute their oligopolistic struggles for access to rents, to define convergent interests, and thereby to forge a sense of common interest. Their interaction in the focal point created information and incentives such that it served wider interests than their own specific ones.

They interacted inside the focal points as they did in the wider society, using informal, personalized rules, but now disciplined by the logic of repeated interaction in the focal point and the emerging sense of a common interest. Their interactions would not score well by the criteria of the good governance agenda.

The involved public officials acted so as to steer the private calculations of private coalitions in the direction of a larger and longer-term national interest. "Steerage" is different from top-down instruction (as in the conventional meaning of dirigisme), as it is also different from bottom-up capture; and it spans the conventional western opposition between private and public elites. It is a notion wholly unfamiliar in the US and the UK civil service, except in the defense industries, where industrial policy flourishes though never named as such.

The basic bargain of the state-business alliance was that business received assistance from the state in finance, technology, and marketing, in return for delivering performance as measured by indicators such as exporting, or import-replacing, or reducing the gap between international and domestic prices, or increasing proportion of local content.

From its role in helping business success, the state gained legitimacy for further interventions, and the circle became virtuous rather than vicious. On the other hand, where the state provided protection and subsidies without performance conditions, failure was more likely and the same circle became vicious. Exhibit A is India for several decades after the Second World War, notably its automobile industry.

One of the tasks of the public officials was to steer the insiders to support measures of inclusionary growth, or growth that was sufficiently inclusionary to offset discontent among outsiders that could be exploited by one or other coalition of insiders in a way that would destabilize the insider system. In East Asia, heavy public spending in rural areas after land reforms helped to buy off discontent,[41] as did social housing in Singapore and the social security system in France (much of which *The Economist* excoriated as "nanny state").

Concrete manifestations of this kind of institutionalized coordination include Japan's MITI, Taiwan's Economic Planning Council and its Industrial Development Bureau, South Korea's Economic Planning Board, Singapore's Economic Development Board; and also numerous industry associations. In France, the Commissariat General au Plan, established in 1946, was another important example. In some countries, sectoral focal points have been more important than national ones: in Brazil, automobiles and aircraft; Colombia, coffee; Chile, several agroprocessing sectors; and Italy, IRI (the giant public-sector holding company) and sector associations of a decentralized kind mainly in the center and north of the country.

In South Korea, the Economic Planning Board acted as the peak state organization, headed by the deputy prime minister, with authority over the other ministries. It was complemented by a dense array of subordinate forums of consultation between state agencies and business groups. Through these forums the big business groups (*chaebol*) sought help from the state in order to assist them to compete internationally and replace imports, and they used corruption as an informal tool of credit allocation.

In the Philippines, by contrast, the big landed families—lacking such institutionalized focal points—used personalized rules of the game to obtain political protection in order to oppose industrial transformation, and used corruption to protect their existing sources of rents and assassinate interlopers.

India's Planning Commission was intended to have a similar peak coordinating and strategizing function, but the offensive against it by business in the 1950s opened the way for ministries to revolt against its authority, and it was never able to function in this way.[42]

Three conditions are important for the coordination mechanism to have prodevelopmental effects. First, the state and the business groups should be relatively evenly balanced. The state must insist that business respect the quid pro quo, which means that in return for political patronage and protection, business does not challenge the government politically or try to directly penetrate the political sphere (e.g., by placing family members in state agencies to act on businesses' behalf). Failure to insist on this separation leads to the Philippines.

Where (as in Korea before the transition to democracy in 1988) a small set of government and business elites, organized in peak organizations and organizationally separate from each other, are evenly balanced, with neither side having the upper hand, political protection and corruption (rent-seeking) can have relatively benign effects. Where one side has the upper hand, the effects may be less benign. Democratization in Korea had the effect of fragmenting the state and strengthening big business, breaking the previous balance. Thereafter the state lost effectiveness as a development agency and big business escaped national discipline (e.g., via borrowing abroad), both of which contributed to the 1997–9 crash. In the Philippines, on the other hand, democratization has somewhat restrained a state that, under Marcos, plundered from the top down, and moved the nation a little way in the direction of a joint state-business project of a developmental state.

The second condition relates to the mindset of public officials. The public officials engaged in governing the market should operate with an activist, public-service-oriented mindset of the kind suggested by the quote displayed in the entrance to the Industrial Development Bureau in Taipei: "The most important thing in life is to have a goal, and the determination to achieve it."[43] In its assumption of activism, this mindset is approximately opposite that of senior British civil servants working on economic issues, as articulated by one who declared in 1930, "If I leave the office on Saturday feeling confident that in the past week I have done no harm, then I am well content."[44] The descendants of this breed of "do no harm" civil servants came to shape the world view of much of the World Bank, and were key to the restoration of "right thinking" in the Bank after the McNamara-Chenery interregnum. One of the early events in this restoration was the Bank's *Accelerated Development in Sub-Saharan Africa: An Agenda for Action* (1981), which portrayed post-colonial policy and performance in Africa as disastrous and ushered in what became the conventional wisdom on the state in Africa: an undifferentiated source of pathologies.[45]

Third, the state should create bifurcated political and economic administrative structures, such that political patronage can be given via political channels without sacrificing economic efficiency. In Korea, the government created in the early 1970s the New Community (Saemaul) Movement, a gigantic hierarchy of offices, budgets, plans, and activities centered in the President's office and extending down to private firms, urban boroughs, government departments, and rural counties.[46] President Park declared it a "national spiritual revolution for a better way of life," "a driving force for nation-building" via increased productivity, community participation in local infrastructure projects, and education in the policies of the government and the thinking of its great leader (himself). Saemaul groups from across the country were brought together periodically at various levels of the hierarchy, culminating in the Saemaul Institute near Seoul, for education and motivation. Through this channel much patronage and protection flowed, rewarding supporters and not rewarding dissidents, separate from the economic departments of government.[47]

Conclusion

Liberal or "new liberal" economics continues to dominate development policy-making. It continues to use misleading policy dichotomies like "import substitution" vs "export orientation," and to load the virtues onto one and the vices onto the other. It is an Old Testament kind of religion. And in its political economy, the new liberal paradigm not only assumes that market failure is less than government failure, but that developing country states are typically "neopatrimonial" and even worse than states-in-general, and therefore to be constrained as much as possible by markets.

The preceding discussion illustrates how we can get beyond such crudities by examining actual states and their configurations with business interests. Such examination suggests rules of thumb for the institutional configurations out of which appropriate development strategies are likely to emerge with some chance of being effectively implemented. The severe global economic crisis that began in 2008 is forcing even liberal market states like the US and the UK to overcome their long aversion to taking responsibility for structural outcomes and take center stage in saving their plunging economies. As they move beyond ad hoc emergency responses toward more strategic responses, their move may open the way for a larger reconsideration of the role of the state in development in places like the World Bank. In a *New Yorker* cartoon, a messenger runs into the castle just as the executioner is about to behead the king and shouts, "Stop! Wait! Government is not the problem, it is the solution."

My argument for pro-active industrial policy designed to accelerate the growth of industry boils down to four testable propositions: (1) Kaldor's growth laws are empirically valid in developing countries with large agricultural or mining sectors; here there is a strong positive correlation between the growth of manufacturing output and the growth of productivity in both manufacturing and non-manufacturing. (2) The "China price" means that manufacturing sectors throughout the developing world are under intense competitive pressure and many are shrinking. (3) Industrial policy can help to accelerate restructuring and diversification of the kind needed to survive Chinese competition. However, (4) the industrial policy must be of the "open economy" kind, not the inward-looking kind used in many developing countries through the 1950s and the 1970s, and it must use "reciprocal control mechanisms," where state assistance is given against performance. Just slapping on protection yields the pre-liberalization Indian automobile industry, which for decades produced replicas of 1955 British Morris cars.

I also stress the need to avoid the trap of thinking that industrial policy equals "picking winners," and that it is like a light switch, either "on" or "off," "present" or "absent." Industrial policy can be big or small, discontinuous or incremental. It can "lead" the market or—less riskily—"follow" the market. Much East Asian industrial policy was of the "followership" kind, and involved nudging private producers to extend their production capabilities by degrees (producing more sophisticated fluorescent lights, for example) and nudging foreign affiliates to switch supplies of intermediate goods from imports to domestic firms. East Asian industrial policy provides concrete examples of how to do small-scale, market-following industrial policy of a nudging kind, which may be relevant in countries with embryonic manufacturing sectors and few highly trained engineers. But before this can be done, politicians and civil servants have to stop being "the slaves of some defunct economist," in Keynes' phrase, or more accurately, the slaves of the new liberal ideas of many very living economists located in or trained in the centers of the discipline in the United States and Britain—not coincidentally the two hegemonic powers of the past 150 years.

Notes

1. I do not use the term "neoliberal" because it has come to be used only with negative valence, which makes it more suitable for rhetoric than for analysis. At the level of policy prescription coming from organizations that purport to "prescribe for national governments what is good for both national economies and the world economy," liberal economics (one of whose expressions is the Washington Consensus) has eclipsed all others since the 1980s – including the model of import-substituting industrialization, the developmental state, and Keynesian economics. For reasons suggested later, it may be better to speak of "new liberal" economics to differentiate it from classical liberalism.
2. Freeman (2009).
3. See Wolf (2004) for this argument.
4. See chapter 7 in Milanovic (2005). See also the discussion below, using a weaker criterion of catch-up growth.
5. Wade (2008, 2004b).
6. Korzeniewicz and Moran (2009).
7. Rodrik (2008).
8. Wade (2009, 2007).
9. *The New York Times*, February 9, 2002, p. 1.
10. Woodall (2006: 3).
11. Mankiw (2006).

12. Lapper (2004). In the late 1990s, Brazil's finance minister declared, "Today there are only two choices: you are either a neoliberal or a neomoron."

13. The government that took power in Mongolia after the end of Communism in 1991 embarked on a program of fast economic liberalization, making it a star pupil of the Washington Consensus. The result was a collapse of the industrial sector, fast-rising urban unemployment, an influx of pastoralism, fall in pastoral yields, and a sharp deterioration in "social indicators," which had been high in the era of protected industry relative to Mongolia's average income. However, the government did want to retain a primitive industrial policy instrument, namely an export tax on unprocessed wool. The Asia Development Bank offered the government a big loan on condition that the government drop the export tax. The government obliged, and Mongolia's wool came to be processed in China and Italy. See Reinert (2004: 157–214). Fast-forward to 2002, when a German Development Bank mission arrived in Ulan Bator to help with Mongolia's WTO accession. The mission discussed Mongolia's situation with the World Bank country director. It floated the idea of restoring an export tax on unprocessed wool. The World Bank country director put his foot down. He said (as recalled by a participant), "That would be going backwards. We don't want the government to intervene in the economy. We want the government to stick to free trade." Most economists dismiss evidence of this kind as mere "anecdote," as though the next observation could reverse the big picture. I predict that a large set of observations of World Bank economics staff and country directors in action would support the picture from the Mongolian case (though with more deference to "political realities" in important borrowers like India and China, without a change in the economics). See also the impact of Fund/Bank conditionality in Cramer (1999).

14. Stanculescu (2007) and personal communication with author.

15. William Easterly, former World Bank economist and author of *The Elusive Quest for Growth*, admits that the big-picture evidence does not support core ideas of the Washington Consensus, and declares the lack of support a "mystery." Interviewed in 2002, Easterly said, "Things had gone very well in the 1960s and 1970s in developing countries. They had grown about as fast as the rich countries, and some of them considerably faster.... [T]here was a huge reversal of fortune just at the time when much of the advice that is standard today was becoming fashionable.... And just as all of these efforts [of reform] should have been bearing fruit, they failed." Asked why the typically developing country did well in the 1960s and 1970s when there was so much government intervention, often in the form of import substituting trade regimes, he said, "It is a bit of a mystery why they did well.... the growth had a lot of mystery for me.... It is mysterious to those [like me] who advocate hands-off markets." See Easterly (2002) "The Failure of Development Economics," *Challenge*, 45 (1): 88–103. By declaring the relative success of developing countries under regimes of import substitution and other forms of "government intervention" a mystery, Easterly protects the Washington Consensus from re-examination, and helps to enable opinion-makers like the World Economic Forum, *The Economist*, Gregory Mankiw and others to continue to advocate liberal economic policies for all. It is an interesting question as to why liberal ideas have such power to replicate themselves in the minds of successive generations of graduate students and journalists and fight off contrary evidence. For a striking example, with very

unfortunate consequences, see the statement of Ben Bernanke, then chairman of the Council of Economic Advisors, in August 2005: "It is important to point out that house prices are being supported in very large part by very strong fundamentals . . . We have lots of jobs, employment, high incomes, very low mortgage rates, growing population, and shortages of land and housing in many areas. And those supply-and-demand factors are a big reason why house prices have risen as much as they have." Quoted in Cassidy (2008).

16. Wolf (2004: 4).
17. Bairoch (1993: 30); Chang (2002).
18. Lee, Mathews, and Wade (2007).
19. Wade (2004a: 319).
20. Wade (2004a: Appendix A); Wade (1990).
21. This comparison comes from Rodrik (2007).
22. See Thirlwall (2006: 117–20). Data presents a problem particularly for the non-manufacturing sectors. The derived hypotheses may be less true today in developed countries than in developing countries with a large, low productivity agricultural sector and a large service sector made up of services of a low productivity "informal" or clientelistic government kind. For developed countries, see McCombie, Pugno, and Soro (2003).
23. Shapiro (2005). See also Wade (2010).
24. Goodacre (2007); Palley (2006).
25. Gomery and Baumol (2000); Krugman and Venables (1995).
26. For an African application see Page (2008).
27. For new arguments for infant industry protection see also Melitz (2005).
28. Wade (2006). WTO agreements (on intellectual property, on industrial subsidies, government procurement, and the like) have become prime weapons by which the North tries to maintain its "levitation" against counter-forces, such as the growing migration to the South of professional jobs formerly concentrated in the North, and the growing migration to the South of professionals trained in the North.
29. Samuelson (2004).
30. Lall (2003: 15).
31. Krueger (1974).
32. Krugman (1987).
33. Beattie (2007).
34. Moran (2006).
35. Note that "80 percent in 10 countries" is from the mid 1990s. See "Symposium on Infant Industries," (2003) with contributions from John Roberts, Robert Wade, Sanjaya Lall, and Adrian Wood, *Oxford Development Studies*, 31(1): 3–20.
36. Ciccone and Matsuyama (1996).
37. Kosacoff (2000: 188).
38. Khan (2006).
39. Meisel (2008).
40. North, Wallis, and Weingast (2006).
41. Wade (1982, 2004).
42. Chibber (2003).
43. Weiss and Thurbon (2004).

44. Allen (1975).
45. Mkandawire (2001).
46. Wade (1982).
47. Wade (2004a); Chen (2008).

References

Allen, G. C. (1975). "Advice from Economists – Forty-Five Years Ago," *Three Banks Review*, 106: 35–50.

Bairoch, P. (1993). *Economics and World History: Myths and Paradoxes*. Chicago: University of Chicago Press.

Beattie, A. (2007). "Ownership is not the Real Problem with China," *Financial Times*, 16 April.

Cassidy, J. (2008). "Anatomy of a Meltdown," *The New Yorker*, 1 December: 54.

Chang, H.-J. (2002). *Kicking Away the Ladder*. London: Anthem.

Chen, L. (2008). "Preferences, Institutions and Politics: Re-Interrogating the Theoretical Lessons of Developmental Economies," *New Political Economy*, 13 (1): 89–102.

Chibber, V. (2003). *Locked in Place*. Princeton, NJ: Princeton University Press.

Ciccone, A. and Matsuyama, K. (1996). "Start-Up Costs and Pecuniary Externalities as Barriers to Economic Development," *Journal of Development Economics*, 59: 33–59.

Cramer, C. (1999). "Can Africa Industrialize by Processing Primary Commodities? The Case of Mozambican Cashew Nuts," *World Development*, 27 (7): 1247–66.

Freeman, A. (2009). "The Poverty of Statistics and the Statistics of Poverty," *Third World Quarterly*, 30 (8): 1427–48.

Gomery, R. and Baumol, W. (2000). *Global Trade and Conflicting National Interests*. Boston: MIT Press.

Goodacre, A. (2007). "What Would Post-Autistic Trade Policy Be?," *Post-Autistic Economics Review*, 41: 2–8.

Khan, M. (2006). *Governance and Anti-Corruption Reforms in Developing Countries*, No. 42. Geneva: UNCTAD.

Korzeniewicz, R. P. and Moran, T. (2009). *Unveiling Inequality: A World-Historical Perspective*. New York: Russell Sage Foundation.

Kosacoff, B. (ed.) (2000). *Corporate Strategies Under Structural Adjustment in Argentina*. New York: St Martin's Press.

Krueger, K. (1974). "The Political Economy of the Rent-Seeking Society," *American Economic Review*, 64 (3): 291–303.

Krugman, P. (1987). "Is Free Trade Passé?," *Journal of Economic Perspectives*, 1: 143.

—— and A. Venables (1995). "Globalisation and the Inequality of Nations," *Quarterly Journal of Economics*, 110: 857–80.

Lall, S. (2003). "Reinventing Industrial Strategy: The Role of Government Policy in Building Industrial Competitiveness." Paper for Intergovernmental Group on Monetary Affairs (G24).

Lapper, R. (2004). "Latin America Quick to Dance to China's Tune," *Financial Times*, 11 November, available at <http://www.ft.com/cms/s/0/0cdbc92c-3350-11d9-b6c3-00000e2511c8.html?nclick_check=1>.

Lee, K., Mathews, J., and Wade, R. (2007). "Rethinking Development Policy: From Washington Consensus to the Beijing-Seoul-Tokyo Consensus," *Financial Times*, 19 October.

Mankiw, N. G. (2006). "Repeat After Me," *The Wall Street Journal*, 3 January.

McCombie, J., Pugno, M., and Soro, B. (2003). *Productivity Growth and Economic Performance: Essays on Verdoorn's Law*. New York: Macmillan.

Meisel, N. (2008). "Is 'Good Governance' a Good Development Strategy?" Working Paper 58. Paris: Agence Francaise de Developpement.

Melitz, M. (2005). "When and How Should Infant Industries be Protected?," *Journal of International Economics*, 66: 177–96.

Milanovic, B. (2005). *Worlds Apart: Measuring International and Global Inequality*. Princeton, NJ: Princeton University Press.

Mkandawire, T. (2001). "Thinking about Developmental States in Africa," *Cambridge Journal of Economics*, 25: 289–313.

Moran, T. (2006). *Harnessing Foreign Direct Investment for Development*. Washington, DC: Center for Global Development.

North, D., Wallis, J., and Weingast, B. (2006). "A Conceptual Framework for Interpreting Recorded Human History," Working Paper 12795. Cambridge: National Bureau of Economic Research.

Page, J. (2008). "Rowing Against the Current: The Diversification Challenge in Africa's Resource-Rich Economies," Global Economy Working Paper 29. Washington, DC: Brookings Institution.

Palley, T. (2006). "Rethinking Trade and Trade Policy: Gomery, Baumol and Samuelson on Comparative Advantage," Public Policy Brief 86. Annandale-on-Hudson, NY: Levy Economics Institute.

Reinert, E. (2004). "Globalization in the Periphery as a Morgenthau Plan: The Underdevelopment of Mongolia in the 1990s," in E. Reinert (ed.), *Globalization, Economic Development and Inequality*. Cheltenham: Edward Elgar.

Rodrik, D. (2007). "The Global Governance of Trade as if Development Really Mattered," *One Economics, Many Recipes*. Princeton, NJ: Princeton University Press.

—— (2008). "The Death of the Globalization Consensus," Policy Innovations, July 30, Carnegie Council.

Samuelson, P. (2004). "Where Ricardo and Mill Rebut and Confirm Arguments of Mainstream Economists Supporting Globalization," *Journal of Economic Perspectives*, 18: 135–46.

Shapiro, H. (2005). "Industrial Policy and Growth," United Nations Department of Economics and Social Affairs (DESA) Working Paper No. 53. Available at <http://www.un.org/esa/desa/papers/2007/wp53_2007.pdf>.

Stanculescu, D. (2007)."Stuck in the Rut of Primary Commodity Production: Why Does Mali Continue to Fail to Industrialize?" M.Sc. dissertation, Development Studies Institute, London School of Economics.

Thirlwall, A. P. (2006). *Growth and Development*. Basingstoke: Palgrave.

Wade, R. (1982). *Irrigation and Agricultural Politics in South Korea*. Boulder: Westview Press.

—— (1990). "Industrial Policy in East Asia: Does it Lead or Follow the Market?" in G. Gereffi and D. Wyman (eds.), *Manufacturing Miracles: Paths of Industrialization in Latin America and East Asia*. Princeton, NJ: Princeton University Press.

—— (2004a). *Governing the Market*. Princeton, NJ: Princeton University Press.

—— (2004b). "On the Causes of Increasing World Poverty and Inequality, or Why the Matthew Effect Prevails," *New Political Economy*, 9 (2): 163–88.

—— (2006). "Goodbye Doha, Hello New Trade Round," *Challenge*, Nov.–Dec. 52 (1): 14–19.

—— (2007). "The Washington Consensus," *International Encyclopedia of the Social Sciences*. Farmington Hills, MI: Gale.

—— (2008). "Globalization, Growth, Poverty, Inequality, Resentment and Imperialism," in J. Ravenhill (ed.), *Global Political Economy*, 2nd edn. Oxford: Oxford University Press.

—— (2009). "Is the Washington Consensus Dead?," *Antipodes*, forthcoming.

—— (2010). "Does Trade Liberalization Promote Economic Prosperity?," in P. Haas, J. Hird, and B. McBratney (eds.), *Controversies in Globalization*. Washington, DC: Congressional Quarterly Press.

Weiss, L. and Thurbon, E. (2004). "Where There's a Will There's a Way: Governing the Market in Times of Uncertainty," *Issues and Studies*, 40 (1): 61–72.

Wolf, M. (2004). *Why Globalization Works*. New Haven: Yale University Press.

Woodall, P. (2006). "The New Titans," *The Economist*, September 16: 3–34.

9

Institutional Capacity and Policy Choices for Latecomer Technology Development[*]

Banji O. Oyeyinka and Padmashree Gehl Sampath

Introduction

In a world of perfect information and perfect competition, institutions may be assumed away. In a perfect market, efficient allocation requires a competitive contracting process with perfectly informed, rational, utility-maximizing individuals, the absence of transaction costs, and the absence of externalities to third parties (Kreps 1995). In the absence of these parameters, transaction costs occur for reasons of information asymmetries, bounded rationality of agents, and uncertainty. All of these factors cause market imperfections and contractual incompleteness, and prevent optimal allocation of resources for innovation.

Most developing countries do not possess formal institutions to support innovation processes (North 1990; Chang 2001) and some do not even have the awareness of the imperative of these institutions. This results in externalities and coordination failures—a situation that takes on new and urgent notes in addressing underdevelopment. "Markets" are among these institutions; in most developing countries markets do not function as they should because of costly and imperfect information and a lack of non-market institutions that could mitigate these inefficiencies (see Stiglitz 1998). The design of appropriate innovation policies is an urgent and immediate concern for overall economic development in developing countries, not the esoteric issue of debate that neoliberal economists have made it.

The failure of markets to provide knowledge inputs—such as extension services for standards setting, testing,[1] metrology, quality and information, intellectual property, vocational, technical and skill training, and scientific and technological laboratories (which could be private or public research organizations)—needs to be corrected through institutional mechanisms created to bridge these gaps.

The work of Stiglitz and Greenwald (1986) demonstrates that whenever markets are incomplete, information is imperfect, or both (which is the case in nearly every latecomer economy, although this is also true, with less severity, of developed economies), governments are required to implement various institutional interventions in order to enhance the efficiency of markets.[2]

The literature on development tells us that market imperfections are pervasive and widespread, particularly in developing environments (Rodrik 2007).[3] To address market imperfections, states in East Asia and Latin America have extensively employed industrial policies in the catching-up process as a means to removing obstacles to structural transformation. More serious for the latecomer,[4] however, is the evident reality that "backwardness has been relatively greater," requiring an even larger dose not only of state action, but also of policy competence. This backwardness manifests in a number of ways: the absence of strong and competent state institutions; weak entrepreneurial business firms; a relatively low level of skilled engineers and technical personnel; and a lack of well-educated and abundant low-cost managers (Amsden 1989; Amsden and Chu 2003). Although Gerschenkron (1962) observes that in catching up, latecomers potentially have access to a basket of proven technologies, much of what development requires is embedded in the realm of tacit knowledge, with significant preconditions for interpersonal learning. In other words, access to such knowledge sources is not automatic and even if it were so, the institutions that mediate knowledge acquisition (whether markets or networks) are largely absent in developing countries. Lastly, as Amsden and Chu (2003: 13) observe, market forces are unkind to the weakly organized economies ("the more backward the country, the harsher the justice meted out by market forces"), with their inherent and often contradictory requirements. In this chapter, we argue that, precisely because of these reasons, latecomer countries need even stronger governmental interventions (a concept not necessarily anathema to free trade) in terms of innovation policies that address the present institutional gaps in their local contexts.

The role of governments is critical in as much as they are the custodians of policies and institutions, as well as the means of enforcement. State actions manifest in the capability to identify market failures and opportunities, and the ways in which policies, regulations, and accompanying apparatus put in place for enforcement affect agents' strategic technology choices and steer economies in particular directions. Here, we focus on the importance of policies and the capacity of governments of latecomer countries to affect technology choices for development. We argue that the application of the state-led development discourse and lessons learned from East Asian successes need to be broadened to include factors specific to latecomer contexts, in order to understand how states can develop the capacity to promote stronger domestic economic integration. The following section centers on the importance of state policy for structural economic transformation, and highlights the differences in institutional and policy capacity for latecomer countries. The next section analyzes the formal and informal institutions that constitute innovation policy frameworks in latecomer countries and argues for a broadening of the state-led development discourse to include country-specific factors. Next, we analyze two cases where distinct policy choices among latecomer countries led to historical success in order to highlight the role of state policy in promoting technological development in latecomer countries.

States and their capacity for policy choices

In order to put policy capacity and policy choices in perspective, we propose, in the tradition of developmental state theory (Johnson 1982) and evolutionary economics, that catch-up will be nigh impossible if the different states do not, through deliberate policy choices, effectively attenuate obstructions to economic structural transformation. Here, we define *innovation policy* as purposive and strategic actions taken by governments and their agents to foster industrial structural transformation by creating new processes, products, markets, sources of supply, and forms of organizations. This follows the Schumpeterian tradition, which holds that the economic capacity of nations derives from the extant modes of organizations, as well as the capabilities and knowledge infrastructure that coordinate actors and systems.

An economy comprises a wide variety of economic and non-economic actors that are coordinated within a system involving both market and non-market transactions. Coordination is effected by means of institutions that are both formal and informal (rules, norms, social conventions, laws, and statutes). Where these institutions are missing or inadequate, industrial and innovation policies must provide institutional compensation to enable parties to engage in socially beneficial exchanges, as if there were no missing institutions. Within the context of a particular country, structuring such institutional compensations involves making choices among a host of contending alternatives.

Institutions for innovation and technological development are extremely important to long-term economic growth precisely because technology mediates the introduction of new products and processes in the economy. In an industrially dynamic context, changes to machinery and equipment and the introduction of new forms of industrial organization will be accompanied by "new institutions [and] the institutionalization of . . . new social technologies may require new law, new organizational forms, new sets of expectations" (Nelson and Sampat 2001: 49). The role of the state in latecomer development is to provide institutions that mimic the market mechanism by creating conditions that minimize uncertainty, socialize risk inherent to industrial activities, and encourage entrepreneurship and local technological advancement. As Johnson (1987) states,

> One of the things a state committed to development must do is develop a market system and it does this to the extent that its policies reduce the uncertainties or risks faced by entrepreneurs, generate and disseminate information about investment and sales opportunities, and instill an expansionist psychology in the people. Once a market system has begun to function, the state must be prepared to be surprised by the opportunities that open up to it, ones that it never imagined but that entrepreneurs have discovered (p. 41).

This involves not only the state regulating political and economic relationships so that they focus on sustained technological development, but also engaging in institutional innovation and adaptations that will enable local entrepreneurs to capitalize on the new opportunities that they have discovered over time.

Policy choices and development: explaining variations in innovation capacities across countries

Latecomer countries possess varying policy and institutional capacities to make the kinds of choices that promote development and face difficulties in transforming knowledge through learning activities to technological capabilities and innovative performance. Myriad questions arise about how best to resolve the latecomers' development conundrum. For instance, why is access to knowledge not sufficient to promote the use of knowledge? Why is technology transfer not an adequate precondition for technology absorption? Why is public-sector research ineffective in promoting product development through the private sector? The answer to most of these very basic, often-assumed-to-be-given constraints lies in the nature and capacity of formal and informal institutions that underlie innovation in latecomer countries.

We suggest that one of the causes of this failure is the lack of an institutional base for innovation, one that is built on local and contextual factors. Rather than drawing on the underlying principles and processes that have generated diverse past and present institutions in their national contexts, most latecomer countries have focused on building organizations without paying much attention to the institutions that sustain them. By this we mean the evolutionary process of making policy choices for institutional design and development, which fitted institutions to differing and changing contexts, while usually embedding individual components within functionally coherent structures. We make a clear distinction between *organizations* and *institutions* (see Oyeyinka and Gehl Sampath 2009), where *institutions* are defined as the "rules of the game"; imply routine behavior and actions; and consist of the "cognitive, normative and regulatory structures and activities that provide stability, coherence and meaning to social behavior" (North 1996). As opposed to the normative and cognitive aspects of institutions, greater emphasis is laid on the structural dimension of the "organization," which is set up to perform one or several of the functions required under the institutional framework.

By simply imitating organizational structures that work for the present context in industrialized countries, a number of latecomer countries have ignored the fact that these structures—or organizations—were products of an organic institution-building process, rather than mechanically given forms. The institutional forms were created, refined, and adapted to given contexts over a long historical period. As a result, problems of functional incoherence were designed into the structure from the beginning. The present institutional structures observed in the industrialized countries were radically different from what they were half a century ago, once again signifying a process of gradual-yet-dynamic evolution—imitating them now would hardly offer a coherent basis for developing innovative capacity elsewhere. Institutions that foster innovative capacity cannot be captured in terms of ideal, ready-to-replicate characteristics. These institutions that have worked or are working were outcomes of deliberate policy choices, often made in difficult and uncertain times. This is further compounded by the fact that many, if not all, latecomer countries have limited state capacity. There are many convincing reasons that point to the necessity of a strong state; however, many latecomer countries lack a strong state for reasons that include corruption and interest-group lobbying, rent-seeking (see Khan and Stiglitz and Noman in this volume), and lack of organizational competence.

Broadening the discourse on state capacity for latecomer development

Government and government agencies were central to creating and nurturing a semiconductor industry in East Asia. The government-business relationship is one of "governed interdependence"—a kind of productive and complementary relationship. Government agencies need the private sector to implement policies, while the private sector needs public agencies to coordinate catch-up activities, particularly in financial allocation, risk-sharing, and technological upgrading.[5] The relationship between the public and private sectors has not been fixed, but has coevolved with the industry over time (Mathews and Cho 2000).

Three important issues arise when analyzing the potential role of the state in the development of latecomer countries. First, latecomer economies do not possess the East Asian economies' elaborate institutional bureaucracies, which were credited as being largely responsible for their successes. In fact, in a situation of economic backwardness, changes to institutions and institutional expansion are just as rare as technological innovation itself.[6] Poor state capacity in latecomer countries is as much a result of low-level information regimes as it is of low-level knowledge and poor skills for policymaking choices. Second, the traditional state capacity discourse needs to be broadened to capture a wider array of issues than those simulated by the East Asian experiences. Much of the East Asian and Japanese experiences of state-led development have focused on the conduits of credit-based financial structures and financial policy, with some labor-related issues on the side (Woo-Cummings 1999).[7] In the context of latecomer development, this needs to be broadened to include labor and human skills, land reforms, and social coalitions that may often have their basis in the unequal distribution of wealth, but are powerful enough to induce socially suboptimal policy choices to retain status quo. In other words, the distribution of power among various interest groups in latecomer societies may not be one conducive to a "developmental embeddedness." As Evans (1995) argued, for the state to be called "developmental," it should be embedded in the society and share a set of connections that "link the state intimately and aggressively to particular social groups with [which] the state shares a joint project of transformation." And third, rather than exploring the role of the state as the controller of economic and financial assets that seizes all power unto itself, the application of the state-led development discourse to latecomer development calls for a nuanced understanding of how the state, business, and society can partner to bring about industrial transformation. How can states in latecomer contexts develop the capacity to promote stronger domestic economic integration? What institutions are needed to promote knowledge-based and innovation-driven development in very latecomers? What sort of policy and institutional capacities would be required to ensure that the gains of such innovation-driven development also address equity?

Formal institutions and incentives for innovation

Latecomer countries exhibit institutional inadequacies that include an absence or poor enforcement of legal and institutional frameworks—a lack of rules of the game. The range of policies that is collectively termed *innovation policy* is extensive. They include those that promote human capital formation, sectoral, science and technology, and general infrastructure policies. All or most of these policies that are needed for innovative capacity are either missing or not enforced in a latecomer context.

Institutional incentives to encourage coordination among the organizations set up to fulfill these mandates form an equally critical part of an environment that enables innovation. These incentives include policies that focus both on primary research and extension services that help to build and foster the enterprise sector's collaboration with public-sector institutions in order to commercialize products based on ongoing inventive activities. Incentives also encompass a range of policy efforts that enhance collaborative research through subsidies, joint research programs, product development initiatives, and intellectual property protection or sharing schemes.

Unfortunately, most latecomer countries that did manage to set up structures for knowledge creation and policies and institutions for innovation have focused on framework policies that laid too much emphasis on science and technology (S&T) and research and development (R&D) institutions. Sectoral policies are admittedly harder to enact and enforce than broader framework policies for S&T, which have tended to be fewer and far between. There are two other reasons why the success of sectoral policies is more difficult to envisage in latecomer contexts. First, sectoral policies require a capable and sophisticated S&T bureaucratic mechanism for enforcement, a mechanism that is weak in latecomer countries. Second, sectoral policies, despite their individual focus, function within the larger innovation context of the country. If the larger context for innovation is constrained and institutionally bankrupt, the impact of sectoral initiatives will be marginal. In this section, we identify in institutional contexts of latecomer countries two problems that are critical to explaining the institutional inadequacies and failures of innovation.

Institutional path-dependent failures

Many of the problems in enactment and coordination of institutions for innovation may in part be traced back to initial conditions—the quality of pre-existing national human and industrial capabilities in latecomer countries—and is well illustrated by persistent educational institutions established several decades prior. Latecomer governments have recorded substantial progress in educational attainment despite the fact that very few changes have been made to the structure of colonial-era education systems. Although comparisons show that despite initial conditions, it is the pace of increase of education across countries that matters (World Bank 1993), the factors that prevented the pace of increase in certain countries as opposed to those countries that achieved it (in East Asia, for example), are important. Although the percentage of GNP that was invested in education by African countries in the 1960s was on par with East Asian countries, over time policymakers had very little influence over the development of the education systems in their countries (King 1991). The donor/client dependency relationship that emerged hindered the capacity of Africans to develop educational policies that were socially relevant and financially feasible (King 1991).[8] It seems that the combination of this legacy and the lack of significant African involvement in education policy formulation resulted in an education system that remains elitist in ethos and does not cater to the employment and skill needs of the continent.

Institutional ineffectiveness and inertia

Institutions in latecomer contexts are ineffective at establishing efficient interlinkages and incentives for agents to engage in learning and knowledge creation activities. As a result, while there is a general agreement that developing countries need to create organizations and institutions where they do not exist and reform those that are functioning poorly, policymaking institutions lack both broad and specific competencies in their coordination functions. This is a serious drawback for developing countries and, in the absence of strong market coordination, leads to a situation in which policy coordination is largely politically driven. Lack of funding for relevant organizations creates additional gaps and exacerbates the consequences. Maintaining these organizations to achieve effective service delivery depends to a considerable extent on available public resources. But poor financial commitment to meeting organizational obligations results in disillusioned scientists and researchers, lack of private-sector trust in collaborating with public-sector institutions, and often even prevents the rise of a private sector since organizations that promote the growth of private-sector firms do not function effectively. Their inefficiencies give rise to the poor coordination of knowledge and economic production functions, which leads to imbalances in the demand and supply for the right kinds of skills, a mix of quantity and quality at sectoral levels. Other institutional gaps arising from a lack of funding for relevant organizations only magnifies the consequences, as discussed earlier in this chapter.

A major factor for this kind of organizational dysfunction lies with government involvement that tends to create its own idiosyncratic lock-in conditions, which happens for two main reasons. First, instead of playing a supportive role in rectifying market imperfections, governments in latecomer contexts have lent strength to the creation of institutions that override market forces, thereby creating alternative institutions to which actors must respond, albeit to promote self-interested, inefficient outcomes. This capture of the entire institution-building process is a commonplace occurrence, in which unofficial (i.e. informal) attitudes of agents within the system get embedded over time. Institutional frameworks in latecomer contexts have several features of embeddedness that prevent competitive pressures of global exports and other conventional market incentives from fostering these linkages locally, despite the obvious gains. Organizations in latecomer contexts may respond too slowly relative to the changes in the local, national, or global contexts. This might well be the case for much of the perceived slow speed in adopting quality standards imposed on firms in the latecomer countries in the wake of the liberalization of financial markets and production. Second, organizations may have too much structural inertia, relative to their internal capabilities, to make even adequate ongoing changes. Structural inertia is the result of informal rules of the game that condition interactions and learning processes and prevent even well-intended policies and market incentives from enhancing the patterns of interaction and learning that are needed for innovation. Through repeated learning, organizations develop and modify the routines by which their legitimacy is established and competencies recognized. If these routines are conditioned by inadequate funding, corruption, a lack of strategic vision, and scope for personal gains, they create an institutional memory that is often difficult to change or that can change only very slowly.

How policy choices made historical differences: a discussion of latecomer experiences

Despite institutional constraints, there are cases in which distinct policy choices at critical turning points led to historical changes in the countries that adopted them. Here we relate the cases of two policy choices and delineate the reasons why they worked in these countries and not in others, in order to explicate the role of state policy in promoting technological development in latecomer countries.

Product patent protection as a policy choice and India's pharmaceutical sector

India's policy choice of denying product patent protection to promote its local pharmaceutical sector, which is now a global success, has come under intense scrutiny as to the lessons it holds for other latecomer environments. The Indian pharmaceutical sector was estimated to be worth US$12 billion in 2006/7 according to its Department of Chemicals and Petrochemicals. Although there are some differences in industry forecasts—the Economist Intelligence Unit predicts it to be worth US$20 billion a year by 2021,[9] a McKinsey analysis (2007) concludes this to be possible by 2015 (KPMG 2006), and the Indian National Pharmaceutical Policy of 2006 sets this as a feasible target for 2010—there is no doubt that the sector is thriving despite India's full-scale compliance with the Agreement on Trade Related Aspects of Intellectual Property (TRIPS) in 2005.[10] In 2005/6 the Indian pharmaceutical industry's share of the global market stood at 1.5 percent (ranked thirteenth) in terms of value but at 8 percent (ranked fourth) in terms of volume (IBEF 2006). The domestic sector meets 70 percent of all local demands for drugs despite the increased presence of multinational companies since 2005.

POLICY CHOICES FOR DEVELOPING CAPACITY

The critical policy changes that led to the growth of the sector can be divided into three broad phases, beginning with key changes initiated in the 1960s. It was in that decade that the Indian government, in an effort to boost local production of pharmaceutical products, introduced three major policy incentives: the Drug Price Control Order (to control the prices of drugs); the Indian Patent Act of 1970 that denied product patent protection to pharmaceutical firms and limited process patents for a period of seven years; and government-held pharmaceutical production companies (Gehl Sampath 2005). As a result of the changes introduced by the Patent Act, the number of patents granted per year within India fell by three quarters from 1970–81 (Lanjouw 1998: 4). By setting a ceiling on the overall profits of pharmaceutical companies, the Drug Price Control Order led to a large-scale exodus of the multinational corporations that had been operating in India. Technology required for reverse engineering skills, specifically those related to imitative process R&D, formulation, and production technologies, was acquired through public-sector efforts and passed on to the private sector. The local industry, a large part of which developed through spin-off entrepreneurship by employees of government-held pharmaceutical firms, was quick to take cue from the conducive environment: entrepreneurs developed extensive skills in chemistry-based reverse engineering, which forms the core of their product and process development skills even today. Indigenous local capacity for production was thus built through a combination of the right policy environment, access to international technology, education, and promotion of entrepreneurship, among other factors, while the main impetus for learning came from learning-by-doing activities (Mashelkar 2005).

A second phase of policy changes was triggered by India's trade liberalization at the end of the 1980s. By this time, the pharmaceutical sector was exporting bulk drugs and formulations and was recognized as being of strategic importance for its technological and export potential. During this phase, several of the policy changes, aimed at enabling the sector to take advantage of India's shift from an import substitution economy to a liberalized one, helped boost the sector's potential as an exporter of generic formulations. This, supported by India's continued policy of minimal intellectual property rights (IPR), created a comfortable and stable economic climate in which several of the larger firms, such as Ranbaxy and Dr Reddy's, acquired facilities in developed countries, including the United States, in the 1990s.

These two phases of policy transformation were responsible for the radical changes in the foreign-versus-local-firm ratio in the Indian market. From a virtually non-existent domestic sector in 1970 (15 percent of Indian firms opposed to 85 percent foreign firms in the local market), the market structure transformed into one in which both Indian and foreign firms held a 50 percent share in 1982, to a 61 percent Indian and 39 percent foreign share in 1999 (OPPI 2000).

A third phase of policy changes was precipitated by India's entry into the World Trade Organization in 1995, resulting in the implementation of the Agreement on Trade-Related Aspects of Intellectual Property Rights (TRIPS) by 2005. From 1999–2005, India radically revised its intellectual property policies for pharmaceutical products and, by granting product patent protection, became fully TRIPS-compliant. Intellectual property protection will cause profound changes, including potential losses to the sector, since Indian firms can no longer produce generic versions of drugs that are patented elsewhere (see Fink 2000; Grace 2004 and 2005; Gehl Sampath 2005). However, the government introduced several other policy changes aimed at enhancing the industry's credibility nationally and internationally in order to strengthen the sector's capacity to deal with foreign competition and potential losses induced by stronger intellectual property protection. One such change was the introduction of good manufacturing practices (GMPs), which applies uniformly across the sector.

Throughout the three phases, knowledge infrastructure policies were implemented that targeted higher education and health research spending, placing an extraordinary emphasis on science-based university educations and specialized public research institutes (PRIs). The government has invested heavily in excellent university facilities in disciplines of key relevance to pharmaceutical research (such as medicine, pharmacology, chemistry, biochemistry, biology, molecular biology, and biotechnology), as well as forming PRIs, such as the Centre for Science and Industrial Research, Indian Drugs and Medical Research Institute, All India Institute of Medical Sciences, Indian Institute of Chemical Technology, and Indian Institute for Science. This points attention to another important strength of Indian policy in this regard, namely, the coherence of the entire policy package, one that was both demand and supply-side consistent, that was developed to support the growth of science and technology for the sector (see more generally Lall 2000; Pietrobelli 2000).

This trend has continued into the present, with the establishment of the Institute for Human Genetics, the Centre for Biotechnology, and the Institute of Microbial Technology, among others with the mandate of conducting research on emerging areas of importance to drug research. Throughout the past four decades, government spending on health research has been extensive, with up to 90 percent of all research funds being sourced internally for the public and private sector (CHRD 1990: 49).[11]

However, as it was initially laid out, the emphatic focus of the sector policy was on encouraging local production of drugs at affordable prices—not on building an innovative industry that could attain global competitiveness. This emphasis remained throughout all policy stages, despite a gradual expansion of industrial and innovation policy incentives. Policy action thus resulted in a strange assemblage of strengths, and significant differences in technological capabilities among small, large, and medium-sized firms.

In hindsight, the strengths of domestic enterprise, built over time, are reflected in the way the sector has been able to thrive and advance beyond mere production of generic pharmaceuticals into innovative territories, expanding into modern technologies such as health biotechnology. However, the key task of plunging into the global market was largely a result of the aspirations of local firms. The local firms were quick to anticipate that India's compliance with TRIPS would fundamentally change the nature of the innovative activities they would be allowed to participate in, and began making large-scale changes several years before India instituted product patent protection in 2005.

Table 9.1 R&D spending as a percentage of total revenues of the top five firms from 2003–6 (excluding Cipla)[1]

Company	2003	2004	2005	2006
Dr Reddy's	7.6%	9.5%	12.9%	9.6%
Ranbaxy	4.5%	5.3%	6.2%	9.4%
Aurobindo	1.2%	2.0%	3.1%	3.6%
Glenmark	4.4%	6.5%	5.3%	4.4%
Sun Pharma	3.4%	5.0%	5.9%	6.3%

[1] Compiled using company annual reports.

In the years leading up to India's compliance with TRIPS, the top Indian firms began investing up to 10 percent of their annual profits into R&D. Table 9.1 shows the R&D spending of the top five firms in the Indian pharmaceutical sector (excluding Cipla). They diversified their activities to expand beyond generics production to (1) generics-based R&D (including developing novel delivery systems, non-infringing processes, and similar activities that feed into the generics business); (2) drug discovery and development; and (3) contract research and manufacturing for global firms, including clinical trials work. Such diversification ensured that they would be able to develop synergies between the need to be competitive in the present and aspirations to build greater innovative capabilities and integrate into the global structure.

The private-sector firms were quicker than the state; they saw opportunities for competitive advantages in contract research and manufacturing, and have used these to solidify their position in the global pharmaceutical market as a powerful global producer of generic drugs. Their main activities today range between generics-based R&D, new drug discovery, and contract research and manufacturing (including clinical trials work) for the global pharmaceutical sector (see Gehl Sampath 2008).

Since the early 2000s, local Indian firms have been actively involved in expanding through foreign acquisitions, setting up global subsidiaries, and hiving off separate R&D companies, all of which point to the emergence of new industrial structures. Indian firms made eighteen international acquisitions between January 2004 and October 2005, including Matrix Labs's acquisition of Belgium's Docpharma for $263 million in June 2005, Dr Reddy's acquisition of Roche's API business for $59.6 million, Ranbaxy's acquisition of a 40 percent stake in Japan's Nihon Pharmaceutical Industry, and Sun Pharma's completion of its purchase of ICN Hungary for an undisclosed sum.[12]

This new industrial dynamism has been strongly influenced by changes in global regulatory structures for pharmaceutical innovation, an influx of newer technologies, and strategies of global players that go far beyond outsourcing. The government, for its part, has done as Johnson (1987) suggested—it has made it possible for firms to capitalize on opportunities that were not anticipated when it began promoting policy changes to enable local production.

DUPLICATING SUCCESS ELSEWHERE: KEY LESSONS

To understand state involvement in promoting innovation in a latecomer context, it is useful to compare India to Bangladesh, where the state initiated a similar set of institutional incentives in an effort to boost local pharmaceutical production (see Gehl Sampath 2007b). Bangladesh's pharmaceutical sector exports a wide range of drugs (therapeutic class and dosage forms) to sixty-seven countries worldwide (field interviews). Local exports have risen from US$0.04 million in 1985 to US $27.54 million in 2006 (Export Promotion Bureau, Bangladesh). The companies include specialized multinational companies, large local companies with international links, and smaller local companies. Approximately 450 generic drugs, in 5,300 registered brands having 8,300 different presentations of dosage forms and strengths, are manufactured by the sector (which includes five multinationals).[13] However, Bangladesh's biggest impediment to expanding into the global pharmaceutical market is its inability to reverse-engineer drugs. The local firms presently are mainly engaged in the formulation of active pharmaceutical ingredients (APIs) requiring manufacturing skills only, and are struggling to build capacity in the more knowledge-intensive processes of reverse-engineering APIs.[14]

A comparison of the institutional incentives that were initiated in Bangladesh and India (which had a similar set of policies to boost pharmaceutical production), as presented in Table 9.2, is revealing in terms of sector performances. In the table, India's policy regime from the 1960s to the 1980s is compared to that of Bangladesh from the 1980s to the 2000s, on the basis of the stage of development of the local pharmaceutical sector. At a first glance, it may seem unreasonable to compare the two countries since the international regulatory context changed substantially between the 1960s and 2000, in terms of industrial and innovation policies. However, Bangladesh is exempt from implementing TRIPS until 2016, owing to its status as a least developed country, and there are significant similarities in the policy apparatus that was put in place in the two countries (see Table 9.2), lending strength to such a comparative exercise.

As the table shows, the same three policy incentives (setting up governmental production companies, drug price control, and PRIs for pharmaceutical research) were initiated in Bangladesh as in India. However, there was no restriction on patenting, the local law allows for both product and process patents, and the public-sector institutes were lacking in funding and vision, rendering them largely dysfunctional. The policy framework also failed to generate the skills necessary for the sector: while there is a large supply of pharmacists in the country, chemical synthesis skills, which is the backbone of reverse-engineering processes, are conspicuously absent. Only in the last few years has the government begun to initiate

Table 9.2 Comparing Bangladesh and India's policy regimes for pharmaceutical self-sufficiency

Bangladesh's Policy Support Regime, 1980s to 2000s	India's Policy Support Regime, 1960s to 1980s
Similarities	
Drug Control Ordinance of 1982	Drug Price Control Order of 1970
Setting up of public research institutes, but lack of funding and vision.	Setting up of government-held companies to boost the local production of drugs.
Setting up of government-held companies for production.	Setting up of extensive public research infrastructure for pharmaceutical research.
Differences	
No restrictions on pharmaceutical patents under the 1911 Act.	Restrictions on patenting of foreign pharmaceutical products under the Patents Act of 1971.
No comparable role of the government or public-sector institutions to help firms acquire reverse-engineering skills.	Proactive role in technology transfer related to reverse-engineering to local firms, through public research institutes.
No funding to public-sector institutions; the Bangladesh Centre for Scientific and Industrial Research is almost defunct.	Extensive funding to public-sector organizations to boost the capacity for pharmaceutical research, especially Centre for Science and Industrial Research, the Central Drug Research Institute, and IDMR.
Lack of vision and funding to reform the university education system.	Introduction of university education to suit industry requirements (in chemistry and pharmaceutical sciences).
	Other industrial policy measures, such as investment and ownership restrictions on multinational companies.

Source: Gehl Sampath India surveys in India (2005) and Bangladesh (2006–7).

new courses in biotechnology at the university level, which means there will still be a shortage of skills necessary for the growth of the sector for some time.

An empirical survey of the local pharmaceutical sector in Bangladesh shows that, contrary to India's experience, the Drug Price Control Ordinance that sought to prevent foreign competition in the local market to boost local capabilities has been perfected over the years to become a system in which firms thrive on local sales (most of the sales for even the largest firms accrue from the local market)[15] at the expense of public health concerns. Instead of generating a highly competitive local sector, there seems to be very little incentive to enhance competitiveness thanks to informal rules for marketing and sales incentives for firms that are structured to extract maximum rents (Gehl Sampath 2007a and 2007b). The protection from imports, which in the case of India gradually emerged to be a decisive factor in the expansion of the local sector (with intense competition among local firms), did not bear the same results in Bangladesh. Even today, the sector has only around 135 active local firms, which includes small and medium enterprises. The failure of policy initiatives to achieve results similar to India's reinforces our earlier point that the policy package required for the development of a sector must be both supply and demand-side coherent in order to ensure sustainable growth and economic development. While this was more the case in India, Bangladesh's policy package was especially lacking in ensuring the growth of the knowledge infrastructure for the sector, enabling price control, and making significant public health guarantees. The survey found numerous instances where firms work around well-intentioned policies to find informal mechanisms that help them to retain their profits, to the detriment of the economy and technological progress, not to mention public health and equality. The informal institutions in the pharmaceutical sector in Bangladesh have paved the way for institutional capture of health concerns by the local firms, as the survey showed. The incumbent firms are interested in keeping the status quo, so they find ways to work around minor policy changes, which undermines potential for real growth.[16]

Knowledge-building as a policy choice and the success of Chinese computer hardware

The growth of China's computer industry and the increasing influence of Chinese firms at the global level have been based on the systematic building of production capabilities that focus on both domestic and export markets. The country has become the number-one producer of hardware components in the world for many product categories. However, Chinese computer firms, most of which operate near the low-technology end of the industrial value chain, lag behind global leaders, such as Taiwanese and American firms, that dominate the global production networks (GPN).[17] One of the keys to success in China was the early focus on mastering core technical components, particularly integrated circuits, chip design, and software mold. While the pursuit of international market standards has been an important stimulus, consistent policy and institutional choices at all stages of development is central in explaining the transformation of the industry. The computer industry in China has its origin in policy actions taken as far back as the mid 1950s.[18] However it took more than twenty years, until 1979, before a formal organization emerged with the State Council's Bureau of National Computer, the first national organization with the sole objective to develop the computer industry. In 1985, the first personal computer, Great Wall 0520, designed for large-scale industrial production, was developed within a PRI. At this time, the few computer users in China used them mainly for basic calculations, while the majority of the population was largely unaware of them.

Building on this foundation, in 1986, the Ministry of Electronics Industry, inspired by the developments in the USA, spelled out key policies and listed four categories of electronics products as priorities for development: integrated circuits, computers, software, and switching boards. The policies contained various incentives, including exemptions from production taxes, tariffs on key equipments and machinery (which constitutes 10 percent of R&D expenses of turnover), and import taxes of significant imported projects. In order to attract highly qualified personnel, engineers and scientists were given competitively high salaries. In addition, new policies were put in place to promote small and medium-scale enterprises, although the efficacy of these policies is a matter for debate.

We identify four major policy focal points: cultivation of industry champions,[19] sustained investment in knowledge-building, systemic linkage promotion, and fostering of special economic zones (SEZs). While all these policies were part of the long-term strategy behind the emergence of the industry, it is beyond the scope of this chapter to discuss all of them. We briefly examine two: the policies behind knowledge-building and the evolution and impact of geographic clusters in the form of SEZs.

SUSTAINED INVESTMENT IN KNOWLEDGE-BUILDING

We found four important measures of knowledge inputs that reflect China's consistent policy emphasis on the computer sector. The first is the sustained and explicit investment in R&D by firms since the middle of the 1990s. R&D investment increased from RMB54.73 million in 1995 to RMB2.48 billion in 2002 (see Table 9.3). The second measure is indicated by an increase in number of S&T personnel, which rose from 8,422 in 1995 to 16,411 in 2002. The third is the number of R&D personnel in the industry, which increased from only 1,355 in 1995 to 3,589 in 2002. The fourth is the number of scientists and engineers, which rose from 4,745 in 1995 to 13,310 in 2002.

At the same time that capabilities were increasing thanks to knowledge investments, product outputs were also evolving, evidenced by steadily increasing investments in technology imports and adaptation. For example, before 1999, the main innovation input was domestic technology adaptation efforts and investment, which was then higher than the expenses for importation. However, investment for technology imports increased from RMB527.44 million in 1999 to RMB1.93 billion in 2002. In the same period, expenses for domestic technology adaptation also increased from RMB359.29 million to RMB453.02 million. This is indicative not only of the changed dynamics of the competitive Chinese markets where efforts were made to meet global demand, but also of rising domestic technological capabilities, which has resulted in more discriminating local consumers.

Table 9.3 Investment in human capital and R&D 1995–2002 (RMB ten thousand)

Indicators	1995	1997	1998	1999	2000	2001	2002
R&D personnel	1355	7660	4028	6139	3941	6683	6589
R&D expenses	5473	72611	44911	76554	115541	107124	248386
S&T personnel	8422	13884	12386	11960	14886	18143	16411
Scientists and engineers	4745	10436	8180	8301	11347	14275	13310

Sources: China High Technology Industrial Statistics Yearbook (2003).

Table 9.4 Comparative R&D intensity in the manufacturing, high-technology, and electronics industry

Sectors	China	USA	Japan	Germany	France	UK	Canada	Italy	SK
	2001	2000	2000	2000	2000	2000	1999	1999	2000
Manufacturing industry	2.6	8.2	9.2	7.8	7.0	6.0	3.7	2.1	5.3
High-tech industry	5.1	22.5	21.7	23.2	27.1	21.2	27.0	13.0	14.8
Electronics industry	6.5	18.6	16.0	33.0	35.1	13.5	26.2	27.2	16.9

Sources: Data of large and medium enterprises from the National Statistics Bureau (ed.), *Chinese High Technology Statistics Yearbook* (2002); data of other countries from the OECD structure analysis database (2003) and enterprises R&D analysis database (2002).

Notes: R&D intensity=science and technology expenses/gross production values
STP=S&T personnel/employees by the end of year.

The numbers of science and technology personnel (STP) also increased steadily in 1990s (see Table 9.4) and China has now notably attained international STP intensity level. This is indicative of the growing depth and input quality of the country's high-tech human capital, which in sheer quantity has outpaced the United States.

PROMOTION OF SPECIAL ECONOMIC ZONES

With the acceleration of globalization and increased competitive pressures, network clusters have emerged as an important form of economic organization to promote firm-level learning anchored on location advantage. One such network formation closely associated with the computer industry is the GPN. Like South Korea and Taiwan before it, China recognized early the need to foster industrial clusters in the form of SEZs as a policy tool to attract flagship firms that are at the center of GPNs.

The literature on East Asia shows that these innovation strategies consistently emphasize global integration with a focus on international trade and investment in technology capabilities.[20] Multinational firms, despite their global reach, are learning to exploit the benefits of geographic agglomeration, which promotes innovative, interaction-rich learning regions. Large firms with the assets to engage in production in a wide range of different locales are drawn to those places. For instance, by the early 2000s, five contract manufacturers—EMS, Solectron, Flectronics, Sanmina SCI, Celestica, and Jabil Circuit—had all established presences in China's coastal regions (see Table 9.5).

As a result of China's huge market, which is distributed among different geographic regions, the clusters vary considerably in size and structural diversity of firms, as well as in the depth of technological knowledge. This is manifested in, for example, the coexistence of small and medium enterprises with flagship firms.

The emergence and growth of high-tech clusters often depends on two key factors: the proximity to strong science and engineering universities and the

Table 9.5 2001 global EMS contract manufacturers' production locations in China

Ranking	EMS manufacturers	Main regions
1	Solectron	Suzhou, Shanghai, Shenzhen
2	Flectronics	Zhuhai, Shenzhen, Shanghai
3	Sanmina SCI	Dongguan, Kunshan, Dingdao
4	Celestica	Dongguan, Suzhou
5	Jabil Circuit	Danshui, Panyu
6	Hon Hai Precision	Beijing, Shenzhen, Suzhou
7	Elcoteq Network	Dongguan, Beijing
8	Viasystems	Beijing, Guangzhou, Nantong, Shanghai, Zhongshan
9	Venture	Shanghai
10	Pemstar	Tianjin
11	Kimball	Dongguan, Kunshan
12	Nam Tai	Shenzhen
13	Delta	Dongguan, Wujiang

Sources: <http://www.ebnchina.com/>, <http://ctnews.yam.com>.

availability of a well-developed infrastructure. Innovative clusters tend to form around sources of knowledge based on a sophisticated infrastructure in which knowledge is developed and exchanged. The network clusters in China have formed around fifty-two high-technology zones that have emerged since 1988.[21] Among these are the information hardware sectors in Zhongguancun Science Park, Shanghai Zhangjiang Hi-Tech Park, and Zhuhai National Hi-Tech Industrial Development Zone, which produce more than 70 percent of total industrial output.

The manufacturing bases are concentrated in the Guangdong, Jiangsu, and Fujian provinces as well as in the cities of Shanghai and Beijing. In these regions, computer manufacturing is mostly concentrated in three locations, the Yangtze River Delta, Pearl River Delta, and Loop Bo Sea Region. These industrial clusters are highly concentrated and demonstrate strong linkages between entrepreneurs, investors, and researchers. They exist within localized geographical areas and interact within larger innovation systems at the regional, national, and international levels. As with the rest of East Asia, clusters in China have become key to the country's ability to attract the international investments that generate new technological expertise; to interest investors in innovation through the use of venture capital, for example; and to benefit from the international mobility of skilled personnel.

THE CASE OF SOUTH AFRICA

China's experience in the hardware sector provides an interesting contrast to that of South Africa's hardware and software sectors, which have been a focal point of innovation policy in the country. The comparison is especially relevant because South Africa, as a science and technology leader in Sub-Saharan Africa (SSA), also demonstrates state capacity to guide technology choices. While China has been very successful in building the sector, South Africa's experience highlights the limitations of the role of the state in SSA and makes a case for rethinking policy.

In South Africa, our empirical work on the hardware and software sectors found that emerging high-tech activities have a strong geographic locus; such firms are concentrated in Gauteng and, to a lesser extent, the Western Cape. Government support is directed equally toward software and hardware firms. There are a few exceptions in the kinds of support structures. Targeted innovation incentives, science park/cluster advantage, and special support for small and medium enterprises (SMEs) are directed specifically towards the software sector,[22] while public-sector R&D institutions for technical solutions and bank loans are mainly directed towards the hardware sector. In other words, government has had a differentiated approach to the two subsectors, in addition to the more general macro-level support. The main sector-specific governmental initiatives are summarized in Box 9.1 below.

In addition to these, there are a number of provincial initiatives, particularly in Gauteng and Western Cape. In the Gauteng province, the government launched

---

Box 9.1 GOVERNMENT INITIATIVES FOR ICTS IN SOUTH AFRICA

The first attempt to develop a sector-specific initiative can be traced back to the South African Information Technology Industry Strategy (SAITIS) in 1995. There were stakeholder meetings conducted on the SAITIS project and the selection of a group of 37 stakeholders as an Advisory Group to the SAITIS Project. They represented key organizations and agencies with interests in the sector. The outcome was a Project Design Document (PDD) to guide the direction of the project and the establishment of a Project Steering Committee (PSC).

The Government of South Africa was also supported by the Canadian International Development Agency (CIDA), under its Country Development Program for South Africa, to develop the *South African ICT Sector Development Framework* in November 2000. Among its numerous goals, the ones relevant for the ICT sector were those related to accelerating growth of the base of ICT SMEs; focusing on regional growth through clusters, particularly in Gauteng and the Western Cape (mainly Cape Town); and upgrading local expertise to compete in the regional and global markets. Special emphasis was placed on creating and supporting new entrants, particularly SMEs. Following the release of the *ICT Sector Development Framework*, the ICT Development Council was established in 2000 by the Department of Trade and Industry. The *Strategic Industrial Projects* (SIP) that started in 2001 and is managed by the Department of Trade and Industry (DTI) provides a 50–100 percent tax allowance to encourage investments from local and foreign investors. To support firms further, import duties on IT hardware and software were abolished on 2003. Presently, the firms importing into South Africa only pay a Value Added Tax to the South African Customs. As hardware firms source technology mostly from abroad, release from import duties highly benefits South African small firms.

Source: Empirical survey by authors (2006)

---

the Blue IQ program in 2002.[23] The first phase of the Blue IQ involved the delivery of eleven strategic projects; the second phase of commercialization is expected to be dependent on private-sector participation. One of these projects was the creation of the Innovation Hub, an information and communication technology incubator and science park. The Innovation Hub and other similar ICT incubating centers are at the nexus of the technology support services strategy directed at small entrepreneurs in Gauteng. But the Western Cape Province has recently started challenging Gauteng's dominance. The Western Cape provincial government, along with the Municipality of Cape Town, is promoting the Western Cape as a growing hub for ICT activities with various policies directly focused on strengthening the sector.

While South Africa has had some success in promoting its hardware and software industries, state policy on the whole has provided certain innovation incentives but not active intervention and state leadership, as in the case of China. This helps to explain the lack of manufacturing depth of the domestic industry, which would need policy initiatives to be consistent with the needs of the firms and sectoral characteristics for there to be growth. Especially, given the dominance of a large number of SMEs in the sector, much more than tax holidays are required for sustaining the growth and enhancing long-term competitiveness. We also find evidence of the limitation of the state in deliberately building knowledge infrastructure, similar to the earlier comparison between India and Bangladesh.

The main actors with the most capabilities in the computer hardware sector are engineers and scientists. The core knowledge infrastructure includes scientific laboratories as well as design and research centers. The availability of scientific infrastructure, firms, universities, and PRIs determine the scope for specialization in any or all stages of the computer hardware industry, in terms of both physical and human capital, which is specific for each substage.[24] To facilitate innovation, each substage requires different combinations of knowledge and skills from various disciplines, some as diverse as physics, informatics, and computer science. This scope of necessary and diverse competencies among industry actors can limit a country's vision and actions. A country like China is able to take advantage of the global knowledge pool in this sector, but this is less feasible for most latecomers, including South Africa.

Policy choices for latecomer development: concluding remarks

The two comparisons—between India and Bangladesh, China and South Africa— highlight the limitations, but also the strengths of the state in deliberately building knowledge infrastructure. The contrasting cases of India and China on one hand and Bangladesh and South Africa on the other show that states have limited resources and specific institutional settings that may not all be amenable to uniform policy intervention. Three major points stand out when the reasons for success are segregated and analyzed. First is the importance of historical investments made in developing basic and advanced knowledge infrastructures. Much of the transformation of the Chinese computer hardware sector has been the result of historical and strategic factors, as well as political choices that were made in the past. For instance, the initial conditions of the country, including vast amounts of scientists and engineers, and the presence of a knowledge infrastructure, have been an important variable. However, the competitive advantages of this high-technology industry were created through strategic policy initiatives that have proved to be successful in other cases of East Asian miracles; one of "governed interdependence" as discussed earlier. Although India does not display the same kind of coordinated interplay as China and the other East Asian miracles, it has similarly benefited from its historical investments in building quality tertiary education institutions, as well as the presence of other knowledge infrastructures. In the wake of its TRIPS compliance, systemic collaboration is boosted by the entire range of institutions, from intellectual property to venture capital, to skilled manpower provision (many of which existed already) and will be decisive for India's potential to competitively offer a wide range of services in the pharmaceutical sector in the future.

In contrast with this, South Africa shows evidence of purposive government intervention in building knowledge infrastructure especially at regional levels, but the outcomes have been far different from China's. For instance, South Africa has had little success in computer hardware manufacturing and export, while China has made major strides as a global exporter. The situation is similar in Bangladesh, where the scattered investments in building knowledge infrastructure are far from strategic. This brings us to the second point: while infrastructure is a necessary condition, it is not sufficient in and of itself. What counts is the combination of factors, as well as the coherence and harmony of institutions and policies that bring about change; a total policy package where the state foresees and pioneers particular technology choices for the agents by making it easier for them to pursue some options over others. The Chinese government deployed innovation policies in a targeted and consistent way that has ensured coevolution with institutional changes that were used to attenuate problems of market failure, and in strategic terms, to change the factor conditions that create competitive advantages. For example, from the 1950s to the 1970s, there were no specific departments responsible for computer industry development in China. The basic institutional framework rested on the instrumentality of science and technology agencies in the departments responsible for research, development, and production of electronics goods. Then the Chinese government took measures to support the development of the computer industry within the backdrop of a planned economy.[25]

Over time, the environment within which the Chinese electronics industry developed also changed significantly as policies evolved. First, market deregulation increased competition. Second, along with the reform of the research system, institutes began to provide services for economic activities rather than being limited to research. Third, open economy and importation of foreign technology, an "exchange technology with market" strategy, was carried out. Fourth, the electronics industry transformed from focusing on military applications to civil applications and technology imitation and adoption. Meanwhile, government simultaneously enacted electronics industry policies that pushed for collaboration among firms and selectively supported the IC, computer, software, and switchboard subsectors.

In the Chinese case, an open-market policy did not mean less intervention, an important lesson for African latecomers seeking economic development trajectories within the multilateral trade regime. A number of measures were taken to support the development of the domestic computer industry including tax policies, and setting up the "Development Fund,"[26] subsidiaries, and licenses as well as the emphasis on national production. This is once again amplified when one considers the Indian pharmaceutical sector—although product patent protection is often projected as the critical choice in sector accounts that have analyzed success, it is clear that merely denying patent protection does not promote a local pharmaceutical sector. The policy choice of denying patent protection was propped up substantially by a range of initiatives aimed at strengthening local production capacity, including restricting foreign companies from setting up subsidiaries in India. Even today, the TRIPS-compliant policy framework in India is seeking to extract TRIPS flexibilities available in the international framework to support the local pharmaceutical firms (Gehl Sampath 2008).

The coevolution of policies and institutions with technological advances in the sector demonstrates the partnership potential between the state and enterprise sector to move toward more productive frontiers. From our analysis of the evolution of policies and the institutions supporting systems that sought to develop the computer industry and the pharmaceutical sector in China and India respectively, it is evident that a process of coevolution of the sector and policy learning had been taking place all along. At the initial stage, policy targets mainly focused on creating basic conditions and environment, including locating technology sources both from domestic R&D efforts and commercialization as well as facilitating international technology transfer. Because the industry was still in its infancy, the government protected domestic industrial firms in the 1980s through a battery of policies. In the 1990s, the targets of policies shifted to increasing production capacity, scaling up of industry and firm size, and more crucially, raising sectoral innovation capacity in order to meet the rapidly growing demands of national economy informatics. Since 2000, industrial structure has reached new and higher levels with indicators showing growth in size and world market share, although it still faces many challenges and bottlenecks. Improvements to the indigenous innovation capabilities of the domestic firms have also become a major issue of industrial development. Thus, since 2000, the policies have shifted to reflect these new targets of industrial innovation capabilities.

The goal to create such cooperative surplus from economic activities has to be promoted by the state in latecomer contexts where observed routines are "the sources of continuity in the behavioral patterns of organizations" (Nelson and Winter 1982: 96), but may embody negative embeddedness. Empirical work in Bangladesh and South Africa, as well as in several other latecomer countries and sectors not presented here, profoundly implicate the role of the state as the champion in latecomer development.[27]

Finally, we identify five roles for the state (only partly articulated here) in the pursuit of technology and innovation-led development in latecomer countries.

(1) States need to formulate a long-term vision or goal and pursue it. This is perhaps the clearest message that other latecomer countries can derive from the East Asian success stories. Both Freeman (1987) and Johnson (1982) allude to the technology imperative that dominated long-term development goals in Japan,[28] as well as Korea and Taiwan (Amsden 1989; Amsden and Chu 2003; Mathews 2000). "MITI and other Japanese ministries saw it as one of their main responsibilities to encourage the introduction of new technologies through new investment" (Freeman 1987: 35). And as quoted by an eminent champion of the topic, "A third problem is achieving optimal resource allocation from a long-term dynamic viewpoint which cannot be accomplished by the market mechanisms alone. These are the areas in which industrial policy can — and should — play a useful role."[29] They did this by using a wide array of instruments and incentives to acquire technology and by building entrepreneurial innovation capacity through targeted and selected intervention in key sectors.

(2) States have to provide coordination in order to bring harmony and efficiency when there are multiple actors in a system.[30] Innovation and production activities involve the actions of a wide variety of economic and non-economic actors that require coordination, which lies at the heart of state mandate. System coordination is conducted by complex sets of formal and informal institutions that come in various forms (Chang 1994).[31] For this reason, states have to build or strengthen institutions (more of this in the next section). As Alexander Hamilton perceptively remarked two centuries ago: "Capital is wayward and timid in lending itself to new undertakings, and the State ought to excite the confidence of capitalists...by aiding them overcome the obstacles that lie in the way of all experiments."[32] Finally the process of industrial transformation involves continuous processes of change (innovation), moving from low- to high-productivity activities and the mobility of human and physical assets (Chang 1994). States are not only regulators and entrepreneurs; they also need to manage conflicts and deal with problems of asymmetric power relations (e.g. small versus large firms, locals versus multinationals engaged in value chain governance).

(3) *States have to put in place institutions where they are missing and strengthen those that are weak.* These institutions include those that foster interactive learning through systemic coordination. Incentive systems tend to develop from more fundamental institutional roots such as labor laws and even national constitutions. Terms of employment and work environments, both tangible (research and teaching facilities) and intangible (possibilities for institutional collaboration, quality of networks and colleagues) play a pivotal role in retaining skilled professionals.[33] States have been involved in promoting academic-industry exchanges by encouraging channels of learning, such as joint publications, mobility of scientists and engineers, cooperative R&D, facility sharing, research training (e.g. capacity development at Ph.D. level, international and local exchange of staff), IPRs (licenses, patents, copyrights), and academic entrepreneurship (spin-off firms) (Brennenraedts et al. 2006).

(4) *States act as guarantors of risks and provide innovation "insurance."* It is not uncommon that entrepreneurs are slow to embrace innovation prospects coming out of the activities in a sector or economy due to risk and uncertainty, especially in sectors and technologies that are new to the local context. In such cases, successful state action has involved the creation of several mechanisms, including newer systems of property rights that insure rents for having taken up the risks of engaging in innovation. The case of data exclusivity in pharmaceutical and biotechnological innovations is one such example. The European Union began granting data exclusivity as a mechanism for protecting rents for biotechnological innovations, at a time when biotechnological patents were not allowed, in order to allow entrepreneurs to engage in such innovation activities. Similarly, the grant of plant breeders' rights for agricultural varieties is a mechanism that evolved to guarantee rents for the creation of new plant varieties when protection of life forms was heavily in debate in both the USA and Europe. Apart from creating alternate property rights structures, state actions can insure innovation in a variety of other ways, including helping to create or protect consumer markets, both local and export-oriented. All these forms of innovation "insurance" tend to play an important role, especially for firms in emerging sectors in latecomer contexts.

(5) *States have to manage conflict and resolve problems of asymmetric power relations.*[34] Recourse to the fundamental nature of innovation (risk and uncertainty) and the problems of incompleteness of contracts that is deeply inherent in large-scale industrialization efforts helps us to explain two of the roles of the state. As we have seen, innovation—as with the execution of large-scale projects involving heavy chemicals, iron and steel, and electronics industries—involve the participation of and, in an ideal situation, collaboration among several actors, all of whom might not be willing participants. This happens when powerful actors with vested interests in an economy stand to lose influence, profits, and markets as a result of emerging new sectors and industries. In other words, some actors might potentially gain while

others potentially lose; and more invidious is the uncertainty of the extent of gains and losses. This raises the prospects for conflict. Where then is the platform for bargaining and mediation? In this scenario, the state could act as the overall coordinator with the mechanisms of institutions.[35] This is not to say that the state in question would always have all the requisite capacity and the willingness to undertake such a task.

Even though we make the case for a stronger state for latecomers, the reality is that most latecomers have weak or non-existent state capacities. Therefore, it is important to consider what comes first in latecomer countries that do not have the state capacity to foster such change. Our empirical work in latecomer countries strongly supports the view that state capacity is the capstone of sustainable development. In resource-constrained frameworks, even a little state capacity can have a significant impact and catalyze the emergence of agent responses in desired forms.

Notes

* The authors are thankful for comments received at the IPD Addis Meeting, July 10–11, 2008 and to Carlo Pietrobelli, who reviewed the paper.

1. 15 European Union (EU) countries spend over €83 billion yearly (approximately 1 percent of EU GDP) on measurement and standardization (Wagner 2005).

2. The state and its role is well recognized in economics (see for example, Coase 1960), although its importance has been limited largely to definition and enforcement of property rights and provision of "rules of the game."

3. Rodrik goes as far to declare that development economics is constructed around resolving the problems of market imperfection.

4. We define "latecomer" as a country that is late in meeting certain key capabilities compared with both the forerunners at the global frontier and the competitors.

5. For instance Korean government efforts were directed "to help the private sector accelerate technological efforts." This effort focused on three dimensions: to induce the private sector to invest in technological efforts by creating a market for innovative products (*the demand side of technology*); to help it enhance R&D activities and acquire technological capabilities (*supply side of technology*); and to "provide an *effective linkage between the demand and the supply sides*, making technological efforts feasible and less risky and costly" (Kim and Lee 1987: 282).

6. Nelson and Sampat (2001) cite North's (1990) rearticulation of the "institutional obstructionist" notion of economic backwardness as being responsible for the failure of poorly performing economies to adopt productive technologies.

7. For example, strong financial incentives were used by Korean governments as instruments to deepen technology and to foster export growth (Chang 1994).

8. For example, at the 1961 Addis Ababa conference, which was one of the first conferences that sought to address the education system in Africa, King notes that the African voice appears to have been "indistinct." This also seems to have been the case for subsequent

conferences, such as the UNESCO/ECLA of 1962, and research reports, such as the Faure Report of 1972, which were all influential in shaping educational policies in Africa. See K. King (1991), "Education and Training in Africa: The Search to Control the Agenda for their Development," in D. Rimmer (ed.), *Africa 30 Years On* (London: Royal African Society), 73–90. In addition, it is interesting to note that it was only in the late 1980s that the World Bank began to make a conscious attempt to include African nationals in analytical work for their various education sector studies. Prior to this, the Bank used its own staff or those of UNESCO for such work. See World Bank (2001: 64–5).

9. The Economist Intelligence Unit Forecast (2007: 9).

10. The Agreement on Trade Related Aspects of Intellectual Property Rights (TRIPS) is an annex agreement of the World Trade Organization that all its member countries have to adhere to, subject to differential timelines. TRIPS prescribes minimum standards of intellectual property rights for all countries, and has several provisions dealing with protection of pharmaceuticals, including product patent protection.

11. A 1986 cross-country comparison of several developing countries including Brazil, Mexico, Philippines, Thailand, and India ranked in the top category of government spenders for health research within developing countries (CHRD 1990: 49).

12. See also KPMG (2006) for a discussion.

13. Although the sector boasts of 237 registered companies, only around 150 are estimated to be in a functional state according to Bangladesh's Directorate of Drugs Administration.

14. Pharmaceutical production can be split up into two components: the knowledge-intensive component is the reverse-engineering process that yields the know-how to produce active pharmaceutical ingredients (APIs) for a drug. The formulation process is mainly a manufacturing activity where the API is mixed with certain exipients to create the final product, in the form of a tablet, injection, or syrup.

15. The largest firm in the market, Square Pharmaceuticals is reported to be exporting only 3 percent of its total production, and Beximco, another firm in the top five, exports only 2.7 percent.

16. Innovation studies on other sectors in the country confirm these findings, see for example World Bank (2007).

17. GPNs are intra- and inter-firm relationships in a given sphere of production, as well as consideration of the forms of coordination that bind the network together. It points attention to the notion of production within a network of relationships at the center of which is the flagship company with varying tiers of subcontractors, service providers, and strategic alliances (Ernst and Kim 2002).

18. See Oyelaran-Oyeyinka and Rasiah (2008, forthcoming) for a full account.

19. The role of industry champions is underlined by the *Large Firm Strategy Document,* issued by the government in order to cultivate and support the industry champions.

20. See Hobday (1995); Lall (2000); Ernst and O'Connor (1989); Ernst and Guerrieri (1998); Mathews and Cho (2000); Borrus, Ernst, and Haggard (2000).

21. According to CCID statistics, 90 percent of the high-technology zones are electronics information industry.

22. The fact that special support for SMEs is mainly directed toward the software sector makes sense as firms in that sector are on average smaller than those in the hardware sector.

23. Through Blue IQ, the Gauteng local government is investing R3.7 billion in eleven projects for "strategic" industries and value-added manufacturing to restructure the composition of the provincial economy.

24. The sub-stages comprise: (1) product design, (2) component manufacturing, (3) assembly, (4) software development, (5) marketing, and (6) distribution.

25. The famous Founder Chinese characters typesetting system evolved from the collaborative development project supported by governmental allocation to the Department of Computer of Peking University and Shandong Weifang Computer factory (renamed Shandong Huaguang Company) in 1974.

26. The "development fund" is a scheme that was started in 1986, wherein the government allocates RMB100 million per year to support technology adaptation, technology, and commercialization of the above four products. Since the 1990s, it has also been used to start up a significant number of projects. Although many other such schemes were abandoned, the development fund is still operational.

27. See Gehl Sampath (2007b), Oyeyinka and McCormick (2007), and Oyeyinka and Gehl Sampath (2009) for empirical work in other latecomer countries.

28. As Woo-Cummings (1999: 64) observed, "Johnson takes the importance of technology to Japanese growth seriously...MITI rode herd on the acquisition of new technologies and how at critical turning points MITI directed advanced technologies and cheap finance to new industrial sectors—especially the shift to heavy and chemical industries in the 1950s."

29. These words are from Fukukawa, the director-general of the International Trade Administration Bureau of MITI in Japan. This quote was from a lecture delivered by Fukukawa titled "Features of the Industrial Policy of Japan," cited in Freeman (1987: 33).

30. See Chang (1999, 1994) for details.

31. Institution-building and adaptation could be complex and costly. Governments in the East Asian Tiger economies showed the ability to devise and implement complex institutional interventions effectively and there is much to learn from their success. Korea and Taiwan emulated Japan and all of these countries devised institutions for trade interventions, export orientation, as well as corporatist discipline that involved both industry and governments.

32. Alexander Hamilton quoted in Johnson (1982), *The Industrial Policy Debate*, Institute for Contemporary Studies, San Francisco.

33. Countries have other incentives such as those in German law that confer ownership of patents on individual researchers, who thereby have full rights to their inventions (Giesecke 2000).

34. Chang (1999) and Vartiainen (1999).

35. "The point is that efficiency may require that the parties can contract on an extremely wide set of variables.... the structure of transactions and property rights may, however, rule out such bargains" (Vartiainen 1999: 211).

References

Amsden, A. H. (1989). *Asia's Next Giant: South Korea and Late Industrialization*. New York and Oxford: Oxford University Press.

—— and Chu, W. W. (2003). *Beyond Late Development Taiwan's Upgrading Policies*. Cambridge, MA: MIT Press.

Borrus, M., Ernst, D., and Haggard, S. (eds.) (2000). *International Production Networks in Asia. Rivalry or Riches?* London: Routledge.

Brennenraedts, R., Bekkers, R., and Verspagen, B. (2006). "The Different Channels of University–Industry Knowledge Transfer: Empirical Evidence from Biomedical Engineering." Eindhoven, The Netherlands, Eindhoven Centre for Innovation Studies.

Chang, H. J. (1994). "State, Institutions, and Structural Change," *Structural Change and Economic Dynamics*, 5 (2): 293–313.

—— (1999). "The Economic Theory of the Developmental State," in M. Woo-Cummings (ed.), *The Developmental State*. Ithaca: Cornell University Press, 182–99.

—— (2001). *The Rebel Within*. London: Wimbledon Publishing Company.

CHRD (Commission on Health Research for Development) (1990). *Health Research: Essential Link to Equity in Development*. New York: Oxford University Press.

Coase, R. (1960). "The Problem of Social Cost," *Journal of Law and Economics*, 3: 1–4.

Economist Intelligence Unit (2007). "Industry Forecast: Health Care and Pharmaceuticals India," EIU, London, November.

Ernst, D. and Guerrieri, P. (1998). *International Production Networks and Changing Trade Patterns in East Asia: The Case of the Electronics Industry*. Oxford Development Studies, 26 (2): 103–21.

—— and Kim, L. (2002). "Global Production Networks, Knowledge Diffusion, and Local Capability Formation," *Research Policy*, 31 (8): 1417–29.

—— and O'Connor, D. (1989). *Technology and Global Competition: The Challenge for Newly Industrializing Economies*. Paris: Organization for Economic Cooperation and Development.

Evans, P. (1995). *Embedded Autonomy, States and Industrial Transformation*. Princeton, NJ: Princeton University Press.

Fink, C. (2000). "How Stronger Patent Protection in India Might Affect the Behavior or Transnational Pharmaceutical Industries," World Bank Working Paper No. 2352. Washington, DC: World Bank.

Freeman, C. (1987). *Technology Policy and Economic Performance: Lessons from Japan*. London: Frances Printer.

Gehl Sampath, P. (2005). "Economic Aspects of Access to Medicine after 2005: Product Patent Protection and Emerging Firm Strategies in the Indian Pharmaceutical Industry." Study Commissioned by the CIPIH, World Health Organization.

—— (2007a). "Innovation and Health in Developing Countries: Can Bangladesh's Pharmaceutical Sector Help Promote Access to Medicines?" A UNU-MERIT Working Paper, Maastricht.

—— (2007b). "Intellectual Property and Innovation in Least Developed Countries: Pharmaceuticals, Agro-Processing and Textiles and RMG in Bangladesh," Background Paper No. 9, Least Developed Countries Report 2007 on Knowledge, Technological Learning and Innovation for Development. Geneva: UNCTAD. Available on <http://www.unctad.org>.

—— (2008). "India's Pharmaceutical Sector in 2008: Implications for Global and Local Access to Medicines." A Study for the DFID. London: DFID. Available at <http://www.dfid.gov.uk/>.

Gerschenkron, A. (1962). *Economic Backwardness in Historical Perspective*. Cambridge, MA: Harvard University Press.

Giesecke, S. (2000). "The Contrasting Roles of Government in the Development of the Biotechnology Industry in the US and Germany," *Research Policy*, 29: 205–23.

Grace, C. (2004). "The Effect of Changing Intellectual Property on Pharmaceutical Industry Prospects in India and China; Considerations for Access to Medicines." London: DFID Health Systems Resource Centre.

—— (2005). "Update on China and India and Access to Medicine," Briefing Paper for DFID, London.

Greenwald, B. C. and Stiglitz, J. E. (1986). "Externalities in Economies with Imperfect Information and Incomplete Markets," *Quarterly Journal of Economics*, 101 (2): 229–64.

Hobday, M. (1995). *Innovation in East Asia*. Cheltenham: Edward Elgar.

India Brand Equity Foundation (2006). *India: Pharmaceuticals*. Report by Ernst and Young for IBEF.

Johnson, C. (1982). *MITI and the Japanese Miracle: The Growth of Industrial Policy 1925–1975*. Stanford: Stanford University Press.

—— (1987). "Political Institutions and Economic Performance: The Government–Business Relationship in Japan, South Korea and Taiwan," in F. C. Deyo (ed.), *The Political Economy of the New Asian Industrialism*. Ithaca: Cornell University Press.

Kim, L. (1997). *Initiation to Innovation: The Dynamics of Korea's Technological Learning*. Boston: Harvard Business School Press.

—— and Lee, H. (1987). "Patterns of Technological Change in a Rapidly Developing Country: A Synthesis," *Technovation*, 6 (4): 261–76.

King, K. (1991). "Education and Training in Africa: The Search to Control the Agenda for their Development," in D. Rimmer (ed.), *Africa 30 Years On*. London: Heinemann, 73–90.

KPMG (2006). "The Indian Pharmaceutical Industry: Collaboration for Growth." Private report.

Kreps, D. M. (1995). *A Course in Microeconomic Theory*. Princeton, NJ: Princeton University Press.

Lall, S. (2000). "The Technological Structure and Performance of Developing Country Manufactured Exports 1985–1998," Queen Elizabeth House Working Paper Series, No. 44, University of Oxford.

—— (2001). *Competitiveness, Technology and Skills*. Cheltenham: Edward Elgar.

Lanjouw, J. O. (1998). "The Introduction of Pharmaceutical Product Patents in India: 'Heartless Exploitation of the Poor and Suffering?'" NBER Working Paper No. 6366. New Haven, CT: Economic Growth Center, Yale University.

Lundvall, B. A. (1988). "Innovation as an Interactive Process: From User-Producer Interaction to the National System of Innovation," in G. Dosi, C. Freeman, G. Silverberg, and L. Soete (eds.), *Technical Change and Economic Geography*. London: Frances Pinter.

Mashelkar, R. A. (2005). "Nation Building through Science & Technology: A Developing World Perspective," *Innovation Strategy Today*, 1: 16–32. Available at <http://www.biodevelopments.org/innovation/ist1hires.pdf>.

Mathews, J. A. (2000). "Accelerated Technology Diffusion through Collaboration: The Case of Taiwan's R&D Consortia," Working Paper No. 106, European Institute of Japanese Studies (EIJS). Stockholm, Sweden: School of Economics.

—— and Cho, D. S. (2000). *Tiger Technology: The Creation of a Semiconductor Industry in East Asia*. Cambridge: Cambridge University Press.

Nelson, R. (1993). *National Innovation Systems: A Comparative Analysis*. Oxford: Oxford University Press.

—— and Sampat, B. (2001). "Making Sense of Institutions as a Factor Shaping Economic Performance," *Journal of Economic Behavior and Organization*, 44 (1): 31–54.

—— and Winter, S. (1982). *An Evolutionary Theory of Economic Change*. Cambridge: Belknap Press.

North, D. C. (1990). *Institutions, Institutional Change and Economic Performance*. Cambridge: Cambridge University Press.

—— (1996). *Economic Performance through Time: Empirical Studies in Institutional Change*. Cambridge: Cambridge University Press.

Organisation of Pharmaceutical Producers in India (OPPI). (2000). "35th Annual Report." Mumbai: OPPI.

Oyelaran-Oyeyinka, B. and McCormick, D. (2007). *Industrial Clusters and Innovation Systems in Africa*. Tokyo: UNU Press.

—— and Gehl Sampath, P. (2009). *Biotechnology and Economic Development: Innovation in Asia and Africa*. New York: Palgrave McMillan. Forthcoming.

—— and Rasiah, R. (2008). Uneven Paths of Development: Learning, Innovation and Catching Up in Asia and Africa. Cheltenham: Edward Elgar.

Pietrobelli, C. (2000). "The Role of International Technology Transfer in the Industrialisation of Developing Countries," in M. Elena and D. Schroeer (eds.), *Technology Transfer*. Aldershot, UK: Ashgate.

Rodrik, D. (2007). *One Economics, Many Recipes: Globalization, Institutions and Economic Growth*. Princeton, NJ: Princeton University Press.

Stiglitz, J. 1998. "Redefining the Role of the State", in H.J. Chang, (ed.), *The Rebel Within*. London: Wimbledon Publishing Company, 94–126.

—— and Greenwald, B. C. (1986). "Externalities in Economies with Imperfect Information and Incomplete Markets," *Quarterly Journal of Economics*, 101 (2): 229–64.

Vartiainen, J. (1999). "The Economics of Successful State Intervention in Industrial Transformation," in M. Woo-Cummings (ed.), *The Developmental State*. Ithaca: Cornell University Press, 200–34.

Wagner, C. S. (2005). "Six Case Studies of International Collaboration in Science," *Scientometrics*, 62 (1): 3–26.

Woo-Cummings, M. (1999). "Chalmers Johnson and the Politics of Nationalism and Development," in M. Woo-Cummings (ed.), *The Developmental State*. Ithaca: Cornell University Press, 1–31.

World Bank (1993). *World Development Indicators, 1991*. New York: Oxford University Press.

—— (2001). *A Chance to Learn: Knowledge and Finance for Education in Sub-Saharan Africa*. Washington, DC: International Bank for Reconstruction.

—— (2007). *Enhancing Agricultural Innovation: How to Go Beyond the Strengthening of Research Systems*, Agriculture and Rural Development Series. Washington, DC: World Bank.

10

State–Business Relations, Investment Climate Reform, and Economic Growth in Sub-Saharan Africa[*]

Kunal Sen and Dirk Willem te Velde

Introduction

Researchers, who have long examined the factors that contribute to economic growth, are now challenged to examine how state–business relations (SBR) affect economic performance in Sub-Saharan Africa (SSA). Critics contend that this is a difficult task because such relations are intangible and immeasurable and their effects are difficult to assess. While we acknowledge that informal aspects of SBRs will be difficult to measure, our research suggests that it is possible to identify and measure key factors behind effective SBRs that are conducive to growth in Africa, but more needs to be done.[1]

The context for SBR research in Africa is rich, diverse, and dynamic. Some countries have long had official relations separating state and business, while in other countries the relations are difficult, complex, and based on mistrust. In many countries a significant portion of business is owned by the state. In some countries, such as Mauritius and South Africa, there is an institutionalized form of state–business relations, while in other countries, such as Malawi, the state and business were brought together through a facilitated forum. Some countries have a developed entrepreneurial business sector; in others this is largely absent. Nearly every African country has seen improvements in the factors associated with good SBRs, so it would be instructive to see whether and how some effective SBRs have facilitated economic performance, accounting for other drivers of growth.

Our motivation for focusing on effective state–business relations as an additional determinant of economic performance is influenced by long-standing literature in political science and political economy that collaborative SBRs can be growth-enhancing (e.g., Amsden 1989; Evans 1995). The literature has argued that sustained economic growth has occurred in contexts where the state has intervened in the economy so as "to provide incentives to private capital and to discipline it" (Harriss 2006) and takes the position that "good growth-enhancing relations between business and government elites are possible" (Maxfield and Schneider 1997). The empirical evidence in support of this view has been mostly from case studies, drawn predominantly from East Asia (e.g. Johnson 1987) or Latin America (Doner and Schneider 2000). In support of this, some recent firm-level studies provide evidence that state support contributes to firm survival and growth (Fajnzylber et al. 2008; Hansen et al. 2009).[2] There is as yet limited knowledge of whether effective SBRs can contribute to economic growth in SSA. This is a significant omission in the literature. The political science literature on Africa has recognized the growth-impeding collusive behavior among weak and fragmented political and economic elites that has characterized most African countries. The political science literature also provides examples of political elites who formed successful "growth coalitions" with economic elites in countries as disparate in initial conditions and geographical characteristics as Botswana, Ghana, and Mauritius (Herbst 1993; Bräutigam et al. 2002; Robinson and Parsons 2006).[3]

There are several unresolved issues in research on SBRs. There is no single definition of SBRs, which makes the topic more difficult to navigate. Questions of more substance relate to how state–business relations are formed, what different forms they take, whether the essence of SBRs can be measured, whether SBRs can have measurable effects at micro and macro levels, and whether different forms or functions of SBRs have different effects on performance. This chapter summarizes ongoing research on the factors associated with effective SBRs, how SBRs can be measured, and what the effects of SBRs are. We conclude with some implications.

The following section discusses the factors that are normally thought to be associated with effective state–business relations, such as transparency, reciprocity and credibility, and how they are expected to affect growth. The next section measures state–business relations at the macro and micro levels. Next, we summarize empirical evidence on the relationships between effective state–business relations and economic performance at both the macro and micro levels. The final section provides policy implications.

Factors associated with effective state–business relations

The literature takes the following elements as essential characteristics of effective SBRs (see Maxfield and Schneider 1997).

- *Transparency:* the flow of accurate and reliable information, both ways, between business and government.

- *Reciprocity:* the capacity and autonomy of state actions to secure improved performance in return for subsidies.

- *Credibility:* when capitalists are able to believe what state actors say.

Effective SBRs, as characterized above, can affect growth by fulfilling a number of economic functions. First, they can help to solve information-related market and coordination failures in areas such as skill development and infrastructure provision. For instance, business associations or government departments may coordinate and disperse information among stakeholders.

Second, effective SBRs provide a check-and-balance function on government policies and tax and expenditure plans (te Velde 2009). Thus, effective SBRs may help to ensure that the provision of infrastructure is appropriate and of good quality. The design of effective government policies and regulations depends, among other things, on contributions from and consultation with the private sector. Regular sharing of information between the state and businesses ensures that private-sector objectives are met with public action and that local-level issues are fed into higher-level policy processes. The private sector can identify constraints, opportunities, and possible policy options for creating incentives, lowering investment risks, and reducing the cost of doing business. More efficient institutions and rules and regulations might be achieved through policy advocacy, which could reduce the costs and risks faced by firms and enhance productivity.

Finally, effective SBRs and membership of business associations may help to reduce policy uncertainty (*op. cit.*). Firms operate in an uncertain environment and frequently face risks and resource shortages. They undertake decisions concerning technology, inputs, and production facilities based on anticipated market conditions and profitability. Uncertainty can have significant negative effects on investment, when it involves large sunk and irreversible costs and there is the option to delay the decision to make the investment until further information becomes available (Dixit and Pindyck 1994). Businesses that have better relations with government may be able to anticipate policy decisions.

Hisahiro (2005) argues that various forms of information and resources, which are dispersed among entities in the public and private sector, need to be integrated in a more sophisticated way to jointly coordinate policies and provide better public services. It is this combination of insulation and connectedness that minimizes the risks and enhances the effectiveness of economic policies. Hence, appropriate government capacity and policy, which are necessary to support private-sector development and promote economic growth, can be enabled by good state–business relations and productive public–private sector dialogue.

Effective SBRs can enhance economic growth by positively affecting the two proximate determinants of growth—the rate of factor accumulation and the growth of total factor productivity (te Velde 2009). Greater transparency in the flow of information between state actors and the business sector leads to both a better allocation of investments by the business sector to their most productive uses and, by reducing policy uncertainty in the minds of investors, a higher rate of investment. Higher credibility of state actions leads to fewer problems of time and dynamic inconsistencies of government policies and provides a more favorable environment for investment to occur. Reciprocity ensures improved performance by private-sector actors in return for subsidies and the provision of public goods, which contributes to higher productivity growth in the economy.

Effective SBRs can mitigate both market failures and government failures, which are pervasive in most developing countries, and by doing so, bring about an increase in economic growth.

There are visible aspects of SBRs, which could be measured. Some would argue that less visible, informal aspects are equally, if not more, important. Trust, for instance, is not always dependent on contracts or visible enforcement mechanisms. This we acknowledge. However, we argue that the visible aspects mentioned previously are important in their own right, and that the informal aspects may influence the links between measurable aspects of SBRs and performance, but this does not deny that there could be a systematic link between formal SBRs and growth. Hence, our hypothesis is on understanding the effects of the measurable aspects of SBRs.

Measuring state–business relations

In-depth discussions of state–business relations have so far focused mostly on Asian countries, such as Korea, Japan, Malaysia, Bangladesh, and Thailand (e.g., Hisahiro 2005), and on Latin America (Doner and Schneider 2000). The measurement of state–business relations is still in its infancy and nearly absent in SSA, despite its potential importance for economic development.[4] Hyden et al. (2004) focus on six governance categories, of which economic society is one, and this includes (deliberately) subjective questions covering perceptions of SBRs. The study covers several developing countries, but only two African countries. The Kaufmann et al. (2005) indicators have become frequently used, but are also centered around perceptions of governance variables, such as government effectiveness and rule of law. Finally, while investment climate measures in the World Bank's *Doing Business* reports are objective (e.g., number of procedures required to obtain a license), these are unlikely to be fundamental drivers of economic performance, and can be seen as outcomes of effective SBRs. There is a lack of description and comprehensive measurement of effective SBRs as potentially fundamental drivers of economic growth in SSA.

Measuring SBRs at the macro level

In order to measure effective SBRs and assess their importance for economic performance, we need to measure the essence of SBRs. Following the discussion in the previous section, we argue that there are four main elements responsible for good SBRs: (1) The way in which the private sector is organized *vis-à-vis* the public sector; (2) the way in which the government is organized *vis-à-vis* the private sector; (3) the practice and institutionalization of SBRs; and (4) the avoidance of harmful collusive behavior.

We construct a composite measure of SBRs based on these four elements for nineteen SSA countries for which we have data for the period 1970–2004. Our measure is similar in principle to those used to measure the restrictiveness of trade policy, in that we are trying to capture the *institutional relations* between states and businesses that may lead to better outcomes for investment and growth, rather than the outcomes themselves.[5] We are interested in the causes of better investment climate outcomes, not in measuring the outcomes.[6] What follows is a discussion of each of the four elements of good SBRs.

THE WAY THE PRIVATE SECTOR IS ORGANIZED *VIS-À-VIS* THE PUBLIC SECTOR

Good SBRs cannot be sustained in the long run without effective private-sector participation. Weiss (1998) indicates that the more firms are involved in business associations, the easier it is to coordinate policy between the government and business. The importance of business associations is further emphasized by Hisahiro (2005), who suggests that they play a significant role in facilitating the formulation, implementation, and monitoring of economic policies and provision of feedback to the government. All-encompassing business associations are more likely to engage in collective action by pressing for policies that bring about economic growth throughout the economy, rather than favoring particular sectors at the expense of others (Olson 1982). A representative umbrella organization for all private-sector associations is present in some countries.[7] We indicate the organization of each country's private sector in a given year by giving it a score of 0 if it did not have a private-sector umbrella organization and giving a score of 1 if it did (for further details, see te Velde 2006).

THE WAY THE GOVERNMENT IS ORGANIZED *VIS-À-VIS* THE PRIVATE SECTOR

A government faces numerous decisions regarding how it may organize itself to interact with business. An important measure is the presence and effectiveness of an investment promotion agency (IPA), which could be seen as indicative of advocacy of private-sector interests as a whole.[8] We measure how the public sector is organized *vis-à-vis* the private sector by the presence and length of existence of an IPA to promote business. A score of 0 for each country in a given year indicates that it did not have an IPA and a score of 1 indicates that it did (for further details, see te Velde 2006).

THE PRACTICE AND INSTITUTIONALIZATION OF SBRS

Effective SBRs require the cooperation of the public and private sectors, but cooperation and willingness may not be effective in and of themselves. To examine these qualities, we investigate whether a country has a mechanism for public–private dialogue. Without such a mechanism, usually a forum, it is more difficult for the state and the private sector to be on agreeable terms in a transparent way, and to avoid harmful collusive behavior.[9] A dialogue mechanism can come in a number of forms: it can be open to all and autonomous of government intervention, as is the case with a formal existing body, or it can be an informal "suggestive" body with no entrenched power. The statistics of a forum, such as when it was founded and how often it meets, provide an idea of the forum's strength. We score 0 for each country in a given year if it did not have an institutionalized public–private dialogue (PPD); 0.5 if a country's PPD comprised one or fewer annual meetings; and 1 a country's PPD comprised two or more meetings per year (see te Velde 2006 for further details).

MECHANISMS TO AVOID HARMFUL COLLUSIVE BEHAVIOR

Competition laws are created to promote business competition and the creation of new businesses. The existence of such laws and their duration will be used as initial indicators of a country's commitment to such competition policies, though it will be important to consider the efficacy of the laws. We measure the presence of *anti-collusive behavior* (COMP) by scoring 0 for each country in a given year if it did not have a competition policy in place, 0.5 if it did have a policy but there is evidence that it was not effective, and 1 if a country had an effective competition policy (for further details, see te Velde 2006).[10]

Each of the four elements can be measured over time, leading to four, time-varying indicators per country. In order to obtain a composite measure, we take the average of the above indicators for the country in question for a given year (attaching the same weight to each indicator). Figure 10.1 plots the averages for four groups of countries, ranging from the fastest growing group over 1970–2005 (group 1) to the slowest growing group (group 4). As expected, countries with higher SBR scores grow faster.

There are two caveats regarding our measure. First, it captures the formal aspects of SBRs, not the informal aspects. The latter are to a large extent "not observable," and cannot be quantified. However, as has been noted by Chingaipe and Leftwich (2007) and Handley (2008), SBRs in Africa are characterized by a high degree of informality. Our measure cannot capture personalized and informal interactions between the state and the business sectors, which may also be growth-enhancing. Second, our measure may not be easily generalized outside of SSA, which does not have a long-standing history of umbrella business associations in contrast to countries such as India. Only recently have the governments of many African countries actively solicited private investment via the creation of IPAs. These features of SBRs in SSA allow for variation in the time dimension and in the cross-section dimension, which may not hold true for other regions, such as East and South Asia.

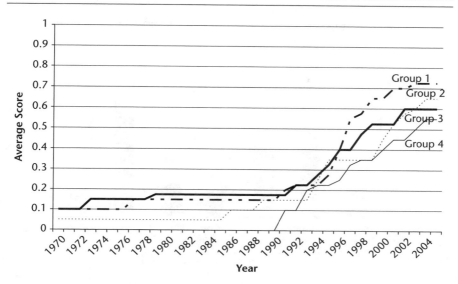

Figure 10.1 Higher SBR scores for groups of faster growing countries

Notes: Group 1 = Botswana, Mauritius, Uganda, Mozambique, Mali; Group 2 = Tanzania, Ghana, Eritrea (part), Senegal, Kenya; Group 3 = Benin, Ethiopia, South Africa, Nigeria, Rwanda; Group 4 = Malawi, Zimbabwe, Madagascar, Zambia, Côte d'Ivoire. Groups based on purchasing power parity GDP per capita growth rates from 1980–2004.

Source: Authors' calculations

Measuring SBR at the micro level

We have argued that one indicator associated with good SBRs is an organized private sector, which can be measured at the micro level by memberships in business associations. This micro-level measure does not take into account other features of effective SBRs, such as an organized public sector, the formalized interactions between the state and business, and absence of collusive behaviors. This micro-level measure captures just one dimension of what we consider to be an effective SBR, and therefore has its limitations. Nevertheless, the advantage of this measure is that it can be operationalized at the firm level and linked to firm performance in a manner that the macro-level measures that we have discussed cannot.

Figure 10.2 presents the distributions of firms that are members of business associations across seven African countries.

Business associations provide different services and the World Bank questionnaire asks firms which services are found to be most important. Lobbying government and information on government regulations are on average the two most important services provided by business associations to the firms covered in the sample (Figure 10.3a–3c). The least important services are resolution of disputes (with officials, workers, or other firms) and accrediting standards or quality of products. We find wide variation in the value of services across the three countries

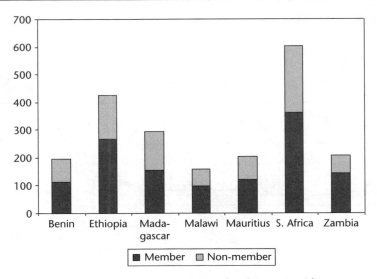

Figure 10.2 Private-sector organizations membership across African countries

Source: Authors' calculations; World Bank Enterprise Surveys

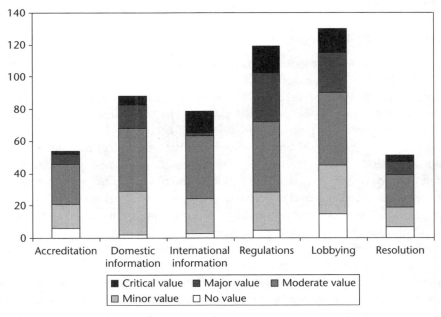

Figure 10.3a Value of services by business associations to firms in Zambia

Source: Authors' calculations; World Bank Enterprise Surveys: Ethiopia, South Africa, and Zambia

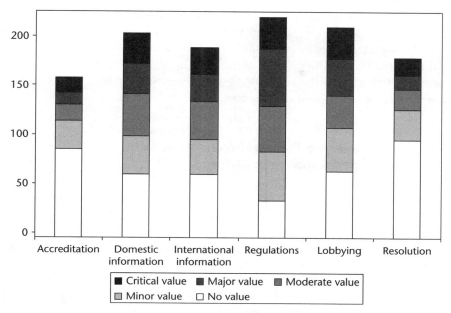

Figure 10.3b Value of services by business associations to firms in Ethiopia
Source: Authors' calculations; World Bank Enterprise Surveys: Ethiopia

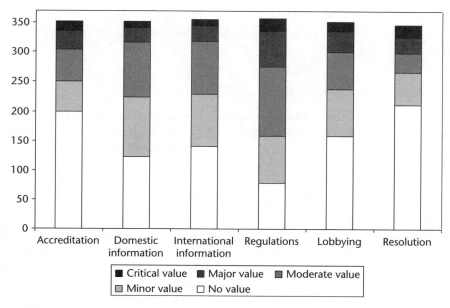

Figure 10.3c Value of services by business associations to firms in South Africa
Source: Authors' calculations; World Bank Enterprise Surveys: South Africa

considered—Ethiopia, South Africa, and Zambia—suggesting that the specific roles that business associations play vary significantly across countries, and may be related to both the effectiveness of the state's interactions with the business sector and the capability of the business association to provide specific services to its members. The research also shows that business membership varies by sector and firm size; but all sectors and sizes are covered.

What we have learned about the effects of SBRs on economic performance in Africa

This section summarizes a number of empirical studies aimed at examining the effects of SBRs in Africa, at both the macro and micro levels. We have argued that effective SBRs can positively impact economic growth by increasing the rates of capital accumulation and productivity growth. In this section, we test this hypothesis in two ways. First, in a direct test of our hypothesis, we estimate reduced-form growth regressions using panel data and examine whether improvements in our macro SBR measure lead to increased economic growth, controlling for other growth determinants. We follow this macro exercise with a more disaggregated analysis of the relationship between effective SBRs and economic growth by using our micro measure of SBRs to examine determinants of productivity growth at the firm level. By moving to the micro level, we can drill down to the constituents of effective SBRs that matter for firm-level performance and address some limitations of cross-country econometric analysis of the determinants of economic growth (Sen et al. 2006).

Effects of SBRs at the macro level

While the importance of SBRs has been acknowledged in the context of SSA, they have not been detailed in the economic growth literature and their effects have never been quantified. Our research has begun to quantify the effects of effective SBRs (Sen and te Velde 2009). We use the index developed by measuring SBRs (as detailed above) and estimate standard growth regressions in dynamic panel form for nineteen African countries over the period 1970–2004 using annual data, controlling for more conventionally used measures of institutional quality in the empirical literature. Previous empirical studies of institutions' role in growth measure institutional quality by the rule of law index (Knack and Keefer 1995; Sachs and Warner 1997), bureaucratic quality (ibid.), incidence of corruption (Mauro 1995), and constraints on the executive (Glaeser et al. 2004). To see whether SBRs can explain economic growth independent of these other institutional variables, we include these variables in our estimated equations along with the SBR measure, as well as standard control variables used in growth regressions,

Table 10.1 Effective state–business relations and economic growth: regression results

VARIABLES	Col. (1)	Col. (2)	Col. (3)
CONSTANT	0.67	0.87	0.87
	(5.13)***	(3.77)***	(3.76)***
ONE-YEAR LAGGED GDP	0.93	0.91	0.91
	(70.80)***	(38.56)***	(38.57)***
SBR	*0.03*	*0.03*	*0.03*
	*(2.67)***	*(2.00)**	*(2.00)**
INFLATION	−0.0003	−0.0002	−0.0002
	(3.48)***	(3.01)***	(3.12)***
GOVT CONSUMPTION	0.001	0.001	0.001
	(1.62)	(1.75)*	(1.84)*
OPENNESS	0.0003	0.0003	0.0002
	(1.77)*	(1.01)	(1.01)
EXECUTIVE CONSTRAINTS	–	0.0003	0.0003
		(2.25)**	(2.25)**
RULE OF LAW	–	0.07	0.07
		(2.15)**	(2.17)**
BUREAUCRATIC QUALITY	–	0.0006	0.0006
		(0.20)	(0.20)
CORRUPTION	–	0.004	0.004
		(1.11)	(1.22)
R-square	0.99	0.99	0.99
ESTIMATION METHOD	ORDINARY LEAST SQUARES, FIXED EFFECTS	ORDINARY LEAST SQUARES, FIXED EFFECTS	INSTRUMENTAL VARIABLE REGRESSION, FIXED EFFECTS
Number of Observations	579	328	328

Notes: (a) *, **, and *** significant at the 10, 5, and 1 percent respectively; (b) t-ratios in brackets, unless otherwise stated. Log Per Capita Income is the dependent variable. In the instrumental variable regression, we use past SBR as an instrument for current SBR.

such as past GDP (to take into account path dependence in country growth experiences) inflation, government consumption, and openness. The results are presented in Table 10.1.

The striking result is that the coefficient on SBRs is positive and significant at the level of 5 percent or less for all estimates presented in columns 1–3. The value of the coefficient on the SBR variable remains remarkably consistent at 0.03 for all the estimates, whether we use ordinary least squares or instrumental variables. The significance of the SBR variable remains even when we include the more commonly used measures of institutional quality, such as the degree of executive constraints, the rule of law, corruption, and the quality of the bureaucracy.[11] Our results suggest that our measure of SBRs captures a different dimension of institutional quality than those ordinarily captured by studies on institutions and growth. Thus, there is strong support for the proposition that effective SBRs matter for economic growth in SSA, independent of other measures of institutional quality and macroeconomic factors.

Also, the index of SBRs advanced significantly and began to improve before the pick-up in growth (though different conditions applied in different countries), suggesting that effective SBRs are causal to growth, rather than the other way around. In further regressions that we have undertaken, we also found that effective SBRs seem to matter more for the growth of the manufacturing sector, and that among the components of the SBR measure, what seems to affect economic growth most are the presence of IPAs and formalized PPD (see Sen and te Velde 2009).

Effects of SBRs at the micro level

The micro-level studies follow a two-stage approach (Qureshi and te Velde 2007a). In the first stage, we estimate a production function for firms in a country by fitting a production function explaining production value added as a function of capital and labor. We used the Levinsohn-Petrin technique to account for endogeneity of the error term and factor inputs labor and capital. In this respect, the data set is rich since we can exploit the fact that there are often three years' worth of firm performance data, as well as variables such as material input costs that can be used as proxies. In the second stage, we estimate a total factor productivity equation, where productivity is based on the residuals in the first stage, and test whether membership is associated with better performance, accounting for other effects.

Some suggest that there might be endogeneity issues, in that good performance leads to membership: firms with higher productivity are more likely to become a member of a business association. However, there are a number of reasons to suspect that the relationship is actually the other way around. Indeed, the literature suggests that it is more likely that firms become a member *because* they expect higher benefits. Doner and Schneider (2000) suggest that the right incentive structure (i.e. benefits of selected firms) is a key driver for membership. Moreover, evidence from the World Bank Enterprise Surveys suggests that firms perceive there to be a high value of services provided by business associations (see for example Figure 10.3a–3c).

The micro-level regressions for Zambia (Qureshi and te Velde 2007a) used the Enterprise Survey data of the World Bank Group for around 200 firms with data on performance, including data that facilitate the calculation of productivity levels, and on the institutional context facing or perceived by firms. Data shows that business association membership enhances Zambian firm performance in the form of productivity improvements in the range of 37–41 percent. This finding is robust to including other variables. Further, joining a business association is particularly useful for small and medium-sized firms. Finally, the results supported the view that foreign-owned firms lobby the government more effectively than their Zambian counterparts.

Subsequent work used the enterprise survey data of the World Bank Group for seven African countries (Qureshi and te Velde 2007b) independently as well as in a panel of African firms (allowing for country- and sector-specific effects). The results

Table 10.2 Effects of different services of business associations on productivity

Variable	Estimated coefficient in productivity equation	Perceived usefulness on scale of 0 (no value) – 4 critical value, mean value
Information on government regulation	0.10*	1.85
Lobbying government	0.08*	1.41
Information on domestic markets	0.07	1.42
Information on international markets	0.07	1.34
Accreditation standards	0.08	1.00
Resolution of disputes	0.02	0.97

Note: This is the coefficient on the business association variable in an equation explaining productivity (TFP) controlling for other factors: based on data available from Ethiopia, South Africa, and Zambia.

show that being a member of a business association improves firm performance in the form of total factor productivity improvements on average between 25–35 percent. This finding is robust to including other variables that are commonly used to describe the investment climate, and robust to using estimates of productivity that account for endogeneity problems.

Detailed findings in Table 10.2 show that the efficacy of business associations works primarily through solving information-related market and coordination failures and lobbying government. The findings confirm that the perceived value of services provided by business associations is in line with the estimated effects. The more important a service is perceived as being, the more important its estimated effect. Thus, business associations affect firm performance by reducing policy uncertainty and by lobbying government over regulations. Membership in business associations can also work through its effect on business climate indicators. For instance, we found that business association membership decreases the size of informal payments by individual firms and improves other investment climate indicators. Finally, membership also increases labor productivity so that positive productivity effects are at least in part captured by labor; most of these benefits are going to the skilled workers providing positive dynamic incentives throughout the economy.

Linking micro and macro levels of analyses

The micro-level work for each of the seven African countries reveals that there are significant differences in the effects of membership across countries, ranging from highly significant and positive effects in Mauritius and Ethiopia to insignificant effects in Benin and Madagascar, with positive and significant effects in Malawi and Zambia.

Importantly, when we compare the estimated coefficients for membership to the overall SBR scores that we computed for these seven countries, we estimate the correlation coefficient to be 0.55 (see Figure 10.4). This suggests that there is a link between the advancement of visible aspects of SBRs at the macro level (SBR

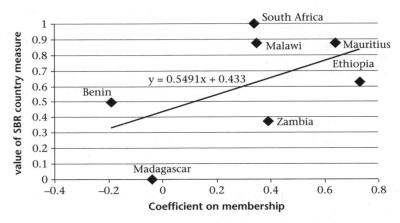

Figure 10.4 The effect of business association membership on productivity is greater in countries that are better prepared for effective state–business relations

Source: Authors' calculations

country measure) and the effects on firm performance at the micro level. In general, the effects of SBRs are more pronounced in countries that have strong institutional set-ups to support and conduct effective SBRs.

Conclusions and implications

Our ongoing research efforts suggest that improvements in formalized institutional relations between the state and the private sector increase economic growth in the African context. These institutional relations could be the creation of umbrella business associations, the setting up of IPAs, formalized PPDs, or the implementation of competition laws. Umbrella business associations can help resolve collective action problems for the private sector and allow them to push for growth-enhancing policies. The development of effective IPAs signals the intention of the government to take the private sector and investment activity seriously. Formalized public–private sector dialogue processes allow for transparency in policy formulation and efficient dissemination of information from both the public and the private sectors. Effective competition laws prevent rent-seeking and collusive behavior on the part of bureaucrats and capitalists. Our research shows that the creation and sustenance of effective state–business relations along these lines may have a stronger impact on economic growth in Sub-Saharan Africa than the conventional measures of governance reform such as improvements in the rule of law and stronger anti-corruption measures that have been stressed in the literature and in the policy debate.

While we have suggested there are certain key principles behind effective SBRs, this does not mean that each country should follow one institutional blueprint. Indeed, this study does not indicate whether certain types of SBRs or business associations work better than others (as explained in Doner and Schneider 2000 for non-African developing countries), which are likely to be context-specific and dependent in part on informal aspects. It does not identify which economic function is most relevant (or binding) in which country, e.g. reduction in policy uncertainty or lobbying government (as suggested in the microeconometric study for Zambia by Qureshi and te Velde 2007a). While this study does show that effective SBRs can be good for enhancing growth—which is an important policy finding given the historically skeptical view toward the African private sector as being solely rent-seeking—there is much left to research at the country level. Perhaps most importantly, the analysis shows that our SBR measure does have empirical meaning, so the nature of SBRs in Africa is worthy of further study.

This new and ongoing research on understanding the key characteristics and effects of SBRs is challenging and yielding preliminary insights and implications as well as unfinished business. SBRs can be measured at micro and macro levels and we can already sketch out some ways through which SBRs affect economic performance theoretically and empirically, but much more needs to be done.

Conceptually, it is important to test the boundaries of what can be measured in terms of SBRs. This is partly about what can be measured per se and partly about whether there are enough data on what can be measured. It is important to test the effects of the measurable aspects of SBRs; we suggested that as a very general conclusion, measurable aspects of SBRs have a positive impact on economic performance in SSA at both micro and macro levels. This provides support for the hypothesis that more open and visible SBRs are good.

However, it is too soon to assess and understand the precise effects of SBRs on development and what the exact channels are. So far, the available evidence points to a number of possible routes. The micro evidence suggested that business associations lobby government (in addition to the lobbying of individual firms) and this is both *perceived* to be important as well as *estimated* to increase firm performance. We need to know why this is so. One possible route is that business associations would be effective in identifying and removing investment barriers by lobbying the government. Such a mechanism would provide for a democratic way of conducting effective SBRs; in fact, membership is associated with a reduction in informal payments by individual firms.

We need to know more about the precise effects on economic performance and on different types of growth and the precise routes through which this is expected to work. A conceptual framework on the effects of SBRs on shared growth is only just emerging. We also need to know more about what leads to the formation of SBRs, what sustains them, and what factors we exclude by focusing on measurement issues. As Leftwich (2009: 4) argues, effective SBRs are more likely to occur when "'growth coalitions' (rather than distributional coalitions or predatory coalitions) can be built." This is a two-way relationship as growth coalitions are more likely to be formed when SBRs "take the form of active cooperation toward the goal of policies that both parties expect will foster investment and increases in productivity" (Bräutigam et al. 2002: 540). There is need for careful case studies of growth experiences in the African context using historical institutionalist approaches that can analyze the origins of "growth coalitions" and the formation of effective SBRs. In our view, the focus on measuring SBRs facilitates a debate between economists and political scientists on what matters for state–business relations to improve growth prospects.

Notes

* The research presented in this chapter has been undertaken for the Research Programme Consortium on Improving Institutions for Pro-Poor Growth (IPPG) and funded by UK DFID. More details of the research are available at <http://www.ippg.org.uk>. Special thanks to Mahvash Qureshi and Max Cali, the co-authors of some of the work summarized in this chapter. We are grateful to the World Bank for providing access to the World Bank Enterprise Surveys, and to an anonymous referee and the editors of this volume for comments. Any errors and opinions expressed are the sole responsibility of the authors.

1. By effective state–business relations, we mean a set of highly institutionalized, responsive, and public interactions between the state and the business sector.

2. Fajnzylber et al. (2008) address aspects of the impact of forms of government support on Mexican micro firms, using various techniques to identify treatment effects of credit, training, and tax payments (as a measure of formality, hence a proxy for potential access to public services) on firm profits, growth, and survival likelihood. They find that, although access to these forms of support does not appear to significantly influence profits, "formality" and access to credit improve the likelihood of survival. They argue that facilitating access to credit and business development services and promoting formalization (which is similar to state–business relations) are all likely to increase firm growth. In this way, there is some evidence that SBRs, at the micro level, can support private-sector development and contribute to growth. A paper in a similar vein by Hansen et al. (2009) explores the effects of direct government assistance during start-up and other forms of interaction with the state (which relates to aspects of SBRs) on the long-run performance of small and medium-sized manufacturing enterprises (SMEs) in Vietnam. They find strong effects on firm dynamics (survival and growth) from interaction with state institutions—providing further micro evidence that SBRs matter for firm performance.

3. There is also a wider literature that discusses the possibility of a developmental state *à la* East Asia in the Sub-Saharan African context; Mkandawire (2001) argues that the institutional relations that governed state–business interactions in East Asia are also possible in Africa.

4. Bräutigam et al. (2002), which examines the nature of "growth coalitions" involving business interest groups and the government in Mauritius, Zambia, and Zimbabwe, is an exception.

5. For example, the restrictiveness of trade policy is best measured using tariff or quotas rather than import penetration ratios, as the latter is an outcome of trade policy changes rather than the measure of these changes.

6. This is an important distinction. The creation of export processing zones or the provision of skills and infrastructure by the government, for example, are outcomes of an effective SBR, rather than a measure of an effective SBR. By making this distinction, we avoid to a large extent the endogeneity problems that are endemic to outcome-based measures of institutions. See Glaeser et al. (2004) for a critique of outcome-based measures of institutions that are used in the literature.

7. Case study evidence also supports the argument that well-organized business associations can be important in pushing for growth-oriented policies. For example, the Ivorian Chamber of Industry played an important role in arguing for policies supporting export-oriented manufacturing (Rapley 1994). The Private Sector Foundation in Uganda is mandated to do policy research and advocacy for the private sector and has achieved improvements in the investment climate such as lower tariffs on key imports, upgrading of infrastructure, and streamlining of public procurement (Badagawa 2008).

8. An example of a successful IPA in the African context is the Rwandan Investment Promoting Agency (RIPA), formed in 1998, but which changed its name six years later to Rwanda Investment and Export Promoting Agency. This semiautonomous agency has made great strides in working with the private sector and gaining its input on reform measures (te Velde 2006).

9. An example of a successful institutionalized public–private dialogue process is the Joint Economic Council (JEC) in Mauritius. As Bräutigam et al. (2002: 526) notes, "over the years, the JEC has become institutionalised as a strong and legitimate 'peak' association for businesses in Mauritius, an encompassing group that represents all the major sectors and works out broadly agreeable positions on economic policy." The JEC discusses with the Minister of Finance a draft budget and presents proposals, which to a varying degree are taken over in the final budget.

10. The mere passage of competition law does not imply that it will be implemented. In 1995, Senegal passed the Decree on Price, Competition and Economic Contentions to prevent the commerce industry from colluding. However, more recent anti-corruption laws while accepted have been accused of being "watered-down" by Parliament (te Velde 2006). By taking into account the functioning of competition laws, and not just their form, we incorporate the possibility that competition laws introduced as a result of donor conditionality may not lead to a deepening of state–business relations.

11. Economic growth is measured by the year-to-year changes in GDP per capita, where the latter is in 1980 constant price in local currency. Data on GDP per capita along with government consumption, inflation, and openness – exports + imports as a ratio of GDP are obtained from the World Bank's *World Development Indicators*. Data on bureaucratic quality, rule of law, and corruption are obtained from the International Country Risk Guide published by Political Risk Services (PRS). These measures were originally constructed by the Center for Institutional Reform and the Informal Sector (IRIS) (see Knack and Keefer 1995 for further details). The variables are only available for the period 1987–2004. Data on executive constraints are obtained from the online database of the Polity IV project hosted by the Center for International Development and Conflict

Management at the University of Maryland. This variable is available for the entire period 1970–2004. Higher values of these indices indicate greater bureaucratic quality, higher rule of law, lower corruption, and higher degree of executive constraints.

References

Acemoglu, D., Johnson, S., and Robinson, J. (2001). "The Colonial Origins of Comparative Development," *American Economic Review*, 91 (5): 1369–401.

Amsden, A. (1989). *Asia's Next Giant: South Korea and Late Industrialization*. New York: Oxford University Press.

Badagawa, G. (2008). "Public–Private Dialogue: The PSFU Experience." Presentation at a PPD workshop in Senegal, April 3, 2008, available at <http://www.publicprivatedialogue.org/workshop%202008/PSFU%20PPD%20process%20-%20Dakar.ppt>.

Bräutigam, D., Rakner, L., and Taylor, S. (2002). "Business Associations and Growth Coalitions in Sub-Saharan Africa," *Journal of Modern African Studies*, 40 (4): 519–47.

Chingaipe, H. and Leftwich, A. (2007). "The Politics of State–Business Relations in Malawi," IPPG Discussion Paper No. 7, available at <http://www.ippg.org.uk>.

Dixit, A. and Pindyck, R. (1994). *Investment under Uncertainty*. Princeton, NJ: Princeton University Press.

Doner, R. F. and Schneider, M. R. (2000). "Business Associations and Economic Development: Why Some Associations Contribute More than Others," *Business and Politics*, 2: 261–88.

Evans, P. (1995). *Embedded Autonomy: States and Industrial Transformation*. Princeton, NJ: Princeton University Press.

Fajnzylber, P., Maloney, W. F., and Montes-Rojas, G. V. (2008). "Releasing Constraints to Growth or Pushing on a String? Policies and Performance of Mexican Micro-Firms," *Journal of Development Studies*, 45 (7): 1027–47.

Glaeser, E., La Porta, R., and Lopez-de-Silanes, F. (2004). "Do Institutions Cause Growth?" *Journal of Economic Growth*, 9: 271–303.

Hall, R. and Jones, C. I. (1999). "Why do some Countries Produce so Much More Output Per Worker than Others?" *Quarterly Journal of Economics*, 114: 83–116.

Handley, A. (2008). *Business and the State in Africa*. Cambridge: Cambridge University Press.

Hansen, H., Rand, J., and Tarp, F. (2009). "Enterprise Growth and Survival in Vietnam Does Government Support Matter?" *Journal of Development Studies*, 45 (7): 1048–69.

Harriss, J. (2006). "Institutions and State-Business Relations," Improving Institutions for Pro-Poor Growth (IPPG) Briefing Note 2, available at <http://www.ippg.org.uk>.

Herbst, J. (1993). *The Politics of Reforms in Ghana 1982–1991*. Berkeley: University of California Press.

Hisahiro, K. (2005). "Comparative Analysis of Governance: Relationship between Bureaucracy and Policy Co-ordination Capacity with Particular Reference to Bangladesh," Institute for International Cooperation, available at <http://www.jica.go.jp/kokusouken/enterprise/chosakenkyu/kyakuin/200509_gov.html>.

Hyden, G., Court, J., and Maese, K. (2004). *Making Sense of Governance: Empirical Evidence from Sixteen Developing Countries*. Boulder, CO: Lynne Rienner.

Johnson, C. (1987). "Political Institutions and Economic Performance: The Government-Business Relation in Japan, South Korea and Taiwan," in F. Deyo (ed.), *The Political Economy of the New Asian Industrialism*. Ithaca: Cornell University Press.

Kaufmann, D., Kraay, A., and Mastruzzi, M. (2005). *Governance Matters IV: Governance Indicators for 1996–2004*. World Bank Policy Research Working Paper Series No. 3630, available at <http://www.worldbank.org>.

Knack, S. and Keefer, P. (1995). "Institutions and Economic Performance: Cross-Country Tests Using Alternative Measures," *Economics and Politics*, 7: 207–27.

Leftwich, A. (2009). "Analysing the Politics of State–Business Relations: A Methodological Concept Note on the Historical Institutionalist Approach," IPPG Discussion Paper No. 23A, available at http//:www.ippg.org.uk.

Maxfield, S. and Schneider, B. R. (eds.) (1997). *Business and the State in Developing Countries*. Ithaca: Cornell University Press.

Mauro, P. (1995). "Corruption and Growth," *Quarterly Journal of Economics*, 60: 681–713.

Mkandawire, T. (2001). "Thinking about Developmental States in Africa," *Cambridge Journal of Economics*, 25: 289–313.

North, D. C. (1990). *Institutions, Institutional Change and Economic Performance*. Cambridge: Cambridge University Press.

Olson, M. (1982). *The Rise and Decline of Nations*. New Haven: Yale University Press.

Qureshi, M. and te Velde, D. W. (2007a). "State-Business Relations and Firm Performance in Zambia," IPPG Discussion Paper 5, available at <http://www.ippg.org.uk>.

——— (2007b). "State-Business Relations, Investment Climate Reform and Firm Productivity in Sub-Saharan Africa," IPPG Discussion Paper 6, available at <http://www.ippg.org.uk>.

Rapley, J. (1994). "The Ivorian Bourgeoisie," in J. B. Berman and C. Leys (eds.), *African Capitalists in African Development*. Boulder, CO: Lynne Rienner.

Robinson, J. and Parsons, Q. N. (2006). "State Formation and Governance in Botswana," *Journal of African Economies*, 15 (Supplement): 100–40.

Rodrik, D. (2003). *In Search of Prosperity: Analytic Narratives on Economic Growth*. Princeton, NJ: Princeton University Press.

—— Subramanian, A., and Trebbi, F. (2004). "Institutions Rule: The Primacy of Institutions over Geography and Integration in Economic Development," *Journal of Economic Growth*, 9: 31–165.

Sachs, J. and Warner, A. M. (1997). "Sources of Slow Growth in African Economies," *Journal of African Economies*, 6 (3): 335–76.

Sen, K. et al. (2006). "Institutions and Pro-Poor Growth: Toward a Framework for Quantitative Analysis," IPPG Discussion Paper No. 3, available at <http://www.ippg.org.uk>.

—— and te Velde, D. W. (2009). "State–Business Relations and Economic Growth in Sub-Saharan Africa," *Journal of Development Studies*, 45 (8): 1–17.

te Velde, D. W. (2006). "Measuring State–Business Relations in Sub-Saharan Africa," IPPG Discussion Paper No. 4, available at <http://www.ippg.org.uk>.

—— (2009). "Analysing the Economics of State–Business Relations: A Summary Guide," IPPG Discussion Paper No. 23B, available at <http://www.ippg.org.uk>.

Weiss, L. (1998). *The Myth of the Powerless State*. Ithaca: Cornell University Press.

11

Africa, Industrial Policy, and Export Processing Zones: Lessons from Asia[*][1]

Howard Stein

Introduction

One of the more remarkable trends associated with the increasing international integration of the economies of developing countries has been the proliferation of free trade and export processing zones or free trade zones (FTZs). In 1959, Irish Shannon Export Free Zone, the first zone of any consequence, was established. The initial success of this experiment led to organizations such as the United Nations Industrial Development Organization (UNIDO) promoting it as a model to be reproduced by developing countries. In 1965, India became the first developing country to organize a zone. By 1980, more than thirty countries had established export processing zones. Ten years later, the number of countries with zones had doubled. While the exact numbers vary in accordance with definitions, most estimates placed the total number of zones at well over 200 in 1990, with total employment exceeding 2.5 million.[2] Over the 1990s, employment and the number of zones rapidly proliferated to around 845, which, in 1997, employed roughly 22.5 million people. By 2006, the number of zones had quadrupled again to 3,500, with worldwide employment reaching nearly 66 million in 130 countries. 3,126 of these zones are in developing or transitional countries, with a total employment of around 64.9 million.[3]

Most zones, and most of the people employed in them, are in China, where there are roughly 900 zones and roughly 40 million people employed. In 1990, Africa accounted for a mere 9 percent of the total number of zones in developing countries. Only three African countries—Egypt, Mauritius, and Tunisia—had zones with any significant employment or exports. In Sub-Saharan Africa, including Mauritius, only eight countries had organized export processing zones (EPZs). By 1996, they had been joined by at least seven other Sub-Saharan countries.[4] The most recent survey for 2006 lists twenty countries in Sub-Saharan Africa (SSA), with employment of 1,043,186 in more than ninety-one zones (roughly 2.6 percent of the total in developing countries including China, or 3.5 percent excluding China). However, 51 percent of total SSA employment is in one country: South Africa.[5] Only Mauritius, Lesotho, Kenya, Nigeria, and Madagascar employ more than 35,000 people in total. Three of these five rely heavily on textile exports and are in danger of significant contraction in the wake of the end of the Multi Fibre Arrangement. Many generate few jobs and have small labor forces (fewer than 10,000 workers) working in the zones (ILO 2007).

The rather slow expansion of EPZs in many African countries has been disappointing, but it provides many African countries with an opportunity to influence their direction at an earlier stage in their development, if they choose this route. Ultimately, the design and operation of zones that can maximize local and regional impact can also provide an environment conducive to the growth of foreign investment; employment opportunities; foreign exchange; backward, forward, and demand linkages; self-generating capital accumulation; training and technological spillovers; and significant local spin-offs and co-ownership opportunities. However, a number of success indicators suggest that zones in Africa have been broadly disappointing, particularly in contrast to the experiences of a number of Asian countries. The main problem is that many zones in SSA have been driven by aid agencies and, frequently, promises of special access to foreign markets through donor programs such as the Africa Growth and Opportunity Act (AGOA) and Everything But Arms (EBA). The benefits have proved to be somewhat ethereal, particularly after the expiration of the Multi Fibre Arrangement in January 2005. Moreover, the vision has been driven by the rather faulty neoclassical notion, frequently embedded in World Bank policy papers, that EPZs are simply second-best solutions to the total liberalization of economies. However, for many Asian countries with successful export zones, EPZs have been part of a broader industrial policy in which zones are not an end of themselves, but a component of broader industrialization strategies.

The paper begins with a taxonomy of the different types of zones before briefly reviewing some of the literature concerned with free trade type zones. The next section of the paper presents the theory of industrial policy and how FTZs can fit into manufacturing strategies. The latter part of the paper contrasts examples from Asia and Africa, which buttress the main theoretical arguments. The final section examines the Onne Free Trade and Gas Zone and how it could be better designed in an industrial policy framework in Nigeria.

Toward a taxonomy of terminology

There are a wide variety of terms to describe open trading and manufacturing areas that operate with custom rules and government policy measures, different from those found in other sections of a country. Given the wide use of imprecise terminology in the literature, it is important to carefully define and differentiate the various types of zones.[6]

Free ports and trade zones

A *free trade zone* (FTZ) is a spatially defined area in a wider political unit and is often next to a port where unrestricted trade with the rest of the world is permitted. Merchandise may be moved in and out of FTZs free of customs, stored in warehouses for varying periods, and repackaged as necessary. The requisite duty is paid on goods imported into the host country. FTZs provide rapid delivery opportunities, while removing the interest costs of custom payments (Hewitt and Wield 1992). *Free ports* (FPs) generally coincide with a political unit where goods are imported without customs regulation and either consumed locally or re-exported. Examples are Hong Kong, Singapore, and Gibraltar (DMS 1996).

Export processing zones and units and special economic zones

Export processing zones (EPZs) generally go beyond the conditions of FTZs to include a variety of measures aimed at encouraging investment in manufacturing exclusively for export.[7] In addition to the exemption from duties on imported intermediate goods, raw materials, and equipment, taxation and industrial regulations are typically more generous than elsewhere in the country. Tax holidays and the guarantee of the repatriation of profit are often provided. Infrastructure is typically well developed and often subsidized. Wages are sometimes lower than elsewhere and unionization is discouraged. Red-tape measures are minimized with approval often on a one-stop basis. A variety of other extension services are typically provided. EPZs are the most widespread examples of zones.

The most wide-scale activity found in EPZs is labor-intensive, non-complex manufacturing processes, with a heavy emphasis on assembly operations (Johansson 1994). Two activities are overwhelmingly dominant in the EPZs: textiles and garment production and electronic assembly. For instance, textiles and garments in the early 1990s accounted for almost 90 percent of employment in zones of Jamaica, Mauritius, and Sri Lanka. In Malaysia, employment in electronics accounted for 74 percent of the total (UNCTAD 1993).

Closely related to the EPZs are *economic processing units* (EPUs), single-firm units that operate as if they were EPZs. They are generally not restricted to a specific area in a country. Imported inputs are held in bond inside the factory and may be subject to continuous verification by officials or to random spot checks (DMS 1996). EPUs have the advantage of firms that fully factor locational variables into their decision-making. The major drawback is the loss of economies of scale, as well as some externalities that can arise from the situational proximity of firms.

Special economic zones (SEZs) include many of the features of EPZs, EPUs, and FPs. Companies receive many of the benefits of firms in EPZs and may locate anywhere within the zone, where the political and spatial unit are coterminous. They also have features that differ from other zones, including a diversity of economic activities that in certain cases have drawn foreign investment into agriculture, manufacturing, construction, communications, trade, catering, housing, public utilities, and other services such as finance and tourism. China, the main proponent of this approach, organized five SEZs from 1979–88.

The SEZs provided a unique opportunity for China to experiment in market reform, which has been slowly emulated in many townships and regions. SEZs also demonstrated the viability of the Chinese two-systems approach for Hong Kong and Macau prior to their annexation. The SEZs were selected for geographical and historical reasons (Shenzhen by Hong Kong; Zhuhai by Macau; Xiamen by Taiwan; Shantou because of its connections to overseas Chinese; and Hainan, which is easily accessible to Singapore, Japan, and Taiwan). The zones have attracted a large amount of foreign investment. By 1994, the accumulated foreign funds attracted for capital construction reached $6.4 billion. While overall, Hong Kong has provided the most important source of investment funds, the origins of funds in each zone have, relatively speaking, generally reflected the original design.[8]

It should be noted that over time, the number of joint ventures and investment sources other than foreign direct investment (FDI) grew appreciably. For example, in Shenzhen, more than half the investment funds came from foreign sources in 1981. By 1993, the figure had fallen to only 13 percent, with most funds from self-raised domestic loans and other sources. In 1981 only 13 percent of FDI was in joint ventures. By 1993, 64 percent of total FDI was in joint ventures (Ge 1999). As discussed below, this is an important conduit for channeling foreign technology and managerial expertise to local companies and was a deliberate aim of China's industrial policy. There are other variations of zone types, such as science and technology (S&T) parks in Taiwan, Korea, and China, which are aimed at increasing research and development (R&D) spending.

In China, the high and new technology industrial development zones (HNTIDZs) have played an increasingly important role in fostering research and applying it to the development of new industrial products, another strategy arising out of the priorities set in China's industrial policy (more on this below). In 1988, after the State S&T Commission announced their Torch Program to assist in organizing the zones, fourteen HNTIDZs were launched by provincial and municipal governments; thirteen more were launched two years later. These were formally approved in 1991 and twenty-five more were approved in 1993. By 1997, the 53rd zone, focusing on agriculture, was organized in Shaanxi.

Through 2001, the numbers have continued to rise to around 150, with 53 central level zones, 68 provincial, and 30 at the university level. The HNTIDZs were provided with an array of incentives, including no import licenses for inputs related to export processing, bonded warehouses and factories, zonal import/export agencies, rights to run a foreign trade business, low income taxes (15 percent across the board), and complete income tax exemption for the first two years after commencing operations. From 1992–4, the central government invested about RMB50 billion to construct the zones. Closely associated with the zones are a series of government-sponsored incubator programs aimed at providing training, consulting, information, exhibition centers, and a one-stop approval service for registration, insurance, commodity inspection, customs-bonded warehousing, and other services.

Enterprises and employment rapidly proliferated. By 1997, there were 15,000 new technology firms, employing 1.4 million people with an annual income of RMB339 billion (US$40 billion at the 1997 exchange rate 8.3 RMB/dollar) and a profit of RMB10.8 billion. The most important areas of product development have been in electronics and information, optics-machinery-electronics integrations, new materials, and bioengineering and pharmaceuticals. In some zones, a number of firms grew to large sizes. In the Beijing zone, three companies (Legend, Stone, and Founder) accounted for RMB20 billion of output in 1996, or roughly half of the total of the zone (Jici and Wang 2002).

The literature: a brief comment

While the literature on export-oriented zones in Sub-Saharan Africa is slowly growing, an extensive set of articles and books, based mostly on the experiences of Asia and Latin America and the Caribbean, has been published. Space precludes an extensive review of the literature, but broadly speaking, it can be divided into four different approaches for evaluating the economic impact of EPZs. These include formal modeling, which is heavily influenced by neoclassical welfare analysis; descriptive case studies; cost-benefit approaches; and policy modeling.

Pioneering neoclassical studies were undertaken by Hamada (1974) and Hamilton and Svensson (1982). The argument is that EPZs will not attract domestic investment since it provides a lower return (given that all prices are assumed to be international) than the protected segment of the economy. Similarly, foreign investors will also be discouraged since they would need to accept a lower return compared to other parts of the economy. Moreover, the neoclassicals argue that zones create distortions and are welfare–reducing, since the inflow of capital into the zones will attract labor from labor-intensive sectors of production (as countries follow their comparative advantage due to large labor endowments) to comparatively more capital-intensive sectors in the zones.

This counter-intuitive argument arises from assumptions embedded in the models. The models focus on tariffs on outputs and ignore the importance of other, capital-attracting factors, including tariff reductions on inputs, reduction in transactions costs due to simplified customs regulation, the ability to repatriate profits and lower taxes. Moreover, the models also assume full employment, which is completely contrary to the conditions of labor surplus that propel countries to organize zones in the first place. Other studies in this vein have been based on somewhat more realistic assumptions, but like most neoclassicals, they focus on the impact of the measures on increasing or decreasing distortions in a hypothetical world (Johansson 1994).

The case study approach has led to a wide variety of conclusions concerning the effectiveness of the zones. Disagreements often exist because case studies focus on different zones, some of which have been failures for reasons that include poor location, inadequate infrastructure, and gross mismanagement. However, there has also been fervent debate in the literature on the effectiveness of specific zones in countries such as the Dominican Republic.[9]

Cost-benefit analysis is aimed at quantifying the more qualitative evaluations of zones by arriving at a bottom-line net present value or internal rate of return. Benefits include the foreign exchange earned as a result of using local inputs, such as labor, including adjustments for the difference between the official exchange rate and the shadow rates (where exchange rates are under- or overvalued); the revenue gained by the government; the employment benefits as measured by the difference between the wage and the social opportunity cost of labor (what labor could earn elsewhere); and the net profits share to local joint partners (taking into account the opportunity costs of the inputs provided). Costs are associated with infrastructural expenditures, administrative costs, and the subsidies and incentives provided by the government.

The results of studies have been generally positive. Chen (1993) has shown strong social benefits for the Chinese SEZ of Shenzhen. Other studies have indicated positive values in zones in Indonesia, Sri Lanka, China, South Korea, and Malaysia, but a negative return for the Philippines Bataan EPZ (UNCTAD 1993; Jayanthakumaran 2003). These results should be qualified because of the weaknesses of the methods used, which include heroic assumptions about shadow prices and discount rates. The studies also miss important aspects of zones, including demonstration effects, technical transfers, linkages, externalities inside the zone, and important features of institution-building (including building relations between foreign and domestic capital, trust between the governments managing the zones and foreign capital, and organizational structures for industrial policy).

A fourth approach in the literature is policy modeling, which relies less on mathematical proofs that use unrealistic assumptions and more on conceptually linking causal factors to explain the varied outcomes of zones. Yuan and Eden (1992) relate eleven measures of zone performance to fourteen causal factors under three general headings: the international environment, domestic conditions, and the role of the state. Amirahmadi and Wu (1995) pinpoint the source of the success of EPZs in the confluence of three well-designed sectoral and spatial policies: free trade zones, industrial policy, and a growth-centered strategy. While policy modeling can seem ethereal compared to case studies, and can lead to varying interpretations of actual events, it does provide one with a set of concepts and issues that can be useful when considering the design of EPZs.

Some literature has pointed to EPZs as being mere enclaves. McMichael (2008) argues that EPZs can be social and economic enclaves cut off from the country and can deny basic human rights to a mostly female labor force, while having few or no linkages to the economy. While this can be the case—particularly in some African countries that have designed EPZs in line with a flawed World Bank vision of zones as second-best solutions to free trade (see discussion below)—the literature cited above points to the importance of industrial policy to help integrate EPZs into the domestic economy. However, within the literature, there is little analysis of what industrial policy means, its content, or the policies that are best suited for the design of zones for developmental purposes. What is meant by the term industrial policy?

Industrial policy and EPZs

The literature in support of industrial policy has frequently emphasized market over state failures. In this view, real world markets are affected by imperfections stemming from a variety of conditions, including public goods, externalities, and monopoly. The problem of designing policies in this manner is that it is captured by a neoclassical vision of markets: if only market failures were not present, industry would prosper. However, industrial transformation is a complex process, one that involves significant institutional transformation and transcends putative attempts to counter imperfections in order to produce a hypothetical world of self-seeking individuals operating in a perfectly competitive market. Instead, we should focus on developing the institutions that will lead to the formation, operation, and evolution of new and existing industries in the context of domestic and international needs.

Industrial policy comprises conscious state interventions designed to transform the structure of industry in order to enhance the "developmental competitiveness" of an economy. *Developmental competitiveness* refers to an institutional continuum that propels a dynamic process of accumulation focused on increasing the diversity, market share, linkages, and depth of an economy. *Diversity* refers the variety or heterogeneity of goods produced. *Market share* means the proportion of global and domestic goods produced locally. Linkages focus on various spillover effects. *Depth* refers to the basic strength of a sector as measured by the number, type, and production conditions of firms.

The state is central to improving developmental competitiveness. In co-operation with private industry, it should help conceptualize the potential of each industrial stage of entry into the global economy and develop dynamic strategies that lead to new stages. Purposive policy intervention should not only fine-tune the institutional continuum, but also alter it to create new directions that enhance the market share, diversity, depth, and linkages of an economy. An institutional continuum involves the transformation of both the private sector and state institutions aimed at supporting industrial accumulation, including the design of EPZs. The state is the central agent necessary for transforming an institutional matrix and set in motion a cumulative process of development. What do we mean by institutions and the institutional continuum? And how can industrial policy, including EPZ strategies, be used to change it?

At the core of industry is a matrix of institutional constructs that shape how people interact as they generate goods for domestic and international markets. The five institutional constructs are capacities, norms, incentives, regulations, and organization. They control the socially prescribed correlative behavior at the heart of a manufacturing sector. *Norms* are behavioral guides, the accumulation of established patterns of life and associated ways of thinking. In manufacturing, norms focus on elements, such as trust and ethical standards, which allow manufacturing business relationships to evolve and the development of clusters and networks.

Incentives are the rewards and penalties that arise from different forms of behavior. Material conditions are one of a broad array of social factors that influence behavior. Unlike the momentary, marginally calculating *Homo economicus* of neo-classical economics, the habits and thoughts of real people are powerfully affected by material rewards and penalties. An institutional approach also recognizes a range of options, including non-material incentives. In addition, the response to incentives is formed gradually and is highly contextualized. Incentives should focus foremost on encouraging investment and production that enhances development.

Regulations constitute the legal boundaries that define the rules of operations in economies. Organizations are entities that concatenate the operations of groups of people with narrowly defined common rules and purposes. In an industrial policy context, organizations include commercial enterprises involved in manufacturing, as well as business and professional groups, which all provide impetus for change and act as conduits for information to their constituents.

Capacities are the levels of abilities of individuals, groups, and organizations to operate effectively under rules in order to reach particular organizational goals. In the industrial context, capacities encompass supply-side dimensions like entrepreneurship, skills, and technological capabilities.

The way forward is the creation of clear industrial policies that are aimed at putting in place a trajectory of institutional change—or a continuum of new norms, capacities, incentives, organizations, and regulations—aimed at fostering private-sector or joint private–state entrepreneurship and accumulation, with the goal of enhancing developmental competitiveness.[10]

In Asia, EPZs have been part of a broader industrial policy and, in some countries, a way for the state to learn how to handle FDI for developmental purposes. African customs and other government bodies have been bureaucratic and at times corrupt. Zones are forums for experimentation. They are a way to develop habits that will lead to efficiencies that can be emulated elsewhere in the country, while at the same time helping to build trust with foreign investors. A successful drive to industrialize requires the development of capacities and policies to foster private-sector investment. The operation of a zone is a good starting point to begin to learn to apply those capacities. African governments have tended to be ambivalent about foreign capital with too many policy shifts. Continuity and stability in the policy of governments can build relationships that can lead to a greater commitment to foreign investment.

The operation of the zones can have other important demonstration effects. Foreign investors often have a well-developed understanding of technology and an ability to synthesize new forms of technology as they appear. These are two capacities that are woefully inadequate in Africa. In general, SSA's share of medium- and high-technology activities in its manufactured value added (MVA) is the lowest in the world and, in contrast to most regions, has been falling over time (Lall 2005). In addition human capital tends to be poorly developed in Africa. Employment can lead to training, which enhances human capital. Even where there is little formal training, a modern industrial setting with quality control, punctuality, organizational discipline, and a spirit of innovation and drive can have lasting consequences to future industrialization (UNCTAD 1993).

A number of examples illustrate how states have used industrial policy strategies to build institutions associated with successful EPZs.

Asian EPZs, industrial policy and institutional transformation

By almost any measure, the most successful export zones in the world have been in South Korea, Taiwan, and China. Taiwan, like many African countries, was searching for ways to enhance export promotion after initially focusing on import substitution. However, complex administrative procedures and a heavy-handed bureaucracy impeded efforts in this area. In 1966, Taiwan established at Kaohsiung the first zone, which was aimed at offering incentives and minimizing administrative procedures. Two more zones were quickly organized and, relative to the criteria described above, they were wildly successful. FDI grew annually at a rate that varied from 10 to 81 percent from 1967–79. Average annual exports increased at an astounding 61.3 percent. Net exports were an impressive 40 percent of total exports between 1966 and July 1980. The zones became increasingly important to Taiwan's trade accounts. Net exports from the zones relative to the total increased from 3.3 percent in 1967 to 53.4 percent in 1976. Employment peaked at more than 80,000 workers in 1986 before declining to about 70,000 in 1990.

Unlike many other zones in other parts of the world, the EPZs were not mere enclaves—they had both significant backward linkages and technology transfer. In 1967 only 2.3 percent of all inputs were of local origin. By 1973 the figures rose to 17 percent and finally reached about one third of the total by 1980. More than 1,000 factories were organized to provide inputs to the zones. There were forty technical cooperation agreements among foreign investors and suppliers that aimed at upgrading the quality of inputs and leading to significant technology transfer. In addition, more than 4,000 people were sent abroad for technical training from 1966–79. Over time, local Chinese technicians and managers replaced expatriates (Yuan and Eden 1992; Amirahmadi and Wu 1995).

Although slightly less significant than Taiwan's, South Korea's zones have also generated high levels of employment, foreign investment, net exports, and significant backward linkages and technology transfers.

The key to the successes in Taiwan, South Korea, and China has been the ability to attract foreign capital and to encourage the zones to undertake activities with greater developmental consequences. All three carefully used zones as part of a broader industrial policy strategy (Kuchiki 2007). Each carefully institutionalized linkages with the local economy, utilizing an array of new norms, incentives, capacities, organizations, and regulations. A staged approach of transformation in line with shifting priorities that was set up in a broader strategic or industrial policy domain[11] was also important. EPZs were seen as part of the overall strategic approach to transform the institutions and structures of the economies for developmental purposes, in marked contrast to the World Bank's conceptualization of EPZs as a second-best solution to free trade (see discussion below). At the core of the strategy has been the utilization of a set of carefully sequenced incentives. In China, for example, tax policy differentiation has been an important instrument of industrial policy, carefully used to reflect the state priorities over time. From the beginning, SEZs in China were seen as a mechanism to attract FDI, not only for export purposes, but also for technology transfers and for spillover effects and backward linkages through joint ownership with local corporations. This was encouraged in a number of ways. Prior to 1994, the corporate tax rate was 55 percent. However, joint enterprises were taxed at a lower rate, which provided a strong incentive for local companies to hook up with foreign enterprises. Regulations were passed, which allowed local companies to receive full rights as foreign enterprises with only 25 percent foreign ownership, thus generating a new type of industrial organization not present in China up to that point (Lai 2006: 46).

Moreover, from the other side, FDI access to local finance was much easier with links to local companies. Earlier, we saw the resulting large increase in percentage of joint ventures in places such as Shenzhen. With this relationship, there was a much higher probability of using local inputs in joint ventures compared to wholly owned foreign operations. Other incentives were used to encourage the purchase of local exports in other zones. South Korea and Taiwan extended duty-free status to local inputs going into the zones (they became indirect exporters), allowing them to compete with the foreign inputs that companies in the zones imported duty-free. Both countries did not rely on market incentives alone to build up capacities. In South Korea, Masan zone officials placed technical experts in local suppliers to upgrade the quality of the products sold to the zone companies. Over time, the percentage of locally used inputs grew from 3 percent in 1971 when the zone was first formed to 44 percent. In Taiwan, common norms emphasizing things such as the importance of quality were built through the placement of officials from zone firms into local companies (Radelet 1999).

As industrial policy priorities evolved, so did the nature of the components of their institutional matrix in order to ensure consistencies between zones and country needs. In keeping with broader industrial policy priorities, they encouraged the development of certain sectors, emphasized value-added production, and provided incentives to encourage the purchase of local inputs. In 1979, for example, South Korea organized a Machinery Purchase Fund to finance the purchase of machinery by EPZs in order to upgrade the capital intensity of production (Yuan and Eden 1992). In another example, when China set up a flat-rate corporate tax of 33 percent in 1994, it also set the level in the HNTIDZs to 15 percent, with companies exempted for the first two years after commencing operations.

As discussed previously, the zones reflected the Eighth Five Year Plan's emphasis on high-tech manufacturing goods (Ding 2002). In Taiwan, as the government encouraged higher value added and technology in EPZs, the capacities of potential workers were also upgraded. The Japanese policy of widespread literacy education was continued by the KMT government, which by 1968 provided children with nine years of free and compulsory education. In keeping with the drive for an increasingly sophisticated industry and a dynamic comparative advantage, educational emphasis was placed on vocational education in high schools, which reached 66 percent of total enrollment in 1980 (from 37 percent in 1950), and scientific and engineering skills in universities (40 percent of total enrollment already by 1972) (Brautigam 1995).[12]

Companies in zones have clear aims, including ease of entry and exit; access to high quality, reliable, and low-cost infrastructure; propitiously located zones (proximity to export facilities and to input and output markets); a low-cost, reliable, and well-trained labor force (educational levels, work habits, wages and benefits, nature and extent of unionization, and the supply of labor); ease of operations (nature and exercise of regulations affecting areas such as production, labor, and the environment have a direct bearing on the ease of operations); political and economic stability;[13] economies and externalities (specialization in operations of a similar nature allowing joint strategies in bargaining, gain from labor force training of similar companies, and capturing significant economies through specialized services and infrastructure); access to domestic markets; flexibility of zone administration; and numerous incentives provided by the government (tax reductions, holidays, subsidies on infrastructure, access to inexpensive credit, extension services). Many of these aims are not in harmony with country developmental interests (for example, companies would like to operate in a footloose manner and leave at the whim of corporate headquarters, etc.). From the previous examples, we see the ability of states to capture FDI through a sequence of contingent incentives that increase the long-term integration into the local economy in line with industrial policy priorities.

In contrast to the experiences of a number of Asian countries, African EPZ initiatives have been constrained by the anti-industrial policy sentiments embedded in World Bank-imposed strategies and in the faulty conceptualization of EPZs by the international financial institutions.

Constraints on linking EPZs to industrial policy in Africa: the World Bank and neoliberal interpretations of EPZs

After 1980, the World Bank deconstructed African state and parastatal agencies dealing with the support of industry while at the same time opposing new industrial policy efforts by restricting the domain of state intervention to avoid distortions. The justification was laid out in the paradigm-shifting World Development Report of 1983, which was the first to be written under the supervision of Anne Krueger.[14] The focus of development should be on creating efficiency, which is best generated through "the pricing of inputs and outputs to reflect relative scarcities." In the view of the report, distortions do not arise from market imperfections but are generally the product of policies "introduced by government directly or indirectly in pursuit of some social or economic objective" (p. 37). The report uses a problematic empirical exercise[15] to point to growth losses from government interventions at the heart of industrial policy strategies (tariffs, interest rates subsidies, less than full cost pricing of infrastructure, exchange rate interventions, etc.).

State industrial support is rejected for other reasons as well. State capacities are too weak and "governments have tried to control too much economic activity." The state should focus on core responsibilities, which should not include attempts to "alleviate market failures," since "all too often the attempted cure has been worse than the disease" (pp. 46, 52). Competition policy should not even be attempted except indirectly through wholesale import liberalization (pp. 53–4). All industrial policies must be discouraged as a likely source of corruption and rent-seeking, which can be best reduced by curtailing administrative interventions including "controls on international trade and payments" (p. 117).

There was little change in World Bank reports over the 1980s and 1990s. The 1989 Africa study linked the poor performance of manufacturing on the continent to industrial policy-type interventions of the 1970s and early 1980s such as "heavy protection, extensive regulation and directed investment," although manufacturing value-added growth was much slower in the 1980s, following the implementation of adjustment, compared to the 1970s.[16] The few manufacturing success cases, such as Mauritius, were presented only as products of orthodox stabilization, exchange rate liberalization, and trade policy, which ignored strong evidence that the country successfully used a number of industrial policy instruments to improve manufacturing[17] (World Bank 1989: 110–11).

The anti-industrial policy sentiment continued with the World Bank's East Asian Miracle Study, which concluded that "the promotion of specific industries did not work" and therefore held "little promise for other developing countries" (World Bank 1993: 24).[18] Following the report, the main World Bank Africa study was unambiguous: "governments should not try to pick 'winners'... Governments can best help entrepreneurs discover and develop competitive exports by getting out of the way..." (World Bank 1994: 192).

By 1997, the Bank recognized that countries may fail to industrialize because of market failures[19] and that industrial policy intervention might be justified because of "information and coordination problems" (World Bank 1997: 72). However, this reasoning is dismissed for the same reasons spelled out in the World Bank Report of 1983: "pursuing this style of investment coordination presupposes levels of public and private institutional capability that are beyond the reach of most developing countries" and would likely lead to rent-seeking and corruption (ibid.: 73).

Along the same lines, the Bank's conception of EPZs completely collapsed into their neoliberal framework and was seen as a surrogate to neoliberal trade reforms, rather than as an extension of industrial policy. This is clearly stated in numerous Bank documents. For example, a lengthy World Bank review of the role and impact of EPZs emphatically states that "an EPZ is not a first best policy choice. The best policy is one of overall liberalization of the economy... Nevertheless, zones can play a long-term dynamic role in their country's development if they are appropriately set up... as an integrated part of a national reform and liberalization program" (Madani 1999: 3). Other World Bank authors argue that EPZs have failed because "of government interference and in the increasing distortions introduced in the operation of free trade and capital regimes" including "labor market distortions" introduced through government interference (Watson 2001: 4–5). Instead of viewing EPZs as a catalyst for development, EPZs should be used "to integrate [their] economies into the global economies" and should be "aimed at a well-defined market" (Watson 2001: 1, 12).

This vision of zones has driven the EPZ agenda in many African countries, with problematic consequences. Countries like Madagascar and Kenya have been able to expand jobs and increase exports by emphasizing unregulated, low-wage, labor-intensive industries such as textiles, and AGOA eligibility largely aimed at the US markets. French and Mauritian capital were particularly attracted to Madagascar in the 1990s, although Asian capital also became interested as countries came up against their multi-fiber ceilings. By 2004 there were over 100,000 employees in Madagascar's Zone Franche (more than 90 percent in textiles). Monthly wages for an unskilled textile industry machine operator were less than one third the equivalent wage in Mauritius, half of that in China, and 60 percent of the average wage in India. Although productivity was lower, unit labor costs are among the lowest in the world. Generally, wages are even lower, with longer working hours compared to industrial jobs outside the zone, although the wages exceed informal-sector levels. There is a very high turnover rate, although the high unemployment levels on the island ensure a ready supply of replacement labor (Cling et al. 2005). However, even these somewhat problematic jobs are being lost because of the end of the Multi Fibre Arrangement and a focus on a single market—the United States. Textile exports to the US have fallen from $324 million in 2004 to $290.3 million in 2007, a decline of nearly 11 percent (USITC 2008).

Kenya also rode the Multi Fibre Arrangement and AGOA to focus on textiles in their FTZs. From 2000–4, the number of jobs in the garment sector of the EPZs went from 5,600 to 34,614. The zones were overwhelmingly in garment production and constituted roughly 92 percent of the total employment in 2004. However, as in Madagascar, the end of the Multi Fibre Arrangement took its toll, with garment exports from the zones to the US falling from $221 million in 2004 to $195 million in 2005, a decline of nearly 12 percent. From 2004–7, overall textile exports to the US from Kenya fell from $277.3 million to $248.4 million, a decline of 11 percent (USITC 2008). The downward trends in Kenya and Madagascar are typical for the African garment field following the end of the Multi Fibre Arrangement. SSA textile and apparel imports to the US fell from $1.8 billion in 2004 to $1.3 billion in 2007—a drop of nearly 30 percent. Over the period, SSA has become even more dependent on oil-product exports to the US. In 2004, 73 percent of all imports to the US from SSA were in energy-related products. By 2007, the figure was up to 80 percent. Excluding South Africa, the figure in 2007 was 93 percent, up from 89 percent in 2004! These are the statistics from the United States, a country that is supposedly helping to create opportunities for SSA to diversify its exports through AGOA (USITC 2007).

EPZs in Africa have generally had poor forward and backward linkages because they have not been designed with an institutional focus relative to the industrial policy priorities of the country. In Madagascar, roughly 75 percent of non-labor inputs in its EPZs are from foreign sources, which is considerably higher than the non-EPZ industrial sector (Cling et al. 2005). Since inputs can be brought in duty-free, it is difficult for developing countries to compete with the high-quality goods available elsewhere. As we saw above, the most successful zones from a develop-mental perspective have been those with significant partnerships between local and foreign capital, not only for technology-sharing benefits, but also because it can lead to higher levels of backward linkages.[20] Much can be learned from foreign investors. Joint ownership arrangements with local capital are more conducive to the spread of technology, which is one of the reasons for the success in China (Ge 1999). In Madagascar, only 11 percent of enterprises had local ownership (Cling et al. 2005). The Kenyan EPZs are also overwhelmingly foreign-owned. Only 28.4 percent were joint ventures (KEPZA 2005).

Based on this discussion, it might be useful to see how an African zone with enormous potential might be developed using an industrial policy framework. The Onne zone in Nigeria, which I first visited in 1997, provides an opportune example.

Onne Oil and Gas Free Zone

Under the Oil and Gas Free Zone Decree No. 8 of March 31, 1996, all approved enterprises operating within the zone are exempt from paying taxes. Any goods imported into the zone are free of customs duties, as long as they are in connection with an approved activity. Under Section 18, other provisions to attract foreign investors include repatriation of capital with appreciation, remittance of profits and dividends earned by foreign investors in the zone, no import or export licenses, rent-free land (only guaranteed at the construction phase), up to 100 percent ownership of business, employment of foreign personnel subject to visa approval by the Authority operating the zone, and no strikes or lockouts for a period of ten years (FRN 1996).

The project was divided into three phases. The first stage, which commenced on March 8, 1997, provided a 220-acre free port/free trade zone at the Onne Port Complex. It included fencing off the territory, streamlining the port facilities to accommodate the traffic, expanding customs and pre-inspection capabilities, and clarifying the procedures for moving cargo from the airports into the zone. The goal was to act as a transshipping point to service the oil and gas industry. The projected second phase would expand the area to cover 730 hectares. The second phase could be aimed at systematically developing an EPZ. A third phase would make available more territory by incorporating the undeveloped Ikpokiri island area into the zone.

There are a number of issues that can be raised. At its initial phase, the developmental potential of the zone was limited. There has since been a significant increase in port activities. However, with the exception of a cement factory, a pre-cast panel factory, and a pipe coating and machine shop, most of the activities are focused on warehousing for oil companies. Still, roughly 7,000 jobs have been generated, with about 112 companies using the site as of January 2007. To date, the main beneficiaries are the oil companies that have a free and secure area with few hindrances for storage. They are able to obtain equipment and parts for expansion or servicing much more rapidly, allowing economies to be gained in shipping and reduced production delays. Nigeria and other regional countries gain largely from the potential increase in oil exports.[21] There are, however, significant institution-building opportunities. The zone could provide the training of organizations that would be needed to operate an EPZ. To upgrade and expand the zone into an EPZ, the FP/FTZ must be successful. This is an ideal chance to solidify relations and build trust with companies that can participate in future assembly/manufacturing activities.

The key to a successful zone is the ability of the overseeing Authority to act efficiently and independently to ensure a harmonization of aims. In a zone organized as a storage and shipping depot, goods must be moved rapidly to accommodate the industry—the oil industry in this case. The organization of the zone, as originally specified in the Decree, created some potential difficulties (many of which have been addressed). The Decree established various government agents in the zone (customs, police, immigration, etc.) and if the experience of other countries is any indication, this created the dangers of red tape and corruption. The ability of the Authority to intervene against representatives of other government agencies was also uncertain in the Act. Under Section 5-1-f, labor disputes could not be settled independently of the Federal Ministry of Labour Productivity.

Also as established in the Decree, the Governing Board was given wide representation from ministries, agencies, and business organizations. The powers of intervention were not clearly specified. This created an opening for patronage or political interference in the running of the zone. The management of the zone, in the Decree, was initially specified as the Nigerian Export Processing Zone Authority, a government organization. Like most successful operations, the zone must implement "one stop" procedures for approving operating licenses, but the procedures were not clearly defined in the Decree.

The Nigerian government began to address some of these concerns early on.[22] Based partially on the poor response to the Calabar zone,[23] which was organized along similar lines, and due to comments by the oil companies planning to participate in the zone, the government moved forward to reconstitute the Governing Board to include broad representation from oil-related companies operating in the zone.[24] The Ministry of Commerce and Tourism signed a five-year technical management contract to run the zone with Intels, a private company, jointly Nigerian and foreign-owned, that has been running three ports in southern Nigeria (Warri, Calabar, and Onne) since 1982. The contract was subsequently extended and Intels was given broad powers to act as the agent dealing with immigration, registration, marketing, and police affairs while acting as the intermediary between customs, shipping, and terminal handling (http:// www.onnefreezone.com).

The infrastructure has been gradually upgraded. Measures included a dual carriageway into the port (which was a two-lane congested mess when I was there in 1997), a fiber-optic cable into the zone, extending the runway at Port Harcourt airport to accommodate larger aircraft, and completing the Federal Ocean Terminal to handle larger ocean-going vessels. The quay length is currently 790 meters, but is being expanded to 1,576 meters to accommodate a vessel of up to 70,000 tons (NPA 2005).

Intels has moved toward simplifying the license-granting procedures in the direction of a one-stop approach. All applicant companies require a Free Zone License and operate in the zone under "Special" or "General" licenses, the former for companies incorporated outside of Nigeria and the latter for companies incorporated in Nigeria. The former companies must use an agent or distributor to conduct business in Nigeria outside the zone. While the management contract gives Intels the right to issue Free Port, Special, and General licenses, all companies must be registered by the Nigerian Department of Petroleum Resources (DPR) to operate in the zone; companies operating under the General License category also need a certificate of incorporation from the Nigerian Registrar of Companies.

Overall, the Nigerian government took early steps to respond to zone participants in keeping with the flexibility associated with successful zones elsewhere. Moreover, they have recognized the need to move slowly and prudently in order to gain experience and credibility.[25]

Ultimately for the zone to have greater consequences for local and national development goals, a careful phasing process must be planned, including the design of proper incentives to encourage more value-added activities, further infrastructure upgrades both within and to the zone, the creation of facilities to train the labor force in line with new production, encouragement of more joint production agreements with local capital, etc. To date, however, there seems to be little understanding of the kind of interventions and industrial policy that is required to transform this zone into a center of oil- and gas-related manufacturing.

Conclusions

This chapter points to the importance of industrial policy interventions in the management of developmentally successful industrial zones. For Africa, there are serious challenges ahead. First, there is the potential for composition problems if too many countries produce the same types of labor-intensive goods (Kaplinsky 1993). Second, competition for a fixed amount of foreign capital might lead to high levels of expenditures on infrastructure and very costly provisions for incentives, which could lead to significantly decreased net benefits for the countries. Third, one of the big incentives of investment in zones in the past has been the Multi Fibre Arrangement and AGOA. However as we saw, since the expiration of the Arrangement in 1994, there has been a precipitous decline in textile imports to the US from SSA.

These caveats point to the need to avoid laissez-faire or second-best solutions to orthodox liberalization approaches to organizing export-oriented zones. One way of addressing these issues is through spatial conceptions that might lead to the specialization of zones by product type in which the design of zones is matched with potential users. Within the Nigerian context, the contrast between Calabar (which employs only 2,000 people) and Onne, which is organizing the zone in close cooperation with oil-related companies, is striking. International or regional bodies can help coordinate efforts to ensure zones encourage economies and regional market access, while avoiding costly duplication and competition. An industrial policy approach using better sequencing and incentives to use local inputs with the encouragement of joint ventures between FDI and local capital must be put in place—something that does not seem to be happening at this time.

Overall the lessons of successful zones are that proper sequencing, design, and incentives within an industrial policy framework can provide an environment conducive to the growth of foreign investment. This can generate employment opportunities; foreign exchange; backward, forward, and demand linkages; and training and technological spillovers with a significant potential impact on the structural and institutional transformation of Africa economies.

Zones should not be seen as a panacea for solving the diverse and complex economic problems of all African countries. However, well-designed zones can contribute to the developmental competitiveness of African countries and ultimately to the standard of living for a population held captive for too long by the false promises of entrenched orthodoxy.

Notes

* This paper draws on Stein (1997, 2007). The first draft was prepared for the Third Meeting of the Africa Task Force, Initiative for Policy Dialogue (Columbia University), Addis Ababa, Ethiopia, July 10–11, 2008. The author is grateful to comments from an anonymous referee.
1. The use of export processing zones (EPZ) in the title broadly refers to an array of zone types, of which the FPZ is but one. See the discussion below.

2. This figure is based on UNCTAD (1993). The number seems to include only export processing zones, which would appear to correspond to free ports or zone areas with the processing of goods. However, this is rather conservative. In China, for example, the UNCTAD figures include seven zones, of which five are the most open special economic zones. However, there are now various types of open zones in China that are similar to EPZs, such as economic and technological development zones, hi-tech development zones and free trade areas. In 1993, the estimates, compiled by various ministries, ran from a total of 1,700 to 9,000 throughout China. See David Wall et al. (1996).

3. The numbers are calculated by adding total regions and deleting Australia and New Zealand from Pacific; Japan, Singapore, Taiwan, and S. Korea from Asia; Europe (except Turkey); and the US (ILO 2007).

4. 1990 the Sub-Saharan countries included Botswana, Ghana, Lesotho, Liberia, Mauritius, Senegal, Swaziland, and Togo (UNCTAD 1993). By 1996, they were joined by Cameroon, Côte d'Ivoire, Kenya, Namibia, Nigeria, Mozambique, and Zimbabwe (Weissman 1996). By 2006, Madagascar, Cape Verde, Mali, Malawi, Gabon, and Seychelles also joined, but Liberia disappeared from the list (ILO 2007).

5. In South Africa, these are mostly known as industrial development zones (IDZs). For a critique of IDZs and other EPZs as part of a neoliberal "race to the bottom strategy," see Jauch (2002). Given the strong South African expertise at the task force meeting, there is little I could add to their knowledge in this paper, so I have largely avoided discussing South Africa in this paper.

6. The imprecision of language use in this area is probably linked to the comparative newness of these zones, the lack of any systematic use of terminology in the zones (zones with similar functions are called by many different names), and the dynamic character of some zones due to shifting government policy. Even the Library of Congress Subject Index refers to all types of zones as "free ports and zones."

7. This export exclusivity seems to be ubiquitous with one prominent exception: Brazil's Manaus Free Zone, where production seems to be aimed largely at the domestic market. This could almost be deemed an "import processing zone." See UNCTAD (1993) for more discussion of this zone. In 2001, Nigeria moved in this direction by abrogating the rule that the EPZs must export at least 75 percent of their production (see note 23 below).

8. For instance in Xiamen, the same number of projects in 1991 were approved for Taiwanese investors compared to Hong Kong investors. In Shenzhen, where you would expect a smaller Taiwanese presence, Taiwan only had 5 percent of Hong Kong's number of projects. Hong Kong's large presence in most of the zones is partly due to the number of Chinese that use Hong Kong as a base for investing in China and who are fully counted in the Hong Kong investment figures in the zones (Wall et al. 1996).

9. See for example the exchange between Raphael Kaplinsky (1993, 1995) and Larry Willmore (1995) over the impact of EPZs in the Dominican Republic on wages, technology transfer, and linkages.

10. This is in contrast to the current World Bank view, aimed at state neutrality and retraction, on how to build private sectors and their exporting capacity. See for example recent World Development Reports that focus on the "business climate" in terms of the number of days and procedures to start a business (World Bank 2006, particularly Table 5.2).

11. For a more detailed analysis of the industrial policies of Korea and Taiwan and their relevance to Africa, see Stein (1995).

12. Of course the breakdown of the total is one indicator. Another is the number per capita. In engineering, for example, in 1985, Taiwan had 767 engineers per 100,000 of the general population. A study of 13 African countries put the number there at 9 per 100,000 (Brautigam 1995). Until Africa can increase the supply of human capital, the emphasis in most countries will need to be on export zones with labor-intensive processing.

13. The political crisis of 2002 led to a nearly 50 percent drop in exports from Madagascar's zone and the departure of a number of key investors (Cling et al. 2005).

14. A detailed and critical review of WDR 1983 including the role of Krueger and its importance in re-conceptualizing the nature of the state in development can be found in chapter 6 of Stein (2008).

15. See Stein (2008) for a critique.

16. SSA MVA annual growth rates were 5.7 percent from 1970–80 and only 2 percent from 1980–90 (Lawrence 2005).

17. See for example Milner (2001) and Lall and Wignaraja (1998) for the role of trade and industrial policy in Mauritius.

18. Literature critical of the study is extensive; Wade (1996: 24) sums it up nicely: "The trouble [with the anti-industrial policy argument], as several of the analysts have shown, is that most of the evidence does not survive serious scrutiny." He provides a good summary of the main critiques and an excellent presentation of the history of the study.

19. See Chang (1996) for a good summary of this literature.

20. As the Mauritian Minister of Industry and Commerce pointed out at a workshop this author organized at a 1991 meeting of the corporate council on Africa, local capital (often from the sugar sector) used joint operations to learn about textile manufacturing. By 1997, more than 60 percent of investment in the export processing units was from local capital. The Minister emphasized that one of the major reasons for the success of the EPUs in Mauritius is their domination by local capital, which has a vested interest in developing linkages to the local economy.

21. Onne is perhaps the most propitiously located port in West Africa, in terms of its centrality and proximity to oil and gas zones in and around Nigeria, while being well sheltered but readily accessible to ocean vessels (up to 10 meters draft).

22. The discussion below is based on interviews in April 1997 in Lagos, Port Harcourt, and Abuja with officials of the Nigerian Port Authority, Customs Authority, oil supply companies, Ministry of Commerce and Tourism, and Intels, the private company contracted to run the port and zone.

23. The Calabar export processing zone, which was constituted in 1992, has been a great disappointment. Although the infrastructure has been well developed there have been a number of operational problems. First, no provision has been made for a free port in Calabar, due to disagreements between ministries. Second, the port is situated far from the ocean, up a river that is in constant need of very expensive dredging. Third, before the zone was organized, little effort was taken to locate potential users. Fourth, mixed signals have been sent. A 1994 Executive Council ruling permitted companies to receive the same benefits as those operating in the zone if they were exporting more than 60 percent of production, thus providing little incentive to participate in the Calabar

zone. By April 1997, only two companies were operating in the zone. Partly to address the failure, Nigeria abrogated the rule that companies must export at least 75 percent of their production, effectively making Calabar a free trade zone. By 2004, 22 firms were located in Calabar with employment of 2,000 workers producing goods mostly for the domestic market. This is still a terrible disappointment by any standard, given what has been invested in the zone (IMF 2005).

24. A business guide for the zone indicates a board structure chaired by the Minister of Commerce and Tourism, with representation from the Nigerian Port Authority, the Nigerian Customs Service, The Ministry of Petroleum Resources, and five representatives from the oil-producing and service companies (Intels 1997: 15). In my interviews in Nigeria, other structures have been discussed including representation from a larger number of ministries and oil companies as well as from regional countries permitting companies operating in their territorial confines to utilize the zone. The latter representation might encourage more regional participation and diminish the possibility of costly duplication and competition.

25. This was very explicit in my discussions with officials at various government levels.

References

Amirahmadi, H. and Wu, W. (1995). "Export Processing Zones in Asia," *Asian Survey*, 35 (9): 828–49.

Brautigam, D. (1995). "The State as Agent: Industrial Development in Taiwan, 1952–1972," in H. Stein (ed.), *Asian Industrialization and Africa: Studies in Policy Alternatives to Structural Adjustment*. New York: St. Martin's Press.

Chang, H.-J. (1996). *Political Economy of Industrial Policy*. Basingstoke: Macmillan/Palgrave.

Chen, J. (1993). "Social Cost-Benefit Analysis of China's Shenzhen Zone," *Development Policy Review*, 11 (3): 261–72.

Cling, J. P., Razafindrakoto, M., and Roubaud, F. (2005). "Export Processing Zones in Madagascar: A Success Story under Threat?" *World Development*, 33 (5): 785–803.

Development and Management Strategies Ltd (DMS) (1996). *Interim Report on a Master Plan for the Development of the Oil and Gas Export Free Zone at Onne/Ikpokiri*. London: DMS.

Ding, L. (2002). "China's Industrial Policy and Long Term Structural Planning," in J. Wong and L. Ding (eds.), *China's Economy in the New Century*. Singapore: Singapore University Press.

Federal Republic of Nigeria (FRN) (1996). "Oil Gas Export Free Zone Decree 1996, Decree No. 8," *Official Gazette*, March, 83 (12). Available at <http://www.babalakinandco.com/resources/lawsnigeria/LAWS/968OIL%20AND%20GAS%20EXPORT%20FREE.htm>.

Ge, Wei (1999). "Special Economic Zones and the Opening of the Chinese Economy: Some Lessons from Economic Liberalization," *World Development*, 27 (7): 1267–85.

Hamada, K. (1974). "An Economic Analysis of the Duty Free Zone," *Journal of International Economics*, 4 (3): 225–41.

Hamilton, C. and Svensson, L. E. O. (1982). "On the Welfare Economics of a Duty-Free Zone," *Journal of International Economics*, 20: 45–64.

Hewitt, T. and Wield, D. (1992). *Industrialization and Development*. Oxford: Oxford University Press.

Intels (1997). *Business Guide, Onne Oil and Gas Free Zone*. London: Intels.

International Labor Organization (ILO) (April 2007). "ILO Database on Export Processing Zones," available at <http://www.ilo.org/public/english/dialogue/sector/themes/epz/epz-db.pdf>.

International Monetary Fund (IMF) (August 2005). "Nigeria: Selected Issues and Statistical Appendix," IMF Country Report No. 05/303.

Jauch, H. (2002). "Export Processing Zones and the Quest for Sustainable Development: A Southern African Perspective," *Environment and Urbanization*, April, 14 (1): 101–13.

Jayanthakumaran, K. (2003). "Benefit-Cost Appraisals of Export Processing Zones: A Survey of the Literature," *Development Policy Review*, 21 (1): 51–65.

Jici, W. and Wang, M. (2002). "High and New Technology Industrial Development Zones," in M. Webber, M. Wang, and Z. Ying (eds.), *China's Transition to a Global Economy*. Basingstoke: Macmillan/Palgrave.

Johansson, H. (1994). "The Economics of Export Processing Zones Revisited," *Development Policy Review*, (December), 12: 387–402.

Kaplinsky, R. (1993). "Export Processing Zones in the Dominican Republic: Transforming Manufactures into Commodities," *World Development*, 21 (11): 1851–65.

—— (1995). "A Reply to Willmore," *World Development*, 23 (3): 537–40.

Kenya Export Processing Zone Authority (KEPZA) (2005). *Annual Report for the Year 2005*. Nairobi: KEPZA.

Kuchiki, A. (2007). "Industrial Policy in Asia," IDE Discussion Paper No. 128, October, available at <http://www.ide.go.jp/English/Publish/Dp/pdf/128_kuchiki.pdf>.

Lai, H. (2006). *Reform and the Non-State Economy in China: The Political Economy of Liberalization Strategies*. Basingstoke: Palgrave/Macmillan.

Lall, S. (2005). "Is African Industry Competing?" Queen Elizabeth House Working Paper No. 121.

—— and Wignaraja, G. (1998). "Mauritius: Dynamizing Export Competitiveness." Commonwealth Economic Secretariat, Economic Paper, 33.

Lawrence, P. (2005). "Explaining Sub-Saharan Africa's Manufacturing Performance," *Development and Change*, 36 (6).

Madani, D. (1999). "A Review of the Role and Impact of Export Processing Zones," Policy Research Working Paper, 138 (November). Available at <http://siteresources.worldbank.org/EXTEXPCOMNET/Resources/2463593-1213887855468/11_A_Review_of_the_Role_and_Impact_of_EPZs.pdf>.

McMichael, P. (2008). *Development and Social Change: A Global Perpective,* 4th edn. Thousand Oaks, CA: Sage/Pine Forge Press.

Milner, C. (2001). "International Trade and Trade Policy," in R. Dabee and D. Greenaway (eds.), *The Mauritian Economy: A Reader*. Basingstoke: Palgrave/Macmillan.

Nigeria Port Authority (2005). "Port and Harbor Development in Nigeria," available at <http://www.pbintel.com>.

Radelet, S. (1999). "Manufactured Exports, Export Platforms, and Economic Growth." Harvard Institute for International Development, August. Available at <http://pdf.usaid.gov/pdf_docs/Pnach178.pdf>.

Stein, H. (ed.) (1995). *Asian Industrialization and Africa: Studies in Policy Alternatives to Structural Adjustment*. New York: St. Martin's Press.

Stein, H. (1997). "Free Trade Zones in Africa: Local and Regional Impact and Possibilities for U.S. Business," in Corporate Council on Africa, *Africa and the American Private Sector, Corporate Perspectives on a Growing Relationship*. Washington DC: Corporate Council on Africa.

—— (2007). "African Development Challenge," CAPORDE lecture, July 10, Cambridge University.

—— (2008). *Beyond the World Bank Agenda: An Institutional Approach to Development*. Chicago: University of Chicago Press.

UNCTAD (1993). *Export Processing Zones: Role of Foreign Direct Investment and Development Impact*. Geneva: United Nations, Trade and Development Board.

—— (various years). *World Investment Report*. Geneva: UNCTAD. Available at www.unctad.org.

USITC (2007). "U.S. Trade and Investment with Sub-Saharan Africa," available at <http://reportweb.usitc.gov/Africa>.

USITC (2008). "U.S. Trade and Investment with Sub-Saharan Africa," available at <http://reportweb.usitc.gov/Africa>.

Wade, R. (1996). "Japan, The World Bank and the Art of Paradigm Maintenance: The East Asian Miracle in Political Perspective," *New Left Review*, 1/217, May–June.

Wall, D., et al. (1996). *China's Opening Door*. London: The Royal Institute of International Affairs.

Watson, P. (2001). "Has Africa Missed the Boat? Not Yet." Africa Region Working Paper Series No. 17, May. <http://siteresources.worldbank.org/INTEXPCOMNET/Resources/Watson_2001.pdf>

Weissman, R. (1996). "Waiting to Export: Africa Embraces Export Processing Zones," *Multinational Monitor*, 17 (7–8).

Willmore, L. (1995). "Export Processing Zones in the Dominican Republic: A Comment on Kaplinsky," *World Development*, 23 (3): 529–35.

World Bank (1989). *From Crisis to Sustainable Growth: A Long-Term Perspect Study*. Washington, DC: World Bank.

—— (1993). *The East Asian Miracle: Economic Growth and Public Policy*. Washington, DC: World Bank.

—— (1994). *Adjustment in Africa: Reforms, Results and the Road Ahead*. Washington, DC: World Bank.

—— (1995). *World Development Report, 1995*. Oxford: Oxford University Press.

—— (1996). *World Development Report, 1996*. Oxford: Oxford University Press.

—— (1997). *The State in a Changing World, World Development Report, 1997*. Washington, DC: World Bank.

—— (2006). *World Development Indicators, 2006*. Washington, DC: World Bank.

Yuan, J. and Eden, L. (1992). "Export Processing Zones in Asia: A Comparative Study," *Asian Survey*, 32 (11): 1026–45.

12

South African Post-Apartheid Policies Towards Industrialization: Tentative Implications for Other African Countries

Nimrod Zalk[1]

Introduction

This article critically reviews South Africa's post-apartheid policies linked to industrialization. South Africa is the African continent's largest and most industrialized economy, with a long history of industrialization going back to the late nineteenth century. It accounts for an overwhelming share of the continent's manufacturing value-added (MVA) and a large share of the continent's exports, as shown in Tables 12.1 and 12.2.

Since 1994—when South Africa attained democracy—it has undertaken a range of Washington Consensus (WC) type economic reforms, including extensive trade liberalization in most sectors of manufacturing and agriculture. Trade liberalization was implemented in the context of a set of internally imposed macroeconomic stabilization policies and microeconomic constraints.

The success or otherwise of South Africa's experience with WC-type economic reforms—as Africa's largest and most industrialized economy—over its post-apartheid

Table 12.1 Regional shares in manufacturing value-added US$ (percent), 2004

Latin America & Caribbean	4.6%
Middle East & North Africa	0.9%
Sub-Saharan Africa	0.9%
South African share in SSA MVA	*60.3%*
East Asia & Pacific	12.0%
South Asia	1.9%
World	100.0%

Table 12.2 Regional shares in world trade US$ (percent), 2006

North America	14.2%
South and Central America	3.6%
Europe	42.1%
CIS	3.6%
Africa	3.1%
South African share in African trade	*15.6%*
Middle East	5.5%
Asia	27.8%
World	100.0%

Sources: World Development Indicators and WTO

period could hold useful policy lessons for other African countries seeking to industrialize.

The article is broken down into five sections. First, the literature around industrialization and the role of industrial and trade policy is covered. Second, the most fundamental of pre- and post-apartheid government policies impacting on industrialization are reviewed. Third, post-apartheid economic performance is examined with a particular emphasis on the real economy. Fourth, the key driving forces of real-economy performance over this period are considered, with a particular focus on manufacturing. Fifth, some conclusions are drawn: both for the South African economy and more tentatively for other African countries.

Industrialization: theory and historical evidence

Theory

Economic development is often understood as a process of catch-up or convergence of developing countries with the per capita living standards of developed countries. Orthodox economic theory in its unalloyed form predicts factor-price equalization across countries where trade increases the return of the abundant factor (assumed to be labor in a developing country) and decreases the return of the scarce factor (capital) (Reinert 2007). This orthodox trade theory predicts that trade liberalization will unlock production and exports of products and services in which countries have an underlying comparative advantage based on a range of assumptions that are rarely met in real-world production and trade. These assumptions include: there are no qualitative differences among economic activities (no sector is more productive or has stronger linkage effects than another); returns to scale are constant or diminishing; there is perfect information about technological possibilities; and the adoption of technology is costless.

As increasing evidence mounts with respect to the failure of Washington Consensus policies influenced by this orthodoxy, additional elements have been added to preserve its core. This so-called WC plus (WC+) focuses mainly on bolting on additional requirements, mostly of an institutional nature. Not only must developing countries get the prices right, they must *also* have good governance and quality institutions of various kinds. In the WC+, the direction of causality is largely predetermined: from institutions to economic growth. However, historical evidence indicates that desirable modern institutions are at least as likely to be the product of economic development processes as their cause (Chang 2002; Khan 2004).

By contrast to the WC (of either vintage), industrialization is conceptualized by structuralist or heterodox economists as a process of learning by developing country firms (Amsden 1989). Developing industrial capacity is a highly costly and risky process of acquiring tacit production knowledge, which involves multiple market and production failures, externalities, and spillover effects (Lall 2004). Rather than relying on their static comparative advantage—which is likely to be in the production of diminishing return primary activities—developing countries and their firms need to learn *how* to produce. Indeed, as Hausmann and Rodrik (2003) observe, developing countries also need to identify *what* to produce, although their proposed "self-discovery" process for unveiling this is somewhat flawed.[2]

Amsden (2003) argues that two factors have been critical in successful episodes of late and rapid twentieth-century industrialization. First, prior manufacturing experience—generally acquired prior to World War II. Second, a number of developing countries were able to utilize the policy space afforded by the decolonization process to leverage these nascent industrial capabilities. This was achieved through allocating economic rents using a set of "reciprocal control mechanisms" (RCMs) which rewarded rapid progress toward industrial learning and punished failure. The ability of different developing countries to exercise reciprocal control mechanisms has of course been uneven. How rapidly countries industrialize is therefore very much a function of how well they wield RCMs.

There are, however, weaknesses in the literature that argue for state intervention in economic development and for industrial policy in particular (often described in short-hand fashion by the term "developmental state"). In the same way that it cannot be assumed that markets will produce rapid catch-up via factor-price equalization, it similarly cannot be assumed that the requisite state capabilities to manage rapid catch-up will emerge automatically (Chibber 2006). The latter critique needs to be distinguished from the much more extreme neoliberal view that such capabilities can *never* emerge. The "growth-enhancing governance" capabilities that a state needs to build to implement an industrial policy agenda are fundamentally different to those espoused in terms of "good governance" capabilities (Mushtaq Khan, this volume). The political economy roots of why such capabilities are built in one state and not another is a sorely neglected area of research.

Thus rapid catch-up requires the state to address considerations of (1) what types of productive economic activities or sectors should be encouraged; (2) which group of existing or emerging capitalists can be induced via conditional economic rents or RCM to engage in these activities; and (3) an RCM that is calibrated to both technical and political economy considerations to ensure that the conditions attached to the economic rents are enforceable within the prevailing "political settlement."

Historical experience

Recent historical analyses illustrate that the now-advanced economies developed through policies, institutions, and instruments far removed from either variant of the WC (Reinert 2007; Chang 2002; Nolan 2001). Almost all of these countries made conscious and extensive use of import and export tariffs, subsidies, and other forms of state intervention to build their manufacturing sectors.

Britain—the first industrializer—developed through colonial conquest and wide-ranging state intervention. Of particular importance was the extensive use of import tariffs over roughly a century-and-a-half between 1721 and 1860. Britain's erstwhile colony—the United States—used the highest levels of protection in the world between 1816 and 1945 to catch up with and indeed surpass its former colonial master and become the world's leading economic power. Other now-industrialized countries similarly adopted interventionist policies in their processes of industrialization including Germany, France, Sweden, the Netherlands, and Switzerland. It is important to note that a number of institutions now supposedly deemed essential for economic development by the WC+ only emerged very late in the industrialization processes of the now-developed countries, such as extensive protection of physical and even intellectual property rights.

Since World War II, Japan and a range of other developing countries experienced very rapid rates of industrialization and convergence of incomes with developed countries, particularly until the end of the 1970s (Johnson 1982; Amsden 1989, 2003; Wade 1990). What was common to all of these countries was the successful deployment of RCMs that exchanged temporary economic rents for entry, learning, and upgrading in specific economic sectors—generally in manufacturing. Although many of these countries are located in East Asia, a number of countries from other regions also experienced rapid industrialization.[3]

It is important to stress the heterogeneity of the development processes of these countries even amongst the so-called "East Asian Tigers." There are important differences in terms of history, sectoral choices, and applications of different forms of RCMs. There have been different mixes of some of the main instruments of industrial policy amongst these countries, with respect to the use of trade policy, subsidies, the development banking system, foreign direct investment, domestic research, and development (Amsden 2003; Lall 2004).

Despite the heterogeneity in experiences, the rate of catch-up of these countries has been unprecedented in economic history. Amsden (2003: 12) states: "Between 1950 and 1973 per capita incomes doubled in some countries and quadrupled in others. In Asia, including India, they again either almost doubled or rose by an even larger factor between 1973 and 1995."

The role of trade and trade policy in industrialization

Trade plays a very important role in industrialization. But the selective use and sequencing of trade policy instruments is critical. As discussed above, industrialization is fundamentally a process of learning how to produce. This occurs predominantly through the importation of existing technologies (in the form of capital goods) which are mastered for local conditions through adaptation and adoption. The need to pay for the imports of capital goods, intermediate inputs, and certain wage goods requires the earning of export revenue so that the growth process does not run into a balance of payments constraint. Exports are also an important source of economies of scale, particularly in countries with relatively small domestic markets.

Shafaeddin (2005) examines the impact of trade liberalization across a range of developing countries since the early 1980s. He finds that the majority of countries experienced "unsatisfactory" performance. Trade liberalization generally led to "re-orientation of the industrial sector in accordance with static comparative advantage" (21). Half of the countries—mostly low income—experienced de-industrialization. Private-sector investment in manufacturing fell. Only industries that were already close to international competitiveness benefited from liberalization, such as the Brazilian aerospace industry. Thus trade policy—rather than being seen as a shift to as low tariffs as soon as possible—must comprise an appropriate tariff regime (as well as other forms of support and intervention).

Industrialization policies under apartheid and democracy

Apartheid era industrialization

South Africa's industrialization has been characterized as dominated by a "minerals energy complex" (MEC) "both as a set of core sectors and as a system of accumulation" (Fine and Rustomjee 1996a). State-owned enterprises have played a central role in the provision of inputs into MEC industries in this process (Clark 1994).

Discovery of diamonds and precious metals—particularly gold—in the late nineteenth century kicked off a process of mining and mining-linked industrialization, largely dominated by English capital. Limited backward linkages from the mining industry and demand for consumer goods generated by predominantly white wage-earners provided the initial impetus for industrial development (Chabane et al. 2006).

South African Railways (SAR) was created around the time of Union in 1910, followed by two critical state-owned enterprises (SOEs) established during the interwar period that would play a fundamental role in shaping South Africa's future industrialization: Eskom (electricity) and Iscor (steel).

The political victory of the white Afrikaner National Party—within a whites-only electoral system—in 1948 ushered in a phase of state-led industrialization aimed at the advancement of white interests in general and Afrikaner interests in particular. The state led a process of integration of Afrikaner capitalists with historically English capital, predominantly mining and finance. SOEs were used as a primary site to create white working-class employment as well as an instrument to rapidly build a nascent Afrikaner capitalist class.

Mining—led by gold—expanded rapidly over the post-war period, reaching its zenith in the late 1970s in the wake of the first oil shocks. Six main diversified conglomerates—comprising a mix of both English and Afrikaner mining and financial capital—increasingly dominated private economic activity and the Johannesburg Stock Exchange (JSE). Growing domestic demand, tariff protection, capital controls, and later economic sanctions saw the scope of these conglomerates expand from their roots in mining into a broad range of activities. For instance, the Anglo American Corporation "diversified (in chronological order) into explosive materials and mining equipment, banking, industrial commodities (steel, paper, and chemical engineering), and consumer goods (including beer and furniture)" (Chabane et al. 2006: 551).

SOEs and the recently established state-owned Industrial Development Corporation (IDC) played the central role in post-war industrialization, aided by other forms of state support such as import tariffs. Using cheap coal as a feedstock, low-priced electricity was used as a policy instrument to create and expand a range of capital and electricity-intensive industries. A range of SOEs were created *inter alia* for the provision of rail, port, and road transport infrastructure (under the South African Railways and Harbours Administration), shipping (Safmarine), telecommunications (under the department of Department of Posts and Telecommunications), and armaments (Armscor).

The IDC took on much of the post-war risk of a number of new ventures and expansions of capital and electricity-intensive resource-processing ventures through large equity stakes and loan financing. Clark (1994: 163) argues that these ventures were established using a similar labor model to that which prevailed in the mining industry, namely a combination of relatively skilled white labor in conjunction with "dispensable" low-skilled black labor, that could easily be disciplined and coerced.

Iscor became a vertically integrated steel producer—including owning its own iron ore mines—and by far the dominant steel producer by the mid 1950s. It went through a series of expansions over the post-war period and well into the post-apartheid period, drawing extensively on IDC financing support. Sasol was established—predominantly with IDC financing—in 1950 to produce oil from coal and a range of industrial chemical products. It went through very large IDC-supported expansions during the 1970s and 1980s. Alusaf began production of aluminum in 1971 with IDC as a joint venture partner. Foskor (a manufacturer of phosphates) was also established under full IDC ownership in 1951.

Thus apartheid-era industrialization proceeded largely on the basis of processing mineral and other natural-resource-based products without sufficient political impetus to develop more labor-intensive and value-adding "downstream" manufacturing sectors. Figure 12.1 illustrates the historical correlation between the performance of three key manufacturing sectors (metal fabrication, capital equipment, and transport equipment) and investment by public corporations. Rather than developing their own growth impetus, these sectors have been historically tied to investment by SOEs as well as the mining sector, relying heavily on unconditional tariff protection until 1994. As SOE and infrastructure investments declined from their peak in 1980, so too did the metal fabrication and equipment sectors. The lack of a coherent strategy to specifically develop the competitiveness of these sectors meant they did not become competitive in export markets.[4] Moreover, their performance has became increasingly de-linked from SOE

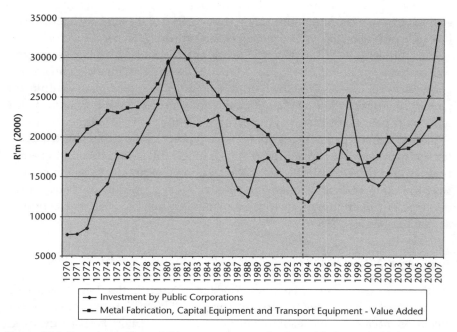

Figure 12.1 Investment by public corporations and value-added in metal fabrication, capital equipment and transport equipment (R'm 2000), 1970–2007

Sources: SARB and Quantec SA Standardized Industry Database

351

investments in the face of very rapid trade liberalization after 1994 as these sectors lost market share against imported goods.

The two SOEs that provided critical sets of inputs into downstream manufacturing, mining, and agriculture (steel, polymers, and other chemical products) were privatized through public listings: Sasol in 1979 and Iscor in 1989.[5] No regulatory checks and balances were put in place to strategically leverage the capabilities developed by these companies under state ownership, or to limit the abuse of dominance of now privately owned natural monopolies. Such a regulatory vacuum, combined with weak competition policy until very recently has allowed the extraction of monopolistic or oligopolistic rents from downstream firms, predominantly in the form of the practice of import parity pricing (IPP)[6] (Roberts and Zalk 2004).

In addition to the role of SOEs and the IDC in supporting mineral processing, there has been a long history of automotives production under relatively poorly designed protection in pre-democracy South Africa, with the first assembly plants installed in the 1920s (Black 2007). In 1961, the first in a long series of local content programs was introduced, which encompassed a number of phases with the last, Phase VI, introduced in 1986. A focus on local content without appropriate attention to economies of scale led to a proliferation of models aimed at serving a limited and almost exclusively white market. This led to attendant diseconomies in both the assembly and components sectors. However, notwithstanding the relative incoherence of apartheid-era automotive policy, the existence of the industry represented a base on which to build a more coherent post-apartheid policy for the sector.

Thus Amsden's RCM was deployed by the apartheid state on a large scale but a narrow scope, predominantly in the form of SOEs and IDC financing, to create a particularly capital- and electricity-intensive industrialization path. Within the narrow confines of its racial objectives, the state ensured certain conditions were met. Trade policy, however, was not deployed in any strategic manner.

Thus, the development of a set of resource-processing industries largely marked for the apartheid government the end-state of its limited industrialization ambitions. This contrasts with the well-known example of Korea's development of a steel industry—against all international advice—as a *necessary condition* for the development of industries such as ship-building, automotives, and consumer appliances (Amsden 1989).

Post-apartheid policies

South Africa's post-apartheid policies related to industrialization have largely been characterized by a set of self-imposed Washington Consensus type reforms, focused chiefly on macroeconomic stabilization and trade liberalization. Post-apartheid economic policy has been fundamentally informed by the 1996 Growth Employment and Redistribution (GEAR) strategy (Appendix: Box 12.1). GEAR predicted two main real-economy outcomes: rapid growth in both investment and employment.

Box 12.1 MAIN ELEMENTS OF THE GEAR STRATEGY

- a renewed focus on budget reform to strengthen the redistributive thrust of expenditure;
- a faster fiscal deficit reduction program to contain debt service obligations, counter inflation, and free resources for investment;
- an exchange rate policy to keep the real effective rate stable at a competitive level;
- consistent monetary policy to prevent a resurgence of inflation;
- a further step in the gradual relaxation of exchange controls;
- a reduction in tariffs to contain input prices and facilitate industrial restructuring, compensating partially for the exchange rate depreciation;
- tax incentives to stimulate new investment in competitive and labor-absorbing projects;
- speeding up the restructuring of state assets to optimize investment resources;
- an expansionary infrastructure program to address service deficiencies and backlogs;
- an appropriately structured flexibility within the collective bargaining system;
- a strengthened levy system to fund training on a scale commensurate with needs;
- an expansion of trade and investment flows in Southern Africa; and
- a commitment to the implementation of stable and coordinated policies.

Source: Department of Finance (1996: 2)

Monetary policy, inflation targeting, and capital account liberalization

The post-apartheid period has been characterized by relatively tight monetary policy, cemented by the adoption of formal inflation targeting in 2000 with a target range of 3–6 percent. This was accompanied by substantial liberalization of the capital account during the 1990s that focused on easing outflows while welcoming inflows: Restrictions were lifted and limits raised for corporate offshore investment and remittance of profits as well as individual portfolio investment.

Relatively high real interest rates have resulted in lower inflation than under most of the apartheid period. However, high real interest rates together with liberalization of the capital account led to a currency that experienced long periods of overvaluation and substantial volatility linked to the fortunes of minerals and semi-processed resources globally.[7] It has—only fairly recently—been widely acknowledged that currency overvaluation and volatility have had a negative effect on the growth and diversification of the tradables sectors, both with respect to exports and ability to compete against imports (Accelerated and Shared Growth Initiative for South Africa (AsgiSA), available at <http://www.info.gov.za/asgisa/asgisa.htm>).

A significant component of capital account liberalization has been to allow a number of major corporations to establish offshore listings. Firms which have shifted their primary listings offshore have included: Billiton (mining/mineral-processing), South African Breweries (brewing), Anglo American Corporation (mining), Old Mutual Life Assurance (financial services), and Dimension Data (information technology).

Fiscal restraint, debt reduction, strengthened revenue collection and weak state capacity

GEAR initiated a process of fiscal restraint based on the argument that lower government expenditure and debt would result in lower interest rates, and thus less "crowding out" of private investment.

Fiscal restraint led to a lower debt burden, but came at the cost of low growth in the immediate post-apartheid period. Low government and SOE expenditure since 1994 on economic infrastructure (until very recently) compounded the failure of the apartheid state to make such investments since the late 1970s. This has limited the productive capacity of the economy. Fiscal restraint, strong tax revenue growth—a major post-apartheid success story—and weaknesses in capacity of other government departments to spend their budgets, culminated in a budget surplus by 2007.

Government's fiscal position has allowed for significant growth in social expenditure, particularly in the areas of health, education, housing, and limited forms of welfare grants (largely child support and old-age pensions). However, growth in expenditure on economic infrastructure and "economic" government functions (largely sector-specific departmental functions) has been weak.

The role of weaknesses in government capacity to spend is under-researched and needs to be better understood. This includes both issues of the adequacy of financing models that emerged under GEAR and the prevalence and reasons for weak capacity of state officials and accountability within government. Von Holdt (2010) argues that a key cause of "dysfunctionalities" in the post-apartheid state is an unresolved ambiguity between the state as provider of services and as a site of black middle-class formation.

Widespread trade-liberalization and narrow industrial policy support

From 1993, the democratic government accelerated the trade liberalization process begun by its apartheid predecessor[8] through the commitments it made when rejoining the World Trade Organization (WTO).[9] These committed the country to substantial unilateral tariff reductions in a range of industrial and agricultural products, with the exception of two "sensitive" industries: automotives and clothing and textiles. South Africa also entered into two main regional free-trade agreements with the European Union (1999) and the Southern African Development Community (1994). Trade liberalization was implemented even more rapidly in terms of South Africa's commitments under the WTO.[10] The average industrial tariff declined from 28 percent in 1990 to 23 percent in 1994 to 8.2 percent by 2006.

Part of GEAR envisaged a range of—largely grant-based—"supply side" measures in order to help small and medium manufacturing firms to adapt to a sharp increase in international competition. In practice these measures were generally of limited scale and widely dispersed across a range of sectors and multiple policy targets (such as investment, SMME, competitiveness, and innovation support).

By contrast, substantial on- and off-budget support was afforded to capital- and electricity-intensive natural-resource-processing industries. Support was afforded at least three important ways. A range of resource-processing firms received generous tax allowances and IDC funding for expansions in the post-apartheid period. This included firms in industries such as: carbon and stainless steel, aluminum, chemicals, and paper and pulp. However, this support was not tied to strong reciprocal conditionalities; in particular, there was no monitoring of the pricing policies of these companies in the domestic market. Weak enforcement of competition policy thus allowed these industries to extract monopoly rents from downstream firms. Finally these firms continued to receive cheap electricity over the post-apartheid period.

In no industry have these arrangements been more generous than in relation to the foreign acquisition by Arcelor Mittal South Africa (AMSA) of majority shareholding in Iscor in 2004. In addition to other forms of support, it inherited an evergreen cost-plus arrangement for the provision of iron ore to Iscor by Kumba, a company established in 2001 by the spin-off of Iscor's mining assets. The launch of the National Industrial Policy Framework and Industrial Policy Action Plan in 2007 marked the start of a more coherent and ambitious approach to industrial and trade policy.

Commercialization of state assets

Although two of the most important privatizations (Sasol and Iscor) had pre-dated democracy in 1994, part of GEAR was a commitment to the privatization of various SOEs. This was only partially carried out. SOEs in a range of sectors were instructed to become self-financing and generally commercialized in preparation for privatization. This often took the form of substantial cost-cutting: of staff, new investment, and maintenance of existing infrastructure. Only where very large rents accrued to new investment, e.g. in telecommunications, did investment take place in the context of a weak regulatory environment that allowed for super-dominance. There was little or no investment in electricity and transport infrastructure, which had last seen investment in the 1970s under the apartheid government. This led to an effective exhaustion of electricity supply by January 2008, when the country experienced an electricity crisis in addition to inefficient transport infrastructure.

Black economic empowerment (BEE), employment equity (EE), and land reform (LR)

The major area where post-apartheid economic policy has departed from WC orthodoxy has been with respect to the promotion of a black capitalist class and the redress of racial imbalances in the labor market. BEE has gone through a few iterations since the mid 1990s. BEE transactions have occurred chiefly in sectors where the state has some direct form of leverage such as the issuing of licenses or undertakes large direct procurement, e.g. in mining and telecommunications (Ernst and Young 2009). Mining policy in particular has been almost overwhelmingly focused on facilitating transfer of ownership of the mining sector into black hands through the introduction of a new licensing regime in 2002.

Most transfers of ownership in terms of BEE transactions have been straightforward mergers or acquisitions. Conditions attached to these ownership transfers have not been linked explicitly to increases in productive capacity or employment.

EE legislation has seen more widespread changes to the patterns of those employed, with greater representivity in the South African workplace. It has also contributed strongly to the creation of a black middle class and increased domestic demand for goods and services. However, the combination of an overvalued exchange rate and trade liberalization has meant that this domestic demand has been serviced increasingly by imports rather than domestic production.

Skills development

There have been major weaknesses with respect to post-apartheid skills development institutions. The previous artisan system was replaced by a skills levy linked to sector education and training authorities (SETAs). This has resulted largely in an oversupply of relatively "shallow" skills and an undersupply of more complex skills required in sectors such as manufacturing.

Post-apartheid economic and industrial performance

Consumption-led growth

South Africa has achieved steady growth since 1994. Annual average GDP growth was 2.7 percent from 1994–9, and accelerated to 3.7 percent from 2000–4 and to 5.2 percent from 2005–7. However, this apparently improving performance masks major weaknesses and is not sustainable.

Growth has been driven predominantly by consumption. This is demonstrated in Figure 12.2a and even more starkly in Figure 12.2b. Growth in consumption has not been matched by a corresponding growth in the production side of the economy. This, coupled with weak export performance, has led to a widening

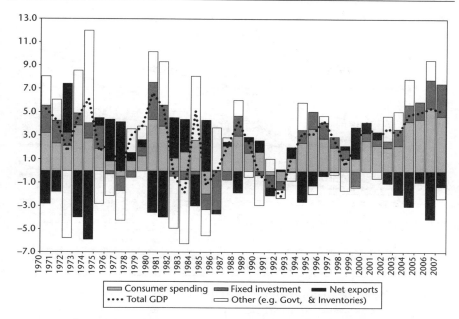

Figure 12.2a Components of annual GDP growth (R'm 2000)
Source: South African Reserve Bank, calculations by IDC

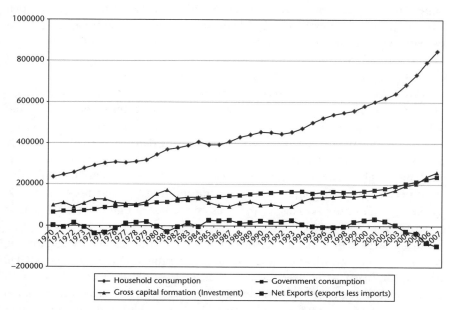

Figure 12.2b Cumulative components of GDP (R'm 2000)
Source: South African Reserve Bank

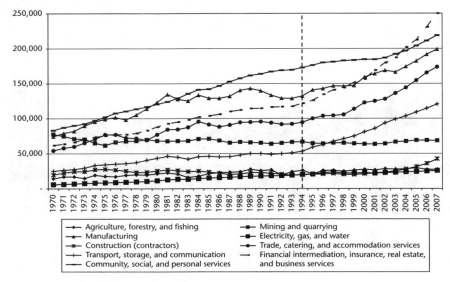

Figure 12.3 Growth in GDP by nine broad sectors (R'm 2000)

Source: Quantec RSA Standardized Industry Database

current account deficit that amounted to 7.3 percent in 2007 and an average of 8.1 percent in the first three quarters of 2008. The ability to externally finance such a consumption-led growth path has been reliant on short-term capital inflows associated with the global commodity boom and with high real interest rates.

While overall growth performance has improved during the post-apartheid period it has been heterogeneous as demonstrated in Figure 12.3. Consumption-led growth has meant that the services sectors of the economy (transport, storage, and communication; finance, insurance, real estate, and business services; and trade, catering, and accommodation) have grown fastest. The construction sector has also grown strongly on the back of rising housing demand, and more recently various forms of public Capital Expenditure (Capex). Thus, services and construction have roughly doubled in size between 1994 and 2007. Manufacturing grew by 50 percent over the same period; agriculture, forestry, and fishing by only 5 percent; and mining—on aggregate—was only 2 percent larger in 2007 than it was in 1994.

Strong growth in financial services has not been accompanied by a corresponding growth in private investment in the economy. Investment as a percentage of GDP has generally been weak over the post-apartheid period, fluctuating around 15 percent of GDP between 1994 and 2002 (Figure 12.4). This suggests that far too much optimism was placed in the ability of the GEAR strategy to raise investment rates. The latter have only begun to rise since 2003, coinciding precisely with the

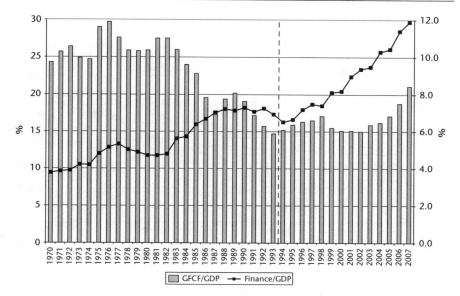

Figure 12.4 Gross fixed capital formation to GDP versus share of finance and insurance sector in GDP (R'm 2000), %
Source: South African Reserve Bank and Quantec RSA Standardized Industry Database

growth in public infrastructure expenditure (Figure 12.1), and rising to 20.6 percent of GDP in 2007. Savings rates have performed even more poorly, declining from 16.9 percent to 14.6 percent between 1994 and 2007 and thus opening an increasing investment-savings gap. Although the share of the finance and insurance sector in GDP has risen dramatically—roughly doubling its share since 1994—investment rates have come nowhere near to those achieved in the 1970s and early 1980s. This raises serious questions about the efficiency of South Africa's private financial sector in terms of aggregating and channeling resources into investment in the real economy, particularly the tradable merchandise sectors of the economy.

Employment growth in the post-apartheid period has been weak and concentrated overwhelmingly in private services sectors (Figure 12.5). While GDP grew by 60 percent from 1994–2007, formal employment grew by only 12 percent over the same period. The official unemployment rate rose rapidly in the post-apartheid period, peaking at 31.2 percent in 2003 before declining to 23 percent in 2007. This official unemployment rate excludes "discouraged workers" who have given up looking for work although it is reflected in relatively low labor force participation rates.

Figure 12.6 zooms in on employment trends in private services. Services employment has been chiefly in the wholesale and retail sectors and business services. The growth in wholesale and retail reflects the surge in imports accompanying trade liberalization and currency overvaluation, and has therefore been in

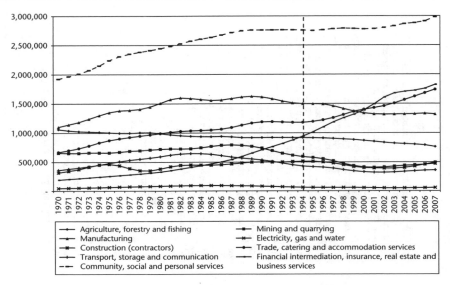

Figure 12.5 Employment growth by nine broad sectors (R'm 2000)
Source: Quantec RSA Standardized Industry Database

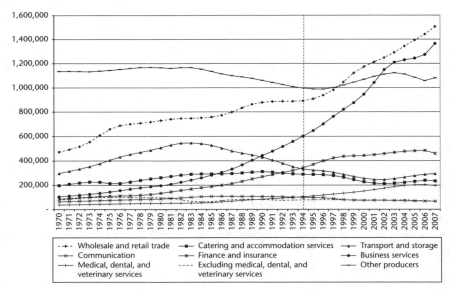

Figure 12.6 Employment growth in private services
Source: Quantec RSA Standardized Industry Database

considerable part at the expense of the manufacturing sector and the trade balance. Employment in these sectors will be difficult to sustain when the credit and consumption boom comes to an end, as is already being seen.

The growth in the share of business services in GDP and employment reflects two problematic trends (Mohammed and Roberts 2008). First, much of this growth has been in the private security sector in response to crime. Second, the catch-all category of business services reflects the outsourcing of a range of activities, such as catering and cleaning services, as well as the rise in the role of labor brokers in arranging formal employment, that was previously undertaken directly in sectors such as manufacturing.

Outsourcing and casualization of employment, with its associated downward pressure on wages and working conditions, goes a long way toward explaining the rising share of profits and declining share of wages in GDP. Profits rose from around 25 percent to more than 30 percent share in GDP between 1994 and 2003, while wages declined over the same period from around 50 percent to 45 percent (Makgetla 2008: 149).

Because of a combination of high unemployment and downward pressure on wages and working conditions, it is unsurprising that poverty and inequality remain high. Some 48 percent of the population lived in poverty in 2005, a decline from 53 percent in 1995 (PCAS 2008: 18).[11] However, inequality increased between 1995 and 2005, as reflected in the rise of the Gini coefficient from 0.64 to 0.69 (ibid.: 101).

Driving forces of growth in the real economy

Limited real-economy growth and diversification

The "real economy" is understood to comprise all sectors of the economy except finance and insurance. However, this section focuses predominantly on the merchandise or tradable sectors of the economy, as the performance of other real-services sectors (such as wholesale and retail and business services), as well as the construction sector have already been discussed.

Figure 12.7 demonstrates the heterogeneity of growth in different groupings of merchandise sectors since 1994. Appendix A, Box 12.2 provides the composition of these sectoral groupings. On an indexed basis, the automotives sector has experienced the most rapid growth between 1994 and 2007, at 93 percent. This is followed by natural-resource-based manufactures at 85 percent and durable manufactures at 56 percent. Labor-intensive and other manufactures both grew by only 22 percent. The fact that agriculture and mining (on aggregate) have experienced virtually no growth has already been noted.

Figure 12.8 demonstrates a somewhat similar composition with respect to real exports. The following features stand out. First, mining continues to dominate

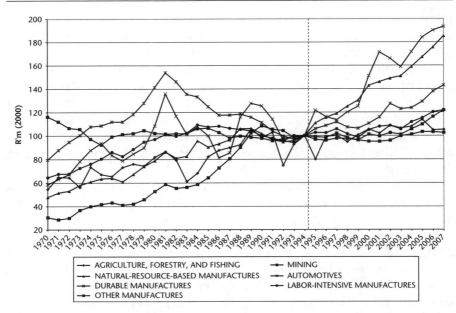

Figure 12.7 Index of real value-added growth of merchandise sectors by sectoral grouping (R'm 1994=100), 1970–2007

Source: Quantec RSA Standardized Industry Database

merchandise exports even though there has been virtually no growth in the aggregate real value of mining exports, going right back to the 1970s. Second, there has been a very rapid growth in the exports of natural-resource-based manufactures. Third, automotive exports have increased substantially from a relatively low base. Fourth, the remainder of the merchandise sectors' exports has been stagnant.

The weak aggregate investment performance of the post-apartheid South African economy has been noted. Figure 12.9 shows that the bulk of investment in merchandise sectors in the post-apartheid period (and going back to the 1970s) has been in the capital-intensive natural-resource-based manufacturing sectors as well as mining. The apparent contradiction between aggregate mining stagnation and sizeable levels of mining investment is partly explained by the sectoral shifts taking place within mining. While gold mining has been on a long-term decline, new investment has been taking place in more profitable mining subsectors, particularly among the Platinum Group Metals (PGMs).

Figure 12.10 shows that formal employment has either declined or stagnated across most merchandise sectors in the post-apartheid period, notwithstanding reasonable levels of value-added growth in sectors such as automotives and natural–resource-based manufactures.

Box 12.2 SECTORAL GROUPINGS

Agriculture, Forestry, and Fishing

MINING
Coal mining
Gold and uranium ore mining
Other mining

Natural-Resource-Based Manufactures

Coke and refined petroleum products
Basic chemicals
Other chemicals and man-made fibers
Rubber products
Non-metallic minerals
Basic iron and steel
Basic non-ferrous metals
Wood and wood products
Paper and paper products

Durable Manufactures

Plastic products
Glass and glass products
Metal products excluding machinery
Machinery and equipment
Electrical machinery and apparatus
Motor vehicles; parts and accessories
Other transport equipment

Labor-Intensive Manufactures

Food
Tobacco
Textiles
Wearing apparel
Leather and leather products
Footwear
Printing, publishing, and recorded media
Furniture

Other Manufactures

Beverages
Television, radio, and communication equipment
Professional and scientific equipment
Other manufacturing

Total formal employment in manufacturing fell during the post-apartheid period from 1.5 million in 1994 to 1.3 million in 2007. The process of de-industrialization—defined as a declining share of manufacturing employment of total employment—that began in 1982 has accelerated since 1994. Manufacturing's

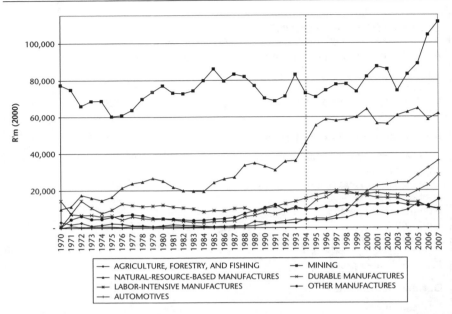

Figure 12.8 Real export growth of merchandise sectors by sectoral grouping (R'm 2000), 1970–2007

Source: Quantec SA Standardized Industry Database

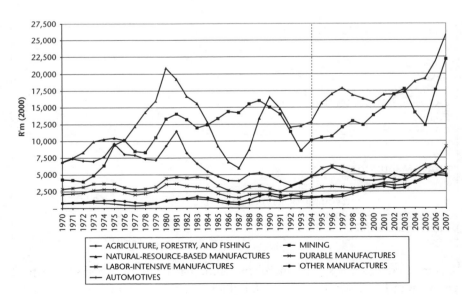

Figure 12.9 Real investment by sectoral grouping (2000), 1970–2007

Source: Quantec SA Standardized Industry Database

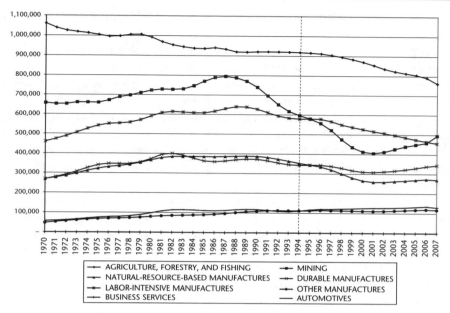

Figure 12.10 Employment by sectoral grouping, 1970–2007
Source: Quantec SA Standardized Industry Database

share of total formal employment thus fell more rapidly than its share in GDP over the post-apartheid period: from 17 percent in 1994 to 13 percent in 2007.

Only mining has experienced somewhat of a reversal of this trend. The precipitous decline of mining employment since its peak in 1987 bottomed out in 2001, but had only recovered 1997/8 levels by 2007.

Where has the manufacturing growth been and why?

As shown in Figure 12.7, only three groups of manufacturing sectors stand out for having achieved anything approximating "respectable" growth over the post-apartheid period; that is growth that equaled or exceeded the average GDP growth rate. These are automotives, natural-resource-processing industries, and durable manufactures. What accounts for the performance of these sectors?

Edwards and Lawrence (2006) argue that the "growth in non-commodity manufactured sectoral exports as a result of liberalization was actually faster than sectoral imports." This leads them to conclude that even more trade liberalization should be prescribed and "could well be part of the strategy to enhance export diversification."

These conclusions arise from econometric correlations derived between trade liberalization and "medium technology" industries using Lall's technological

365

classification. But what comprises these medium technology industries? Lall's "Medium Technology Manufactures" are broken down into three categories: MT1: Automotive; MT2: Process (which includes the processing of primary steel and chemical products); and MT3: Engineering (which includes a broad range of machinery and equipment). Thus medium technology manufactures captures a large part of the three industries identified above.

Relying on orthodox trade theory, and omitting any detailed account of the historical evolution of these industries, Edwards and Lawrence arrive at misleading conclusions both with respect to explaining the performance of the industries themselves, as well as what might be appropriate policy recommendations for the broader economy.

As demonstrated above, the natural-resource-based sectors emerged through the conscious industrial policy of the apartheid state, in which the use of state owner-ship and IDC financing played the fundamental role. By 1994 they corresponded closely to Shafaedin's "mature industries" that are close enough to competitive-ness not to be destroyed by full international competition. Thus, trade liberaliza-tion may have been appropriate for these sectors, *but only once they reached a particular stage of development.*

The automotive industry has had a long history of tariff protection, which was particularly incoherent in the late-apartheid period, with attendant diseconomies of scale and scope. The 1995 MIDP introduced a much more coherent policy for the industry. Although automotive import tariffs have been substantially reduced since 1995, the IRCC system has been one of directed and conditional economic rents, not a case of trade liberalization. This highlights the limitations of analyses that fail to engage with industry detail and only examine high-level data.

Durable manufactures had a long correlation with the fortunes of investment in mining and state-owned enterprises during the apartheid period. This occurred without any coherent strategy for their further development and behind uncritical trade protection. A combination of low infrastructure investment after 1994 and trade liberalization provided a double-blow. Conversely, as infrastructure expen-diture has accelerated since 2002, so has the performance of these sectors, although subject to much higher levels of competition than during the pre-democracy period.

For the remainder of manufacturing sectors and parts of agriculture, trade liber-alization has arguably been premature and has led to stagnation or de-industriali-zation in various subsectors.

Conclusions

South Africa is the largest and most industrialized economy on the African conti-nent. Thus, in terms of orthodox economic theory it would be the African economy most likely to benefit through the gains from much greater openness to trade and broader economic liberalization of the economy.

Growth has steadily improved since 1994, particularly since 2000. However, this growth has been unsustainably consumption-led. Because of insufficient dynamism and diversification of the production side of the economy, consumption has outstripped production, leading to an ever-larger current-account deficit. This in turn is dependent on short-term portfolio capital inflows that are only sustainable on the basis of continued high commodity prices. A combination of unfavorable macro- and microeconomic policies has further damaged productive competitiveness, particularly in manufacturing. These include exchange rate appreciation and volatility associated with short-term capital inflows; high real interest rates; wide, deep, and poorly sequenced trade liberalization; low investment in economic infrastructure; monopolistic provision of key inputs; a poorly performing skills system; and transfers in economic ownership not linked to productive capacity and employment.

Notwithstanding improvements in growth, and more recently investment performance, both have been lower than in peer countries (Mohammed and Roberts 2008). Export performance in particular has been extremely weak. Therefore convergence has been limited. Further, growth has occurred in the context of exceptionally high unemployment rates and worsening inequality.

The introduction of trade liberalization simultaneously with deficiencies and unfavorable conditions in a range of other markets has ignored the theory of the second-best (Fine and Rustomjee 1996a). That is, if conditions for pareto optimality are not simultaneously present in all markets, then proposed reforms in one market need to be revisited.

Liberalization of trade has been coupled with substantial continuity in support for natural-resource-based manufactures, although with little or no reciprocal conditions imposed. This has strengthened South Africa's reliance on mining and natural-resource-based industries, particularly with respect to exports. The major exception has been the automotives industry, where prior protection—however incoherent—created manufacturing capabilities that were susceptible to being leveraged in a more coherent way since 1995. There has been a moderate improvement in the performance of durable manufactures, particularly since 2003. This correlates closely to the upturn in investment by public corporations. However, much lower import tariffs mean that these sectors have benefited far less than in the previous surge of public investment (peaking in 1980). Thus what limited dynamism there has been in South African manufacturing since 1994 largely represents a combination of (1) the legacy of apartheid-era industrial policies; (2) the single significant post-apartheid piece of sectoral policy: for automotives; (3) and the limited but important impact of rising public investment since 2002.

Recognizing the heterogeneity of African countries, some tentative conclusions can be drawn with respect to efforts of other African countries to industrialize.

Industrialization and trade policy

Without manufacturing, African countries will remain dependent on diminishing return activities in agriculture and mining with little prospect of developing advanced services without first going through an industrialization phase.

South Africa's experience with trade liberalization is largely in line with Shafaeddin's hypothesis. Even in Africa's most industrialized economy, "big bang" unilateral liberalization (combined with other unfavorable policies) destroyed nascent industrial capabilities and pushed South Africa back toward its natural resource advantage. Only industries already close to international competitiveness or enjoying industrial policy support i.e. automotives survived this process.

Thus, to the full extent that policy space allows, African countries should be circumspect about liberalizing trade, particularly in their manufacturing sectors. There is such a phenomenon as too rapid trade liberalization too soon.

Prior manufacturing experience and the RCM

Amsden's periodization of a phase of "prior manufacturing experience" followed by a more coherent industrialization drive using the RCM finds very limited expression in post-apartheid industrial policy.

However, the automotives industry provides an interesting and useful case study. Post-apartheid South Africa inherited a highly uncompetitive automotives industry, which had been the product of a long history of poorly designed protection. This prior experience, however, formed the base on which to develop a more coherent strategy with the MIDP as its "reciprocal control mechanism" and provide much needed diversification and growth in the South African manufacturing sector.

This underscores the need for African countries to nurture and leverage nascent manufacturing capabilities they have thus far acquired as well as to seek to develop new capabilities.

Resource management, financing for industrialization, and external balance

For countries rich in natural resources, rents associated with these activities will play a fundamental role in shaping their development trajectory. How these rents are deployed and managed will depend on whether they have positive or negative developmental effects. Negative potential effects included the squandering of resource rents and the possibility of "Dutch disease" currency appreciation, rendering manufactures relatively less competitive.

South Africa's continued reliance on primary and semi-processed commodities, in conjunction with the global commodity boom, has generated substantial negative effects. These included the overvaluation and volatility of the currency and the provision of the external financing necessary for an unsustainable consumption-led period of growth. It appears that currency appreciation over the post-apartheid period has not been the product of Dutch disease per se but rather the openness of the capital account to short-term portfolio flows associated with the commodity boom, namely in the shares of listed companies producing commodities.

However, natural-resource rents can be deployed and managed in more development-friendly ways. Given that mineral and petroleum resources in particular are non-renewable, there is a strong case for taxing these rents and deploying them toward building industries that are more sustainable in the long term, as well as physical infrastructure. Countries have found ways of managing resource-related capital inflows so as to minimize disruptive currency movements.[12]

Notes

1. This article reflects the author's personal views.
2. They raise a legitimate and under-researched (and indeed underconceptualized) part of industrial policy literature. The economy is viewed as a suboptimal equilibrium but they expect that answers for structural change will come from within the same group of sectors and entrepreneurs who are engaged in such suboptimality. There is no recognition that large and more powerful firms and interests may dominate such processes and might entrench rather than change the current development path.
3. The countries identified by Amsden are Argentina, Brazil, Chile, Mexico, Turkey, China, India, Indonesia, South Korea, Taiwan, and Thailand.
4. To some extent, growing economic sanctions and poor political relations with other African states may also have played a role. However, successful apartheid-era companies proved adept at bypassing sanctions as well as trading with African partners.
5. Although government held significant equity stakes through the IDC and continue to hold small stakes.
6. This is the pricing of a product up to the point that it would cost to import. This practice results in uniquely high rents in the South African economy due to a confluence of factors: high weight/value ratios of intermediate products, relative underindustrialization of the subregion, and long distances and high transport costs of alternative sources of import supply.
7. Overvaluation and volatility appear to have been driven predominantly by financial rather than trade flows, particularly movement in and out of highly liquid currency and stock markets. The relatively small size of SA's financial sector combined with high levels of openness leaves it highly vulnerable to external financial shocks.
8. This largely involved the removal of quantitative restrictions and surcharges.
9. Although South Africa's rejoining of the WTO in 1993 slightly pre-dated the first democratic elections in 1994, South Africa's offer to unilaterally lock in widespread trade liberalization reflected the decision of the incoming political order and not the apartheid regime.
10. This has placed South Africa at a significant disadvantage in the Doha round of negotiations where unlike a range of other developing countries, bound rates are generally low and there is little "water" between bound and applied rates.

11. Using the more realistic R322 per person per month poverty line (2000 prices).
12. For instance, holding them offshore in a Sovereign Wealth Fund or other structure, the introduction of "Tobin Taxes" to slow speculative portfolio inflows, etc.

References

Amsden, A. (1989). *Asia's Next Giant: South Korea and Late Industrialization*. New York: Oxford University Press.

—— (2003). *The Rise of "The Rest": Challenges to the West from Late-Industrializing Economies*. New York: Oxford University Press.

Black, A. (2007). *Automotive Policy and the Restructuring of the South African Industry, 1990–2005*. Ph.D. dissertation, University of Cape Town, South Africa.

Chabane, N., Goldstein, A., and Roberts, S. (2006). "The Changing Face and Strategies of Big Business in South Africa: More Than a Decade of Political Democracy," *Industrial and Corporate Change*, 15 (3): 549–77.

Chabane, N., Machaka, J., Molaba, N., Roberts, S., and Taka, M. (2003). "10 Year Review: Industrial Structure and Competition Policy," Corporate Strategy and Industrial Development research project, School of Economic and Business Sciences, University of the Witwatersrand. Available at <http://www.sarpn.org.za/documents/d0000875/docs/10yerReviewIndustrial-Structure&CompetitionPolicy.pdf>.

Chang, H.-J. (2002). *Kicking Away the Ladder: Development Strategy in Historical Perspective*. London: Anthem Press.

Chibber, V. (2006). *Locked in Place: State-Building and Late Industrialization in India*. Princeton: Princeton University Press.

Clark, N. (1994). *Manufacturing Apartheid: State Corporations in South Africa*. New Haven: Yale University Press.

Department of Finance, Republic of South Africa (1996). "Growth and Redistribution: A Macro-Economic Strategy," available at <http://www.treasury.gov.za>.

Edwards, L. and Lawrence, R. (2006). "South African Trade Policy Matters: Trade Performance and Trade Policy," CID Working Paper No. 135, Cambridge, MA.

Ernst and Young (2009). *Mergers and Acquisitions: A Review of Activity for the Year 2009*. Johannesburg: Ernst and Young.

Fine, B. and Rustomjee, Z. (1996a). *The Political Economy of South Africa: From Minerals-Energy Complex to Industrialization*. London: Hurst & Company.

—— (1996b). "Debating the South African Minerals-Energy Complex," *Development Southern Africa*, 15 (4): 689–70.

Hausmann, R. and Rodrik, D. (2003). "Economic development as self-discovery," *Journal of Development Economics*, 72 (2): 603–33, 14th Inter-American Seminar on Economics.

Hirsch, A. (2005). *Season of Hope: Economic Reform Under Mandela and Mbeki*. Scottsville, SA: University of KwaZulu-Natal Press.

Johnson, C. (1982). *MITI and the Japanese Miracle: The Growth of Industrial Policy, 1925–1975*. Stanford: Stanford University Press.

Khan, M. (2004). "Governance and Anti-Corruption Reforms in Developing Countries: Policies, Evidence and Ways Forward," G24 Discussion Paper Series No. 42, United Nations Conference on Trade and Development, New York.

—— (2007). "Governance, Economic Growth and Development since the 1960s," United Nations Department of Economic and Social Affairs (DESA) Working Paper No. 54. Available at <http://www.un.org/esa/desa/papers/2007/wp54_2007.pdf.>

Lall, S. (2004). *Reinventing Industrial Strategy: The Role of Government Policy in Building Industrial Competitiveness*, QEH Working Papers qehwps111. Oxford: Queen Elizabeth House, University of Oxford.

Makgetla, N. (2008). "A Developmental State for South Africa?" in B. Turok (ed.), *Wealth Doesn't Trickle Down: The Case for a Developmental State in South Africa*. Cape Town: New Agenda.

Mohammed, S. and Roberts, S. (2008). "Questions of Growth, Questions of Development," in B. Turok (ed.), *Wealth Doesn't Trickle Down: The Case for a Developmental State in South Africa*. Cape Town: New Agenda.

Nolan, P. (2001). *China and the Global Business Revolution*. Houndsmill: Palgrave.

Reinert, E. (2007). *How Rich Countries Got Rich . . . and Why Poor Countries Stay Poor*. London: Constable.

Roberts, S. and Zalk, N. (2004). Addressing Market Power in a Small, Isolated, Resource-Based Economy: The Case of Steel in South Africa. CRC Third International Conference, "Pro-Poor Regulation and Competition: Issues, Policies, and Practice," September 7–9.

Policy Coordination and Advisory Services (PCAS) (2008). *Towards a Fifteen Year Review: Synthesis Report—A Discussion Document*, The Presidency, Republic of South Africa.

Shafaeddin, S. M. (2005). "Trade Liberalization and Economic Reform in Developing Countries: Structural Change Or De-Industrialization?" UNCTAD Discussion Paper 179. Geneva: UNCTAD.

Von Holdt, K. (2010). "The South African Post-Apartheid Bureaucracy: Inner Workings, Contradictory Rationales and the Developmental State," in O. Edigheji (ed.), *Constructing a Democratic Developmental State in South Africa: Potentials and Challenges*. Cape Town: Human Sciences Research Council Press.

Wade, R. (1990). *Governing the Market: Economic Theory and the Role of Government in Taiwan's Industrialization*. Princeton: Princeton University Press.

13

Issues in Africa's Industrial Policy Process

Matsuo Watanabe and Atsushi Hanatani[1]

Introduction

Recent years have seen increasing attention to growth in the development discourse, following the emphasis on poverty reduction in the last decade. The economies of Sub-Saharan Africa (hereafter Africa) have performed well in recent years. However, the income level of the continent as a whole is still behind other developing regions and the growth pattern is subject to world commodity prices despite considerable aid inflows over the last three decades.[2] African policymakers seek sustained growth through diversification of economic structures by promoting new activities (in manufacturing as well as service and agro-industries). In this context, international development discourse finds renewed interest in industrial policy and the Asian industrialization experience, which is often attributed to Asia's interventionist approach (for example, Rodrik 2007; Stiglitz 2008a; Wade 1990).

The reevaluation of industrial policy reflects skepticism about the effectiveness of the policies under the guidance of international financial institutions (IFIs). The post-Washington Consensus school advocates industrial policy for developing countries, allowing broader policy space for governments and diverse development strategies reflecting the local context of individual countries. The orthodox economics school contends that industrial policy is hazardous, especially for developing countries, because of the lack of sufficient information for government to design effective intervention, as well as rent-seeking and corruption. The validity of industrial policy for latecomers is still an open question.

There is a large volume of literature on Asia's economic success. Export-oriented industrialization led by foreign direct investment (FDI) has been a model for latecomers. The authoritative style of governance, which was disapproved for being "undemocratic," has also seen a revaluation in terms of its prudent economic management, Weberian bureaucracy, and its contribution to economic performance.

However, the development paths of Asian economies are diverse and based on unique socioeconomic conditions; there is no single formality perceived as being an Asian model. Is the Asian experience relevant to other developing economies?

This chapter explores these issues and suggests a policy direction in industrial development and in constructing a foundation for sustainable growth, but it is not within our scope to provide an account of the disappointing past performance of Africa *vis-à-vis* East Asia. The following section briefly reviews the recent economic performance of Africa. Next, we discuss industrial policy for latecomers, with an overview of past discourse on industrial policy and the problems faced by developing countries pursuing industrial policy. Subsequently, the argument of the post-Washington Consensus is presented. We then discuss the factors that allowed Asia's industrial policy to function, before turning to issues of donor assistance in the industrial policy implementation of latecomer countries.

Sustained growth is needed for Africa

Over a decade beginning in the mid 1990s, most African economies have had good opportunities to grow like other developing regions (except East Asia and Latin America at the end of the 1990s due to the 1997 financial crisis). The real GDP growth rate has been positive since 1993 in Sub-Saharan Africa as a whole, and has steadily increased since 1998. In particular, the years after 2004 saw an annual average rate of nearly 6 percent, which was above the rates of Latin America and the Middle East (Figure 13.1). This growth has not been confined to resource-rich countries. Except

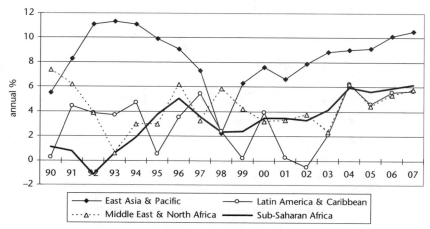

Figure 13.1 GDP growth of developing regions, 1990–2007
Source: World Development Indicators
Note: Based on constant 2000 USD

for the conflict or post-conflict countries, countries with few natural resource endowments also enjoyed an annual growth rate exceeding 5 percent during the period (Figure 13.2). Even landlocked, non-resource exporters, such as Rwanda and Uganda, grew as fast as Nigeria. While these performances are largely accounted for by the commodity boom, African efforts to improve the business climate (e.g. the resolution of a number of protracted conflicts, macroeconomic management, and the expansion of trade and investment opportunities) have also been essential to growth (JICA/JBIC 2008).[3]

However, there is another side to this story. The income level of Africa is still low compared to other developing regions (Figure 13.3). Africa's average GDP per capita from 2000–7 was USD542, while that of the Middle East and North Africa was USD1,684 and that of East Asia and the Pacific USD1,240. For Africa's real per capita GDP to reach that of present-day Thailand or Malaysia within the next twenty years, for example, per capita GDP would have to grow at 7.8 percent or 9 percent, respectively, on an annual basis—that is, a GDP growth rate of at least 11 percent per annum.

The perception that economic growth contributes to poverty reduction is becoming a "consensus" (Nelson 2007). Many empirical studies (e.g. Dollar and Kraay 2000) show a robust correlation between growth and poverty. For African countries to overcome economic challenges including poverty reduction, sustained growth is needed. The post World War II development paradigm has been swinging between

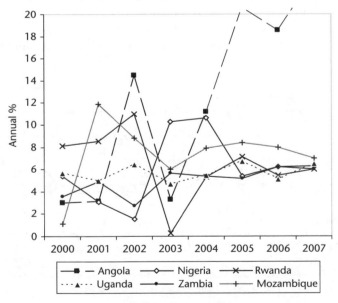

Figure 13.2 GDP growth of African countries
Source: World Development Indicators
Note: Based on constant 2000 USD

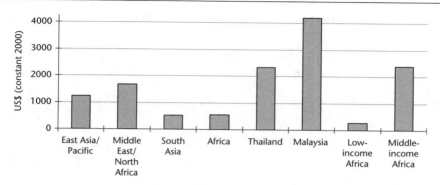

Figure 13.3 Income level: 2000–7 average
Source: World Development Indicators

growth and poverty (or basic human needs). The recent international discourse on African development finds a renewed interest in the growth agenda, as can be seen in the Commission on Growth and Development (2008) and the "Growth Diagnostics" advocated by Hausmann et al. (2005) *inter alia*.

The pattern of Africa's economic performance has remained subject to volatile world commodity prices (Figure 13.4).[4] Stiglitz (2008b) points out that even those countries that have done well in macroeconomic management and governance have still not managed to attract much "non-extractive" FDI or attained

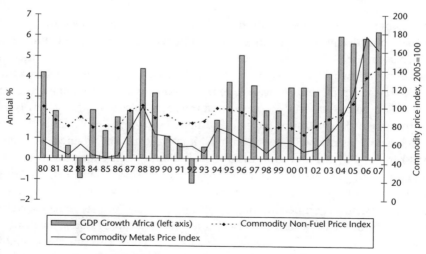

Figure 13.4 Africa's growth and commodity prices
Sources: World Development Indicators, IMF Commodity Prices
Note: GDP growth rate based on constant 2000 USD

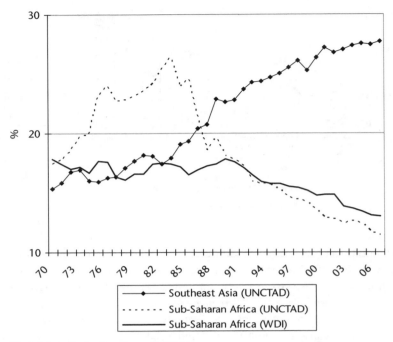

Figure 13.5 Manufacturing share in GDP

Sources: World Development Indicators, UNCTAD *Handbook of Statistics*

Note: There is a large deviation between WDI and UNCTAD data on Africa especially for the 1970–80s. Nevertheless they both indicate the declining trend in the 1990s afterwards

significant structural transformation. The share of Africa's manufacturing in GDP has been practically stagnant since 1960, while its Southeast Asian counterparts (which accounted for less than Africa in the early 1970s) saw a remarkable increase during the last two decades (Figure 13.5). In other words, no substantial structural change has taken place in African economies (*vis-à-vis* other developing regions, such as Southeast Asia), and it appears that the economies may have to be diversified through industrialization to realize sustained growth.[5]

How can such sustained growth through industrialization be attained? Watanabe (2008) argues that African countries have made decades-long efforts to reform their economies and governance. Such efforts have not necessarily borne expected fruits when it comes to promoting new industries. Insufficient reforms, civil wars, and their negative effects on neighboring countries partly account for setbacks. Nevertheless, the current low levels of infrastructure and other capital stocks, the disparity between the productivity and wages of labor, the costs associated with public administration, and the lack of efficient financial systems have all contributed to reducing business profitability in Africa, and so placed limits on economic growth (JICA/JBIC 2008). In addition, it is still open to question whether reform efforts to improve the environment (e.g. strengthening market mechanisms, macroeconomic balance, best practices in governance) are enough to promote industrialization, or whether economic success is likely to be confined to resource-related sectors, which have fewer ripple effects on the entire economy and less scope for productivity growth and sustainable development. Our position is that government should play a more active role beyond the "improvement of the environment," and industrial policy measures may be considered as a means to this end, especially for long-term changes in economic structure.[6]

Industrial policy for latecomers

Proponents and opponents of industrial policy

The efficacy of industrial policy has been subject to controversy in development economics literature. Schmitz (2007) offers a classification of industrial policy as the combination of *support* and *challenge* to entrepreneurs. The former refers to preferential access to scarce resources (credit, technology) and to protection from foreign competition by trade barriers. The latter includes targets set by government that enterprises must meet to qualify for preferential access and foreign and domestic competition through the lowering of trade barriers and freer entrance into sectors (Table 13.1).

High-challenge, *low*-support policies—in which enterprises are exposed to international competition under transparent domestic rules—characterize those adopted by many developing countries in the 1980s and afterward under the Washington Consensus. *Low*-challenge, *high*-support policies characterize the protectionist policies typically adopted during the import substitution industrialization of the 1950–70s, which mostly failed because of the low incentive for domestic enterprises to increase productivity. Those "disillusioned" with the protectionist and Washington Consensus policies have shown interest in *high*-challenge, *high*-support policies, which involve integration in the world economy but provide support in the form of tax incentives for investment or low-interest

Table 13.1 Classification of industrial policies

		Support	
		Low	High
Challenge	High	Washington Consensus	Active industrial policy
	Low	No policy	Protection under import substitution industrialization

Source: Schmitz (2007: Figure 1)

credit for developing new technologies, among others (ibid.: 419). An exemplar of this policy type is the Korean case, in which a limited number of enterprises had access to a profitable domestic market upon meeting export targets.

"INDUSTRIAL POLICY IS NECESSARY AND POSSIBLE"

Latsch (2008) characterizes the three views on industrial policy in terms of necessity and possibility for latecomers. First, the school that sees industrial policy as both necessary and possible for latecomers finds successful cases in East Asia (i.e. *high* challenge, *high* support in Table 13.1). Lall and Teubal (1998) argue that the countries in the region, South Korea and Taiwan in particular, adopted industrial policy measures and achieved rapid economic growth, diversification of manufacturing, and capture of overseas market shares through a set of technology policies that stimulated markets. In their account, the nature of such policies is *horizontal* in that they promote certain activities *across* sectors, improve markets, and may target particular (sub)sectors, rather than merely *selective* (i.e. "picking winners," identifying relevant firms, sectors, or markets that are subject to market imperfection) or *functional* (addressing such market failures as narrowly defined in the neoclassical sense).[7] Rodrik (2004) supports industrial policy in terms of informational externalities. The benefits of entrepreneurs' comparative advantages in the market are not captured by themselves, and the level of entrepreneurship tends to be suboptimal in developing countries. To address this problem, discretionary intervention by government can be rational as it is responsive to changing circumstances and sensitive to the feedback from (the consequences of) government policies. Chang et al. (2002) look to "learning and innovation rents" created by discretionary industrial policy instruments (e.g. subsidies to activities of research and development) under the market imperfections inherent in the process of technological development, particularly in developing countries.

"INDUSTRIAL POLICY IS NEITHER NECESSARY NOR POSSIBLE"

The second view rejects both the necessity and the possibility of industrial policy. The conventional objections are concerned with the abilities of governments and with rent-seeking and corruption. It is often stated that governments are not good at picking winners properly, because they do not have adequate information to design welfare-increasing industrial policies (hence industrial policy is not possible).[8] Provision of governmental support to specific enterprises (e.g. directing credit from the banking system and protecting with trade barriers) tends to distort competition, and the private sector tends to spend its time asking for favors rather than improving their operations and expanding markets. For this school, Asian countries are not an exception. Yusuf (2001) argues that industrial policy is not cost-effective. By listing the unsuccessful cases in Asian countries, he asserts that the investments under government control have been wasteful, and have ended up directing credit to the less efficient parts of the economy, retarding the maturation of the financial sector, and bringing about a steady accumulation of non-performing assets.[9]

Other industrial policy opponents believe in the market mechanism that they assume functions in developing countries. To achieve economic growth (through unleashing entrepreneurship, promoting investments, increasing productivity and per capita output, for example), this school stresses that domestic and international barriers should be abolished, that competition should be promoted, and that government's role should be minimal and limited to providing purely public goods, such as law and order, within a rule-based, non-discretionary framework of well-designed property rights so that technological externalities can be captured (e.g. Parente and Prescott 2000; Baumol 2002).

SKEPTICISM TO THE NECESSITY AND POSSIBILITY
The third and "intermediate" view, according to Latsch, represents skepticism about the necessity and possibility of industrial policy. This school, while recognizing the East Asian growth performance, does accept the justification of the use of industrial policy to address market failure, yet finds little empirical evidence for active government policy (Pack and Saggi 2006). Noland and Pack (2003), by examining the total factor productivity growth and externalities generated by leading sectors, attribute a large part of Asian success to macroeconomic management of the governments in the region (e.g. controlling public deficits and inflation and maintaining stable real exchange rates).[10]

UNSETTLED DEBATE ON INDUSTRIAL POLICY
The debate on industrial policy appears not to be settled; Everest-Phillips (2008: 165) puts it as a "dialogue of the 'deaf' using selective evidence to assert market failure or government failure, while ignoring politics and giving short shrift to history." Rodrik (2008b) points out that proponents mostly rely on successful case evidence, whereas opponents largely rely on cross-industry econometric studies, most of which conclude that industrial policy instruments do not contribute to productivity increase. The drawback is that model specification does not distinguish between policy instruments that are used to compensate declining industries for political reasons (and where productivity is not the target) and those intended to support the most deserving sectors.

The "ideal" policies that the negative views on industrial policy commend— such as barrier-free international trade and investment, elimination of vested interests of insiders, and rule-based, non-discretionary regulatory framework (i.e. *high* challenge, *low* support)—are hard to actualize in developing countries. "Evolving and dynamic ability of private actors and competitive markets to maximize the benefits and minimize the cost of the peculiarity of knowledge and technology" cannot be the benchmark for current African development (Latsch 2008: 33).[11] These are goals obtained in the process of development, and more fundamentally, are a matter of political economy rather than a constitutive deficiency. The Korean case, in which rent-seeking was effectively checked, was a product of a strong and disciplined state commitment to growth, as Pack and Saggi (2006) recognize. Asian governments with politically independent technocrats managed to control rents and even used rents or subsidies to upgrade technological levels of their economies. The next section explores the possibility that latecomers can catch up by introducing the recent discourse of the post-Washington Consensus, which looks to the necessity and possibility of industrial policy.

Post-Washington Consensus: more role of government and policy space

DEVELOPMENT PATHS AND STRATEGIES IN ASIA AND AFRICA

Globalization processes, such as significant reductions in telecommunication and transport costs, which have been accelerating since the 1980s, have provided new opportunities for countries worldwide, including developing countries. Following the members of the Association of South East Asian Nations (ASEAN), a number of developing economies, notably China and India, have taken advantage of these opportunities and achieved remarkable growth in recent years.

Export-oriented industrialization has been regarded as a banner of Asia's development strategy, together with a set of common features observed in the Asian experience (JICA/JBIC 2008). First, economic institutions (e.g. enforcement of contracts and protection of property rights) were not strong at the outset; they gradually improved once economic growth began to accelerate, under stable developmentalist regimes lasting fifteen to twenty years.[12] Second, agricultural and rural development allowed the price of agricultural products to fall and improved the economic welfare of the poor before the industrialization phase. The productivity increase in the agricultural sector created excess workers who moved to urban areas and worked for the manufacturing sector—which contributed to further industrialization, the alleviation of demographic pressure, and eventually to political stability. Third, there existed regional economic networks among Muslim, Indian, and Chinese traders that connected the capitals and markets within the region during the recent industrialization period. Fourth, Asian countries managed to stabilize their macroeconomies by controlling inflation and keeping the exchange rate competitive. They managed to realize a positive linkage between maintenance of positive real interest rates and high saving rates, which enabled domestic capital accumulation and the creation of capital mobilization mechanisms that channeled accumulated capital into investment in industries and infrastructure. Fifth, the governments attached great importance to budget allocation for education, including education for females—which promoted participation in the growing industrial sector and a decline in the birthrate, and realized the demographic dividend.[13] While having these commonalities with more or less active governments, development policies and growth paths taken by Asian countries have been diverse and reflect their own particular socioeconomic conditions (JICA/JBIC 2008).

In Africa, however, approaches to industrial development have been more or less identical. African countries have made efforts to rectify macroeconomic imbalances through structural adjustment and stabilization in the 1980s. During the subsequent decade, they pursued reforms in governance and institutions, under the guidance of IFIs that observe the Washington Consensus. African countries have been required to meet uniform standards with little consideration for particular socioeconomic situations. Amsden and Hikino (2000) contend that the problems bedeviling latecomers today are not formal legal constraints but informal political pressures exerted by North Atlantic economies adamantly in favor of market liberalization. Latecomers lack vision to guide them in responding to this pressure, especially politically supported vision grounded in relevant science and technology.[14] As a result, economic growth and industrial development strategies in most African countries have converged with the search for a silver bullet of export-oriented industrialization through FDI.

Under this condition, the scope of governments in pursuing economic policies has been limited. African governments are hindered from designing their own policies or institutions, or enhancing their capacities through experiments and are recommended to follow the norms and best practices of international development (Watanabe 2008). African governments today face stricter discipline of international trade and investment under the regime of the World Trade Organization (WTO) than their Asian counterparts did in the 1980s (when the Uruguay Round of the General Agreement on Tariffs and Trade (GATT) was not yet concluded). Akyüz, Milberg, and Wade (2006) point out that developing countries' industrial tariffs are unbound (or bound at relatively high levels) under the WTO, while actual tariffs applied are lower and imposed by the IMF and World Bank through conditionality. In addition, WTO regulations, such as Trade-Related Intellectual Property (TRIP) and Trade-Related Investment Measures (TRIMs), limit, if not prohibit, pursuing many policy instruments, which have been widely used in the past by industrial countries. Africa's efforts to follow and comply with the international regulatory regimes have not only failed to bring about the development of new industries, but also the efforts themselves could limit the scope of development in the future.

CRITIQUE OF THE WASHINGTON CONSENSUS: LEGITIMATIZATION OF GOVERNMENT INTERVENTION

Stiglitz (2008a) argues that Washington Consensus policies often "assume the worst about the nature and capability of *all* governments, and, in its quest to find a 'one-size-fits-all' policy," solely commend the market mechanism. This has resulted in a strong bias against basing policy advice on an analysis of what interventions are appropriate in certain contexts, or building institutions, or the capacity of states to intervene effectively. The recent "policy space" discourse in the global economy and development (e.g. Chang 2006; Hoekman 2005; Stiglitz 1998) argues that the rules and norms of international economic regimes have narrowed the policy options in trade, macroeconomic management, and industrial development for "regime takers," including developing countries, and that this limitation has led to constraints on economic growth opportunities for developing countries.[15]

The argument of this post-Washington Consensus points to legitimatization of government intervention and industrial policy. While recognizing the costs of flawed policies can be high, the school acknowledges that "there are systematic ways to improve the performance of the government . . . actually often playing an important role" in addressing market failures particularly in developing countries (Stiglitz 2008a: 46). In this view, the policy prescriptions have not been adequately informed by the lessons of East Asia in getting the right balance between the state and the market. When it comes to realizing sustained growth in Africa, it is hard to imagine (and is politically unrealistic) that the issues, such as inadequately distributed production factors and rigid economic structures, are solved through mere liberalization in the short or medium term. For latecomer economies in general, there is a strong reason for government involvement because of externalities. It is the government that leads investment projects with large spillovers, which the private sector would not calculate when making the decision to invest—particularly for enterprises in developing countries whose financial base is too small and fragile to make large investments in uncertainty, even if economy-wide, intersectoral spillover is expected. (Even developed countries do not hesitate to coordinate information on specific sectors, to subsidize research and development, or to provide incentives to targeted sectors.) Given the weakness of the private sector and the lack of competitiveness seen in Africa, it appears that expansion of the range of policy measures adopted by the governments can be justified.

The following discussions elaborate on some of the specific factors—namely, observation of country specificity, experiment, and public-private partnership—which corroborate the post-Washington Consensus argument. These factors can guide latecomers (which often lack sufficient institutional capacity and a Weberian-type bureaucracy to perform, for example, the Korean-style industrial policy) in designing and implementing effective industrial policies as well as in addressing anticipated problems, such as information deficiency of government and rent-seeking.

Country specificity: different policies for different countries

Although Asia's development is commonly characterized as export-oriented industrialization, the development paths have been diverse among the region in practice; individual economies pursued different development strategies according to their different endowments and circumstances. For example, Japan, Korea, and Taiwan financed development projects domestically, while the ASEAN economies have mainly depended on FDI. There are both resource-rich countries (Indonesia and Malaysia) and resource-poor countries, such as Singapore, Thailand, and the Philippines. The governments of Korea, Singapore, Indonesia, Malaysia, and the Philippines have had active records of intervening in the economy, while those of Taiwan (after the 1980s) and Thailand have made modest interventions. Although the "flying geese" model—transformation from labor-intensive to capital/techno-logical-intensive industries—was mentioned in general, the leading sectors have also varied among countries, e.g., heavy industry, electric appliances, agro-industry, or textiles.

A recent report commissioned by the World Bank (Commission on Growth and Development 2008) stresses that each country has specific characteristics and that historical experiences must be reflected in designing a growth strategy. The Yokohama Declaration of the Tokyo International Conference on African Develop-ment (TICAD IV 2008) and JICA/JBIC (2008) also call for country-specific industrial development strategies that look to identify and support prospective growth indus-tries with a focus on the latent potentialities of individual economies. This attention to local context has increasing support in the international development discourse. Weiss (2008), who examines the post-Washington Consensus paradigm for develop-ment assistance for its validity and effectiveness, contends that aid strategies will have to respect specific conditions and be adaptable to local context to reduce poverty effectively. African countries, where geographical conditions and endowments are as diverse as Asia, would have adopted different economic policies and growth strategies with different prioritized measures and sequences reflecting their diverse conditions.

Past policy prescriptions made by donors to Africa have had dismal outcomes. Rodrik (2008a: 359, 364) contends that the best practices (e.g. political and eco-nomic stability, protection of property rights, integration into the world economy, among others) "do not map into unique, well-defined policy recommendations" and that as such, the first-best solutions are impractical or take a long time to implement in low-income economies. Although individual best practices are legit-imate, East Asia's experience suggests that desired objectives—supply incentives, effective property rights, integration into the world economy, saving mobiliza-tion—can be achieved in a variety of ways.

In designing government interventions, consideration must be given to the uniqueness of individual economies and their (sub)sectors. For instance, con-straints on growth vary among economies: It needs to be determined whether the root problem is low return on investment or high costs of access to capital, as each of these problems calls for different prescriptions (Hausmann et al. 2005). There is no single measure that would improve the business environment in every economy. It is necessary to consider the unique conditions of each country and sector to identify individual constraining factors and adopt appropriate measures. No development strategy can be viable without reference to the embedded politi-cal, social, and economic institutions of a country.

Experiment: trial-and-error, leading-by-doing

Even if broader policy space is given and the government's active role is legitimatized, governments (those of developed, as well as developing, countries) do not necessarily possess adequate conditions to pursue effective industrial policy. Even if they do, all industrial policy instruments may not obtain the intended results. In fact, industrial policy attempts in Asia did sometimes fail. Malaysia, with a reputation of successful industrial policy, has seen disappointing results in, for example, the auto industry (Maseland and Peil 2008). For opponents of industrial policy, this is the primary problem with it.

Latecomers at lower technological levels have chances to grow via technology transfer from technologically advanced countries. Then, for growth to be sustained, there must be an increase in efficiency of production factors. It is uncertain how this is to be accomplished, however, and is obtained only by trial and error (Aghion and Durlauf 2008). In addition, specificity of individual countries/firms presents challenges to latecomers in the process of technology transfer, because countries/firms cannot be certain whether an imported technology is transferable (applicable) to their local context. The catching-up process faces less uncertainty than technological frontiers do, because there are tangible targets to follow. Nevertheless, the catching-up process is costly for latecomers, as it is inevitably experimental, and experiment involves certain failures in practice. While this is the very reason for governmental involvement in developing countries, designing and implementing industrial policies also inevitably involve experiment and failures. The capacity to pursue effective industrial policy can be developed only through a learning-by-doing process.

The logical solution to address this challenge would be institutions to monitor the impacts of policy measures, and to correct them if necessary, so that social costs are mitigated. This is tough to accomplish in practice, however, because it is hard for developing countries to establish and maintain a functioning monitoring system. Additionally, timely policy changes are difficult to make, as vested interests tend to persist once government support is given to a sector/firm. Efforts to abolish such wasteful rents have immense political implications. The international community should be tolerant of (and provide support for) experimental failures of developing countries. When providing assistance, donors should encourage the efforts of developing countries to configure such institutions.

Close partnership between government and the private sector

Closer collaboration between government and the private sector is the key to addressing government's information deficiency problem in order to design and implement effective industrial policy measures. Public-private partnership (hereinafter PPP) refers to an institution in which the two sectors share information on production and markets, identify bottlenecks in business, elicit the private sector's needs and priorities, design effective interventions, and monitor and evaluate policy outcomes (Rodrik 2008b; JICA/JBIC 2008; Nelson 2007). In other word, PPP is an essential platform that facilitates the process of successful industrial policies.

Traditionally, PPP takes the form of a deliberation council, which is a consultative committee whose members include government officials and representatives from the private sector—usually from industry and academia, sometimes from consumer groups and labor (Campos and Lien 1994). Councils are often hosted by governments, and are organized by industries or sectors by theme (as with the Industrial Structure Council of Japan, which has subcommittees on specific industrial sectors and cross-cutting issues) or by function as with Thailand's Joint Public Sector–Private Sector Consultative Committee, for example. Other forms may include supplier development forums, search networks, investment advisory councils, sectoral round tables, and private-public venture funds.

The advantage of PPP is straightforward. The institution helps government to identify spillovers, market failures, and obstacles of economic structural changes—essential information to design industrial policy interventions, as discussed previously—through dialogue with the private sector (Rodrik 2004, 2008b). When it comes to the industrial policy of developing countries (where the levels of information asymmetry, uncertainty, and risk are high), the conventional principal-agent assumption does not work because a government (principal) does not know exactly what to do, how to do it (which instrument), or how much it should do for the agents (target sectors/activities). An effective PPP allows government to elicit this information. In the Asian development experience, the advantage of politically independent, autonomous technocrats is often mentioned. In practice, however, close information-sharing networks between public and private, as well as among private sectors, is observed in many cases, such as those of Japan, Korea, Malaysia, Singapore, and China. PPP also helps to reduce rent-seeking. Campos and Lien (1994) argue that a deliberation council reduces uncertainty to the extent that it generates exchange of information, and rent-seeking is hence expected to decrease. Such exchanges reduce the transaction cost discussed in North (1984) and improve efficiency. In addition, Campos and Lien's two-stage incomplete information game model suggests that the council induces participation (government officials, industry, and labor) to reveal the truth, as the participants (firms) are better off if they can communicate their true valuations to competitors. This shows that PPP can function effectively in developing country settings.[16]

For PPP to function in the intended manner, the institution must be deliberately designed for African contexts. JICA/JBIC (2008) points out that in many countries, there exists a "less than warm" relationship between the public and the private sectors. This may reflect the past dismal record of corruption and exploitation of resources.[17] In constructing an effective PPP, the entire process has to be transparent: appointment of members, agenda-setting, the minutes, and decision-making should be open to the public so that the institution is not abused by insiders and does not become another hotbed of vested interests, in order to gain confidence in and support for PPP and the industrial policy process.

Everest-Phillips (2008) and Rodrik (2004, 2007) argue that industrial policy, rather than being about picking winners, is a process whereby the state and the private sector jointly arrive at diagnoses through trial and error about the sources of blockage in new economic activities and propose solutions for them. In this sense, it appears that the notion of industrial policy needs to be relaxed. The process of industrial policy contains most issues of development. Successful industrial policy involves improvement of institutional capacity and social changes—in other words, development itself.

The relevance of Asia's experience to Africa's industrial policy

Diversities in Asian experience

The Asian experience has been cited as a successful case of industrial policy. Its growth record since the 1980s has also attracted the attention of policymakers in developing countries, and various academic disciplines have analyzed the reasons for the remarkable economic performance. This section briefly notes the points that are understood to be the factors of the successful industrial policy.

Despite certain commonalities, the idea of an "Asian Model" was also inspired by the notion that context mattered (Maseland and Peil 2008). The endowments and paths of industrialization have been highly diverse throughout the region. Each country adopted its own industrialization strategy to correspond with the endowment and changes in exogenous conditions. For example, sources of development financing vary. Korea, Japan, and Taiwan largely financed domestically, whereas the ASEAN members, Singapore in particular, relied on foreign capital. The shares of FDI in gross fixed capital were less than 5 percent in the former group, while the Philippines and Thailand saw increases in their shares from the 1980s on, excluding the financial crisis period beginning in 1997 (Figure 13.6). There are also variations among resource-rich countries (China, Indonesia, and Malaysia) and resource-poor ones (Japan, Korea, Singapore, Taiwan, and Thailand).

In addition, the growth-leading industries are also diverse—heavy industry (Korea), consumer electronics (Malaysia), agro-processing (Thailand), textiles and garments (Bangladesh), and information and communication technology (ICT) (India).[18] In general, capital- or technology-intensive industries (e.g. heavy industry, machinery, and consumer electronics) became more competitive than labor-intensive ones (typically textiles and garments). This shift was propagated from Japan to the newly industrialized economies (NIEs), then from the NIEs to ASEAN members (i.e. flying geese formation). This take-off pattern of development has now given way to the international "horizontal division of labor" (where

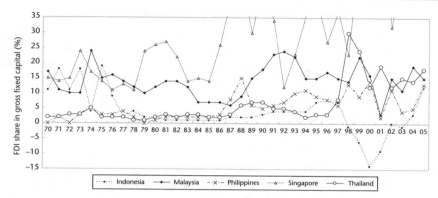

Figure 13.6 ASEAN dependence on foreign capital
Sources: UNCTAD, FDI database

production processes are segmented into different countries), which further accelerates diversities. Commonalities, such as the prevalence of authoritarian developmentalist regimes, can be explained by regional emulation of plausible development strategy of neighbors (Ohno 2008), and diversities partly reflect different endowments (as well as fortuities to some extent), *inter alia*. However, one key factor has been deliberate efforts by Asian governments to seek viable ways to attain economic development under the given political, economic, and social conditions.

Exploitation of policy space

INSTITUTION- AND POLICY-MAKING

The interventionist approach of Asian governments, often referred to as "developmental states," has been allowed to exist by the competence of development administration. While Indonesia (up to the 1990s), Korea (up to the 1980s), Malaysia, the Philippines (up to the mid 1980s), Singapore, and Taiwan (up to the early 1980s) have taken more interventionist approaches than other Asian countries, the degrees of intervention among them are highly diverse (JICA/JBIC 2008). On one hand, Korea and Taiwan were highly authoritarian, whereas Hong Kong never employed such a regime. Malaysia has not been as prominent as Korea and Taiwan, but this country and even Thailand (which has been classified as liberal in Asia) have duly executed interventionist policies.

Ohno and Shimamura (2008) and Everest-Phillips (2008) stress that political leaders' determination to achieve economic development and the existence of technocrats who realized leaders' development visions have been universal characteristics of the successful East Asian governments. In particular, central economic agencies (CEAs) played a vital role during the early stages of development. The technocrats of CEAs translated the vision into concrete actions. Their tasks included formulating development plans and strategies, articulating priority policies, programming public investments, and managing resources within hard budget constraints. They also coordinated among various stakeholders (line ministries, state agencies, local governments, donors, and private sector) so that coherence among short- to long-term policies was assured. Their role further extended to the management of incoming foreign resources, such as modern technologies and capitals through aid, trade, and FDI.

The institutional arrangements of government across East Asia, however, have been highly varied. Although CEAs in both Thailand and Malaysia acted as strategic core centers for development policy management in the 1970–80s, there were differences in the approaches to division of labor among ministries and CEAs, in the relationships between top leadership and technocrats, and in the relationships between the executive and legislative branches. In Thailand the elite technocrats of CEAs—namely, the National Economic and Social Development Board, Bureau of Budget, the Fiscal Policy Office, the Public Debt Management Office of the Ministry of Finance, and the central bank—had authority delegated to them by political leaders and jointly formulated and implemented policies. By contrast, the Malaysian style is top-down and centralized. The prime ministers of Malaysia have exercised strong leadership in setting out policy directions, and the role of CEA technocrats is to transform the leaders' ideas into policy measures. The Economic Planning Unit (EPU) in the Prime Minister's Department has played the role of CEA, functioning as the "super-ministry" at top of the line ministries, leading the formulation of mid- and long-term plans and controlling the budget process (especially the allocation of the development budget) with the finance ministry.[19] Regardless of the styles of policy formulation, these countries have had strong intra-governmental coordination mechanisms that ensured policy coherence and effectiveness of development policies despite fiscal pressure.

NON-LINEAR DEVELOPMENT POLICY
The countries managed to ensure intra-governmental consistency of development policies in each period in history. The development of trade and investment regimes, however, has not necessarily been "linear" toward liberalization; rather, it fluctuated frequently between import substitution (IS) and export orientation (EO) in a cyclical manner during 1960–80s (JICA/JBIC 2008) (Table 13.2).

The first wave of IS (mainly for protecting light industries) took place in the NIEs, excluding Hong Kong, in the 1960s and in the ASEAN countries in the 1970s. This was followed by EO. Subsequently, the second wave of IS (for heavy industries) was observed in the NIEs in the 1970s and in ASEAN countries in the 1980s. During periods of IS, countries fostered targeted sectors' domestic production capacities and then gradually lifted trade barriers and shifted to EO. Some

Table 13.2 Transformation of trade and investment regime

	59	60	61	62	63	64	65	66	67	68	69	70	71	72	73	74	75	76	77	78	79	80	81	82	83	84	85	86	87	88
Malaysia		1st IS														EO									2nd IS					EO
Event							'65 Consumer goods			'68 IPL			'71 FTZ									'80 Malaysia Heavy Industry Public Co. Cement, steel, automotive, chemical products						'86 IPL, 100%		
Intervene																														
Thailand							IS							'72 IPL		EO						IS + EO			'83 100%				EO	
Event						Light industries													Heavy industry (intermediate and capital goods)											
Intervene																														
Indonesia																1st IS									2nd IS					EO
Event										Foreign capital selectively invited								Industry protection enforced					Heavy Industry Project						'86 Rupiah devalue	
Intervene																														
Korea	1st IS								EO							2nd IS								EO						
Event											IS for intermediate goods				Heavy chemical industry						Knowledge and information industry promotion			Economy stagnated			Economy maturing			
Intervene		Consumer goods																												
Taiwan	1st IS						EO																			EO				
Event							'65 EPZ launched					'70 IPL																		
Intervene																														
Singapore				1st IS																									EO	
Event			'61 Industrial Estate Establishment Law						'67 Economic Expansion Promotion Law												'79 High Wage Policy		Capital/technology intensive industry Export-oriented SMEs promoted			Upgrade of industrial structure			Non-manufacturing sector promoted		
Intervene																	Capital/technology-intensive Electronic industry & heavy industry				'79 Heavy chemical industrialization									

Source: JICA/JBIC (2008: Tables 1–7), Kuchiki (2007)

Note: IS: Import Substitution, EO: Export-oriented, FTZ: Free Trade Zone, IPL: Investment Promotion Law, 100%: 100% Foreign ownership approved, EPZ: Export processing zone countries (e.g. Thailand) simultaneously pursued both IS and EO during the second IS period, in which heavy and chemical industry was protected, while the exports of already competitive sectors were promoted. After the second IS, most countries have shifted to EO since the 1990s (Kuchiki 2007; JICA/JBIC 2008).

The shifts in trade policy orientation were the reflection of the countries' intentions to promote specific industries in accordance with the stages of industrialization by employing policy measures in a strategic manner. The EO that followed in the later 1980s is considered to be a response to changing circumstances and opportunities, including the globalization process and the international trade regimes of the GATT Uruguay Round and the WTO, as well as the worldwide renewed interest in free trade agreements.[20] Ohno (2008) contends that the countries' primary goal was not poverty reduction, but gaining the status of advanced countries with higher living standards by industrialization. The seeming fluctuation of trade policy has been the consequence of this clear and consistent policy objective. The message here is meant to acclaim not IS, but rather the countries' efforts to muddle through the changing international and domestic circumstances with flexible policy management to pursue their goals.

Policy-driven industrialization and collaboration with the private sector

While the rapid expansion of trade among Asian countries has been mainly the result of industrialization and industrial collaboration in the form of production sharing, it has not been driven through the operation of market forces alone (Shafaeddin 2008). Trade can also be used as a policy-driven vehicle for industrialization in lower-income countries, and is linked to the principle of dynamic comparative advantage. Everest-Phillips (2008) points out that coordination of public and private initiatives and flexibility in adapting policy instruments to changing circumstances are among the distinctive features of industrial policy in East Asia, as well as efficient local linkages fostered by governments concerned with promoting innovation and technological upgrading.

The PPP institutions have been the vehicle for industrialization programs in Asian countries (GRIPS Development Forum 2008; Iwasaki 2006; Jegathesan and Ohno 2008; Ohno 2008; Woo-Cumings 2001). The PPP is also embedded in an intraregional project, the Greater Mekong Subregion (GMS) Development Program, by Thailand, Vietnam, Laos, Cambodia, China, and Myanmar, as the GMS Business Forum, which sponsors workshops for the private sector and proposes private investment projects for industrial clusters.[21]

Policy-driven industrialization efforts in Asia saw mixed results. In fact, there are a number of failures, such as the pre-1995 large-scale export processing zones in the Philippines, largely due to politically biased decision-making in the selection of location and target industries, as well as red tape in customs procedures (JICA/JBIC 2008). In contrast, Malaysia's experience is an example of government policies having propelled the breakaway from a resource-dependent economy, and diversification through export-oriented industrialization.

Until the early 1980s, Malaysian exports had relied on a few commodities such as crude oil and natural rubber.[22] In 1981, the Malaysian government launched a policy initiative to diversify its economic structure by developing heavy industries as well as domestic part suppliers.[23] In 1986, the government announced a ten-year industrialization plan for 1986–95 and a five-year development plan for 1986–90. To promote the twelve product groups proposed in the ten-year plan, policy proposals were called for with concrete measures to attract FDI and regulations for each group. The five-year plan advocated private-led growth, and called for mobilization of domestic capital, deregulation on foreign capital, the revitalization of agriculture, and the creation of an enabling environment for developing the twelve industries.[24] During the course of these initiatives, in 1983, the government adopted the "Malaysia Incorporated" concept as the core policy to provide a framework for public–private cooperation. The government launched the Malaysian Business Council, chaired by the prime minister with members of the government and private sector. Under the council, several committees were set up to deal with specific issues (infrastructure, monetary and financial issues, human resource development, and most importantly, trade and investment) (Economic Planning Unit 2004; Jegathesan and Ohno 2008).

These policy initiatives and the 1985 Plaza Accord caused Malaysia to see a robust increase in FDI, especially from Japan, through which new export industries (mainly in the machinery sector) emerged.[25] At this point, however, exporting manufacturers largely relied on foreign imports for most of the intermediate inputs, and hence the linkage with domestic firms was weak. To address this problem, the Malaysian government pressured industries to increase local content and simultaneously unveiled a "vendor development program." The program was intended to increase the capacities of local parts suppliers and to upgrade the economy through strengthening linkages between SMEs, large-scale companies, transnational companies, and financial institutions. For these developments to happen, local large and multinational companies, referred to as "anchor companies," were required to provide vendor companies with machinery and equipment as well as advice on technologies and management, under the coordination of the Ministry of International Trade and Industry.

These initiatives allowed the country to transform from a raw material producer to the world's largest producer of electric semiconductors and the third largest exporter of room air conditioners, with the creation of over 150,000 jobs by the sectors alone. FDI increased from USD420 million in 1987 to USD5.2 billion in 1992, while GDP constantly grew until 1997 (Figure 13.7). The shares of export and import in GDP, around 60 percent in the 1980s, expanded to 124 and 105 percent in 2000, respectively (Figure 13.8). The manufacturing sector also expanded more than five times during the 1989–2005 period (Figure 13.9). In

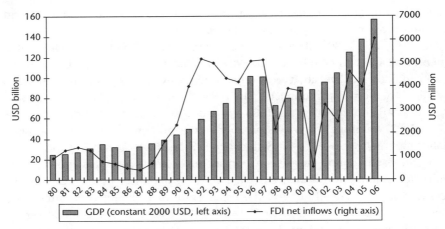

Figure 13.7 Malaysia growth of GDP and FDI
Source: World Development Indicators

particular, the production of electrical machinery and electronics increased from RM3.8 billion to RM31.2 billion in the same period.

This experience demonstrates the determination of the government to restructure the economy through industrialization. The effort materialized through the strong state initiative to identify priority sectors through a set of explicit criteria and to upgrade the technological level of domestic firms. The private sector is invited to the

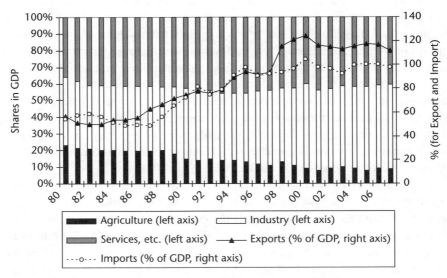

Figure 13.8 Malaysia GDP structure and trade
Source: World Development Indicators Database

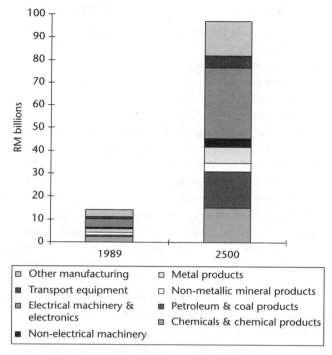

Figure 13.9 Development of manufacturing
Source: Central Bank of Malaysia

policy planning process as the essential ingredient: this allows industrialization plans, including the (relatively) sensible selection of target sectors. Next, we explore the factors that allowed the public–private institution to work in Asian economies.

Confidence-building and growth: Zeitgeist, sense of national purpose

Asian countries' successful economic management and industrial policies often have been attributed to the leaders' determination to deliver economic growth and to the fact that state autonomy—the capability of Weberian technocrats to autonomously make and implement policies beyond the pressures of interest groups—was secured (Iwasaki 2006). State legitimacy was enhanced by remarkable economic growth, which was shared by the public as a sense of national purpose. Everest-Phillips (2008: 169) suggests that "[T]he politics of economic growth, by legitimating contentious policy and motivating individuals and social groups behind a shared vision of long-term development, is the least understood dimension to development."

In fact, nearly all successful latecomers have experienced some political settlement around the elites' use of nationalism and the politics of economic growth to ensure social cohesion. Malaysia's active policies can be explained in this context. Maseland and Peil (2008) point out that the widening income gap between the Malay ethnic group and others, especially Chinese, needed to be resolved for social stability in postcolonial Malaysia. Besides affirmative action for the Malay, economic development was used as the national vision (the Vision 2020, set out by Prime Minister Mahatir, which purported to unite the people and to achieve economic growth so as to build an advanced economy by 2020) to address this problem. In constructing such a vision, a Malay nationalism (and anti-British sentiment) was harnessed, and sublimated into the "Look East Policy," which turns to Japan and Korea as an example for cultivating an Eastern work ethic.[26,27] As such, Asian countries tailored economic development to be a political, nationwide ethos.

Such an ethos may account for part, if not all, of the viability of developmentalist policies by the authoritarian regimes in the region.[28] Iwasaki (2006) implies that this developmental state model, with the combination of authoritarian regime and technocrats, was only viable in the specific context of the 1970–80s and may not be possible to duplicate today, as the state autonomy of the period underpinned by the non-democratic authoritarian regime is no longer allowed to exist. If such a system of authoritarian regime coupled with ethos represents the lesson of the Asian model, other regions, such as Africa, have no chance to learn from and emulate it. Instead, the ethos is best understood as a vehicle for establishing a sense of national purpose underpinned by unity of the people. Everest-Phillips (2008) identifies slogans of economic nationalism (and national unity): Bismarck's ideology of "Blood and Iron," Japan's Meiji era slogan "Fukoku Kyohei" (prosperous country, strong military), South Korea's "defeat communism and achieve unification" in the 1960s, and Taiwan's "Retake the mainland." Setting aside the way in which nationalism was built, the facts that leaders of Asian countries managed to create unity and a sense of national purpose, and that such unity was directed toward economic growth, account for the politics of this period. In these processes, the belief that "hard work pays off" was embedded in the societies as the *zeitgeist* that was translated to the motivation of technocrats and to the pursuit of prosperity in the private sector—the latter may be observed in Shanghai, Bangalore, and garment factories in Dhaka today.

Donor assistance for industrial policy

The preceding sections show that the process of industrial policy is equivalent to the issues of development, which includes social change. The public and private sector jointly seek new economic activities, find solutions through trial and error, and improve capacities via learning-by-doing. To assist this process, the international community needs a more holistic approach and flexible ideas for Africa to integrate in the global economy and realize sustained growth.

First, donors are urged to revise assistance strategies to encourage African countries to pursue their own initiatives. Assistance policies need to reflect the importance of diverse strategies and policy measures, to redefine the role of government, and to allow necessary experimental failures in leaning-by-doing. In employing other regions' successful cases (as well as technologies and know-how), simple transplant has to be avoided. For example, under the competition with Asian counterparts, conventional labor-intensive manufacturing may not always be a viable option for landlocked countries with low population density and poor transportation infrastructure.[29] The applicability should always be examined in accordance with the local context.

Second, assistance approach and practices should reflect the grim reality of Africa. We have seen numerous policy initiatives with no implementation on the continent. Many second-generation poverty reduction strategy papers look to economic growth and set out industrialization strategies, which duly identify specific sectors to promote, but often end up being a wish list with no priority or budgetary corroboration. Past donor practices are partly owing to this. Many donors, if not all, send teams of development experts into developing countries, produce stylized reports, hand them over to the client governments, summon ministers to one-day seminars, and walk away. Policymakers in the developing countries review the donor reports on their desks and end up saying, "We know the problem and what to do, but not how to do it." The gap has to be filled by working with client governments and demonstrating how policy measures can be implemented until tangible results are duly obtained, at least in the initial stages.

Third, to help African governments configure effective industrial policy, advice needs to be realistic and critical. The problems in industrial policy, such as rent-seeking, corruption, or discretionary policymaking, are the reality in many parts of Africa. As an impartial outsider, donors are expected to support clients to arrive at solutions (rather than direct clients to follow desktop prescriptions) to address the problem. PPP institutions can be an entry point for donor support. The participation of donors and foreign investors can strengthen the validity of the institution (and ultimately leverage the institutional capacity of the country) not just as objective observers but as involved collaborators with ideas, skills and technologies, markets, and financial resources.

International development agendas have been fluctuating in the past decades between growth and poverty/basic human needs, and so have the target sectors of donor support. (The last couple of years have seen another shift to growth from poverty reduction.) Donors' commitment to specific projects and subjects has not necessarily been sustained. Industrial policy process involves a long period of time before goals are attained. For example, the agglomeration of the automotive industry in the Eastern Seaboard of Thailand, emerged at least several years after the infrastructure projects were completed and the Thai government enacted investment promotion laws (Watanabe 2003). Donors must maintain the commitment once they intervene. For this, their system of project evaluation as well as internal personnel management may require revisions.

Concluding remarks: implications of Asia's experience to Africa

The growth performance of African economies largely remains subject to world commodity prices. Africa's quest for sustained growth—through industrialization, redressing the technological and marketing gaps with advanced economies, and participation in the global value chain—is yet to be fully materialized. The reform efforts in the past decades, complying with prescriptions based on the international development norms, have not seen the intended results. Although it is tempting to ascribe this to "unfinished" reforms, there are grounds for rethinking the viability of the assumptions of the Washington Consensus's first-best solution in Africa.

The Asian experience of the 1970–90s cannot be simply transplanted to today's Africa. The policy instruments of Asian governments and their successes have to be understood in the context of the domestic and international political economy of the time. Nevertheless, Asia's experience suggests that industrial policy can be effective for latecomers where the markets are imperfect and risks are high for nascent private enterprises. Government intervention can be legitimate when it is designed and tuned to reflect local contexts—social, economic, and political conditions of individual countries—underwritten by state autonomy and national unity. For this, the institution of PPP is the necessary bedrock for implementing an effective industrial policy and minimizing the costs thereof (losses of rent-seeking, corruption, or moral hazard, among others). A successful industrial policy thus involves social and institutional changes; the process of industrial policy represents *development*.

The international community ought to allow plural development strategies, a broader role of government (depending on the institutional capacities of individual countries), and inevitable experimental failures in view of learning-by-doing in the process of industrial policy implementation. African countries are encouraged to have a long-term vision of their development, while donors support their African counterparts, working *with* them to find ways to accelerate the process.

Appendix: An industrial complex development plan in changing circumstances, Thailand

The Eastern Seaboard (ESB) Development Plan was a large-scale industrial development plan of the 1980s by the Thai government with assistance from Japan and the World Bank. The plan aimed (1) to boost competitiveness through FDI in the export-oriented industry sector and (2) to ease the overconcentration of economic activities in the Bangkok area. The ESB project consists of two industrial complexes with deep seaports, Leam Chabang and Map Ta Phut, with infrastructure development (roads, railways, dams, and utility facilities). The former was intended for labor-intensive, export-oriented industries, while heavy chemical industry was planned for the latter. The planning started in the 1970s and was formally announced in 1982. Due to the subsequent economic slump, however, the implementation was put on hold until 1986.

Leam Chabang, which originally planned for SMEs in textiles and shoes, instead saw concentrations of machinery industry (general and electronic machinery, followed by transportation equipment) and domestic and foreign investments in various sectors from large-scale manufacturing to small-scale vendors. This was the result of the large-scale development projects which facilitated a synergy of production chain and transportation.

In Map Ta Phut, the development of petrochemical industry duly took place as the core of this complex in the 1990s. However, as the originally planned fertilizer plants were not built, the petrochemical industry took the spare space and expanded in response to the expanding domestic demand. This, however, faced criticism that the construction of the port with such a scale was too large for domestic demand in the end and hence money-wasting. In the later 1990s, however, Map Ta Phut succeeded in absorbing investments overflowing from the unexpectedly congested Leam Chabang zone. Today, the two zones have been integrated as a major export base for machinery (automotives, in particular) and supporting industries in the region.

The keys to success of ESB include: (1) that the technocrats who were independent from political pressures maintained the commitment to the ESB plan; (2) that the plan was flexibly conducted—the government managed to negotiate with the two dominant donors with workable solutions at the time of macroeconomic imbalances caused by the external shocks (i.e. oil shocks, global stagflation, and commodity price slump), and managed to handle the unexpected cancellation of factory construction; and (3) the check provided by the domestic media pressed the government to address problems, and consequently made the ESB process transparent and open (JICA/JBIC 2008; Shimomura 2005; Watanabe 2003).

Notes

1. This chapter is based on a joint study of Japan International Cooperation Agency (JICA) and Japan Bank for International Cooperation (JICA/JBIC 2008). The views expressed herein are those of the authors and do not necessarily reflect the position of the two organizations. We thank Masafumi Kuroki, Takaaki Oiwa, Taichi Sakano, Kensuke Shimura, Keiichi Tsunekawa, and anonymous reviewers for their comments in developing these ideas.

2. The per capita GDP of East Asian countries was lower than Africa's in the 1940–50s, while the present level is three times that of Africa. The income level of East Asia grew at a rate of 5.5 percent per annum from 1981–2003, while the size of the population living on less than USD1 a day decreased by 400 million. In the meantime, the total Official Development Assistance inflow to East Asia and Africa from 1981–2003 amounted to USD1,079 trillion and 2,089 trillion respectively, according to the Organization for Economic Co-operation and Development statistics (*Geographical Distribution of Financial Flows to Aid Recipients*). That is, Asian economies achieved such growth with half the volume of ODA of Africa (Watanabe 2008; MOFA 2005).

3. For example, Sub-Saharan Africa as a whole saw increasing foreign trade and FDI inflows. The share of trade in GDP increased from 2 percent in 2000 to 3.4 percent in 2007, while the share of FDI in GDP increased from 63.4 percent to 71.3 percent in the same period (numbers taken from the World Development Indicators).

4. In Figure 13.4, the Pearson's coefficient of correlation for the 1980–2007 period between (a) GDP growth and Commodity Non-Fuel Price Index and (b) GDP growth and Commodity Metals Price Index are (a) 0.577 and (b) 0.652, respectively, and significant at 0.01, where (a) $t = 3.7342$, $p = 0.00093142$, and (b) $t = 4.5536$, $p = 0.000109211$.

5. UNCTAD (2008: 1) states, "the level and composition of the continent's exports have not substantially changed... African countries have not diversified their exports towards more dynamic primary commodities and manufacturing goods..." In this chapter, "industrialization" does not merely refer to manufacturing but also includes the agriculture (agro-industry) and service sectors.

6. The literature largely regards industrial policy as selective government interventions for structural transformation of national economies. In general the goals of industrial policies are either to promote certain industries (or firms) or to soft-land declining industries (e.g. coal). The former looks to providing public goods and services and to market imperfection and externalities, for example, while the latter is intended to address the imperfections of production factor mobilization and sank cost problem. (This chapter is concerned with the former case.) While "direct," major measures of industrial policies include subsidies, tax concessions, soft loans, preferential procurement, import restrictions, and export promotions, even "indirect" policies such as in exchange rates and education can be considered as measures of industrial policy.

7. Stiglitz (1994) and Lall (2004) argue that markets for information and technology cannot function like standard competitive markets; hence, corrective intervention can be rationalized. The corrective intervention should be selective because of the peculiarity of technology (in tacit nature and externalities and in the way of spillover being technology-specific); as such the mere (narrow) functional correction of the neoclassical sense is not appropriate.

8. Pack and Saggi (2006) list the required information for industrial policy: information on firms and industries that generate knowledge spillovers; information on sectors that have a long-term comparative advantage; information on the size of scale economies; information on firms' learning abilities and amounts thereof; information on capital market failures; and information on potential effects of FDI/international trade on coordination problems and on spillover effects, among others.

9. Such as the auto, aircraft, and plywood industries in Indonesia, state-owned basic metals, machinery, petrochemicals, paper, building materials, and car manufacturing in Malaysia, according to Yusuf (2001).

10. Pack and Westphal (1986) and Everest-Phillips (2008) argue that Korean industrial policy was successful without substantial efficiency losses. Government support to the private sector is always time-bound, and assessed by transparent performance criteria often linked to export orientation that provides market discipline through learning international competitiveness. Subsequently, Pack (2000) still admits the Korean (and Japanese) cases, but notes that they are exceptional. See Woo-Cumings (2001) for the description of Korean industrial policy implementation.

11. Relating to this, proponents' discourse that learning and innovation rents are created by policy instruments appears to be a distant dream in the face of the reality of African governments and ordinary private sectors in Africa. If not "devisal" or "twists" emerging from daily operations, it is implausible that the private sector can effectively respond to (absorb) such (rather sophisticated) "innovation" rent that only government can provide.

12. For example, Suehiro (2000) lists the administrations of Korea (Park Chung-hee, 1961–79; and Chun Doo-hwan, 1980–7), Taiwan (Chiang Kai-shek, 1961–75; and Chiang Ching-kuo, 1978–88), Indonesia (Suharto, 1967–98), Singapore (Lee-Kuan-yew, 1965–90; and Goh Chok-tong, 1990–4; and afterwards), Malaysia (Mahatir, 1981–2003), and Thailand (Sarit, 1958–63; and Thanom, 1963–73). Ohno (2008) and Everest-Phillips (2008), recognizing the criticism of authoritarian regimes as undemocratic, point out that the regimes should be understood as a matter of survival as a nation state under the internal and external security threats at the time, and ultimately in terms of the needs for speedy resource mobilization for economic takeoff.

13. The demographic dividend is represented by an increase in economic growth rate and output per capita through an increasing share of working-age population. The phenomenon takes place in the late stage of demographic transition from a largely rural agrarian society with high fertility (and mortality) rates to a predominantly urban industrial society with low fertility (and mortality) rates as well as low youth dependency rate (Lee and Mason 2006). According to Bloom and Williamson (1998), this dividend accounts for 25 to 40 percent of the remarkable growth of East Asian economies.

14. Maseland and Peil (2008: 1181) argue from the politico-historical viewpoint that the European experience as the future goal of the less developed world was inextricably connected to the political dominance of 19th-century Europe over the world, and to the 20th-century dominance of the US. It was "not only informed by this dominance, but also legitimatized and reproduced it, denying the other societies the possibility to speak with their own voices . . . " The increasing prevalence of the post-Washington Consensus discourse might imply that the US model itself is questioned, reflecting declining US supremacy, if any, and the multi-polarizing world (or non-polarization, according to Haass 2008). This issue, however, is out of this chapter's scope, and no further discussion is presented.

15. Skepticism toward the broader role of government from the orthodox view remains, such as Lawrence (2007).

16. Evans (1995; 1997) argues that "embedded autonomy," a combination of Weberian bureaucratic institutions with close ties to business, is the key to the developmental state's effectiveness in pursuit of a joint public–private project of economic transformation, as typically seen in Asia, but not in Brazil or India. The embeddedness allows state actors to structure full information (i.e. addressing the information asymmetry) on businesses. The autonomy refers to the state capacity to formulate selective interventions so as to lower risk and enable individual businesses to pursue more Schumpeterian entrepreneurship, and to monitor and discipline individual enterprises to prevent rent-seeking. While the government–business relations are divergent depending on the internal structure of the state (and hence the patterns of industrialization have been divergent in Asia), he stresses embedded autonomy can function only when the two components are combined.

17. See the patrimonial state discourse, such as Medard (2002) and Reno (1995).

18. According to the Thai government statistics (Office of the National Economic and Social Developing Board 2007), the manufacturing sector grew from 28.9 percent (average 1980–99) to 37.8 percent (average 2000–6) of Thai GDP. In the manufacturing sector, agro-processing (food, beverages, and tobacco altogether) accounts for the largest part (19.2 percent for average 1980–99 and 16.9 percent for average 2000–6), followed by textile and apparel (17.8 percent and 11.5 percent, respectively). Machinery and equipment accounted for 6.4 percent and 4.7 percent, and transport equipment (motor vehicles) for 7.9 percent and 8.8 percent, respectively. When it comes to export, machinery accounts for 43.6 percent of the country's total export (average 2001–8), while food, beverages, and tobacco altogether account for 12.7 percent in the same period.

19. When it comes to macroeconomic policy management, Thailand went for strong fiscal conservatism and prudent debt management, whereas Malaysia took an activist approach. The debt service of the latter was covered by the rapid economic growth, and the fiscal balance duly saw a surplus in 1993 (Ohno and Shimamura 2008). These variations in government institutions and policies reflected the individual countries' conditions. Malaysia's expansionist fiscal policy was partly accounted for by the need to address the income gap between ethnic groups, as discussed later in this section.

20. The Appendix discusses Thailand's experience in industrial park planning under changing circumstances.

21. The program was launched by the Asian Development Bank in 1992 in the areas of transportation, energy, communication, tourism, environment, human resource development, trade and investment, and agriculture. The program encourages industrial development of inland areas in particular, by establishing intraregional corridors to provide access to ports. Plans also include free trade zones and industrial parks with infrastructures. See <http://www.adb.org/GMS/>.

22. In 1984, primary goods accounted for 68.5 percent of total exports, of which the share of crude oil was 22.6 percent, followed by LNG (4.6 percent), palm oil (11.7 percent), round timber (7.1 percent), rubber (9.5 percent), and tin (3 percent).

23. In the course of this, the government reviewed the *Bumiputra Policy*—an affirmative action that gave preference to the Malay ethnic group and virtually discouraged domestic and foreign investment including Chinese investors—to promote foreign capital inflows in 1982. This decision was a direct response to the recession in the same year, and the

government took short-term adjustment policies, including monetary relaxation and bail-outs of financial institutions, stimulation of domestic demand encouraging housing construction, an emergency loan to the tin-mining industry, and cutting power rates for industry use.

24. In support of the private sector and local capital, a credit scheme for small and medium enterprises (particularly those owned by ethnic Malays) and an investment fund were created.

25. By the Accord, the value of the Japanese currency rose from its average of JPY239 per USD in 1985 to JPY128 in 1988, doubling its value relative to the USD.

26. For example, in the early 1980s a "Buy British Last" campaign was instigated. Mahatir boycotted Commonwealth meetings and gave anti-Western speeches at the UN General Assembly, among others (Maseland and Peil 2008: 1177).

27. Morishima (1982) points out that a strongly held national ethos played an important role in the creation of Japanese capitalism. By interacting with ethical doctrines, especially the Japanese Confucian tradition of complete loyalty to the firm and to the state, it minimized the internal distributional (often asocial) conflicts, self-centered interests (at the expense of others), and the distributive bias in favor of politically powerful groups. Maseland and Peil (2008) also identify that communitarian values like filial piety, collectivism, consensus, discipline, and respect for authority as the basis for Singapore's socioeconomic success.

28. Jenkins (1995) and Evans (1997) argue that effective intervention in industrial promotion requires a degree of state autonomy and unity. Taiwan's rare failure case in automobile industry development is largely attributed to the strong opposition by key economic actors whose interests would have been violated if the state program has been enacted. This is an industry-specific problem, as the state did not see such objections to other intervention programs.

29. Wade (2008) points out that Chinese manufacturing goods come to the markets at about 50 percent cheaper than other developing country counterparts, which induces sustained competitive pressure on developing country manufacturing sectors.

References

Aghion, P. and Durlauf, S. (2008). "From Growth Theory to Policy Design." Paper presented at Workshop on Macroeconomic and Financial Policies for Growth, Commission on Growth And Development, 9 April, New York. Available at <http://www.growthcommission.org/storage/cgdev/documents/aghion-durlauf-wbapr3fin.pdf>.

Akyüz, Y., Milberg, W., and Wade, R. (2006). "Great Controversies: Developing Countries and the Collapse of the Doha Round: A Forum," *Challenge*, 49 (6): 9–16.

Amsden, A. and Hikino, T. (2000). "The Bark is Worse Than the Bite: New WTO Law and Late Industrialization," *Annals of the American Academy of Political and Social Science*, 570 (1): 104–14.

Baumol, W. J. (2002). *The Free-Market Innovation Machine*. Princeton, NJ: Princeton University Press.

Bloom, D. E. and Williamson, J. G. (1998). "Demographic Transitions and Economic Miracles in Emerging Asia," *World Bank Economic Review*, 12: 419–55.

Campos, J. E. and Lien, D. (1994). "Institutions and the East Asian Miracle: Asymmetric Information, Rent-Seeking, and the Deliberation Council," World Bank Policy Research Working Paper, 1321.

Chang, H. J. (2006). "Policy Space in Historical Perspective—With Special Reference to Trade and Industrial Policies," *Economic and Political Weekly*, February, 41(7): 18–24.

—— Cheema, A., and Mises, L. (2002). "Conditions For Successful Technology Policy In Developing Countries—Learning Rents, State Structures, And Institutions," *Economics of Innovation and New Technology*, 11 (4/5): 369–98.

Commission on Growth and Development (2008). *The Growth Report: Strategies For Sustained Growth And Inclusive Development*. Washington, DC: World Bank.

Dollar, D. and Kraay, A. (2000). "Growth is Good for the Poor," *Journal of Economic Growth*, 7 (3): 195–225.

Economic Planning Unit, Malaysia (2004). *Development Planning in Malaysia*, 2nd edn. Putrajaya, Malaysia: Economic Planning Unit. Available at <http://www.epu.gov.my/new%20folder/publication/dev.%20planning(pdf)web.pdf>.

Evans, P. B. (1995). *Embedded Autonomy: States and Industrial Transformation*. Princeton, NJ: Princeton University Press.

—— (1997). "State Structures, Government-Business Relations, and Economic Transformation," in S. Maxfield and B. R. Schneider (eds.), *Business and the State in Developing Countries*. Ithaca, NY: Cornell University Press.

Everest-Phillips, M. (2008). "Governance for Growth: Improving International Development through Anglo-Japanese Cooperation," in GRIPS Development Forum (ed.), *Diversity and Complementarity in Development Aid: East Asian Lessons for African Growth*. Tokyo: GRIPS Development Forum.

GRIPS Development Forum (2008). "An Overview: Diversity and Complementarity in Development Efforts," in GRIPS Development Forum (ed.), *Diversity and Complementarity in Development Aid: East Asian Lessons for African Growth*. Tokyo: GRIPS Development Forum.

Haass, R. N. (2008). "The Age of Nonpolarity: What Will Follow U.S. Dominance," *Foreign Affairs*, 87 (3): 44–56.

Hartmann, A. and Linn, J. F. (2007). "Scaling Up: A Path to Effective Development," *2020 Focus Brief on the World's Poor and Hungry People*. Washington, DC: IFPRI.

Hausmann, R., Rodrik, D., and Velasco, A. (2005). *Growth Diagnostics*. Cambridge, MA: John F. Kennedy School of Government, Harvard University, available at <http://ksghome.harvard.edu/~drodrik/barcelonafinalmarch2005.pdf>.

Hodler, R. (2009). "Industrial Policy in an Imperfect World," *Journal of Development Economics*, 90: 85–93.

Hoekman, B. (2005). "Operationalizing the Concept of Policy Space in the WTO: Beyond Special and Differential Treatment," *Journal of International Economic Law*, 8(2): 405–24.

Iwasaki, I. (2006). "Singapore no Kaihatsu to Good Governance," ("The Development of Singapore and Good Governance"), in Y. Shimomura (ed.), *Asia No Governance*. Tokyo: Yuhikau.

Japan International Cooperation Agency and Japan Bank for International Cooperation (2008). *Report of the Stocktaking Work on the Economic Development in Africa and the Asian*

Growth Experience, IIC-JR-08-02. Tokyo: JICA. Available at <http://www.jica.go.jp/english/publications/reports/study/topical/aid/aid_01.pdf>.

Jegathesan, D. J. and Ohno, M. (2008). "Strategic Action Initiatives for Economic Development: Trade and Investment Promotion in Zambia," in GRIPS Development Forum (ed.), *Diversity and Complementarity in Development Aid: East Asian Lessons for African Growth*. Tokyo: GRIPS.

Jenkins, R. (1995). "The Political Economy of Industrial Policy: Automobile Manufacture in the Newly Industrializing Countries," *Cambridge Journal of Economics*, 19 (5): 625–45.

Kuchiki, A. (2007). *Asia Sangyo Cluster Ron: Flow Chart Approach no Kano-sei (Industrial Clusters in Asia: Possibility of Flow Chart Approach)*. Tokyo: Shoseki-Kobo-Hayayawa.

Lall, S. (2004). "Reinventing Industrial Strategy: The Role of Government Policy in Building Industrial Competitiveness," United Nations Conference on Trade and Development, G-24 Discussion Paper Series, No. 28.

——— and Teubal, M. (1998). "'Market-Stimulating' Technology Policies in Developing Countries: A Framework with Examples from East Asia," *World Development*, 26 (8): 1369–85.

Latsch, W. (2008). "The Possibility of Industrial Policy," *Oxford Development Studies*, 36 (1): 23–37.

Lawrence, R. Z. (2007). "A True Development Round? A Review of Joseph E. Stiglitz and Andrew Charlton's *Fair Trade for All: How Trade Can Promote Development*," *Journal of Economic Literature*, 45 (4): 1001–10.

Lee, R. and Mason, A. (2006). "What Is the Demographic Dividend?" *Finance and Development*, 43 (3): 5. Available at <http://www.imf.org/external/pubs/ft/fandd/2006/09/basics.htm>.

Maseland, R. and Peil, J. (2008). "Assessing the New Washington Pluralism from the Perspective of the Malaysian Model," *Third World Quarterly*, 29 (6): 1175–88.

Medard, J. F. (2002). "Corruption in the Neo-Patrimonial States of Sub-Saharan Africa," in A. J. Heidenheimer and M. Johnston (eds.), *Political Corruption: Concepts & Contexts*, 3rd edn. Piscataway, NJ: Transaction Publishers.

Ministry of Foreign Affairs (MOFA), Japan (2005). *Japan's Official Development Assistance White Paper, 2006*. Tokyo: MOFA.

Morishima, M. (1982). *Why Has Japan "Succeeded"?: Western Technology and the Japanese Ethos*. Cambridge: Cambridge University Press.

Nelson, J. (2007). *Building Linkages for Competitive and Responsible Entrepreneurship*. United Nations Industrial Development Organization.

Noland, M. and Pack, H. (2003). *Industrial Policy in an Era of Globalization: Lessons from Asia*. Washington, DC: Institute for International Economics.

North, D. C. (1984). "Government and the Cost of Exchange in History," *Journal of Economic History*, 44 (2): 255–64.

Office of the National Economic and Social Developing Board, Thailand (2007). *National Income of Thailand*, available at <http://www.nesdb.go.th/Portals/0/eco_datas/account/ni/ni_2007/Book_NI2007.pdf>.

Ohno, I. and Shimamura, M. (2008). "Diverse Models of Development and Aid Management: Experiences of Thailand, Malaysia, and the Philippines," in GRIPS Development Forum (ed.), *Diversity and Complementarity in Development Aid: East Asian Lessons for African Growth*. Tokyo: GRIPS.

Ohno, K. (2008). "The East Asian Growth Regime and Political Development," in GRIPS Development Forum (ed.), *Diversity and Complementarity in Development Aid: East Asian Lessons for African Growth*. Tokyo: GRIPS.

Pack, H. (2000). "Industrial Policy: Growth Elixir or Poison?," *World Bank Research Observer*, 15 (1): 47–67.

—— and Saggi, K. (2006). "Is There a Case for Industrial Policy? A Critical Survey," *World Bank Research Observer*, 21 (2): 267–97.

—— and Westphal, L. E. (1986). "Industrial Strategy and Technological Change: Theory and Reality," *Journal of Development Economics*, 22: 87–128.

Parente, S. L. and Prescott, E. C. (2000). *Barriers to Riches*. Cambridge, MA: MIT Press.

Reno, W. (1995). "Reinvention of an African Patrimonial State: Charles Taylor's Liberia," *Third World Quarterly*, 16 (1): 109–20.

Rodrik, D. (2008a). "A Practical Approach to Formulating Growth Strategies," in N. Serra and J. E. Stiglitz (eds.), *The Washington Consensus Reconsidered: Towards a New Global Governance*. New York: Oxford University Press, 356–66.

—— (2008b). *Normalizing Industrial Policy*, Commission on Growth and Development, Working Paper 3. Washington, DC: World Bank.

—— (2007). "Industrial Development: Some Stylized Facts and Policy Directions," in Department of Economic and Social Affairs, *Industrial Development for the 21st Century: Sustainable Development Perspectives*. New York: United Nations Publications.

—— (2006). "Goodbye Washington Consensus, Hello Washington Confusion? A Review of the World Bank's Economic Growth in the 1990s: Learning From a Decade of Reform," *Journal of Economic Literature*, 44 (4): 973–87.

—— (2004). "Industrial Policy for the Twenty-First Century," Centre for Economic Policy Research, Discussion Paper 4767. Available at <http://www.cepr.org/pubs/dps/DP4767. asp>.

Schmitz, H. (2007). "Reducing Complexity in the Industrial Policy Debate," *Development Policy Review*, 25 (4): 417–28.

Shafaeddin, M. (2008). *South-South Regionalism And Trade Cooperation on The Asia-Pacific Region*, UNDP Regional Centre, Colombo, Sri Lanka. Available at <http://www.gdnet.org/ fulltext/1221041110_final.pdf>.

Shimomura, Y. (2005). "Export Capacity Building in Thailand: Managing Donors and the Development Process toward a Self-Reliant Economy," in I. Ohno (ed.), *True Ownership and Policy Autonomy: Managing Donors and Owning Policies*. Tokyo: GRIPS Development Forum.

Stiglitz, J. E. (1994). *Whither Socialism?* Cambridge, MA: MIT Press.

—— (1998). "More Instruments and Broader Goals: Moving Toward the Post-Washington Consensus," UNU-WIDER Annual Lecture, available at <http://www.wider.unu.edu/publications/annual-lectures/en_GB/AL2>.

—— (2006). "Some Lessons from the East Asian Miracle," *World Bank Research Observer*, 11 (2): 151–77.

—— (2008a). "Is There a Post-Washington Consensus Consensus?" in N. Serra and J. E. Stiglitz (eds.), *The Washington Consensus Reconsidered: Towards a New Global Governance*. New York: Oxford University Press.

—— (2008b). "Video Message," in TICAD IV International Symposium on "Economic Development in Africa and Asian Growth Experience," JICA, Tokyo. Available at <http://www.jica.go.jp/english/publications/reports/study/topical/ticad/>.

—— and Charlton, A. (2005). *Fair Trade for All*. New York: Oxford University Press.

Suehiro, A. (2000). *Catchup-gata Kogyoka-ron (Catch-Up Type Industrialization)*. Nagoya, Japan: Nagoya University Press.

Tokyo International Conference on African Development (TICAD IV) (2008). *Yokohama Declaration: Towards a Vibrant Africa*, available at <http://www.mofa.go.jp/region/africa/ticad/ticad4/doc/declaration.pdf>.

United Nations Conference on Trade and Development (UNCTAD) (2008). *Economic Development in Africa 2008—Export Performance Following Trade Liberalization: Some Patterns and Policy Perspectives*. Geneva: United Nations.

Wade, R. H. (1990). *Governing the Market: Economic Theory and the Role of Government in East Asian Industrialization*. Princeton, NJ: Princeton University Press.

—— (2008). "How Can Low-Income Countries Escape Gravity and Begin to Catch Up With High-Income Countries? The Case for Open-Economy Industrial Policy." Conference Background Paper, *Africa Task Force Meeting, Initiative for Policy Dialogue*, July 10–11, Addis Ababa, available at <http://www0.gsb.columbia.edu/ipd/pub/WadeRob.pdf>.

Watanabe, M. (2008). "Japan's Foreign Aid Policy in Transition: An Interpretation of TICAD IV," *Japan aktuell*, 3: 7–26. Available at <http://www.giga-hamburg.de/dl/download.php?d=/content/publikationen/archiv/ja_aktuell/jaa_0803_fokus_watanabe.pdf>.

—— (2003). "Official Development Assistance as a Catalyst for Foreign Direct Investment and Industrial Agglomeration," in H. Kohama (ed.), *Asian Development Experience, Vol.1, External Factors for Asian Development*. Singapore: Institute of Southeast Asian Studies.

Weiss, J. (2008). "The Aid Paradigm for Poverty Reduction: Does it MakeSense?" *Development Policy Review*, 26 (4): 407–26.

Woo-Cumings, M. (2001). "Miracle as Prologue: The State and the Reform of the Corporate Sector in Korea," in S. Yusuf and J. E. Stiglitz (eds.), *Rethinking The East Asian Miracle*. New York: Oxford University Press.

Yusuf, S. (2001). "The East Asian Miracle at the Millennium," in S. Yusuf and J. E. Stiglitz (eds.), *Rethinking The East Asian Miracle*. New York: Oxford University Press.

14

Tiger, Tiger, Burning Bright?[1] Industrial Policy "Lessons" from Ireland for Small African Economies

David Bailey, Helena Lenihan, and Ajit Singh[2]

> ...capitalism is not a system given to stasis. What works in one period is
> unlikely to work in the next; and even when it 'works,' its distribution of
> costs and benefits is never socially equal. So when deciding which tiger to
> ride, it is worth remembering that the choice is only between tigers, and that
> if a safe ride is what you want, you would do well not to ride tigers at all (Coates
> 2007: 193).

Introduction

There is a growing consensus in the development field that industrial policy really
does matter and that the global crisis suggests both the necessity and the opportunity
for change (UNCTAD 2009b). Taking a longer historical perspective, experience over
the last half century indicates that whereas industrial policy has been highly successful in some countries, it has been equally unsuccessful in others, and that African
countries need to draw appropriate lessons from both sets of experience. As latecomers to industrialization, the African countries are actually well placed to carry out
such an exercise. Accordingly, this paper explores potential industrial policy "lessons" for small African countries (both negative and positive) from the experience of
Ireland, as we feel researchers have relatively neglected such a comparison. In so
doing, we reject a "one size fits all" approach and instead aim to add to the discussion
on what range of policy tools are available to such countries so that an appropriate—
and holistic—selection can be made according to local needs.

There is, however, a prior question that obviously needs to be considered: should such countries have an industrial policy at all? The East and South East Asian countries' experience indicates that industrial policy has played a key role in the extraordinary success of these economies in recent decades.[3] In addition, there is another related and powerful reason for African countries to examine the Asian story. Many countries in the two regions at the time of independence from colonial rule had broadly similar economic structures and income levels. To illustrate, in the 1950s, around the time of the country's independence, Malaysia's economy was much like that of Ghana, based on exports of primary agricultural commodities: rubber in the case of Malaysia, and cocoa in relation to Ghana. Both countries shared the common legacy of British colonial rule. However, today, Malaysian per capita income is nearly US$5,000 at current exchange rates and US$10,000 at PPP rates, while the Ghanaian per capita income has risen very little over the same period. It is legitimate to ask how one can account for such a difference in the evolution of the two economies. Was it, for example, simply due to the fact that the Ghanaian economy was subject to greater economic shocks than Malaysia's? There is little empirical support for this hypothesis. Moreover, a large number of other East and South Asian countries also did very well using industrial policy and outperformed most African countries. For these reasons, comparisons of African countries with East and South Asian countries are commonly made and are often useful. However, in this paper we instead give detailed attention to *Ireland* as a comparator.

Close attention to the Irish case does not of course imply that other countries' experiences are not significant or relevant, but we believe that Ireland's experience with industrial policy has particularly useful and significant lessons for Africa, and that this needs more attention. Nevertheless, for African countries, at a practical policy level, it is essential to be cautious. As Aiginger (2007) notes, "industrial policy is one of the most controversial policy fields. Its scope, instruments and rationale vary across countries, changing over time; intentions and outcomes often differ" (143).

The following sections will discuss in detail the political economy of development in Africa; the need to view industrial policy in a broad sense, taking a holistic approach, before detailing the role of industrial policy in the development of the Irish economy, together with the lessons for African countries. In so doing, we make reference to East Asian countries where such comparisons are useful in highlighting particular points of difference or similarity with experience elsewhere.

Why is Ireland a useful reference point for small African states?

There are, in fact, a number of reasons for using Ireland as an interesting reference point. First, when Ireland joined the then "Common Market" in 1973, the economy was in many senses a small, poor, peripheral, and agriculturally dominated economy with an overdependence on links to its former colonial master, the UK.

Trade was limited given ongoing protectionism (the European Union in particular had yet to fully open up). In fewer than three decades, however, the Irish economy has transformed itself from being one of the four cohesion countries of the EU to being considered an advanced high-tech enclave of the EU.

In addition, Ireland, like most African countries, is a small economy. It has the geographical size of Sierra Leone, as well as a similar population. Given its small size, clearly membership in the EU has played a major role in the evolution of the Irish success story. Apart from providing a far bigger market for Irish products so as to be able to reap the economies of scale, the EU has also provided Ireland with very large direct assistance for the development of its infrastructure. What could take the place of the EU even in a limited sense in the present context of small African countries? This issue will be taken up in this paper.

Furthermore, although Ireland is far from being a laissez-faire economy it is by no means as "dirigiste" as the East and the South Asian countries. It is more corporatist than the East Asian countries; various social partners, including unions, have played a major role in the determination of wages and prices. Compared with the East Asian model it is therefore more likely to be directly relevant to the African countries given the need for a "social contract" to underpin successful industrial policy. In addition, the East and South Asian pattern of development is heavily dependent on the outstanding qualities of the civil service. Such qualities are not simply inherited but are developed alongside the expansion of the economy (see Chang 2006). Nevertheless, the corporatist model makes comparatively fewer demands on administrative capacity.

It can also be argued that African countries potentially have more to learn from the experience of the operation of industrial policies in Ireland than in the East and South Asian countries. Irish industrial policy did not involve measures of coercion in the allocation of resources in the way it did in the case of East Asian countries during the prime of their industrial policy: for example, Japan between 1950 and 1973, and Korea between 1970 and 1990.[4] It will be recalled that in Japan during this period, the government used the allocation of foreign exchange in coercive ways as a principal weapon to meet government's targets for specific firms and industries. Similarly in Korea during its main industrial policy period, there is evidence of coercion in the expansion and upgrading of country's exports by the large conglomerates that the government itself had created (see Amsden 1989, 1994; Amsden and Singh 1994; Singh 1995, 1998; and Chang 2006). It should not be forgotten that during the operation of industrial policy in a number of East Asian countries, industrial "peace" was ensured through the suppression of trade union rights. Some would argue that this alone makes the Irish example suitable as a role model for African countries.

Finally, the development of small and medium-sized enterprises (SMEs)—given their importance in both Ireland and small African states—suggests as well that

Ireland can be regarded as a worthwhile case study. Certain characteristics of Irish SMEs are of particular relevance here:

(1) Irish SMEs were focused primarily upon the home market. Indeed, export-oriented SMEs were an uncommon occurrence in the Ireland of the 1970s.

(2) Ireland's small manufacturing firms in the past were mostly found in traditional industries such as food, beverages and tobacco, textiles, and wood products. These industries were characterized by low productivity, skills, and research and development (R&D).

(3) Small firms in Ireland were then faced with barriers similar to those facing small firms in Africa today (albeit on a different scale), namely financial barriers (particularly at the business start-up stage), poor macroeconomic conditions, and a poor business environment.

On the latter point, several studies on the barriers encountered by small firms in Ireland have pointed to access to finance as being the single most critical issue (Forfás 1994; Goodbody Economic Consultants 2002; Fitzsimons et al. 2001). Very recent work on the Irish case shows that small businesses continue to experience difficulties in obtaining appropriate levels of finance for start-up and growth (Small Business Forum 2006). This finding has been reiterated in recent work with regard to small firms in Africa (see below).

Until recently, there has also been no well-defined, structured, or focused policy for support of SMEs in Ireland. As we shall see below, industrial policy in Ireland has mostly been geared toward foreign direct investment (FDI) and it could reasonably be argued that this has been at the expense of indigenous companies. This has some similarities to Africa, where an adverse business environment (with little support from government agencies, the regulatory offices, and the managers of state enterprises) is an additional impediment for small firms.

Despite these apparent similarities, one key aspect missing in the African case is the benefit of European integration in the form of the single market. When Ireland joined the Common Market, there were lacunae of developed common policies outside the Common Agricultural Policy (which at the time absorbed three quarters of the European Community's budget). Over time, though, there have been two major ways in which EU economic integration has brought substantial opportunities for small firms: (1) through the *Acquis Communautaire* and (2) through the benefits emanating from structural funding, particularly in the sphere of infrastructural development. The latter has brought significant benefit to Ireland. Beyond the costs associated with the *Acquis*, it can generate many advantages to small firms in the medium to long run. These firms will be able to benefit from the entire (completed) internal market of about 450 million consumers. The Single Market and deregulation in the EU will also ameliorate cross-border trade by small firms engaging in flexible specialization. The Single Market can also be helpful in attracting market-seeking FDI, an element that is very much missing from the African case, in which thirty-one countries have a population of ten million or less, and most less than five million (UNCTAD 2009a).

From its post-Second World War beginnings, the EU has evolved into an integrated single market of some 450 million people. Many of its member states have also adopted a common currency and a common monetary policy together with many other measures of deep political integration. Such far-reaching integration is clearly beyond the capacities of Sub-Saharan African (SSA) countries. However, there are substantial benefits, economic as well as political, even from the limited regional integration that some countries have attempted. There are also a few reasonably well-functioning examples of integration in African countries, notably in Southern Africa. The emphasis in the more successful of these late integration projects has been less on trade integration and more on integration of transport, as well as in other spheres of infrastructure. Over time these countries may be able to cooperate on monetary matters as well as on trade and investment. The possibilities of African economies being able to benefit from the kind of assistance that Ireland received from the EU may not appear to be a practical proposition for African countries.

The political economy of African development

The African economies, particularly those in Sub-Saharan Africa, stand today at an important crossroads. During the 1980s, for the average African country, GDP per capita fell at a rate of 0.5 percent per annum; in the 1990s it rose slightly at a rate of 0.3 percent per annum (see Table 14.1). However, in the last four years, the average growth rate of this variable has been a respectable 3 percent per annum. In 2007, the GDP growth rate in Africa was estimated to be 6 percent per annum, one of the highest rates recorded during any year over the last quarter century. Apart from indicating the recent recovery in African economic growth, the table also highlights the poor long-term performance of the African economies relative to other developing countries. Over the entire twenty-six-year period, 1981–2007, for which the data are presented in the table, per capita GDP in African countries rose only by 16 percent compared with a more than 100 percent rise for all developing countries. For the East and South Asian economies, the growth in GDP per capita has been spectacular, a rise of well over 300 percent.

It is very much a moot point whether this recent reversal of fortunes for the African countries has been due to the late success of structural adjustment programs (SAPs) of the World Bank and the IMF, as is implicitly claimed by the two Bretton Woods institutions (World Bank 2007; IMF 2008). These programs, which have been the dominant influences on SSA economies during much of the 1980s and all of the 1990s, have embodied the Washington Consensus and its aftermath.

Table 14.1 Per capita GDP growth by region and economic grouping, 1981–2007 (percent)

	Average Annual Growth			Overall Growth
	1981–1989	1990–2002	2003–2007	1981–2007
World	1.4	1.2	2.3	41.4
Developed economies	2.5	1.8	2.1	67.5
Economies in transition	1.9	–4.0	7.3	–25.8
Developing economies of which:	1.7	3.0	5.0	112.5
Africa	0.5	0.3	3.0	16.4
America	–0.3	1.1	3.5	22.7
West Asia	–1.7	1.1	4.1	16.0
East and South Asia	5.1	5.3	6.3	317.5

Source: UNCTAD (2007).

Table 14.2 World primary commodity prices, 2002–6 (percentage change)

Commodity group	2002–6
Food and Tropical Beverages	48.4
Agricultural raw materials	62.3
Minerals, ores and metals	219.9
Crude petroleum	157.6

Source: UNCTAD Secretariat calculations, based on UNCTAD *Commodity Price Bulletin*, various issues, and UNSD, *Monthly Bulletin of Statistics*, various issues. Adapted from UNCTAD (2007).

According to independent economists (UNCTAD 2005, 2007; ILO 2007; McKinley 2005; and Lall 2005), although many countries implemented these programs, there has not been much success in enhancing their economic growth on a sustained basis. Indeed Thandika Mkandawire (2005), a leading scholar of African economies, argues persuasively that the SAPs were in fact counterproductive and often led to the wrong kind of structural change, which would hinder rather than help economic development.

The most plausible reason for the fast growth of African economies in the last four years would appear to be the huge increase in international commodity prices up to 2008–9. Information provided by UNCTAD (2007) reveals how the prices of various commodities have changed over this period (see Table 14.2).

The increased value of SSA exports as a result of the commodity price rise helped to relax the balance of payments constraint, which in turn led to faster growth. The central issue is whether or not the African countries can translate this recent improved performance into sustained, fast, long-term economic growth. Here the economic history of these countries in the last half century does not provide much ground for optimism. The good record of African economic growth between 1950 and 1973, when these economies expanded at a rate of nearly 5 percent per annum, could not subsequently be sustained. Similarly, during the 1990s, a number of countries were successively selected as the "African success stories" by the Bretton Woods institutions, none of which could actually maintain fast growth for more than two or three years (Mkandawire 2005). Such economic history invites skepticism about the ability of African countries to convert their recent favorable changes in the terms of trade into lasting progress. The case of the skeptics is straightforward. Apart from all the other handicaps, the African countries have been further debilitated by two decades of stagnation or worse, and are therefore unlikely to achieve fast long-term growth.

There are however important counter arguments that are equally an essential part of the story. The African countries are today much better equipped for initiating and sustaining fast growth, with a far greater endowment of human and material resources than they were twenty-five years ago.

- The educational level of Africa's citizens is much higher today than it was in the early 1970s. This is particularly notable at the tertiary level. There were for example only seven university graduates in Tanzania in 1964 at the time of the country's independence from British colonial rule. Today, after independence there are literally thousands, as a result of the establishment of the University of Dar-e-Salam, a splendid institution of higher education.

- There is a network of science and research institutions and engineering colleges throughout the continent. A number of business schools have also been established and they are in close collaboration with the best business schools in the US and the UK (Pfeffermann 2008).

- There are signs of an emerging middle class in the African countries. There is evidence also of the evolution of entrepreneurship in these countries (ibid.).

- Moreover, as *The Economist* (2008) notes, "an unexpected and overlooked continent may benefit from its very isolation" (33). It suggests by way of illustration that African banks are normally regarded as being very conservative and excessively regulated. "Now, however," observes *The Economist* (2008), "this very de-linkage from the Western financial system has turned out to Africa's advantage. Its banks have almost no exposure to the sub-prime market causing such havoc elsewhere . . . " (33).

Finally, it is also worth noting that countries such as Mauritius, Botswana, and Uganda have demonstrated that late development is indeed feasible (Rodrik 2007; UNCTAD 2009b).

Viewing development in the Round: the need for a holistic approach to policy

In line with UNCTAD (2009b), we suggest that commonly adopted definitions of industrial policy are too narrow, especially when looking at countries embarking on major structural change in the economy.[5] The focus has too often been on providing grant aid to firms and intervention with respect to particular sectors, even with a more recent focus on policies directed at the promotion of R&D and innovation and FDI and SMEs. Rather, we argue that good practice in industrial policy is in fact much more "holistic" in its approach and focuses *simultaneously* on both demand and supply-side factors of industrial development; on microeconomics as well as macroeconomics.[6] Such an approach is in line with that suggested by the Culliton Report (1992) in the context of Irish industrial policy. Culliton (1992) emphasized the provision of infrastructural needs; reform of the tax system; a refocusing of the education and training system; increased funding for science and technology (coupled with greater involvement by industry in steering the use of these funds); and a greater emphasis on technology acquisition. In so doing, the report stressed that the role of the industrial promotion agencies should be kept under review, and the desirability of fostering clusters of related industries building on "leverage points" of national advantage was also highlighted.

As for indigenous industry, Culliton saw the widespread existence of grants as being often counterproductive (the argument being that it encourages a hand-out mentality). In this vein, more emphasis should be placed on the increased use of equity finance as opposed to non-repayable cash grants; an emphasis on the need for the expansion of the indigenous sector; a reorganization of grant-awarding agencies into two main agencies, one of which would address the needs of foreign-owned industries, the other the needs of indigenous ones. Culliton was also at pains to stress that the Irish Department of Industry and Commerce was overly focused on operational matters and needed to place industrial policy formulation and evaluation at the centre of its activities. We argue that a "good practice" definition of industrial policy includes all of these but also needs to encompass other dimensions such as support for well-functioning labor and credit markets, an appropriate macro-environment, and attempts to build consensus over appropriate policy direction.

We broadly agree with Hitchens and Birnie (1992) that the real challenge is to try to weigh the importance of the above factors with regard to the overall "competitiveness problem" (we would however be more inclined to see this as the industrial or economic development challenge). With reference to improving competitiveness (or in our case industrial or economic development) the authors correctly point out that there is little point calling for the need to improve competitiveness "without any satisfactory definition that can be operationalised" (29). They proceed to argue that "this lack of identification of its causes and hence effective solutions is an impediment to a satisfactory industrial development policy" (ibid.). Therein of course lays the challenge for policymakers regardless of country.

Thinking back to Ireland's less favorable times, the preface to the Culliton Report (1992) opens its narrative with the following comment: "Over the past six months we have considered industrial policy bearing in mind the 260,000 people who are unemployed. We have concluded that there are no short-term solutions, no quick fixes and no soft options left" (7). In addition, it notes, "Ireland's economic problems are deep-rooted and persistent. Their resolution will require patience, determination and a fundamental re-appraisal of our strengths and weaknesses" (7).

Following on from this broad and holistic view of what industrial policy should comprise, in the Irish case we can identify a range of factors that played a significant part in Ireland's recent catch-up:

(1) Currency devaluations in both 1986 and 1993 which were then locked into the single currency; the Euro's post-2000 depreciation in turn benefited outward-orientated states such as Ireland.

(2) A series of corporatist social pacts from 1987 when trade unions limited wage increases in return for income tax cuts. These have allowed rapid growth without inflation raising too high and have also enabled rapid employment growth.

(3) A rapid expansion in labor supply, in part through net in-migration.[7] More widely, the demographic shifts Ireland has experienced are unique within the EU, with an even balance between natural growth and migration (Salt 2005: 49).[8]

(4) An interventionist industrial policy that has targeted certain sectors for FDI but has also recognized the limitations of FDI-based growth and—somewhat belatedly—has sought to better link foreign plants with domestic firms and has also tried to develop indigenous capabilities and improvements in entrepreneurship, labor skills, and research and development.

This analysis has implications for the design of industrial and other policies in other small, open, and peripheral economies. We suggest that whilst important lessons may be learned, they may not be those picked up by mainstream commentators such as Sapir et al. (2003). Furthermore, it should be noted that a range of factors came together: some more by luck than by judgment, and that the Irish catch-up should have happened much earlier, had it not been for previous policy mistakes, particularly at the macro level (Bailey et al. 2007).

Indeed, on the macroeconomic side, stabilization was an important part of finally "getting things right" in Ireland. By the mid 1980s, the fiscal deficit in Ireland had grown to more than 12 percent of GDP and the public debt ratio was approaching 120 percent. The recognition of the need to address these imbalances led to both the social pacts after 1986 and a process of fiscal consolidation achieved by the government reducing expenditure; over the two-year period 1988–9, the ratio of expenditure to GDP was reduced by 9 percent (see Bailey et al. 2007). The pain of this adjustment was eased both by EU funding and an improved external environment with reduced interest rates and improving demand (Lynch 2005).[9]

Of key relevance, the impact of EU structural funding assistance starting in 1988 should not be underestimated: one study suggests that the cumulative effects of funding may have been to raise the level of GDP by more than 4 percent (Schweiger and Wickham 2005: 50). Another suggests at least approximately 0.5 of a percentage point to GNP growth during the 1990s (Barry et al. 2001: 549). In other words, external funding gave Ireland just enough room to stabilize its economy and to make investments (especially in infrastructure) designed to boost competitiveness; this may be relevant for African economies in the context of overseas development assistance. Similarly, in the Africa case, UNCTAD (2005: 34) notes that overseas development assistance (ODA) could trigger such a "growth process if it is focused on financing pro-growth public investment such as economic infrastructure."

In addition, in the Irish case, currency depreciations, which took place in 1986 and 1993, assisted Irish competitiveness; the latter in particular was a 10 percent depreciation, which was then locked into Euro entry. Whilst there was a revaluation of the Punt before Euro entry in 1998, the depreciation of the Euro after its launch delivered a further 20 percent boost to Irish competitiveness given its external orientation in trade toward non-Eurozone economies. That this did not feed through into higher inflation is in part due to the corporatist social pacts.

Such corporatism has been a long-standing central feature of Irish economic policy, with the establishment of the National Economic and Social Council (NESC) in 1973. As noted, by the early 1980s, Ireland faced a crisis as the government had embarked on deficit-financed expenditure programs after the oil price rise of the early 1980s (and indeed the early 1970s). The existing development strategy based on attracting FDI was also criticized for its failure to support domestic industry (Telesis 1982; Culliton 1992). Transnational firms responded to the crisis by cutting investment and repatriating profits, contributing to a deficit on the balance of payments amounting to around 10 percent of GNP. Meanwhile, unemployment rose to around 20 percent of the labor force.

At this crisis point, the major political parties recognized that an expansionary fiscal policy was no longer an option for Ireland as a small open economy. A social consensus for change emerged. Key to this was the proposal by the trade unions in 1984 for a coordinated approach involving restrictive income policies, or "partnership agreements." Indeed, Kennedy (2001: 135) argued that without partnership agreements, it is unlikely that unions would have tolerated a rise in the profit share of national income (see below). Developing a shared view of what needs to be done certainly seems to have been a key element in enabling the Irish catch-up.[10] Given UNCTAD's (2009a) reflection that successful industrial policy is an expression of the social contract and a partnership of different segments of society, this Irish experience would seem to be especially relevant to developing countries. Senegal, for example, is seen as one country in which the lack of a social contract contributed toward undermining industrial policy efforts (ibid.).

Between 1988 and 2005, there were six social partnership agreements between government, unions, and employers. The first, the Programme for National Recovery (PNR), ran from 1987 to 1990.[11] The PNR set out a strategy to raise competitiveness with four main components, which have been retained and developed over time in each of the subsequent partnership agreements, with later agreements having broader coverage (including chapters on greater social inclusion, equality, enterprise culture, small business, agriculture, public-service modernization of and a commitment to support partnership at the enterprise level):

- A commitment to reduce the level of public debt and maintain the internal and external stability of the Irish currency. This has focused on creating low inflation and interest rates and a positive climate for investors. From the mid 1990s onward, this has tied into the EU's Maastricht Criteria and Stability and Growth Pact (SGP).

- Restraining wage rises in order to improve cost competitiveness. An incomes policy became an essential part of the "new development strategy." Through the pacts, the government has compensated for wage restraint by lowering income taxes, although recently this has perhaps reached the limits of what is achievable.

- To boost competitiveness, the pacts have included structural reforms in several areas, such as industrial policy and taxation. The latter was seen as needing reform to encourage employment creation, being seen as biased toward capital and property.

- Social justice has been seen as important and there have been improvements in welfare payments for the least well-off.

The Irish experience, then, would suggest the importance of strong institutional arrangements in fostering sound economic performance and social cohesion around development objectives. In addition to this, as Andreosso-O'Callaghan and Lenihan (2006) detail, a range of other factors came together to enable Ireland to catch up with other European economies, including:

- Developing a modern telecommunications network reduced the real costs associated with firm location in a peripheral economy such as Ireland.

- Human capital accumulation: in contrast to other peripheral host countries for foreign investment, Ireland had a relatively skilled (and English-speaking) labor force. Yet it is worth noting that rapid economic growth in Ireland has taken place without much investment in innovation. By EU and international standards, and in spite of its relative current wealth, Ireland still suffers from a low R&D to GDP ratio (and R&D/GNP ratio). In contrast with one of the key lessons advocated by mainstream commentators, modern economic growth in Ireland does not owe much to innovation.

- Competition policy and deregulation: the introduction of competition policy and deregulation in the early 1990s was important in terms of delivering on cost competitiveness for firms using Ireland as an export platform (see Braunerhjelm et al. 2000).

- A shift in the type of products being traded internationally: geographical disadvantage may not count as heavily anymore. As Krugman outlined, "changes in both the nature of what nations trade and in how they carry out that trade have shifted the balance of geographical advantage in a way that is favourable to Ireland" (Krugman 1997: 44).

In referring to this well-trodden ground on Irish growth, we simply wish to highlight that there were many factors that contributed to the success of the Irish economy, particularly from the mid 1990s onward. The industrial policy approach adopted by the Irish government was only one feature in the myriad of factors that contributed to the Irish success story. Almost all of the factors alluded to above would have impacted to a very large extent on the Irish business environment at the time. We would still suggest (see below) that there might be potential for government intervention in the SME sector in small African economies to lead to significant improvements in the key growth indicators of these countries. Indeed, the example of industrialization in Mauritius is seen as a good exemplar of combining selective industrial policies with broader support for SMEs and entrepreneurship, thereby setting the scene for job creation and a more inclusive growth pattern (UNCTAD 2009b).

Using foreign direct investment—and involvement—intelligently

It is recognized that FDI flowing into Africa, although increasing, remains too limited—both in geographical coverage and by being focused narrowly on extractive industries—to bring significant benefits in terms of employment creation and poverty alleviation (UNCTAD 2009a; UNCTAD 2007). A key cause of this is the high degree of risk and poor business environment, which deters FDI. According to UNCTAD (2007: 46), these impediments include "(a) poor infrastructure, (b) high entry costs, (c) labour market constraints, (d) low investor protection, and (e) high taxes and a cumbersome tax system." On the tax front, UNCTAD (ibid.) notes that a typical firm in sub-Saharan Africa pays the equivalent of 71 percent of its profits in taxes, some 15 percent higher than the second-highest rate, paid in Europe and Central Asia.

In contrast, FDI, notably from the United States, has been a major trigger for economic growth in Ireland. Indeed, relative to the size of the economy, Ireland has one of the highest levels of FDI inflows in the world. Whilst successive Irish governments have welcomed FDI ("industrialization by invitation") since the 1950s, from the early 1970s onward, the government approach shifted toward a greater emphasis on selectivity and careful targeting, with pharmaceutical and electronics especially targeted as possessing promising opportunities. These industries were ideal for peripheral locations in that they were characterized by relatively low transportation costs and high growth rates (Braunerhjelm et al. 2000). Furthermore, the US was targeted as the most probable market for such projects given the likely benefits that would accrue to US companies using Ireland as an export base within the EU. It is important to note that the promotion and assistance of particular sectors was well timed. For example, the extension by the Irish government of financial incentives to internationally traded services, just as they were about to grow in importance, was a particularly timely intervention. Later, during the 1990s, industrial clusters in such sectors began to develop that involved linkages, spillovers, and sub-supply relationships with SMEs (see below). There was also a demonstration effect in operation, whereby the positive experiences of foreign investors in Ireland stimulated further FDI. If strategic targeting and a more focused approach to FDI were a key part of the success of FDI, this raises the question as to what sectors small African countries should now be targeting.[12]

Whilst the high levels of FDI were largely brought about by a corporate-friendly environment offering the lowest corporate tax rate in the EU, it should be noted that these tax breaks had existed for decades with limited impact on economic success; indeed the corporate tax rate on manufactured exports was zero from 1957 to 1981, then 10 percent and later 12.5 percent. Furthermore, other European economies have had such rates without attracting such levels of US FDI; in part, this may be because of the cultural links between Ireland and the US, where many citizens trace their ancestry back to Ireland, a factor that cannot be replicated or seen as a "lesson" for others. In a similar vein, House and McGrath (2004) note that the emphasis on education and training and the favorable corporate tax environments were both already in place before the mid 1980s when the economy was still stagnant (ibid.).

Of particular note was the recognition by the Irish government in the late 1970s and early 1980s that foreign transnationals were in effect branch plant operations and that the policy of heavily subsidizing FDI was producing little in the way of wider spillovers for the economy. Because of this, policy began to adopt an even more selective approach to FDI, focusing more on high-tech and higher-value-added firms. This is a key problem in terms of African development; as UNCTAD (2009b) notes, a failure to design appropriate policies runs the risk of FDI-led enclave development. Policy should instead be more "balanced and strategic" and tailored to the needs of local economic conditions. In the Irish case, it should be noted that problems and challenges remain and the picture of FDI-induced "transformation" is challenged by some. As Honohan and Walsh (2002) noted, "the huge profits recorded by the Irish affiliates have very little to do with the manufacturing activities being conducted in Ireland." A key lesson, as we show below in more detail, would actually be that spillovers from FDI are *not* generated automatically and that an industrial policy that targets and positions FDI is vital to ensure wider spillovers and to benefit the domestic sector. The case is not anti-FDI per se; indeed we recognize the value of high-quality FDI in assisting economic development. Rather, it needs to be stressed that this should not come at the expense of ignoring domestic firms. In a related vein, Buckley et al. (2006) argue that the contribution of transnationals to the Irish economy can also be over-estimated by failing to take account of the high level of imports (including payments for patents, royalties, and other tangible inputs) and also repatriated profits.

Attracting high-quality FDI and positioning it seems crucial. Here, lessons with FDI experiences in peripheral regions of the EU seem highly relevant in taking on board elements of good practice. This includes targeting strategic sectors and linking FDI to cluster development, building trust with local managers in order to try to upgrade local plants, undertaking sector-specific research on the strengths and weaknesses of local industry, providing aftercare support, targeting financial assistance at specific upgrading needs (e.g. investment in R&D rather than general support), and the monitoring of performance (see Amin and Tomaney 1995; Bailey et al. 1998). The Irish experience of selectively targeting FDI seems very relevant here and raises the issue more generally of using selective as well as horizontal industrial policy.[13]

There was a general belief, hope, and anticipation in Irish industrial policy circles that indigenous SMEs would "grow from foreign firms through linkages and spillovers" (Andreosso-O'Callaghan and Lenihan 2006: 280). This "spillover argument" is often used by governments to justify subsidies for FDI, but such spillovers are not guaranteed. It is to this issue that we now turn, asking how successful (where they existed) were Irish government policy interventions in achieving successful linkages and spillovers between incoming transnationals and indigenous (largely SME) firms. This is significant as some see this link as a key element of the Irish success story. For example, Pike et al. in their well-balanced review of local and regional development (2006: 233) suggest that, "the role of industrial policy . . . seems important, with the Irish state and its governance institutions proving adept at providing the kinds of territorial assets that attract the sorts of TNCs that will contribute to development. Ireland may provide an example of a somewhat 'strategic coupling' between domestic and foreign owned firms . . . ."

The wider FDI literature tells us that, if present, positive spillovers from transnationals can lead to increases in the productivity of domestic firms. This can happen via three main routes: (1) demonstration effects; (2) competition effects; and (3) labor market effects. As noted, spillovers are not an automatic occurrence but are in essence driven by the characteristics of the host economy, such as its degree of economic development, its ability to assimilate imported technology, and more generally, its absorptive capacity (see Blomström and Kokko 1996 and Blomström et al. 2000). The lack of absorptive capacity in Africa has been noted by a number of researchers (UNCTAD 2009a). In this section we briefly highlight the key evidence regarding the prevalence of such linkages and spillovers in Ireland. Most notably, despite the rhetoric of "FDI-led adjustment," there is significant evidence to suggest that the Irish economy operates according to a Lewis-type dualism "with little relationship/interdependence between MNEs and (local enterprises) and each developing according to its own pattern" (Ugur and Ruane 2004: 3). As such, each sector appears to have developed according to its own pattern. Such problems of dualism of course remain a major problem in many developing economies; for example UNCTAD (2007: 6) notes that in Africa, FDI is "relatively volatile and tends to focus on extractive industries with very few linkages to the domestic economy."

In the Irish case, there is evidence from some sectors at least of improved linkages over time, such as in electronics (see Görg and Ruane 2000, 2001), even if foreign (particularly large) firms have lower linkages—perhaps due to the necessary scale needed to supply such firms (ibid.). For high-technology sectors, the evidence of spillover effects is even more evident (Görg and Strobl 2002, 2003 and Barry and Van Egeraat 2008). Here, there is evidence to suggest that the presence of transnationals in high-technology sectors has had a "life-enhancing" effect on indigenous plants in Ireland, improved indigenous entry rates, and has improved links between manufacturers and components suppliers in sectors such as IT. Other contributions (Heanue and Jacobson 2003; Forfás 2004; Lenihan and Sugden 2008) have explored the issue of linkages in Ireland. Lenihan and Sugden (2008) argue that the National Linkages Programme introduced in 1985 was partly in response to criticism of an industrial policy approach by the Irish government that relied on transnationals and was subsequently restructured by Enterprise Ireland with a focus surrounding the issue of the globalization of local supply industry. This approach resulted in a move toward the building of supply networks and chains as opposed to actual direct local company linkages. Forfás (2004) in analyzing the impact of the National Linkages Programme argued that it stopped short of reaching its potential, while Heanue and Jacobson (2003) argued that there was some success up to the 1990s, but thereafter the impact was insignificant. In terms of more traditional sectors, Culliton (1992: 31) argued that only a small proportion of potential linkages between foreign and traditional firms were being realized; and that "[i]n general . . . policy to promote industrial linkages has not lived up to its expectations. It is only a mild exaggeration to say that most of the newer foreign firms operate here as essentially an industrial enclave" (ibid.). The overall conclusion on the success or otherwise of linkages in Ireland is succinctly summed up by Ruane (2001): "it is hard to either totally prove or disprove" whether linkage policies have been successful.

Related to this, how successful was the creation of clusters in Ireland? A focus on creating sectoral and spatial clusters in Ireland really only began in earnest in the

1980s (Buckley and Ruane 2006). Such efforts were focused around two key high-technology sectors, namely, electronics and chemicals/pharmaceuticals. More specifically, four segments of the electronics sector were targeted: microprocessors, software, computer products, and printers. In line with this strategy, some of the key players in these sectors, namely Intel and Microsoft, were attracted to establish operations in Ireland (ibid.). With the location of such firms, and subsequently Hewlett Packard in printing, Ireland to all purposes had an "electronics hub" and the "spokes" were soon populated by dozens of smaller enterprises (ibid.: 1620). Ireland could thus be said to have been a significant beneficiary of the formation of clusters (Krugman 1997); with the presence of the above-named firms contributing to the average share of US FDI in electronics to Ireland increasing to 27 percent between 1994 and 2001, compared to a rate of less than 12 percent for Irish manufacturing as a whole (Buckley and Ruane 2006). The two other key sectors where industrial clusters were created are the chemicals and pharmaceutical sectors, with these firms clustering primarily in the Cork region of Ireland. However, in contrast to experience in the electronics sector, where production linkages between firms developed, this was not the case with the chemicals and pharmaceuticals clusters.

In general, the empirical evidence on the impact of clusters in Ireland is, however, limited, with what evidence there is suggesting that there has been relatively little sectoral clustering between transnationals and local firms, at least in low-tech sectors and manufacturing overall (Gleeson et al. 2005; Buckley and Ruane 2006). There does however, appear to have been some clustering between transnationals and local firms in certain high-tech sectors such as IT (ibid.). The Irish government (Report of the Small Business Forum 2006) has recognized, however, that as more low-value-added activities migrate to lower-cost countries, a greater proportion of GNP will have to be produced by indigenous firms (predominantly SMEs). Other reports commissioned by the Irish government (e.g. a study by Goodbody Economic Consultants 2002) have also focused on the importance of entrepreneurship and more specifically on eliminating the barriers to entrepreneurship in Ireland. Whilst welcoming this focus, we would argue that this should have come much earlier in Ireland's development, and we see this as an important "lesson" for other states as they look for lessons to be learned in terms of industrial policy trajectory. It is interesting that in looking at policy experience in Uganda, for example, the United Nations (UNCTAD 2009b) concludes that policy was not as effective as it could have been if policy had been more orientated toward the needs of domestic firms rather than foreign investors. An implication of this was that the potential benefits of FDI failed to properly materialize. Ireland offers important lessons in this respect.

This review only serves to reiterate our point that a holistic industrial policy needs to account for the limitations and fragilities of FDI-led growth and hence also promote measures to grow domestic capacity, and to deliver a variety of growth drivers for the economy. It is accurate to say that the limitations of FDI-led growth have been increasingly (if belatedly) recognized. Ireland became vulnerable because of the downturn in the US economy, given its overwhelming reliance on US-based FDI. Ireland faces increasing competition for FDI from emerging economies, and Ireland is no longer a cheap country in which to do business, due to rises in wages and raw material costs, and declining price competitiveness. This has most recently been reflected in a wave of plant closures and downsizing by foreign transnationals. We suggest that a more holistic approach to policy development at the outset could have avoided some of these problems, thereby enhancing economic development, a point that small, peripheral economies elsewhere may wish to note.[14]

The discussion of this section will be seriously incomplete without reference to the fact that in the practice of industrial policy in East Asia, both Japan and South Korea discouraged FDI rather than sought it. Singh (1995) noted that among developing countries, the Republic of Korea was second only to India in its low reliance on FDI inflows (see UN 1993 for figures). In the view of World Bank economists, this discouragement was a self-imposed handicap, which was compensated for by the fact that both countries remained open to foreign technology through licensing and other means (Singh 1998: 21). Singh, however, noted that World Bank economists did not ask the following question: if the governments of Japan and the Republic of Korea were as efficient and flexible in their economic policy as they themselves suggested (to account for their long-term, overall economic success), why did they persist with this apparently wrong-headed approach for so long?

An alternative interpretation is that the approach was perhaps not so wrong-headed after all. It was "functional" within the context of the overall industrial policies that the two countries were pursuing. First, it would have been difficult for MITI or the authorities of the Republic of Korea to use "administrative guidance" to the same degree with foreign firms, as they were able to do with domestic ones. Second, as UN (1993) rightly emphasized, there was a link between the national ownership of large firms and their levels of investment in research and development. The Republic of Korea had, in relative terms, by far the largest expenditure on R&D among developing countries.[15] Korea's performance in this area outstripped that of many developed countries—for example Belgium (1.7 percent in 1987), Denmark (1.5 percent in 1987), and Italy (1.2 percent in 1987). It was, of course, still below that of industrial superpowers: Japan (2.8 percent in 1987) and Germany (also 2.8 percent in 1987).

Third, Freeman (1989) stressed another important advantage of the policy of mainly rejecting foreign investment as a means of technology transfer. This, he argued, automatically placed on the enterprise the full responsibility for assimilating imported technology. This was far more likely to lead to total system improvements and broader spillovers than the "turn-key plant" mode of import or the foreign subsidiary mode.

It is important to emphasize that Japan and South Korea's rejection of FDI for long periods did not mean that these countries were not interested in importing foreign technology. Quite the contrary. Japan after all has been attempting to obtain technology from abroad for a hundred years. The reason why it did not favor FDI as a source of technology was that it was *inter alia* comparatively much more expensive than licensing. The latter was a policy pursued by Japan up to the 1980s, when under pressure from the US, it began finally to dismantle such barriers and started to allow in FDI without requiring a Japanese joint venture partner (Bailey and Sugden 2007).

The above considerations may also be valid for those South Saharan African countries that prefer to import technology through licensing rather than through the medium of FDI.

Indigenous firms and domestic entrepreneurship

Some commentators, such as Bailey et al. (2007), have argued that the Irish government, on recognizing the limitations of solely focusing on FDI as an engine of growth, also sought to develop indigenous SMEs and entrepreneurship more generally. Whilst acknowledging the merits of this opinion, we would also suggest that the focus on indigenous SMEs and entrepreneurship by Irish policymakers should have come much earlier. Despite the fact, as outlined by Andreosso-O'Callaghan and Lenihan (2006: 282), that "even as far back as 1979, some 95 percent of all manufacturing units could be classified as SMEs," it is nevertheless quite astonishing that there was no formal focus by the Irish government on the small firms sector per se until the mid 1990s.[16] The "SME story" in Ireland is an indigenous one as a majority of all indigenous firms in Ireland are classified as SMEs.

One could justifiably argue that the Irish government to a large degree overlooked the indigenous (largely SME sector) until the mid 1990s. As such, this represents a key policy "failure" and should be avoided by small African states. Admittedly, in the Irish case there were grants available to indigenous firms to start up and expand—but the focus on indigenous and SME firms was overshadowed by the prime focus of the Irish government on FDI. This is evident in comments from various reviews of industrial policy over the decades, most notably the Telesis Consultancy Group (1982), which highlighted an overemphasis on foreign industry. The Culliton Report noted above also emphasized the need to expand the indigenous sector, noting that "the focus instead must shift decisively to indigenous companies. The view of . . . Porter and his colleagues . . . is that in Ireland the shift has been 'too little too late' and that there has not been a full commitment to the slow process of developing a broader base of indigenous firms" (67). However, it was not until the "Task Force on Small Business Report" was published in 1994 that the focus on the SME sector by Irish policymakers truly began in earnest.

Some of the problems facing small firms in Ireland are similar, albeit in a much more intense form, in Africa, most notably the issue of access to finance. As UNCTAD (2007: 15) notes, this is especially the case for the small domestic enterprises in the informal sector that represent the vast majority of firms. Indeed, it is thought that firms in SSA fund between one half and three quarters of their new investments from their informal savings. In order to address this, microfinance systems have emerged in recent years in order to rectify some of the shortcomings of the financial system in Africa. However, further action is needed with respect to the financial system in the African economies, as a poorly functioning financial system will continue to keep investment at low levels.[17]

More generally, Acs et al. (2007) suggest that entrepreneurs in Ireland are held in high esteem, and that this has been beneficial for the economy. This is questionable. Indeed, Culliton (1992) highlighted "the negative attitude toward enterprise that is prevalent in this country" (22) and proceeded to outline "a deep-rooted prejudice against failure in business. The stigma that attached to a failed enterprise very often inhibits the individual from ever trying again" (22). Perhaps it could be argued that such a negative attitude no longer exists. However, ten years after Culliton, Goodbody Economic Consultants (2002), although acknowledging an improvement, still noted that the "non-acceptance of 'failure,' both on the part of financial institutions and the general public is still perceived to be an issue by Irish entrepreneurs" (iv). They do, however, admit that "these attitudes are somewhat at variance with recent international studies which indicate that the general public's attitude toward entrepreneurship in Ireland is now highly favourable" (iv).

The role for policy evaluation

In view of the previously noted types of market failures that are likely to arise in the SME sector (e.g. the finance gap), a realistic route to help improve the efficiency of such markets is through the services provided by industrial development agencies. The extent to which development agencies in Ireland have produced the expected effects is an issue of significant and ongoing debate. One key issue that emerged in discussions (particularly pertaining to the 1990s) is that of agency duplication of services provided. The Industrial Evaluation Unit (1999) found that around 39 percent of firms that received support from more than one agency took up such support within the same time period. The prime lesson to be learned in this regard is that the support environment provided by government to firms needs to be clearly targeted and focused in its delivery. A clear underlying rationale for a specific type of intervention should be provided in all cases.

One of the outcomes of EU funding in the case of Ireland is that over time, there was increased pressure to engage in an evaluation of industrial policies (primarily to begin with for reasons of accountability). Indeed, guidelines from the European

Commission, as a result of Ireland being a Structural Fund beneficiary, were definitely a key driving force behind the much greater emphasis placed on evaluation in Irish policy from the early 1990s onwards. This is outlined by Andreosso-O'Callaghan and Lenihan (2006) in the context of the smaller, new EU member states, but here we argue that the same issues are also pertinent to small African states. A number of possible strategies can be adopted in the context of industrial policy evaluation (options 1–3 are not mutually exclusive and a mixed approach is possible):

(1) Wait until pressure comes from outside to evaluate. In Ireland's case this was from the EU. In the case of the African economies, the impetus may come from agencies providing overseas development aid. This was the stance largely adopted by Ireland from around 1993 onwards.

(2) Familiarize themselves with "best practice" or at least "good practice" evaluation frameworks and methodologies adopted internationally (reflecting on the key issues learned) so that they are in a position to know how (deciding on the methodological approach to be adopted is one of the key challenges for evaluators) to evaluate when requested to do so by external donors or organizations.

(3) View evaluation as a useful tool in its own right. This would involve adopting a proactive approach whereby evaluation would take place at the three stages of the industrial policy process: policy formulation (*ex-ante* evaluation focusing on the market failure argument as a rationale for intervention and fundamental economic principles such as opportunity cost); policy implementation; and policy accountability (*ex-post* evaluation) (Rist 1995). Such an approach not only sees evaluation as something that must be undertaken due to an external pressure (e.g. donor or funder) but rather sees evaluation as a worthwhile activity in terms of lessons to be learned that can subsequently be incorporated into future policy interventions. There is no doubt that many would regard evaluation as a "luxury" in African economies where resources are already scarce. We would argue however, that if robust evaluations are carried out (which ask the right questions relating to issues such as deadweight, displacement,[18] multipliers, and linkages) this may lead to improved future industrial policy interventions which in the long run could prove to be extremely cost-effective and efficient. Clearly, this is an area that merits further investigation.

Whilst Lenihan et al. (2005: 14) note that the "methodological rigor" of Irish industrial policy evaluations has been improving in recent years, it was not until pressure came from the European Commission that Irish policymakers and academics alike truly began to take industrial policy evaluation seriously. This is somewhat difficult to comprehend given that an interventionist approach to industrial policy has been a feature of the industrial policy stance by successive governments in Ireland since the 1950s, with the first grant to firms actually being awarded as far back as 1952. In this regard, Storey (2000) argues that a prerequisite to any evaluation is that clear objectives be specified. More precisely, he highlights the "impossibility of conducting an evaluation in the absence of clearly specified objectives for the policy concerned" (177). This calls for a clearly defined set of policy objectives from the outset, and to allow for trial and error as an important part of policy development. As UNCTAD (2007: 87) notes, referring in particular to East Asian experience:

> A simple replication of the East Asian developmental State, even if there were such a thing, would not do...Indeed, the intrinsic differences among the Asian experiences underscore the importance of "trial and error" as an important ingredient of policy formulation and implementation in developmental States. This process should benefit from constant monitoring and the feeding of the lessons learnt from monitoring into new policies to overcome earlier shortcomings.

An additional challenge (as with all calls for evaluation) is who should actually carry out such evaluations. The follow-on question is who should evaluate the evaluators. Clearly, in the face of the level of corruption and lack of resources to carry out some evaluations in some of the African economies, this issue is particularly pertinent.

Concluding thoughts

As outlined in this paper, there are indeed some interesting similarities and lessons to be learned (both good and bad) by the smaller African economies from Irish industrial policy experiences. Key amongst these is the concern expressed in this paper that industrial policy should not be seen purely in narrow terms; that is, with a sole focus on attracting FDI. We argue here that there is need for a more holistic approach to economic development that *inter alia* focuses on the development of domestic entrepreneurship and indigenous firm expansion more generally, as well as emphasizing the importance of other supply-side factors (e.g. infrastructure, well-functioning labor markets). It may be argued that this more comprehensive view of industrial policy and economic development could take a longer time to materialize. This is a difficult dilemma for African economies to face, given the extremely high levels of poverty and deprivation witnessed in many of these economies. We do, however, argue that such a holistic growth trajectory could lead to a more sustainable industrial development path, in contrast to that of Ireland, which because of its (over)dependence on US firms, is now suffering severe reverberations from the recent downturn in the US.[19]

This paper has provided some novel insights by showing a detailed comparison between Ireland and the small African economies. As argued earlier, when comparisons are made in terms of industrial policy lessons to be learned, these tend mainly to rely on the East Asian experience (which, as indicated earlier, undoubtedly provides interesting economic development insights, but with certain caveats). The paper suggests that a very important contribution of the Irish model is its emphasis on corporatism rather than state direction of industrial policy. The Irish model can also be considered more democratic, having protected workers' rights during the development process to a greater extent than in the highly dirigiste East Asia model. Bearing in mind the small size of the African economies, the paper recommends regional integration and sufficient ODA for infrastructural development.

Last but not least, it is important to bear in mind that the various small African economies each face their own industrial and economic development challenges, therefore we do not suggest a one-size-fits-all approach. As outlined by UNCTAD (2007), referring to East Asian experience, the path to sustainable growth and development is derived from "a pragmatic mix of markets and state action, taking into account the country-specific development challenges" (UNCTAD 2007: 61). It concludes:

> The challenge for Africa (as for other developing countries), therefore, is not how to copy any model, but how to create "capitalisms" adaptable to the unique opportunities and development challenges in each country . . . . (UNCTAD 2007: 88)

Notes

1. From a poem by William Blake (1757–1827).
2. Lenihan is based at the Department of Economics, Kemmy Business School, University of Limerick, Ireland. She worked on this paper during her sabbatical leave as a Visiting Fellow at the CBR at Judge Business School, University of Cambridge, while concurrently a Visiting Fellow at Wolfson College, University of Cambridge, UK, and finally as a visiting academic at the CSME, Warwick Business School, University of Warwick, UK. Bailey is Professor of International Business Strategy and Economics at Coventry University Business School, UK. Singh is Emeritus Professor of Economics, University of Cambridge and Director of Research with CERF at the Judge Business School in Cambridge.
3. Amsden (1989) and Wade (1990) are two well-known representative studies from the huge literature on this subject.
4. These were the high-growth periods for the two countries. In 1973, Japan was still more like a developing country than it has been since (see Singh 1995).
5. The UN (2009) identifies a range of dynamic objectives a "new developmental industrial policy" should aim for, such as creating a dynamic domestic comparative advantage in a more complex and sophisticated range of goods and services; upgrading human capital; upgrading productive capacity; building industrial policy capability; creating conditions

for inclusive growth; fostering the transformation from agrarian to post-agrarian socie-ties; raising labor productivity through improved public inputs; diversifying natural-resource activities; and promoting learning and knowledge diffusion among firms and workers.

6. Singh (1995) comments on the interrelationship between industrial policy and macro-economic stability with particular reference to the experience of East Asian countries. To the extent that industrial policy was effective in Japan or the Republic of Korea in relieving the balance of payments constraint, it will also have aided macroeconomic stability. A current-account balance at the desired growth rate can help to avoid the stop-go cycles that many economies experience. This, in turn, will lower the cost of capital since for a given savings rate in the economy, other things being equal, the more variable and unstable the economic performance, the higher the interest rate. Similarly, faster economic growth also leads to faster growth of real wages, and hence enhances social stability and the political legitimacy of the socioeconomic order. Thus, macroeconomic stabilization and industrial policy interact with each other in a virtuous circle of cumula-tive causation.

7. Ireland has the highest fertility rate in the EU, and between 1981 and 2001 experienced a population increase of 15 percent, from 3.5 million to just over 4 million in 2004 (NESC 2005: 1).

8. UNCTAD (2007: 25) notes that monetary or non-monetary resource transfers by migrants to their home countries are increasingly recognized as an important source of financing for development in Africa, being the second largest source of development capital flows to developing countries.

9. Quite why the Irish economy prospered at this time when the state pursued a very restrictive fiscal policy has been the subject of much debate. The European Commission saw it as an "expansionary fiscal contraction," which led to improved confidence and greater consumption and investments (EC Commission 1991; McAleese 1990). Others have stressed the Lawson boom in Britain, which raised demand for Irish products and fall of the oil prices: "Irish policy makers were just lucky that their adjustment was carried out at a time when world growth became buoyant and world interest rates were falling" (Bradley et al. 1993). Kennedy (2001: 131–2) also suggests that growth in the US econ-omy and the advent of the Single Market after 1993 were important factors.

10. MITI (the Ministry of International Trade and Industry) in Japan may have played a similar consensus-building role after the Second World War through to the 1980s (see Bailey and Sugden 2007).

11. The pattern applied in the PNR was followed in successive pacts. Successive social pacts have broadened stakeholders involved in the negotiation as well as the focus of agreements.

12. Here, the selection of target industries needs to be realistic and related both to the country's technological capabilities and world market conditions. The success of East Asian countries for example "owe a lot to the fact that they did not attempt to make too big a step" (Chang 2006: 126).

13. See Bailey and Cowling (2006), who note that industrial policy in the US and Japan has involved both vertical measures in targeting new technologies and emerging industries, and horizontal measures to support all industries, suggesting that the current focus in

Britain and the EU with the horizontal aspects of industrial policy has been largely misplaced.

14. The role of large indigenous firms in the development process also needs to be noted here. In many countries, such firms, which are large by developing countries' standards but rather puny in international terms, are the spearheads of spreading technical change and productivity growth. Amsden (1989) is the leading exponent of the critical role of large indigenous firms in late industrialization. What is, therefore, required in industrial policy for developing countries is the right balance between the promotion of large and small firms. To illustrate this point, Indian industrial policy in the period 1950 to 1980 is an example of a policy that encouraged small firms at the expense of large firms in order primarily to safeguard employment. Despite its good economic rationale, this policy is generally regarded as being a failure as it stopped the growth of large firms and thwarted their role in the development process. See further Joshi and Little (1994), Ahluwalia (1992), and Singh (forthcoming). The UN (2009a) notes that African firms tend to be mainly small firms, which in general do not network with other firms or organizations.

15. At 1.9 percent of GNP in 1988, compared with 1.2 percent for Taiwan Province of China (1988), 0.9 percent for India (1986) and Singapore (1987), 0.5 percent for Argentina (1988), 0.6 percent for Mexico (1984), and 0.4 percent for Brazil (1985) (UN 1993).

16. See the *Task Force on Small Business Report* (1994) and the *Small Business Operational Programme* (1995).

17. On the development of stock markets and banks in Africa, see further Singh (1999b) and Singh (forthcoming).

18. For a discussion of the concepts and estimation of deadweight and displacement, in the context of Ireland, see Lenihan (1999 and 2004) and Lenihan and Hart (2004).

19. In 2001, the number of US companies in Ireland reached a peak at 531. This information is derived from the combined sources of UNCTAD WID (2005) Country Profile Ireland and various Annual Report from IDA Ireland (various years).

References

Acs, Z., O'Gorman, C., Szerb, L., and Terjesen, S. (2007). "Could the Irish Miracle be Repeated in Hungary?" *Small Business Economics*, 28: 123–42.

Ahluwalia, I. J. (1992). *Industrial Growth in India*. Oxford: Oxford University Press.

Aiginger, K. (2007). "Industrial Policy: Past, Diversity, Future. Introduction to the Special Issue on the Future of Industrial Policy," *Journal of Industry Competition and Trade*, 7: 143–6.

Amin, A. and Tomaney, J. (1995). "The Regional Development Potential of Inward Investment in the Less Favoured Regions of the European Community," in A. Amin and J. Tomaney (eds.), *Behind the Myth of the European Union*. London: Routledge.

Amsden, A. (1989). *Asia's Next Giant: South Korea and Late Industrialization*. Oxford: Oxford University Press.

Amsden, A. (ed.) (1994). "Reviews of World Bank, 1993," *World Development*, 22 (4): 627–33.

Amsden, A. H. and Singh, A. (1994). "The Optimal Degree of Competition and Dynamic Efficiency in Japan and Korea," *European Economic Review*, 38 (3/4): 941–51.

Andreosso-O'Callaghan, B. and Lenihan, H. (2006). "Is Ireland a Role Model for SME Development in the New Member States?" *Journal of European Integration*, 28 (3): 277–303.

Bailey, D. and Cowling, K. (2006). Industrial Policy and Vulnerable Capitalism, *International Review of Applied Economics*, 20 (5): 537–53.

Bailey, D., de Ruyter, A., and Kavanagh, N. (2007). "Lisbon, Sapir and Industrial Policy: Evaluating the Irish Experience," *International Review of Applied Economics*, 21 (3): 453–67.

—— and Sugden, R. (2007). "*Kūdōka*, Restructuring and Possibilities for Industrial Policy in Japan," in D. Bailey, D. Coffey, and P. Tomlinson (eds.), *Crisis or Recovery in Japan? State and Industrial Economy*. Cheltenham: Edward Elgar.

—— Thomas, R., and Sugden, R. (1998). "Inward Investment in Central and Eastern Europe: The Compatibility of Objectives and the Need for an Industrial Strategy," in M. Storper, S. Tomadakis, and L. Tsipouri (eds.), *Industrial Policy for Latecomers in the Global Economy*. London: Routledge.

Barry, F. (ed.) (1999). *Understanding Ireland's Economic Growth*. London: Macmillan Press.

Barry, F., Bradley, J., and Hannan, A. (2001). "The Single Market, the Structural Funds and Ireland's Recent Economic Growth," *Journal of Common Market Studies*, 39 (3): 537–52.

—— and Van Egeraat, C. (2008). "The Decline of the Computer Hardware Sector: How Ireland Adjusted," *Quarterly Economic Commentary*, Spring 2008, ESRI: 38–57.

Blomström, M. and Kokko, A. (1996). "Multinational Corporations and Spillovers," CEPR Discussion Paper 1365.

Blomström, M., Kokko, A., and Globerman, S. (2000). "The Determinants of Host Country Spillovers from Foreign Direct Investment," in N. Pain (ed.), *Inward Investment, Technological Change and Growth*. Basingstoke: Palgrave.

Bradley, J., Wright, J., and Whelan, K. (1993). *Stabilization and Growth in the EC Periphery: A Study of the Irish Economy*. Avebury: Aldershot.

Braunerhjelm, P., Faini, R., Norman, V., Ruane, F., and Seabright, P. (2000). *Integration and the Regions of Europe: How the Right Policies can Prevent Polarisation*. London: Centre of Economic Policy Research.

Buckley, P. J. and Ruane, F. (2006). "Foreign Direct Investment in Ireland: Policy Implications for Emerging Economics," *The World Economy*, 29 (11): 1611–28.

Buckley, R. (2005). *Multinational Enterprises, Productivity Spillovers and the Growth and Development of the Irish Software Industry*, Unpublished Ph.D. dissertation, University of Limerick, Ireland.

—— Leddin, A., and Lenihan, H. (2006). "An Assessment of the Contribution of MNEs to the Irish Economy," *ILL Foro de Economia Regional*, FPRG Economico de la Rioja, Logrono, May 9–11, La Rioga, Spain.

Chakravarty, S. and Singh, A. (1988). "The Desirable Forms of Economic Openness in the South," World Institute for Development Economics Research (WIDER), Helsinki.

Chang, H.-J. (2006). "Industrial Policy in East Asia—Lessons for Europe," *EIB Papers*, 11 (2): 106–33.

Coates, D. (2007). "The Rise and Fall of Japan as a Model of 'Progressive Capitalism,' " in D. Bailey, D. Coffey, and P. Tomlinson (eds.), *Crisis or Recovery in Japan? State and Industrial Economy*. Cheltenham: Edward Elgar.

Culliton, J. (1992). *A Time for Change: Industrial Policy for the 1990s (Report of the Industrial Policy Review Group)*, Stationery Office, Dublin.

European Commission (1991). *The Regions in the 1990s,* Fourth Periodic Report on the Social and Economic Situation in the Regions of the Community, Commission of the European Community, Brussels.

Fitzsimons, P., O'Gorman, C., and Roche, F. (2001). *Global Entrepreneurship Monitor: The Irish Annual Report.* Dublin: Enterprise Ireland.

Forfás (1994). *Technological Innovation in Irish Manufacturing Industry: Report for the Policy and Advisory Board for Industrial Development in Ireland.* Dublin: Forfás.

—— (2004). *Innovation Networks.* Dublin: Forfás.

Freeman, C. (1989). "New Technology and Catching-Up," *European Journal of Development Research,* 1 (1): 85–99.

Gleeson, A. M., Ruane, F., and Sutherland, J. (2005). "Successfully Promoting Industrial Clusters: Evidence from Ireland," Discussion Paper No 89. Paper presented at "Multinationals, Clusters and Innovation: Does Public Policy Matter?" April 30, University of Porto, Portugal.

Goodbody Economic Consultants (2002). *Entrepreneurship in Ireland.* Dublin: Goodbody Economic Consultants.

Görg, H. and Ruane, F. (2000). "An Analysis of Backward Linkages in the Irish Electronics Sector," *The Economic and Social Review,* 31 (3): 215–35.

—— —— (2001). "Multinational Companies and Linkages: Panel-Data Evidence for the Irish Electronics Sector," *International Journal of the Economics of Business,* 8 (1): 1–18.

—— and Strobl, E. (2002). "Multinational Companies and Indigenous Development: An Empirical Analysis," *European Economic Review,* 46 (7): 1305–22.

—— —— (2003). "Multinational Companies, Technology Spillovers and Plant Survival," *Scandinavian Journal of Economics,* 105 (4): 581–95.

Greenspan, A. (1998). Testimony Before the Committee on Banking and Financial Service, US House of Representatives, January 30. Available at <http://www.federalreserve.gov/boarddocs/testimony/1998/19980130.htm>.

Heanue, K. and Jacobson, D. (2003). "Low Tech Policy," *PILOT—Newsletter 1,* May, DCU Business School, Dublin City University.

Hitchens, D. and Birnie, E. (1992). "Evaluating the Culliton Report," *The Irish Banking Review,* Summer: 28–40.

Honohan, P. and Walsh, B. (2002). "Catching Up With the Leaders: The Irish Hare," *Brookings Papers on Economic Activity,* 1: 1–77.

House, D. and McGrath, K. (2004). "Innovative Governance and Development in the New Ireland," *Governance: An International Journal of Policy, Administration and Institutions,* 17 (1): 29–58.

ILO (2007). *World Employment Report.* Geneva: ILO.

IMF (2008). *World Economic Outlook, October 2008.* Washington, DC: IMF.

Industrial Development Authority (IDA) (various years). Ireland Annual Reports. Dublin: IDA.

Joshi, V. R. and Little, I.M.D. (1994). *India: Macroeconomics and Political Economy.* Oxford: World Bank and Oxford University Press.

Kearns, A. and Ruane, F. (2001). "The Tangible Contribution of R&D-Spending Foreign-Owned Plants to a Host Region: A Plant Level Study of the Irish Manufacturing Sector (1980–1996)," *Research Policy,* 30: 227–44.

Kennedy, K. (2001). "Reflections on the Process of Irish Economic Growth," *Journal of the Statistical and Social Inquiry Society of Ireland*, 30: 123–39.

Krugman, P. R. (1997). "Good News from Ireland: A Geographical Perspective," in A. W. Gray (ed.), *International Perspectives on the Irish Economy*. Dublin: Indecon Economic Consultants.

Lall, S. (2005). "Is African Industry Competing?" QEH Working Paper Series, No. 121, Queen Elizabeth House, Oxford University.

Lenihan, H. (1999). "An Evaluation of Regional Development Agency's Grants in Terms of Deadweight and Displacement," *Environment and Planning C: Government and Policy*, 17 (3): 303–18.

—— (2004). "Estimating Irish Industrial Policy in Terms of Deadweight and Displacement: A Quantitative Methodological Approach," *Applied Economics*, 36 (3): 29–252.

—— and Hart, M. (2004). "The Use of Counterfactual Scenarios as a Means to Assess Policy Deadweight: An Irish Case Study," *Environment and Planning C: Government and Policy*, 22 (6): 817–39.

—— —— and Roper, S. (2005). "Developing an Evaluative Framework for Industrial Policy in Ireland: Fulfilling the Audit Trail or an Aid to Policy Development?" *Quarterly Economic Commentary*, Summer 2005, ESRI: 69–85.

—— and Sugden, R. (2008). "Policy on Business Networking in Ireland: A Review, and Prospects for Evaluation," in M. Araguren, C. Iturrioz, and J. Wilson (eds.), *Networks, Governance and Economic Development: Bridging Disciplinary Frontiers*. Cheltenham: Edward Elgar.

Lynch, C. (2005). "Can We Learn from Ireland's Experience? An Irishman's Perspective," *Policy Backgrounder*, No. 6, June. Wellington: New Zealand Business Roundtable.

McAleese, D. (1990). Ireland's Economic Recovery, *Irish Banking Review*, Summer: 18–32.

McKinley, T. (2005). "Economic Alternatives for Sub-Saharan Africa: 'Poverty Traps,' MDG-based Strategies and Accelerated Capital Accumulation," *UNDP Draft Paper for G-24 Meeting*, 15–16 September, New York.

Midelfart-Knarvik, K. H. and Overman, H. G. (2002). "Delocation and European Integration: Is Structural Spending Justified?" *Economic Policy*, 17 (35): 323–59.

Mkandawire, T. (2005). "Maladjusted African Economies and Globalisation," *Africa Development*, 30 (1/2): 1–33.

National Economic and Social Council (NESC) (2005). "Strategy 2006: People, Productivity and Purpose," Report No. 114, December, Dublin. Available at: <http://www.nesc.ie/press/press_detail.asp?newsId=82&zoneId=4&catId=19>.

Pfeffermann, G. (2008). "Into Africa," available at <http://www.elmg.org/globalfocus>.

—— (2008). "African Business Schools," available at <http://www.mercnetwork.org>.

Pike, A., Rodríguez-Pose, A., and Tomaney, J. (2006). *Local and Regional Development*. London: Routledge.

Rist, R. C. (1995). *Policy Evaluation Linking Theory to Practice*. Cheltenham: Elgar Reference Collection.

Rodrik, D. (2007). *One Economics, Many Recipes*. Princeton, NJ: Princeton University Press.

Ruane, F. (2001). "Reflections on Linkage Policy in Irish Manufacturing—Policy Chasing a Moving Target." Paper presented at the UNECE/ERBD Expert Meeting, "Financing for

Development," Geneva, available at <http://www.unece.org/ead/ffd2001papers_new.htm>.

Salt, J. (2005). *Current Trends in International Migration in Europe*. Strasbourg: Council of Europe.

Sapir, A., Aghion, P., Bertola, G., Hellwig, M., Pisani-Ferry, J., Rosati, D., Viñals, J., and Wallace, H. (2003). "An Agenda for a Growing Europe: Making the EU Economic System Deliver," Report for the President of the European Commission, European Commission, Brussels.

Schweiger, C. and Wickham, J. (2005). "Is the Tiger Eating Its Children? The Two Sides Of the Irish Employment Model," *Dynamics of National Employment Models (DYNAMO) Project*, Country Study (Draft), <http://iat-info.iatge.de/projekt/2005/dynamo/publications.html>.

Singh, A. (1995). "The Causes of Fast Economic Growth in East Asia," *UNCTAD Review*, Geneva: UNCTAD.

—— (1997). *Catching Up With the West: A Perspective on Asian Economic Development into the XXI Century*. Washington, DC: Inter-American Development Bank.

—— (1998). "Savings, Investment and the Corporation in the East Asian Miracle, Study 9," *The Journal of Development Studies*, 34 (6): 112–37.

—— (1999a). "Asian Capitalism and the Financial Crisis," in J. Michie and J. Grive-Smith, *Global Institutions*. London: Routledge.

—— (1999b). "Should Africa Promote Stock-Market Capitalism?" *Journal of International Development*, 11 (3): 343–67.

—— (forthcoming). "The Past, Present and Future of Industrial Policy in India: Adapting to the Changing Domestic and International Environment," in M. Cimoli, G. Dosi, and J. Stiglitz, *Policies and Development*. Oxford: Oxford University Press.

—— Singh, A., and Weisse, B. (1999). "The Asian Model: A Crisis Foretold?" *International Social Science Journal*, 160: 203–15.

Small Business Forum (2006). *Small Business is Big Business: Report of the Small Business Forum*. Dublin: Small Business Forum.

Storey, D. (2000). "Six Steps to Heaven: Evaluating the Impact of Public Policies to Support Small Business in Developed Countries," in D. L. Sexton and H. Landström (eds.), *The Blackwell Handbook of Entrepreneurship*. Oxford: Blackwell.

Summers, L. H. (1998). Quoted in an Article by Gerard Baker, "US Looks to G7 Backing on Asia Crisis," *Financial Times*, February 19.

Telesis Consultancy Group (1982). "A Review of Industrial Policy," Report 64, National Economic and Social Council, Dublin.

The Economist (2008). "Africa's Prospects," October 11–17: 33.

Ugur, A. and Ruane, F. (2004). "Export Platform FDI and Dualistic Development," Institute for International Integration Studies Discussion Paper, No. 28, July.

UN (1993). Transnational Corporations from Developing Countries: Impact on their Home Countries. New York: United Nations.

United Nations Conference on Trade and Development (UNCTAD) (2005). *UNCTAD WID Country Profile Ireland*. New York: United Nations.

—— (2007). *Economic Development in Africa: Reclaiming Policy Space. Domestic Resource Mobilization and Developmental States*. New York: United Nations.

—— (2009a). "Economic Development in Africa: Rethinking the Role of Foreign Direct Investment." New York: United Nations.

—— (2009b). *The Least Developed Countries Report 2009: The State and Development Governance*. New York: United Nations.

Wade, R. (1990). *Governing the Market: Economic Theory and the Role of Government in East Asian Industrialization*. Princeton, NJ: Princeton University Press.

World Bank (2007). *World Development Report 2007*. Washington DC: World Bank.

Part IV
Employment and Human Capital

15

Employment in Sub-Saharan Africa: Lessons to be Learnt from the East Asian Experience

Azizur Rahman Khan[1]

Introduction: Lessons for Sub-Saharan Africa from the East Asian Experience

High employment intensity is perhaps the most important characteristic of poverty-alleviating growth. People who are poor are better endowed with labor than any other resource. The most direct contribution that economic growth can make to poverty reduction is to create productive and remunerative employment as rapidly as possible. Other attributes—for example, the redistribution of assets in favor of poor people through egalitarian land reform and improved access to human capital—undoubtedly facilitate poverty reduction. Typically though, these policies help poverty reduction by increasing opportunities for more productive employment, not by opening escape routes that are independent of employment.

Rapid poverty reduction through high and highly employment-intensive growth is best illustrated by the experience of the East Asian pioneers.[2] The employment intensity of growth is measured by the *gross* output elasticity of employment (OEE), the ratio of proportionate growth in employment to proportionate growth in value added.[3] For a developing country, characterized by a large subsistence sector, it is difficult to measure the elasticity for traditional sectors, such as agriculture and informal services, because employment is hard to measure meaningfully. Nor is a high elasticity for such sectors always desirable as economic development should lead to a relative, and ultimately absolute, fall in employment in these activities. However, the OEE in industries and modern services should be high enough to permit a gradual transfer of employment from the low-productivity traditional sectors to high-productivity industries and services. To illustrate with reference to an East Asian country for which estimates are available, in the Republic of Korea, the OEE in industries was approximately 0.7 during the 1970s.[4] Assuming that this was the OEE for the entire modern sector, which at the time probably employed half the labor force and achieved something like 10 to 12 percent annual growth, the annual labor absorption in these sectors alone accounted for 3.5 to 4 percent of the entire employed labor force, close to twice the annual increase in labor supply (which had started declining because of an early demographic transition that these East Asian countries had achieved). The result was a dramatic restructuring of the composition of employment away from agriculture and other traditional activities and an annual growth rate in the real wage rate that matched the annual growth rate in per capita GDP. Wide access to human capital helped the process by steadily contributing to increased productivity of labor. It was not only growth by itself, but also its high employment intensity that explains the continued equality of income distribution and the extraordinary rapid poverty reduction. Some of the contemporary cases of equally or even more rapid growth, as in China and India, have failed to prevent rising inequality. The low OEE is an important cause of the differences in outcome.

East Asia also had a high ratio of employment to population from the early years of its being launched on the development path. On the supply side, this was because of a quick demographic transition that brought about a decline in the dependency ratio, the ratio of children to population, as well as a high labor force participation rate (LFPR), the ratio of labor force to population in economically active age group. On the demand side, this was made possible by the high employment intensity of growth. The high LFPR was the result of the very high participation rate among women, which was facilitated by the absence of social and cultural impediments.[5]

What can one say about Sub-Saharan Africa's (SSA) performance in making growth adequately employment-intensive *in the cases where growth has occurred* and its potential performance in doing so if and when growth takes place in the rest of the region? Attempts to find answers to such questions are severely constrained by the limitation imposed by the inadequacy of employment data. The International Labour Organization's (ILO) documentation shows that between 1990 and 2005, only twenty-four of the forty-two SSA countries, each with more than one million people, had any kind of employment survey; only ten had more than one survey during this period; and only eleven have had such a survey since 2000. Mauritius and South Africa are the only countries that have had regular annual surveys in recent years.

Estimates and projections of *labor force* are available from the ILO for most countries. While they shed useful light on aspects of employment characteristics and problems, they are of limited value in dealing with the issues under review.

A further problem is with the quality of the data that are available. As discussed below, attempts at understanding the employment consequences of growth have often proved frustrating because of the doubtful quality of the employment data.

Some features of SSA's labor force and employment characteristics

Some of the important features of SSA's labor force and employment characteristics are highlighted in Table 15.1 with comparative data for the two largest and rapidly growing contemporary developing regions, South Asia and East Asia. In this table, East Asia represents the developing East Asia of today; it excludes the East Asian pioneers whose experience is described above—they have all graduated to the category of high-income countries. The contemporary East Asian developing countries, however, share the important employment characteristics of the East Asian pioneers during the period of their rapid development: high LFPR, low

Table 15.1 Some aspects of labor force and employment in Sub-Saharan Africa and contemporary developing Asia

Region/ Country	Dependency Rate (100D)	LFPR	Unemployment Rate (u)	Employment/ Population Ratio (w)	Labor Force Growth Rate
SSA	43.5	74.2	9.8	37.8	2.55
Kenya	45.5	71.8	10.4	35.1	2.54
Tanzania	42.2	69.3	5.1	38.0	2.12
Uganda	50.7	83.1	3.2	39.7	3.21
Botswana	44.8	55.1	18.6	24.8	−0.46
South Africa	31.6	61.4	26.8	30.7	0.39
South Asia	33.4	59.7	5.4	37.6	1.96
East Asia	30.0	74.2	4.2	49.8	1.45

Definitions: E = Employed labor force   U = Unemployed labor force
L = Labor force = E + U   WAP = Working-age population
NWAP = Non-working-age population   P = Population = WAP + NWAP
LFPR = L/WAP, Labor force participation rate
D = NWAP/P, Dependency rate = 1 − (WAP/P)
e = E/L, Employment/labor force ratio
u = U/L, unemployment rate = 1-e
w = Employment/population ratio = LFPR (1 − D)(1 − u)

Note on data sources: Data for Kenya are from Pollin et al. (2007) and are based on a 2005–6 Labor Force Survey. For others, WAP (for 2006) is from ILO, April 2007; P (for 2006) is from the *WDI 2008*; U, defined as those "who did not work at all in a 'survey' week, either for pay or assisting in a family business . . . and, most importantly, were actively seeking work" (ILO 2007a: 6) is from ILO (2007a). The estimates of D for countries from the ILO data count only the children below 15 as dependents and it is believed that the denominator of the LFPR from the same source also includes in the working-age group all persons age 15 and older. For Kenya, the latter refers to people between the ages of 15 and 64 and the LFPR is estimated accordingly. Labor force growth is annual average growth rate between 2000 and 2006 according to data in ILO, April 2007. The definition of unemployment excludes the "discouraged" workers (ILO 2007a: 6). It is well known that these labor force and employment measurements are notoriously subject to errors, even in countries with good systems of statistical reporting, due to the effects of seasonality in unemployment surveys that extend over as short a period as a week; the failure to ensure intertemporal consistency of the criteria of defining labor force; and other such problems. It is likely that in many SSA countries these problems are more than usually acute.

rates of unemployment, and a low ratio of dependent children to people of working age—characteristics that led to a high ratio of employment to population.

There are important differences between South Asia and East Asia with respect to these employment characteristics.[6] South Asia has the disadvantage of a high dependency ratio, represented in the table by a low ratio of employment to population, as compared to East Asia. This translates a given output per worker into a smaller product per person, in addition to indicating the need to commit more resources for educational and health infrastructure in order to bring up children. This is because of a low LFPR, largely caused by a much lower participation of women in the labor force as compared to East Asia, and a high ratio of children to people of working age, the result of a much slower demographic transition than the one that East Asia experienced. As shown in Table 15.1, the outcome for SSA as a whole, with respect to the ratio of employment to population, is similar to that for South Asia rather than for East Asia: it too has the disadvantage of a low value of this ratio.

While the above characteristics are widespread among the SSA countries, a small group of middle-income countries in Southern Africa seem to be exceptions. These are Botswana, South Africa, Namibia, Lesotho, and Swaziland, as well as a few other countries characterized by low female LFPR, most importantly, Mauritius, Nigeria, and Côte d'Ivoire. Table 15.1 provides examples of countries in both the mainstream SSA category and the exceptional category.

The mainstream category consists of the vast majority of SSA countries. Three examples of this category are shown in Table 15.1. These countries overwhelmingly belong to the low-income category though they include a handful of middle-income countries (Angola, Cameroon, and the Republic of Congo). The LFPR for these countries is as high as in East Asia and their unemployment rate is as low as in East Asia. However, the ratio of employment to population in these countries is as low as in South Asia because of the high ratio of children to people of working age (low ratio of working-age population to total population). The latter is due to the fact that these countries did not experience the demographic transition of the type that East Asia experienced when it launched on its growth path, a transition that quickly brought about a radical change in the age structure in favor of the working-age population.

Another feature of the employment scene in these countries is that being "employed" in these low-income SSA countries often does not provide protection from poverty because of high dependency ratio and low productivity of employment. Employment in these countries is typically dominated by self-employment (89 percent in Tanzania and 59 percent in Uganda, ILO reported in April 2007) and low incidence of wage-employment (7 percent in Tanzania and 15 percent in Uganda, according to the same source). Thus in these countries, self-employment in family and subsistence activities hides much of unemployment, which is low according to time criterion but almost certainly very high according to income criterion, to use a distinction that Amartya Sen has proposed.[7] That employment can coexist with low productivity and low income, leading to the widespread phenomenon of working poor, is well known, of course. In SSA, its incidence seems to be very high. A recent study for Kenya finds that the median wage in the informal sector is well below the official urban poverty line, which, assuming that such a worker supports a family member, means that almost all such workers would be below the poverty line.[8]

Much of the low productivity of employment is associated with the very high proportion of employment in agriculture, a sector with much lower output per worker than industrial and services sectors. For 2006, the ILO estimates that 63 percent of employment in SSA is in agriculture as compared to 51.7 percent for South Asia, the region with the next highest concentration of employment in agriculture (ILO, January 2007). The World Bank estimates that of all the developing regions, productivity per worker in agriculture is lowest in SSA (at 2000 prices: US$335 for the period 2003–5 as compared to US$406 in South Asia, the region with the next lowest productivity) and that it has experienced the lowest rate of growth in recent decades.[9]

Let us briefly turn to the small number of countries that are characterized by a low LFPR. This small group consists of two distinct subcategories: the *middle-income countries of Southern Africa*—Botswana, South Africa, Lesotho, Namibia, and Swaziland—and the few countries, such as Mauritius, Nigeria, and Côte d'Ivoire, that have a much lower female LFPR than is characteristic of SSA as a whole. The difference between the latter group and mainstream SSA appears to be the result of cultural differences that are not entirely tractable. The difference between the middle-income Southern African countries and the low-income mainstream SSA countries is, however, not due to sex difference in LFPR between the two groups. In these countries both the male and female LFPRs are low *relative* to those in the mainstream SSA countries.

As Table 15.2 illustrates, the ratio of employment to population is even lower in the middle-income Southern African countries than in the rest of SSA. This derives from both a low LFPR, more like South Asia than East Asia, and an astronomical rate of open unemployment.

The LFPR in the middle-income Southern African countries is intriguingly low in comparison with the very high LFPR in the poor SSA countries. One source of the difference seems to be the much lower LFPR among people ages 15–24, perhaps signifying a greater enrollment in secondary and tertiary education in the higher-income countries than in the rest. It also seems possible that a much higher rate of HIV prevalence in Southern Africa also contributes to the difference in LFPR; however, not enough information is available to evaluate the impact of HIV on the LFPR. Table 15.2 does provide some tantalizing hints. While the HIV prevalence is high throughout Southern Africa, the low LFPR is limited to the middle-income countries. It is possible that part of the reason that the LFPR in the low-income

Table 15.2 HIV, income level, and LFPR, circa 2006

Country	HIV Prevalence	LFPR	Income Per Capita (Income $)
Southern Africa: Middle Income			
Botswana	24.1	55.1	5570
Lesotho	23.4	57.1	980
Namibia	19.6	53.0	3210
South Africa	18.8	61.4	5390
Swaziland	33.4	49.0	2400
Southern Africa: Low Income			
Malawi	14.1	87.3	230
Mozambique	16.1	83.1	310
Zambia	17.0	77.2	630
Zimbabwe	18.1	72.2	340
Non-Southern: Middle Income			
Angola	3.7	80.6	1970
Congo	5.3	77.1	1050

Note: HIV prevalence rates are measured as percent of population ages 15 to 49 and are from *WDI 2008*. Income per capita is in current US$ equivalent at exchange rate and is from *WDI 2008*. LFPR is from ILO, April 2007.

Southern African countries is high, despite the high HIV incidence, is that the HIV incidence in these countries, though much higher than the SSA average, is not as high as in the middle-income Southern African countries. But it also seems partly because of the lower enrollment in secondary and tertiary education in these poor countries, as suggested by their high LFPR for the 15–24 age group. It is, however, unlikely that the high HIV incidence has not affected people's ability to work. Instead it appears likely that poverty in these low-income countries has forced many more workers who have the disease to continue to be in the labor force than their counterparts in the higher-income countries. That relatively high income by itself may not lead to low LFPR is suggested by the very high LFPR of those middle-income countries that are outside Southern Africa with low HIV incidence: LFPR in the examples in this category shown in Table 15.2 is as high as in the low-income mainstream countries of SSA. It would appear that the small number of cases of deviation from the high LFPR in the SSA countries is the result of either the combination of relatively high income and high HIV prevalence or cultural differences from the mainstream SSA countries.[10]

The other difference between the middle-income Southern African countries and the rest is the very high unemployment rate in the former (31 percent in Namibia, 27 percent in South Africa, 19 percent in Botswana, 25 percent in Swaziland, and 39 percent in Lesotho) as compared to the latter (3 percent in Uganda and 5 percent in Tanzania). This is certainly because of very different labor market conditions between the two groups of countries. A correlate of this difference between the two groups is their difference with respect to the ratio of wage-and-salary employment to total employment: it is very high in the middle-income countries (83 percent in Botswana, 82 percent in South Africa, 80 percent in Mauritius, and 62 percent in Namibia) and very low in the poorer countries

(7 percent in Tanzania and 15 percent in Uganda). Self-employment and family labor hide unemployment far better than does a labor market dominated by wage labor.[11]

Thus, excluding a handful of exceptional cases, the countries of SSA are characterized by a very high LFPR, low open unemployment, and a very high ratio of employment to working-age population. The latter is higher than what it is in most other developing regions. By this measure SSA would compare favorably with East Asia during the latter's historical takeoff into the high-growth trajectory. However, much of this advantage is offset by the low ratio of working-age population to total population in SSA, so that in terms of the ratio of employment to total population, SSA does no better than contemporary South Asia, a region with much lower LFPR than SSA.

Quite apart from the disadvantage of high dependency ratio, much "employment" in SSA is characterized by low productivity and low remuneration. Estimates of working poor—the ratio of those workers who earn less than PPP$1 per day to all employed workers—are available from the ILO. This ratio for SSA is far higher than in the other developing regions: 55 percent as compared to 12 percent in East Asia, 11 percent in South-East Asia and the Pacific, 34 percent in South Asia, 11 percent in Latin America, and 3 percent in the Middle East. The ratio is as high as 89 percent in Uganda and 80 percent in Nigeria.[12]

Between 1990 and 2005, the labor force in SSA increased at a significantly faster rate than in either of the two Asian regions. This growth rate has also been higher than the historical growth rate in the East Asian pioneers during the period of their takeoff. The labor force in SSA grew at a significantly faster rate than the labor force in the rest of the developing world taken together and in the low-income countries taken together, although not as fast as the labor force in Latin America, the Middle East, and North Africa. This means that the required rate of increase in employment in the mainstream SSA countries must be higher than in contemporary developing Asia or the East Asian pioneers.

It should be noted that labor force growth rates in the Southern African countries have turned much lower in the period 2000–6 than the SSA average. Besides the two cases shown in Table 15.2, the other countries in the region experienced the following growth rates: for the middle-income countries, the fall in growth rate was very sharp (growth rates during 2000–6 being –0.39 percent in Lesotho, 0.99 percent in Namibia, and 0 in Swaziland); for the low-income countries, the difference was very modest (Malawi 1.97 percent, Mozambique 1.56 percent, Zambia 1.71 percent, and Zimbabwe 1.15 percent). Unlike the decline caused by "healthy" demographic transition (such as a fall in birth rate preceding the decline), this particular decline was almost certainly because of the "unhealthy" demographic fact of high HIV prevalence. Unlike a fall in birth rate, which reduces the denominator of the LFPR, the increased HIV prevalence reduced the numerator of the LFPR. Thus the reduced rate of growth in labor force in the

Southern African countries is hardly a desirable phenomenon. Once again, it is hard to determine what has caused a far slower decline in the growth of the labor force in the lower-income countries of Southern Africa than in the higher-income countries. It could be the lower incidence of HIV prevalence or a difference in the time path of HIV spread. It is impossible to settle these puzzles without a great deal more reliable information.

The meaning of employment-intensive growth for poverty reduction in SSA

What are the priorities for poverty-reducing employment-intensive growth in the context of the labor force and employment characteristics of the SSA countries analyzed above? There are two links in the process. The first is to increase the ratio of employment to population from the current South Asian level to the East Asian level in order to increase the income per capita from a given output per employed worker. The second is to increase the output per employed worker.

Consider the first, the increase in the ratio of employment to population (w) which, as explained at the bottom of Table 15.1, is the product of three things: the employment rate ($1 - u$, where u is the unemployment rate); the LFPR; and the ratio of working-age population to total population ($1 - D$, where D is the dependency ratio). In the overwhelming majority of the countries that we have chosen to call mainstream SSA—all except the handful of middle-income Southern African countries and the few culturally different countries with low LFPR—it would clearly not make sense to try to seek a further increase in the LFPR, which is already very high. Indeed, it would be natural for the LFPR to decline in these countries as enrollments in secondary and tertiary education increase with economic progress. There is also a very limited scope for reducing the rate of open unemployment, which is already quite low in these countries. The way to bring about an increase in the ratio of employment to population in these countries is to focus on the third element, the ratio of working-age population to total population. Unfortunately this change can only come gradually by inducing the appropriate kind of demographic change, principally through declining birth rates. For the middle-income Southern African countries, focus must also be concentrated on improving the numerator of the LFPR by blunting the effect of HIV on the ability to work through wider access to antiretroviral treatment and, in the longer run, by arresting and reversing the spread of HIV. Furthermore, the big challenge in these countries is to bring down the astronomical rate of open unemployment that prevails in them. We have identified a third category comprising a small number of countries with low female LFPR. Policy for improving the ratio of employment to population in these countries must focus on improving the female

LFPR. This paper has little to say on this subject, which involves the analysis of intractable sociocultural factors.

By their nature, policies for increasing the ratio of employment to population are difficult to implement, slow to produce results, and unlikely to accomplish the objective of poverty reduction by themselves. Thus, much of the focus of employment-intensive growth for poverty reduction must concentrate on improving the productivity and remunerability of employment for the working poor.

The problem of low productivity is nowhere greater than in agriculture, the sector that is the home for an overwhelming proportion of people in SSA. The World Bank estimates the share of agriculture in GDP in 2006 to be only 15 percent, while the ILO estimates the share of agriculture in employment to be 63 percent in SSA.[13] The spread between the two may be even greater for the poorer SSA countries. This is probably the highest spread between employment and output shares of agriculture of all the regions of the world economy.[14] Most alarmingly, this spread has been increasing over time: the same data sources indicate that the ratio of employment share to output share for agriculture increased from about 3.6 in the mid 1990s to about 4.2 a decade later. Productivity per agricultural worker in SSA is lowest among all the developing regions. It is a quarter lower than in contemporary East Asia (again, excluding the pioneers) and 17 percent lower than in South Asia, despite the fact that arable land per agricultural worker is probably twice as high in SSA as in East Asia and two thirds as much more as in South Asia.[15]

Historically, this problem has been overcome by a structural change in the composition of output and employment. As noted earlier, this is also a lesson of the experience of the East Asian pioneers: rapid growth of industries and modern services with high OEEs facilitates this process both by increasing the proportion of workers employed in activities with higher levels of productivity and remuneration and by helping to increase the productivity of the declining proportion, and ultimately the declining absolute number, of workers who are left behind in agriculture and other traditional activities.

The enormity of the required magnitude of this transformation in SSA is reflected in the very high and steadily increasing spread between agriculture's shares of employment and output. Furthermore, the shares of industries in both output and employment have fallen over time. The share of services in total employment has increased; but little is known about the kind of services that account for the sector's increased shares of employment. Can SSA achieve the required rate of industrialization (broadly interpreted to include the growth of the higher-productivity tertiary activities as well) with high enough employment intensity that would enable it to deal with the problem of its working poor within a reasonable time frame?

There is an interesting twist in the experience of the East Asian pioneers that is worth noting at this stage. As these countries started on their growth path,

445

agriculture remained substantially more employment-friendly than in the traditional cases of industrialization. The work of Shigeru Ishikawa, and a large number
of case studies by others following his lead, established that the pattern of agricultural growth in Japan and the East Asian pioneers was substantially different from
both the historical experience of past industrial revolutions and other more contemporary development experiences as in South Asia.[16] The main features of this
experience can be summarized as follows: in pre-World War II and the immediate
post-World War II period in East Asia, labor use per hectare of land was much
higher than in South Asia and this higher labor input per hectare was associated
with a larger proportionate difference in yield per hectare.[17] There is evidence that
labor input per hectare over time in the early growth phase of the East Asian
pioneers increased and this was accompanied by more than proportionate yield
per hectare. This productive absorption of increased labor in agriculture made the
task of structural transformation easier, quite apart from creating a broadly positive role for agriculture in helping the growth process. Can the SSA countries
follow this East Asian lesson?

There are reasons to believe that some of the principal preconditions for East
Asian agriculture's high and productive absorption of labor do not prevail in SSA.
Research has highlighted two principal sets of such preconditions. The first relates
to agro-climatic factors. Even rainfall in East Asia made it possible to prepare land
with little assistance from non-human sources of power and made multiple crop-
ping easier. The second set of factors relates to the highly egalitarian distribution of
landholdings in East Asia. Even before land reforms in the post-World War II
period, operational landholdings in East Asia have by and large been small family
farms with a low incidence of hired labor. Land reforms solidified this feature. In
family-labor-based farming the "cost" of labor input is lower than the market cost
of hired labor, a feature that promotes greater labor use both in direct farming and
in capital construction for land improvement for which peasant ownership provides ample incentive. The SSA countries lack both these preconditions.

Not only are the employment-friendly East Asian environmental conditions
absent, but much of the SSA has rather harsh environmental conditions characterized by uncertain rainfall. These adverse natural conditions are exacerbated by the
dismally low level of infrastructure and input use: of all the developing regions,
SSA has the lowest irrigation intensity (3.5 percent of cropland as compared to the
average of 18.6 percent for the low-income countries and 20.4 percent for all
developing countries), the lowest rate of fertilizer use (119.2 grams per hectare
as compared to the average of 448.7 grams for the low-income countries and
1,090.7 grams for all developing countries), and the lowest level of mechanization
(thirteen tractors per 100 square kilometer of arable land as compared to the
average of forty-seven for the low-income countries and 163 for all developing
countries). Worse still, the low level of agricultural input use in SSA has often
declined further in recent times: between 1990–2 and 2003–5 fertilizer use

per hectare fell by 8 percent and tractors per square kilometer fell by 32 percent, while irrigation intensity remained virtually unchanged.[18]

The author has very limited access to information about the agrarian systems of the SSA countries; however, it does not seem that these countries are characterized by the prevalence of peasant agriculture with secure and egalitarian access to land. Attempts have been made to reform the land system (e.g. in Ethiopia), but they have not gone far enough to create an agrarian system in which individual households are the principal entrepreneurs in agriculture that is principally dependent on family labor.

And yet there is evidence to suggest that SSA agriculture can productively absorb labor and make this a major instrument for poverty reduction, even though there is far too little information and research to document opportunities along this path. An example of how the absence of the East Asian agro-climatic conditions can at least be partly compensated for by land abundance is provided by the case of Sudan, which is characterized by the coexistence of different agrarian systems: irrigated agriculture (IA) in the Gezira project area; mechanized rain-fed cultivation (MRFC), under which large tracts of land are leased out to large farms; and traditional rain-fed farming (TRFF), which encompasses most of the rural households under a system of cultivation in which land is assigned to the tribe or the community, which parcels it out in roughly equal amounts to its members. The community has only the right to use, not the full right of ownership, which vests in the government. These traditional farms are the closest thing that Sudan has to family farms, although they do not have the right to ownership or to transfer the lease. During the 1990s Sudanese agriculture achieved remarkably rapid growth. Of the three systems, growth was most rapid in TRFF and virtually absent in MRFC. During this period, Sudanese agriculture experienced a further decline in the rate of use of already scarce agricultural inputs like fertilizer. Much of the remarkable growth of the traditional family farms was achieved, despite the reduced use of fertilizer and other inputs, by the more intensive use of labor. The outcome was that output per person increased and, at least in certain crops, output per unit of land also increased. As an explanation of the phenomenon, we can hypothesize that increased labor use in the traditional family farms was driven by distress caused by the loss of part-time wage employment in irrigated agriculture because of a large shift from more labor-intensive crops to less labor-intensive crops. As part of their response for survival, households increased their labor use in the family farms, a process that was facilitated by the relative land abundance and the consequent elastic supply of land.[19] This story points to the far more dynamic possibility of productive absorption of labor under appropriate conditions to incorporate greater resources for agriculture and more conducive institutions to enable the household farms to become full-fledged entrepreneurs endowed with necessary rights and access to resources and services.

Another example of the possibility of productive absorption of labor—more appropriately, more productive use of the labor force in agriculture—is Ethiopia. It implemented villagization with access of individual households to land, but fell short of converting the peasant households into a dynamic entrepreneurial class by withholding the full usufruct right to land; allowing the continuation of some of the past disincentives; and letting the severe resource starvation of the sector to continue. Once these deficiencies are removed, Ethiopian agriculture should be able to have far greater productive absorption of labor both in direct farming and in much-needed labor-intensive capital construction.[20]

It is perhaps unlikely that the headcount of employment in agriculture would rise except in a very limited number of cases. But there is the possibility of much greater intensity of use and productivity of the sector's existing labor, a process that would reduce the enormous gap between agriculture's shares of employment and output.[21]

Regardless of the ultimate potential for the productive expansion of employment in agriculture, there is no alternative to an accelerated industrial growth (broadly defined to include the growth of modern tertiary activities) with high employment intensity. The current share of agriculture's employment is inconsistent with an acceptable level of development. This paper will now address the issue of employment-intensive growth of the non-agricultural activities, which has been the hallmark of the poverty-alleviating and equality-preserving growth in East Asia.

The SSA experience of the employment intensity of growth

So far, we have discussed several interrelated links in the East Asian experience of employment-intensive growth. First, there was rapid economic growth. Second, growth was even more rapid in high-productivity sectors, industries, and modern services. The elasticity of these sectors with respect to GDP was as high as 1.5 or higher. Third, the OEE in these sectors was high. The broad orders of magnitude of these elements were a 7 percent GDP growth associated with a 10–12 percent growth of "industries" and an OEE of 0.7 in this sector. With an initial share of labor force in these sectors of about half, this meant an annual growth of employment in these sectors alone that amounted to 3.5 percent or more of the labor force, leading to a net transfer of labor from traditional agriculture and related sectors.

In the case of the typical SSA countries, a similar growth pattern would have a less dramatic effect on the structural distribution of employment because, compared to East Asia at the end of the 1960s for example, the initial share of the industries and modern services in their output and employment is smaller and the growth rate in their labor force is faster (except in a handful of as-yet untypical

Table 15.3 Growth in the SSA countries, 2000–6 (annual percent)

Country	GDP	Industry	Manufacturing
Countries that Attained 5% or Higher Annual Growth During 1996–2006			
Angola	11.5	12.2	17.1
Botswana	5.1	4.8	2.1
Burkina	6.2	7.3	6.3
Mozambique	8.2	9.6	12.4
Rwanda	5.0	6.2	3.0
Sudan	7.0	14.2	8.8
Uganda	5.6	6.3	11.4
Additional Countries that Failed to Average 5% Annual Growth During 1996–2006 *But Succeeded in Averaging 5% Annual Growth During 2000–6*			
Chad	14.1	41.7	>5.0
Ethiopia	5.7	7.0	4.4
Ghana	5.3	7.5	>5.0
Mali	5.7	4.8	5.3
Mauritania	5.0	4.0	−2.5
Nigeria	6.0	5.5	8.8
Sierra Leone	12.3	low	low
Zambia	5.0	9.2	5.4
SSA	**4.7**	**5.4**	**3.4**

Note: Growth rates are from *WDI 2008*. For manufacturing in Chad and Ghana growth rates are not shown in the WDI. Their upper limits have been estimated by using the change in the sector's share in GDP between 2000 and 2006 shown in WDI. The qualitative rates of growth for industries and manufacturing for Sierra Leone are similarly arrived at. Industries include manufacturing, mining, construction, electricity, gas, and water. The identification of countries which attained 5 percent or higher annual growth between 1996 and 2006 is based on growth rates shown in ILO, April 2007.

cases). For the SSA countries to benefit from a more modest version of the East Asian type of poverty-reducing employment-intensive growth, it would be necessary to attain something like the East Asian growth and its structural composition and an incentive structure that is conducive to the East Asian type of OEE.

Table 15.3 provides information on the recent growth performance of SSA. Even as recently as the 1990s, GDP in SSA as a whole increased at the annual rate of 2.5 percent (not shown in Table 15.3), a shade lower than the rate at which population increased (WDI 2008). This was preceded by the 1980s, during which the per capita GDP of SSA as a whole declined. In the first six years of the twenty-first century, SSA as a whole achieved an annual growth rate of 4.7 percent, reversing the fall in per capita GDP that had occurred during at least the preceding two decades. From 1996–2006, only seven of the forty-two SSA countries with a minimum population of a million averaged an annual growth rate of 5 percent or more. During the shorter period from 2000–6, another eight countries averaged annual growth rates of 5 percent or more. Notice, however, that while for the entire decade 1996–2006 only Angola, Mozambique and Sudan averaged a minimum of 7 percent growth, over the shorter period 2000–6 the number of such countries increased to five (with the addition of Chad and Sierra Leone), representing less than 12 percent of the population of SSA. The vast majority of the SSA countries, which account for more than 88 percent of the continent's population, do not come close to reaching the most basic of the elements of East Asian performance.

How employment-intensive has growth been in those few countries that have succeeded in attaining decent growth? Lack of information prevents us from analyzing the issue in necessary detail, with the exception of just two countries—Ethiopia and Uganda—and even then, the quality of data is so poor that not much sense can be made of the suggested findings. However, indications are that the composition of output growth in these countries is far from conducive to high employment intensity.

Table 15.3 shows growth rates for both industries and manufacturing. Industries include activities that are uncertain indicators of the dynamic sectors that are of critical importance in the present context. In our view, growth of manufacturing better represents the kind of dynamism that is our concern. The elasticity of industries with respect to GDP in SSA has been less than one for the period 1990–2006. In particular, the growth of *manufacturing* industries has significantly lagged behind the already anemic overall economic growth. During the 1990s, the elasticity of manufacturing value-added with respect to GDP was 0.76. While the overall GDP growth rate increased during the first six years of the twenty-first century, the elasticity of manufacturing value-added with respect to GDP actually fell to 0.72. The share of manufacturing in GDP has fallen from 17 percent in 1990 to 14 percent in 2005 and 2006.[22] Without a reversal of this relative de-industrialization, poverty reduction through employment-intensive growth will remain beyond the reach of the region.

Of the fifteen cases of decent growth in recent years, manufacturing growth was significantly higher than GDP growth in only six—Angola, Mozambique, Sudan, Uganda, Nigeria, and Zambia.[23] Of these six, growth in Angola, Sudan, and Nigeria was driven by the growth of oil with no evidence of dynamic industrialization. Indeed, Nigeria is a classic case of Dutch disease: growth of the oil industry since the 1970s killed off its agricultural and light industrial exports. The case of Uganda, along with Ethiopia, is discussed in detail later. Mozambique and Zambia probably are lone examples of possibilities that, under proper conditions, might develop into broad-based growth. Mozambique's growth has been associated with the export of bulk electricity, aluminum, and agricultural goods; and a relatively broad group of industries have developed. But so far the employment data, imperfect as they are, indicate that only 6 percent of employment is in industries that account for 26 percent of GDP. Zambia's growth, both in terms of output and exports, has been stimulated by the growth of minerals and non-traditional agriculture (floriculture). The abundant supply of arable land, of which it is estimated that only 20 percent is used, points to the opportunity of increasing productivity in agriculture, which currently directly and indirectly engages 85 percent of the labor force. Paucity of data makes it difficult to analyze the issue of the employ-ment intensity of growth in these two countries with any confidence. It would be useful to know if the East Asian type of growth-employment poverty reduction has been working in these countries. Unfortunately, even less is known about the employment characteristics of these two countries than the rest of the SSA; neither of them have had an employment survey since 1990.

The ILO has carried out a number of country case studies on the relationship between the employment intensity of growth and the poverty alleviation effect of growth. Two African countries, Ethiopia and Uganda, have been included in these case studies.[24] Uganda averaged 7.1 percent annual growth during the 1990s and 5.6 percent in the first six years of the twenty-first century. Ethiopia emerged in the early 1990s from a long period of stagnation and misrule and has averaged an annual growth of 4.4 percent in the decade ending in 2006. What do the two case studies tell us?[25]

Ethiopia

Ethiopia stagnated during the 1980s, the decade preceding the emergence of the new regime, with an annual average GDP growth of just 2.3 percent, below the rate of population growth, which is estimated to have been above 2.5 percent. During the 1990s, following extensive economic reform, growth increased, but still no more than about 2 percent per year in terms of per capita income. That this rate of growth was inadequate for poverty reduction is evident from the fact that from 1995–2000, the only period for which poverty estimates are reported in the case study, per capita real consumption in rural Ethiopia actually fell by 4 percent and per capita real urban consumption increased by just 3 percent. The poverty out-come was determined by the change in the distribution of income and consump-tion: rural Gini ratios fell a little and the incidence of rural poverty, by all the standard measures, fell a little. Urban Gini ratios increased, substantially for con-sumption expenditure, and urban poverty increased. At the national level, there was no appreciable change in the incidence of poverty.[26] It is noteworthy that the poverty outcome would have been far more favorable if the growth rate in per capita consumption was the same as the growth rate in per capita GDP. In Ethiopia, the incremental share of the government in GDP was higher than its average share for well-known imperatives and so might have been the case with the income shares of business. The incremental share of households was conse-quentially less than their average share.

Employment data are available at discrete intervals and they do not coincide with the pre-reform or post-reform periods. From 1984–94, employment increased at a rapid annual rate of 5.9 percent, at similar rates across sectors, far outpacing the rate of output growth. During 1994–9, roughly coinciding with the period over which poverty estimates are available, employment growth for the economy as a whole was dismal, –0.6 percent per year. The largest sector of employment, agriculture and allied activities, recorded a 2.9 percent annual decline in employment. For a number of reasons, these employment data seem implausible. Poverty data show that for the farming population, the incidence of poverty declined between 1995–6 and 1999–2000. It is hard to imagine this happening with a large decline in employment. It is also difficult to imagine where all the laid-off agricultural workers went. The "allied activities" seem to indicate much of the informal rural employment categories. It is possible that the sources of employment data at the two points were not comparable.

Employment in manufacturing, reported by a separate annual data source, recorded an annual trend growth of 1.8 percent from 1992–3 to 1999–2000. During the same period, the annual trend growth in manufacturing output was 5 percent. These indicate a "trend" estimate of the gross output elasticity of employment of 0.36, which must be considered low for a labor-abundant economy like Ethiopia.

Uganda

The Uganda case study analyzes the relationship among growth, employment, and poverty over the period 1992–2002, during which Uganda attained close to 6 percent annual growth in GDP. Uganda's growth was poverty-alleviating until the turn of the century. Between 1992–3 and 1999–2000, six distinct annual observations showed steady decline in the incidence of poverty. In the early years of the new century—between 1999–2000 and 2002–3—this trend was reversed, with a rise in the incidence of poverty in both rural and urban areas.

The immediate explanation is that growth in the new century slowed, and, more significantly, inequality in the distribution of income, which had remained steady during the 1990s, had risen sharply by 2002–3. Thus the poverty-alleviating character of growth during the 1990s appears to have been due largely to its avoidance of increased inequality.

The attempt of the study to link growth to poverty reduction via the employment performance of the economy has not been successful because of the poor quality of employment data. "Comparable" data on employment are available only for 1992–3 and 1997; but these data also suffer from a lack of standardization of the amount of work time per worker. These data show that over this period, agriculture's share of employment increased, industry's share fell, and services' share increased. Over the period, employment in agriculture increased at 7.86 percent per year and real value-added increased at 3.54 percent per year, indicating an OEE of 2.22. On the same basis, the elasticity turns out to be 0.42 for industries, 1.04 for services, and 1.06 for the economy as a whole. Except for industries, output per worker fell everywhere, drastically so in agriculture, while output per person increased significantly. It is almost certain that the lack of comparability over time of the average intensity of work per person in agriculture and traditional services accounts for these extraordinary estimates. If one takes the estimates literally, then one must conclude that over time an average agricultural household of a given size was allocating more individuals to the labor force and causing strong diminishing returns, which sharply reduced the output per worker but still allowed the output per person to rise.

While the elasticity estimates for agriculture and services are not enlightening, it is unlikely that industrial employment estimates, largely in a wage-based market environment, would suffer from these problems. One would thus conclude that Uganda's industries were not particularly employment-intensive, a fact that is confirmed by the detailed, though often erratic, estimates of these elasticities for individual manufacturing industries reported by the study. It also seems likely that agriculture absorbed much of labor, if not at the stratospheric rate suggested by the data.

Be that as it may, it seems fairly certain that the "agricultural" population increased at least at the same rate as the growth of aggregate population. This would imply that output per person in agriculture increased very little. The study reports poverty incidence by the occupational sector of the head of the household and it shows a significant decline in the incidence of poverty over the period for agricultural households. How could that be consistent with very modest, if any, increase in output per person? The explanation seems to lie in an improvement in agriculture's terms of trade brought about by the rising export prices of agricultural crops during this period. Indeed, the study reports a much faster reduction in poverty among households dependent on cash crops than among households dependent on food crops. One of the major explanations of the reversal of poverty reduction in the early twenty-first century is the adverse movement in export prices of agricultural crops during that period.

Thus Uganda's poverty-alleviating growth during the 1990s was largely the result of a reasonably rapid income growth in agriculture, facilitated by a modest rate of growth in physical output per capita and an improvement in terms of trade; stable inequality; and large-scale labor absorption in the sector, possibly including ancillary services. Industrial growth was rapid, but not particularly labor-intensive. This limited the prospect for migration of labor out of agriculture. Even without the benefit of large-scale emigration, agriculture experienced significant poverty reduction as long as its rising income continued to be distributed with unchanged inequality. The process came to an end when the rate of income growth slowed and inequality increased. It would be interesting if the details of the story behind the evolution of income distribution could be disentangled and the role that employment had in it could be spelled out. Currently, inadequate data render this impossible.

The case studies of Ethiopia and Uganda show that employment data are not sufficiently reliable to provide useful estimates of OEE, especially for agriculture and possibly for services as well. However, it seems unlikely that data on industrial employment suffer from as many problems of measurement as employment in other sectors. Thus one should take these estimates more seriously than estimates for other sectors. In both Ethiopia and Uganda, the industrial OEE was low, far lower than what it was in the East Asian pioneers at comparable levels of development.

The case studies do not analyze why the industrial OEEs are low. Was it because industries in the pre-reform period suffered from the widely observed phenomenon of "excess employment," which reforms dispelled partially or completely? Was it because the incentive system is biased against appropriate labor intensity? One needs to find the answers in order to judge whether the restoration of growth in SSA would be accompanied by high employment intensity so that growth would be adequately proverty alleviating.

The "incentive system"

If the recent trend of stagnation reversal continues and growth in SSA accelerates with an appropriate composition of incremental output, will the OEE be high enough to expand employment as rapidly as is warranted by the poverty reduction targets? Is the "incentive system" consistent with a degree of labor use that is dictated by SSA's relative factor endowments? It is not possible to provide a convincing answer to the question. But there are concerns suggested by the meager empirical evidence and some ongoing debate about the employment friendliness of SSA's labor market.

As already noted, reliable empirical estimates of OEE are virtually non-existent in the SSA countries. But among the available estimates, there are none that can be taken to suggest high employment intensity of industries. The low estimates for Ethiopia and Uganda have been previously mentioned. For South Africa, estimates are available for the incremental ratio of formal employment to GDP, which fell rapidly in the decade following the early 1990s, during the period of transition to democracy.[27] While these estimates hardly form a reliable basis for conclusion, they are not contradicted by any estimate of equivalent credibility to indicate a different outcome with respect to the employment intensity of growth.

The World Bank has strongly argued that the organization of SSA's labor market is not conducive to either growth or high employment intensity of growth.[28] The points that this particular line of argument makes include the following: wages in SSA's formal sector are set too high by policies such as minimum wage regulations and are buttressed by a regulatory environment that prevents entry into the formal sector; SSA has the highest index of employment rigidity of all developing regions (43 in a scale of 0 to 100, as compared to 21 for contemporary East Asia, 27 for South Asia, and 36 for the entire developing world; see WDI 2008); and high indices of difficulty of hiring and firing.

The experience of the East Asian pioneers suggests that high mobility of labor is of great importance for the right kind of industrialization and high OEE. One of the requirements of this high mobility is the ease with which labor can move between the traditional and modern sectors; between the informal and formal

Table 15.4 Median monthly incomes/wages in Kenya (in Ksh), 2005–6

Sector/Employment Type	National	Rural	Urban
Informal Sector			
Paid employee	2880	2000	4000
Self-employed worker	2600	2000	4000
Working employer	6000	4083	7800
Formal Sector			
Paid employee: Private	6160	4800	9000
Paid employee: Public	15,375	14,672	16,132

Note: See Pollin et al. (2007: Table 2.4).

sectors; and between the rural and urban areas. In the cases of the typical East Asian pioneers, this was reflected in the low differential between urban/rural and formal/informal wages. The difference was often as low as 20 percent.

Table 15.4 shows some estimates from a recent survey in Kenya that are probably representative of formal/informal and urban/rural wage/earning differences in the SSA countries. Admittedly the urban/rural difference is much higher than it was for the East Asian pioneers, although it is doubtful if it is any higher than in China and other contemporary East and South Asian countries. Furthermore, it needs to be discovered what is behind these differences. A simple-minded view, often peddled in World Bank analysis and policy advice, is that these are created by the rigidities of state regulation: minimum wages in the formal sector, labor market regulations, and trade union power. In the Kenyan case, as analyzed by Pollin et al., it seems that these differences have continued even during a period of rapidly declining unionization of labor. Furthermore, there is little evidence to suggest that minimum wage regulations were effective.

An important point, which is almost ignored, but which is strongly supported by the experience of the East Asian pioneers, is that labor mobility may be inhibited more by the absence of enabling factors—such as education, knowledge, ease of transport, and access to working capital—than by obstacles like regulations. Consider, for example, that in Kenya, the urban/rural difference in *informal* wages and earnings is proportionately nearly as high as the difference in those between the formal and informal sectors. State regulations could not have been responsible for preventing the movement of labor between rural and urban informal sectors; rather, it was the absence of enabling factors.

Similarly attention needs to be focused on non-discrimination between small employers and poor self-employed workers on the one hand and large enterprises on the other, in terms of access to credit, technology, inputs, and market access. This is another important lesson of the East Asian pioneers in general and Taiwan in particular. This requires a focus on providing access to enabling factors, rather than removing regulations.

This is not a defense of the mindless regulations that exist in many SSA countries: complex and multiple minimum wages that in any case are ineffective;

and requirements for too many permits; and too many rules that discriminate much more against small entrepreneurs. There is a case for the removal or simplification of these regulations. But East Asia has shown that the hope that much benefit can result from the removal of what are at best minor irritants can be misplaced. Consider the case of the Republic of Korea, where the fundamental law of the country made it virtually impossible to terminate workers.[29] But this proved to be no obstacle to the dramatic shift in the composition of labor that the Korean economy frequently underwent in order to conform to the constantly evolving pattern of comparative advantage. Workers had little incentive to cling to their current occupations when retraining costs were low and the rewards of greater productivity and better earnings were high.

Conclusions and policy priorities

Sub-Saharan Africa is not a homogenous region. The countries do not have similar employment characteristics or problems. It is not possible to meaningfully analyze SSA employment in a single short paper. It is hardly possible to begin to understand the vastly different problems that afflict the employment scene in these countries by individual effort. Even a large-scale effort to thoroughly analyze the subject will face many more difficulties of data limitation than is the case for any other major developing region. SSA countries need to improve the quality of employment data by institutionalizing regular labor force surveys and periodically integrating them with comprehensive household surveys.

Despite these obstacles, certain broad issues stand out with relative clarity. On the supply side, the SSA countries, with a few exceptions, have a high labor force participation rate, associated with a high participation rate among women. This is a characteristic that they share with the East Asian countries, both the pioneers and the contemporaries. This is an advantage that SSA has over certain other developing regions, notably South Asia and the Middle East and North Africa. Unlike East Asia, this advantage does not translate into a high ratio of labor force to population (the inverse of the dependency ratio). This is because of SSA's demographic disadvantage in having a high ratio of children to population, which reflects these countries' failure to achieve a significant demographic transition. A small number of SSA countries do not have the high LFPR that characterizes the region. This small group is further divided into two categories: the middle-income Southern African countries and the culturally different countries. Although the middle-income Southern African countries have a high incidence of HIV consistent with their neighbors, they have a greater incidence of secondary and tertiary education, a degree of social protection, and conditions that allow for at least some people who are ill with HIV to withdraw from the workforce. The overall LFPR of culturally different countries like Mauritius, Nigeria, and Côte d'Ivoire is affected by a low female LFPR. Supply-side policies must focus on hastening the process of demographic transition, the success of which will translate into a higher ratio of workforce to population only with time, and on dealing with the incidence of HIV, by reducing its prevalence and by improving access to antiretroviral therapy.

On the demand side, the problem is primarily the absence of rapid, dynamic growth. Only recently has SSA succeeded in reversing decades of decline and stagnation. During the first six years of the twenty-first century, only a handful of countries achieved decent growth and only three have sustained growth of East Asian magnitude over a decade. The problem is not merely one of low overall growth rate; of the handful of countries that have succeeded in achieving reasonable rates of growth in recent years, few, if any, have achieved the kind of industrial and tertiary growth that enabled the East Asian pioneers to dramatically transform the employment scene within a short period. Furthermore, it is uncertain if the "incentive system" that guides the employment decisions of entrepreneurs and households is of the kind that promotes a high employment intensity of growth.

The myriad aspects of the growth strategy for the SSA countries constitute a subject that is well outside the scope of this paper. Many of these are dealt with by other chapters of the present volume. It is, however, useful to highlight certain important priorities of SSA's growth strategy that are implied by the analysis in this paper.

A high proportion of SSA's labor force, and an even higher proportion of its working poor, is employed in agriculture where the focus must be on making employment more productive and more remunerative. Policymakers in SSA can benefit from the East Asian experience of productive absorption of labor in agriculture in the early phase of their rapid growth. The SSA countries do not have the agro-climatic advantage of East Asia that was an enabling factor behind this feature of the latter's development; but this can be compensated for by large capital investment in land. Another relevant lesson in this area is the promotion of family-labor-based farms as the principal form of entrepreneurship in agriculture. Even though the East Asian type of land reform may not be widely replicable in the SSA countries, appropriate modifications to traditional institutions can go a long way toward approximating the East Asian characteristic in this regard. Non-discriminatory terms of trade, adequate access to inputs, and publicly funded technology research are some of the other priorities suggested by the East Asian experience.

Agriculture cannot, however, provide productive employment for all the labor that is now located in the sector. One of the most important lessons of East Asian development is the rapid structural change, which led to a transfer of labor from agriculture to industries and modern services by means of the high growth rates of these sectors promoted by support on a broad front. Given the generalized infancy that characterizes industries in SSA, this would require similar action on a broad front: improving infrastructure, including the skill endowment of the labor force, and creating an overall environment that is conducive to entrepreneurship; and, since these developments produce results slowly, providing more direct incentive to help develop industries that have potential comparative advantage. International constraints to industrial promotion and protection are far stricter today than they were during the period of industrialization of the East Asian pioneers. It is questionable to what extent the World Trade Organization's regulations would allow the replication of the direct export subsidies used by the Republic of Korea to promote its industries, even if they are carefully targeted and limited in duration. The SSA countries must make full use of the opportunities that the existing international order still permits and preserve and expand them during the forthcoming negotiations under the Doha round.

Another important issue is that the accelerated growth of the SSA countries would require a massive public investment. It has been noted that agriculture in SSA needs a great deal of investment and that a major prerequisite for overcoming the generalized industrial infancy is the provision of infrastructure and human capital, activities in which investment is bulky, indivisible, and embodying large externality. These activities are unlikely to attract much private investment. Thus, large public investment is a critical precondition for accelerated growth of the SSA, perhaps even more than it was in the case of East Asia. Obstacles to successful implementation of public investment of the indicated magnitude are many: resources would need to be attracted and governments would need to increase their administrative capacities in order to handle the massive investment programs, even as the increase in the public sector's handling of resources expands the opportunity for corruption—already a big impediment to development. Compared to East Asia, SSA's governance capability is meager and this perhaps is the single largest obstacle to growth in the region.

The final point emerging from this analysis is that labor market institutions and policies need to be made more employment-friendly. Too frequently, the focus is on deregulation and the reform of arbitrary and inefficient institutions and policies, of which SSA has its share. Such reform may have a role to play. But the principal focus of reform for greater employment friendliness of the labor market must be on the enabling factors: endowing the members of the labor force with more human capital, greater access to credit, improved market information, and better infrastructure.

Notes

1. The author is Professor Emeritus of Economics, University of California, Riverside. He would like to express his gratitude to Rizwanul Islam of the International Labor Office, for making available many documents including ones that were unpublished; and to Robert Pollin, John Weeks, and Eva Kaplan for many useful comments on an earlier draft.
2. The East Asian pioneers are: The Republic of Korea, Taiwan, Hong Kong, Singapore, and, in a slightly earlier period, Japan. Egalitarian growth with high employment intensity is a characteristic that is not present, certainly not to the same degree, in the later rapid growth of other East Asian countries, such as China, Thailand, and most others. See

Mazumdar and Basu (1997) for an analysis of the East Asian experience in employment-intensive growth.

3. This *observed* ratio is called the *gross* OEE to distinguish it from what might be construed as the *net* OEE, showing the *true causal relation between growth and employment expansion under appropriate incentives, institutions, and policies*. The gross OEE can diverge from the net OEE if incentives, institutions, and policies are inappropriate. While a higher gross OEE is generally more desirable than a lower one, there are clear limits to this in so far as a high OEE indicates a very low productivity growth. See Khan (2005: 16) for more on the concept and Islam (2006: 75) for a discussion of the relationship between the magnitude of OEE and productivity growth. OEE in this paper refers to gross OEE unless otherwise specified.

4. See Islam (2006: 77–80) for the estimate and the method of estimation for the Republic of Korea.

5. According to the *World Development Indicators 2009* (Table 2.2), female labor force participation, as percent of ages 15 and over, for 1990 was 69 percent for East Asia and the Pacific, 38 percent for Latin America and the Caribbean, 21 percent for Middle East and North Africa, and 36 percent for South Asia.

6. See Mazumdar and Basu (1997) and Khan and Muqtada (1997: ch. 7) respectively for accounts of East Asian and South Asian experience.

7. See Sen (1975).

8. See Pollin et al. (2007: ch. 2).

9. For example, between 1990–2 and 2003–5 it increased at 1.47 percent per year after having fallen between 1980–94 at an annual rate of 0.72 percent. Combining the two, one finds that productivity per worker in agriculture in 2003–5 was barely 9 percent higher than a quarter century before! Figures for 1990–2 and 2003–5 are from the *WDI 2008* and those for the productivity change between 1980–94 from Khan (1997: Table 3).

10. A further explanation of the low LFPR in countries like South Africa may be the relatively generous social protection transfer payments. Although these payments are not intended for non-disabled people of working age, such people could benefit from payments made to their elderly and young family members, raising their reservation wage above what it would otherwise be. The author is indebted to Robert Pollin for pointing this out.

11. The source of most of the information in this paragraph is ILO, April 2007.

12. See ILO (2005). Note that all the PPP$1 poverty estimates must be considered out of date because of the recent drastic revision of PPP$ multiplier by the World Bank (see *WDI 2008*). These figures must be treated as indicators of orders of magnitude with some (perhaps not much) validity for regional relativities.

13. These figures respectively are from *WDI 2008* and ILO, April 2007.

14. We do not have comparable estimates for the East Asian pioneers during their early growth phase; but indications are that they were lower and falling. This spread has also been very high, and growing over time, in *contemporary* East Asia because of the strongly discriminatory policies against agriculture practiced in, but not only, China, the overwhelmingly dominant economy in the region. But while the ratio of employment share to output share in East Asia's agriculture in recent years has been about 3, it is 4.2 for SSA if one can trust the output and employment data shown above.

15. Productivity figures are estimates of agricultural value added per worker for 2003–5. See *WDI 2008*.

16. See ILO (ARTEP) (1980), especially the final chapter titled "An Interpretative Summary" by Ishikawa for an account of the experience in Japan and Taiwan. Also see Ishikawa (1981).

17. Although direct comparison is made with South Asia, it seems that it might be extended to a similar comparison between East Asia and the rest of the developing world where labor use per hectare was almost certainly lower than in Asia.

18. All these figures are from *World Development Indicators 2009*, Table 3.2. The levels of input use refer to the period 2003–5.

19. The case is documented in Khan (2004).

20. While Ethiopia implemented the most comprehensive land redistribution, it is not the case that the rest of SSA has done nothing by way of land reform. Redistributive policies have sought to give more land to landless Africans in Malawi, Namibia, South Africa, and Zimbabwe. Land titling has also been attempted in Côte d'Ivoire, Cameroon, and Uganda. The point is that the totality of efforts has nowhere succeeded in creating a system in which the egalitarian peasant farmers are the principal entrepreneurial class in the rural economy. See Nkurunziza (2006) for some details on reforms.

21. Another important factor explaining low agricultural *revenue* product per worker that may be very important in many SSA countries is the agricultural protection practiced by the advanced industrial countries. The recent increase in world food prices has probably weakened some of these disincentives at least temporarily. But the problem seems to continue in the case of cash crops like cotton and, even in the case of food, it is hard to know if the recent increase in food prices would hold.

22. The estimates in this paragraph are based on the data in different issues of the *WDI*.

23. In addition, in Burkina Faso the growth of manufacturing was about the same as of GDP.

24. These are respectively chapters 7 and 10 in Islam (2006).

25. The summaries that follow are based on the case studies and are largely derived from Khan (2005). In addition to these two, the ILO has also made case studies of Mozambique and Ghana. In the absence of overall and sectoral employment data, the Mozambique study takes a microeconomic approach, based on household-level data, to determine the importance of access to employment for poverty reduction (as expected, the effect is found to be positive). It does not provide estimates of the employment intensity of growth. See Bruck and van den Broeck (2006). The Ghana study (see Baah-Nuakoh 2006) does not shed useful light on the issue of employment intensity of industries and the employment data are older than the period of growth under review.

26. The case study calls the official estimate of the slight decline in rural poverty "a statistical myth" since "the growth rate of real agricultural per capita output has been negative and real per capita rural income has declined."

27. See Pollin et al. (2006: xiii).

28. Prominent World Bank documents on the subject include: Alby et al. (2005) and World Bank (2005).

29. See Islam (1994: ch. 2) for the documentation of the Korean case.

References

Alby, P., Azam, J. P., and Rospabe, S. (2005). "Labor Institutions, Labor-Management Relations, and Social Dialogue in Africa." Washington, DC: World Bank.

Baah-Nuakoh, A. (2006). "Economic Growth, Poverty and Employment Linkages in Ghana," Draft Final Report prepared for ILO, Dakar, September.

Bruck, T. and van den Broeck, K. (2006). *Growth, Employment and Poverty in Mozambique*, Issues in Employment and Poverty Discussion Paper 21, January.

International Labour Office (2005). *Key Indicators of the Labour Market*, 4th edition. Geneva: ILO.

—— (2007a). *Global Employment Trends Brief*, January. Geneva: ILO.

—— (2007b). *African Employment Trends*, April. Geneva: ILO.

ILO (Asian Regional Team for Employment Promotion) (1980). *Labour Absorption in Agriculture: The East Asian Experience*. Bangkok: ILO.

Ishikawa, S. (1981). *Essays on Technology, Employment and Institutions in Economic Development*. Tokyo: Kinokuniya.

Islam, R. (ed.) (1994). *Social Dimensions of Economic Reforms in Asia*. New Delhi: ILO SAAT.

—— (2006). *Fighting Poverty: The Development-Employment Link*. Boulder, CO and London: Lynne Rienner Publishers.

Khan, A. R. (1997). "Reversing the Decline of Output and Productive Employment in Rural Sub-Saharan Africa," Issues in Development Discussion Paper 17. Geneva: ILO.

—— (2004). "Agriculture, Development, and Poverty Reduction in Sudan: An Analysis of Performance and Policies," Background Paper for a UNDP project on "Macroeconomic Policies for Poverty Reduction in Sudan." Available at <http://www.azizkhan.net>.

—— (2005). *Growth, Employment and Poverty: An Analysis of the Vital Nexus Based on Some Recent UNDP and ILO/SIDA Studies*, Issues in Employment and Poverty Discussion Paper 19, October. Geneva: ILO.

Khan, A. R. and Muqtada, M. (eds.) (1997). *Employment Expansion and Macroeconomic Stability Under Increasing Globalization*. London: Macmillan.

Mazumdar, D. and Basu, P. (1997). "Macroeconomic Policies, Growth and Employment: The East and South-East Asian Experience," in A. R. Khan and M. Muqtada (eds.), *Employment Expansion and Macroeconomic Stability Under Increasing Globalization*. London: Macmillan.

Nkurunziza, J. D. (2006). "Generating Rural Employment in Africa to Fight Poverty." Paper presented at ECOSOC's High-Level Segment, New York, May 9, 2006. Yaounde: United Nations Economic Commission for Africa Sub-Regional Office for Central Africa.

Pollin, R., Epstein, G., and Heintz, J. (2006). *An Employment-Targeted Economic Program for South Africa*. New York: UNDP.

—— wa Githinji, M., and Heintz, J. (2007). *An Employment-Targeted Economic Program for Kenya*. New York: UNDP.

Sen, A. (1975). *Employment, Technology and Development*. Oxford: Clarendon Press.

World Bank (2005). "Jobs in Kenya: Concept Note," draft manuscript. Washington, DC: World Bank.

—— (relevant years). *World Development Indicators* (WDI).

16

Skills Development for Economic Growth in Sub-Saharan Africa: A Pragmatic Perspective

Yaw Ansu and Jee-Peng Tan[1]

Introduction

Sub-Saharan Africa (SSA) is acknowledged to be the critical development challenge of our time. Average per capita income in 2007 was $478 (in constant 2000 US$) compared to the average of $766 (in constant 2000 US$) for non-SSA low-income countries.[2] Among nine countries with the relevant survey data for 2000–5, poverty rates are as high as around 70 percent in Sierra Leone and Zambia, and no lower than around 35 percent in the remaining countries.[3] Underlying the low per capita income and widespread poverty are high rates of unemployment or underemployment and low levels of productivity. Across the continent, policymakers feel under pressure to provide productive job opportunities, particularly to the youth. To do this, the economies have to grow faster. Faster economic growth would require a number of preconditions which are now familiar—a stable macroeconomic environment, good governance, an environment supportive of the private sector, higher capital investment, etc.

Among the conditions, skills development—to increase productivity, to make economies more competitive, and to motivate investors to provide capital and engage in economic activities that will propel growth—is critical, but usually gets less attention than it deserves.[4] Unfortunately, however, skills development is expensive, and to be able to afford it on a sustained basis, countries have to grow in order to generate the resources and government revenues required. So, in a sense countries face a "chicken-and-egg" problem, at least in the short term: they need more skills to help accelerate growth and employment; but they also need growth in order to finance skills development. Furthermore, although African countries are, relative to other parts of the world, deficient in skilled manpower, they are also confronted with the irony that significant numbers of their trained people end up unemployed, working in areas unrelated to their (specialized and typically expensive) training or emigrating to other countries—a misallocation and waste of resources that these countries can ill afford.

This paper explores an approach to skills development aimed at helping to inform African countries' efforts to address the chicken-and-egg problem and also to reduce the waste currently involved in skills development. It entails pursuing two distinct strategies in parallel—one oriented toward results in the short term and the other toward reforms and capacity building that produce results in the medium to long term. The short-term strategy is embedded in FDI-led industrial development, and relies to a large extent on targeted training of people who already have a certain level of education (e.g., unemployed high-school or university graduates or even those already employed) in order to meet the needs of industries that the country is trying to attract or expand. The medium-term strategy involves reforming the educational system to enhance access and quality, and, more importantly, to increase its scientific and technical orientation as well as its overall responsiveness to the needs of private investors and employers. Although distinct, the two strategies are mutually reinforcing and tend to converge in the long term. They both emphasize skills development as a key for supporting national development, for attracting investment, and for supporting economic growth, export competitiveness, and industrialization. As such, the effectiveness and success of the two strategies become the concern and pursuit of the whole government, including, in particular, the Ministries of Finance and Planning, of Trade and Industry, rather than just that of the Ministries of Education or of Labor.

The paper is organized as follows. The second section outlines the rationale for and approach of a skills-intensive development strategy. The third highlights the challenges that African countries face in terms of their current low levels of skills and the pressure to create productive employment, especially for the growing populations of young people. The short-term and longer-term strategies are discussed in the fourth and fifth sections, respectively, with the latter section also pointing out how the two strategies reinforce each other over time. We then discuss some key lessons from successful education and training reformers and conclude the paper in the last section.

A skills-intensive strategy for economic development

Confronting Africa's multifaceted development challenges requires an explicit consideration of the issue of skills and human capacity.[5] The continent's weakness in this regard constrains the ability of African countries to thrive in a global trading environment where competition has intensified with the emergence of Asian economies that have been faster to build their capacities in manufacturing and services. It restricts the potential for diversification into higher-return agricultural or industrial products by reducing the ability to break into global supply chains and networks and to meet the requirements set by buyers for higher-order participation in these markets where profit margins are more lucrative. Africa's weak skills base also hampers countries' attempts to leverage on the unfolding knowledge and technology revolution to enter and compete successfully in the markets for new services and products (e.g. IT-enabled services and biotechnology). In the continent's many natural-resource-rich countries, the lack of a sufficiently well-qualified workforce narrows the scope for adding value through domestic processing of the resources and through the generation of spillover benefits to the local input-supplying industries. It also means a weaker capacity to negotiate and monitor the kinds of contracts with foreign companies that would maximize the returns to the country and minimize the adverse impacts on the environment.

Besides affecting the performance of firms, skills constraints also hamper African countries' capacity to create and manage the conditions required to foster faster growth. In particular, the capacity to plan, build, operate, and maintain physical infrastructures (i.e. transportation networks, power plants, etc.) and other capital assets is seriously compromised, as is the ability to manage the broader challenges posed by impending climate change and by the pressures of rapid population growth and urbanization. A thin skills base also makes it harder to run a civil service that can create and implement effective regulatory and governance frameworks adapted to the complexities of economic and political transactions, including decentralization, in today's world. Taken together, in both the public and private spheres of economic and social activity, a lack of adequate managerial, organizational, and administrative skills and experience, in addition to the dearth of scientific and technological skills, reduces the capacity to support industrialization and to cope with the demands of modern government.

While Africa's skills gaps are very real and deep-seated, solving them will require more than a call to increase investments in skills development. Such investments must deliver results in the short run as well as prepare a reliable and steadily growing supply of trainable (and retrainable) workers with diverse skills. In countries with mature education and training systems both needs are typically met as a matter of routine, albeit to varying degrees of excellence. Such systems have had more time to experiment with and regularize the management and operational arrangements for all parts of the whole system to work together seamlessly. In the best systems, an integrated qualifications framework exists that provides a roadmap for learners to acquire skills that are recognized by employers and qualifications that are accepted by the admissions officers of more advanced training programs. Such a system offers learners the possibility to acquire and build skills throughout life, thus enhancing their productivity and employability in a context of changing labor market conditions.

In the less well-developed context of African countries, the formal education and training system also aims, at least in rhetoric, to supply the modernizing economy with educated and skilled workers. In reality, however, most systems lack the speed, nimbleness, and capacity to provide the just-in-time and ready-to-use skills required for the pressing needs at hand. And the costs associated with training are often prohibitive. As a result, a more strategic evaluation of the short-run opportunities for skills development must be developed while the longer-term goal of reforming the whole system is addressed as a parallel, though separate, agenda. The latter will be discussed in more detail later in this paper. The shorter-term goal of investing in skills development to achieve immediate results presents a more novel challenge, in part because it often lacks ownership by a single government ministry or agency and requires a certain capacity for innovation, risk management, and networking outside of one's normal sphere of interactions. Two potential channels that can be leveraged for skills development to benefit Africa's growth and competitiveness are the inflows of foreign direct investment (FDI) and official development aid (ODA). This paper focuses mainly on the first channel.

Every foreign company that sets up operations in a country does so to take advantage of favorable local conditions for its business (see Figure 16.1). These conditions include the policy environment and its impact on the security of investments, on the ease of doing business, on the availability of state incentive packages, and on the company's after-tax profitability. They also pertain to domestic endowments in the form of physical infrastructure, connectivity, and human capital. Countries that have successfully pursued FDI-led development strategies, such as the Asian Tigers and Ireland, have been persistent in manipulating these conditions to attract the most desirable firms. From the perspective of the host country, desirable firms are those that bring the largest number of well-paying jobs, contribute to government revenue, strengthen the balance of payments position, create the best opportunities for technology transfer, and generate other spillover benefits for the domestic economy. By technology transfer we mean not just knowledge about production methods, but also knowledge about business processes and practices. The most astute host countries see the foreign firms as a source of learning that can help them step onto and climb the techno-logical ladder. Training workers according to the specifications of the foreign firm using equipment provided by the firm is a common approach. Even if the host country does not start with very highly qualified workers, the arrangement can be developed as the relationship with the foreign company evolves. As the experiences of the most successful developing and some late-industrializing countries suggest, a skills development strategy embedded in FDI-led industrialization can make a significant contribution to growth, provided it is pursued strategically to

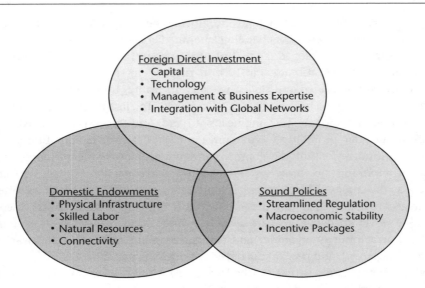

Figure 16.1 Skills development to support FDI-led industrialization
Source: Authors' construction.

build the capability of the indigenous workforce. In Ireland, the process has worked so well that Irish multinational firms have emerged and begun investing overseas, so much so that in 2004, outward FDI exceeded the inward volume (Sweeney 2008).

With regard to ODA, in addition to the direct funding of education, the inflow of funds for projects, particularly in infrastructure, to a recipient country could also be associated more consciously and aggressively with skills development. In an ODA-financed power project, for example, the capacity development component might include training for project staff to oversee the procurement of goods and services for project implementation, to process the use of funds, and to monitor progress. It might also involve training for the staff who will eventually manage the operations of the capital assets and infrastructure created by the project. In a roads or buildings project, it might involve twinning with domestic subcontractors (and suppliers) that could develop to become lead contractors. A desirable outcome of ODA-financed investments—one that warrants close attention by governments and donors alike—would be the facilitation of technology and knowledge transfer to a degree that is sufficient to equip indigenous counterparts with the skills and capacity to prepare, plan, and implement other similar operations. The extent to which ODA investments in fact do so depends on many factors, including the nature of the contracts mediating the relations between the foreign and local firms and other entities involved at all phases of project activities. An assessment of the conditions under which ODA-financed investments contribute to skills and capacity development of the recipient countries would therefore be very useful. Unfortunately, because the relevant data are scattered and not easily mobilized for such an assessment, we focus below on the opportunities for skills development embedded in FDI-led industrialization, leaving to future work an assessment of skills development in the context of ODA-funded activities.

The challenge of skills development and employment in Africa

A skills-intensive strategy for growth and competitiveness poses many practical challenges in Sub-Saharan Africa. First, it needs to take into account the sheer size of the population of young Africans, estimated at 200 million in the 12–24 age range, roughly four times the number in 1950 and yet only half the projected count in 2050; not surprisingly, most of the estimated 7–10 million Africans who enter the labor force each year are also concentrated in this age range. Second, the educational profile of the population, even in the younger cohorts who are generally better educated than their parents, reflects a weak human capital base (see Figure 16.2).[6] On average across SSA countries, fewer than 7 percent of workers between ages 25 and 34 have an upper secondary education, and only about 2 percent have received either technical/vocational training or have acquired tertiary education. While there is great diversity across countries, the picture is

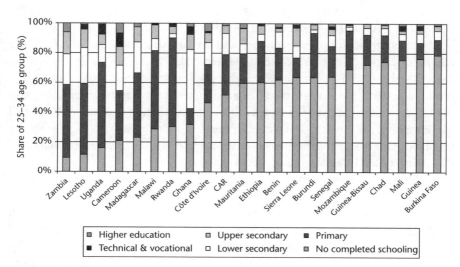

Figure 16.2 Education profile of the non-school population ages 25–34, circa 2003
Source: Authors' construction based on data in Majgaard and Mingat (forthcoming).
Note: Based on population in the age group 25–34 that are not in school at the time of survey.

Table 16.1 Percentage distribution of out-of-school population ages 15–59 by employment status, 23 SSA countries, circa 2003

		Not active: **14.0**			
		Unemployed: **6.9**			
Total population 15–59: **100**	Economically active: **86.0**	Employed: **79.1**	Informal sector: **71.0**	Farming: **51.3**	
				Non-farm: **19.6**	
			Modern sector: **8.2**	Private: **4.3**	Skilled: **4.8**
				Public: **3.9**	Unskilled: **3.4**

Source: Majgaard and Mingat (forthcoming).

one of a thin educational base on which technology-related skills might be built. Third, the current economies of SSA provide few opportunities for skills utilization (see table 16.1). Averaging across a group of twenty-three countries for which data are available, subsistence farming or the informal sector provide a livelihood to more than 70 percent of working-age adults, while the modern sector offers it to only 8 percent. Of the latter, less than 60 percent are in what might be characterized as a skilled job.

Most African businesses, even those in the modern sector, invest little in developing the skills of their workers; and among those that do, there is a strong tendency to favor the more educated among their workers. Paradoxically, with the low level of education in the general population, one might have expected businesses to snap up the available educated labor. Yet the data suggest that the demand for educated workers is in fact quite weak in Africa today. Sizable shares of educated youth with upper secondary and tertiary education find it difficult to obtain jobs when they finish their studies (see Table 16.2). The most able among the graduates find jobs abroad, but many eventually take up jobs, often in the informal sector, that do not take full advantage of their formal schooling and the implied human capital investment. The weak demand for educated labor and the limited investment in skills development of workers is consistent with the small industrial bases of African economies, their scarcity of large-scale enterprises, and their limited integration into global markets.

Breaking out of the current vicious cycle of low skills and low employment will require creative solutions. In this paper, as noted earlier, we suggest a two-track solution with one being a short-term approach that sees the existing pool of educated but unemployed or underemployed labor as a resource to be harnessed under an industry-oriented growth strategy, particularly one supported by FDI that is adapted to a country's comparative advantage and that can benefit from the opportunities created by the global economy. In parallel, we suggest a medium-to-long-term strategy of reform of the educational system to enable it to build up the pipeline of future workers whose education and training equip them

Table 16.2 Employment status by age cohort and educational attainment, average for 23 African countries, circa 2003

	25–34 years		35–49 years		50–59 years	
	Upper secondary	Higher education	Upper secondary	Higher education	Upper secondary	Higher education
Employed:						
Modern sector (%)	36	55	46	76	53	74
Informal sector (%)	46	20	47	19	41	22
Unemployed (%)	18	26	7	6	6	4
Inactive (%)	8	3	5	3	9	9
Total (%)	100	100	100	100	100	100

Source: Majgaard and Mingat (forthcoming).

to meet the economy's evolving needs as it diversifies into higher-value activities. Ideas for both tracks are elaborated below.[7]

Skills development to produce results in the short term

Foreign firms constantly review the location of their operations and have little time to wait for reforms in the whole training system to start producing the workers they seek. Thus, rather than starting by attempting to change the existing system, some of the countries that have been most successful in engendering a mutually reinforcing process of FDI flows and skills development for economic transformation and growth typically followed a more pragmatic solution which consisted of creating new institutions with explicit industry linkages, or even *ad hoc* training centers or programs linked to specific employer needs. For a time, the approach may produce what looks like an array of unconnected activities and responses. Yet with the proper strategic vision, the disparate patchwork lends itself to upgrading and consolidation, so that it can, in time, be institutionalized as an integral part of the formal system of education and training. Indeed, the interface with industry would at that point become a routine and natural *modus operandi* of the formal system. The experience of such countries as Ireland, Malaysia, and Singapore among others—all late starters in the 1960s—exemplifies the approach.

Examples of successful skills development

Singapore's experience with skills development bears recounting because the details reveal the underlying process of refining and adapting through learning-by-doing to build what is today recognized worldwide as a world-class system of technical training. The main agency in Singapore spearheading industrial development was the Economic Development Board (EDB), which was created in 1961 as a statutory board under the Ministry of Finance with the mission of attracting foreign direct investment to the country.[8] By the end of EDB's first decade, some of the key elements of its skills development strategy had been laid, including the establishment of firm-based worker training programs.[9] The effort started off with the establishment, by 1968, of six training-cum-production workshops run in parallel to the school system[10] under the Engineering Industry Development Authority (EIDA), with funding from the United Nations Development Program and technical assistance and contributions of machinery from Japan, Britain, and France (Chiang 1998). It was an inauspicious beginning, however. The six centers were an administrative headache to the EIDA which underwent three changes of management in as many years; and they were not cost-effective. At the end of four years, the government had spent $12 million on EIDA, but only 86 people had graduated. This expensive scheme was ended in 1973.

The EDB also experimented with worker retraining schemes, an effort occasioned by Britain's announcement in 1968 of its intention to close its naval base in Singapore by 1971. The implications were ominous, as the 38,000 people (or more than 5 percent of the total workforce of 717,200 in 1970) who depended on the base for employment suddenly faced the prospect of joblessness.[11] The EDB worked with the Ministry of Education to offer, on the premises of existing educational facilities, retraining courses in technical subjects, such as metalwork, machine turning and fitting, radio maintenance and repairs, and plumbing. The intention was to equip the workers who were going to lose their jobs with what was thought to be employable skills. The uptake was limited, however (only 1,749 trained in four years), and those trained only reached an elementary level of qualification. Clearly, this approach was not going to equip Singapore's labor force with the skills required for the country to succeed in its drive for industrialization.

The experience with these early starts convinced EDB's leaders that the kind of training needed to accompany its investment promotion work could not be provided within the regular technical education institutions. The programs offered in these institutions were seen as "remedial" options meant for students who did poorly in their studies; they were in any event also not producing quickly enough the skilled workers for the kinds of jobs in the foreign firms that the EDB was trying to attract. The agency therefore eschewed tinkering with the formal system of technical and vocational training, and decided instead on a leapfrogging and mission-oriented approach designed to go hand-in-hand with the EDB's investment promotion and industry development effort. The strategy was to affiliate with leading international industry partners with proven training systems, to learn the training business from them, to train to their needs, and to adapt and improve the methods to meet local needs.

The pattern set by the arrangement with the first company, the Tata Group (India's largest engineering firm at the time that made trucks, excavators, locomotives, machine tools, etc.), is instructive because it provided the prototype for scaling up a successful model of company-affiliated training. Around 1970, the EDB was trying to attract Tata to set up a precision engineering plant in Singapore and offered to partner with the company to set up a training facility that would produce workers trained in the way Tata required (i.e. that would be similar to the training schools that supplied Tata's workers in India). The government provided the land and buildings, contributed 70 percent of the operating costs of the center, and paid the stipends of the trainees (all of whom signed a bond to serve the EDB or any company as directed by the government for a period of five years).[12] The training center opened in 1972 and trained twice as many people as Tata required. Tata hired the cream of the crop of graduating trainees while EDB retained the rest as a marketing asset to attract other engineering firms to Singapore. In effect, the strategy was to build a pipeline of skills to grow a whole industry rather than to meet the needs of a single company.

By the end of the 1970s, the EDB had set up three company-affiliated training centers (besides Tata, the other companies were Rollei-Werke and Philips; see Figure 16.2). A good start had been made, but EDB felt that the centers were not yet producing the higher levels of technical skills to put the country on a path to technology-intensive development. The agency's next move was to enlist the help of foreign governments to upgrade the various training centers. Its efforts paid off, so that by end of the 1980s, five EDB Institutes of Technology were established, one of them by consolidating and upgrading three of the centers set up in the 1970s (see Figure 16.3 and endnotes). At the same time, the EDB won commitment from leading foreign companies to participate in joint training programs through a "transnational" partnership. The arrangement avoided the proliferation of new institutions—each tied to a particular company—and introduced the idea of pooling training resources to serve companies in an industry cluster. The new collaborative approach contained key ingredients for Singapore to acquire the advanced skills for growing its new technology-intensive industries: the secondment of experts to Singapore on request, the training of EDB lecturers and technical staff at the participating firms' overseas locations, assistance with curriculum and program development, donation or loan of equipment, commitment to upgrade equipment and software, and commitment of participating companies to remain in the scheme for at least three years (Chiang 1998).

Given the success of the EDB institutions, it would have been tempting to continue using them to assure a steady supply of skilled workers. Yet a decision was taken in 1993 to bring the various EDB institutes into the mainstream by integrating them into the formal education and training system, which by this time had been rationalized through consolidation and made more efficient. In this way, many of EDB's innovative concepts and practices in industry-responsive skills development found their way into the mainstream, thus benefiting the whole system. Today, the country has five polytechnics with a combined

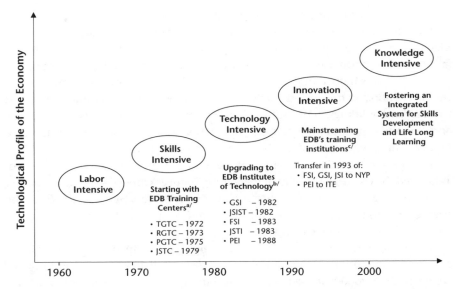

Figure 16.3 Evolution of Singapore's industrial phases and skills development, 1960–2000

Source: Authors' construction based on Chiang (1998) and Chan (2008).

[a] The acronyms refer to the Economic Development Board (EDB), the Tata-Government Training Center (TGTC), the Rollei-Government Training Center (RGTC), the Philips-Government Training Center (PGTC), the Japan-Singapore Training Center (JSTC). The TGTC, the RGTC, and the PGTC centers produced between 100 and 140 trainees a year after the initial settling-in period; while the JSTC produced about 200 a year.

[b] The acronyms refer to the German-Singapore Institute (GSI), the Japan-Singapore Institute of Software Technology (JSIST), the Japan-Singapore Technical Institute (JSTI, later upgraded to Japan-Singapore Institute, JSI), the French-Singapore Institute (FSI), the Precision Engineering Institute (PEI), an amalgamation of the TGTC, the Brown-Boveri-Government Training Center (which replaced the RGTC), and the PGTC.

[c] The acronyms refer to the Nanyang Polytechnic (NYP), established in 1992 as Singapore's fourth polytechnic) and the Institute of Technical Education (ITE, established in 1992 as the result of the restructuring and upgrading of the Vocational and Industrial Training Board).

enrollment of 60,000 students in 2006 and a three-college Institute of Technical Education (ITE) with 25,000 full-time students and 30,000 working adults in part-time courses in 2007. The structure of the system is such that close to two-thirds of secondary school graduates pursue job-related training in the polytechnics and the ITE, most of them in engineering and technology fields, while the remaining third enter junior colleges that prepare them for a university education. Nearly 60 percent of the first degrees awarded by the universities in the early 2000s were in science and engineering (National Science Board 2008). The system provides for permeability across institutions, so that the best ITE students can compete for places in the poly-technics, and the best among the polytechnics students, for places at the universities.

In Singapore, skills development is seen as part of a package used to attract FDI to help drive the country's industrialization and employment growth. Other ele-ments of the package, in addition to an overall private-sector-friendly and stable macroeconomic policy environment, included fiscal incentives, and use of an industrial park—e.g. Jurong Town Corporation—to provide first-rate infrastructure to meet the requirements of foreign firms. Although conditions have evolved over the years and the role of FDI has changed, Singapore's leaders continue to place great importance on strengthening skills development through the polytechnics and technical institutes.[13] The move to a knowledge-based economy has not diminished the role and relevance of practice-oriented learning while the context of rapid economic growth has not reduced the potential for skills mismatches and the continued need for effort to reduce them.

Ireland is another country that has successfully harnessed the FDI-skills development linkage as part of a national strategy to achieve high rates of economic growth. The Irish equivalent of Singapore's EDB was the Irish Development Authority (IDA), which was established in 1949 and given the job of attracting foreign investment in 1952. That it has played a crucial role in transforming Ireland from what was considered a "basket case" in the 1980s to economic miracle from the early 1990s onward is widely acknowledged (see Sweeney 2008). IDA targeted key sectors—ICTs, pharmaceuticals, chemicals, financial services, chemicals, among others—and developed incentive packages to attract leading foreign firms to the country. A key selling point, in addition to IDA's portfolio of incentives, was Ireland's well-educated population and the government's explicit effort to increase the output of skilled apprentices and technicians through the creation, beginning in the early 1970s, of new regional technical colleges (RTCs, eventually numbering thirteen).

These colleges greatly supplemented the modest capacity of four existing institutions to train mid-level technicians in science, engineering, business, and art and design. Perhaps more important was the change they brought about in the way educational institutions related to the business sector (O'Hare 2008). Created to serve as sources of innovation and responsiveness to the needs of firms, the RTCs offered courses with an applied orientation and they developed close ties to businesses from the outset. Their first presidents were all appointed at a young age (28–34 years old) and were chosen for their dynamism, creativity, experience in foreign countries, and freedom from the culture and ethos of the traditional institutions. They were embedded in IDA's strategy to convince foreign companies that the Irish education system was responsive to their needs to a greater degree than in other countries. Their presidents, professors, and staff participated regularly and actively in IDA's promotional functions to support the claims made by the agency to foreign firms. Because of these interactions, the new institutions were able to offer new and innovative programs in response to emerging market trends, for example, software engineering (with computer science), communications (combining business studies with linguistics), biotechnology (not biological sciences), and so on.

IDA's successful efforts to attract leading foreign companies produced a virtuous cycle of skills upgrading. The cutting-edge nature of these companies' businesses meant that they functioned, knowingly or otherwise, as educational institutions transferring knowledge—about manufacturing techniques, organization of production, management practices, marketing strategies, etc.—to national institutions (e.g. local firms, universities, colleges, and research centers). The story of Ericsson, the Swedish telecom company, in Ireland is illustrative in this regard.[14] The company initially set up a plant to build a modern telecom infrastructure for the state and had planned to leave when the job was done, leaving a skeleton staff of only ten people. Yet five years later, it was employing 1,000 people. The company's Irish managers had the foresight to learn "everything about the Ericsson business model" during their initial association with the company and (aided by the lure of state grants) succeeded in persuading the company to remain in Ireland, with a new business model directed at servicing the markets that were less attractive to the Swedes. Ericsson Ireland had the pick of the crop each year from the technical colleges and used the skilled workforce to move methodically up the value chain. It progressed from assembling and wiring electronic boards to programming and then to electronics.

Malaysia offers yet another example where skills development was organized in response to short-term industry needs, the earliest effort being in the state of Penang which hosts the country's first skills development center. Home to 1.5 million people and the country's second largest airport and its third largest seaport, Penang has undergone a dramatic economic transformation over the past few decades, as reflected in the increase in manufacturing's share of output from 12.7 percent in 1970 to 42.9 percent by 2005 (Somchit 2008). To supply the skills required to expand and upgrade the manufacturing sector, the Penang Skills Development Center (PSDC) was set up in 1989 as a tripartite collaboration between the government, industry, and academia. The government's contribution was to provide the authorizing environment (e.g. recognition of the training qualifications), to offer tax incentives for participating firms, and to contribute modest block grants for equipment and facilities (which amounted to less than $2 million in the Sixth Malaysia Plan, $2.8 million in the Seventh Plan, and $7.2 million in the Eighth Plan). The center's industry partners supplied the trainees, generated ideas and content for the training programs, identified training needs, provided equipment, and paid the fees for the trainees they sent to the center. Academia completed the tripartite collaboration by supplying the trainers and academic advisors and by developing and delivering the training programs.

Since inception, PSDC has trained more than 100,000 individuals, and is a financially self-sustaining operation with a portfolio of more than 500 courses. Its main mission continues to center on proactive human development initiatives to help the manufacturing and service industries based in Malaysia become more competitive globally. Its industry partners now comprise 142 companies, among them internationally recognized brands such as Agilent, Bosch, Braun, Dell, Fairchild, Grundig, Motorola, etc., many of which are represented on the PSDC's decision-making management council. The PSDC has progressed from a small operation in the early years offering only basic training (e.g. radio repair, basic machining, basic electronics) through several phases of maturation and it is now able to provide graduate-level engineering courses. The Malaysian government sees the PSDC as a successful model of job-oriented training and has replicated it in other states in the country.

Emerging examples from Africa

In Africa, some public–private partnerships are now underway to introduce job-related training designed to meet the short-term needs of employers. One example is the Ghana Industrial Skills Development Center (GISDC), which was launched in 2005 to provide training in mechanical, electrical, and process engineering. The seeds for this initiative were sown when TexStyles Ghana Limited, a local subsidiary of the international firm Vlisco Helmond B.V., found that other factories shared its chronic problem of being unable to find and retain employees who could service their machines. As a result, many of the factories often had to fly in troubleshooters from abroad, which added to their operating costs. To overcome the problem, the governments of Ghana and the Netherlands joined forces with the Association of Ghana Industries to set up the GISDC in 2005. Located on the premises of Tema Technical Institute (an existing government facility) but run independently, the GISDC is now operational with a governance arrangement that includes industry representatives on its decision-making board and an impressive list of firms among its partners (e.g. Guinness, Unilever, Nestle, Coca Cola, etc.).

Mozambique is another country that is attempting to set up industry-responsive training. One example is an ICT technicians training program, which again features a tripartite arrangement involving the government, an existing public training center, and industry representatives on the institution's decision-making body. As in Ghana, the program is being set up in response to a felt need by industry, in this case, for computer technicians to install and service the electronic equipment used in modern industrial facilities.

In Nigeria, concern with equipping youth with employable skills has also motivated recent efforts to augment opportunities for skills development (Yacuba 2008). Policymakers realize that many of the country's youth are leaving primary and lower secondary school without adequate skills for employment and that the country's tertiary-level institutions can absorb only about 30 percent of the 1 million candidates that each year seek entrance to the universities, polytechnics, or other tertiary-level institutions. To provide more options, the government has started to process the certification and accreditation of private providers that meet certain criteria (including a governance structure that includes industry representation) to qualify as Vocational Enterprise Institutions (VEIs targeting those with nine years of schooling) or Innovation Enterprise Institutions (IEIs targeting those with twelve years of schooling). These institutions provide practical training in target areas, among them ICT, telecommunications, computer hardware engineering, refrigeration and air-conditioning, welding and fabrication, petroleum geosciences, building technology, film and TV production, paralegal studies, fashion design, hospitality and tourism, etc. So far, seventy-five institutions have been licensed to operate, with more in the pipeline to be certified and accredited.

The foregoing examples reflect emerging interest among African countries and attempts to provide market-responsive options for technical and vocational training. In all three countries, the initiatives are still very new and will therefore require a period of experimentation and adaptation to local conditions before they can prove their worth and relevance to the countries' industrialization strategy. Given the well-known failures of many training schemes in Sub-Saharan Africa and elsewhere in the developing world, skepticism about these new initiatives is understandable. While their success is not guaranteed, they nonetheless inspire hope in light of the lessons from other low-income economies that have prospered by developing skills as an explicit part of their industrialization and economic growth strategy. These lessons suggest three features that are salient to the new models for training: (a) a tight alignment between the agenda for skills development and the broader strategy for industrialization and economic growth, with FDI helping to facilitate the process; (b) training institutions that are outside of the traditional education system and that are thus more able to react quickly, flexibly, and innovatively to industry needs; and (c) governance arrangements in training institutions that encourage close involvement by industry (e.g. through representation on the boards of the training institutions) in defining training curricula, in providing equipment and trainers, in finance, in the exposure of students and faculty to industry-driven projects e.g. work placements, etc.

Longer-term reform of the education and training system

The experience of countries that have succeeded with a skills-intensive path to development suggests that the short-term strategy discussed above needs to be accompanied by sustained effort over the longer term to improve the entire education system, by expanding enrollments, by raising the quality and relevance of learning, and by preparing a pipeline of trainable entrants into the labor market. Policymakers in these countries attended to the immediate needs of industrialization while simultaneously keeping an eye on the longer-term goal of raising the technological sophistication of the whole economy and diversifying its scope of activities. By ensuring coherence and mutual reinforcement between the short and longer-run strategies for skills development, these policymakers made it possible for their countries to "climb the technology ladder while raising the floor" (IDB 2006). Below we take stock of Africa's current situation and identify some of the key challenges for the reform agenda.

Overcoming a flawed legacy

African countries that seek a skills-intensive path out of poverty struggle with a legacy of inadequate investment in education in the past. A comparison of South Korea and Ghana, for example, exemplifies the big gaps that now separate them after decades of divergent paths in the education sector (Figure 16.4). South Korea pursued a policy of sustained investment to universalize primary education, while progressively expanding secondary and tertiary education. As a result, the share of the Korean population age 15 and older with secondary education rose from 17 percent in 1960, to 49 percent in 1980, and 55 percent in 2000, while the corresponding shares for tertiary education were 3 percent, 9 percent, and 26 percent. In Ghana, the educational profile of the population age 15 and older also improved, but mostly between 1960 and 1980; thus, while the share with secondary education rose from less than 2 percent in 1960 to 26 percent by 1980, the increase was followed by two dismal decades of stagnation, reflecting the general stagnation in the country's economy. As a result, forty years after starting from 1960 with a slight disadvantage *vis-à-vis* Korea, Ghana had fallen far behind

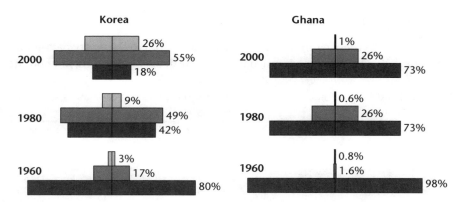

Figure 16.4 Education profiles of the working population in Korea and Ghana, 1960–2000

Source: World Bank (2005), *Expanding Opportunities and Building Competencies for Young People: A New Agenda for Secondary Education* © by The International Bank for Reconstruction and Development/The World Bank 1818 H Street, NW, Washington, DC 20433, USA.

Note: The working population refers to the population aged 15 and over; for each year, the top block refers to the share with tertiary education, the middle block to the share with secondary schooling, and the bottom block, to the share with primary or no schooling.

by 2000. The data for other African countries paint a similar picture of serious lags in the educational profile of the population.

Expanding educational coverage

In recent years, the situation has improved as African countries make progress in expanding coverage. A key turning point was the 2000 World Education Forum in Dakar, Senegal, at which 164 governments worldwide, among them those of African countries, joined with partner organizations to make a collective commitment to dramatically expand educational opportunities for children, youth, and adults. That African countries acted on this commitment is evident from the data on enrollment (Table 16.3). In primary education, the gross enrollment ratio for a group of thirty-three low-income Sub-Saharan countries gained an average of 3.1 percentage points a year between 2005 and 2009 and an average of 2.8 points a year between 1999 and 2005, compared with a rate of only 0.8 points a year between 1990 and 1999. More tellingly, while the primary school completion rate was practically unchanged between 1990 and 1999, it grew by an average of 1.9 points a year between 1999 and 2005 and 2.1 points a year between 2005 and 2009. The pace of increase was even faster in secondary and higher education. Even with the rapid pace of increase, however, Africa continues to lag behind other world regions (see Figure 16.5). An important part of Africa's challenge is therefore to continue expansion of educational opportunities to equip today's children and youth with the human capital they need to improve their future livelihoods.

Improving learning outcomes

Hanushek and Woessmann (2008) in their analysis of cross-country data found that economic growth depends much more on the quality of learning than on the

Table 16.3 Indicators of educational coverage in low-income Sub-Saharan Africa, 1990, 1999, 2005, and 2009

	1990	1999	2005	2009
Primary education				
Gross enrollment ratio (%)	67.8	75.7	92.5	105.0
Grade 1 gross intake rate (%)	74.0	80.9	105.4	118.9
Completion rate (%)	42.4	43.0	54.6	63.1
Secondary education				
Lower secondary gross enrollment ratio (%)	18.8	25.4	35.5	45.4
Upper secondary gross enrollment ratio (%)	8.3	11.3	15.4	21.2
Higher education				
Gross enrollment ratio (%)	2.2	3.1	4.0	4.6
Students per 100,000 inhabitants	160	245	291	450

Source: Majgaard and Mingat (forthcoming).

Note: Data reflect the simple averages of indicators for 33 low-income countries in Sub-Saharan Africa.

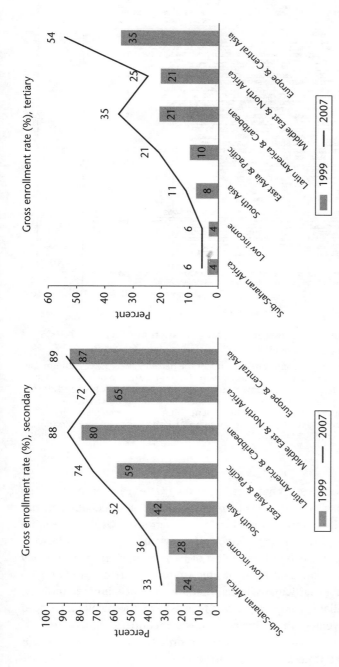

Figure 16.5 Coverage in secondary and tertiary education in Sub-Saharan Africa and other world regions, 1999 and 2007

Source: Authors' construction based on World Bank EdStats data available at <http://databank.worldbank.org/ddp/home.do?queryId=189> (accessed March 28, 2011).

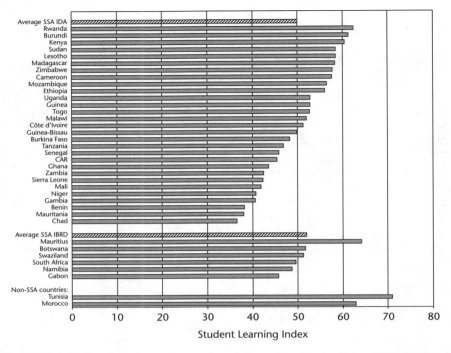

Figure 16.6 Student learning outcomes in primary education in Africa, 1996–2005

Source: Majgaard and Mingat (forthcoming).

Note: The student learning index is a composite measure of the percentage of the curriculum that students have mastered at the time of testing. It ranges from 1–100 and is based on a consolidation of the results of regional or international assessments tests administered between 1996 and 2003 to students at various grades in primary school (in some instances in lower secondary grades). These tests include UNESCO's Monitoring Learning Achievement (MLA), the *Programme d'Analyse des Systèmes Educatifs de la Confemen* (PASEC), and the Southern African Consortium for Monitoring Educational Quality (SACMEQ). See Majgaard and Mingat (forthcoming) for additional details on the index.

extent of educational coverage. What this implies is that expansion of coverage is only part (perhaps not even the most important part) of the challenge that African countries face. If tomorrow's workers are to perform jobs that are more skills-intensive than the jobs of their parents, and if they are to do their jobs well, today's students will need a strong foundation of basic competencies in literacy and numeracy, and many of them must be able to build on this foundation to acquire higher-order skills, particularly in mathematics, science, and technology. Piecing together the available comparative data reveals a worrisome picture indeed (see Figure 16.6): on average, the primary or lower secondary student in low-income Sub-Saharan Africa countries has mastered only half of what he or she is expected to know at the time of testing; and their peers in the middle-income countries in Sub-Saharan Africa did not fare much better.

Table 16.4 Eighth graders' performance on international tests in Africa and other selected countries, 2003 and 2007 (percentage scoring below 400)[b]

Country[a]	Mathematics		Science	
	2003	2007	2003	2007
Korea	2	3	5	3
Singapore	1	2	2	7
International Average	**20**	**33**	**22**	**25**
Malaysia	7	18	5	20
Jordan	40	39	20	9
Indonesia	45	52	39	35
Egypt	48	53	41	45
Botswana	68	68	65	65
Ghana	91	83	87	81
South Africa[c]	90	–	87	–

Sources: Martin et al. (2004) and Mullis et al. (2004), respectively, for South Africa's 2003 scores on science and mathematics; and Martin et al. (2008) and Mullis et al. (2008) for the 2007 scores for all countries shown. Detailed reports are available online at <http://timss.bc.edu/>.

[a] The data are from the International Mathematics and Science Study (TIMSS) which periodically administers standardized tests to students. Average scores are available from the sources cited above. Here the data show the percentage failing to reach the lowest of the four TIMSS performance benchmarks, these being scores of 625, 550, 475, and 400 denoting, respectively, advanced, high, intermediate, and low levels of performance. A score of 400 suggests that the test taker has "only some basic mathematical knowledge" and "recognizes some basic facts from the life and physical sciences."

[b] A total of 49 and 59 countries, respectively, participated in the 2003 and 2007 TIMSS.

[c] Did not participate in the 2007 TIMSS.

Test scores from the Trends in International Mathematics and Science Study (TIMSS) in which three African countries—Botswana, Ghana, and South Africa—participated along with other generally more developed countries confirm the scale of the challenge (Table 16.4). Botswana and Ghana participated in both the 2003 and 2007 TIMSS while South Africa participated only in the 2003 study. Over time Ghana's performance in both mathematics and science appears to have improved while Botswana's scores have stagnated. In all three countries, however, the scores are among the lowest in the sample of participating countries, with very high shares of eighth graders failing to attain even a basic level of knowledge in mathematics and in science. Clearly, these countries' education systems are not yet producing future workforces with the skills required to compete in the global marketplace. A key objective of system reform should therefore be to strengthen the foundational skills at the primary- and secondary-school levels, by focusing particularly on curriculum reform, textbook development, teacher training, and school leadership programs.

Building a pipeline of technical and scientific personnel

Given the weak foundations in primary and secondary education, many African countries find it difficult to boost tertiary-level enrollments in science and technology (Table 16.5). These fields of studies are deemed to be particularly important to enable Africa to climb out of their low-skill trap. In 2003–4, the share of university students in

Table 16.5 Share of tertiary students enrolled in science and technology disciplines, Africa, 1980–2003/4

	1980	1986–9	2003–4
Angola	54	64	38
Benin	27	21	30
Botswana	22	9	23
Burkina Faso	20	32	32
Burundi	31	30	26
Cameroon	29	32	33
Central African Republic	17	27	36
Chad	n.d.	12	17
Congo, Republic of	18	13	16
Ethiopia	57	40	31
Ghana	46	42	35
Kenya	44	32	47
Lesotho	12	10	13
Madagascar	40	43	35
Malawi	34	17	59
Mali	24	42	33
Mozambique	47	61	37
Niger	44	31	29
Nigeria	41	39	58
Rwanda	34	26	34
Senegal	33	39	26
Togo	33	24	12
Uganda	46	22	18
Average	34	31	31

Sources: Brossard and Foko (2008); Saint (1992); Teferra and Altbach (2003) cited in World Bank (2008b).
Note: n.d. denotes no data.

these disciplines averaged only 31 percent, similar to the shares in the 1980s and 1990s.[15] The weak pipeline of scientific, engineering, and technological skills is consistent with Africa's meager contribution to the world's science and engineering publications (about 1.37 percent for all of Africa in 2005–6, of which South Africa's contribution alone was 0.37 percent and with the small number of patent applications filed by residents in Africa (UNESCO Science Report 2005). Many African governments see the scarcity of scientists, engineers, and technologists as an obstacle that frustrates their countries' access to the world's storehouse of scientific and technical knowledge; reduces the ability of their public agencies and private enterprises to apply this knowledge to raise productivity; and impedes their country's success in seeking a competitive edge in the global economy. A momentum is being built up under the aegis of the African Union's NEPAD initiative to rectify the situation and countries are also beginning to make their own efforts in this regard.

Clearly, building a pipeline is not the same as producing the skilled workers that employers seek. An important challenge is therefore to ensure that those who graduate from the system leave equipped with employable skills. Experience in many countries suggests that training institutions which develop close ties with prospective employers and which regularly seek employers' input to develop the curriculum enjoy the best results. In the most developed countries, such as

Sweden, employers' input is sought even for decisions about the content of what is taught in high schools (IDB 2006).

Strengthening technical and vocational training

An important challenge is creating a quality technical and vocational training subsystem within the educational system. In many countries, this subsystem is the weakest part. There are many difficulties that countries have to face in overcoming this weakness. For example, clear choices have to be made regarding the relationship between the technical and vocational system on the one hand and the secondary and tertiary systems on the other. Will the technical and vocational system be pre-secondary, integrated with secondary education, run parallel with the secondary education system, or will it be a post-secondary system? If a post-secondary system, how does it relate to the universities; will they be degree-granting? Another difficulty is the often-times negative image of technical and vocational education which makes it difficult to attract bright and ambitious students.

Regarding the positioning of the technical education system, countries have successfully applied different options. However, one option that seems not to work well is the one that introduces additional technical or vocational-oriented courses into a secondary-school curriculum; it leads to neither a good secondary-school system nor a good technical/vocational system. For one thing, a technical and vocational education system done well is expensive—up to three times as costly as general secondary education and in the industrial training programs, about as costly as an academic university course in the social sciences (Mingat, Ledoux, and Rakotomalala 2010). This is mainly because high-quality programs require skilled teachers with industry experience and up-to-date equipment used in industry to ensure students are getting the relevant training. In addition, students need internships or apprenticeships in industry. For many countries, it is simply not possible to afford the cost of quality technical education or find meaningful internships for all secondary-school students. It therefore makes sense to focus on a subset of the student population, train them to high standards, and ensure that other requisite government economic growth and industrialization policies are in place so they can get jobs when they graduate.

Also, the prospects of well-paying jobs upon graduation, combined with a sustained promotional campaign involving the high leadership, not just the Minister responsible for Technical and Vocational Education or for Labor, could be used to change the public's image of technical and vocational education for the better. It is important to emphasize that promotional campaigns and exhortations not backed by demonstrated enhanced job prospects for technical and vocational school graduates are unlikely to be successful. Another way to address the challenge is to build "bridges and ladders" into the educational system to enable movement, both ways, between the technical and vocational part of the system and the general/academic part.

Strengthening universities' applied research capabilities and their links to industry

A skills-intensive strategy for growth in Africa cannot ignore the potential contribution of the universities.[16] Yet bringing about the desired improvements will present difficult reform challenges. On the supply side, governments need to focus on several tasks, among them strengthening the governance of these institutions by granting them more autonomy and fostering greater competition among them; encouraging a more diverse mix of institutions, particularly self-financing private ones; subjecting all institutions to quality assurance mechanisms; improving the qualifications of the academic staff; providing incentives for collaborative research between tertiary institutions and firms in key strategic areas relevant to the growth agenda; fostering collaboration across institutions; and introducing measures to put tertiary institutions on a path to sustainable financing, including the mobilization of other sources of funding to supplement government budgetary allocations. At the same time, demand-side policies will be needed to forge stronger links between tertiary education and industry, so as to foster productivity-led growth and development of the leading sectors of the economy. Promising actions by the government include: the provision of incentives for knowledge-intensive industries and the creation of science parks in the vicinity of leading universities; the offer of seed capital for high-tech start-ups, coupled with funding for R&D by public and private firms and other entities; and support for public–private mechanisms to facilitate student and faculty involvement in collaboration with firms on research, design, testing, or product development.

Easing financial constraints

Given that most African countries face an unfinished business of providing adequately in terms of access and quality for basic and secondary education, an increased focus on scientific and technical education, which would require more resources for tertiary education, would certainly present funding challenges. With education expenditures of 4 to 5 percent of GDP, and around 20 percent of budget expenditures, many governments in Africa are already spending on par, if not more, than those in East Asia and elsewhere (UNESCO 2007). Certainly they should make additional efforts to contribute more, but realistically (particularly for the countries that already devote substantial resources to the sector) the scope for such efforts is not that wide. Where will the needed extra resources come from?

First, through reforms to promote efficiency, governments could try to achieve more with what they spend. Second, students in the tertiary stream could be asked to contribute more to their education. This will not be easy, but it would be more manageable if students face enhanced prospects of securing well-paying jobs after graduation. This is one area where the strategy aimed at generating FDI investment, economic growth, and employment growth in the short term could facilitate the medium-term strategy of systemic change. This strategy, if successful, can powerfully change expectations of students and their parents. Seeing the expansion of well-paying jobs in the economy, they are more likely to dip into their own resources or go into debt (through well-designed student loan schemes) to invest in education. Another way in which the short-term strategy could ease the funding constraint and facilitate medium-term systemic change is for private firms that have set up or are expanding operations in the country to be encouraged and incentivized to play a more active role in improving the existing training arrangements. As has been the case elsewhere, such firms could be a source of equipment, expertise, and finance. Furthermore, a growing economy, spurred by the short-term strategy, could increase government revenue, making available more resources, even at the same GDP or budget shares, to the education sector.

Lessons from successful education and training system reformers

African countries must naturally find their own paths for building and reforming their education and training system to support a skills-intensive development strategy. Yet the experience of countries that have achieved some measure of success in this regard yields some useful lessons for consideration. Three mutually reinforcing ingredients seem essential: (i) the exercise of strategic and visionary leadership by top-level policymakers, including those outside the education sector; (ii) the use of longer time horizons for policy development and implementation; and (iii) systematic and persistent effort to create and maintain backward and forward linkages within the education sector as well as between the sector and the economy. The experience of East Asian countries in particular demonstrate how these elements have worked together to foster sustained development of the education system, which in turn contributed to the dramatic transformation of their economies since the 1960s. Below we elaborate briefly on each of them.

Exercising strategic and visionary leadership

Reforming the education and training system will often be difficult. In particular, achieving the objectives of expanded access, improved quality at the primary and secondary levels, and also building up the tertiary levels within a severely constrained budget envelope will likely require trade-offs—not only between education and other sectors, but also among and within education subsectors. In the early years of East Asia's development, public spending for education as a share of the GDP was modest but rose as the economy grew, reflecting a commitment to invest in building up the system. In 1960, for example, it was 2 percent in Korea, 2.8 percent in Singapore, and 2.3 percent in Thailand; by 1989, the figure had risen to 3.6 percent in Korea, 3.4 percent in Singapore, and 3.2 percent in Thailand; and by 2004, it had risen to 4.6 percent in both Korea and Thailand (Fredriksen and Tan 2008).[17] Within the education sector, expenditures were typically prioritized to enroll all children in primary school followed by expansion to universalize eight to ten years of basic education. The bias of public expenditures towards primary education usually meant that other levels of education, where society's elites are typically over-represented, had to rely relatively more on fees as a source of financing.[18] It also meant that access to post primary levels was managed carefully to avoid expanding the system beyond its capacity to provide services of reasonable quality. In the meantime, the emphasis on primary education did not eliminate support for other levels of the system or careful deployment of the resources and hard choices within the primary subsector. Korea, for example, decided initially to concentrate subsidies on rural schools and tolerated, for a time, huge class sizes (sometimes exceeding 90 pupils per class) in order to stretch the budget; Singapore operated almost all its schools on double shift well into the late 1990s; and Vietnam prioritized support to enable all schools to meet a national minimum standard of quality for inputs.

While most policy trade-offs are politically difficult, they are generally a bit easier to make in a growing economy (where both government revenues and personal incomes would be growing) than in a stagnant one, as the experiences of some East Asian countries attest. Yet even in the relatively favorable context of these countries, it took exceptional leadership to envision a future of shared growth in which as many citizens as possible would have a fair chance to acquire the knowledge and skills to make a decent living. It also took perseverance to convince the skeptics of the advantages of the approach and their self-interest in supporting it (World Bank 1993). To an important extent, the results achieved by the most successful East Asian countries reflect their leaders' commitment to raising living standards for everyone, their clarity of vision about the role of education in nation-building and economic development, their political savvy in mobilizing public support for policies that may overturn long-standing arrangements, and their ability to organize and coordinate the implementation of evolving reform agendas that are at once complex and fragile.

Using longer time horizons

The main consideration is a practical one: It takes time to transform the entire system and gear it to prepare today's students for tomorrow's job market. In the 1960s, no one could have foreseen that poor countries in East Asia would one day join the ranks of developed nations and become, in certain fields, industry leaders themselves. Yet their leaders took the long view, envisioned where the country could be in ten to twenty years' time, and concluded that the education system must equip all students with a good foundation in mathematics, science, and language skills, in order for the students and the country to prosper in tomorrow's labor market and global economy. Details of the vision may differ across countries, but the leaders invariably appreciated the strong influence of science, technology, and ICTs on economic competitiveness and realized that technical skills were essential for productive engagement in the emerging landscape of foreign direct investment, exports, transnational business partnerships, global supply chains, niche markets, lean manufacturing, etc.

Once a broad consensus emerged on the need for technically competent workers with good communications skills, East Asian policymakers adopted a suitably long horizon to align the education system accordingly. This approach provides stability for the system, allows time to assemble ideas and technical resources to guide the reforms, encourages learning-by-doing, and offers a framework to plan a proper sequencing of implementation steps. In Singapore, for example, when policymakers realized that moving production up the technology ladder would be frustrated by insufficient numbers of students with the relevant technical skills, they revamped the system to give all children a basic education of ten years with an emphasis on mathematics and science, so that even the weakest students in each cohort could keep up with the courses in the technical and vocational training institutes that trained technicians for the country's emerging industrial sectors during the late 1980s and early 1990s (Law 2008).

Strengthening the foundational skills takes time because investments in curriculum and textbook development, teacher training, and school leadership programs produce results only with a lag. Several of the reforming Asian countries, such as Singapore, Korea, and Hong Kong (China) nonetheless achieved continuous gains in their standing in international tests over a period of many years, moving from a fair level of performance in the mid 1980s in the case of Singapore and Hong Kong (China) to nearly top ranking by 2000 onwards (Mourshed, Chijioke, and Barber 2010; Woessmann with Hanushek 2010).[19] A common element across these countries is the use of external validation and benchmarking to track performance and motivate reform for sustained improvement. Especially noteworthy is that test scores rose as a result of systemic reforms that focused on different challenges at each stage of progress.[20] The experience suggests that it is never too early to expect education systems to improve learning outcomes, even if results show up only after a lag.

The long time horizons involved in reforming education and training systems make even more salient the two-prong strategy proposed in this paper. The strategy recognizes that it will take time to design and implement sustained reforms to change the character of the entire system, not only in terms of its ethos and mission, but also in its operational functions, so as to align the system with the country's national development agenda. In the meantime, the country will need a parallel, just-in-time, and highly responsive mechanism to provide the skilled labor that industry requires now in order to improve productivity and competitiveness and to expand into new markets.

Fostering backward and forward linkages

This is the third essential ingredient for sustained development of the whole education system. The underlying idea is simple: if the goal is to prepare students for tomorrow's jobs, it makes obvious sense to establish close collaboration between educators, employers, and economic policymakers and others whose job is to scan the horizon for future trends and evaluate their implications for the economy. In the upper levels of the education system where the majority of students may be just one or two years away from entering the labor market, this collaboration in the most successful countries takes such forms as having industry representatives help define and shape the curricula, promoting student participation in industry projects as a routine part of their studies, encouraging student internships with employers, and so on. Graduating students thus leave the system with ready-to-use skills and even job offers in hand.

For the system as a whole, however, alignment with the growth agenda requires a deeper collaboration between educators and employers and economic policy makers, one that extends farther into the system where students are possibly still many years away from entering the labor force. A recent study that compared several Latin American countries (Costa Rica, El Salvador, and Recife, Brazil) with Sweden illustrates what it means for an education system to prepare students for jobs of the future (IDB 2006). In Sweden, policymakers expect nearly all 19-year-olds to have learnt mathematics, science, and technology up to a specific level, so that the economy can count on having a critical mass of youth with the technical preparation to succeed in further studies or in challenging jobs. The researchers found that Swedish youth are taught mathematics and science as disciplines for problem-solving (for applied purposes), not as ends in themselves. These subjects are thus not academic studies for the elite few but essential skills that expand options in life for all students. By contrast, in Latin America, the education system values abstract and theoretical learning at all levels, including the university. Mathematics and science are taught as free-standing subjects with little appeal and relevance to the majority of students. Many students drop out early and among those who stay, very few choose mathematics and science for further studies. As a result the school system is failing to produce the critical mass of people with core skills to help the economy become more technologically sophisticated.

Conclusion

Skills development for economic growth is a daunting yet indispensable task in Sub-Saharan Africa. Without a skilled workforce, countries blunt their competitive edge in today's global trading environment, reduce their ability to benefit from the global progress in science and technology, and hamper their capacity to cope with the serious environmental, health, and social challenges that they face. The lack of a skilled workforce also makes countries less attractive to potential investors who might provide capital, bring know-how, and serve as bridges to connect the domestic economy more closely to global networks of markets, all of which can help to spur growth. While there is little doubt that skills development is desirable, it remains an elusive goal because the costs are high and typically beyond the capacity of Sub-Saharan governments to finance to the extent and quality required. Thus, instead of enjoying a virtuous cycle in which economic growth generates the resources for investment in skills development which in turns helps boost economic productivity and growth, Africa's policymakers face a chicken-and-egg dilemma in which the lack of skills stifles economic growth which in turn reduces countries' financial capacity to invest in skills development, thus reinforcing their economic disadvantage.

In this paper, we have proposed a two-prong strategy to get out of the chicken-and-egg stalemate, inspired to a large extent by the strategies followed by some of the most successful East Asian economies during the early years of their development experience. The strategy recognizes that in order to be sustainable, skills development to foster growth in low-income economies must deliver results in the short run to meet industry needs and spur growth, while at the same time addressing the longer-run agenda of enhancing the pipeline of future workers. The short-run prong of the strategy contains three salient features: tight alignment with the country's economic development plan, especially plans to attract skills-using FDI; institutional arrangements (possibly, initially outside the formal education system) that allow quick, nimble, and flexible responses to employers' requirements for skilled labor, particularly employers in the leading economic sectors; and close engagement of employers in designing curricula, in defraying costs, and in fostering links between industry and the training institutions. The longer-run prong of the strategy involves the more traditional task of improving the performance of the whole system, a priority being to enable as many children as possible to acquire a strong foundation in literacy and numeracy skills as a basis for future learning and skills acquisition. While the two prongs may proceed initially as separate agendas, they would converge over time through a process of consolidation, mainstreaming, and streamlining. Ideally, the result would be a system of education and training that is sensitive to demand signals and that uses the information to equip today's children and youth with the knowledge and competencies required for success in tomorrow's job market. Achieving this dynamic relationship between the supply of and demand for skills is a major challenge, but as the policymakers and educators of other fast-developing countries have shown, it can be attained with the exercise of visionary and strategic leadership coupled with a learning-by-doing approach to implementation in order to achieve results in both the short and long run.

Notes

1. At the time of writing the authors were respectively Sector Director of the Africa Region Human Development Department and Advisor of the Human Development Network, of the World Bank. Currenty, they are, respectively, Chief Economist, Africa Center for Economic Transformation (ACET), Accra, Ghana; and Advisor, Education Department, Human Development Network, World Bank. The views expressed are their own and should not be attributed to the World Bank or to its Board of Directors. The authors wish to thank, without implication, Paul Mahler, Kirsten Majgaard, and Petra Righetti for their help in preparing this paper. In addition, they acknowledge the insightful comments from Akbar Noman and two anonymous reviewers that have helped to improve the paper. All remaining errors are the sole responsibility of the authors.
2. The data for Sub-Saharan Africa refer to 38 countries (excluding South Africa and five other countries with per capita GDP exceeding South Africa's), while the data for non-African low-income countries refer to 16 Asian countries plus Haiti and Yemen. All data are from the World Development Indicators published by the World Bank at <http://ddp-ext.worldbank.org/ext/DDPQQ/member.do?method=getMembers&userid=1&queryId=135>.
3. Data are from World Bank (2008a).
4. The human capital framework provides the basis for our making the link between skills development and growth. Our purpose here is neither to revisit this framework nor to add to the vast empirical evidence (see, for example, the survey by Krueger and Lindhal 2001) on the relation between education and skills (typically proxied by educational attainment) and growth or productivity. Our view is that the accumulated evidence, from both microeconomic and macroeconomic studies, supports, on balance, the existence of such a link. The most recent studies address the data shortcomings in previous studies that find no link (e.g. Cohen and Soto 2007; Baten and Zanden 2008); they also add important clarifications showing, for example, that the quality of education matters more than its quantity (e.g. Hanushek and Woessmann 2008); that the impact on growth depends on a country's ability to make productive use of schooling investments (e.g. Rogers 2008); and that the contribution of human capital depends on a country's distance to the technological frontier, and the extent of skills-biased technical change in the economy (e.g. Vandenbussche, Aghion, and Meghir 2006; Kaboski 2009).
5. See World Bank (2008b) for a more detailed discussion.
6. As various writers have noted, the human capital base of African countries is also compromised by the wide educational disparities among population groups within countries, especially between boys and girls and between rural and urban groups (see, for example, Sender, Cramer, and Oya 2005) and by the burden of the HIV/AIDS epidemic and other diseases (see for example, Schultz 2004).
7. The potential role of the diaspora has received attention in recent years, given the preponderance of the highly educated among the stock of the some 16 million African emigrants in 2005 (Ratha and Xu 2008). While it is beyond the scope of this paper to develop the theme in more detail, the diaspora is clearly a source of finance, skills and entrepreneurial talent that could, if appropriately linked to home country institutions and businesses, make a contribution to a skills-intensive development in the home country, as exemplified by the experience of Taiwan (China), and more recently by

that of China and India (see, for example, Hsueh, Hsu, and Perkins 2001 and Kuznetsov 2006). This paper also does not address the issue of vocational training for the informal sector in Africa; for a recent treatment of the subject, see Walther with Filipiak 2007, which reports on the experience in seven African countries.

8. The EDB is now a statutory board under the Ministry of Trade and Industry.

9. It is noteworthy that in evaluating three decades of the EDB's contribution to economic development in Singapore, Low et al. (1993) concluded that the organization's manpower and skills development schemes were its greatest innovation in supporting the country's industrialization effort. Over time, these schemes probably improved the country's ability to emulate what the then Minister of Finance felt was an important strength of its competitors in the 1960s, namely, "an aggressive importation of foreign know-how and its adaptation to local conditions, frequent cases of the separation of imported know-how from imported capital or management participation" (Hon 2004).

10. These workshops included: the Prototype Production Training Centre, the Metal Industries Development Centre, the Electromechanical Training Centre, the Electrochemical Training Centre, the Woodworking Industries Development Centre, and the Precision Engineering Development Centre.

11. Data from Chiang (1998) and from Government of Singapore (1996).

12. The principles underlying this approach to meeting the skills needs of companies that invested in Singapore was not limited to the higher-level technical skills. As retold in a personal encounter with P.Y. Huang, chairman of the EDB during 1982–5, the provision of a job-ready pipeline of workers also formed part of the package of incentives to attract the labor-intensive garment companies that were attracted in the 1960s to help create jobs.

13. See for example, the Distinguished Guest Speaker presentation by Singapore's Minister for Finance, Tharman Shanmugaratnam (a former Minister for Education), at the July 15–17, 2009 Conference in Tunis that was organized by the World Bank, the African Development Bank, and the Association for the Development of Education in Africa for African Ministers of Finance and of Education on the theme of "Sustaining the Education and Economic Momentum in Africa Amidst the Current Global Financial Crisis" (see <http://www.adeanet.org/adeaPortal/programs/en_MinConf-EducationFinance-July-2009.jsp>).

14. See Sweeney (2008: ch. 3) for additional details on the story of Ericsson in Ireland.

15. Internationally comparable data are scarce, but the following comparison offers an indication of Africa's lagging enrollments in science and technology: in Malaysia, 53 percent of tertiary-level graduates in 2006 graduated with degrees in science and technology-related fields (i.e. agriculture, engineering, manufacturing, construction, health and welfare, and science); in South Africa, Sub-Saharan Africa's most advanced economy, the corresponding figure was only 27 percent (UNESCO Institute for Statistics in EdStats 2009, available at <www.worldbank.org/education/edstats>).

16. See World Bank (2008b).

17. The corresponding figure for Singapore, 3.1 percent, pertains to 2005. In Sub-Saharan African countries, public spending on education as a percentage of the GDP also rose, from an average of 2.4 percent in 1960 to 4.1 percent in 1989. However, the stagnant economic conditions in the 1980s and 1990s reduced the real value of the expenditures and made it very difficult to manage the trade-offs.

18. In Korea in 1989, for example, the share of total expenditures paid by families was 2 percent for primary education, 42 percent for junior secondary education, and more than 70 percent for senior secondary and college and university education (Fredriksen and Tan 2008).

19. Mourshed, Chijioke, and Barber (2010) classify the performance of 17 school systems based on the results of various international and national tests administered over the years across multiple subjects, including the Trends in International Mathematics and Science Study (TMSS), Program for International Student Assessment (PISA), Progress in International Reading Literacy Study (PIRLS), National Assessment of Educational Progress (NAEP). The scores on these tests were normalized into a single universal scale which is equivalent to the 2000 PISA test. On this scale, a difference of 38 points is equivalent to about one school year; school systems were classified into 5 levels of performance as follows: Excellent >560 (achieved so far only by Finland); Great 520–60; Good 480–520; Fair 440–80; Poor <440.

20. Mourshed, Chijioke, and Barber (2010) note in their analysis the following patterns among the 17 systems in the progress from one level of performance to the next. Going from poor to fair performance levels, reforms typically prioritized supporting students to attain literacy and math basics, by providing "scaffolding for low-skilled teachers, fulfilling all basic student needs, and bringing all schools up to a minimum threshold of quality." Going from fair to good, reforms focused on consolidating system foundations, by producing "high quality performance data, ensuring teacher and school accountability, and creating appropriate financing, organization structure, and pedagogy." Going from good to great, reforms emphasized making teaching and school leadership a full-fledged profession, by "putting in place the necessary practices and career paths to ensure the profession is as clearly defined as those in medicine and law." Going from great to excellent, the reforms focused on decentralizing the locus of improvement in the schools, by introducing peer-based learning through school-based and system-wide interaction, as well as supporting system-sponsored innovation and experimentation."

References

Baten, J. and Luiten van Zanden, J. (2008). "Book Production and the Onset of Modern Economic Growth," *Journal of Economic Growth*, 13 (3): 217–35.

Brossard, M. and Foko, B. (2008). "Costs and Financing of Higher Education in Sub-Saharan Africa." Washington, DC: World Bank.

Chan, C. B. (ed.) (1998). *Heart Work: Stories of How EDB Steered the Singapore Economy from 1961 into the 21st Century*. Singapore: Singapore Economic Development Board and EDB Society.

Chan, L. M. (2008). "Polytechnic Education," in S. K. Lee, C. B. Goh, B. Fredriksen, and J. P. Tan (eds.), *Toward a Better Future. Education and Training for Economic Development in Singapore since 1965*. Singapore: The World Bank and National Institute of Education.

Chiang, M. (1998). *From Economic Debacle to Economic Miracle: The History and Development of Technical Education in Singapore*. Singapore: Times Edition.

Cohen, D. and Soto, M. (2007). "Growth and Human Capital: Good Data, Good Results," *Journal of Economic Growth*, 12 (1): 51–76.

Fredriksen, B. and Tan, J. P. (2008). "East Asia Education Study Tour: An Overview of Key Insights," in B. Fredriksen and J. P. Tan (eds.), *An Africa Exploration of the East Asian Education Experience*. Washington, DC: World Bank.

Government of Singapore (1996). *Singapore, 1965–1995 Statistical Highlights. A Review of 30 Years' Development*, Department of Statistics, Ministry of Trade and Industry, SNP Corporation Ltd, Singapore.

Hanushek, E. A. and Woessmann, L. (2008). "The Role of Cognitive Skills in Economic Development," *Journal of Economic Literature*, 46 (3): 607–68.

Hon, S. S. (2004). *Strategies of Singapore's Economic Success*, arranged and edited by L. Low and B. L. Lim. Singapore: Marshall Cavendish.

Hsueh, L.-M., Hsu, C.-K., and Perkins, D. H. (2001). *Industrialization and the State: The Changing Role of the Taiwan Government in the Economy, 1945–1998*. Cambridge, MA: Harvard University Press.

Inter-American Development Bank (IDB) (2006). *Competitiveness and Science and Math Education: Comparing Costa Rica, El Salvador and Brazil (Recife) to Sweden*. Sweden: Hifab International and Washington, DC: The Inter-American Development Bank.

Kaboski, J. P. (2009). "Education, Sectoral Composition, and Growth," *Review of Economic Dynamics*, 12 (1): 168–82.

Krueger, A. B. and Lindahl, M. (2001). "Education for Growth: Why and for Whom?" *Journal of Economic Literature*, 39 (4): 1101–36.

Kuznetsov, Y. (ed.) (2006). *Diaspora Networks and the International Migration of Skills: How Countries can Draw on Their Talent Abroad*, WBI Development Studies. Washington, DC: World Bank.

Law, S. S. (2008). "Vocational Technical Education and Economic Development: The Singapore Experience," in S. K. Lee, C. B. Goh, B. Fredriksen, and J. P. Tan (eds.), *Toward a Better Future. Education and Training for Economic Development in Singapore since 1965*. Washington, DC: World Bank and Singapore: National Institute of Education.

Lee, S. K., Goh, C. B., Fredriksen, B., and Tan, J. P. (eds.) (2008). *Toward a Better Future. Education and Training in Singapore since 1965*. Washington, DC: World Bank and Singapore: National Institute of Education.

Lin, C. T. (1998). "Training a New Breed of Technologists," in C. C. Bok (ed.), *Heart Work: Stories of How EDB Steered the Singapore Economy from 1961 into the 21st Century*. Singapore: Singapore Economic Development Board and EDB Society.

Low, L., Toh, M. H., Soon, T. W., Tan, K. Y. and Hughes, H. (1993). *Challenge and Response: Thirty Years of the Economic Development Board*. Singapore: Times Academic Press.

Majgaard, K. and Mingat, A. (forthcoming). *Education in Sub-Saharan Africa: A Comparative Analysis*. Washington, DC: World Bank.

Martin, M. O., Mullis, I. V. S., and Foy, P. (with Olson, J. F., Erberber, E., Preuschoff, C., and Galia, J.) (2008). *TIMSS 2007 International Science Report: Findings from IEA's Trends in International Mathematics and Science Study (TIMSS) at the Fourth and Eighth Grades*. Chestnut Hill, MA: TIMSS & PIRLS International Study Center, Boston College, available at <http://timss.bc.edu/isc/publications.html>.

—— —— Gonzalez, E. J., and Chrostowski, S. J. (2004). *Findings From IEA's Trends in International Mathematics and Science Study (TIMSS) at the Fourth and Eighth Grades*. Chestnut

Hill, MA: TIMSS & PIRLS International Study Center, Boston College, available at <http://timss.bc.edu/timss2003i/scienceD.html>.

Mingat, A., Ledoux, B., and Rakotomalala, R. (2010). *Developing Post-Primary Education in Sub-Saharan Africa: Assessing the Financial Sustainability of Alternative Pathways*, African Human Development Series. Washington, DC: World Bank.

Mourshed, Mona, Chijioke, Chinezi, and Barber, Michael (2010). *How the World's Most Improved School Systems Keep Getting Better*. McKinsey & Company.

Mullis, I. V. S., Martin, M. O., and Foy, P. (with Olson, J. F., Erberber, E., Preuschoff, C., Arora, A., and Galia, J.) (2008). *TIMSS 2007 International Mathematics Report: Findings from IEA's Trends in International Mathematics and Science Study (TIMSS) at the Fourth and Eighth Grades*. Chestnut Hill, MA: TIMSS & PIRLS International Study Center, Boston College, available at <http://timss.bc.edu/isc/publications.html>.

—— —— Gonzalez, E. J., and Chrostowski, S. J. (2004). *Findings from IEA's Trends in International Mathematics and Science Study (TIMSS) at the Fourth and Eighth Grades*. Chestnut Hill, MA: TIMSS & PIRLS International Study Center, Boston College, available at <http://timss.bc.edu/timss2003i/mathD.html>.

National Science Board (2008). *Science and Engineering Indicators 2008,* available at <http://www.nsf.gov/statistics/seind08/c2/c2s5.htm#c2s52>.

O'Hare, D. (2008). "Education in Ireland: Evolution of Economic and Education Policies since the Early 1990s," in B. Fredriksen and J. P. Tan (eds.), *An Africa Exploration of the East Asian Education Experience*. Washington DC: World Bank.

Ratha, D. and Xu, Z. (2008). *Migration and Remittances Factbook*. Washington, DC: World Bank, available at <http://siteresources.worldbank.org/INTPROSPECTS/Resources/334934–1199807908806/SSA.pdf>.

Rogers, M. L. (2008). "Directly Unproductive Schooling: How Country Characteristics Affect the Impact of Schooling on Growth," *European Economic Review*, 52 (2): 356–85.

Saint, W. (1992). "Universities in Africa: Strategies for Stabilization and Revitalization," World Bank Technical Paper 194. Washington, DC: World Bank.

Schultz, T. P. (2004). "Evidence of Returns to Schooling in Africa from Household Surveys," Working Papers 875. New Haven: Economic Growth Center, Yale University.

Sender, J., Cramer, C., and Oya, C. (2005). "Unequal Prospects: Disparities in the Quantity and Quality of Labor Supply in Sub-Saharan Africa," Social Protection Discussion Paper Series #525. Washington, DC: World Bank.

Somchit, B. (2008). "PSDC Model: Application to the SSA Scenario." Presentation at the Workshop on Leaders in Education and Training for Sustained Growth in Sub-Saharan Africa (LETSGA), Singapore, January 30, available at <http://www.psdc.orb.my>.

Sweeney, P. (2008). *Ireland's Economic Success. Reasons and Prospects*. Dublin: New Island.

Teferra, D. and Altbach, P. G. (eds.) (2003). *African Higher Education: An International Reference Handbook*. Bloomington, IN: Indiana University Press.

UNESCO (2005). *UNESCO Science Report 2005*. Paris: UNESCO Publishing.

—— (2007). *UNESCO Global Education Digest 2007*. Paris: UNESCO Institute of Statistics.

Vandenbussche, J., Aghion, P., and Meghir, C. (2006). "Growth, Distance to Frontier and Composition of Human Capital," *Journal of Economic Growth*, 11 (2): 97–127.

Walther, R. with Filipiak, E. (2007). *Vocational Training in the Informal Sector*, Notes and Documents, 33. Paris: Agence Française de Dévéloppement.

Woessmann, Ludger with Hanushek, Eric A. (2010). "The Economics of International Differences in Educational Achievement," in E. A. Hanushek, S. Machin, and L. Woessmann (eds.), *Handbook of the Economics of Education*, Vol. 3. Amsterdam: North Holland.

World Bank (1993). *The East Asian Miracle: Economic Growth and Public Policy*. Washington, DC: World Bank.

—— (2005). *Expanding Opportunities and Building Competencies for Young People: A New Agenda for Secondary Education*. Washington, DC: World Bank.

—— (2008a). *African Development Indicators 2007*. Washington, DC: World Bank.

—— (2008b). *Accelerating Catch-Up: Tertiary Education for Growth in Sub-Saharan Africa*. Washington, DC: World Bank.

Yacuba, N. (2008). "New Initiatives for Expansion of Access to Post-Basic Education Through Skills Development in Partnership with Private Sector Providers in Nigeria." Paper presented at the World Bank Group International Colloquium on Private Education, May 14, Washington, DC.

Part V
International Context

17

Economic Liberalization and Constraints to Development in Sub-Saharan Africa

Jomo K. S. and Rudiger von Arnim[1]

Growth and poverty reduction in a shifting policy environment

This chapter critically reviews the impact of globalization on Sub-Saharan Africa (SSA) since the early 1980s. The large gains expected from opening up to international economic forces have been limited. Instead, there have been significant adverse consequences. Continuing capital flight has reduced financial resources available for productive investments. Premature trade liberalization has undermined prospects for economic development. Most importantly, foreign direct investment (FDI) in SSA has been confined largely to resources, especially mineral extraction. Global demand for raw materials, particularly from China, over the last business cycle upswing has undermined African efforts to diversify production and exports. Extractive industries are especially ill-suited to generate technology and skill diffusion, and have limited potential for poverty reduction. Before focusing on these matters, we provide an introductory discussion of the shifting policy environment.

Indeed, the African development policy landscape has changed radically over the last three decades. Liberalization and privatization measures aimed at attracting private investment have replaced state intervention and public investment aimed at building infant industries. Policy debates during the developmental era seriously considered the interactions between external and internal factors, but the subsequent liberalization era has tended to focus almost exclusively on the *domestic* determinants of economic performance and assumes that external market forces are benign and price-perfecting.[2]

The policy shift dates back to 1981, when the World Bank published the influential *Accelerated Development in Sub-Saharan Africa: An Agenda for Action*, often referred to as the Berg Report, after its principal author, Elliot Berg, from the

University of Michigan's Department of Economics. The report recommended a more outward-oriented program, the elimination of subsidies and controls, and allowing market forces to determine the prices for exports of raw materials. The international sovereign debt crises of the early 1980s provided an opportunity for the Bretton Woods institutions (BWIs) to broaden this agenda and impose it upon recalcitrant governments through policy conditionalities in exchange for providing desperately needed credit. The International Monetary Fund (IMF) was initially responsible for short-term macroeconomic stabilization programs, and the World Bank for medium-term structural adjustment programs (SAPs). With "cross-conditionalities," these converged around what was subsequently dubbed the Washington Consensus, which is generally seen as having spearheaded the global trend toward greater economic liberalization since the 1980s. While its policy priorities have changed over time (responding, in part, to poorer-than-expected economic performances in implementing countries), it has remained at the core of economic policymaking across most of the African continent.[3]

Without a doubt, the developments in the world economy in the late 1970s and early 1980s had a profound impact on SSA economic prospects. Profitability of private firms was undermined, state revenues collapsed, and debt accumulation accelerated. A vicious downward spiral followed in many countries; with little prospect of raising export earnings to maintain import levels, macroeconomic policies were tightened further, which in turn increased the constraints on investment, diversification, and growth. Debt further mushroomed and compromised some of the most essential conditions for sustainable growth and poverty reduction.

The BWIs have generally been quick to claim responsibility for economic success stories during the subsequent period, even as they have continued to deny the adverse consequences that have arisen from their recommended (or imposed) policies that have been pursued by SSA governments. Rather, they have insisted that the slow growth is best explained by African policymakers' reluctance to undertake governance reforms and to open up quickly enough, which they claim results in only partial implementation of adjustment programs.[4] However, the link between the structural adjustments required by the BWIs and economic growth has been weak: of the fifteen countries identified as core adjusters by the World Bank in 1993, only three were subsequently classified by the IMF as strong economic performers, while few of the original fifteen are among the current crop of strong performers. In fact, the recent cases of rapid growth by a few strong performers can be explained by circumstances unrelated to SAPs.

Between 1970 and 2000, real income growth failed to keep pace with population growth in Sub-Saharan Africa. After posting a modest average annual growth rate in real per capita income of about 0.7 percent during the 1970s, these rates turned negative during the 1980s and 1990s (−1.0 and −0.5 percent respectively). SSA

Table 17.1 GDP per capita in constant 2000 US$

Annual average compound growth rates	1960 to 1969	1970 to 1979	1980 to 1989	1990 to 1999	2000 to 2006
World	*3.4%*	*2.1%*	*1.4%*	*1.2%*	*1.7%*
East Asia & Pacific	1.3%	4.4%	6.1%	7.1%	7.6%
Europe & Central Asia				−2.0%	5.5%
Latin America & Caribbean	2.4%	3.1%	−0.8%	1.5%	1.7%
Middle East & North Africa		2.8%	−0.4%	1.8%	2.4%
South Asia	1.8%	0.3%	3.2%	3.3%	5.1%
Sub-Saharan Africa	2.0%	0.7%	−1.0%	−0.5%	2.1%
Averages per decade					
World	*2806*	*3659*	*4177*	*4780*	*5446*
East Asia & Pacific	140	210	358	696	1184
Europe & Central Asia			2296	1847	2270
Latin America & Caribbean	2277	3099	3446	3643	3994
Middle East & North Africa	923	1295	1372	1464	1720
South Asia	201	224	274	373	510
Sub-Saharan Africa	475	577	552	504	536

Sources: World Development Indicators, World Bank, and authors' calculations

countries have posted improved growth rates since 2000, largely because of commodity-driven recoveries (see Table 17.1).

Even so, real per capita income is still barely higher than in 1970. Furthermore, this weak and erratic growth performance has been accompanied by regressive trends in income distribution (Geda and Shimeles 2007), with a particularly marked drop in the average per capita income for the poorest 20 percent of SSA countries (UNCTAD 2001: 53). Not only is this likely to undermine efforts to develop human resources and strengthen political cohesion in SSA, it is also likely to restrict future growth prospects. Real GDP growth rates suggest that SSA is beginning to recover after the "lost" last quarter of the twentieth century (see Table 17.2). The upturn appears largely due to strong commodity demand. Despite this growth experience, the region is mired in poverty, faces a dire lack of infrastructure, and retains a narrow export base, none of which are conducive to rapid and sustainable development.

Recent estimates by the World Bank[5] include a substantial upward revision of the numbers of people living in poverty worldwide as measured by a poverty line of $1.25 per day at 2005 purchasing power parity (PPP), equivalent to $1 per day in 1996 US dollars (Chen and Ravallion 2008: tables 4, 5, 7, 8). About 1.4 billion people lived in poverty in 2005 (Table 17.3). The new World Bank figures give a total of 384 million people living below the new poverty line in SSA. More than half of the population of SSA lives in poverty, the highest percentage in the world for any region. The period since the early 1980s has also seen rising income inequality, as measured by the Gini index, reversing the trend of previous decades (Nel 2003). Real wages have fallen for many in the formal economy, including the nascent middle class in SSA, contributing to greater inequality and undermining

Table 17.2 Real GDP growth

Annual average growth rates of real GDP, 1970–2005; and 2005, 2006

Selected regions	1970 to 1980	1980 to 1989	1992 to 2000	2000 to 2005	2005	2006
World	3.8	3.3	3.1	2.8	3.5	4.1
Developing economies	5.8	3.8	4.9	5.4	6.5	7.0
Economies in transition	5.0	3.6	−2.0	6.1	6.6	7.1
Developed economies	3.3	3.1	2.8	2.0	2.4	3.0
Developing economies: Africa	4.5	2.3	3.2	4.9	5.5	5.3
Developing economies: America	5.7	1.8	3.1	2.4	4.4	5.1
Developing economies: Asia	6.3	5.6	5.9	6.5	7.4	7.8
LDCs: Africa and Haiti	2.3	1.7	4.3	6.0	7.9	8.2
Major petroleum exporters: Developing Africa	5.9	1.3	2.8	6.2	6.5	5.8
Sub-Saharan Africa	3.3	2.0	3.3	4.8	5.9	5.4
Sub-Saharan Africa excluding South Africa	3.4	2.3	3.6	5.2	6.2	6.2

Sources: UNCTAD *Handbook of Statistics* and authors' calculations (8.2 annual average growth rates of real gross domestic product)

Table 17.3 Percentage of population below poverty line, 1981–2004

"1 PPP$ a day"	1981	1984	1987	1990	1993	1996	1999	2002	2004
By geographical region									
East Asia and Pacific	58%	39%	28%	30%	25%	16%	15%	12%	9%
Europe and Central Asia	1%	1%	0%	0%	4%	4%	4%	1%	1%
Latin America and the Caribbean	11%	13%	12%	10%	8%	9%	10%	9%	9%
Middle East and North Africa	5%	4%	3%	2%	2%	2%	2%	2%	1%
South Asia	50%	45%	45%	43%	37%	36%	35%	33%	31%
Sub-Saharan Africa	**42%**	**46%**	**48%**	**47%**	**46%**	**48%**	**46%**	**43%**	**41%**
By income level									
Low income	49%	46%	46%	44%	39%	39%	37%	35%	33%
Lower middle income	44%	30%	22%	24%	20%	13%	13%	11%	8%
Upper middle income	3%	4%	4%	2%	4%	5%	4%	4%	3%

Source: World Bank PovcalNet, see <http://iresearch.worldbank.org/PovcalNet/>

prospects for a stable growth environment. Higher growth in the last half decade is believed to have raised incomes and reduced poverty levels in some SSA countries. However, growth based on resource extraction has contributed to rising inequality and limited its employment effects, thereby dampening the impact on poverty reduction. In some cases, the combination of slower growth, rising inequalities, and vulnerability to exogenous shocks has contributed to civil conflict, further trapping these countries in a vicious spiral of economic decline.

In the following section, we review the progress—or lack thereof—of capital formation and economic diversification in Africa, and discuss the impact of foreign (FDI, portfolio flows, aid) and domestic (public and private saving) sources of funds to finance development. We proceed with a discussion of the trade and development nexus, with a focus on trade diversification—or lack thereof—and the potential gains from agricultural specialization and liberalization.

Resource mobilization for development

Strong and sustained growth is necessary to address the development and poverty challenges across SSA; most observers put the target figure in the 6–8 percent range annually. It is very difficult to reduce poverty through redistribution when average income levels are low, as in SSA. Further, political stability and prospects for development decrease with elevated economic insecurity (United Nations 2008).

Leaving markets to mobilize and allocate financial resources and determine interest rates is a central objective of the liberal policy agenda. Doing so should not only mean an increased willingness of households to save and hold financial assets, but also that scarce resources will be employed by the most productive firms regardless of their location. Financial liberalization promised to remove distortions arising from an artificially repressed financial sector and also to strengthen the productive sector and ease the constraint on external payments by channeling global savings to the most profitable investments in the capital-scarce poorer countries of the world.

Particular attention has been paid to FDI as a driving force in such a process and a more reliable source of financing trade deficits. In the next section, we discuss the often-limited contribution in Africa of FDI, which has remained small compared to other developing regions, as well as highly concentrated in extractive industries. Portfolio flows, on the other hand, are negative. Capital owners in Africa with access to liquid assets prefer to transfer them abroad. Unlike other developing regions, net portfolio flows have been consistently negative over longer time periods.

What remains as a potential source of finance? Aid, it turns out, is not necessarily as ineffective as many critics have suggested (Minoiu and Reddy 2008), but it is unpredictable and, importantly, does not necessarily promote economic development goals. Increasingly, aid aims to alleviate the effects of disasters or to strengthen welfare programs and social services, rather than to promote industrialization or infrastructure development.

Successful resource mobilization begins at home. However, statistics indicate that savings and investment rates are still low in SSA by international comparison, and reaching a high, sustainable growth path will have to include changing this— as part of creating a dynamic that reverses capital flight and increases more diversified, "developmental" FDI, supported by tangible, predictable aid flows.

FDI flows: small and highly concentrated

Most African governments accepted the BWIs' policies and expected the promised "catalytic effect" on foreign capital inflows after receiving the BWI stamp of approval. The actual response of private capital has, in the words of the World Bank, "been disappointing" (quoted by Mkandawire 2005: 6). Even though rates of return on FDI have generally been much higher in Africa than in any other region (Bhattacharya, Montiel, and Sharma 1997; UNCTAD 1995, 2005), this has not made Africa much more attractive to foreign investors, ostensibly due to ill-specified and often intangible "risk factors." Political instability certainly plays a role here, as Africa is systematically rated as more risky than warranted by economic indicators.

Even the recent surge in FDI into Africa, mostly in minerals, has had only a negligible impact on Africa's share of global FDI flows. Indeed, the share of global FDI to all African developing countries is still far below the 5 percent share it received in the 1970s; the recent increase to 2.4 percent only marks a return to Africa's more modest share in the 1980s (see Table 17.4).

Table 17.5 shows country FDI shares for the top five (of forty-seven) SSA countries, by volume of FDI in the 2000s. The top five countries—Nigeria, South Africa, Angola, Equatorial Guinea, and Chad—are, except for South Africa, highly dependent on petroleum exports and foreign investment in this sector. Since 1990, these five countries have absorbed an average of 64 percent of all FDI going to all forty-seven SSA economies. The exception here might be South Africa, which appears in the top five primarily because of the size of its economy, relative to other SSA countries.[6]

Table 17.4 Africa's share in inward foreign direct investment

Percentage share, US Dollar at current prices	1970 to 1979	1980 to 1989	1990 to 1999	2000 to 2006
Share of world FDI				
Developed economies	75%	75%	68%	68%
Developing economies	25%	25%	31%	29%
Developing economies: Africa	5.1%	2.5%	1.9%	2.4%
Developing economies: America	12%	8%	10%	9%
Developing economies: Asia	8%	14%	19%	18%
Addendum: China	n/a	2%	8%	7%
Economies in transition	n/a	0%	1%	3%
Share of developing country FDI				
Developing economies: Africa	24%	10%	6%	8%
Developing economies: America	50%	36%	32%	30%
Developing economies: Asia	26%	54%	62%	62%
Addendum: China	n/a	8%	24%	23%

Sources: UNCTAD *Handbook of Statistics* and authors' calculations
(Table 7.3 Major FDI indicators (WIR 2007))

Table 17.5 SSA economies with the highest share in the region's total FDI

	1970 to 1979	1980 to 1989	1990 to 1999	2000 to 2006
Nigeria	35.4%	3.0%	40.6%	21.7%
South Africa	7.1%	0.7%	13.3%	16.8%
Angola	0.3%	13.1%	9.8%	9.7%
Equatorial Guinea	0.0%	0.2%	1.9%	8.9%
Chad	1.2%	1.2%	0.5%	4.8%
Subtotal	*44.0%*	*18.2%*	*66.1%*	*61.9%*
United Republic of Tanzania	0.5%	0.4%	1.9%	3.0%
Ethiopia	1.1%	0.1%	1.1%	2.8%
Cameroon	2.2%	12.2%	0.1%	2.7%
Botswana	2.1%	8.9%	0.2%	2.3%
Congo, Democratic Republic of	4.7%	7.3%	4.1%	2.2%
Namibia	0.0%	0.3%	2.5%	2.2%
Mozambique	0.1%	0.3%	1.6%	2.0%
Congo	3.2%	3.8%	2.4%	2.0%
Uganda	0.0%	0.2%	1.3%	1.9%
Zambia	3.3%	5.5%	3.9%	1.9%
Mauritania	0.2%	1.5%	0.2%	1.6%
Ghana	2.3%	1.1%	2.3%	1.5%
Mali	0.2%	0.2%	0.4%	1.4%
Gabon	4.6%	6.9%	−2.1%	1.0%
Madagascar	0.4%	0.4%	0.5%	0.9%
Total	*68.9%*	*67.4%*	*86.3%*	*91.4%*

Sources: UNCTAD *Handbook of Statistics* and authors' calculations
(Table 7.3 Major FDI indicators (WIR 2007))

Increased FDI in SSA since the late 1990s has been cited as evidence that the economic tide is turning in SSA (Pigato 2000). However, there is little evidence that the pattern of FDI in Africa is likely to bring sustained, broad-based economic growth and significantly increased employment (UNCTAD 2005). Much of that FDI has gone to mining, which is hardly influenced by macroeconomic policy considerations. Some new investments have gone to expand or improve existing capacities in sectors where monopolistic rents are high, such as beverages, cement, and the refining of oil into gasoline and petroleum products. FDI has also been drawn by one-time opportunities associated with privatization. For example, FDI to Ghana—hailed by the BWIs as a "success story"—peaked with privatization, with subsequent negative outflows. Moreover, much recent FDI through acquisitions has often been on heavily discounted "fire sale" terms. Such investments accounted for about one sixth of FDI flows into Africa in the 1990s. In 1998 alone, privatization in SSA attracted $684 million in FDI (UNCTAD). Such one-off sales explain the jump in FDI in the 1990s, but by the end of the decade, privatization-related FDI had slowed. "Brownfield" FDI acquisitions through privatization do not enhance economic capacities; rather, they merely signify a change in ownership.

505

The end of the Multi Fibre Arrangement (MFA) in 1995, and of its successor, the Agreement on Textiles and Clothing (ATC), in 2005, has reduced new investments in this sector. Many such industries now survive only because of remaining, but eroding, trade preferences enjoyed in US and European markets. Similarly, logging and agricultural expansion have been especially encouraged in recent years as the Washington Consensus effectively discourages (import-substituting) industrialization for Africa. While generating temporary, albeit dangerous (owing to the high incidence of accidents), work locally, logging has exacerbated water supply problems, floods, droughts, and desertification. More generally, corruption and ongoing resource conflicts in Africa have been fuelled by such foreign interest in the continent's natural resources.

Portfolio flows mainly speculative and negative

Highly speculative portfolio investment has been attracted by often temporary "pull factors" such as high real domestic interest rates on treasury bills to finance budget deficits as well as temporary export price booms that have attracted large export pre-financing loans (Kasekende, Kitabire, and Martin 1997). Mkandawire (2005) notes with concern the predominance of portfolio over direct investments, and of brownfield acquisitions over "greenfield" investments, as consequences of the FDI policies adopted. Moreover, the overwhelming majority of portfolio flows—in the order of nine of every ten dollars invested in the region—goes to South Africa.

Despite growing poverty, Africa has been a net exporter of capital. In 1990, 40 percent of privately held wealth was invested outside Africa (Collier and Gunning 1997; Collier, Hoeffler, and Patillo 1999; quoted by Mkandawire 2005). In the period 1970–96, capital flight from SSA came to $193 billion; with imputed interest, the value goes up to $285 billion (Boyce and Ndikumana 2000), compared to SSA's combined debt of $178 billion in 1996 (Mkandawire 2005). Ndikumana and Boyce (2002) argue that capital flight from Africa has been largely debt-fueled, though Collier, Hoeffler, and Patillo (2004) claim that serious financial capital flight from Africa has started to be reversed. The most recent estimates of net external assets are probably from Ndikumana and Boyce (2008: 6) who report that

[r]eal capital flight over the [1970–2004] period amounted to about $420 billion (in 2004 dollars) for the 40 countries as a whole. Including imputed interest earnings, the accumulated stock of capital flight was about $607 billion as of end-2004...Their net external assets (accumulated flight capital minus accumulated external debt) amounted to approximately $398 billion over the 35-year period. To give a sense of the relative magnitude of the region's net external position, the region's external assets are 2.9 times the stock of debts owed to the world. For some individual countries, the results are even more dramatic: for Côte d'Ivoire, Zimbabwe, Angola, and Nigeria the external assets are 4.6, 5.1, 5.3, and 6.7 times higher than their debt stocks, respectively.

Even World Bank economists concede that the effects of financial liberalization have been "very small" (Devajaran, Easterly, and Pack 1999). Incredibly, it is argued that capital flight may be good for Africa because of a perceived "overinvestment" in Africa: "The much-denigrated capital flight out of Africa may well have been a rational response to low returns at home... Indeed, Africans are probably better off having made external investments than they would have been if they invested solely at home!" (Devajaran, Easterly, and Pack 1999: 15–16). Devajaran, Easterly, and Pack (1999: 23) argue that

> [W]e should be more careful about calling for an investment boom to resume growth in Africa... [and] about Africa's low savings rate... [p]erhaps... due to the fact that the returns to investment were so low. Also, the relatively high levels of capital flight from Africa may have been a rational response to the lack of investment opportunities at home.

These claims can be contested on both methodological and econometric grounds. First, in the standard approach in growth empirics, investment should be measured in international prices. However, the study used domestic prices, which generally overestimate investment rates because of the high cost of doing business in Africa. Second, they used cross-sectional regressions that do not account for country-specific effects. Such an omission can lead to inconsistent estimates.[7] But, more importantly, as Mkandawire (2005) notes, the social benefits—to the national economy—of citizens investing in their own country exceed the private benefits accruing to individual investors.

Aid: unpredictable and welfare-oriented

The role of aid for development has been debated for decades. Rosenstein-Rodan (1943, 1944) laid the foundations for the idea of an externally funded "big push" for development of the so-called "backward areas" through the realization of scale economies. Subsequently, in the post-war development paradigm, substantial foreign aid was seen as necessary to provide financing and balance-of-payments support for such large-scale industrialization and development programs. This broadly structuralist development literature and its derivative policy recommendations have been challenged by more market-friendly economists who worry that aid would crowd out more efficient private investment, and undermined by the economic policy conditionalities and recommendations of the multilateral institutions during the 1980s. Currently, that debate echoes in the context of African development challenges through the conflicting positions of Jeffrey Sachs (2005) and William Easterly (2001, 2007), with the former arguing for a new "big push," requiring much more plentiful and reliable aid flows, and the latter arguing that the private investment needed has been crowded out by large aid flows to the region.

Aid statistics are notoriously controversial. As noted by the United Nations Conference on Trade and Development in its report on "Making the Big Push Work" (UNCTAD 2006), it is well known that a large percentage of aid—as reported by donor countries to the Organisation for Economic Co-operation and Development (OECD) Development Assistance Committee (DAC)—never actually reaches the intended recipients. UNCTAD (2006: 14) quotes a study from the non-governmental organization Action Aid, which reports that about 60 percent of bilateral donor assistance in 2003 "never materializes for poor countries, but is instead diverted for other purposes within the Aid system."

The statistics available also indicate that aid to Africa has been highly volatile. Figure 17.1 shows the regional composition of total aid flow among the four major developing country regions—Oceania, Asia, America, and Africa. Africa's share rose in the 1970s to almost 40 percent, and remained fairly stable until the mid 1990s, before falling off precipitously to 20 percent in 1999; its share then rose to more than 60 percent in 2003, only to fall back to 39 percent in 2005.[8]

To what extent, though, does aid reach its target? In fact, for many countries, much aid is for debt relief and debt repayment, meaning that it does not help to finance development in any way. The old idea—that aid is supposed to help finance a balance of payments deficit in the face of imports of machinery and technology necessary to start a virtuous circle of growth and development on the

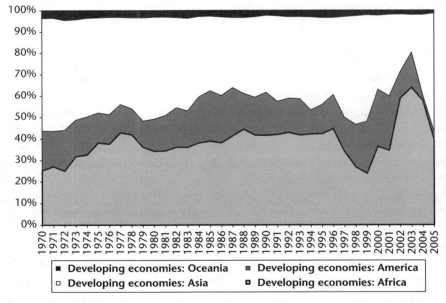

Figure 17.1 Total offical aid flows: regional composition, 1970–2005
Sources: UNCTAD *Handbook of Statistics* and authors' calculations

Table 17.6 Net debt transfers of selected regions*

Ratio to GDP	1990 to 1994	1995 to 1999	2000 to 2004
Developing economies	0.0%	−0.1%	−1.1%
Developing economies: Africa	−0.5%	−1.3%	−1.0%
Eastern Africa	1.7%	0.2%	1.2%
Middle Africa	1.6%	−2.3%	−1.7%
Northern Africa	−1.8%	−2.1%	−2.0%
Southern Africa	0.2%	−0.5%	0.0%
Western Africa	−1.2%	−1.6%	−1.5%
Developing economies: America	−0.4%	0.2%	−2.1%
Developing economies: Asia	0.3%	−0.1%	−0.6%
Developing economies: Oceania	−0.9%	−0.9%	−1.2%
LDCs: Africa and Haiti	0.9%	−3.1%	−1.3%
Major petroleum exporters (Africa)	0.3%	−1.4%	−0.8%
Africa excluding South Africa	−0.7%	−1.6%	−1.4%
Sub-Saharan Africa	0.6%	0.2%	0.4%
SSA excluding South Africa	−1.5%	−1.9%	−2.0%

Sources: UNCTAD *Handbook of Statistics* and authors' calculations
(Table 7.7 External long-term debt of developing economies)
Note: Net transfers are disbursements of loans less debt service (principal plus interest payments) from all sources of creditors.

one hand, and volatile and structurally declining commodity export revenues on the other—appears turned on its head, as many African countries become net exporters of capital. See Table 17.6 for statistics on net debt transfers, which are disbursements of loans less debt service (principal plus interest payments) from all sources of credit. However, a critical review of the IMF argument that aid is ineffective—in terms of promoting growth—suggests that the conclusion is reversed once politically driven aid is factored out (Minoiu and Reddy 2008).

As mentioned before, much of the developing world consists of net capital exporters, but the aggregate statistics in Table 17.6 mask the differences among regions. Asia and, much more recently, Latin America freed themselves from the Washington-led aid nexus, with good export performances, as well as exchange rate and reserve strategies. The drain of capital from a host of countries in Africa, however, does not appear to be based on sustainable development strategies, and thus the ability to afford repayment, but rather on a combination of increased debt service and the slow trickle of real resource transfers from the developed world.

Trade and development

Consistent with the 1981 Berg Report, World Bank research has suggested that Africa would gain most if it specializes in agriculture. Removal or reduction of subsidies and protection in the North would give farmers in SSA the opportunity to significantly increase their share of these markets. This section reviews the structure of African trade, particularly the potential of agricultural trade and problems for African development prospects related to the terms of trade and

"Dutch disease." What and with whom does Africa trade, and how might that help or hinder development? The structural features of the region's trade are an important starting point for trade policy, industrial policy, and development policy.

African countries have experienced volatile and, by and large, unfavorable movements in their terms of trade for much of the post-independence period. First, except in recent years, prices of primary commodities have declined against those of manufactures, as suggested by Hans Singer and Raul Prebisch more than half a century ago (see Ocampo and Parra 2006). Second, prices of tropical agricultural products have continued to decrease relative to temperate agricultural goods, as observed by W. A. Lewis (1969) decades ago. Third, recent decades have also seen the decline of the prices of generic manufactures where entry into industries (e.g., most clothing) has not been inhibited—unlike those activities protected by technological barriers, scale economies, and strong intellectual property rights. Although Africa has experienced de-industrialization over recent decades, a few countries have developed garment industries that still enjoy trade preferences, though reduced, and may at least survive, even if their expansion is hindered because of the erosion of trade preferences stemming from greater trade liberalization.

Table 17.7 underscores Africa's declining marginal role in overall world trade. Africa's share of world trade has long been small, but even this has declined in recent decades. African exports of manufactured goods and food have declined during this period, while exports of minerals and other agricultural products have risen, reflecting the pressures of de-industrialization and changes in agricultural production, and also a heavier reliance on mineral exports, particularly petroleum.

De-industrialization and the investment climate

Exchange rate, monetary, and other policies in East Asia have ensured relative prices favorable to export industries (instead of non-tradables), with preferential

Table 17.7 African shares of world manufacturing exports, 1995–2006

Africa's relative position: World trade Share of world manufacturing exports, 1995–2006**	1995 to 2000	2001 to 2006
Developing economies: Africa	0.702%	0.820%
Developing economies: America	3.6%	3.8%
Developing economies: Asia	21.9%	26.3%
Major petroleum exporters: Developing Africa	0.037%	0.038%
Major petroleum exporters: Developing America	0.102%	0.102%
Major petroleum exporters: Developing Asia	0.422%	0.627%
Sub-Saharan Africa	0.458%	0.558%
Sub-Saharan Africa excluding South Africa	0.158%	0.225%
SADC*	0.394%	0.487%

Sources: UNCTAD Handbook of Statistics and authors' calculations
(Table 2.2 Trade structure of country groupings by partner and product group)

Notes: *SADC includes 15 Sub-Saharan African nations. **Data includes SITC 5 through 8 less 68.

interest rates supporting investment and economic restructuring. Export promotion strategies have generally involved an investment–export nexus, including measures to promote public investment, subsidized inputs (from state-owned enterprises and with preferential special exchange rates), direct subsidies (including tax incentives), selective credit allocation, and other industrial policy instruments (Akyüz 1996). Government instruments for stimulating investment and industrial development have been severely eroded by economic liberalization measures.

African countries had largely "adjusted" by the 1990s, in that they had adopted market-friendly economic policies and made corresponding institutional changes. Most African countries undertook currency devaluations, trade liberalization, and privatization as well as various other investor-friendly reforms, particularly toward foreign investors. Improvements in the terms of trade and favorable weather conditions have recently corrected for the deflationary bias of macroeconomic policies to bring about improvements in economic performance.

African savings rates are generally much lower than in the fast-growing Asian economies; the failure of Africans to raise their savings rate to finance higher investment and growth rates is often emphasized in accounts of the policy challenges facing the region. However, causation is disputed. Keynesians argue that the causal chain runs from growth to investment to savings, and not the other way round. Elbadawi and Mwega (2000) and Mlambo and Oshikoya (2001) have found that causality runs from growth to investment in Africa as well. Capital needs are essentially determined by expected output—investment demand is driven by expected growth. Meanwhile, "endogenous growth theories" also suggest that some "determinants of growth" may themselves be dependent on growth.

The investment patterns following economic liberalization cannot be associated with high economic growth. Historically, investment, growth, and productivity have evolved together; for instance, investment was associated with relatively high growth and significant total factor productivity gains in the pre-adjustment era (Rodrik 2001). Instead, economic liberalization has brought economic stagnation, de-industrialization, and agricultural decline, rather than structural change induced by productivity gains and stronger domestic demand from increasing incomes (Mkandawire 1988; Singh 1987; Stein 1992; Stewart 1994). The two countries that performed well were Botswana and Mauritius, both high-growth economies not pursuing orthodox adjustment programs.

De-industrialization in SSA has been severe,[9] as reflected in Table 17.8, which shows the GDP composition of SSA economies excluding South Africa, both by expenditure and broad categories of value added. First, "adjustment" orchestrated by the BWIs has insisted on reducing government expenditure, which fell from an average 20 percent of GDP in the 1970s to 13 percent of GDP during 2000–6! Even the initial level was low, compared to the developed world, and such spending cuts have not only affected social spending, but also economic expenditure on things such as infrastructure. With strong crowding-out effects linked to these declines in public investment, it is not surprising that the average share of industry in value added fell from 21 percent in the 1970s to 9 percent in the years since 2000.

De-industrialization has been worse for the region's major petroleum exporters where the share of manufacturing in value added fell from 21 percent in the 1960s to 5 percent between 2000 and 2006. See Table 17.8 for statistics on GDP composition for Africa's major petroleum-exporting countries. However, the decrease in government spending has been less drastic in these countries, presumably because of greater fiscal space thanks to natural-resource extraction.

When most other developing economies embarked on import substitution industrialization in the 1950s, Africa was still under colonial rule and remained so well into the 1960s. Consequently, the import substitution phase in most of SSA was relatively short, lasting barely a decade in many countries because of the lateness of independence and the early onset of economic slowdown due to the oil shocks of the 1970s (Mkandawire 1988). Import compression following the debt crisis led to lower utilization of existing capacity and a fall in investment, and prevented many countries in SSA from making a positive adjustment to the changed global environment. In this context, trade liberalization, beginning in the 1980s, prematurely exposed African "infant" industries to global competition with comparatively mature industries, which precipitated de-industrialization. UNIDO notes that African countries had been increasingly gaining comparative advantage in labor-intensive manufacturing before such forced import liberalization. Given the BWI presumption that import substitution was bad, there was no attempt to see how such industries could form bases for new export initiatives.

Table 17.8 GDP components of SSA excluding South Africa, 1970–2006

Sub-Saharan Africa excluding South Africa Averages of percentage shares in GDP	1970 to 1979	1980 to 1989	1990 to 1999	2000 to 2006
Consumption	68%	73%	74%	69%
Government expenditure	20%	19%	14%	13%
Investment	17%	13%	16%	17%
Exports	33%	30%	33%	34%
Imports	38%	36%	37%	32%
Agriculture, hunting, forestry, fishing	**30%**	**28%**	**31%**	**29%**
Industry	40%	40%	32%	35%
Mining, manufacturing, utilities	34%	36%	28%	31%
Manufacturing	21%	22%	12%	9%
Construction	6%	4%	4%	4%
Services	**30%**	**32%**	**38%**	**36%**
Wholesale, retail trade, restaurants, and hotels	12%	12%	14%	13%
Transport, storage, and communications	5%	5%	5%	6%
Other activities	14%	15%	18%	17%

Sources: UNCTAD *Handbook of Statistics* and authors' calculations
(Table 8.3 Gross domestic product by type of expenditure and by kind of economic activity)

Presuming that African import-substituting industries had been protected for far too long, and would never become viable, let alone internationally competitive, the policy was to simply abandon existing industrial capacity.

The growth rates of manufacturing value added have fallen from the 1970s, and actually contracted by an average of 1 percent annually during 1990–7 (UNIDO 1998: 245, quoted in Mkandawire 2005). UNIDO found that in ten industrial branches in thirty-eight African countries, labor productivity declined by 7 percent between 1990–5. The decline in the measure of total factor productivity can also be attributed to de-industrialization.

Gains from trade liberalization?

As discussed earlier, agriculture and agricultural trade present a conundrum for Africa. Africa is at a comparative disadvantage with agricultural exports, relative not only to the developed world, with its protected "green pastures," heavy subsidies, and industrial farming, but also with much of Asia and Latin America as well.

A basic premise of the Berg Report was that Africa's supposed comparative advantage lay in agriculture. If only the state would stop "squeezing" agriculture through marketing boards and price distortions,[10] the supply-side response to agricultural producers would drive export-led growth. Subsequent changes in Africa's exports indicate no significant increase in activities in which African countries ostensibly had comparative advantage. Indeed, after two decades of reforms, Africa's share of global non-oil exports fell to less than half what it was in the early 1980s (Ng and Yeats 2000).

Recent high growth in large Asian economies, especially China, has probably contributed most to the recent increase in primary commodity prices, especially for minerals, inducing strong supply responses from many SSA countries helped by FDIs from these same big Asian developing countries. However, and despite this upsurge, the African share of world exports still remains well below its previous level. Moreover, the damaging consequences for sustainable development and food security have become apparent, and as food prices began to raise sharply in late 2007, renewed attention is now being given to the issue.

Official development rhetoric continues to imply that small farmers in Africa would benefit greatly if agriculture were liberalized under a comprehensive Doha trade agreement. However, this is not an obvious conclusion: many food-importing African countries would be worse off without subsidized food imports while very few economies are likely to be in a position to significantly increase their output and exports in the near term. African agricultural production and export capacities have been undermined by the last three decades of economic contraction and neglect.

Severe cuts in public spending under structural adjustment have caused a significant deterioration of infrastructure (roads, water supply, etc.) and have undermined the potential supply response.[11] Even World Bank estimates (Anderson and Martin 2005) of the overall welfare effects from multilateral agricultural trade liberalization do not suggest significant gains for SSA, but on the contrary, the likelihood of some losses. Gains from agricultural trade liberalization would largely accrue to existing major agricultural exporters, mainly from the Cairns Group,[12] again of little benefit to most of SSA. Greater trade liberalization in manufactures with a non-agricultural market access (NAMA) agreement would further undermine the potential for African industrialization. African access to markets in developed countries is secured through preferential market access agreements, rather than through past trade liberalization per se. Further trade liberalization threatens to erode this advantage.

Next we will look at some of the issues related to trade liberalization and development in Africa in more detail. Trade liberalization results in an immediate loss of tariff revenue, which can be very significant in developing countries, especially the poorest ones, where tariffs have accounted for up to half of total tax revenue. Reducing these revenues severely reduces their fiscal capacities, and can severely aggravate debt problems, creating the need for new and increased borrowing in financial markets.

Referring to rich countries' claims that developing countries ought to repeal manufacturing tariffs before they can reduce agricultural subsidies, Dani Rodrik has asked "[w]hy they need to be bribed by poor countries to do what is good for them is an enduring mystery."[13] Similarly, one might ask why poor countries should agree to multilateral trade liberalization that they need to be compensated for.

"Aid for Trade" was initially proposed as a means to promote and finance trade facilitation. However, the debate over this proposal has recognized that trade liberalization generally involves "winners" and "losers," even if the overall outcome is welfare-enhancing. Several important policy implications follow from this. First, developing countries should be compensated for their loss of productive and export capacities. Less productive enterprises, including small farmers facing subsidized agribusiness competition from G7 and Cairns Group countries, can be expected to go out of business following trade liberalization. In many industrialized countries, many losers have been protected to varying degrees, such as manufacturing workers receiving welfare, unemployment support, retraining programs, and the like. Second, most developing-country governments cannot make up for such lost tariff revenues, and need to be compensated by the richer countries. Third, developing countries—especially the least developed in Africa, the Caribbean, and small island states in the Pacific—need to be compensated to accept the erosion of existing preferences because of further multilateral trade liberalization. Fourth, and most importantly from a development point of view, there are considerable and uncertain costs involved in developing alternative and internationally competitive productive and export capacities and capabilities. Fifth, developing countries have been emphatic that aid for trade must truly be additional to promised official development assistance, which has never been delivered despite being in existence since the 1960s; otherwise, aid for trade risks becoming another excuse for imposing new conditionalities promoting trade liberalization.

The World Bank has long supported the World Trade Organization (WTO) in promoting trade liberalization, often citing projections made using a computable general equilibrium (CGE), the so-called LINKAGE model. A CGE model is essentially a system of equations, describing the behaviors of firms, households, governments, and so on. LINKAGE happens to be a particularly large CGE model with more than 40,000 equations. As in any economic model or system of equations, the number of equations matches the number of variables. The data requirements for parameters and base year variables are tremendous, and trade elasticities in particular are often mere guesstimates, which nonetheless have crucial implications. The effects of trade liberalization then are estimated by removing tariffs and subsidies, which enter the price equations affecting demand decisions.

World Bank projections of ostensible gains from complete trade liberalization (Anderson and Martin 2005) have been significantly revised downward from earlier estimates made just a few years before, presumably owing to the observed effects of trade liberalization in the interim. More than 70 percent of these gains accrue to rich countries, including two thirds of the global benefits from agricultural trade liberalization, and even more for non-textile manufacturers. More than two thirds of the static gains to developing countries from trade liberalization accrue to Argentina, Brazil, and India in the case of agriculture, and to China and Vietnam in the case of textiles and garments.

As full trade liberalization is not under negotiation in the Doha Round, Anderson and Martin (2005) also considered several possible Doha Round scenarios of trade liberalization. Their most realistic scenario projects welfare gains by 2015 of $96 billion, a third of their estimated gains from full trade liberalization, most of which, some $80 billion, or 83 percent, flows to rich countries.

Crucially, the LINKAGE model presumes that governments do not, cannot, or do not want to increase either borrowing or expenditure, which means that the public deficit in the model remains constant. In order to achieve this, governments must raise taxes after tariff removal. Thus, crucial issues—a thin tax base and a large informal sector—are assumed away, implying that taxes can be raised easily. Obviously, if taxes on household consumption are raised, private demand decreases. On the positive side, consumption increases because the prices of imports fall following tariff removal.

An overall positive estimate of gains from trade liberalization relies crucially on a large positive export supply response—which is a heroic assumption when internationally competitive productive and export capacities do not already exist, as in most developing countries, especially the poorest ones. Additional real income—from increased exports and higher consumption—is presumed to out-weigh the impact of increased taxes on households in developing countries.

Most African governments cannot fully substitute lost tariff revenues with new and higher taxes. The main concessions African developing countries are expected to get from a Doha deal are reduced agricultural subsidies and tariffs in OECD countries, but the neglect of both infrastructure and agricultural development over two decades of BWI structural adjustment programs has left these countries with little capacity to respond to such export opportunities. What, then, can Africa gain from a Doha deal? How likely are African countries to realize even the paltry $16 billion projected by this model for developing countries? Developing economies' aggregate nominal GDP, according to the *UNCTAD Handbook of Statistics 2008*, was just above $14 trillion in 2007—making $16 billion, or one tenth of 1 percent, seem fairly negligible and not the big boost to development that the Doha Round is touted to be.

Another World Bank study analyzed the effects on SSA countries of "complete" trade liberalization under a Doha agreement. Its estimates suggest that SSA could gain substantially because "farm employment, the real value of agricultural output and exports, the real returns to farm land and unskilled labor, and real net farm incomes would all rise substantially in capital-scarce SSA countries with a move to free merchandise trade" (Anderson, Martin, and van der Mensbrugghe 2005: 26). According to the simulation results (Anderson, Martin, and van der Mensbrugghe 2005: 38, table 2), SSA excluding South Africa could gain as much as $3.5 billion. SSA GDP in 2007, excluding South Africa, was roughly $550 billion (*UNCTAD Handbook of Statistics 2008*), implying total welfare gains of a little more than half of 1 percent of 2007 GDP. This is much more than the tenth of 1 percent in expected gains for all developing countries relative to 2007 GDP discussed above— but neither is it a lot. Some of the poorest and least developed countries in SSA are also expected to be net losers under "realistic" Doha scenarios (Anderson, Martin, and van der Mensbrugghe 2005: 48, table 12).

To be sure, such gains from trade liberalization are one-time increases attribut-able to theoretical static comparative advantage gains. Such calculations ignore the realities behind the decline of, for example, African food agriculture in recent decades. As previously discussed at length, World Bank structural adjustment programs helped undermine the meager competitiveness of African smallholder agriculture. A comprehensive Doha agreement that lowers agricultural subsidies in the North would raise many imported food prices for developing countries, at least in the short-to-medium term, further reducing many of the long-term welfare improvements these models predict. Hence, it is important to consider the implications of reduced subsidies for food-importing countries as well as non-food farmers in all countries.

A more recent large-scale investigation, based on the MIRAGE model (Bouët 2008), produced similar results: Rich countries will receive 74 percent of total gains, while middle-income and LDCs will get 24 percent and 2 percent respectively. These welfare gains represent increases—in real income by 2015 relative to the base year level—of three tenths, two fifths, and four fifths of 1 percent respectively. SSA, excluding Zambia, South Africa, and members of the Southern African Customs Union, should experience an increase in welfare of three fifths of 1 percent by 2015 relative to initial GDP. It is not surprising that these numbers are so close to those produced by LINKAGE, as the MIRAGE model is structurally comparable and utilizes the same data set.

Bouët (2008) also summarized estimates for full trade liberalization from a variety of other CGE models. First, all the research papers reviewed by him expect trade liberalization to increase world GDP. However, Bouët (2008: 56) cautions that

> [t]his conclusion does not mean that all countries or all economic agents are better off. Liberalizing trade creates a "larger cake", but some can get smaller pieces than others; if efficient redistribution mechanisms are put in place, all agents could experience increased welfare.

This also supports the case for the need to compensate losers. Several studies reviewed by Bouët (2008: table 4.2) suggest that SSA will be one of the losers in terms of welfare. Bouët et al. (2005) found that rich countries would gain $19 billion and China and South Asia $1 billion each, while other developing countries would lose $3 billion.

The likely contribution of such different scenarios toward poverty reduction varies greatly and is further limited by the declining contribution of economic growth toward poverty reduction because of rising inequality. In view of the historically critical role of trade policy reforms favoring growth and employment for economic development—as opposed to trade liberalization—the consequences of trade liberalization for sustainable development are dubious.

Other estimates—not discussed by Bouët (2008)—suggest even more modest gains, with their impacts on poverty and inequality very sensitive to assumptions, definitions and data quality (e.g. Ackerman 2002). Using a simplified, but structurally similar model, Taylor and von Arnim (2006) show how heavily trade liberalization simulation results depend on assumptions. With the benefit of a bit more realism—considering unemployment, for example—it becomes clear that Africa will *not* gain, on balance, from trade liberalization. Their exercise suggests that SSA is likely to experience welfare losses, even assuming the absence of macroeconomic shocks. The region is likely to experience a worsening trade balance, debt problems are likely to increase, and any short-term gains in employment and GDP could evaporate quickly under the pressure of such strained balances.

517

Even though his model's details differ, Kraev's (2005) alternative analysis of the effects of trade liberalization on GDP has a methodology and aims compatible with those of Taylor and von Arnim. By endogenizing output, employment, and the current account in a CGE framework, he estimates future risks and past losses resulting from trade liberalization. With the current account and employment endogenized, trade liberalization is found to induce macroeconomic volatility—with mostly negative effects for developing regions. Kraev considers two different scenarios. In the first, it is assumed that the trade balance remains unchanged, but that the level of demand is variable (implying the possibility of underemployment of resources). With trade liberalization, imports increase and domestic demand must decrease to satisfy the external balance constraint. Results in this scenario suggest losses in the order of 10 percent of GDP (Kraev 2005: 14, table 3) for SSA. The second scenario holds GDP constant, and varies the trade balance. As the level of demand remains unchanged, the trade balance worsens considerably, resulting in growing external deficits (Kraev 2005: 15–16, tables 4 and 5).

Polaski (2006) introduces unemployment and separates agricultural labor markets from urban unskilled labor markets in an otherwise standard CGE model. She concludes that: (1) global gains from further trade liberalization will be very modest; (2) in sharp contrast to the World Bank's full employment models, developing countries' gains come overwhelmingly from market access for manufactured exports; and (3) the largest gains will accrue to countries such as China, while the poorest countries (mainly in SSA) will be net losers. Thus, global gains from any realistic negotiated agreement are close to negligible. "Full liberalization" would bring growth of about half a percent. A "central Doha scenario" could be expected to increase base year global GDP by 0.19 percent,[14] and a "central Doha scenario with 'Special Products' for Developing Countries" by 0.18 percent (Polaski 2006: 22, table 3.1). In contrast to the previously discussed studies, Polaski found that developing countries' aggregate GDP would *decrease* by $6.3 billion, while developed countries' GDP would increase by $5.5 billion with an agreement dominated by agriculture. On the other hand, developing countries' GDP would *increase* by $23 billion, while developed countries would increase by $30.2 billion with an agreement focusing on manufactures.

Crucially, these gross developing-country aggregates obscure the likely impact of trade liberalization on Africa. SSA (excluding South Africa) would lose $122 billion with an agreement focusing on manufacturing trade liberalization, despite the gains for developing countries as a whole (Polaski 2006: 26, figure 3.4). SSA (excluding South Africa) would lose $106 billion with an agreement focusing on agricultural trade liberalization (Polaski 2006: 28, figure 3.8). Polaski's findings appear to more accurately reflect the widespread problems of lack of infrastructure, export capacities, and diminished competitiveness in *both* industry and agriculture in SSA.

Recent advances in international trade theory do not support the case for trade liberalization in SSA either (see Bernard et al. 2007). "New trade theories" and evolutionary studies of technological development suggest that countries risk being "locked" into permanent slow growth by pursuing static comparative advantage. It is now generally acknowledged that economic growth—particularly the accumulation of capacities and capabilities—precedes export growth. In that sense, trade can foster a virtuous circle, but cannot trigger it. Meanwhile, UNCTAD has long pointed to the importance of growth for trade expansion, and, more specifically, to the weakness of the investment–export nexus, that accounts for the failure of many countries to expand and diversify their exports. Also, rapid resource reallocation is not generally feasible without high rates of growth and investment.

Africa's export collapse in the 1980s and 1990s involved "a staggering annual income loss of US\$68 billion—or 21 percent of regional GDP" (World Bank 2000; quoted by Mkandawire 2005). However, "Africa's failures have been developmental, not export failure per se" (Helleiner 2002a: 4). Rodrik (1997) has also argued that Africa's "marginalization" is not due to trade performance per se, although this may be seen as low by international standards. Another view suggests that Africa trades as much as is to be expected, given its geography and per capita income level. Indeed, "Africa overtrades compared with other developing regions in the sense that its trade is higher than would be expected from the various determinants of bilateral trade" (Coe and Hoffmaister 1999; Foroutan and Pritchet 1993).

Mkandawire (2005) notes that the advent of the WTO trade regime was expected to entail losses for Africa from the outset, especially with the loss of preferential treatment (from erstwhile colonial rulers and the European Union under the Lome Convention). Trade liberalization under WTO auspices has significantly reduced the policy options available to developmental states, especially for trade, industrial, or investment policy (Adelman and Yeldan 2000; Panchamukhi 1996; Rodrik 2000a), though some (e.g. Amsden 1999) argue that the WTO regime still leaves room for industrial policy initiatives.

There is considerable controversy concerning structure, assumptions, and resulting estimates from particular models. Overall, though, there is broad agreement that gains for SSA countries from any realistically achievable Doha agreement are, with near certainty, negligibly small, if not negative. It is also important to remember that neither CGE models nor theoretical debates about trade liberalization are directly relevant to the WTO negotiations.

What and with whom does Africa trade?

Africa is less dependent on developed-country demand for its exports today than when the debt crisis hit in the early 1980s (Table 17.9). Asia has emerged as a major

Table 17.9 GDP components of major petroleum exporters in developing Africa, 1970–2006

Major petroleum exporters: Developing Africa Averages of percentage shares in GDP	1970 to 1979	1980 to 1989	1990 to 1999	2000 to 2006
Consumption	59%	64%	64%	53%
Government expenditure	22%	21%	16%	13%
Investment	20%	18%	18%	18%
Exports	39%	32%	36%	43%
Imports	40%	35%	35%	27%
Agriculture, hunting, forestry, fishing	**22%**	**19%**	**20%**	**20%**
Industry	52%	52%	46%	52%
Mining, manufacturing, utilities	45%	45%	41%	48%
Manufacturing	21%	22%	10%	5%
Construction	7%	7%	5%	4%
Services	**26%**	**29%**	**34%**	**28%**
Wholesale, retail trade, restaurants, and hotels	11%	11%	13%	11%
Transport, storage, and communications	4%	5%	5%	5%
Other activities	11%	13%	16%	12%

Sources: UNCTAD *Handbook of Statistics* and authors' calculations
(Table 8.3 Gross domestic product by type of expenditure and by kind of economic activity.) Includes Angola, Congo, Equatorial Guinea, Gabon, Algeria, Libya, Sudan, Nigeria.

trading partner while increased SSA trade integration has reduced the share of exports to the developed world from 74 percent in the 1970s to 59 percent in 2000–6. The export share to East Asia—which includes the ten Association of Southeast Asian Nations (ASEAN) members plus China, Japan, and South Korea—nearly tripled from 5 percent to 14 percent.

However, most of this trade expansion is fairly recent. The share of exports for East Asia averaged 5 percent from 1970–89, grew to 8 percent in the 1990s, and has since jumped to 14 percent. The growth of China's demand for commodities since the late 1990s has been the driving force behind this trend. Notably, intra-SSA exports increased strongly from 5 percent of total exports in the 1960s to 12 percent in 2000–6. Intraregional trade also has significant potential for development, if it relies on and strengthens developmental linkages. The declining importance of industrialized countries' markets for African commodity exporters may have reduced the continent's direct vulnerability to the business cycles of the Western economies compared with the emerging economies of Asia.

Second, sourcing from emerging countries has increased. The lower part of Table 17.9 shows that the decline in the share of imports from developed countries is even more pronounced than for exports, with its share falling from 80 percent in the 1970s to 53 percent in 2000–6. Similarly, as above, both Asian and intraregional import sources have become more important, with the former rising from 7 percent to 20 percent, and the latter from 5 percent to 12 percent.

The apparent diversification in terms of the origin and destination of imports and exports decreases dependence and improves economic integration in some respects, but the greater reliance on minerals is worrying. Also, the developmental implications of diversifying primary commodity export markets and import sources, with greater trade through neighboring transit economies, should not be exaggerated. The persistent reliance on exports of primary commodities, especially minerals, is telling, especially for SSA countries. Table 17.10 shows the share of primary commodity exports in total world exports and selected African country groups. The global share of commodity exports rose slightly from 1995–2000 to 2000–6.

The upturns for a wide range of commodity prices, especially petroleum-related products, have had important consequences. The share of these exports for all developing countries in Africa increased from 71 percent in 1995–2000 to about 73 percent in 2001–6, and from an overwhelming 96 percent to 97 percent for the major petroleum exporters in the region. This picture—aggregating all primary commodities—obscures the declining role of agricultural exports, as reflected in the lower part of Table 17.10. For all developing economies in Africa, the average share of agricultural exports in total exports fell from 18 percent to 12 percent between 1995–2000 and 2000–6. The fall in the share of agricultural exports is likely due to a combination of much higher oil and other mineral prices—in excess of also rising agricultural commodity prices—and continued structural change toward services.

This is underlined by the fact that Africa, particularly SSA, did not significantly increase the exports of manufactured goods in 2001–6 as compared to 1995–2000 (Table 17.11). While developing economies in Asia export as much as 26 percent of total manufactured goods in the world, Africa's share of world manufactured exports does not reach 1 percent. This is even more pronounced for petroleum-exporting countries in Africa—compared to petroleum exporters in other regions of the world—but holds for all of SSA, including South Africa.

Table 17.10 Destinations and sources of SSA trade with selected regions, 1960–2006

Destination and origin of SSA trade Export shares, selected regions, 1960–2006	1960 to 1969	1970 to 1979	1980 to 1989	1990 to 1999	2000 to 2006
To developed countries	74%	69%	64%	62%	59%
To ASEAN+3*	5%	6%	6%	8%	14%
Intra-Sub-Saharan Africa	5%	5%	4%	10%	12%
To rest of the world	16%	20%	26%	20%	15%
Import shares, selected regions, 1960–2006					
From developed countries	80%	80%	71%	64%	53%
From ASEAN+3	7%	10%	11%	18%	20%
Intra-Sub-Saharan Africa	5%	5%	6%	10%	12%
From rest of the world	8%	4%	12%	8%	15%

Sources: UNCTAD *Handbook of Statistics* and author's calculations

Note: *ASEAN+3 includes the ASEAN members plus China, Japan and South Korea.

Table 17.11 Africa's export composition, 1995–2006

Africa's export composition Share of primary commodity exports, 1995–2006*	1995 to 2000	2001 to 2006
World	22.04%	23.67%
Developing economies: Africa	70.99%	72.86%
Major petroleum exporters: Developing Africa	96.44%	97.39%
Sub-Saharan Africa excluding South Africa	85.48%	83.27%
Share of agricultural exports, 1995–2006**		
World	10.38%	8.57%
Developing economies: Africa	18.15%	12.64%
Major petroleum exporters: Developing Africa	3.27%	1.51%
Sub-Saharan Africa excluding South Africa	27.90%	18.45%

Sources: UNCTAD *Handbook of Statistics* and author's calculations
(Table 2.2 Trade structure of country groupings by partner and product group)
Notes: *Data includes SITC 1 through 4 plus 68; **Data includes SITC 0+1+2-27-28+4; food items plus agricultural raw materials.

More pronounced trade specialization or dependence is principally the result of economic liberalization strategies pursued under the auspices of the BWIs. The period since the 1980s has seen a general neglect of agriculture, especially for food security—often in the form of reduced public spending for infrastructure, agricultural research and development, extension services, and agricultural subsidies—and some encouragement of export-oriented agriculture. Such policies undermined earlier commitments and efforts in the interest of food security, rural development, and even urban-rural redistribution, further weakening the viability of small-scale farming, increasing reliance on food imports, and inadvertently creating the conditions for the food crisis that began late in 2007.

Developed countries, on the other hand, strengthened their efforts to ensure their own food security and support their own farmers. More recently, they have begun promoting biofuels, ostensibly for energy security and climate change mitigation, but which has had the effect of precipitating the food price spikes. Indeed, the possibility of many developing countries gaining from increased agricultural exports has been frustrated by such increased protection and subsidies in rich economies. Trade preferences ensure better market access, particularly for former colonies, least developed countries (LDCs), and African, Caribbean, and Pacific economies. As we will discuss further, erosion of such preferential market access is of particular concern to African countries in negotiations over further trade liberalization. (See Anderson, Martin, and van der Mensbrugghe (2005: 37, table 1, for evidence.)

Trade concentration, tropical fate, and resource curse

By the end of the 1990s, it had become clear that the few acknowledged gains from trade for SSA were of a one-off character, often reflecting switches from domestic to foreign markets without much increase in overall output (Helleiner 2002a, 2002b; Mwega 2002; Ndulu, Semboja, and Mbelle 2002). In some cases, manufactured exports increased even as the manufacturing sector contracted.

> No major expansion occurred in the diversity of products exported by most of the Sub-Saharan African countries... Indeed, the product composition of some of the African countries' exports may have become more concentrated. Africa's recent trade performance was strongly influenced by exports of traditional products which appear to have experienced remarkably buoyant global demand in the mid-1990s (Ng and Yeats 2000: 21; quoted by Mkandawire 2005).

The World Bank (1993: 77) noted that temperate countries grew, on average, by 1.3 percentage points more than tropical countries during the 1965–90 period, after controlling for other factors. The study explains this significant tropical-zone shortfall in terms of the greater prevalence in the tropics of disease, poor soils, typhoons, and other natural calamities.

Surprisingly, the study seems to be oblivious to W. A. Lewis's (1969, 1978) pioneering work, which sought to explain economic performance in the tropics. Lewis (1978) argued that the tropics did not industrialize and grew slower than temperate settlements during the last period of globalization beginning at the end of the nineteenth century. However, his data do not confirm this assertion in his chapter synopsis that "the trade of these new [temperate] settlements accelerated at about the same time as tropical trade, but grew much faster than tropical, U.S. or European trade" (Lewis 1978: 194). Exports from both the new temperate settlements and tropical countries grew faster than either US or European trade.

The tropics generally had more modest export bases than the temperate zone to begin with, suggesting that the tropics were better able to respond to export demand despite the disadvantages they faced.[15] Lewis emphasized that not all tropical countries have been able to take advantage of opportunities from increased export demand. He suggested that the exports in greater demand were largely water-intensive; hence, only those areas with enough water to substantially increase their exports were able to take advantage of the new opportunities. Thus, the more arid tropical areas, such as those in SSA, could not benefit from the increased demand for tropical products.

Some newly industrializing countries in Southeast Asia and some other tropical countries have grown rapidly since the 1960s; but most tropical countries have fared badly, especially in the last two decades of the twentieth century. It is not enough to simply attribute the tropical growth shortfall to "pests, diseases, typhoons and other natural calamities," though such factors may have been important. As mentioned earlier, Lewis observed that the terms of trade for tropical commodity exports have deteriorated badly against temperate commodity exports. In the half century between 1916 and 1966, for example, the index for natural rubber fell from 100 to 16. This suggests that productivity gains in the tropics were largely lost to worsening terms of trade, with the situation worse where few productivity gains were made.

Many observers (e.g., Intal 1997) have suggested that SSA has lagged behind in terms of agricultural development since the 1960s because of inadequate agricultural research and development (R&D) and infrastructure, crop, and agronomic considerations, as well as macroeconomic conditions. Higher temperate-zone agricultural productivity has partly been due to large and sustained investments in agricultural R&D, of which temperate-zone developing countries have been better able to take advantage. The tropical Green Revolution in rice farming since the 1960s has benefited mainly irrigated farms in Southeast and South Asia, while arid-zone agriculture in Africa has generally been left behind. The Southeast Asian success with tree crop agriculture may offer some opportunities for equatorial Africa. Significant investments in tree crop agricultural R&D (in rubber, oil palm, and cocoa for instance) as well as rural infrastructure may have made possible productivity gains in tree crop agriculture as well.

Sachs and Warner (1997) suggests that natural resource wealth is bad for growth. Curiously, the study defines natural-resource abundance in terms of the ratio of net primary product exports to GDP in 1971, without distinguishing extractive non-renewable natural resources (especially minerals) from agricultural products. So-called Dutch disease mainly involves the former, which tends to be very capital-intensive and only involves a small proportion of the population in extraction of the resource. Consequently, additional income from resource extraction accrues mainly to a few while appreciation of the country's currency affects the entire population.

Agricultural exports generally involve much more of the population, and increased income usually accrues to all involved, diffusing the adverse consequences of currency appreciation. Most Southeast Asian high-performing economies have been major agricultural exporters, which has helped to offset problems associated with the mineral exports of Malaysia and Indonesia, in sharp contrast to, say, Nigeria. Generally better macroeconomic management—including undervalued exchange rates—has also helped, especially to check the tendency to indulge in expenditure on imports or non-tradables.

Conclusions

Circumstances since the 1980s have fundamentally changed the environment and conditions for developing states attempting to pursue selective industrial or investment policy. Most importantly, economic liberalization—at both national and international levels—has seriously constrained the scope for government policy interventions, including selective industrial promotion efforts. This is especially apparent in international economic relations, but is also true of the domestic policy environment, where World Bank and IMF policy conditionalities as well as WTO and other obligations have radically transformed the scope for national economic development policy initiatives.

There has been a widespread and rapid opening up of trade, investment, finance, and other flows. Very often, such liberalization has been externally imposed by the BWIs as conditions to secure access to emergency credit during the debt crises of the 1980s and, more recently, in the wake of currency and financial crises. This has been especially true of much of Latin America and Africa, which experienced a "lost decade" of economic growth in the 1980s. The 1990s were only slightly better, with sporadic, but not sustained, growth spurts. While the Washington Consensus has been challenged, if not discredited, in academic and even policy circles, revised versions continue to provide the ideological basis for economic analysis and policymaking in developing countries, especially in African, Latin American, and other smaller economies.

Invariably, the circumstances of such policy changes as well as the limited policy capabilities of the governments concerned have meant that little preparation—in terms of a proactive strategy or transitional policies to anticipate and cope with the implications of sudden exposure to new international competition—has been undertaken. Few of the investment policy instruments of the past are viable or feasible options today, including many used successfully in post-war East Asia. Most of the main industrial policy tools were used by the advanced industrial economies, including those that now deny such selective industrial promotion to others. Indeed, most advanced economies still have a plethora of policies and institutions involved in R&D, skills training, investment promotion, and infrastructure provision, such as those for new information and communication technologies (ICT) and export promotion.

Such policies and institutions are probably necessary, but certainly not sufficient for stimulating and sustaining economic growth and structural change for developing countries to try to "catch up." Additional initiatives are urgently needed to prevent such economies—already at a historical disadvantage in various respects—from falling further behind the industrially more developed economies of the North, as well as the other newly industrialized economies that have emerged in recent decades.

The preceding discussion strongly suggests that much of the conventional wisdom regarding African development and poverty is not only misguided, but also often harmful. International financial liberalization has not improved growth, but has instead exacerbated volatility. For Africa, net capital outflows, facilitated by such liberalization, have exceeded official development assistance (ODA) inflows—not only on a net, but also even on a gross basis. Worse still, there is strong evidence that some of the economic policy advice given to, and the conditionalities imposed upon, SSA governments have reflected vested interests and prejudices. In recent years, much emphasis has been given to promoting FDI, even though experiences elsewhere show that FDI generally tends to follow, rather than lead domestic investments. Not surprisingly, there continues to be limited FDI, mainly confined to the minerals sector, with limited employment and other benefits. Nonetheless, economic policy reforms have enhanced the profitability and protection of FDI while reducing the trickle-down benefits to domestic economies of such enclave investments.

Available evidence suggests that the gains from trade liberalization will be modest for the world economy, and even more so for developing countries, while gains for Africa are even less assured. There is considerable evidence that the main winners from agricultural trade liberalization will be the existing big agricultural exporters from North America, Australasia, Southeast Asia, and the Southern Cone of Latin America. Nonetheless, many well-meaning advocates have joined in the chorus calling for agricultural trade liberalization as if it will boost development in Africa.

In view of the pervasive influence of such erroneous and harmful policy advice and conditionalities, it is crucial to increase "policy space" for governments to be able to pursue policies for development. Countries need to be able to choose or design their own development strategies as well as elaborate and implement more appropriate development policies. Besides enhancing policy space, it is necessary to increase financial resources for development. The removal of the huge debt overhangs of the poorest countries through debt relief has been an important step in this direction. Massive and sustained increases in ODA are needed to kick-start investments and growth and, in the longer term, to reduce the continent's resource gap and dependence on aid (UNCTAD 2006). Over two decades of economic stagnation, contraction, and increased poverty, corruption, abuse, as well as disease, conflict, and other scourges have also taken a huge toll on the continent's economic, social, and political fabric, and proactive efforts are urgently required to build new capacities and capabilities for development.

As economic growth and development do not necessarily reduce poverty and inequalities, special efforts are needed to ensure such outcomes. The United Nations' Millennium Development Goals (MDGs) provide some specific welfare targets and indicators for this purpose. Enhanced social expenditure should be universal as far as possible to ensure broad public support and, thus, sustainability, but selective targeting—including affirmative action measures—may be needed to overcome long-term discrimination, marginalization, and neglect. After all, progress toward achieving the MDG indicators may still bypass the poor, as even the rising tide of economic growth does not raise all boats.

The MDGs are important for and mutually reinforce the UN's broader Development Agenda of internationally agreed-upon development goals derived from the UN's global summits and conferences, especially since the 1990s, such as the Earth Summit in Rio de Janeiro in 1992, the Population and Development Conference in Cairo in 1994, the Fourth World Conference on Women in Beijing in 1995, the

Copenhagen Summit in 1995, the Monterrey Conference on Financing for Development in 2002, and the World Conference on Sustainable Development in Johannesburg in 2002, among others. This agenda has been reiterated and given greater coherence by the Millennium Declaration of 2000 and the Outcome Document of the World Summit in September 2005. It is now up to African governments to follow through with meaningful reforms to reinstitute sustainable development processes, and for the international community of donors and the BWIs to provide the financial means, other resources, and policy space for them to do so.

Notes

1. Jomo K. Sunderam is Assistant Secretary-General for Economic Development in the United Nations Department of Economic and Social Affairs (UN-DESA). Rudiger von Arnim is Assistant Professor in the Department of Economics, University of Utah, UT, and completed this work while working for the G24 Intergovernmental Group on International Monetary Affairs and Development. We are grateful to Richard Kozul-Wright as well as two anonymous referees for suggestions to improve this paper and to Miriam Rehm and Sheba Tejani for their editorial assistance, but implicate none of them.

2. More recently, this domestic focus has gone beyond economic policies to include institutions, governance, the role of rent-seeking elites, ethnic diversity, geography, etc. This chapter is concerned with macroeconomic developments, and will not delve into this literature. For a theoretical discussion of rents and rent-seeking, see Khan and Jomo (2000). For a discussion of corruption, see Jomo (2009).

3. See, for example, Stiglitz (1998) and Stein (2008).

4. See Alassane Ouattara (1997) and World Bank (2000). Commenting on the continuing stagnation of African per capita incomes, *The Economist* (2001: 12) argued that "it would be odd to blame globalization for holding Africa back. Africa has been left out of the global economy, partly because its governments used to prefer it that way."

5. According to earlier World Bank figures, the number of poor people in the developing world had decreased slightly from 1179 million in 1987 to 1120 million in 1998 (Chen and Ravallion 2010). Meanwhile, the number of poor in SSA rose from 217 million in 1987 to 291 million in 1998, averaging around 46 percent of the SSA population over the period (World Bank 2001b: 17, 23). The proportion of the population with less than $1 a day in the least developed African countries was still higher and rising, increasing from an average of 55.8 percent in 1965–9 to 64.9 percent in 1995–9 (UNCTAD 2002: tables 19, 20).

6. Angola, Equatorial Guinea, and Chad are three of the four highest ranked countries if recipient country FDI is related to recipient country GDP. South Africa ranks low in that list.

7. We owe these observations to Carl Gray and Oumar Diallo, who have also provided other valuable comments and suggestions.

8. Note that both Latin American and African developing countries experienced this decline after 2003. The increase in Asia's share of total aid may have been due to large amounts of emergency aid in the wake of severe natural disasters, such as the Indian Ocean tsunami.

9. See, as well, Jalilian and Weiss (2000) on the issue of SSA de-industrialization.

10. Also see Bates (1981).

11. Numerous studies have confirmed the importance of good infrastructure for production capacity enhancement and trade facilitation (see Badiane and Shively 1998; Abdulai 2000).

12. The Cairns Group is a group of 19 agriculture exporting countries, comprising Argentina, Australia, Bolivia, Brazil, Canada, Chile, Colombia, Costa Rica, Guatemala, Indonesia, Malaysia, New Zealand, Pakistan, Paraguay, Peru, the Philippines, South Africa, Thailand, and Uruguay.

13. Dani Rodrik, "Don't cry for Doha," *Daily Star* (Egypt), August 5, 2008.

14. The "central Doha scenario" assumes that developed and developing countries decrease tariffs on agricultural (manufactured) products by 36 percent (50 percent) and 24 percent (33 percent) respectively. Export subsidies are eliminated completely, and domestic support is reduced by a third in all regions.

15. For the period 1883–1913, for example, French Indochina, Thailand, British Ceylon, West Africa, French West Africa, and Madagascar all had average annual export growth rates of 5 percent or more, while Brazil had 4.5 percent. Among the new *temperate* settlements—Canada, Australia, New Zealand, Argentina, Chile, South Africa, and Uruguay—only Argentina and South Africa featured export growth rates above 5 percent (see Lewis 1978: 195, tables 8.1 and 8.2).

References

Abdulai, A. (2000). "Spatial Price Transmission and Asymmetry in the Ghanaian Maize Market," *Journal of Development Economics*, 63: 327–49.

Adelman, I. and Yeldan, E. (2000). "Is this the End of Economic Development?" *Structural Change and Economic Dynamics*, 11: 95–109.

Akyüz, Y. (1996). "The Investment-Profit Nexus in East Asian Industrialization," *World Development*, 24 (3): 461–70.

Amsden, A. (1989). *Asia's Next Giant*. New York: Oxford University Press.

——(1999). "Industrialization Under New WTO Law," UNCTAD X High Level Round Table on Development Directions for the Twenty-First Century, Bangkok.

Anderson, K. and Martin, W. (eds.) (2005). *Agricultural Trade Reform and the Doha Development Agenda*. Washington, DC: World Bank.

Anderson, K., Martin, W., and van der Mensbrugghe, D. (2005). "Would Multilateral Trade Reform Benefit Sub-Saharan Africans?" Policy Research Working Paper. Washington, DC: World Bank.

Ariff, M. and Hill, H. (1985). Export-*Oriented Industrialization: The ASEAN Experience*. Sydney: Allen and Unwin.

Badiane, O. and Shively, G. (1998). "Spatial Integration, Transport Costs, and the Response of Local Prices to Policy Changes in Ghana," *Journal of Development Economics*, 56: 411–31.

Bates, R. (1981). *Markets and States in Tropical Africa*. Berkeley: University of California Press.

Bernard, A. B., Jensen, J. B., Redding, S. J., and Schott, P. K. (2007). "Firms in International Trade," *Journal of Economic Perspectives*, 21 (3): 105–30.

Bhagwati, J. (1988). "Export-Promoting Trade Strategy: Issues and Evidence," *World Bank Research Observer*, 3 (1): 27–57.

Bhattacharya, O., Montiel, P., and Sharma, S. (1997). "Can Sub-Saharan Africa Attract Private Capital Flows?" *Finance and Development*, June, 34 (2): 3–6.

Bird, G. (2001). "IMF Programmes: Do They Work? Can They Be Made to Work Better?" *World Development*, 29 (11): 1849–65.

Bouët, A. (2008). "The Expected Benefits of Trade Liberalization for World Income and Development: Opening the 'Black Box' of Global Trade Modeling," *IFPRI Food Policy Review*. Available at <http://www.ifpri.org/publication/expected-benefits-trade-liberalization-world-income-and-development>.

——Mevel, S., and Orden, D. (2005). "More or Less Ambition? Modeling the Development Impact of US-EU Agricultural Proposals in the Doha Round," IFPRI Information Brief. Washington, DC: International Food Policy Research Institute.

Boyce, J. K. and Ndikumana, L. (2000). "Is Africa a Net Creditor? New Estimates of Capital Flight from Severely Indebted Sub-Saharan African Countries, 1970–1996," Political Economy Research Institute, University of Massachusetts, Amherst.

Bradford Jr., C. I. (1990). "Policy Interventions and Markets: Development Strategy: Typologies and Policy Options," in Gary Gereffi and Donald Wyman (eds.), *Manufacturing Miracles: Paths of Industrialization In Latin America and East Asia*. Princeton, NJ: Princeton University Press.

Chang, Ha-Joon (1994). *The Political Economy of Industrial Policy*. Basingstoke: Macmillan.

Coe, D. and Hoffmaister, A. (1999). "North-South Trade: Is Africa Unusual?" *Journal of African Economies*, 8 (2): 228–56.

Collier, P. (2004). "Africa's Exodus: Capital Flight and the Brain Drain as Portfolio Decisions," *Journal of African Economies*, 13: 15–54.

——(2007). *The Bottom Billion: Why the Poorest Countries are Failing and What Can Be Done About It*. New York: Oxford University Press.

——Elliott, V. L., Hegre, H., Hoeffler, A., Reynal-Querol, M., and Sambanis, N. (2003). *Breaking The Conflict Trap: Civil War And Development Policy*. New York: Oxford University Press, 11–50.

——and Gunning, J. W. (1997). *Explaining African Economic Performance*. Oxford: Centre for the Study of African Economies, Oxford University.

————(1999). "Why Has Africa Grown Slowly?" *Journal of Economic Perspectives*, 13 (3): 3–22.

——Hoeffler, A., and Patillo, C. (1999). "Flight Capital as Portfolio Choice," International Monetary Fund, Washington, DC.

Collins, S. M. and Bosworth, B. P. (1996). "Economic Growth in East Asia: Accumulation Versus Assimilation," *Brookings Papers on Economic Activity*, 2: 135–203.

Darity, Jr, W. A. (2005). "Africa, Europe and Origins of Uneven Development: The Role of Slavery," in C. Conrad, J. Whitehead, P. Mason, and J. Stewart (eds.), *African Americans in the U.S. Economy*. Oxford: Rowman and Littlefield, 14–19.

——and Davis, L. (2005). "Growth, Trade and Uneven Development," *Cambridge Journal of Economics*, 29 (1), January, 141–70.

Devajaran, S., Easterly, W., and Pack, H. (1999). "Is Investment in Africa Too Low or Too High? Macro and Micro Evidence." Washington, DC: World Bank.

Easterly, W. (2000). "The Lost Decades: Developing Countries Stagnation in Spite of Policy Reform, 1980–1998," *Journal of Economic Growth*, 6: 135–57.

——(2001). *The Elusive Quest for Growth: Economists' Adventures and Misadventures in the Tropics*. Cambridge, MA: MIT Press.

——(2007). *The White Man's Burden: Why the West's Efforts to Aid the Rest Have Done So Much Ill and So Little Good*. New York: Penguin Press.

——and Levine, R. (1995). "Africa's Growth Tragedy: A Retrospective 1960–89," Policy Research Working Paper 1503. Washington, DC: World Bank.

ECA (2004). *Economic Report on Africa, 2004: Unlocking Africa's Trade Potential*. Addis Ababa: Economic Commission for Africa.

The Economist (2001). "Globalisation and its Critics: A Survey of Globalisation," *The Economist*, September 29: 5–6.

Elbadawi, I. and Mwega, F. M. (2000). "Can Africa's Saving Collapse Be Reversed?" *World Bank Economic Review*, 14 (3): 415–43.

Fischer, S., Hernàndez-Catà, E., and Khan, M. S. (1998). "Africa: Is This the Turning Point?" Washington, DC: World Bank.

Foroutan, F. and Pritchet, L. (1993). "Intra-Sub-Saharan African Trade: Is It Too Little?" *Journal of African Economies*, 2 (1): 74–105.

Geda, A. and Shimeles, A. (2007). "Openness, Trade Liberalization, Inequality and Poverty in Africa," in Jomo K. S. (ed.), *Flat World, Big Gaps*. London: Zed Books.

Gerschenkron, A. (1962). *Economic Backwardness in Historical Perspective*. Cambridge, MA: Harvard University Press.

Helleiner, G. K. (2002a). Introduction, in G. K. Helleiner (ed.), *Non-Traditional Export Promotion in Africa: Experience and Issues*. London: Palgrave.

——(2002b). *Non-Traditional Export Promotion in Africa: Experience and Issues*. New York: Palgrave.

Hernández-Catá, E. (2000). "Raising Growth and Investment in Sub-Saharan Africa: What Can Be Done?" Washington, DC: International Monetary Fund.

Intal Jr, P. S. (1997). Comments on Chapter 2 of the Emerging Asia Study: "Economic Growth and Transformation," "Emerging Asia" Seminar, Asian Development Bank, Manila, September, 1–2.

Jalilian, H. and Weiss, J. (2000). "De-Industrialization in Sub-Saharan: Myth or Crisis?" in H. Jalilian, M. Tribe, and John Weiss (eds.), *Industrial Development and Policy in Africa*. Cheltenham: Edward Elgar.

Jomo K. (2009). "Good Governance, Anti-Corruption, and Economic Development," in Robert Rotberg (ed.), *Corruption and Global Security*. Cambridge, MA: American Academy for the Advancement of Science, 457–68.

Kasekende, L., Kitabire, D., and Martin, M. (1997). "Capital Inflows and Macroeconomic Policy in Sub-Saharan Africa," in G. K. Helleiner (ed.), *Capital Account Regimes*. London: Macmillan.

Khan, M. H. and Jomo K. S. (eds.) (2000). Rents, Rent-Seeking and Economic Development: Theory and Asian Evidence. Cambridge: Cambridge University Press.

Killick, T. (1992). "Explaining Africa's Post Independence Development Experiences," Biennial Conference on African Economic Issues, Lome.

Kim, Jong-Il and Lawrence, L. (1994). "The Sources of Economic Growth of the East Asian Newly Industrialized Countries," *Journal of the Japanese and International Economies*, 8 (3): 235–71.

Kraev, E. (2005). "Estimating GDP Effects of Trade Liberalization on Developing Countries." London: Christian Aid.

Krugman, P. (1994). "The Myth of Asia's Miracle," *Foreign Affairs*, 73 (6): 62–78.

Lewis, W. A. (1969). "Aspects of Tropical Trade, 1883–1965," *Wicksell Lectures*. Stockholm: Almqvist & Wicksell.

——(1978). *Growth and Fluctuations, 1870–1913*. London: Allen & Unwin.

Lindauer, D. L. and Valenchik, A. D. (1994). "Can African Labor Compete?" in D. L. Lindauer and M. Roemer (eds.), *Asia and Africa Legacies and Opportunities in Development*. San Francisco: ICS Press.

Little, I. (1994). "Trade and Industrialization Revisited," *Pakistan Development Review*, 33 (4i), Winter: 359–89.

——Scitovsky, T., and Scott, M. (1970). *Industry and Trade in Some Developing Countries: A Comparative Study*. New York: Basic Books.

Loayza, N., Schmidt-Hebbel, K., and Servén, L. (2000). "Saving in Developing Countries: An Overview," *The World Economy Review*, 14 (3): 393–414.

Madavo, C. and Sarbib, J. L. (1997). "Africa on the Move: Attracting Private Capital to a Changing Continent," *The SAIS Review*, 7 (2): 111–26.

McPherson, M. F. and Goldsmith, A. A. (2001). "Is Africa on the Move?" Belfer Center for Science & International Affairs, John F. Kennedy School of Government, Harvard University, Cambridge, MA.

——and Rakovski, T. (2001). "Understanding the Growth Process in Sub-Saharan Africa: Some Empirical Estimates of African Economic Policy," Belfer Center for Science & International Affairs, John F. Kennedy School of Government, Harvard University, Cambridge, MA.

Milanovic, B. (2002). "The Two Faces of Globalization: Against Globalization As We Know It," May. Washington, DC: World Bank.

——(2005). *Worlds Apart*. Princeton, NJ: Princeton University Press.

Minoiu, C. and Reddy, S. (2008). "Aid Does Matter After All: Revisiting the Relationship Between Aid and Growth," in J. A. Ocampo, K. S. Jomo, and R. Vos (eds.), *Growth Divergences: Explaining Differences in Economic Performance*. London: Zed Books, 236–59.

Mkandawire, T. (1988). "The Road to Crisis, Adjustment and De-Industrialization: The African Case," *Africa Development* 13 (1): 5–32.

——(2002). "The Terrible Toll of Post-Colonial 'Rebel Movements' in Africa: Toward an Explanation of the Violence Against the Peasantry," *Journal of Modern African Studies*, 40 (2): 181–215.

——(2005). "Maladjusted African Economies and Globalization," *Africa Development*, 30: 1–33.

——(2007). "Universalism versus Targeting," United Nations Research Institute for Social Development, Geneva, in J. A. Ocampo, Jomo K.S., and S. Khan (eds.), *Policy Matters*. London: Zed Books.

——and Soludo, C. C. (1999). *Our Continent, Our Future: African Perspectives on Structural Adjustment*. Trenton, NJ: African World Press.

Mlambo, K. and Oshikoya, T. W. (2001). "Macroeconomic Factors and Investment in Africa," *Journal of African Economies*, 10 (2): 12–47.

Mosley, P., Subasat, T., and Weeks, J. (1995). "Assessing Adjustment in Africa," *World Development*, 23 (9): 1459–73.

Mwega, F. M. (2002). "Promotion of Non-Traditional Exports in Kenya," in G. K. Helleiner (ed.), *Nontraditional Export Promotion in Africa: Experience and Issues*. New York: Palgrave.

Myrdal, G. (1968). *Asian Drama*, 3 vols. New York: Pantheon.

Naya, S., Sandhu, K. S., Plummer, M., and Akrasanee, N. (eds.) (1989). *ASEAN-US Initiative: Assessment and Recommendations for Improved Economic Relations*. Singapore: Institute of Southeast Asian Studies.

Ndikumana, L. and Boyce, J. K. (2002). "Public Debt and Private Assets: Explaining Capital Flight from Sub-Saharan African Countries," Working Paper No. 32. Amherst: Political Economy Research Institute, University of Massachusetts.

——(2008). "New Estimates of Capital Flight from Sub-Saharan African Countries: Linkages with External Borrowing and Policy Options," Working Paper No. 166. Amherst: Political Economy Research Institute, University of Massachusetts.

Ndulu, B. J., Semboja, J., and Mbelle, A. (2002). "Promotion of Non-Traditional Exports in Kenya," in G. K. Helleiner (ed.), *Non-Traditional Export Promotion in Africa: Experience and Issues*. New York: Palgrave.

Nel, P. (2003). "Income Inequality, Economic Growth and Political Instability in Sub-Saharan Africa," *Journal of Modern African Studies*, 41 (4): 611–39.

Ng, F. and Yeats, A. (2000). "On the Recent Trade Performance of Sub-Saharan African Countries: Cause for Hope or More of the Same?" Washington, DC: World Bank.

Ocampo, J. A. and Parra, M. A. (2006). "The Commodity Terms of Trade and Their Strategic Implications for Development," in Jomo K. S. (ed.), *Globalization Under Hegemony: The Changing World Economy*. New Delhi: Oxford University Press.

Ouattara, A. (1997). "The Challenges of Globalization for Africa," Southern African Economic Summit, organized by the World Economic Forum, Harare. Available at <http://www.imf.org/external/np/speeches/1997/052197.htm>.

Panchamukhi, V. (1996). "WTO and Industrial Policies." Geneva: UNCTAD.

Perkins, D. (1994). "There are at Least Three Models of East Asian Development," *World Development*, 22 (4): 655–61.

Pigato, M. (2000). "Foreign Direct Investment in Africa: Old Tales and New Evidence." Washington, DC: World Bank.

Polaski, S. (2006). "Winners and Losers: Impact of the Doha Round on Developing Countries," Carnegie Endowment for International Peace, Washington, DC.

Przeworski, A. and Vreeland, J. (2000). "The Effects of IMF Programs on Economic Growth," *Journal of Development Economics*, 62: 385–421.

Reddy, S. and Miniou, C. (2006). "Real Income Stagnation of Countries, 1960–2001," DESA Working Paper No. 28, September. New York: United Nations.

Rodrik, D. (1994). "Getting Interventions Right: How South Korea and Taiwan Grew Rich," NBER Working Paper No. 4964, December. Cambridge, MA: National Bureau of Economic Research.

——(1995). "Trade Strategy, Investment and Exports: Another Look at East Asia," Working Paper No. 5339, November. Cambridge, MA: National Bureau of Economic Research.

——(1997). "Trade Policy and Economic Performance in Sub-Saharan Africa." Stockholm: Swedish Foreign Ministry.

——(2000a). "Can Integration into the World Economy Substitute for a Development Strategy?" World Bank ABCDE-Europe Conference, Paris. Available at <http://www.hks.harvard.edu/fs/drodrik/publications.html>.

——(2000b). "Saving Transitions," *World Bank Economic Review*, 14 (3): 481–507.

——(2001). "The Global Governance of Trade as If Development Really Mattered," Cambridge, MA: Kennedy School of Government, Harvard University. Available at <http://www.wcfia.harvard.edu/node/587>.

Rodrik, D., Subramanian, A., and Trebbi, F. (2002). "Institutions Rule: The Primacy of Institutions Over Integration and Geography in Economic Development," IMF Working Paper No. 02/189, African Department, November. Washington, DC: International Monetary Fund.

Rosenstein-Rodan, P. N. (1943). "Problems of Industrialisation of Eastern and South-Eastern Europe," *The Economic Journal*, 53: 202–11.

——(1944). "The International Development of Economically Backward Areas," *International Affairs*, 20: 157–65.

Sachs, J. (2005). *The End of Poverty: Economic Possibilities for our Time*. New York: Penguin Press.

——(2008). *Common Wealth: Economics for a Crowded Planet*. New York: Penguin Press.

——and Warner, A. (1995). "Natural Resource Abundance and Economic Growth," HIID Discussion Paper No. 517A. Cambridge, MA: Harvard Institute for International Development.

Sender, J. (1999). "Africa's Economic Performance: Limitations of the Current Consensus," *Journal of Economic Perspectives*, 13 (3): 89–114.

Singh, A. (1982). "Industrialization in Africa: A Structuralist View," in M. Fransman (ed.), *Industry and Accumulation in Africa*. London: Heinemann.

——(1986). "The IMF-World Bank Policy Programme in Africa: A Commentary," in P. Lawrence (ed.), *The World Recession and the Food Crisis in Africa*. London: James Currey and Review of African Political Economy.

——(1987). "Exogenous Shocks and De-Industrialization in Africa: Prospects and Strategies for Re-Industrialization," in RISNODEC, *African Economic Crisis*. New Delhi: RIS.

——(1999). "Should Africa Promote Stock-Market Capitalism?" *Journal of International Development*, 11 (3): 343–67.

Stein, H. (1992). "De-Industrialization, Adjustment and World Bank and IMF in Africa," *World Development*, 20 (1): 83–95.

——(2008). *Beyond the World Bank Agenda: An Institutional Approach to Development*. Chicago: University of Chicago Press.

Stewart, F. (1994). "Are Short-Term Policies Consistent with Long-Term Development Needs in Africa?" in G. A. Cornia, and G. K. Helleiner (eds.), *From Adjustment to Development in Africa: Conflict, Controversy, Convergence, Consensus?* London: Macmillan.

Stiglitz, J. E. (1998). "More Instruments and Broader Goals: Moving Toward the Post-Washington Consensus," UNU/WIDER Lecture, World Institute for Development Economics Research, United Nations University, Helsinki.

Taylor, L. and von Arnim, R. (2006). "Computable General Equilibrium Models of Trade Liberalization: The Doha Debate," Paper for Oxfam UK, January 8. New York: Center for Economic Policy Analysis, New School University.

Toye, J. (1987). *The Dilemma of Development.* Oxford: Blackwell.

UNCTAD (1987). "Handbook of Trade Control Measures of Developing Countries, Supplement: A Statistical Analysis of Trade Control Measures of Developing Countries." Geneva: United Nations Conference on Trade and Development.

——(1995). "Foreign Direct Investment in Africa, 1995." Geneva: United Nations Conference on Trade and Development.

——(1998). "Trade and Development Report, 1998." Geneva: United Nations Conference on Trade and Development.

——(2000). "World Investment Report, 2000: Cross-border Mergers and Acquisitions and Development." Geneva: United Nations Conference on Trade and Development.

——(2001). "Economic Development in Africa: Performance, Prospects and Policy Issues," UNCTAD/GDS/AFRICA/1. Geneva: United Nations Conference on Trade and Development.

——(2002). "Economic Development in Africa: From Adjustment to Poverty Reduction: What is New?" UNCTAD/GDS/AFRICA/2. Geneva: United Nations Conference on Trade and Development.

——(2005). "Economic Development in Africa: Rethinking the Role of Foreign Direct Investment." Geneva: United Nations Conference on Trade and Development.

——(2006). "Doubling Aid: Making The 'Big Push' Work." Geneva: United Nations Conference on Trade and Development.

UNECA (1999). "The ECA and Africa: Accelerating a Continent's Development." Addis Ababa: United Nations Economic Commission for Africa.

UNIDO (1998). "Domestic Capacity-Building for Enhancing Productivity and Competitiveness in Africa," in A. Sall (ed.), The Future Competitiveness of African Economies. Paris: Karthala.

United Nations (2005). "The Inequality Predicament: Report on the World Social Situation, 2005." New York: United Nations Department of Economic and Social Affairs.

——(2008). "World Economic and Social Survey, 2008: Overcoming Economic Insecurity." New York: United Nations Department of Economic and Social Affairs.

Wade, R. (1990). *Governing the Market.* Princeton, NJ: Princeton University Press.

Weisbrot, M., Baker, D., Kraev, E., and Chen, J. (2001). "The Scoreboard on Globalization, 1980–2000: Twenty Years of Diminished Progress." Washington, DC: Center for Economic and Policy Research (CEPR).

——————Naiman, R., and Neta, G. (2000). "Growth May Be Good for the Poor – But are IMF and World Bank Policies Good for Growth?" Washington, DC: Center for Economic and Policy Research (CEPR).

————and Rosnick, D. (2005). "Scorecard on Development: 25 Years of Diminished Progress," CEPR Reports and Issue Briefs 2005–30. Washington, DC: Center for Economic and Policy Research (CEPR).

——Naiman, R., and Kim, J. (2000). "The Emperor Has No Growth: Declining Economic Growth Rates in the Era of Globalization." Washington, DC: Center for Economic and Policy Research (CEPR). Available at <http://www.cepr.net/images/IMF/The_Emperor_Has_No_Growth.htm>.

Wolfensohn, J. (1997). "The Challenge of Inclusion, Address to the Board of Governors, Hong Kong." Washington, DC: World Bank.

——(1999). "A Proposal for a Comprehensive Development Framework." Washington, DC: World Bank.

World Bank (1981a). "Accelerated Development in Sub-Saharan Africa: An Agenda for Action." Washington, DC: World Bank.

——(1981b). "World Development Report, 1981." New York: Oxford University Press.

——(1983). "World Development Report, 1983." New York: Oxford University Press.

——(1993). *The East Asian Miracle: Economic Growth and Public Policy*. New York: Oxford University Press.

——(1994). *Adjustment in Africa: Reforms, Results and the Road Ahead*. Washington, DC: World Bank.

——(1997). "World Development Report, 1997: The State in a Changing World." New York: Oxford University Press.

——(2000). *Can Africa Claim the 21st Century?* Washington, DC: World Bank.

——(2001a). "Global Development Finance, 2001." Washington, DC: World Bank.

——(2001b). "Global Economic Prospects." Washington, DC: World Bank.

Yeats, A. J., Amjadi, A., Reincke, U., and Ng, F. (1997). *Did Domestic Policies Marginalize Africa in International Trade? Directions in Development*. Washington, DC: World Bank.

Young, A. (1994). "Lessons from the East Asian NICs: A Contrarian View," *European Economic Review*, 38 (3–4): 964–73.

——(1995). "The Tyranny of Numbers: Confronting the Statistical Realities of the East Asian Growth Experience," *Quarterly Journal of Economics*, 110 (3): 641–80.

18

The Emerging Asian Giants and Economic Development in Africa

Deepak Nayyar

The last two decades of the twentieth century, beginning *circa* 1980, witnessed rapid economic growth in China and India. In the first decade of the twenty-first century, the rapid growth has sustained in China and accelerated in India. This remarkable growth performance provides a sharp contrast to the world economy over the same period and to the preceding hundred years in these two Asian giants. Indeed, except for Japan and the East Asian Four, economic history provides few parallels of such rapid and sustained growth. The past quarter of a century has thus witnessed the return of the forgotten dragon and the vanishing tiger to the world economy. So much so that it is no longer possible to consider prospects for the world economy in 2025 or 2050 without placing China and India at center stage. During the period since 1980, Africa provides a sharp contrast. Its economic performance ranged from retrogression to stagnation.

The object of this essay is to analyze the economic implications of the rise of China and India for Africa, situated in the wider context of the world economy. The first section sketches a profile of China, India, and Africa in the world economy. It sets the stage by outlining the broad contours of their significance in the past, present, and future. The following section considers the main forms of engagement and channels of interaction for China and India with Africa. Its focus is on international trade with some discussion on international investment, international aid, and international migration. The next part examines the implications of rapid economic growth in China and India for economic development in Africa. In doing so, it asks whether these two Asian giants could be the new engines of growth, touches upon the underlying economic causation, and explores their possible impact on Africa. The final section draws together some conclusions.

China, India, and Africa in the world economy

The significance of China, India, and Africa in the global context has changed over time. This section provides a historical perspective of the past and a snapshot of the present. It also sets out an extrapolated scenario of the future for China and India.

The past

The emerging significance of China, India, and Africa in the world economy must be situated in historical perspective. Table 18.1, which is based on estimates made by Angus Maddison (2003), presents evidence on the shares of China, India, and Africa in world population and in world income for selected years from 1820–2001. It shows that in 1820, China and India accounted for 57 percent of the world population and 49 percent of world income.[1] A dramatic change took place in the next 150 years. In 1973, the share of China and India in world population was significantly lower at 37 percent, but their share in world income had collapsed to less than 8 percent, a small fraction of what it was 150 years earlier. Over the same period, the significance of Africa in the world economy also changed, but nowhere near as much. In 1820, Africa accounted for 7 percent of world population and 4.5 percent of world income. In 1973, the share of Africa in world population was distinctly higher at 10 percent although its share in world income was somewhat lower at 3.4 percent. The next thirty years witnessed some recovery in China and India but not in Africa. While the share of China and India in world population remained in the range of 37 percent, their share in world income rose to almost 18 percent in 2001. On the other hand, the share of Africa in world population rose further to 13 percent, while its share in world income remained almost

Table 18.1 China, India, and Africa in the world economy (percentage share in population and income)

Year	Share of World Population			Share of World GDP		
	CHINA	INDIA	AFRICA	CHINA	INDIA	AFRICA
1820	36.6	20.1	7.1	32.9	16.0	4.5
1870	28.1	19.9	7.1	17.1	12.1	4.1
1913	24.4	17.0	7.0	8.8	7.5	2.9
1950	21.7	14.2	9.0	4.5	4.2	3.8
1973	22.5	14.8	10.0	4.6	3.1	3.4
2001	20.7	16.5	13.4	12.3	5.4	3.3

Source: Maddison (2003)

Note: The percentages in this table have been calculated from estimates of population and GDP in Maddison (2003). The data on GDP are in 1990 international Geary-Khamis dollars, which are purchasing power parities used to evaluate output that are calculated based on a specific method devised to define international prices. This measure facilitates inter-country comparisons over time.

unchanged at 3.3 percent. The essential contours of this story are clear enough. Beginning in 1820, China and India's share in world population declined steadily until 1973 but, over the same period, the decline in their share of world income was much more pronounced. Consequently, during the period from 1820 to 1973, there was a sharp increase in the asymmetries, or disproportionalities, between the shares of China and India in world population and in world income. The partial recovery in their share of world income from 1973–2001 has reduced the asymmetry, but the disproportionality remains significant. However, this trend suggests that China and India have reentered the world economy. For Africa, this asymmetry increased throughout the period. In 2001, its share in world population had nearly doubled, while its share in world income was less than three fourths what it was in 1820. This trend suggests a decline in the significance of Africa in the world economy, which was clearly discernible during the last quarter of the twentieth century.

The present

It is possible to juxtapose this past with the present. Table 18.2 outlines a profile of GDP, population, and GDP per capita in China, India, and Africa, as compared to developing countries, industrialized countries, and the world, in 2000 and 2005. It shows that the population of the world is more than six billion, of which a little less than one billion people live in industrialized countries, while somewhat more than five billion people live in developing countries. Of the latter, 1.3 billion live in China, 1.1 billion live in India, and 0.9 billion live in Africa. Thus, 51 percent of the population in the world and 60 percent of the population in developing countries live in China, India, and Africa. There are two sets of figures on GDP and GDP per capita: at constant prices with market exchange rates and in terms of purchasing power parities (PPP). Consider each in turn. At market exchange rates, from 2000–5, in world GDP, the share of China increased from 3.8 percent to 5.2 percent, the share of India increased from 1.4 percent to 1.8 percent, and the share of Africa increased from 1.9 percent to 2 percent. The share of China, India, and Africa taken together increased from 37 percent to 42 percent of the GDP of developing countries. Over the same period, at market exchange rates, GDP per capita in China was about the same as, GDP per capita in India was less than half, while GDP per capita in Africa was more than half the average GDP per capita in developing countries. It is worth noting that China, India, and Africa are far below the GDP per capita of the industrialized countries and significantly below GDP per capita in the world as a whole. The picture is somewhat different if the comparison is in terms of PPPs. From 2000–5, in world PPP-GDP, the share of China increased from 11 percent to 14.4 percent, the share of India increased from 5.3 percent to 6.2 percent, and the share of Africa changed little from 3.6 percent to 3.7 percent. The share of China, India, and Africa, taken together, increased from 48 percent to

Table 18.2 GDP, population, and GDP per capita China, India, and Africa, 2000 and 2005

Country	GDP				Population		PPP GDP			
	$billion		$per capita		million		$billion		$per capita	
	2000	2005	2000	2005	2000	2005	2000	2005	2000	2005
China	1198	1890	949	1449	1263	1305	4973	7842	3939	6012
	(3.8)	(5.2)			(20.8)	(20.3)	(11.0)	(14.4)		
India	460	644	453	588	1016	1095	2402	3362	2364	3072
	(1.4)	(1.8)			(16.8)	(17.0)	(5.3)	(6.2)		
Africa	588	727	731	810	804	897	1635	2016	2033	2247
	(1.9)	(2.0)			(13.3)	(13.9)	(3.6)	(3.7)		
Developing Countries	6058	7813	1191	1440	5085	5427	18818	25322	3701	4666
Industrialized Countries	24542	27148	27304	29251	899	928	25157	27898	27988	30058
World	31756	36352	5241	5647	6060	6438	45144	54573	7450	8477

Source: World Bank (2007)

Notes: (a) GDP and GDP per capita are measured in constant 2000 dollars. (b) PPP-GDP and PPP-GDP per capita are measured in constant 2000 international dollars. (c) Figures in parentheses are the totals for China, India, and Africa as a percentage of totals for the world economy.

52 percent of the PPP-GDP of developing countries. Over the same period, in PPP terms, GDP per capita in China surpassed GDP per capita in developing countries by a significant margin, whereas GDP per capita in India was about two thirds, and GDP per capita in Africa was less than one half, of GDP per capita in developing countries.

This snapshot situates China, India, and Africa in the world economy at the present. However, the observed reality has been shaped by their economic performance in the past. Table 18.3 sets out rates of growth in GDP and GDP per capita, from 1951–80 and 1981–2005, for China, India, and Africa in comparison with the developing countries, the industrialized countries, and the world economy.[2]

It is worth noting that time-series data on GDP and GDP per capita for the entire period from 1951–2005 are not available from a single source. The figures for the period 1951–80 are based on Maddison data because United Nations data are not available for years prior to 1971. The figures for the period 1981–2005 are based on United Nations data because Maddison data are not available for years after 2001. These two sources are not strictly comparable. However, it is possible to resolve the problem, as data are available from both sources for the period 1981–2000. To

Table 18.3 Growth performance of China, India, and Africa: 1951–80 and 1981–2005. Comparison with country groups (percent per annum)

	Maddison Data 1951–80	Maddison Data 1981–2000	United Nations Data 1981–2000	United Nations Data 1981–2005
	GDP			
China	5.03	7.36	9.80	9.73
India	3.57	5.68	5.54	5.79
Africa	4.12	2.42	2.60	2.97
Developing Countries	4.84	2.65	2.74	3.04
Industrialized Countries	4.40	2.56	2.59	2.50
World	4.77	2.64	2.72	2.95
	GDP per capita			
China	3.01	6.01	8.46	8.51
India	1.40	3.62	3.50	3.83
Africa	1.66	−0.17	−0.06	0.39
Developing Countries	2.19	0.39	0.42	0.80
Industrialized Countries	3.50	2.04	2.06	1.96
World	2.40	0.66	0.69	0.99

Sources: Maddison (2003), United Nations (2006b, 2006c)

Notes:
(a) The growth rates for each period are computed as geometric means of the annual growth rates in that period.
(b) The Maddison data and the United Nations data on GDP and GDP per capita are not strictly comparable.
(c) The Maddison data on GDP and GDP per capita, which are in 1990 international Geary–Khamis dollars, are purchasing power parities used to evaluate output which are calculated based on a specific method devised to define international prices. This measure facilitates inter-country comparisons.
(d) The United Nations data on GDP and GDP per capita are in constant 1990 US dollars.
(e) The figures in this table for the world economy cover 128 countries, of which 21 are industrialized countries and 107 are developing countries.
(f) Latin America includes the Caribbean.

facilitate a comparison, Table 18.3 also presents figures on growth rates from 1981–2000, computed separately from Maddison data and United Nations data. A comparison of the two sets of growth rates during the period 1981–2000, for which both sources are available, shows that the numbers correspond closely, except in the figures for China, where UN data suggest much higher growth rates than Maddison data. Even so, it is reasonable to infer that the growth rates for the periods 1951–80 and 1981–2005, even if computed from different sources, are comparable, with the exception of China. In interpreting the data on China, where the step-up in growth rates between these two periods is probably overstated, some downward adjustment might be needed.

A study of Table 18.3 shows that growth in GDP and GDP per capita during 1981–2005 was much slower than it was during 1951–80. This was the case for the world economy, for industrialized countries, and for developing countries. Growth in GDP was in the range 5 percent per annum from 1951–80 and in the range of 3 percent per annum from 1981–2005 almost everywhere, including Africa, except in China and India where it was much higher. Growth in GDP per capita slowed considerably even in the industrialized countries, from 3.5 percent per annum to 2 percent per annum, but the slowdown was more pronounced for developing countries, from 2.2 percent per annum to 0.8 percent per annum. In Africa, however, during 1981–2005, growth in GDP per capita was less than 0.4 percent per annum.[3] It is worth stressing that China and India were the exceptions to this worldwide slowdown in growth. In both countries, growth rates in the second period were much higher than the perfectly respectable growth rates in the first period. So much so that, between 1951–80 and 1981–2005, average annual growth in GDP per capita almost trebled in both China and India. This was attributable in part to higher GDP growth rates and in part to lower population growth rates.

The future

Most growth scenarios for the future are based on an extrapolation of growth from the past. The construction of future scenarios began with the Goldman Sachs study that attempted to project levels of GDP and GDP per capita for Brazil, Russia, India, and China in 2050.[4] In attempting such projections, most exercises assume that growth rates in China and India, as in the industrialized countries, would remain at levels observed in the recent past. In a more sophisticated exercise that uses simple convergence equations, Robert Rowthorn (2008) projects that, in 2050, at purchasing power parity, the per capita income in China will be 63 percent of per capita income in the United States, while per capita income in India will be 45 percent of per capita income in the United States. It is also projected that both China and India should comfortably overtake the United States in GDP measured at purchasing power parity. This catch-up is not confined to PPP-GDP comparisons. The Rowthorn projections show that, even at market exchange rates, by 2050 total output in China will be 60 percent larger than in the US, while total output in India and the US will be roughly equal.[5]

It needs to be said that these projections suggest broad orders of magnitude rather than precise predictions. Even so, such projections highlight the power of compound growth rates—for growth rates do indeed matter. If GDP grows at 10 percent per annum, national income doubles in seven years. If GDP per capita grows at 7 percent per annum, per capita income doubles in ten years. If GDP grows at 7 percent per annum, national income doubles in ten years. If GDP per capita grows at 5 percent per annum, per capita income doubles in fourteen years. Growth rates in China and India have been in this range for some time. And growth rates in India have accelerated in the early 2000s. If such growth rates are sustained, their cumulative impact over time is no surprise. However, growth is not simply a matter of arithmetic. In fact, it is about more than economics; therefore, it is necessary to consider the economic determinants of growth.

In principle, China and India may be able to sustain high rates of economic growth for some time for the following reasons. First, their populations are large and income levels are low. Second, their demographic characteristics, which indicate an increase in the workforce for some time to come, are conducive to growth.[6] Third, in both countries, wages are significantly lower than in the world outside and there are large reservoirs of surplus labor. In practice, however, China and India may not be able to sustain their high growth rates because of constraints that are already discernible. In China, the declining productivity of investment at the margin and the sustainability of the political system are both potential constraints. In India, the crisis in agriculture, the bottlenecks in infrastructure, and the limited spread of education are potential constraints. In a longer-term perspective, environmental degradation and climate change could impose serious constraints on growth in both countries. Of course, these constraints are illustrative rather than exhaustive. And there are many others in both countries, which could slow down the process of growth. Even if growth slows down, however, a catch-up scenario is still plausible but it would require a longer period of time.

It is far more difficult to construct future scenarios for Africa, in part, because it is a continent comprising a large number of countries that are significantly different from each other in geographical size, level of income, and stage of development. What is more, there are substantial differences in growth performance across countries. Thus, meaningful analyses or projections are possible only at a disaggregated level for particular countries. Even so, in principle, Africa has a considerable potential for economic growth. Its population is large and income levels are low. Its demographic characteristics, in particular a young population, are a possible advantage. It has low wages combined with surplus labor. And it is abundant in natural resources. Yet, there are dominant constraints: the infrastructure is poor; the spread of education in society is limited; institutions are missing or underdeveloped; and political systems are not conducive to good governance. But these constraints are neither insurmountable nor immutable. Economic policies and development strategies, appropriately designed and effectively implemented, could transform outcomes. Much would depend on what African countries and governments do. Indeed, both China and India, as with most latecomers to development, started with constraints that were similar, if not as acute or binding. It should also be possible for Africa to overcome these constraints—that is what development is about.

Channels of engagement

The preceding discussion was largely in terms of macroeconomic aggregates. It is also necessary to consider the forms of engagement with the world economy, through which the impact of rapid economic growth in China and India, whether positive or negative, is transmitted elsewhere, in particular to Africa. The obvious, and most important, channels of transmission are international trade, international investment, international aid, and international migration.

International trade

International trade is, perhaps, the most important form of engagement with the world economy for China, India, and Africa. It is, however, worth noting that the rapid expansion in their trade with each other is a more recent phenomenon. Thus, the focus of the discussion that follows is on the period 1990–2005. In order to reduce the volume of data to manageable proportions, the tables in this section relate to four selected years: 1990, 1995, 2000, and 2005.

Table 18.4 outlines the trends in China and India's trade with Africa. It presents data on exports to and imports from Africa in comparison with exports to and imports from developing countries and the world. The data show that the expansion in trade was phenomenal. From 1990–2005, China's trade with Africa increased from $1 billion to $37 billion, while India's trade with Africa increased from $1 billion to $11 billion. Starting from a small base, the growth in trade valued at current prices is almost bound to appear impressive. But the expansion in trade with Africa was faster than the expansion in China and India's exports to and imports from developing countries and the world. For China, the share of Africa in exports to the world rose from 1 percent to 2 percent, while it rose from less than 1 percent to more than 3 percent in imports from the world, between 1990 and 2005. Over the same period for India, the share of Africa in exports to the world rose from 2 percent to 6 percent, while it rose from 2 percent to 3 percent in imports from the world.

Table 18.5 outlines the trends in Africa's trade with China and India. It also compares exports to and imports from China and India with exports to and

Table 18.4 China and India: trade with Africa

	1990	1995	2000	2005
China's Exports to Africa in $million	615	1386	4202	16670
as a percentage of				
Exports to Developing Countries	1.7	2.0	4.1	5.2
Exports to the World	1.0	0.9	1.7	2.2
China's Imports from Africa in $million	351	720	5453	20851
as a percentage of				
Imports from Developing Countries	1.5	1.4	4.9	5.4
Imports from the World	0.7	0.6	2.4	3.2
India's Exports to Africa in $million	353	1158	2051	6296
as a percentage of				
Exports to Developing Countries	8.6	9.6	11.1	11.2
Exports to the World	2.0	3.7	4.5	6.1
India's Imports from Africa in $million	541	1672	2067	4673
as a percentage of				
Imports from Developing Countries	7.7	13.6	14.6	9.4
Imports from the World	2.3	4.6	4.0	3.1

Source: UNCOMTRADE, Statistical Database

Table 18.5 Africa's trade with China and India

	1990	1995	2000	2005
Exports to China in $million	128	245	1719	6207
as a percentage of				
Exports to Developing Countries	1.9	2.4	4.7	11.3
Exports to the World	0.3	0.6	1.4	3.5
Imports from China in $million	551	1344	3679	13572
as a percentage of				
Imports from Developing Countries	5.9	8.7	9.4	15.4
Imports from the World	1.1	2.0	3.4	6.7
Exports to India in $million	366	802	5404	3445
as a percentage of				
Exports to Developing Countries	5.5	8.0	14.8	6.3
Exports to the World	0.8	2.0	4.4	1.9
Imports from India in $million	275	1096	1650	4460
as a percentage of				
Imports from Developing Countries	2.9	7.1	4.2	5.1
Imports from the World	0.5	1.6	1.5	2.2

Source: UNCOMTRADE, Statistical Database

imports from developing countries and the world. Once again, the data show a remarkable expansion in trade. From 1990–2005, Africa's trade with China increased from $0.7 billion to $20 billion, while Africa's trade with India increased from $0.6 billion to $8 billion. This expansion in trade was faster than the expansion in Africa's exports to and imports from developing countries and the world. For Africa, the share of China in exports to the world rose from 0.3 percent to 3.5 percent, while it rose from 1.1 percent to 6.7 percent in imports from the world, from 1990–2005. Over the same period for Africa, the share of India in exports to the world rose from 0.8 percent to 2 percent, while it rose from

0.5 percent to 2 percent in imports from the world, although these shares were higher in the intervening years.

A comparison of the evidence in Tables 18.4 and 18.5 reveals a puzzle and suggests a conclusion. The puzzle is that the figures on China and India's exports to and imports from Africa are significantly higher than the corresponding figures on Africa's imports from and exports to China and India. This deserves explanation. International trade statistics are characterized by such differences for two reasons. For one, exports are recorded FOB (Free on Board) while imports are recorded CIF (Cost, Insurance, and Freight). For another, there are time lags in reporting between the country-of-origin and the country-of-destination. But these factors cannot explain such large differences. There are two other plausible explanations. It is almost certain that the international trade statistics for Africa are incomplete and often reported with a time lag. It is also possible that the difference is attributable in part to trade in armaments, which is not recorded in the statistics. But these explanations are in the nature of a conjecture. The conclusions that emerge from a comparison of Tables 18.4 and 18.5 are clear. First, for Africa, China was more important as a market for exports and as a source of imports than Africa was for China. Second, for Africa, India was less important as a market for exports and as a source of imports than Africa was for India throughout the period.

In order to obtain a clear picture of the division of labor between China and India on the one hand and Africa on the other, it is necessary to consider the structure and the composition of their trade as well as the changes in it over time. For this purpose, it is appropriate to divide the trade flows into three categories: primary commodities, fuels, and manufactures. While such a classification is aggregative, and merges Standard International Trade Categories at one-digit level, it is sufficient for analysis.[7]

Table 18.6 outlines the changes in the composition of China's trade with Africa as compared to developing countries and the world. From 1990–2005, the share of primary commodities and fuels, taken together, in China's exports to Africa, dropped sharply from 33 percent to less than 5 percent, while the share of manufactures rose sharply from 66 percent to 94 percent. This composition was somewhat asymmetric in comparison with the composition of China's exports to developing countries, where the share of manufactures rose from 76 percent to 87 percent, and to the world, where the share of manufactures rose from 72 percent to 93 percent. Between 1990 and 2005, the share of primary commodities and fuels, taken together, in China's imports from Africa increased from 70 percent to 86 percent, while the share of manufactures decreased from 30 percent to 12 percent. This composition was much more skewed than the composition of China's imports from developing countries, where the share of primary commodities and fuels increased from 19 percent to 25 percent, and from the world, where the share of primary commodities and fuels increased from 19 percent to 23 percent

Table 18.6 Composition of China's trade with Africa and the world (in percentages)

	1990			1995			2000			2005		
	P	F	M	P	F	M	P	F	M	P	F	M
China's exports to												
Africa	30.9	2.4	66.6	8.7	0.4	89.4	10.3	1.5	87.8	3.8	0.7	93.7
Developing Countries	13.8	4.6	76.3	10.7	3.6	78.6	7.1	4.4	82.6	3.9	3.6	86.8
World	17.4	8.4	72.3	10.8	3.6	85.3	7.0	3.2	89.6	4.1	2.3	93.4
China's Imports from												
Africa	69.7	0.9	29.5	46.4	35.8	17.1	17.5	66.8	9.8	15.6	70.1	12.1
Developing Countries	14.0	4.5	74.2	15.0	8.9	61.4	10.0	16.6	59.2	10.6	13.9	64.6
World	16.3	2.4	80.8	14.4	3.9	81.1	11.4	9.2	78.6	12.7	9.8	77.3

Source: UNCOMTRADE, Statistical Database

Note: P (Primary Commodities), F (Fuels), and M (Manufactures)
Primary commodities include SITC categories 0, 1, 2, and 4; Fuels are SITC category 3; Manufactures include SITC categories 5, 6, 7, and 8, so that non-ferrous metals, SITC category 68, are included in manufactures; SITC category 9 (commodities and transactions not included elsewhere) is excluded from the classification but included in the total. Therefore, percentages in the table do not add up to one hundred.

over the same period. The contrast is just as striking in manufactures. Between 1990 and 2005, the share of manufactures in China's imports from developing countries decreased somewhat from 74 percent to 65 percent, while this share in imports from the world remained in the range of 80 percent.

Table 18.7 outlines the changes in the composition of India's trade with Africa as compared with developing countries and the world. From 1990–2005, the share of manufactures in India's exports to Africa fluctuated between 70–90 percent, while primary commodities and fuels made up the residual. This composition was similar to the composition of India's exports to the world, where manufactures accounted for 70–75 percent, although it was a little different from the composition of exports to developing countries, where manufactures accounted for 64–79 percent because the share of fuels was higher in some years. From 1990–2005, in India's imports from Africa, the share of primary commodities and fuels, taken together, was mostly in the range of 30–40 percent (except in 1995 when it was much higher on account of fuels), while the share of manufactures was mostly in the range of 30–35 percent (except in 1990 when it was much higher). It is worth noting that these statistics on the composition of India's imports from Africa are incomplete because there is a large unaccounted residual of about 30 percent in 2000 and 2005. The data on the composition of India's imports from the rest of the world are more complete as the unaccounted residual is small. Between 1990 and 2005, the share of manufactures in India's imports from developing countries increased from 36 percent to 68 percent, while this share was in the range of 50 percent in imports from the world.

Table 18.8 outlines the changes in the composition of Africa's exports to China and India as compared to developing countries and the world. From 1990–2005, the share of primary commodities and fuels, taken together, in Africa's exports to China increased from 60 percent to 86 percent, while in exports to India it increased from 19 percent to 52 percent, but this share decreased from 62 percent to 56 percent in exports to developing countries and from 81 percent to 59 percent in exports to the world. Over the same period, the share of manufactures in Africa's exports to China and India registered a corresponding decrease, while this share in exports to developing countries and the world fluctuated over time.

Table 18.9 outlines the changes in the composition of Africa's imports from China and India as compared with developing countries and the world. It shows that, between 1990 and 2005, the share of manufactures in Africa's imports from China registered a continuous increase from 62 percent to 95 percent, while the share of manufactures in Africa's imports from India remained in the range 75–80 percent. In contrast, the share of manufactures in Africa's imports from developing countries was in the range of 50 percent while the share of manufactures in Africa's imports from the world was in the range of 60 percent.

The evidence on the composition of trade between China and India on the one hand and Africa on the other, presented in Tables 18.6 to 18.9, highlights some

Table 18.7 Composition of India's trade with Africa and the world (in percentages)

	1990			1995			2000			2005		
	P	F	M	P	F	M	P	F	M	P	F	M
India's exports to												
Africa	8.7	0.0	90.4	27.0	0.0	72.2	6.8	0.1	92.3	12.6	14.7	71.7
Developing Countries	29.0	0.1	68.4	29.6	0.6	69.1	19.4	0.5	78.7	20.0	14.8	63.9
World	24.8	2.9	70.3	23.0	1.7	73.7	16.1	4.3	77.4	15.8	11.5	71.6
India's Imports from												
Africa	31.4	0.0	68.2	22.1	42.8	34.7	30.6	7.3	32.3	27.0	4.8	33.4
Developing Countries	20.9	42.4	35.7	21.2	32.9	43.7	26.2	8.8	58.8	16.9	8.2	68.2
World	12.7	27.3	53.8	11.6	23.7	56.2	10.1	34.8	45.1	8.0	33.8	50.0

Source: UNCOMTRADE, Statistical Database

Note: P (Primary Commodities), F (Fuels), and M (Manufactures)
Primary commodities include SITC categories 0, 1, 2, and 4; Fuels are SITC category 3; Manufactures include SITC categories 5, 6, 7, and 8, so that non-ferrous metals, SITC category 68, are included in manufactures; SITC category 9 (commodities and transactions not included elsewhere) is excluded from the classification but included in the total. Therefore, percentages in the table do not add up to one hundred.

Table 18.8 Composition of Africa's exports to China, India, and the world (in percentages)

		1990	1995	2000	2005
Exports to					
CHINA					
	Primary Commodities	60.2	66.1	26.4	28.3
	Fuels	0.1	9.3	57.6	57.4
	Manufactures	39.7	23.7	15.2	14.1
INDIA					
	Primary Commodities	16.9	18.0	8.4	28.2
	Fuels	1.8	3.9	77.5	24.1
	Manufactures	81.3	78.1	13.9	43.8
DEVELOPING COUNTRIES					
	Primary Commodities	24.9	33.4	20.3	22.7
	Fuels	37.4	23.7	48.8	33.0
	Manufactures	37.7	42.6	29.8	40.1
WORLD					
	Primary Commodities	16.7	35.0	16.9	19.6
	Fuels	64.0	31.0	48.9	39.4
	Manufactures	19.8	32.0	29.8	37.9

Source: UNCOMTRADE, Statistical Database

Note: Primary commodities include SITC categories 0, 1, 2, and 4; Fuels are SITC category 3; Manufactures include SITC categories 5, 6, 7, and 8, so that non-ferrous metals, SITC category 68, are included in manufactures; SITC category 9 (commodities and transactions not included elsewhere) is excluded from the classification but included in the total. Therefore, percentages in the table do not add up to one hundred.

Table 18.9 Composition of Africa's imports from China, India, and the world (in percentages)

		1990	1995	2000	2005
Imports from					
CHINA					
	Primary Commodities	36.1	20.4	14.2	4.0
	Fuels	1.4	0.2	2.0	0.7
	Manufactures	62.3	79.1	83.8	94.8
INDIA					
	Primary Commodities	22.5	27.2	14.0	14.9
	Fuels	0.2	0.1	0.7	5.4
	Manufactures	77.3	72.7	85	78.8
DEVELOPING COUNTRIES					
	Primary Commodities	33.7	31.7	18.5	17.1
	Fuels	22.3	20.8	29.6	25.3
	Manufactures	43.9	47.4	51.1	56.2
WORLD					
	Primary Commodities	25.7	26.4	18.4	15.2
	Fuels	7.5	7.7	12.8	13.8
	Manufactures	62.8	58.4	59.1	60.8

Source: UNCOMTRADE, Statistical Database

Note: Primary commodities include SITC categories 0, 1, 2, and 4; Fuels are SITC category 3; Manufactures include SITC categories 5, 6, 7, and 8, so that non-ferrous metals, SITC category 68, are included in manufactures; SITC category 9 (commodities and transactions not included elsewhere) is excluded from the classification but included in the total. Therefore, percentages in the table do not add up to one hundred.

striking asymmetries. An overwhelmingly large proportion of China's exports to Africa, as also Africa's imports from China, were made up of manufactures. Similarly, an overwhelmingly large proportion of China's imports from Africa, as also Africa's exports to China, were made up of primary commodities and fuels. This pattern of trade was exactly the same as that between industrialized countries and Africa during the colonial era. Both China and Africa's trade with developing countries and the world had a more diversified composition. The pattern of trade between India and Africa was not characterized by so much asymmetry. The proportion of manufactures in India's exports to Africa, as also in Africa's imports from India, was somewhat higher than it was in India's exports to developing countries and the world, as also in Africa's imports from developing countries and the world, but the difference was not so large. At the same time, the share of primary commodities and fuels, taken together, in India's imports from Africa, as also in Africa's exports to India, was more often than not lower than the share of primary commodities and fuels in India's imports from developing countries and the world, as also in Africa's exports to developing countries and the world.

International investment

The picture of international investment is much more difficult to sketch because the necessary data are not available. Table 18.10 sets out evidence on foreign direct investment, inward and outward, in China, India, and Africa compared to developing countries, industrialized countries, and the world. The figures on stocks are for 2000 and 2005, while the figures on flows are annual averages for the period 2001–5. In the early 2000s, of the inward stock of foreign direct investment in developing countries, China accounted for about 12 percent, India for about

Table 18.10 Foreign direct investment: China, India, and Africa: stocks and flows ($billion)

| | Stocks | | | | Flows (average per annum) | |
| | Inward | | Outward | | Inward | Outward |
	2000	2005	2000	2005	2001–2005	2001–2005
China	193	318	28	46	57	4
	(11.4)	(12.0)	(3.2)	(3.7)	(25.4)	(5.6)
India	18	45	2	10	6	2
	(1.0)	(1.7)	(0.2)	(0.8)	(2.5)	(1.9)
Africa	151	264	45	54	20	0.4
	(8.9)	(10.0)	(5.2)	(4.3)	(8.8)	(0.4)
Developing Countries	1697	2655	856	1268	225	80
Industrialized Countries	4035	7219	5593	9278	476	602
World	5803	10130	6471	10672	727	691

Source: UNCTAD Foreign Direct Investment Online Database (http://stats.unctad.org/fdi)

Note: Figures in parentheses represent the total for China, India, and Africa as a percentage of the total for developing countries.

2 percent, and Africa for about 10 percent. During the period 2001–5, of the inward flows of foreign direct investment in developing countries, China accounted for 25 percent, India for 2.5 percent, and Africa for 9 percent. In the early 2000s, of the outward stock of foreign direct investment from developing countries, China accounted for 3–4 percent, India for less than 1 percent, and Africa for 4–5 percent. During the period 2001–5, of the outward flows of foreign direct investment from developing countries, China accounted for 5.6 percent, India for about 2 percent, and Africa for 0.4 percent. It is possible to draw two inferences from this evidence. First, inward foreign direct investment in China, India, and Africa is significant as a proportion of that in developing countries, but small as a proportion of both stocks and flows in the world. Second, outward foreign direct investment from China, India, and Africa is small as a proportion of both stocks and flows even among developing countries.[8]

It is difficult to assess the significance of foreign direct investment from China and India in Africa because data on inward stocks and flows of foreign direct investment in Africa are not available by country-of-origin. Information compiled for thirteen countries in Africa suggests that in 2005, China accounted for 0.6 percent and India accounted for 0.7 percent of the inward stock of foreign direct investment, while, from 1995–2005, China accounted for 0.6 percent and India for 1.1 percent of average annual inflows of foreign direct investment.[9] More complete information and more recent data may suggest an increase in the significance of China and India in foreign direct investment in Africa, at least from the developing world. For example, it is reported that Chinese foreign direct investment increased from $28 million in 1998 to $6 billion in 2005.[10] There are no comparable statistics for India. But it is reported that, during the period 2000–6, of the 309 acquisitions abroad by Indian firms, thirteen were in Africa, of which six were in the petroleum sector, while the others were in pharmaceuticals, chemicals, fertilizers, and consumer goods.[11]

International aid

Information in the sphere of foreign aid and development assistance is also scarce. Even so, it would seem that both China and India are emerging as donors, with a significant presence in Africa. Development finance is the core of China's aid programs, whereas the focus of India's aid programs is technical assistance.[12] For both countries, economic assistance for development in Africa is strategic in terms of political interests. It is portrayed as South-South cooperation, a partnership based on political equality and mutual trust, and one that is depicted as being different from foreign aid to Africa provided by industrialized countries. There was a China–Africa Summit at Beijing in November 2006 and an India–Africa Summit at New Delhi in April 2008, both of which had a large presence of heads of governments from African countries. Unfortunately, evidence on foreign aid flows from China and India to Africa is not readily available. It is reported that foreign aid from China to Africa increased from $107 million in 1998 to $2.7 billion in 2004.[13] Similarly, it is reported that foreign aid from India to Africa was $2.7 billion during the period 2003–8.[14] It is clear, however, that foreign aid from China and India is relatively small as compared with foreign aid provided by the industrialized countries.[15] Yet, it is possible that the multiplier effects of aid from China and India, as also from other emerging donors such as Korea, Brazil, and South Africa, may be significant for two reasons. For one, technical assistance may alleviate infrastructural constraints in developing countries. For another, emerging donors could be a catalyst for aid flows from the industrialized countries in much the same way that foreign aid from the socialist countries was a catalyst during the cold war era.

International migration

International migration is a significant form of engagement with the world economy for China and even more so for India. Both India and China have always been, and continue to be, important countries-of-origin for international migration. The traditional category is emigrants. But globalization has introduced the cross-border movement of guest workers and professionals.[16] The engagement of India and China with developing countries, particularly African countries, through international migration is attributable in part to the diaspora and in part to globalization. For India in Africa, this is attributable to the diaspora embedded in history. For China in Africa, this is attributable to the recent engagement through aid and investment.

The diaspora has historical origins. Following the British Empire's abolition of slavery, for a period of fifty years starting around the mid 1830s, about 50 million people left India and China to work as indentured labor in mines, plantations, and construction in the Americas, the Caribbean, South Africa, South East Asia, and other distant lands.[17] This was probably close to 10 percent of the total population of India and China *circa* 1880. The migration from India and China continued, in somewhat different forms, during the first half of the twentieth century, particularly in the period between the two World Wars. There is, consequently, a significant presence of people from India and China across the world, not only in the industrialized countries but also in the developing countries. This is associated with entrepreneurial capitalisms, both Chinese and Indian, in developing countries where the migration stream has aged. The diaspora from India in Africa engaged in trade and business, an example of such entrepreneurial capitalism, which was the subject of resentment in some nationalist movements and in early post-colonial Africa, but that has since diminished.

The second half of the twentieth century also witnessed significant waves of international migration from India, comprising permanent emigration to the industrialized countries and temporary migration to the oil-exporting countries in the Middle East.[18] The international migration from China was limited during this period, but the gathering momentum of globalization during the past two decades has led to a significant increase in the new categories of cross-border movements of people. In this sphere, the engagement of India with the world economy is much more than that of China. The advent of globalization, which has made it easier to move people across borders, is associated with managerial capitalisms, especially with professionals from India who can migrate permanently, live abroad temporarily, or stay at home and travel frequently for business. These people are almost as mobile across borders as capital. Such an Indian presence is now discernible in Africa, attributable partly to technical assistance provided by the government and partly to investment by firms from the private sector. Such a Chinese presence is now significant in Africa (though the evidence is anecdotal rather than precise), attributable partly to the use of Chinese workers in aid-financed infrastructure construction, people who may not be repatriated after project completion and who may enter into trade or commerce, and partly to Chinese companies that bring their personnel to run business.

Implications for Africa

Globalization is associated with increasing economic openness, growing economic interdependence, and deepening economic integration in the world economy. In such a world, growth prospects would be significantly influenced, if not shaped, by the growth performance of lead economies. The following discussion asks whether China and India could be new engines of growth for the developing world, considers the underlying mechanisms, and examines the possible impact on Africa.

Engines of growth

History provides obvious examples. Britain in the nineteenth century and United States in the twentieth century were engines of growth for the world economy. Statistical analysis since the early 1960s provides confirmation.[19] It is widely accepted that GDP growth in the United States leads GDP growth in the world. A statistical analysis of long-term trends in economic growth, for the period 1963–2001, with five-year moving averages for both sets of growth rates, yields a correlation coefficient of 0.82, while a simple lead-lag analysis shows that the US economy leads the world economy by one year. Available evidence also reveals that developing countries, excluding China, follow the trends in world economic growth and, hence, trends in economic growth of the United States. It is worth noting that economic growth in developing countries follows economic growth in the United States with a lag but with more pronounced swings in cyclical ups and downs.[20]

Rapid economic growth in China and India, if it is sustained at the projected rates, is bound to exercise considerable influence on prospects for the world economy, the industrialized countries, and the developing countries. The consequences for the world economy could be positive in so far as these two mega-economies from Asia turn into engines of growth. The impact could also be negative in the form of environmental consequences[21] and labor market consequences. It would be too much of a digression to enter into a discussion of these possibilities here. Similarly, rapid economic growth in China and India would have an impact on the industrialized countries, which could also be either positive or negative. Such an analysis is also beyond the scope of this essay. In any case, the possible consequences of the rise of China and India for the industrialized countries have been considered in the emerging literature on the subject.[22] Therefore, the thrust of the discussion that follows is on the implications and consequences for developing countries, with a focus on Africa.

In considering the future, is it possible to think of China and India as engines of growth for the developing world, even if not for the world economy? The answer largely depends on the size of the two economies and their growth rates. There are some pointers from recent experience. Statistical analysis shows that since 1980, the Chinese economy has also led world GDP, with a lag of one or two years, although the correlation coefficient is much smaller than that for the United States. This is not surprising. For one, in 2005, China accounted for 5 percent of world GDP at market exchange rates and 14 percent of world GDP in PPP terms. For another, GDP growth in China has been in the range of 9 percent per annum for twenty-five years. By these criteria, India is not an engine of growth, at least not yet. This is also not surprising. Its economic size is smaller than that of China and its growth rate is not as high. In 2005, India accounted for only 2 percent of world GDP at market exchange rates and 6 percent of world GDP in PPP terms. For another, GDP growth in India has been in the range of 6 percent per annum for twenty-five years. Even so, India is a potential engine of growth in terms of both attributes.

Rapid economic growth in lead economies drives economic growth elsewhere in the world by providing markets for exports, resources for investment, finances for development, and technologies for productivity. The classic examples—Britain in the nineteenth century and the United States in the twentieth century—provide confirmation of the suggested economic causation and the possible transmission mechanisms. Indeed, during their periods of dominance in the world, both Britain and the United States were engines of growth, in so far as they provided the rest of the world not only with markets for exports and resources for investment, but also with finances for development and technologies for productivity. At this juncture, China is not quite an engine of growth in every dimension. Economic growth in

China provides a stimulus to economic growth elsewhere mostly as a market for exports. So far, India cannot be characterized as an engine of growth in any dimension, perhaps not even as a market for exports. But, along with China, India has some potential in terms of markets for exports, resources for investment, and technologies for productivity. In this context, it is worth noting that China and India could ultimately be a significant impetus to the growth process in the developing world as an important complement to, even if they cannot be a substitute for, the United States in driving global growth. And, given their strengthening economic relationship with Africa, particularly through trade but also through investment and aid, the emerging Asian giants could also provide a significant impetus to the growth process in Africa if linkages develop appropriately.

Causation and mechanisms

The economic causation outlined above is necessary but not sufficient. The overall effects of economic growth in lead economies on economic growth elsewhere depend upon: (1) whether such growth is complementary or competitive; (2) whether the direct effects are reinforced or counteracted by the indirect effects; and (3) whether, on balance, the impact is positive or negative.[23]

In principle, economic growth in lead economies may be complementary or competitive to economic growth elsewhere. It may be complementary in that it increases the demand for exports, but it may be competitive in that it develops alternative sources of supply. It may be complementary if it provides resources for investment or finances for development, but it may be competitive if it preempts such resources for investment or finances for development. It may be complementary if it provides technologies to others, but it may be competitive if it stifles the development of technologies elsewhere. The distinctions between the complementary and the competitive aspects are widely recognized. However, the distinction between direct effects and indirect effects is less clear because the latter sometimes are difficult to discern, let alone measure. In situations in which direct effects are complementary, indirect effects could be reinforcing if complementary, but counteracting if competitive. For example, the direct effects may be complementary if the lead economies, say China and India, provide cheap wage goods to developing countries in Africa, but the indirect effects may be competitive if competition from firms in lead economies, say China and India, squeezes out local firms in African countries. The direct effects may be complementary if firms from the lead economies, China and India, invest in African countries, but the indirect effects may be competitive if firms from industrialized countries relocate production and invest in China and India rather than in African countries. The direct effects may be complementary if the lead economies provide cheaper inputs for manufactured exports from African countries, but the indirect effects may be competitive if competition from China and India squeezes out manufactured exports from African countries in the markets of industrialized countries. In principle the impact of economic growth in lead economies on economic growth elsewhere could be positive, or negative, or some combination of both and on balance, such impact can be either positive or negative. The outcomes may differ across space and change over time so that generalizations are difficult.

In this context, it is worth noting that macroeconomic policies in China and India, once they become lead economies, may exercise an important influence on economic growth elsewhere. If such policies are counter-cyclical, which has been the case for the United States, these would be supportive of economic growth elsewhere. But if these policies are pro-cyclical, which is common in developing countries, these could be disruptive for economic growth elsewhere. Similarly, exchange rates in lead economies could exercise a significant influence, either positive or negative, on economic growth elsewhere in the world. For example, an undervalued exchange rate in China, which has persisted for quite some time, could constrain the prospects for labor-intensive manufactured exports from developing countries in Africa, thereby limiting the potential demand stimulus to economic growth that could be provided by exports. In fact, it is already doing so.[24]

Possible impact

During the first quarter of the twenty-first century, economic growth in China and India could have a positive impact on developing countries in Africa if it improves terms of trade, provides appropriate technologies, and creates new sources of finance for development, whether investment or aid.

It is clear that, for some time to come, the positive impact on developing countries would be transmitted through an improvement in their terms of trade.[25] Given the abundance of natural endowments in Africa, rapid economic growth in China and India is bound to boost the demand for primary commodities exported by African countries. The reasons are simple enough. Both China and India have large populations and in both countries, levels of consumption per capita in most primary commodities are low, while income elasticities of demand for most primary commodities are high. This burgeoning demand will almost certainly raise prices of primary commodities in world markets and improve the terms of trade for African countries. In this context, Africa is perhaps the most important source of primary commodities in the world economy. What is more, China already is, and India is likely to become, a source of manufactured goods in the world market. Such manufactures, particularly wage goods, from China and India, are likely to be cheaper than competing goods from industrialized countries. This would also improve the terms of trade for African developing countries. Such terms of trade gains would raise real incomes in Africa. But the impact on development, in terms of the well-being of people, would depend on the nature of asset ownership, the quality of mediating institutions, and the effectiveness of government policies in African countries.[26]

The positive impact of China and India on African countries through the other potential channels of transmission is not as clear. We do not yet have either the evidence or the experience. In principle, it is possible that China and India would develop technologies that are more appropriate for the factor endowments and the economic needs of Africa. But it is too early to make a judgment.

Similarly, China and India are potential sources of finance for development. Their foreign aid programs, particularly in Africa, constitute a modest beginning. As has been discussed, much of Chinese aid is directed toward building infrastructure[27] and much of Indian aid is in the form of technical assistance and both are reported to have increased significantly since 2005. Insofar as this infrastructure development and technical assistance ease supply constraints in Africa, such aid should have a positive impact on economic growth through an increase in the productivity of public and private investment. The benefits to recipient countries in Africa would depend in part on the terms of the assistance. In larger part, however, the benefits would depend upon whether such aid supports projects that could not have been financed by domestic resources or Western donors, as also on the design and implementation of government policies in African countries. On balance, there can be little doubt that the emergence of China and India as sources of foreign aid or technical assistance for African countries has enlarged their choices and options, even if it has not improved the terms or enlarged the volume of development assistance from the traditional donors.

In comparison, the contribution of China and India in terms of foreign direct investment is so far limited. It is worth noting, however, that China and India are different from each other in the nature and purpose of such investment. Foreign direct investment from China is through state-owned firms, directed toward natural resource extraction, mostly petroleum and non-ferrous metals, and is concentrated in a few countries.[28] Some diversification in sectors and countries of destination is discernible but the concentration remains. Foreign direct investment from India is through private-sector firms, mostly in manufacturing or services, and is more distributed across countries.[29]

The emergence of China and India in the world economy could also have a negative impact on African countries if the two mega-economies provide African countries with competition as markets for exports or as destinations for investment.

At this juncture, China is clearly the largest supplier of labor-intensive manufactured goods in the world market. Even though it is not as large as China, India is also a significant supplier of labor-intensive manufactured goods in the world market. There is little doubt that manufactured exports from China and India nearly span the entire range of manufactured exports of which other developing countries could have a potential comparative advantage. Hence, it is plausible to argue, though impossible to prove, that on balance, China, and possibly, India have a negative impact on manufactured exports from African countries, which have to compete with China and India for export markets in industrialized countries.[30] This can change if and when China and India vacate their space in the international trade matrix, in much the same way that latecomers to industrialization in Asia, such as Japan, Korea, Hong Kong, Taiwan, and Singapore, vacated their space in the market for simple labor-intensive manufactures for countries that followed in their footsteps. This is not likely, at least in the medium term, because China and India both have large reservoirs of surplus labor at low wages, not only in the rural hinterlands, but also in the urban informal sectors.

The evidence presented earlier showed that China and India absorb a significant proportion of inward foreign direct investment in developing countries both in terms of stocks and flows. Given that the two Asian giants are now among the most attractive destinations for transnational firms seeking to locate production in the developing world, it is once again plausible to suggest, though impossible to prove, that foreign direct investment in China and India might be at the expense of developing countries, particularly in Africa. It would seem that, at present, China and India represent competition for, rather than a source of, foreign direct investment for other developing countries. The share of China and India in outward foreign direct investment in the world economy, as also from developing countries, is modest in both stocks and flows, so that firms from China and India do not, at least so far, compensate with foreign direct investment in African countries.

The less discernible, but more significant negative impact of the Asian mega-economies, particularly China, on Africa is implicit in the unchanged division of labor. It is striking that China's present division of labor with Africa, reflected in the composition of trade flows, is not different from the old North-South pattern of trade, in so far as Chinese imports from Africa are mostly primary commodities while an overwhelming proportion of Chinese exports to Africa are manufactured goods.[31] The evidence presented earlier in Table 18.6 shows that this composition, particularly in imports, is far more skewed than that for China's trade with developing countries or the world economy as a whole. Indeed, when this composition of trade is juxtaposed with Chinese aid to, and investment in Africa, which is concentrated in the extraction of natural resources motivated by a strategic sourcing of raw materials, China's pattern of economic transactions with Africa conforms even more closely to the caricatural neo-colonial pattern. Such traditional patterns of trade can neither transform the structure of production in African countries nor make for a new international division of labor. Indeed, such trade can only perpetuate the dependence of African countries on exports of primary commodities without creating possibilities of increasing value-added before export or entering into manufacturing activities characterized by economies of scale. Such path-dependent specialization can only curb the possibilities of structural transformation in developing countries. Trade with China can sustain growth and support industrialization in African countries only if there is a successful transition from a complementary to a competitive pattern of trade, so that intersectoral trade is gradually replaced by intrasectoral or intra-industry trade and specialization.

Conclusions

It is clear that the rise of China and India in the world economy will have important implications for economic development in Africa. The consequences could be positive if China and India provide markets for exports, resources for investment, and finances for development, which would stimulate the process of growth in Africa. The emerging mega-economies of Asia may also provide African countries with more options, choices, and space in formulating policies that are conducive to national development objectives. Their growing presence would almost certainly reduce the enormous influence that Western countries and multilateral institutions have exercised on development policies and strategies in Africa. This could create more scope for African leaders to evolve their own approaches to development. On the other hand, the consequences could be negative if growth in China and India is competitive rather than complementary to growth in Africa. The economic engagement of the Asian giants with Africa, through trade and investment, may also perpetuate traditional patterns of specialization, which inhibit rather than foster industrialization in African countries. The impact, on balance, will depend upon how reality unfolds. It will depend on the nature of China and India's interactions with Africa. Even more so, it will depend on what African countries do, in terms of initial conditions, better bargaining, and appropriate policies, to maximize the benefits and minimize the costs associated with the process of increasing economic interaction with China and India.

The international arena will also matter. From the perspective of Africa, China and India together may be able to exercise significant influence through multilateralism in the global context. The United Nations, the World Bank, the International Monetary Fund, and the World Trade Organization are among the most important multilateral institutions.[32] In the United Nations, China is a permanent member of the Security Council with a right to veto. But India is knocking at the door, seeking permanent membership in the Security Council, with or without a veto. In the Bretton Woods Institutions, the World Bank and the International Monetary Fund, China and India are permanent members of the Executive Boards. In the World Trade Organization, India has been a long-standing advocate of developing countries. China has a low profile, possibly because of its recent accession. It would seem that China and India have a considerable potential for articulating a collective voice, on behalf of smaller countries, in the world of multilateralism. Coordination and cooperation among them carry a significant potential for exercising influence on multilateral institutions, which could reshape rules and create policy space for countries, particularly in Africa, that are latecomers to development. Such coordination and cooperation, which are possible, have not yet surfaced. China and India have neither articulated a collective voice, nor exercised collective influence. There could be two reasons for the near absence of coordination and cooperation so far. For one, in the early stages of change, these countries might not have recognized their potential for exercising collective influence. For another, their relationship with each other may be characterized more by rivalry, economic or political, and less by unity. It is difficult to predict how reality might unfold in times to come.[33]

It is worth noting two important limitations of the analysis in this paper. First, it considers China and India together, which may be somewhat deceptive insofar as China is much larger than in India in almost every dimension of engagement with Africa. But the analysis does recognize and highlight the important differences. Second, it considers China and India as a composite, which may not be entirely appropriate because an economic and political rivalry between China and India could significantly shape the impact on Africa. It is important to analyze the implications and consequences of this rivalry for economic development in Africa, but such an exercise would require another paper. Even so, this essay constitutes an important beginning in a relatively unexplored subject.

Notes

* The author would like to thank Jonas Shaende for valuable research assistance. Ananya Ghosh-Dastidar and Xuan Zhang helped in the search for information.
1. Such dominance went back a long time. From 1000–1700, China and India, taken together, accounted for 50 percent of world population and 50 percent of world income. And 2000 years ago, in 1 AD, China and India accounted for almost 60 percent of both world population and world income. For a more detailed discussion, see Nayyar (2008a).
2. The evidence in Table 18.3, and the discussion that follows, draws upon earlier work by the author; see Nayyar (2008b).
3. This growth performance in Africa was worse than in other regions of the developing world including Latin America. In fact, during the period 1981–2000, Africa fared even worse as growth in GDP per capita was negative in the range –0.06 to –0.17 percent per annum. It was the revival in growth during the early 2000s that made the growth in GDP per capita positive, even if modest, during the period 1981–2005.
4. For the methodology and the conclusions, see Wilson and Purushothaman (2003).
5. For a detailed discussion on the model, the data and the results, see Rowthorn (2008).

6. In this context, it is worth noting that the proportion of young people in the population is significantly higher in India than in China, so that the potential demographic dividend would be available to India for a longer period of time.

7. In this context, it is worth noting that such a classification probably overstates the share of manufactures in exports and imports from Africa because the definition of manufactures as Standard International Trade Classification (SITC) 5+6+7+8 includes non-ferrous metals, SITC 68, which are often classified as primary commodities. But this does not affect comparisons of the composition of Africa's trade across countries or country groups, which are the focus of the discussion that follows.

8. The share of Africa in the outward stock of foreign direct investment from developing countries was surprisingly higher than that of China essentially because of outward investment from South Africa in earlier years (Nayyar 2010).

9. The selected countries are Algeria, Egypt, Ethiopia, Madagascar, Malawi, Mauritius, Morocco, Mozambique, South Africa, Tanzania, Tunisia, Uganda, and Zambia. In 2005, the total inward stock of foreign direct investment in these countries was $270,984 million, of which $1,595 million was from China and $1,969 million was from India. During the period 1995–2005, the total inflow of foreign direct investment in these countries was $18,394 million per annum, of which $103 million per annum was from China and $209 million per annum was from India. Over the same period, the inflow from developing countries was $1257 million per annum, so that China's share was 8 percent while India's share was 16 percent. These figures have been calculated from figures reported for each of the selected 13 countries from <http://www.stats.unctad.org/fdi> . It is, however, worth stressing that these figures are indicative rather than precise because they relate to only 13 countries in Africa and are reported for only some of the years in the period, which are not the same for all the selected countries.

10. See Toye (2008: 103).

11. This is reported in a study by the Federation of Indian Chambers of Commerce and Industry, *India Inc.'s Acquisitions Abroad* (New Delhi, 2006). For analysis of investment and acquisitions abroad by Indian firms, see Nayyar (2008a).

12. The object of India's technical assistance to Africa is to provide low-cost, affordable, adaptable, and appropriate technologies for infrastructure development. Sharing information and communication technologies to bridge the digital divide is also an important part of this endeavor. In addition, the development of human resources through skill development and capacity building, supported by training and consultancy, is woven into such technical cooperation.

13. See Toye (2008: 104).

14. At the India-Africa Summit in New Delhi, in April 2008, it was announced that aid to Africa, the composite financial package to support development, would double to $5.4 billion over the next five years.

15. During the period 2001–5, net ODA disbursements from DAC countries were US$73,200 million per annum, while net ODA disbursements from non-DAC donors were a mere US$575 million per annum. For the annual statistics, see <http://stats.oecd.org/wbos>. It is worth noting that non-DAC donors include Saudi Arabia, Korea, Turkey, Kuwait, United Arab Emirates, Czech Republic, Hungary, and Poland, among others, but net ODA

disbursements from China and India are not even reported in these OECD statistics on foreign aid.

16. The changing nature of international migration is analyzed, at some length, in Nayyar (2002).

17. Cf. Tinker (1974) and Lewis (1977). See also Nayyar (2002a).

18. For a discussion of, and evidence on, international migration from India, see Nayyar (1994).

19. For a more detailed discussion on the statistical evidence and analysis cited in this paragraph, see United Nations (2006a).

20. The financial crisis and the economic downturn in the United States that began in late 2008 provides clear confirmation, as growth slowed down everywhere in the developing world.

21. Negative environmental consequences could also slow down the process of growth in China and India.

22. See, for example, Freeman (2005), Singh (2007), Rowthorn (2008), and Nayyar (2010).

23. For a detailed discussion, see Kaplinsky (2006). The literature on this subject is limited. But the implications and consequences of rapid growth in China and India, for the developing world, particularly Africa, are analyzed in Kaplinsky and Messner (2008).

24. Evidence cited later in the paper confirms that the size and growth of China's manufactured exports pose serious problems for exports of manufactures from, and industrial growth in, Sub-Saharan Africa.

25. This proposition is stressed by Kaplinsky (2006), Singh (2007), Nayyar (2008a), and Rowthorn (2008).

26. For a detailed discussion, see Toye (2008).

27. For an analysis and evaluation of Chinese aid to Sub-Saharan Africa, based on qualitative rather than quantitative evidence, see Toye (2008).

28. For example, China has acquired stakes in oil companies in Africa at a cumulative cost of $15 billion. Of its petroleum imports from Africa, Angola alone provides 50 percent while Sudan provides another 20 percent. There is a bundling of aid, investment, and trade, not very different from that practiced by the USSR in the past, which is concentrated in a small number of countries in Africa such as Angola, Chad, Congo, Kenya, Nigeria, Sudan, Zambia, and Zimbabwe. The economic ties are often associated with strategic political interests. For a detailed discussion, see Toye (2008).

29. There are two exceptions: ONGC, a public-sector firm from India, acquired a 25 percent share in the Greater Nile Oil Project in Sudan for $766 million in 2002 and a 50 percent share in the Greater Plutonio Project in Angola for $600 million in 2004, both in the petroleum sector (Nayyar 2008a). In this context, it is worth noting that the sectoral composition and geographical distribution of outward foreign direct investment from India provides two sharp contrasts with that from developing countries. For one, three fifths of international investment from India is in manufacturing activities, while this proportion is about one eighth for developing countries. For another, almost three fourths of international investment from India is in industrialized countries, while this proportion is less than one fifth for developing countries. The proportions for China are similar to those for developing countries as a group. In fact, foreign direct investment

from China is probably even more concentrated in primary commodities and developing countries. For a discussion, see Nayyar (2008a).

30. In a recent study, Kaplinsky and Morris (2008) show that the entry of China (and to a lesser extent India) into the global economy as a significant exporter of manufactures poses severe problems for export-oriented industrialization and growth in Sub-Saharan Africa.

31. This pattern is characteristic of China's trade with developing countries except for Southeast Asia. An unpublished study by Rhys Jenkins and Chris Edwards, cited in United Nations (2006a: 22), on China's trade with 18 developing countries (6 in Asia, 6 in Africa, and 6 in Latin America) shows that countries that had significant trade with China were exporting mostly agricultural or extractive primary commodities. A study on China's economic interaction with Latin America and the Caribbean also confirms the traditional pattern of trade, importing mostly primary commodities and exporting mostly manufactured goods (Inter-American Development Bank 2005).

32. For a detailed discussion on the possibilities of reform and change in these multilateral institutions, in the wider context of global governance, see Nayyar (2002a).

33. For a more detailed discussion of this issue, see Nayyar (2010). It is important to recognize that once these countries become major players, there is a danger that they might opt for the pursuit of national interest rather than the spirit of solidarity or the logic of collective action among developing countries.

References

Freeman, R. B. (2005). "What Really Ails Europe and America: The Doubling of the Global Workforce," *The Globalist*, 3 June.

Inter-American Development Bank (2005). *The Emergence of China: Opportunities and Challenges for Latin America and the Caribbean*. Washington, DC: IADB.

Kaplinsky, R. (ed.) (2006). *Asian Drivers: Opportunities and Threats*, IDS Bulletin, Vol. 37, No. 1.

Kaplinsky, R. and Messner, D. (2008). "The Impact of the Asian Drivers on the Developing World," *World Development*, 36 (2): 197–209.

—— and Morris, M. (2008). "Do the Asian Drivers Undermine Export-Oriented Industrialization in Sub-Saharan Africa?" *World Development*, 36 (2): 254–73.

Lewis, W. A. (1977). *The Evolution of the International Economic Order*. Princeton, NJ: Princeton University Press.

Maddison, A. (2003). *The World Economy: Historical Statistics*. Paris: OECD.

Nayyar, D. (1994). *Migration, Remittances and Capital Flows: The Indian Experience*. Delhi: Oxford University Press.

—— (2002a). "Cross-Border Movements of People," in D. Nayyar (ed.), *Governing Globalization: Issues and Institutions*. Oxford: Oxford University Press.

—— (2002b). "The Existing System and the Missing Institutions," in D. Nayyar (ed.), *Governing Globalization: Issues and Institutions*. Oxford: Oxford University Press.

—— (2008a). "The Rise of China and India: Implications for Developing Countries," in P. Artesis and J. Eatwell (eds.), *Issues in Economic Development and Globalization*. London: Palgrave Macmillan.

—— (2008b). "The Internationalization of Firms from India: Investment, Mergers and Acquisitions," *Oxford Development Studies*, 36 (1): 111–31.

—— (2008c). "Learning to Unlearn from Development," *Oxford Development Studies*, 36 (3): 259–80.

—— (2010). "China, India, Brazil and South Africa in the World Economy: Engines of Growth?" in A. Santos-Paulino and G. Wan (eds.), *Southern Engines of Global Growth*. Oxford: Oxford University Press.

Rowthorn, R. (2008). "The Renaissance of China and India: Implications for the Advanced Economies," in P. Artesis and J. Eatwell (eds.), *Issues in Economic Development and Globalization*. London: Palgrave Macmillan.

Singh, A. (2007). "Globalization, Industrial Revolutions in India and China and Labour Markets in Advanced Countries: Implications for National and International Economic Policy," Working Paper No. 81, Policy Integration Department, March. Geneva: ILO.

Tinker, H. (1974). *A New System of Slavery: The Export of Indian Labour Overseas: 1830–1920*. Oxford: Oxford University Press.

Toye, J. (2008). "China's Impact on Sub-Saharan African Economic Development: Trade, Aid and Politics," in P. Artesis and J. Eatwell (eds.), *Issues in Economic Development and Globalization*. London: Palgrave Macmillan.

United Nations (2006a). *Diverging Growth and Development, World Economic and Social Survey 2006*. New York: United Nations.

—— (2006b). National Accounts Main Aggregates Database, Department of Economic and Social Affairs, New York, available at <http://unstats.un.org/unsd/snaama/introduction.asp>.

—— (2006c). Demographic Yearbook System, Department of Economic and Social Affairs, New York, available at <http://unstats.un.org/unsd/demographic/products/dyb/dyb2.htm>.

Wilson, D. and Purushothaman, R. (2003). "Dreaming with BRICS: The Path to 2050," Global Economics Paper No. 99. New York: Goldman Sachs.

World Bank (2007). *World Development Indicators 2007*. Washington, DC: World Bank.

Index

Bold entries refer to tables.

Abacha, Sani 193
Acemoglu, D 68–70
Action Aid 508
adverse redistribution 185–6, 192–3, 202
affection,
  economy of 124
Africa:
  and complexities of development 5–7
  and contrast with East Asian economic
    performance 3–4
  and development strategy 381
  and developmental regimes 5
  and developmental state 34–5
  and diversity of 5
  and economic growth 7–9, 175
    1960 to mid 1970s 183–4
    commodity prices **375**, 411
    constraints on 542–3
    factors favoring 412
    future projections of 542–3
    heterogeneity in patterns 181, 205
    impact of Chinese and Indian
      growth 556–9
    inability to sustain 411–12
    mid-1970s to early 1990s 184–9
    potential for 542
    record of 176–82, 204–5, 373–6, 410,
      500–1, **540**–1
    since mid-1990s 187–90
    variations in 182
  and explanations of economic record 4, 13,
    182, 190, 376–7
    adverse redistribution 185–6, 192–3, 202
    analytic studies 17–19
    commodity booms 185, 202, 411
    external treatment of Africa 15–16
    geography 13–15
    governance 16–17, 30–1, 115, 199–201
    policy syndromes 117–18, 185
    political instability 186, 187, 203, 204
    resource opportunity set 202
    state controls 190–2, 203
    state failure 194, 202–3, 205–6

    structural adjustment programs 188
    suboptimal intertemporal resource
      allocation 193–4, 202
    supply shocks 185, 202
    syndrome-free regime 194–9, 203–**4**, 205,
      210n15
    terms of trade 186, 187, 510
    total factor productivity growth 188–9, 205
  and foreign direct investment **504**, **505**,
    550–1
  and migration 552–3
  and policy options for:
    developmental state 34–5
    growth-enhancing governance 32
    industrial policy 25–6
  and poverty in 175–6
  and share of world population and income:
    current situation 538, **539**, 540
    historical perspective **537**–8
Africa Growth and Opportunity Agreement
    (AGOA) 251, 323, 335, 339
Africa Task Force 4, 13, 22, 39
African culture 124
African Economic Research Consortium
    (AERC) 17–18, 182, 205
African Financial Community (CFA) 192
African socialism 22
Afrikaner National Party 350
Agreement on Textiles and Clothing
    (ATC) 506
agriculture:
  and developed countries 522
  and East Asia 445–6
  and economic growth 39
  and employment in 441
  and employment-intensive growth 445–8
  and Green Revolution 524
  and lack of investment in 8
  and neglect of 522
  and productivity 35, 441, 445, 446–7
  and stagnation in 8
  and state controls 191
  and trade in 509–10, 513, 521, 522

agriculture: (*cont.*)
  and trade liberalization 513–14,
    516, 526
aid 39
  and aid for trade 514–15
  and Chinese assistance to Africa 551–2
  and debate over role of 507
  and debt relief and repayment 508
  and donor assistance and industrial
    policy 394–6
  and failure to finance development 508–9
  and foreign presence in African
    institutions 99
  and functions of 99
  and Indian assistance to Africa 551–2
  and inflows into Africa 398n2
  and institutional reform overload 101–2
  and Japanese aid development strategy 235
    align assistance to existing development
      strategies 235–7
    policies for industrial promotion **236**
    policy dialogue 237–9
    providing conditions for foreign
      investment 241
    regional development around core
      infrastructure 239–40
  and market-enhancing ('good') governance 65
  and need for increases in 526
  and regional composition of **508**
  and role of 503
  and skills development 465, 466–7
  and unreliability of statistics 508
  and volatility of 508
Aiginger, K 407
Amin, Idi 193
Amsden, A 253, 349, 368
Anderson, K 516
Anglo American Corporation 350
Angola:
  and economic growth, explanations for 187
  and natural resources 126
anti-growth syndromes 17–18, 117, 205
  and explanations of 200
    experience of initial leaders 201
    group identity rivalry 202
    initial conditions 201
    reigning international paradigms 201
Arap Moi, Daniel 193
Arcelor Mittal South Africa (AMSA) 355
Argentina 89, 261
Arnim, R von 517
Arrow-Debreu model 81
Arrow, K 81
Asian Development Bank 240, 268n13
Association of South East Asian Nations
    (ASEAN) 380
  and dependence on foreign capital **387**

Austin, G 72
authoritarianism 105n14
  and East Asia 228
autonomous state, and developmental state
    167–8

Bairoch, P 252
Bajpai, J N 92
Bangladesh, and pharmaceutical industry
    285–7
Bardhan, P 105n14
Baumol, W 256
Benin:
  and economic growth, explanations for 184,
    186, 187
  and state controls 192
  and structural adjustment program 188
Berg, Elliot 499–500
Berg Report (1981) 265, 499–500, 509, 513
Berkowitz, D 100
Bernanke, B 269n15
Béteille, A 91, 97
bifurcated state 72
binding constraints 131
Birnie, E 413
Blair Commission 23, 115
Blyth, M 89
Boskin, Michael 42n39
Botchwey, Kwesi 40n3
Botswana:
  and economic growth 5, 181
    explanations for 184, 186, 187
  and natural resources 126
Bouët, A 517
Boyce, J K 506
Brautigam, D A 101
Brazil, and import-substitution policy 12
Bretton Woods institutions (BWIs):
  and explanations of Africa's slow
    growth 500
  and Washington Consensus 500
  see also International Monetary Fund;
    World Bank
Burkina Faso:
  and economic growth, explanations for 184,
    186, 187
  and structural adjustment program 188
Burundi:
  and adverse redistribution 193
  and economic growth 188
    explanations for 184, 186, 187
business, *see* state-business relations
business associations, and state-business
    relations 309–12, 314–15,
    316, 317
Business Environment and Economic
    Performance surveys 65

Cairns Group 514
Callaghy, T 82
Cambodia 224, 239
Camdessus, Michael 85
Cameroon:
  and economic growth, explanations for
    184, 186
  and structural adjustment program 188
Campos, J E 385
Cape Verde 186, 187
capital flight 127, 499, 503, 506–7
capitalism, and motivation of economic
  actors 145
capture:
  and growth-enhancing governance 61
  and industrial policy 28–9
Carruthers, B G 92
'catch-up':
  and divergence in global income levels 246–7
  and problem of 246
Central African Republic 184, 188
central banks:
  and functions of 98
  and industrial policy 98
  and institutional reform 98
central economic agencies (CEAs) 387–8
Chabal, P 123
Chabane, N 350
Chad:
  and economic growth, explanations for
    184, 186
  and structural adjustment program 188
Chang, H-J 42n37, 87–8, 93, 98, 378
Chicago School 92
China:
  and Africa 37–8
    aid assistance to 551
    impact of growth on 556–9
    international trade with 543, **544**, 545,
      546, 547, **549**, 550
  and computer industry:
    clustering 289–90
    development policy 287–90
    investment in knowledge-building 288–9
    promotion of special economic
      zones 289–90
  and development strategy 232–3
  and economic growth 37, 536, **540**–1
    constraints on 542
    factors favoring 542
    future projections of 541–2
    impact on Africa 556–9
    world impact of 555–6
  as engine of world growth 553–5
  and export processing zones 322, 330
  and foreign direct investment 224, 232–3,
    331, 332, **550**–1

and high and new technology industrial
  development zones (HNTIDZs)
  325–6, 332
and institutions 92–3
and international influence 559–60
and international migration 552–3
and property rights 92–3
and regulation 18
and share of world population and income:
  current situation 538, **539**, 540
  historical perspective **537**–8
and special economic zones 289–90, 325,
  331–2
civil conflict 502
civil service 96
Clague, C 83
classical economics, and role of the state 140–1
climate change 39
climate zones, and economic performance 523–4
clustering 151–2, 256
  and Chinese special economic zones 289–90
  and Ireland 420–1
Coase, R 20
Coates, D 406
coercion, and industrial policy 408
Collier, P 116–18
colonial history, and governance and
  growth 68–73
Commission for Africa (Blair Commission)
  23, 115
commodity booms 185, 202, 411
Communaute Financiere Africaine (African
  Financial Community, CFA) 192
Comoros 186
comparative advantage:
  and factor endowments 158–9
  and short-term nature of 257
  and skills and technological capabilities 158
competition law 308, 316, 319n10
competitiveness:
  and free markets 58
  and industrial policy 328–9
  and labor costs 158
  and skills and technological capabilities
    158, 159
computer industry, and innovation policies:
  China 287–90
    clustering 289–90
    investment in knowledge-building 288–9
    promotion of special economic
      zones 289–90
  South Africa 290–2
conditionality 84, 104n8, 500
Congo Republic 186
contracts:
  and fulfilling obligations 145–6
  and state enforcement mechanisms 146

Copenhagen Summit, (United Nations Climate Change Conference 2009) 39
corporatism 408
corporatist social pacts, and Ireland 408, 414, 415–16
corruption, and difficulties in fighting 120
Côte d'Ivoire, and economic growth 184, 188
credibility:
  and institutions 84
  and state-business relations 305
credit:
  and government's role in provision of 38–9
  and lack of access to in Africa 38
Culliton, J 413, 420
Culliton Report (1992) 413–14, 420, 423, 424
culture, African 124

Daloz, J-P 123
Debreu, Gerard 81
debt relief 526
deindustrialization 16, 29, 211n25, 349, 363, 510–11
  and trade liberalization 511–12
democracy:
  and development 242n3
  and developmental state 168–9
  and fragility of 121
  see also governance
Democratic Republic of Congo:
  and adverse redistribution 193
  and economic growth 188
    explanations for 187
democratization 122–3
  and effects of 265
  and property rights 105n14
  see also governance
demography, and Africa's youth population 467
Deng Xiaoping 232–3
de Soto, Hernando 13
Devajaran, S 507
development:
  and dynamic nature of 7
  and historical experiences of 348–9
  and institutions 56–7
  and lack of blueprint for 55–6
  and policy autonomy 54–5, 167–8, 393–4
  and theory of 346–8
development economics, and institutions 80–1
development policy:
  and debate over role of the state 20–2
  and disagreements over 20
  and learning from past growth trajectories:
    developed countries 252
    East Asia 252–4
    East Asia vs Latin America 254–5
development state 40n6

developmental competitiveness, and industrial policy 328–9
developmental state 4, 33
  and Africa 34–5
  and construction of 33–4
  as continuum 34
  and coordination of economic agents 263–4
    bifurcated economic and political structures 265–6
    institutionalized coordination 264
    public officials' mindset 265
    state-business alliance 263–4
    state-business balance 264–5
  and creation by social and political action 169
  and democracy 168–9
  and embedded in society 278
  and establishment of 262–6
  and historical evolution of concept 164–7
    characteristics of industrialization 164–5
    policy implementation 166
    political transformation 166–7
    tariffs 165
  and inclusionary growth 264
  and nature of 167–9
    avoidance of wasteful rent-seeking 169
    common characteristics 169
    guidance of private sector 168
    ideology 167
    state autonomy 167–8
    structure 167
    support for development agenda 168–9
  see also industrial policy
developmentalist state 4, 12
Diamond, Jared 14
discovery 59
disease control 116
distribution, and inequality in developing countries 247
Do Muoi 237
Doha trade agreement 258, 515, 516
Doing Business surveys 65, 133
donor assistance, and industrial policy 394–6
Dr Reddy's 282, 284
Dunning, T 87, 104n5
Dutch disease 368, 369, 450, 510, 524
dynamic capacity development:
  and East Asia 228–9, 242
    China 232–3
    enhancing unique strengths 230
    goal orientation 229–30
    growth-enhancing governance 230–1
    Japan 231–2
    Malaysia 233
    real-sector pragmatism 229
    Thailand 234

and Japanese aid development strategy 235
   align assistance to existing development
      strategies 235–7
   policies for industrial promotion **236**
   policy dialogue 237–9
   providing conditions for foreign
      investment 241
   regional development around core
      infrastructure 239–40

East Asia:
   and agriculture 445–6
   and development strategy 231, 242, 380–1
      China 232–3
      Japan 231–2
      Malaysia 233
      Thailand 234
   and diversity of experiences within 222–5,
      373, 382–3, 386–7
      foreign direct investment 224
      government intervention 224
      growth in real income **223**–4
      manufacturing 224
   and education:
      long-term approach to 486–7
      spending on 485–6
   and employment characteristics 439–40
   and employment-intensive growth 438, 448
   and export processing zones 330–3
   and factors responsible for economic
      success 3
   and flying geese 222, 383
   and growth-enhancing governance 74, 75,
      128, 230–1
   and income growth 398n2
   and industrial policy 29–30, 228–9, 252–4,
      378, 407
      diversity of 382–3
      enhancing unique strengths 230
      export processing zones 330–3
      goal orientation 229–30
      growth-enhancing governance 230–1
      real-sector pragmatism 229
   and initial low capabilities 224–5
   and institutions 97
   and interaction of politics and economics
      225–8
      authoritarian leadership 228
      critique of good governance argument 226
      dynamic capacity development 228
      foreign advisors 225–6
      growth diagnostics 226–7
      need for interdisciplinary research 227
      policy-capability matching 227
      policymaking 225
   and labor force participation rate 438
   and Latin America, comparison with 254–5

and methodology of policy formulation
      221–2
and mobility of labor 454–5
and public-private partnership 385
and regulation 18
and relevance of experience for Africa
      221, 396
   changes in trade policy 388, **389**, 390
   collaboration with private sector 390,
      392–3
   diversity of experience 386–7
   harnessing of nationalism 393–4
   institution- and policy-making 387–8
   national purpose 393–4
   policy-driven industrialization 390–2
and state-business relations 277
East Timor 224
Easterly, W 268n15, 507
economic growth:
   and Africa's record 7–9, 175, 176–82,
      204–5, 373–6, 410, **449**–50,
      500–1, **540**–1
      1960 to mid 1970s 183–4
      commodity prices **375**, 411
      constraints on 542–3
      factors favoring 412
      future projections of 542–3
      heterogeneity in patterns 181, 205
      impact of Chinese and Indian
         growth 556–9
      inability to sustain 411–12
      mid-1970s to early 1990s 184–9
      potential for 542
      since mid-1990s 187–9
      variations in 182
   and anti-growth syndromes 17–18, 117,
      200, 205
      experience of initial leaders 201
      group identity rivalry 202
      initial conditions 201
      reigning international paradigms 201
   and China 37, 536, **540**–1
      constraints on 542
      as engine of world growth 553–5
      factors favoring 542
      future projections of 541–2
      impact on Africa 556–9
      world impact of 555–6
   and complexities of African development
      5–7
   and cross-national analysis of reasons for
      success 9–13
   and determinants of 542
   and diversity of African performance 5
   and explanations of Africa's record 4, 13,
      182, 190, 376–7
      adverse redistribution 185–6, 192–3, 202

Index

economic growth: (*cont.*)
    analytic studies 17–19
    commodity booms 185, 202, 411
    external treatment of Africa 15–16
    geography 13–15
    governance 16–17, 30–1, 115, 199–201
    policy syndromes 117–18, 185
    political instability 186, 187, 203, 204
    resource opportunity set 202
    state controls 190–2, 203
    state failure 194, 202–3, 205–6
    structural adjustment programs 188
    suboptimal intertemporal resource
      allocation 193–4, 202
    supply shocks 185, 202
    syndrome-free regime 194–9, 210n15
    terms of trade 186, 187, 510
    total factor productivity growth
      188–9, 205
  and future projections of 541–3
  and globalization 246
  and governance 51, 86–8, 199–201
    lack of relationship between 32, 58–63,
      226, 262
  and government's role, debate over 20–2
  and growth-enhancing governance 32, 51,
    53–4, 74–5, 127–8
    avoiding over-ambitious approach 128–9
    East Asia 128
    exit strategies 130, 131
    focus on limited priority sectors 131–4
    governance capabilities 54, 74–5
    identifying binding constraints 131
    identifying priorities 57
    incremental approach 62–3, 115, 129–34
    industrial parks 120
    investment 134–5
    labor skills and training 135–6
    lack of blueprints for 55–6
    land allocation 136–7
    methodological approach to 53
    national growth strategy **132**
    pragmatic approach 129–33
    property rights 119
    rent management 121
    responding to market failures 55, 60–1
    theoretical support for 55
    variety in 54
  and Growth/Spence Commission 10–12
  and India 37, 536, **540**–1
    constraints on 542
    as engine of world growth 553–5
    factors favoring 542
    future projections of 541–2
    impact on Africa 556–9
    world impact of 555–6
  and institutions 56–7, 86

  and Kaldor's growth laws 255
  and lack of blueprint for 55–6
  and learning from past growth trajectories:
    developed countries 252
    East Asia 252–4
    East Asia vs Latin America 254–5
  and market-enhancing ('good') governance
    51, 52, **62**
    assumptions of 55
    causality 66–7, 116
    challenges to approach 115–19
    colonial history 68–73
    constraints on achieving 119–21
    lack of relationship between 67
    methodological approach to 52
    minimal state 116–17
    natural resources 127
    not precondition for development 53
    as obstacle to development 31, 33, 55
    over-ambitious strategy 57, 114–15
    problems with evidence for 66–73
    theoretical thinking behind 63–6
  and necessity for 503
  and neoclassical model of, Solow
    model 149–50
  and policy autonomy 54–5, 167–8, 393–4
  and policy syndromes approach 182
    policy environment 205–6
    syndrome-free regime 182, 203–**4**, 205
  and potential for improving 8
  and poverty reduction 375
  and preconditions for 462
  and production structure 258
  and requirements for 54
  and role of the state, debate over 20–2
  and skills development 462, 489
  and social development 147–8
  and state-business relations 303–4,
    305, **313**
    contribution of 305–6, 316
    effects at macro level 312–14
    effects at micro level 314–15
  and structural adjustment programs 188
    impact of 410–11
    weak link between 500
  and syndrome-free regime 194–6,
    197, **198**
  see also employment-intensive growth; gross
    domestic product
economic processing units (EPUs), and
    definition of 324–5
Economist 248–9, 412
Economist Intelligence Unit 281
education:
  and advances in Africa 412
  and development of systems 279
  and East Asian expenditure on 485–6

and education profile of 25–34 age group **467**
and employment status by age and educational attainment **469**
and expanding coverage of 478, **479**
and expanding scientific and technical personnel 481–3
share of student in science and technology **482**
and financing of 484–5
and focus on primary education 16
and foreign direct investment 37
and Ghana and South Korea compared **477**–8
and inadequacies of systems 279
and lack of investment in 477–8
and learning outcomes 478–81
international comparisons **481**
primary education **480**
and lessons from successful reformers 485
backward and forward linkages 488
longer time horizons 486–7
strategic and visionary leadership 485–6
and national innovation systems 155, 156
and reform of 37
and technical and vocational training 37, 483
and universities 484
and weak demand for educated workers 468
see also skills development
Edwards, L 365, 366
Egypt 96, 322
El Salvador, and Japan 240
Ellerman, D 95
employment:
and agriculture 441
and characteristics of African 439–44
and characteristics of South/East Asia 439–40
and distribution of 15–59 age group by employment status **468**
and export processing zones 322, 323, 335
and growth of labor force 443
HIV prevalence 443–4
and labor force participation rate 438, 440, 441, 456–7
HIV prevalence 441–**2**
and low income 441, 443
and low productivity 440, 441, 443
and poverty reduction 35, 437
and self-employment 440
and South Africa 359, **360**, 361, 362–3, **365**
and status by age cohort and educational attainment **469**
and unemployment 440–1, 442–3
and weak demand for educated workers 468
and working poor 441, 443
see also employment-intensive growth; labor markets

employment-intensive growth:
and agriculture 445–8
and Ethiopia 451–2
and mobility of labor 454–6
and non-agricultural sectors 448–51
and output elasticity of growth 437–8
and policy priorities 457–8
and poverty reduction 437, 444–8
increasing productivity 445
increasing ratio of employment to population 444–5
South Korea 438
and South Korea 438
and Uganda 452–3
endogenous growth theory 150, 153–4, 163, 511
and assumptions of 150
entrepreneurial development 129–30
Epstein, G 98
Equatorial Guinea 187
Ericsson 474
Eritrea 5, 187
Eskom 350
Ethiopia:
and agriculture 448
as developmental state 34
and economic growth 5, 18
explanations for 184, 186
and economic policy 14
and employment-intensive growth 451–2
and industrial policy 25
and Japan 237
and leather industry 25
and structural adjustment program 188
ethnic fragmentation 124–5
European Union:
and economic integration 409–10
and Ireland:
impact of membership 408, 409–10
structural funding assistance 415
evaluation, and industrial policy 424–6
Evans, Peter 81, 88, 90–1, 92, 278, 400n16
Everest-Phillips, M 379, 386, 387, 390, 394
Everything But Arms (EBA) 323
exchange rate regime 192
executive, and constraints on 118, 199–200, 206
export processing zones (EPZs):
and advantages for companies in 332–3
in Africa 322–3
experiences with 335–6
Onne Oil and Gas Free Zone (Nigeria) 336–8
in Asia 330–3
in China 322, 331–2
and definition of 324
and demonstration effects 330
and employment in 322, 323, 335

571

export processing zones (EPZs): (*cont.*)
  as experimental forum 330
  and foreign direct investment 331, 332
  and industrial policy 330
  and lessons from successful zones 339
  and literature on economic impact of
      case studies 327
      cost-benefit analysis 327
      neoclassical studies 326–7
      policy-modeling 327–8
  and most active industries within 324
  and Nigeria:
      Calabar export processing zone 337,
          341n23
      Onne Oil and Gas Free Zone 336–8
  and opportunities offered by 323
  and proliferation of 322
  in South Korea 330, 331, 332
  in Taiwan 330–1, 332
  and World Bank's conceptualization of 331,
      334–5
  see also free trade zones (FTZs); industrial
      policy; special economic zones (SEZs)
extractive industries, and economic growth 8
Eyadéma, Gnassingbé 193

factor endowments, and comparative
      advantage 158–9
Federal Express 24
finance 38–9
Financial Times 251
flying geese 222, 383
food security 522
foreign advisors, and development 225–6
foreign direct investment (FDI)
  and Africa's share of **504**, **505**, **550**–1
  and attracting 37, 88–9
  and China 224, 232–3, 331, 332, **550**–1
  and concentration of 260
  and confined to natural resources 499
  and discouragement of 422–3
  and East Asia 224
      discouraged by 422–3
  and export-oriented FDI 260–1
  and export processing zones 331, 332
  and harmful effects of 261–2
  and import-substituting FDI 259–61
  and India **550**–1
  and institutions 93
  and Ireland 417–19
      spillover effects 420
  and limitations of FDI-led growth 421, 422
  and limited contribution of 504–6
  and limited scale of 6, 417
  and little success in attracting 8
  and management of 259–62
  and motives for 465

and privatization 505
and providing conditions for 241
and skills development 465–**6**
    Ireland 473–4
    Singapore 469–73
and spillover effects 419–20
and technical training 37
and technology transfer 465
and Washington Consensus 259
foreign exchange controls 191
Fosu, A K 191
France 264
free markets:
  and competitiveness 58
  and harmful effects in developing
      countries 58
  and market-enhancing ('good') governance,
      theoretical thinking behind 63–6
free ports (FPs), and definition of 324
free trade zones (FTZs):
  and definition of 324
  and proliferation of 322
  see also export processing zones (EPZs)
Freeman, C 422

genocide, and colonialism 70–1
geography, and economic growth 13–15
Germany:
  and industrialization 166
  and legal reform 99–100
  and national innovation system 155, 156–7
      diffusion of technology 157
      exploiting existing technology 157
Gerschenkron, Alexander 80–1, 164–5, 274
Ghana:
  and economic growth 5, 189
      explanations for 184, 186, 187
  and economic reform 189
  and education, comparison with South
      Korea **477**–8
  and Ghana Industrial Skills Development
      Center (GISDC) 475
  and institutional reform 96
  and natural resources 126
  and skills development 475
  and state controls 192
  and structural adjustment program 188
Glaeser, E L 105n14
globalization:
  and developing countries 246
  and divergence in income levels 246–7
  and impact of 37, 499
  and international migration 553
  and opportunities offered by 380
Go, Delphin 18–19
goal-setting, and industrial policy 229–30, 295
Goldman Sachs 541

Gomery, R 256
Goodbody Economic Consultants 424
Gordon, D 84
governance 4
　and alternative methodological approaches
　　52–3
　and constraining executives 118, 199–20, 206
　and constraints on progress toward good
　　governance 119
　　attitudes towards rents 120–1
　　fighting corruption 120
　　fragility of democracy 121
　　property rights 119–20
　and conventional governance agenda 32
　and corporate governance 106n18
　and different approaches to 7, 51–2
　and economic growth 51, 58–63, 86–8,
　　199–201
　　causality 66–7, 116
　　characteristics of growth economies **68**
　　governance capabilities 74–5
　　growth-enhancing governance 74–5
　　lack of relationship between 32, 58–63,
　　　67, 226, 262
　　problems with evidence for link
　　　between 66–73
　and enforcement capabilities 56–7
　as explanation of Africa's poor economic
　　record 16–17, 30–1, 115
　and growth-enhancing governance 32, 51,
　　53–4, 74–5, 127–8
　　avoiding over-ambitious approach 128–9
　　East Asia 74, 75, 128, 230–1
　　exit strategies 130, 131
　　focus on limited priority sectors 131–4
　　governance capabilities 54, 74–5
　　identifying binding constraints 131
　　identifying priorities 57
　　incremental approach 62–3, 115, 129–34
　　industrial parks 120
　　investment 134–5
　　labor skills and training 135–6
　　lack of blueprints for 55–6
　　land allocation 136–7
　　methodological approach to 53
　　national growth strategy **132**
　　pragmatic approach 129–33
　　property rights 119
　　rent management 121
　　responding to market failures 55, 60–1
　　theoretical support for 55
　　variety in 54
　and institutions 56–7
　and liberal economic analysis of Africa 115–19
　and market-enhancing ('good') governance
　　51, 52, **62**, 262, 347
　　assumptions of 55

　　ceiling on development of 115
　　challenges to approach 115–19
　　colonial history 68–73
　　constraints on achieving 119–21
　　critique of 226
　　institutions 83–4
　　judicial reform 89–90
　　methodological approach to 52
　　minimal state 116–17
　　narrow view of 89
　　natural resources 127
　　not precondition for development 53
　　as obstacle to development 31, 33, 55
　　over-ambitious strategy 57, 114–15
　　policy syndromes 117–18
　　problems with evidence for 66–73
　　theoretical thinking behind 63–6
　and market failures 55, 117
　and meaning of 52
　and policy autonomy 54–5
　and problems attributed to Africa 122
　　African culture 124
　　ethnic fragmentation 124–5
　　fragmented polities 123–4
　　neo-patrimonialism 122–3
　　resource curse 126–7
　and weaknesses in 51
　and World Bank ranking of countries 226
　see also institutions and institutional reform
government:
　and debate over role of 20–2
　and developmental state 4
　and legitimization of intervention by 381–2
　and role in promoting development 4, 274
　see also industrial policy; state; state-business
　　relations
Grabel, I 108n31
Gramsci, A 108n33
Green Revolution 24, 524
Greenwald, B 28
gross domestic product:
　and African, Chinese and Indian share of
　　world GDP:
　　current situation 538, **539**, 540
　　historical perspective **537**–8
　and annual growth rates **10**, **15**, **177–8**,
　　449, **501**, **502**
　and components of **511**
　and growth in developing regions **373**
　and growth per worker **183**, **207–8**
　and half-decadal mean annual growth
　　rates **181**
　and manufacturing's share of 8, **376**
　and per capita growth **179–80**
　and regional comparison of growth rates
　　10, **11**
　and trends in Africa **9**, **374**, **411**

growth diagnostics 226–7, 375
Growth/Spence Commission 10–12, 13
Guinea 184
Guinea Bissau 186, 188

Haggard, S 88
Hague, S 101
Haiti 254–5
Halliday, T C 92
Hanushek, E A 478
Harrison, G 95
Harriss, J 304
Hausmann, R 92
Helleiner, G K 519
higher education 36–7
Hirschman, A 129, 130–1
historical change, and alternative
    methodological approaches to 52–3
Hitchens, D 413
HIV:
  and labor force growth rates 443–4
  and labor force participation rate 441–2
Honohan, P 418–19
Houphouet-Boigny, Felix 201
House, D 418
human capital:
  and national innovation system 156
  and public investment 36
  see also education; skills development

ideology:
  and developmental state 167
  and subjective perceptions 145
import-substitution, and Brazil 12
inclusionary growth 264
income levels:
  and Africa compared with other developing
    regions 374, 375
  and drop in per capita income 501
  and East Asian growth 398n2
  and employment 441, 443
  and fall in real wages 501–2
  and global divergence in 246–7
  and income differentials 455
  and increase in inequality 501
  and inequality in developing countries 247
India:
  and Africa 37
  aid assistance to 551–2
  impact of growth on 556–9
  international trade with 543, 544, 545, 547,
    548, 549, 550
  and economic growth 37, 536, 540–1
    constraints on 542
    factors favoring 542
    future projections of 541–2
    impact on Africa 556–9

world impact of 555–6
as engine of world growth 553–5
and export processing zones 322
and foreign direct investment 550–1
and institutions 92
and international influence 559–60
and international migration 552–3
and pharmaceutical industry 281
  development policy 281–5
and Planning Commission 264
and regulation 18
and share of world population and income:
  current situation 538, 539, 540
  historical perspective 537–8
as successful state 125
indigenous populations, and colonialism 70–1
indirect taxation 191
Indonesia 18, 383
industrial parks, and growth-enhancing
    governance 120
industrial policy:
  and African use of 25
  and arguments for 266–7, 378
  and bad reputation of 24
  and Big Push argument 256
  and central banks 98
  and central economic agencies 387–8
  and challenge/support classification of 377–8
  and classification of 377
  and coercion 408
  and computer industry:
    China 287–90
    South Africa 290–2
  and country specificity 382–3
  and critique of 27–8, 378–9
    capture by special interests 28–9
    creating rents 28
  and developed countries 252
  and developmental competitiveness 328
    depth 329
    diversity 328
    market share 328–9
    spillover effects 329
  and dimensions of 24
  and dismissal of 249
  and donor assistance 394–6
  and East Asia 228–9, 252–4, 378, 407
    China 232–3
    diversity of 382–3
    enhancing unique strengths 230
    export processing zones 330–3
    goal orientation 229–30
    growth-enhancing governance 230–1
    Japan 231–2
    Malaysia 233, 384, 390–3
    real-sector pragmatism 229
    Thailand 234

and features of 24
and foreign direct investment, management
    of 259–62
and goals of 398n6
and holistic approach to 413, 421–2
and infant industry argument 28, 257
and information requirements of 398n8
and institutional approach 329
    capacities 329–30
    incentives 329
    norms 329
    organizations 329
    regulations 329
and institutional compensation 275
and Ireland 30
    clustering 420–1
    Culliton Report (1992) 413–14,
        423, 424
    foreign direct investment 417–20
    holistic approach 413, 421–2
    policy evaluation 424–6
and Kaldor's growth laws 255
and learning-by-doing 384
and legitimization of government
        intervention 381–2
and literature supporting 255–9, 328
and macroeconomic policy 428n6
and market failure as rationale for 26–7
and market imperfections 274
and monitoring impact of 384
and narrow interpretations of 412–13
and nature of 267
and need for 377
and neglect of 24
and pharmaceutical industry:
    Bangladesh 285–7
    India 281–5
and potential benefit for Africa 25–6
and poverty 36
and public-private partnership 384–6, 390
and relevance of Asian experience for
        Africa 221, 396
    changes in trade policy 388, **389**, 390
    collaboration with private sector 390,
        392–3
    diversity of Asian experience 386–7
    harnessing of nationalism 393–4
    institution- and policy-making 387–8
    national purpose 393–4
    policy-driven industrialization 390–2
and relevance of Irish experience for
        Africa 406, 407–10
    attitudes towards enterprise 424, 426–7
    clustering 420–1
    foreign direct investment 417–20
    holistic approach 413, 421–2
    limitations of FDI-led growth 421, 422

    orientation towards domestic firms 421,
        423–4
    policy evaluation 424–6
    social contracts 415–16
    spillover effects from foreign investment
        419–20
and renewed interest in 372
and risk amelioration 27
and risks of absence of 29
and role of the state 295–7
    conflict management 296–7
    formulation of long-term vision 295, 387–8,
        393–4
    guarantor of risks 296
    institution building 296
    providing coordination 295
and spillover effects 28, 29
and state-business relations 277
and successes with 29–30, 407
and theoretical support for 255–9
and trade policy 257–8
and trial-and-error approach 384
and uneven success of 406
and United States 252
and unsettled debate over 379–80
and views on 377
    as necessary and possible 378
    neither necessary nor possible 378–9
    skepticism over necessity and
        possibility 379
    unsettled debate 379–80
and widespread use of 24
and World Bank's opposition to 333–4
see also developmental state; export
        processing zones (EPZs); state-business
        relations
industrialization:
    and characteristics of 164–5
    and historical experiences of 348–9
    and learning 347, 349
    and literature on 255–7
    and reciprocal control mechanisms 347, 348
    and role of trade and trade policy 349
    and tariffs 165
    and theory of 346–8
    and Washington Consensus 346–7
    see also industrial policy
inequality 36
    and developing countries 247
    and increase in 501
    and South Africa 361
infant industry protection 28, 257
inflation targeting:
    and central bank reform 98
    and South Africa 353
information asymmetry, and technological
        change 153

infrastructure:
 and deterioration in 514
 and Japanese aid development strategy
  239–40
 and need for investment in 116
 and public investment 36
Initiative for Policy Dialogue, and Africa Task
  Force 4, 13, 22, 39
innovation:
 and absence of institutional support 273, 276
 and economic structure 154
 and incentives for 278
 and institutions 275
 and learning 154
 and rent creation 140–1
 and variation in capacities across
  countries 276–7
 see also national innovation systems
innovation policies:
 and computer industry:
  China 287–90
  South Africa 290–2
 and definition of 275
 and extensive nature of 278
 and incentives for innovation 278
 and institutional compensation 275
 and latecomer countries 274
  institutional ineffectiveness and inertia
   279–81
  institutional path-dependence
   failures 279
  lack of institutional support 273, 276
  sectoral policies 279
 and pharmaceutical industry:
  Bangladesh 285–7
  India 281–5
 and role of the state 295–7
  conflict management 296–7
  formulation of long-term vision 295
  guarantor of risks 296
  institution building 296
  providing coordination 295
 and sectoral policies 279
 and urgent need for 273
institutions and institutional reform 84–5,
  102–3
 and adoption of good governance
  agenda 85
 and central bank reform 98
 and contextual nature of 277
 and coordinating function 275
 and credibility 84
 and development 33, 80–1
 and distinction from organizations 276–7
 and economic growth 56–7, 86
 and foreign ownership 99–101
 and good governance agenda 83–4

and governance 56–7
and industrial policy, East Asia 387–8
and ineffectiveness of 85
and institutional dualism 93–5
and institutional instability and sclerosis
  95–6
and institutional monocropping 88
 meaning of 81
and institutional monotasking 88–91
 meaning of 81
and investment 88–9
and judicial reform 89–90
and learning-by-doing 107n30
and legitimacy 103
and measurement problems 86–7
and mismatch between institutions and
  tasks 101–2
and non-economic role of 91
and rational choice institutionalism 81
and reform overload 101–2
and relabelling of existing activities 85
and restraining vs transformative institutions 96–8
and rule-based policies 84
and uncertainty 145
and undermining of development 97–8
and weak conceptual underpinnings 86
and wrong institutions 91–3
intellectual property policies, and Indian
  pharmaceutical industry 281–2
Intels 337–8
interest rates 38, 191–2
International Development Association
  (IDA) 249
International Labour Organization 438
International Monetary Fund 6
 and conditionalities 104n8
 and ineffectiveness of aid 509
 and institutional reform 85
 and shortcomings of policy advice 226
 and stabilization programs 500
international organizations, and shortcomings
  of policy advice 225–6
 see also International Monetary Fund; World
  Bank; World Trade Organization (WTO)
international trade:
 and African shares of world manufacturing
  exports **510**
 and agriculture 509, 510, 513, 521, 522
 and Chinese-African trade 543, **544**, 545,
  546, 547, **549**, 550
 and climate zones 523–4
 and collapse of Africa's exports 519
 and commodities 521, **522**
 and declining importance of developed
  country markets 519, 520
 and destination and sources of **521**

and development 509–10
with East Asia 519–20
and GDP components of **520**
and import sources 520
and Indian-African trade 543, **544**, 545, 547, **548**, **549**, 550
and industrialization 349
and intra-African trade 520
and one-off gains from 522–3
and patterns of 519–22
and regional shares in world trade **346**
and terms of trade 186–7, 510
and trading partners 519–20
see also trade liberalization
investment:
  and attraction of 88–9
  and authoritarian regimes 105n14
  and growth-enhancing governance 134–5
  and institutional reform 88–9
  and limited scale of 6
  and low rates of 503, 511
  and market failures 59
  and portfolio flows 506–7
  and productivity 58–9
  and South Africa 358–9, 362, **364**
  see also foreign direct investment (FDI)
investment promotion agency (IPA) 307, 308, 314, 316, 319n9
Ireland:
  and corporatist social pacts 408, 414, 415–16
  and currency depreciation 415
  and European Union:
    impact of membership 408, 409–10
    structural funding assistance 415
  and factors favoring economic success 414, 416–17
  and fertility rate 428n7
  and fiscal stabilization 414
  and foreign direct investment 417–19
    spillover effects 420
  and industrial policy 30
    clustering 420–1
    Culliton Report (1992) 413–14, 420, 423, 424
    holistic approach 413
    policy evaluation 424–6
  and Irish Development Authority 473–4
  and National Economic and Social Council 415
  and National Linkages Programme 420
  and nature of economy 407–8
  and Programme for National Recovery 416
  and relevance of experience for Africa 406, 407–10
    attitudes towards enterprise 424, 426–7
    clustering 420–1
    foreign direct investment 417–20

holistic approach to industrial policy 413, 421–2
  limitations of FDI-led growth 421, 422
  orientation towards domestic firms 421, 423–4
  policy evaluation 424–6
  social contracts 415–16
  spillover effects from foreign investment 419–20
  and Shannon Export Free Zone 322
  and skills development 473–4
  and small and medium-sized enterprises 408–9, 423–4
    access to finance 409
Iscor 350, 352, 355
Ishikawa, Shigeru 237, 446
Italy, and industrialization 166
Iwasaki, I 394

Japan:
  and development aid strategy 229, 235
    align assistance to existing development strategies 235–7
    policies for industrial promotion **236**
    policy dialogue 237–9
    providing conditions for foreign investment 241
    regional development around core infrastructure 239–40
  and development strategy 231–2, 382
  and discouragement of foreign investment 422–3
  and El Salvador 240
  and Ethiopia 237
  and goal-oriented development strategy 230
  and industrial policy, coercion 408
  and Industrial Structure Council 385
  and industrialization 166, 348
  and institutionalized coordination 264
  and Mozambique 240
  and public-private partnership 385
  and Thailand 241
  and Tunisia 236–7
  and Vietnam 237–9, 241
  and Zambia 239
Japan International Cooperation Agency (JICA) 23, 231, 236–7
Johnson, C 275–6
Johnson, S 68–70
judicial reform 89–90

Kaldor, N 255
Kaufmann, D 116
Keita, Modibo 201
Kennedy, K 415
Kenya:
  and adverse redistribution 193

Kenya: (*cont.*)
   and economic growth, explanations for 184
   and export processing zones 335, 336
   and industrial policy 25
   and state controls 192
   and working poor 441
Kenyatta, Jomo 201
Keynes, J M 267
Khama, Seretse 201
Khan, M H 230
Knack, S 101
knowledge, as public good 26
knowledge gap 21
Kosacoff, B 261
Kraev, E 518
Krueger, A 258, 333
Krugman, P 256, 259, 417
Kydland, Finn 84

labor costs, and competitiveness 158
labor markets:
   and agriculture 441
   and characteristics of African 439–44
   and features of 35
   and growth-enhancing governance 135–6
   and growth of labor force 443
      HIV prevalence 443–4
   and labor force participation rate 438, 440,
      441, 456–7
      HIV prevalence 441–**2**
   and low income 441, 443
   and low productivity 440, 441, 443
   and mobility of labor 454–6
   and national innovation systems:
      diffusion system 156
      mission-oriented systems 155–6
   and self-employment 440
   and technological change 152–3
   and unemployment 440–1, 442–3
   and working poor 441, 443
Lall, S 258, 365–6, 378
land reform 39
   and growth-enhancing governance 136–7
Laos 224
latecomer countries:
   and definition of 297n4
   and features of 274
   and innovation 274
      institutional ineffectiveness and inertia
         279–81
      institutional path-dependence
         failures 279
      lack of institutional support 273, 276
      sectoral policies 279
   and institutional inadequacies 278
   and limited state capacity 277
   and organizational dysfunctions 280–1

and power distribution 278
and role of the state 275–6, 277–8, 295–7
   conflict management 296–7
   formulation of long-term vision 295
   guarantor of risks 296
   institution building 296
   providing coordination 295
Latin America:
   and East Asia, comparison with 254–5
   and education system 488
   and foreign direct investment, harmful
      effects of 261–2
   and the 'Volcker shock' 12
   and Washington Consensus 254–5
Latsch, W 378, 379
law reform:
   and development 107n28
   and German aid 99–100
   and market-enhancing ('good') governance
      90–1
Lawrence, R 365, 366
learning 8
   and absence from neoclassical models 21
   and accumulation of technological capability
      160–1
   and development 7
   and economic policy 28
   and economic structure 154
   and importance for development 21
   and industrial policy 384
   and industrialization 347, 349
   and innovation 154
   and market failures 59
   and technological change 258
learning, industrial and technology (LIT)
      policies, *see* industrial policy
legitimacy, and institutions 103
Leontief, W 258
Lesotho 184, 187
Levy, Brian 106n18
Lewis, W A 510, 523
liberal economics 246, 267n1
   see also neoliberalism; Washington
      Consensus
liberalization:
   and adverse effects of 23
   and Arrow-Debreu model 82
   and constraining effects of 524–5
   and external imposition of 525
   and failure of 251
   and failure of adjustment 82–3
   and impact of 349, 511, 525
   and market-enhancing ('good')
      governance 62
   see also trade liberalization; Washington
      Consensus
Liberia 5, 186, 187

Lien, D 385
Lieven, M 70
Limongi, F 105n14
Lindauer, D L 86
logging 506
Lome Convention 519

McGrath, K 418
macroeconomic policy, and industrial
    policy 428n6
Madagascar:
    and economic growth 186
    and export processing zones 335, 336
    and state controls 192
Maddison, A 537
Mahathir bin Mohamad 233, 394
Malawi:
    and economic growth 184
    and state-business relations 303
Malaysia:
    and Bumiputra Policy 400n23
    and central economic agencies 388
    and development strategy 233, 383
    and economic growth **392**, 407
    and Economic Planning Unit 388
    and foreign direct investment 391, **392**
    and GDP structure and trade **392**
    and industrial policy 233, 384, 390–3
    and macroeconomic policy 400n19
    and regulation 18
    and skills development 474–5
    and speed of catching up 224
    and *Vision 2020* 233, 394
Mali:
    and economic growth 186
    and structural adjustment program 188, 251
Mamdani, M 72
Mankiw, G 250–1
manufacturing:
    and African shares of world manufacturing
        exports **510**
    and decline in 29
    and East Asia 224
    as engine of growth 255
    and necessity for 368
    and regional shares in manufacturing
        value-added **345**
    as share of GDP 8, **376**
    and South Africa 358, 363–6, 367
market economy:
    and contractual obligations 145–6
    and individual norms and values 146
    and institutional underpinning of 144–8
    and market as social institution 145, 147
    and motivation of economic actors
        144–5, 147
    and property rights 145

and social capital 147
    characteristics of 147
    and state enforcement mechanisms 146
    and uncertainty 145
market failure:
    and financing discovery 59
    and governance 55, 117
    and growth-enhancing governance 55,
        127–8
        avoiding over-ambitious approach
            128–9
        exit strategies 130, 131
        focus on limited priority sectors 131–4
        identifying binding constraints 131
        incremental approach 129–34
        investment 134–5
        labor skills and training 135–6
        land allocation 136–7
        pragmatic approach 129–33
        responses of 60–1
    and investment 59, 134–5
    and knowledge inputs 273
    and learning 59
    and market-enhancing ('good')
        governance 62
    as rationale for industrial policy 26–7
    and technological change 150–4, 163
    and technology 150
    and theoretical literature on 255–6
market fundamentalism:
    and market-enhancing ('good')
        governance 62
    and role of the state 20
    and Washington Consensus 3–4
markets:
    and debate over role of the state 20–2
    and imperfect markets 273, 274
    as social institution 145, 147
Martin, W 516
Maseland, R 394
Matrix Lab 284
Mauritius:
    and economic growth 5
        explanations for 186, 187
    and export processing zones 322
    and industrial policy 25, 417
    and Joint Economic Council 319n9
    and state-business relations 303
    and state controls 192
Maxfield, S 304
Médard, J-F 122
Mexico 261
middle class, and emergence in Africa 412
migration 552–3
Millennium Development Goals 40, 526
Miyaji, Masaki 231
Mkandawire, Thandika 411, 506, 507, 519, 523

Mobutu, President 193
Mongolia 251, 268n13
Moore, B 166, 168
moral hazard, and correcting market
    failures 61
Moran, T 248, 259–61
Mozambique:
    and economic growth 5
        explanations for 186
    and Japan 240
    and skills development 475
    and state controls 192
Multi Fibre Arrangement 323, 335, 339, 506
multinational corporations, and myth
    of 257
multiple equilibria theory 256, 257
Myanmar 224
Myrdal, Gunnar, and Asia's poor prospects 3

Naím, M 105n10
Namibia 186, 187
nation-building 125
national identity 125
national innovation systems 154–9
    and definition of 154
    and diffusion system 155
        diffusion of technology 157
        exploiting existing technology 157
        Germany 156–7
    and economic structure 158
    and mission-oriented system 155
        creation of new technologies 157
        diffusion of technology 157
        United States 155–6
    and requirements for 154–5
    and utilization of new ideas:
        Germany 157
        United States 157
nationalism, and harnessing of 393–4
natural resources:
    as impediment to growth 13–14
    and management of 368–9
    and rents 126, 127
    and resource curse 126–7, 524
Ndikumana, L 506
Ndulu, Benno 15, 18
Nelson, R 275
neo-patrimonialism 122–3
neoclassical growth theory 20
    and institutions 105n12
    and Solow model 149–50
    and technological change 149–50, 163
neoliberalism:
    and Arrow-Debreu model 81–2
    and economic growth:
        Solow model 149–50
        technological change 149–50

and homogenous goods 153
and nightwatchman state 140, 141
    as theoretical impossibility 143
and rational choice theory 143
and rent creation 140–1
and rent-seeking 141
and role of the state 20, 140, 141
and self-interest-maximizing behavior
    141, 143
and technological change 153–4, 163
    inconsistency with 164
see also Washington Consensus
New Institutional Economics 63, 83
New Public Management 95
    and institutional reform 101
Newai Gebre-Ab, Ato 14
Ng, F 523
Niger 186
Nigeria:
    and adverse redistribution 193
    and Calabar export processing zone 337,
        341n23
    and economic growth 188, 374
        explanations for 186
    and Onne Oil and Gas Free Zone 336–8
    and skills development 475–6
    and state controls 192
nightwatchman state 140, 141
    and rational choice theory 143, 144
    as theoretical impossibility 143
Nkrumah, Kwame 201
North, Douglass 56, 83, 86, 95, 107n26, 263,
    276
North Korea 224
Nyerere, Julius 201

O'Connell, S A 191
official development aid (ODA), see aid
Ohnesorge, J 90, 106n19
Ohno, I 387, 390
Olson, M 123
Olympio, Sylvanus 201
Onne Oil and Gas Free Zone (Nigeria) 336–8
Organization for Economic Co-operation and
    Development 98, 508
organizations, and distinction from
    institutions 276–7
Osaka Spinning Company 232
output elasticity of growth (OEE), see
    employment-intensive growth

Pack, H 380, 398n8, 507
Page, John 18–19
Park Chung-hee 265–6
patents:
    and dynamic and static efficiency 26
    and Indian pharmaceutical industry 281–2

path dependence, and institutions for
innovation 279
patron-client politics 122–3
Peil, J 394
pharmaceutical industry, and innovation
policies:
  Bangladesh 285–7
  India 281–5
Philippines 264, 265
  and development strategy 383
  and export processing zones 390
Pike, A 419
Polaski, S 518
policy autonomy:
  and economic growth 54–5
  and state autonomy 168, 393–4
policy-capability matching 227
policy evaluation, and industrial policy
424–6
policy implementation 166
  and state autonomy 168
policy modeling, and export processing
zones 327–8
policy reform:
  and economic growth 18–19
  and sequencing of policies 22–3
policy syndromes 210n9
  and adverse redistribution 192–3, 202
  and Africa's poor performance 117–18
  and anti-growth syndromes 17–18, 117, 200,
205
    experience of initial leaders 201
    group identity rivalry 202
    initial conditions 201
    reigning international paradigms 201
  and economic growth 185
  and evolution of 190
  and policy environment 205–6
  and resource opportunity set 202
  and state controls 190–2, 203
  and state failure/breakdown 194, 202–3,
205–6
  and suboptimal intertemporal resource
allocation 193–4, 202
  and supply shocks 202
  and syndrome-free regime 182, 197, 198,
205, 210n15
    effects of 197–9
    evolution of 203–4
    explaining economic growth 195–7
    trends in 194–5
political fragmentation 123–4
political instability 186, 187, 203, 204, 504
  and state failure/breakdown 194, 202–3,
205–6
political institutions, and economic
growth 184

political transformation, and industrialization
166–7
Pop-Eleches, G 87, 104n5
portfolio flows 503, 506–7
Posco 253
poverty:
  in Africa 175–6, 501
  and population below poverty line 502
  and South Africa 361
  and working poor 441, 443
poverty reduction:
  and agricultural productivity 35
  and economic growth 375
  and employment 35, 437
  and employment-intensive growth 437,
444–8
    agriculture 445–8
    Ethiopia 451–2
    increasing productivity 445
    increasing ratio of employment to
population 444–5
    non-agricultural sectors 448–51
    policy priorities 457–8
    South Korea 438
    Uganda 452–3
  and human capital investment 36
  and industrial policy 36
  and market-enhancing ('good')
governance 65
  and pro-poor growth 36
  and rapid growth 35–6
  and rates of 176
  and structural change 35–6
Prasad, E S 107n30
Prebisch, R 510
Prescott, Edward 84
price controls 185, 202
Pritchett, L 86
privatization:
  and foreign direct investment 505
  and institutional reform 101
  and South Africa 355
productivity:
  and agriculture 35, 441, 445, 446–8
  and employment 440, 441, 443
  and employment-intensive growth 445
  and investment 58–9
property rights 12–13, 84
  and China 92–3
  and colonial history 68–73
  and constraints on achieving 119–20
  and growth-enhancing governance 119
  and judicial reform 89–90
  and market economy 145
  and political implications 90–1
protection, and infant economy argument
for 28, 257

Przeworski, A 105n14
public expenditure, and reduction in 510–11
public goods:
  and good governance 53, 54
  and social capital 147
  and social development 148
  and technology 150
public-private partnerships (PPPs):
  and industrial policy 384–6, 390
  and skills development 475–6

Rajan, R G 107n30
Ranbaxy 282, 284
rational choice institutionalism 81
rational choice theory:
  and economic motivation, self-interest
    143, 144
  and neoliberalism 143
  and the state 143–4
reciprocal control mechanisms (RCMs)
    347, 348
reciprocity, and state-business relations 305
redistribution 191
  and adverse redistribution 185–6, 192–3
regulation, and economic growth 18
rents 141
  and beneficial effects of 120, 258–9
  and growth-enhancing governance 60–1
  and industrial policy 28
  and innovation 59
  and learning 59
  and management of 120–1
  and natural resources 126, 127
  and neoliberal reforms 29
  and rent creation 140–1
  and rent-seeking 141
    endogenizing 142–3
  and technology acquisition 120–1
research infrastructure, and national
    innovation systems 155, 156–7
resource curse 126–7, 524
resource mobilization 503
resource opportunity set 202
revolution from above, and industrialization
    166–7
Rhine model of development 92
risk amelioration, and industrial policy 27
risk, and technological change 152
Robinson, J A 68–70
Rodrik, D 92, 105n9, 105n11, 105n12, 167–8,
    378, 379, 383, 386, 514, 519
Rowstow, W W 80
Rowthorn, R 541
Ruane, F 420
rules:
  and enforcement capabilities 56–7
  and judicial reform 89–90

Russia, and 'shock treatment' 104n5
Rwanda:
  and economic growth 374
    explanations for 184, 187
  and structural adjustment program 188

Sachs, J D 92, 105n9, 115–16, 507, 524
Saggi, K 380, 398n8
Sampat, B 275
Samuelson, P 258
Sandbrook, R 102
Sasol 350–1, 352, 355
Saudi Arabia 126
savings rates 359, 503, 511
Schettkat, R 88
Schmitz, H 377
Schneider, B R 304
Scott, J 124
self-interest, and neoliberalism 141
Sen, A 440–1
Senegal 184
sequencing, and policy reforms 22–3
Seychelles, and economic growth 188
Shanker, D 92
Shannon Free Zone 322
Shapiro, I 90
Shibusawa, Eiichi 232, 243n5
Shimamura, M 387
Sierra Leone:
  and adverse redistribution 193
  and economic growth 187
  and state controls 192
Silicon Valley 152, 256
Singapore 37
  and development strategy 383
  and Economic Development Board 261, 264,
    469–71
  and Engineering Industry Development
    Authority (EIDA) 470
  and foreign direct investment 469–70
  and skills development 469–73
    company-affiliated training 470–1
    evolution of **472**
    higher education 471–2
Singer, H 510
Singh, A 422
skills development:
  and comparative advantage 158
  and consequences of weak skills base 463–4
  and economic growth 36–7, 462, 489
  and educational reform 476–7
    expanding coverage 478, **479**
    expanding scientific and technical
      personnel 481–3
    financing of 484–5
    learning outcomes 478–81
    legacy of low investment 477–8

strengthening technical and vocational
training 483
universities 484
and foreign direct investment 37, 465–**6**
Ireland 473–4
Singapore 469–73
and Ghana 475
and growth-enhancing governance 135–6
and Ireland 473–4
and lack of opportunity for skills
utilization 468
and lessons from successful reformers 485
backward and forward linkages 488
longer time horizons 486–7
strategic and visionary leadership 485–6
and limited investment in 468
and Malaysia 474–5
and mature training and education systems
464–5
and medium-term strategy 463, 468–9, 489
and Mozambique 475
and national innovation systems 155, 156
and need for 488–9
and Nigeria 475–6
and official development aid (ODA) 466–7
and short-term strategy 463, 465, 468, 489
and Singapore 469–73
company-affiliated training 470–1
evolution in **472**
higher education 471–2
and South Africa 356
and technological change 152–3
and unemployment amongst skilled
manpower 463
and weak demand for educated
workers 468
and weak educational base 467–8
small and medium-sized enterprises (SMEs):
in Africa, access to finance 424
and Ireland 408–9, 423–4
access to finance 409
and support for 417
Smith, Adam 81, 140–1, 250
social capital:
and characteristics of 147
and market economy 147
as public good 147
social development 147–8
as public good 148
social pacts, and Ireland 404, 414, 415–16
Solow, R M 21, 24, 149–50
Somalia 5
South Africa:
and apartheid era industrialization policies
349–52
and automobile industry 352, 354, 361, 362,
365, 366, 367

and black economic empowerment
(BEE) 356
and budget support for resource processing
firms 355
and capital account liberalization 353–4
and computer industry 290–2
and debt reduction 354
and economic and industrial performance:
business services 361
components of GDP growth **357**
construction sector 358
consumption-led growth 356–8, 367
employment trends 359, **360**, 361,
362–3, **365**
GDP growth by sector **358**
growth by sectors **362**
investment rates 358–9, 362, **364**
limitations of 367
limited real-economy growth 361–5
manufacturing 358, 363–6
mining 358
profits 361
savings rates 359
service sector 358
wages 361
and economic growth 181
explanations for 187
and employment equity 356
and export processing zones 323
and exports 361–2, **364**, 367
and fiscal restraint 354
and Growth Employment and Redistribution
(GEAR) strategy 352, **353**
and Industrial Development Corporation
(IDC) 350, 351
and industrial policy 30
and inequality 361
and inflation targeting 353
and limited real-economy growth and
diversification 361–5
and manufacturing 358, 363–6, 367
and mining conglomerates 350
and monetary policy 353
and natural resources 368–9
and post-apartheid industrialization
policies 352–6
and poverty 361
and privatization 355
and skills development 356
and social expenditure 354
and state-business relations 303
and state-owned enterprises 350, 351,
352, 355
and supply-side reforms 355
and tax revenue growth 354
and trade liberalization 345, 354–5, 365–6,
367, 368

South Africa: (*cont.*)
 and Washington Consensus type economic
  reforms 345–6, 352
South African Breweries 43n54
South Asia, and employment characteristics
 439–40
South Korea:
 and central bank 98
 and democratization 265
 and development strategy 382, 383
 and Economic Planning Board 264
 and education, comparison with
  Ghana **477**–8
 and employment-intensive growth 438
  poverty reduction 438
 and export processing zones 330, 331, 332
 and foreign direct investment 260
  discouragement of 422–3
 and industrial policy 253, 378
  coercion 408
 and initial low capabilities 224–5
 and insider system 263
 and New Community Movement 265–6
 and speed of catching up 224
 and technological development 297n5
Spain, and industrialization 166
special economic zones (SEZs):
 and China 289–90, 325, 331–2
 and definition of 325
 see also export processing zones (EPZs)
Spence Commission 10–12, 13
spillover effects:
 and foreign direct investment 419–20
 and industrial policy 28, 29
state:
 and debate over role of 20–2
 and latecomer development:
  limited capacity 277
  role in 275–6, 277–8
 and legitimization of intervention by 381–2
 and minimal state 116–17
 and neoliberal view of 140, 141
  rent-seeking 141
 and nightwatchman state 140, 141
  rational choice theory 143, 144
  as theoretical impossibility 143
 and rational choice theory 143–4
 and rent-seeking 141
  endogenizing 142–3
 and role in promoting development 295–7
  conflict management 296–7
  formulation of long-term vision 295
  guarantor of risks 296
  institution building 296
  providing coordination 295
  see also industrial policy; state-business
   relations

state autonomy, and developmental state
 167–8, 393–4
state-building 125
state-business relations 277, 303–4, 316–18
 and characteristics of effective:
  credibility 305
  reciprocity 305
  transparency 304
 and coordinating role 305
 and definition of 318n1
 and economic growth 305, **313**
  contribution to 305–6, 316
  effects at macro level 312–14
  effects at micro level 314–15
 and future research 304, 317–18
 and influence on government
  policies 305
 and measurement at macro level 306–7,
  308, **309**
  avoidance of harmful collusive
   behavior 308
  dialogue mechanisms 307–8
  private sector and government
   organization 307
 and measurement at micro level 309,
  310–11
  business associations 309–12
 and public-private partnership 384–6
 and reduction of policy uncertainty 305
 and solving market failures 305, 306
state controls, and economic growth
 190–2, 203
state failure 194, 202–3, 205–6
state-owned enterprises 192
Stiglitz, Joseph E 104n4
 and *The East Asian Miracle* 3, 9, 12
 and factors responsible for Asian success 3
 and inconsistency of neoliberal theory with
  technological change 164
 and institutions 85
 and learning 28
 and rents 120
 and role of government 382
 and Washington Consensus 381
Storey, D 426
structural adjustment programs 500
 and Arrow-Debreu model 81–2
 and economic growth 188
  weak link between 500
 and failure of 82–3, 251
 and impact of 410–11
 and market-enhancing ('good') governance,
  theoretical thinking behind 64–6
 and weakening of the state 16
suboptimal intertemporal resource allocation
 193–4, 202
subordinate state 167–8

Sudan:
    and agriculture 447
    and economic growth 184, 187
    and structural adjustment program 188
Sun Pharma 284
supply shocks, and economic growth 185, 202
Sweden, and education system 488
Swedish International Development
        Cooperation Agency 100
syndrome analysis, *see* policy syndromes

Taiwan:
    and development strategy 230, 382, 383
    and export processing zones 330–1, 332
    and Industrial Development Bureau
        (IDB) 261, 264
    and industrial policy 253–4, 378
    and insider system 263
    and speed of catching up 224
Tanzania:
    and economic growth 5
    and education 412
    and national identity 125
    and New Public Management 95
    and state controls 192
tariffs:
    and industrialization 165
    and loss of income from 514
    and United States 252
Tata Group 470–1
Tata Industries 37
Taylor, L 517
technological capability, accumulation of
        159–62
    and absorption 159, 160–1
    and centrality to developing countries 163
    and diffusion 159, 162
    and elimination of rent-seeking 161
    and external requirements 161, 162
    and identifying needs 160
    and innovative capability 159
    and investment capability 159
    and learning 160–1
    and moving on to complex technology 162
    and production capability 159
    and starting at low end of market 162
    and steps in process of 159
technological change and development:
    and clustering 151–2
    and computer industry:
        China 287–90
        South Africa 290–2
    and economic structure 158
    and endogenous growth theory 150
    and externalities 151
    and heterogeneous nature of new
        technology 153
    and inconsistent with perfectly competitive
        markets 154
    and increasing returns to scale 151
    and institutions 275
    as learning process 258
    and market failures 150–4, 163
    and national innovation systems 154–9
        creation of new technologies 157
        definition of 154
        diffusion of technology 157
        diffusion system 155, 156
        exploiting existing technology 157
        Germany 156–7
        mission-oriented systems 155–6
        requirements for 154–5
        United States 155–6
    and neoclassical growth theory 149–50, 163
    and pharmaceutical industry:
        Bangladesh 285–7
        India 281–5
    and risk of entry 152
    and role of the state 295–7
        conflict management 296–7
        formulation of long-term vision 295
        guarantor of risks 296
        institution building 296
        providing coordination 295
    and trained labor 152–3
    and utilization of new ideas 157
    see also national innovation systems
technology acquisition 8
    and absence from neoclassical models 21
    and importance for development 21
    and rents 120–1
technology, and public good
        characteristics 150
technology transfer:
    and clustering 151–2
    and foreign direct investment 465
    and industrial policy 384
Telesis Group 423
temperate zones, and economic performance
        523, 524
terms of trade, and economic growth 186–7
Teubal, M 378
TexStyles Ghana Limited 475
textile industry, and export processing
        zones 335
Thailand:
    and central economic agencies 388
    and development strategy 234, 383
    and Eastern Seaboard (ESB) Development
        Plan 395, 396–7
    and infrastructure projects 239
    and initial low capabilities 225
    and Japan 241
    and macroeconomic policy 400n19

Thailand: (*cont.*)
  and manufacturing 400n18
  and nation-building 125
  and public-private partnership 385
  and regulation 18
  and speed of catching up 224
Thaksin Shinawatra 234
Tinbergen's principle 102
Togo:
  and adverse redistribution 193
  and economic growth 188
    explanations for 186
  and state controls 192
Tokyo International Conference on African
    Development 383
total factor productivity growth (TFPG) 41n10,
    188–9, 205
  and Solow model 149
Toure, Sekou 201
Toye, J 80
trade, *see* international trade
trade liberalization:
  and agriculture 513–14, 516, 526
  and aid for trade 514–15
  and benefits for rich countries 515, 517
  and computable general equilibrium (CGE)
    model 518
    LINKAGE 515
    MIRAGE 517
  and deindustrialization 511–12
  and estimates of effects of 515–19, 526
  and impact of 349, 499, 513–19
  and loss of tariff revenue 514
  and reduction of policy options 519
  and South Africa 345, 354–5, 365–6,
    367, 368
  and sustainable development 517
  and unsupported by 'new trade theory' 519
  see also international trade
trade policy:
  and Doha trade agreement 258,
    515, 516
  and East Asia, changes in 388, **389**, 390
  and industrial policy 257–8
  and industrialization 349
  see also international trade; trade liberalization
Trade Related Aspects of Intellectual Property
    Rights (TRIPS) 281, 282, 298n10, 381
trade theory:
  and infant industry protection 257
  and orthodox view of 346
  and trade liberalization 519
training:
  and foreign direct investment 37
  and growth-enhancing governance 135–6
  and national innovation systems 156

  and technological change 152–3
  see also education; skills development
transaction costs:
  and inefficient markets 63, 273
  and reduction of 146, 147, 148, 155, 156
transparency:
  and good governance 89
  and state-business relations 304
tropical zones, and economic performance
    523–4
Tunisia 236–7, 322
Tuozzo, M F 89

Uganda:
  and adverse redistribution 193
  and economic growth 5, 189
    explanations for 187
  and economic reform 189
  and employment-intensive growth 452–3
  and industrial policy 421
  and New Public Management 95
uncertainty, and market economy 145
unemployment 440–1, 442–3
  and skilled manpower 463
United Kingdom, and industrialization 348
United Nations:
  and Copenhagen Summit (1995) 526–7
  and Development Agenda 526–7
  and Earth Summit (Rio, 1992) 526
  and Fourth World Conference on Women
    (Beijing, 1995) 526
  and industrial policy, objectives of 427n5
  and Millennium Declaration (2000) 527
  and Monterey Conference on Financing for
    Development (2002) 527
  and Population and Development
    Conference (Cairo, 1994) 526
  and World Conference on Sustainable
    Development (Johannesburg, 2002) 527
United Nations Conference on Trade and
    Development (UNCTAD) 412, 415, 417,
    424, 426, 427, 508, 519
United Nations Economic Commission for
    Africa (2003) 96
United Nations Industrial Development
    Organization (UNIDO) 322
United States:
  and central bank 98
  and industrial policy 252
  and industrialization 348
  and learning, industrial and technology (LIT)
    policies 24
  and national innovation system 155–6
    creation of new technologies 157
    diffusion of technology 157
universities, and skills development 484

van der Mensbrugghe, D 516
Venables, A 256
Vietnam 254–5
  and infrastructure projects 239
  and Japan 241
    development assistance from 237–9
  and regulation 18
vocational training 483
see also skills development
'Volcker shock' 12
Von Holdt, K 354

Wade, Robert 40n6
wages, see income levels
Walsh, B 418–19
Warner, A 524
Washington Consensus:
  and adverse effects of 22
  and assumptions of 20
  and constraining effects of 524–5
  and continued influence of 22, 248–52,
    259, 525
  and contrast with East Asian policies 3–4
  and criticism of 250, 381
  and emergence of 499–500
  and failure of 16, 346, 511
  and failure of adjustment 82–3
  and foreign direct investment 259
  and good governance agenda 16–17, 262, 347
  and Latin America 254–5
  and limitations of 8
  and power to survive evidence
    against 268n15
  and public expenditure reduction 510–11
  and role of the state 20
  and sequencing of policies 22–3
  and Washington Consensus plus 347
  and weakening of the state 16, 22
  see also neoliberalism
Watanabe, M 376
Weiss, J 383
Whitehead, L 95
Williams, D 89
Williamson, John 40n3
Woessmann, L 478
Wolfensohn, J 84
Wolseley, Lord Garnet 70
World Bank 6
  and Accelerated Development in Sub-Saharan
    Africa (1981) 265, 499–500, 509, 513
  and Adjustment in Africa (1994) 83, 334
  and Arrow-Debreu model 81–2
  and business environment surveys 65
    regulation 18
  and Commission on Growth and
    Development 375, 383

  and corporate governance 106n18
  and Country Policy and Institutional
    Assessment (CPIA) 249
  and From Crisis to Sustainable Growth
    (1989) 82
  and The East Asian Miracle 3, 9, 12, 334
  and Economic Growth in the 1990s 23,
    249–50
  and export processing zones, as second-best
    solution 331, 334–5
  and governance 82
    Anglo-Saxon model 91–2
  and government employment in Africa 96
  and inapplicability of East Asian strategies
    elsewhere 114
  and industrial policy, opposition to 333–4
  and judicial reform 90
  and Knowledge for Development 250
  and Mali 251
  and Mongolia 251, 268n13
  and neglect of industrialization and
    technology 250
  and neoliberal view of 333–4
  and official mindset 265
  and policy-capability matching 227
  and poverty estimates 501, **502**
  and shortcomings of policy advice 226
  and stability 95
  and state intervention 96–7
  and structural adjustment programs 500
  and trade liberalization 515, 516
  and The World Development Report 1980 36
  and The World Development Report 1983 333
  and The World Development Report 1997 227
  and The World Development Report 1998 36
  and Worldwide Governance Indicators
    (WGI) 226
World Education Forum (Dakar, 2000) 478
World Trade Organization (WTO) 282, 354,
  381, 515, 559–60

Yamanobe, Takeo 232
Yanagihara, T 229
Yeats, A 523
Yokohama Declaration (2008) 383
Young, T 89
Yusuf, S 378–9

Zaire 5
Zambia:
  and economic growth 184
  and Japan 239
  and state-business relations 314
  and state controls 192
Zenawi, Meles 14
Zimbabwe 5, 186, 188